READER'S DIGEST

BOOK OF SKILLS AND TOOLS

READER'S DIGEST
BOOK OF SKILLS AND TOOLS

PUBLISHED BY THE READER'S DIGEST ASSOCIATION LIMITED
LONDON • NEW YORK • SYDNEY • CAPE TOWN • MONTREAL

The publishers would like to thank the
following people for their contributions

EDITOR
Jill Steed

ART EDITOR
Jane McKenna

DESIGNERS
Clare Marshall
Keith Miller
Austin Taylor

RESEARCHER
Michaella Standen

PICTURE RESEARCHER
Rosie Taylor

ARTISTS
Precision Illustration

PHOTOGRAPHERS
Martin Cameron
Vernon Morgan (Cover)

INDEXER
Laura Hicks

CONSULTANT EDITOR
Tony Wilkins

SPECIALIST CONSULTANTS

Geoff Allen, Luxcrete Ltd

K. Baden-Powell,
Paint Magic by Jocasta Innes

Bob Baldwin HNC Bldg

John Cordory BSc

Andrew R. Dunstan NCHLC,
Merrist Wood College

Robin Harold-Barry
BSC CEng MICE MASCE MICT,
Concrete Consultancy Ltd

Brian Howard MA,
The British Concrete Masonry Assoc

Terry Knight AADipl ARIBA

Jeff W.H. Laverack BA DipM,
Marshalls Mono Ltd

Michael L. Rowley AADipl RIBA

Ronnie Rustin, Rustins Ltd

Jeremy Turtle, L.H. Turtle Ltd

Michael White,
The Art Veneers Company

READER'S DIGEST GENERAL BOOKS

EDITORIAL DIRECTOR
Robin Hosie

ART DIRECTOR
Bob Hook

EXECUTIVE EDITOR
Michael Davison

MANAGING EDITOR
Paul Middleton

EDITORIAL GROUP HEADS
Julian Browne
Noel Buchanan
Cortina Butler
Jeremy Harwood

RESEARCH EDITOR
Prue Grice

PICTURE RESEARCH EDITOR
Martin Smith

BOOK OF SKILLS AND TOOLS was edited and designed by The Reader's Digest Association Limited, London.
First edition Copyright © 1996 The Reader's Digest Association Limited, Berkeley Square House, Berkeley Square, London W1X 6AB.
Copyright © 1996 Reader's Digest Association Far East Limited.
Philippines Copyright © 1996 Reader's Digest Association Far East Limited.

Printed in Great Britain

ISBN 0 276 42197 3

The information in this book has been adapted from
Book of Skills and Tools, published in 1993 by Reader's Digest, USA.

ACKNOWLEDGMENTS

The editors wish to thank the following organisations and individuals for the assistance they provided:

Amari Plastics Ltd
American Hardwood Export Council
The American Tool Company
C. Blumsom Ltd
John Boddy's Fine Wood and
    Tool Store Ltd
Buck & Ryan Ltd
A.W. Champion Ltd
Concraft Ltd
Draper Tools Ltd
Fitchett and Woollacott
Footprint Tools Ltd
Formica Ltd

Freeman Distribution Ltd
Henkel Ltd
Hitachi Power Tools (UK) Ltd
HSS Hire Shops
Ibstock Brickwork Design Centre
Douglas Kane Hardware
John Lewis Partnership
Marshalls Clay Products
Mitutoyo (UK) Ltd
Mona Precast (Anglesey) Ltd
Moore and Wright
Mosley-Stone Ltd
The Newson Group

Sainsbury's Homebase
Sandvik Ltd
Skarsten Manufacturing
    Company Ltd
Stanley Tools
Top Layer
TRADA Technology Ltd
Trend Machinery and Cutting
    Tools Ltd
TubeHeat Ltd
L.H. Turtle
Vitrex Ltd
H.S. Walsh and Sons Ltd

PHOTO CREDITS: p.12 (bottom, left) Draper Tools Ltd; p.287 (bottom, left) Jane Legate/Robert Harding Picture Library; p.287 (bottom, right) Ideal Home /© IPC Magazines Ltd/Robert Harding Picture Library.

MAIL ORDER CATALOGUES

Some of the tools and hardware shown in this book are not commonly found in DIY centres and tool shops. Many specialist tools and materials may be obtained through mail order catalogues, such as those listed below.

CRAFT SUPPLIES
A wide range of woodturning tools, machinery and wood blanks.
Tel. 01298 871636 for a catalogue.

JOHN BODDY'S FINE WOOD AND TOOL STORE LTD
More than 9000 woodworking tools, accessories, wood blanks and timber.
Tel. 01423 332370 for a catalogue.

MACHINE MART
A wide range of tools and equipment.
Tel. 0115 956 5555 (24-hour service) for a catalogue.

H.S. WALSH AND SONS LTD
Tools, material and equipment for watch and clock-making, gold and silver work, jewellery-making and associated skills.
Tel. 0181 778 7061 for a catalogue.

WOODFIT LTD
Furniture fittings and accessories.
Tel. 01257 266421 for a catalogue.

ABOUT THIS BOOK

The BOOK OF SKILLS AND TOOLS is made for you if you enjoy working with tools or if you want to improve your home. Whether you are thinking about paving your patio, putting up shelves, painting or papering a wall or simply having the enjoyment and satisfaction of building something useful and beautiful, this book will fill a dual purpose. It will tell you how to do the job, and show you what tools and materials you will need.

The book is divided into eight major sections. The first two, 'Tools' and 'Hardware', consist of galleries of colour photographs of well over a thousand tools and articles of hardware, with explanations of how to use each item. Included are all the standard hammers and saws, pliers and screwdrivers and nails and hinges, but there are also unusual, specialised tools, such as a textured paint roller, a screw pitch gauge and a variety of router templates.

On each double-page spread the tools and hardware are photographed in the same perspective so that their sizes, relative to one another, are accurate – except for tools enclosed in a ruled box, which are either much larger or much smaller than the other items on the page.

Each of the remaining six sections is devoted to the skills you will need to use these tools and hardware when working with particular types of material. Colour photographs show either the raw materials or the effects that can be created with them – woods, metals, mouldings, concrete and concrete blocks, bricks, stones, pavers, ceramic and vinyl tiles, plastic laminates, glass fibre, glass and glass blocks, paints and wall coverings and flooring of every type.

Each picture gallery is followed by full, step-by-step instructions on working with the materials, giving all the information a beginner needs, and including advanced techniques as well. In the tradition of other Reader's Digest do-it-yourself books, these instructions are brought to life with hundreds of full-colour drawings.

The BOOK OF SKILLS AND TOOLS is not a project book that provides detailed blueprints for specific jobs, but it can teach you how to work with a wide variety of tools and materials, giving you the skills and confidence to create your own projects. At the same time, you will be able to indulge your creative impulses and derive a great deal of satisfaction from the completed work.

This book is not intended as a manual for very large construction jobs and it contains no information on electrical or plumbing work. However, the skills it teaches can help you to save money by doing much of the work in even the largest of projects, leaving only the heavy-duty and highly technical work to the professionals.

Completing the book are sections on organising a safe workshop, working safely with tools, planning a project and, finally, useful conversion charts.

This edition of the BOOK OF SKILLS AND TOOLS has been adapted from the original US version, specifically for readers in the United Kingdom. Particular care has been taken to use the appropriate terminology, to show standard UK practices and to ensure that all the tools and items of hardware shown in the book are available in the UK – even if under a different brand name or with minor superficial differences.

THE EDITORS

CONTENTS

SAFE WORKSHOP PRACTICES

TOOLS

HARDWARE

WOODWORKING

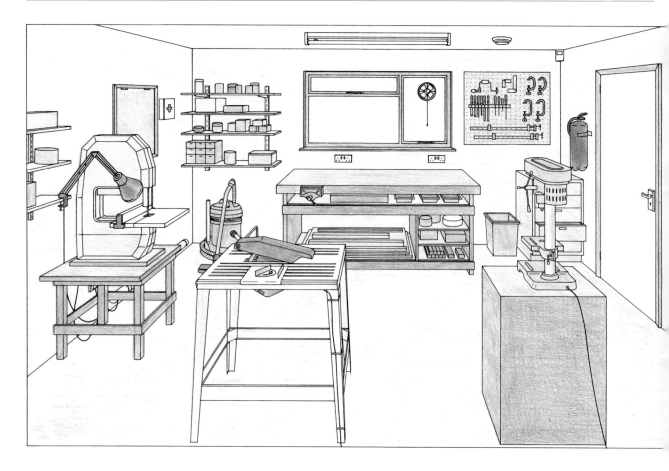

Many projects around the house and garden require workshop facilities – as do hobbies such as wood-turning and furniture-making. The ideal is a self-contained workshop which is warm and dry, and where unfinished work can be left undisturbed and secure. The bigger the space, the better, as lengths of wood or sheet materials may need space in which to be manoeuvred while being cut to size.

Choosing the space If there is no spare room available, consider buying a prefabricated workshop which is at least 3 m × 2.4 m (10 × 8 ft), with plenty of windows to let in daylight. If you choose one with a single-slope roof, make sure that the headroom at the lower part of the slope (usually where there is a window) is adequate.

If the workshop has no floor, it can be placed on a prepared concrete base which incorporates a damp-proof membrane. The concrete should be sealed with floor paint which will ensure that no abrasive dust is released.

A timber floor will prove warmer to the feet, and if you choose one, make sure that the floorboards are supported adequately. A springy floor is not ideal for bench-mounted power tools. To make a firm base, lay heavy gauge polythene on compacted earth, then place paving slabs on top, to give firm support to the timber joists.

Timber walls are best lined with bitumen-impregnated building paper to keep out the damp. This can be fixed between the main timbers, then the walls lined with sheet plasterboard or oil-tempered hardboard. If possible, an openable flap on one of the short walls is useful, as it allows for the handling of timbers longer than the workshop, as well as offering an easy point of entry for other materials.

Electrical supply Have the power supply professionally installed, using either an overhead cable or a special metal-clad cable buried in the soil. Ideally, incorporate a residual current device (known as an RCD) so that, should any fault develop, the circuit is broken immediately.

Have ample power sockets installed at a comfortable working height. This will avoid the danger of having long flexes trailing across the workshop.

A fluorescent light may be useful for general illumination, but tungsten lights should be used in conjunction with moving machinery such as wood-turning lathes. (A fluorescent light can have a disturbing stroboscopic effect.) Make sure that all portable lights are correctly earthed.

Heating will be required during the winter months. Choose tubular heaters which supply a steady background

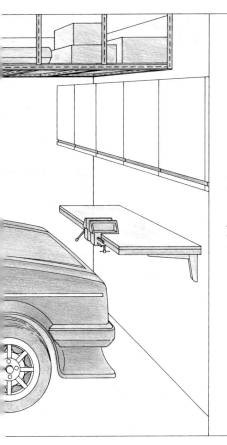

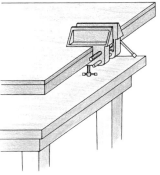

Kitchen-table cover A made-to-fit work surface that slips over your kitchen table must overlap sufficiently to allow you to clamp on a portable vice. Never leave tools unattended if children are about.

Lay out your workshop so that the main bench is convenient to your large power tools and major storage areas. If you have a table saw, leave enough space round it to handle large sheets of plywood. If you mount your large power tools on tables with locking castors, you'll be able to store them out of the way when not in use. If necessary, install a fold-down work surface, or one that fits over the bonnet of your car, in your garage. Store materials overhead, above a false ceiling.

warmth without getting red hot. They are controlled by switches with pilot lights so that you can see when the heating is on. During the warmer months an extractor fan will be useful.

Where dust-producing tools are used, provide some form of extraction unit which can be connected by a flexible tube to most power tools. A wet-and-dry vacuum cleaner that can be attached to a power tool is adequate in a small workshop (p.12).

Equipment A sturdy workbench is essential. Ideally it should be sited under a main window and have a woodworking vice plus a small engineer's vice of the type which can be clamped in place at any point. Plan for the bench top to be kept clear. Tools like a vertical drill stand and a small turning lathe are best positioned elsewhere – preferably on their own benches, if space permits.

Adequate shelving is important in a workshop. Brackets on slotted uprights are best, as the shelf-height can be adjusted to suit the items stored.

A large sheet of pegboard, mounted on a simple timber frame to hold the board away from the wall, can be fitted with pegboard clips designed to hold various tools and attachments. An outline painted round each tool stored will show you, at a glance, which tools are missing at the end of a day.

Storing timber is often a problem. If possible, use existing rafters or install extra battens within the roof space to support long timbers.

Safety Mount a fire extinguisher on the wall. A dry-powder type (which is usually coloured blue) is suitable, but make sure it carries the BS number 5423 or 6165 and the British Standard kitemark. A smoke alarm should be installed to give warning of fire.

Also have a first-aid kit close at hand and remember to replace any item that is used, as soon as possible.

The workshop floor should be kept free of mess at all times, so a broom is useful, plus a large metal bin for wood shavings and other debris. Wood dust can ignite and many hardwood dusts are a health hazard (p.12).

Where a workshop is not covered by the security system of the house, install an alarm system. And if there are children about, keep the workshop locked when not in use. If it is open, ensure that all power tools are unplugged from the power supply.

If the power tools are being used, keep small children right out of the workshop. See that older ones in the area are supervised at all times.

Other locations If a separate workshop is not feasible, it may be possible to utilise the end of a garage, installing a bench which either folds away or is just high enough to allow the car bonnet to fit under it.

There may be sufficient headroom to make a false ceiling, above which you can store materials.

Coat the floor with garage floor paint to prevent the creation of dust and to make cleaning easy.

A wet car driven into the garage will raise the humidity, and will almost certainly lead to tool rust. Extra ventilation will help, but tools are best stored in closed cupboards and drawers rather than on wall-mounted racks. Silica gel sachets are useful in small, enclosed spaces. The crystals inside absorb moisture and then need to be reactivated regularly in a warm oven to drive off the accumulated moisture.

Using the kitchen If, as a last resort, the kitchen table has to serve as your workbench, make up a sturdy worktop from a sheet of medium density fibreboard (MDF) mounted on a simple timber frame which fits neatly over the table top. Make sure that its structure allows a portable vice to be clamped to the frame.

Choose tools that suit your budget, space, experience and the type of work you plan to do. Quality tools are expensive, but you needn't buy a lot of them at first. Start with a few basic hand and power tools, learn to use them, and as you gain experience, add others. Rent tools that you will use only once. For advice on finding the tools you need, see pages 348-53.

Tool maintenance Take care of your tools to keep them effective and safe. Sharpen, clean or replace blades, bits and other cutters before they become damaged or dull. A sharp tool cuts smoothly, accurately and safely.

Follow the maker's instructions to keep power tools in good condition. Most power tools are permanently lubricated and sealed and require no oiling. You may have to oil certain parts of some tools, however, and you may be able to replace worn brushes or power flexes or defective switches. Check your owner's manual.

To clean a power tool, unplug it and wipe it with a damp cloth or sponge.

Never submerge the tool in water or clean it with solvents. If a tool's air vents become clogged, remove the debris with compressed air from a foot pump or with a vacuum cleaner.

If you have cordless tools, use only the battery and charger that came with the tool. Never charge or store a tool where the temperature is below 5°C or above 40°C. Batteries rely on chemical reactions that slow down in the cold and stop altogether at freezing point. High temperatures release vapours from the battery and diminish its capacity.

Tool storage Store cutting tools where their sharp edges won't be damaged, cause injury or damage other tools. To prevent rust from forming on tools, store them in a dry place. Spray a rust-inhibiting oil on steel tools or put camphor tablets or rust-preventive paper in toolboxes and cabinets. The camphor vapour coats the tools with a rust-preventive film, and the paper gives off a protective vapour or absorbs moisture.

Toolboxes come in a variety of sizes. A small or medium-sized box with removable tray is used to store small tools and to transport them to a job site. Larger boxes with drawers, trays and compartments store a variety of tools and hardware.

When working outside, use a carpenter's pouch or a tool belt to carry basic tools and hardware. A canvas nail apron holds nails, screws, other fasteners and small tools.

Clothing Dress appropriately in your workshop and have any helpers do the same. Wear proper footwear, preferably sturdy leather shoes or boots with nonslip soles. Roll long sleeves up above the elbows, tie long hair back, and never wear dangling jewellery or loose-fitting clothing, especially when operating power tools; they can become entangled in the tool and cause serious injury. Wear gloves to protect your hands when working with rough materials, sharp edges, hot metal or broken glass and when unloading supplies or cleaning up.

Do not wear gloves when handling most tools. A hand tool may slip from your grasp or twist around and injure you; a power tool's cutter may catch a glove and drag your hand in with it.

Wear kneepads when installing tiles, doing masonry work or working on other projects that require kneeling for long periods. If you don't have kneepads, kneel on a folded blanket or thick newspaper while working.

Eye and ear protection Wear adequate eye protection whenever you saw, grind, file, chisel or do any other work that involves dust, flying chips or harmful liquids that might splash into your eyes. Safety glasses give good general protection, but goggles are more efficient and can be worn over prescription eyeglasses. For full protection, use a face shield.

When operating power tools or performing noisy tasks such as driving nails, wear hearing protectors or earplugs. They filter out damaging noise but allow you to hear voices.

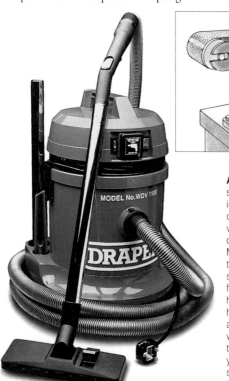

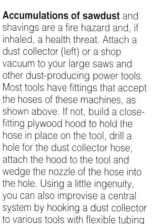

Accumulations of sawdust and shavings are a fire hazard and, if inhaled, a health threat. Attach a dust collector (left) or a shop vacuum to your large saws and other dust-producing power tools. Most tools have fittings that accept the hoses of these machines, as shown above. If not, build a close-fitting plywood hood to hold the hose in place on the tool, drill a hole for the dust collector hose, attach the hood to the tool and wedge the nozzle of the hose into the hole. Using a little ingenuity, you can also improvise a central system by hooking a dust collector to various tools with flexible tubing and rigid PVC drainpipes and fittings.

Safe work habits Whether you are working with hand or power tools, think about safety before and with every move you make. Keep your mind on your work, avoid distractions, work at a comfortable pace and stop before you get tired. Avoid potentially dangerous operations that you don't feel totally comfortable performing. Don't smoke in the workshop.

Keep children, visitors and pets out of your workshop, especially when you are operating power tools. They could cause an accident by distracting you or getting in your way.

Tools can be dangerous if used improperly. To ensure safety, always read and follow the owner's manual or instructions that came with the tool. Be careful to use the right tool for the job; never force a tool to work beyond its capacity or your ability. When working with power tools, observe the safety rules listed at right.

When using power tools out of doors, plug them into an RCD (Residual Current Device) adapter. This will be activated should any fault develop or the flex be cut accidentally and will perhaps prevent a serious electric shock.

Clearing the air Wood, metal, concrete and other types of workshop dust are hazardous when inhaled. In addition, dust created from sanding some woods, including pressure-treated woods, and some stains and finishes can cause harm if they come into contact with the skin and eyes.

Open doors and windows or turn on a fan to ventilate your workshop. Use a dust mask for jobs that generate dust and a respirator for work that involves toxic fumes (such as using glues and strippers) or when working with insulation.

Most dust-producing power tools have an exit nozzle, to which a vacuum-cleaner hose can be connected. So use a dust collector or vacuum cleaner as often as possible to keep dust and debris from accumulating, and attach one to all the machines you can.

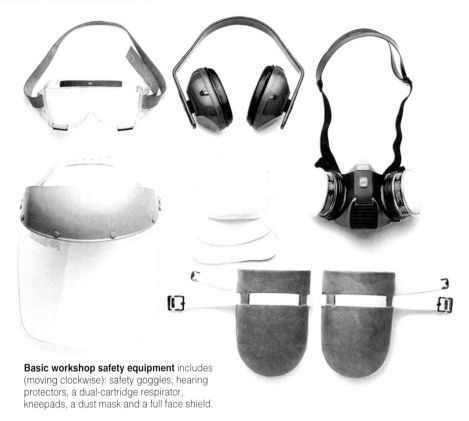

Basic workshop safety equipment includes (moving clockwise): safety goggles, hearing protectors, a dual-cartridge respirator, kneepads, a dust mask and a full face shield.

SAFETY WITH POWER TOOLS

To promote safety when working with power tools, always take the following precautions:
▷ Make sure that the tool you are using is double insulated and properly earthed.
▷ Don't operate a tool if you are tired or under the influence of medication, drugs or alcohol.
▷ Mentally run through the procedures for using a tool before switching it on.
▷ Never ignore, override or remove safety devices, such as blade guards, splitters and antikickback mechanisms on saws.
▷ Don't saw wet wood, and be especially careful when sawing warped or knotty wood.
▷ Check wood for nails, screws and loose knots before cutting or drilling.
▷ Support large workpieces during operations. When cutting long stock or large plywood panels, get an assistant or use a roller stand to support the stock at the outfeed side of a saw.
▷ Clamp all work securely in place.
▷ Use feather boards, push sticks or jigs to move stock past a whirling cutter.
▷ Leave no foreign items on the tool's table.
▷ Remove adjusting keys and wrenches from a tool before turning on the power.
▷ Before plugging in a tool, make sure the power switch is off, tighten all of its clamps, knobs, nuts and levers, and make sure its cutters are securely attached.
▷ Never operate a power tool while standing on a wet surface.

▷ Keep children and pets out of the workshop when operating power tools.
▷ Keep your fingers, hands and other parts of your body well out of the path of cutters.
▷ Keep power cords away from cutters.
▷ Maintain a firm footing; never reach so far with a portable tool that you over-balance. Don't reach over the cutter of any tool.
▷ Stand to one side of a saw in case the blade binds and causes the tool to kick back.
▷ When you finish making a cut, turn off the tool and let the cutters stop naturally if the machine has no brake; never slow down or stop a cutter with a piece of wood.
▷ Never touch a moving cutter.
▷ If a cutter stalls, switch off the power and unplug the tool before trying to free the cutter.
▷ If you are interrupted while using a power tool, finish the operation you are working on and switch the tool off before responding.
▷ Never clear scraps from a saw table with your fingers; instead, use a long stick.
▷ Turn off and unplug tools when not in use or when making adjustments, performing maintenance or changing accessories.
▷ Sharpen or replace any dull or damaged cutters as soon as possible.
▷ Never use the power flex to carry a tool or to pull its plug out of the wall socket.
▷ Don't be overconfident, or you will become careless and have an accident.

TOOLS

For any job that requires accuracy – from making a simple wooden box to installing a built-in home-entertainment centre – a good set of measuring tools is important for working out lengths, widths and angles. Even a small miscalculation can make a difference in the appearance or operation of the finished work; improperly measured pieces will not fit together smoothly when assembled. And if the first step is inaccurate, the error can compound itself as you continue, resulting in a significant blunder. A basic assortment of rules, gauges and calipers is a must for any workshop.

Micrometer, an extremely precise metalworking tool, measures dimensions in metric or imperial. Some models combine both. Most indicate outside dimensions, but some also show inside dimensions.

Steel rule has imperial and metric graduations. An accurate straightedge makes the rule useful as a guide for scribing and cutting when straight lines are important. It comes in lengths from 300 to 1200 mm (12-48 in).

Folding rule, also called a surveyor's rule, useful where a rigid rule is needed. Hinged sections fold for easy storage. One side shows metric and the other imperial. Usually 2 m (6 ft 6 in) long.

Retractable tape stores a spring-loaded metal rule in a small case. The rule is usually replaceable. A hook on the end of the rule makes long measurements a one-person job. Most models feature a metal case with a belt clip and a locking mechanism to prevent retraction. Some retractable tapes have a case that can be used as a square (right). Standard lengths are available from 1 to 15 m (3-50 ft).

Screw pitch gauge offers an easy way to identify the number of threads on a screw, bolt, nut or in a threaded hole. Notched metal blades are held in a case and correspond to the shape and spacing of the threads. Hold various blades against the threads until a perfectly snug fit is achieved. The number on the blade indicates the correct size.

Gauge plate comes in different gauge systems to check the thickness of sheet metal or of wire. To use one, push the wire or sheet metal edge into the slots until you find the right size. The number beside the slot shows the gauge.

Long tape is made of glass fibre (it may stretch a small amount) or a more accurate flexible rust-resistant steel. For one-person measuring, hook the metal loop on the end of the tape over a nail. A manual crank retracts the tape – which can be up to 100 m (about 300 ft) long for large measuring jobs such as house exteriors, landscaping and fencing.

Wrap tape around odd-shaped object; align edges. Start measuring at 2 in, then subtract 2 in from total.

Electronic distance measurer sends an ultrasonic pulse up to 75 m (250 ft) away. When it hits a flat surface, the pulse returns to the tool, which displays the distance. For best results, measure in still air and avoid obstructions such as furniture or trees. Look for a model that can also do calculations.

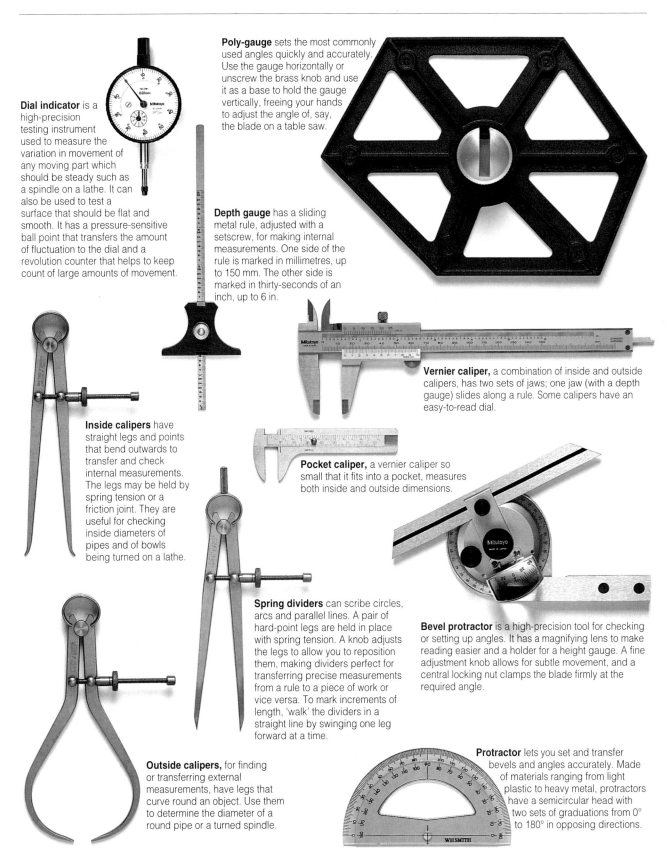

Dial indicator is a high-precision testing instrument used to measure the variation in movement of any moving part which should be steady such as a spindle on a lathe. It can also be used to test a surface that should be flat and smooth. It has a pressure-sensitive ball point that transfers the amount of fluctuation to the dial and a revolution counter that helps to keep count of large amounts of movement.

Poly-gauge sets the most commonly used angles quickly and accurately. Use the gauge horizontally or unscrew the brass knob and use it as a base to hold the gauge vertically, freeing your hands to adjust the angle of, say, the blade on a table saw.

Depth gauge has a sliding metal rule, adjusted with a setscrew, for making internal measurements. One side of the rule is marked in millimetres, up to 150 mm. The other side is marked in thirty-seconds of an inch, up to 6 in.

Inside calipers have straight legs and points that bend outwards to transfer and check internal measurements. The legs may be held by spring tension or a friction joint. They are useful for checking inside diameters of pipes and of bowls being turned on a lathe.

Vernier caliper, a combination of inside and outside calipers, has two sets of jaws; one jaw (with a depth gauge) slides along a rule. Some calipers have an easy-to-read dial.

Pocket caliper, a vernier caliper so small that it fits into a pocket, measures both inside and outside dimensions.

Spring dividers can scribe circles, arcs and parallel lines. A pair of hard-point legs are held in place with spring tension. A knob adjusts the legs to allow you to reposition them, making dividers perfect for transferring precise measurements from a rule to a piece of work or vice versa. To mark increments of length, 'walk' the dividers in a straight line by swinging one leg forward at a time.

Bevel protractor is a high-precision tool for checking or setting up angles. It has a magnifying lens to make reading easier and a holder for a height gauge. A fine adjustment knob allows for subtle movement, and a central locking nut clamps the blade firmly at the required angle.

Outside calipers, for finding or transferring external measurements, have legs that curve round an object. Use them to determine the diameter of a round pipe or a turned spindle.

Protractor lets you set and transfer bevels and angles accurately. Made of materials ranging from light plastic to heavy metal, protractors have a semicircular head with two sets of graduations from 0° to 180° in opposing directions.

Many jobs involve laying out angles and curves as well as straight lines. To lay out a design properly, you will need specialised tools and gauges. Protractors and compasses are most commonly used for drawing curves, but other tools are available. A number of combination tools are handy for multiple uses. To transfer points and cutting lines on your work, you will need various scribers, awls, punches, chalk lines and gauges.

French curves, made of clear acrylic, are used to draw irregular shapes and perspective details. Simply trace along the desired edge to make matching curves in as many locations as you wish.

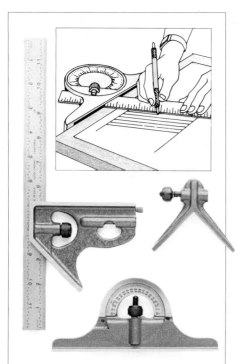

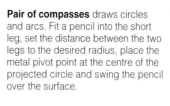

Sliding T-bevel is an adjustable gauge for setting, testing and transferring angles. The handle is made of wood or plastic. The metal blade pivots and can be locked at any angle by loosening and tightening the wing nut. Set the angle from an existing one or set it using a protractor. The end of the blade is angled at 45 degrees for use on mitred corners.

Pair of compasses draws circles and arcs. Fit a pencil into the short leg, set the distance between the two legs to the desired radius, place the metal pivot point at the centre of the projected circle and swing the pencil over the surface.

Combination tool set consists of a rule, protractor head, squaring head and centre finder. To use protractor, lock it onto rule at correct angle, set flat face of head along edge of work and scribe line, as shown. To use centre finder, lock it onto rule, position its ends on circle and draw line using rule; reposition and repeat.

Another combination tool has multiple uses for measuring and constructing angles. The steel rule can be used on its own and with the metal scribing pin incorporated in the head. The head and rule together are used as inside and outside try squares, a mitre square, depth gauge and a height and marking gauge. The angle finder can read unknown angles as well as check for plumb and 45 and 90 degree angles.

Flexible curve is a vinyl-wrapped bundle of lead strips for forming, transferring and duplicating unusual shapes. Bend the tool into any shape, hold it in position and trace the design in as many places as you wish.

Jenny caliper is used to scribe lines, usually on metal. The 'toe' on the straight leg is fitted to the edge of an object, and the point on the bent leg scribes a line the required distance away.

Trammel points draw large circles and arcs. Attach them to a yardstick, board or bar so that the distance between them is equal to the radius of the circle or arc you wish to draw and use the assembly like compasses.

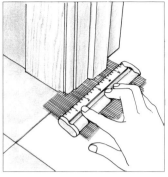

Profile gauge duplicates and transfers an irregular design to a template or piece of stock. The tool is made of a series of movable metal or plastic pins that take on the contour of whatever object they are pressed against.

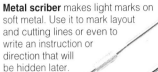

Metal scriber makes light marks on soft metal. Use it to mark layout and cutting lines or even to write an instruction or direction that will be hidden later.

Awl makes small holes for starting nails, drill bits and screws, and can be used in place of a pencil for marking very fine layout and cutting lines. The steel shank is sharpened to a point; the tool's handle is plastic or wood. An awl also punches holes in leather or vinyl.

Punches are steel marking instruments that are used by striking them with a hammer. The centre punch (top) and the sharper prick punch (centre) have bevelled points for starting holes in metal and wood. The pin punch (bottom) has a straight flank and flat tip for knocking out the small pins sometimes used to assemble parts.

Automatic punch operates on a spring so that you need not hit it with a hammer. Simply grasp the tool in one hand and push down firmly where you want a mark.

Chalk line, a case filled with chalk and 15 or 30 m (50 or 100 ft) of line on a reel, marks a long straight line between two points. Pull the line from the case, hold it taut and snap it to leave a chalk mark as a guide. The tool can also be used as a plumb bob.

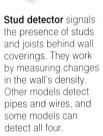

Carpenter's marking knife is used for marking out wood. Hold the knife like a pencil with the flat face of the blade against a try square and the bevelled edge facing the waste. Draw the knife firmly across the wood towards you.

Stud detector signals the presence of studs and joists behind wall coverings. They work by measuring changes in the wall's density. Other models detect pipes and wires, and some models can detect all four.

Marking gauge scribes a line on wood parallel with the edge. Set the distance you wish to mark from the edge of the stock by sliding the gauge's fence to the correct point on the beam. Some models have a graduated scale on the beam. Place the face of the fence against the edge of the wood and draw the pin along the stock (p.132).

Mortise gauge has a single pin for marking and two pins for scribing double lines on the ends of wood for laying out mortises. Lock the fence at the exact measurement, hold the face of the fence against the side of the stock and draw the pin or pins across it.

Pantograph copies a design and enlarges it or reduces it in the process. Clamp the tool to a drawing table or flat board, set it up as shown and adjust it to get the desired scale. Use one hand to trace over the original design with the stylus and the other hand to guide the pencil as it draws the copy.

SQUARES

The square is a layout and measuring tool and is essential for marking and assembling a project accurately. If it is made in two pieces, the metal or wood handle is called the stock; on a one-piece model, the metal handle is called the tongue. To lay out and mark cuts, place the handle parallel with the object and draw a line against the blade. Models with the blade set at 90 degrees to the handle can also check squareness after cutting and assembling the workpiece. Some models have blades set at different angles and others incorporate a spirit level.

Mitre square has a blade set at a 45 degrees angle for laying out and marking lines. It is especially useful for mitre cuts. The opposite angle is set at 135 degrees.

Engineer's square, a metalworking version of the try square (below), has a notch cut into the handle near the blade to make room for burrs when scoring metal.

Dovetail square comes in two ratios: 8:1 for hardwood, 6:1 for softwood. Use it to set angled lines for both the pins and the tails of a dovetail and to lay out vertical lines.

Carpenter's try and mitre square has a lightweight, impact-resistant plastic stock which combines the advantages of both try and mitre squares. The blade is 15 cm (6 in) long, graduated in imperial units.

Combination square combines several features of measuring and marking tools. Its blade and sliding adjustable head incorporate a try square, a 45 degrees mitre square and a spirit level in one compact unit.

Try square for woodworking lets you lay out cutting lines at 90 degrees angles and check the squareness of adjoining surfaces and of planed timber. The most useful model has a 228 mm (9 in) long blade.

T-square is used for marking up large workpieces. Made of aluminium, it shows both metric and imperial measurements up to 61 cm and 24 in. In addition, useful linear, weight, volume and area conversion formulas are shown. The crosspiece is used to steady the square against the end of the work.

Carpenter's square, or roofing square, is useful for laying out many types of projects. It's made from one piece of steel and incremented in inches, divided into eighths, tenths, twelfths and sixteenths. A metric version is also available with 2 mm increments. Both show rafter tables.

Framing square is a specialised version of the carpenter's square, has tables and formulas imprinted on it for making quick calculations, including those required for working out both area and volume.

LEVELS AND PLUMBS

Whether you are fitting a sink, setting a fence post or putting up a wall, keeping surfaces level and plumb is vital. A spirit level has one or more clear vials filled with a liquid. When you rest the level on a surface, a bubble in the liquid shows that the surface is true when it floats within an area marked on the vial. Longer levels are usually more accurate than shorter ones.

Digital level (right) does everything that other levels do, but does it electronically. On some models lights flash red for not level or green for level. Others feature a simulated bubble display plus a digital readout of degrees of slope, rate of rise and run of stairs and roofs and a percentage of slope for drainage problems on patios and masonry.

Torpedo level (below), a shorter 300 mm (12 in) version of a carpenter's level, is preferred by plumbers because it can fit into most restricted places and the grooved base allows it to rest on pipes. It usually has three bubble vials, which can be read through both top and side windows, to show level, plumb and a 45° angle.

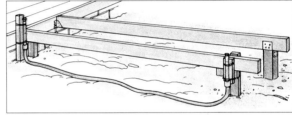

Carpenter's level (left, centre) comes with a varying number of vials to check horizontal level and vertical plumb and may be adjustable or replaceable. The frames are usually made of aluminium, brass, plastic or wood. Some frames are magnetised to keep hands free for moving the workpiece. Before buying a level, test it on a known level surface. Standard lengths are 600 mm and 1200 mm (2 ft and 4ft). To check the drop of a sloped surface, place a 1200 mm level on the surface; use wood blocks 25 mm thick to level the tool. Each wood block represents a one in fifty drop; so if it takes two wood blocks, you have a two in fifty drop.

Artisan level (left), similar to a carpenter's level, includes special features such as heavy-duty bubble vials, including a plumb vial, and protective rubber end plates. The frame can be up to 1800 mm (about 6 ft) for checking across concrete and brick. Some frames are made of wood, others are aluminium.

Water level, when attached to a garden hose and filled with water, establishes level heights at a distance or when out of line of sight. To use it, screw a tube on to each end of the hose; then fill the hose with water. Hold up one tube until the liquid reaches the desired height; the water in the tube at the other end will adjust itself to the same height.

Plumb bob is a weight attached to a line. To establish plumb, which is a straight vertical line, suspend the line from a height and drop the weight to the ground. Do not allow the weight to touch the ground. Give the weight time to steady before checking plumb. It is useful when aligning wall coverings or panelling, as doors and ceilings are not always true.

 Line level is a miniature level with hooks that attach to a taut line stretched between two points. It is very useful in masonry, fencing and landscaping projects.

Angle setter can also be used to determine an unknown angle. To set an angle, select it on the dial, lay the instrument on the workpiece and adjust the piece until it reads level. To determine an angle, turn the dial until it shows level and read off the angle displayed.

Circular level, a 360 degrees disc-shaped level, is also called a bull's-eye level. It is useful when levelling boats, caravans, furniture and appliances. The bubble is centred in a circle when level.

HAMMERS AND MALLETS

Most hammers come in a variety of head weights and handle lengths. Choose a quality tool that is precision-balanced, fits your hand, matches your strength and is designed for the work you are doing. A quality hammer will have a forged steel head and a hardwood, glass fibre, graphite or steel handle. Avoid dangerous cast heads and softwood handles. Faces may be milled (corrugated) to prevent glancing blows and flying nails, but a milled face cannot be used on finished work or it will mark the surface. Most handles are contoured for comfort and some have slip-resistant grips.

Ball-pein hammer has two faces. One is flat, for striking cold chisels and punches. The other, the pein, is rounded, or ball-like, for bending and shaping soft metal. The ball-pein hammer generally has a wood or glass fibre handle. Heads weigh 225-300 g (8-48 oz). For general use, choose a 550 g (20 oz) hammer.

Claw hammer, the most familiar of all hammers, can be used for driving common or finishing nails, but not masonry nails, which can split. The head can weigh from 450 to 680 g (16-24 oz) and has a sharply angled claw to extract nails. The handle may be made of wood or tubular steel.

Ripping hammer is similar to a claw hammer except that its claw is almost straight. Although not as effective a nail puller as the claw hammer, it is excellent for prising apart or tearing out boards, battens or sheet materials. The head weighs 280-675 g (10-22 oz). Some heads are magnetised to hold nails.

Soft-faced hammer will not mark surfaces because its steel head – which weighs 40-900 g (1½-32 oz) – has replaceable soft and hard plastic faces. The hammer is used for joining, seaming and assembling or disassembling wood or soft metal projects.

Tack hammer, a small lightweight tool, holds and sets tacks, small nails and brads. It usually has a wooden handle about 250 mm (10 in) long. The head, which weighs 140-225 g (5-8 oz), has a magnetic face on one end and another striking face or a small claw on the other. The tack hammer is used on cabinetwork, moulding, trim and upholstery.

Brick hammer usually has a square flat face for setting bricks in mortar and a sharpened, chisel-shaped face for scoring and cutting bricks and chipping away excess mortar. The head can weigh 280-675 g (10-24 oz) and the handle may be made of wood or tubular steel.

Cross-pein, or Warrington, hammer has a head with a flat face and a tapered pein. This carefully balanced hammer is a traditional cabinet-maker's tool. You can hold a nail in place with two fingers and start tapping it in with the pein face without hurting your fingers. The head weighs 100-450 g (3½-16 oz). The handle is about 300 mm (12 in) long.

Nail punch, a short, blunt steel punch, countersinks nails in wooden cabinets, furniture, mouldings and trim. Position its point over the head of the nail and strike the top with a hammer. Points range in diameter from 1 to 5 mm to cover most nailhead sizes.

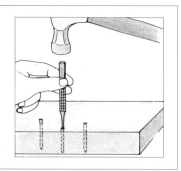

Jeweller's hammer is a lightweight tool that is ideal for working on models, miniatures and jewellery. Its head can weigh as little as 25 g (1 oz).

Sledgehammer breaks up concrete or drives heavy spikes, stakes or chisels into stone, brick or the ground by the sheer power of the weight of its solid steel head, which weighs 1.8-6.3 kg (4-14 lb). The handle can be made of wood or glass fibre. The heavier, long-handled sledgehammers are used primarily for demolition tasks.

Rubber mallet is used primarily in assembling components and pounding out dents in metal. The barrel-shaped head can be made of solid black rubber or nonmarking white rubber, and weighs 550-900 g (20-32 oz). The handle is generally wood and measures 250-330 mm (10-13 in).

Heavy-duty framing hammer, a construction tool for assembling and dismantling framing members, has an even narrower and straighter claw than the standard framing hammer. The long hatchet handle gives more leverage and is less likely to twist in your hand. It may be made of wood or metal. The head weighs about 650 g (23 oz). The model shown here has a milled face.

Club hammer, a broad, double-faced hammer, is used for striking star drills, hardened nails, punches, cold chisels and brick chisels. The metal head weighs 0.9-1.8 kg (2-4 lb) and the handle (generally wood) is about 250 mm (10 in) long.

Carpenter's wooden-head mallet, used mainly for assembling woodworking components and striking chisels, is also good for installing metal parts on equipment without marking them. Its head weighs 175-850 g (6-30 oz) and is usually made of beech or lignum vitae.

Dead-blow hammer head is filled with steel shot that adds to the weight and prevents any rebound in demolition and assembly work. The head can weigh 0.4-1.8 kg (1-4 lb).

Carver's mallet drives chisels and other carving tools into wood or stone with its 400-1180 g (14-42 oz) head. Made from a single piece of lignum vitae wood. Store it in a plastic bag to keep it from drying out.

Two-faced mallet, sometimes called a bossing mallet, has a round face for shaping sheet metal into bowls or other concave shapes when hammered inside a wooden form. The pointed face shapes or raises metal over a solid stake.

Soft-faced hammer set consists of a strong aluminium-alloy head with interchangeable rubber faces. Flat, dome, cone and wedge-shaped faces screw in easily. Heads weigh from 400-1300 g (14-48 oz).

Rawhide mallet consists of a round head of seasoned, compressed rawhide, weighing about 350 g (12 oz) with a long wooden handle. It has the same uses as a carpenter's wooden-head mallet.

METALWORKING HAMMERS AND HAMMERING SURFACES

Because so much metalworking involves hammering, a large number of specialised metalworking hammers are available. Before using a hammer to shape metal, be sure that the face is clean and free of pits or scale; the tiniest defect in the hammer head can be imprinted on the work many times over. It is a good idea to keep a piece of emery cloth handy to wipe off the face of the hammer as you work. Before storing a metalworking hammer for a long period of time, coat the face with petroleum jelly or oil.

Chasing (or repoussé) hammer drives chisel-like tools into the surface of sheet metal to indent decorative designs. The work is done in a pitch-filled bowl. The head of the hammer generally weighs 55-225 g (2-8 oz).

Embossing hammer, despite its name, is used in raising metal, to get into hard-to-reach areas and to imprint decorative bulges in the metal.

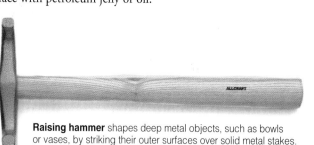

Raising hammer shapes deep metal objects, such as bowls or vases, by striking their outer surfaces over solid metal stakes. Standard and extra-narrow heads are available.

Planishing hammer flattens and toughens sheet metal as it adds texture to it. The head can weigh 55-140 g (2-5 oz). Some models have one square and one round face.

Setting (or scaling) hammer has a flat face for flattening seams without marking the surface of the metal and an angled face for forming and bending sheet metal. Can also be used for removing scale from boilers and welds.

Forging hammer is used to shape metal rods or bars. The head can weigh 85-500 g (3-18 oz). It generally has one slightly domed or flat face and one wedge-shaped face.

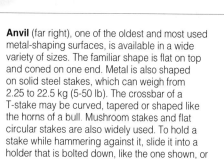

Blacksmith's hammer, the traditional tool for shaping heated metal on an anvil, is also used for driving spikes, stakes, rivets and hardened nails, for striking cold chisels and for any job that requires a heavy striking face. The head can weigh up to 1.8 kg (4 lb). One of its faces is flat and the other is wedge-shaped.

Anvil (far right), one of the oldest and most used metal-shaping surfaces, is available in a wide variety of sizes. The familiar shape is flat on top and coned on one end. Metal is also shaped on solid steel stakes, which can weigh from 2.25 to 22.5 kg (5-50 lb). The crossbar of a T-stake may be curved, tapered or shaped like the horns of a bull. Mushroom stakes and flat circular stakes are also widely used. To hold a stake while hammering against it, slide it into a holder that is bolted down, like the one shown, or into a special opening in your workbench or anvil. Rectangular blocks and cone-shaped mandrels are also used as hammering surfaces.

HATCHETS, NAIL PULLERS AND MECHANICAL FASTENERS

There are many other hammer-like tools and driving tools that are related to the hammer. The hatchet, of course, is used for chopping rather than driving or shaping, but many hatchets have a hammer face opposite the cutting face. Other hand and power tools are used for driving brads and staples, and large wrecking bars or pry bars and nail pullers do the work that is too difficult for the claws on standard hammers.

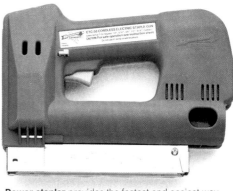

Power stapler provides the fastest and easiest way to staple large or thick materials. Simply place the unit against a surface and pull the trigger to drive in a staple. There are cordless and standard models.

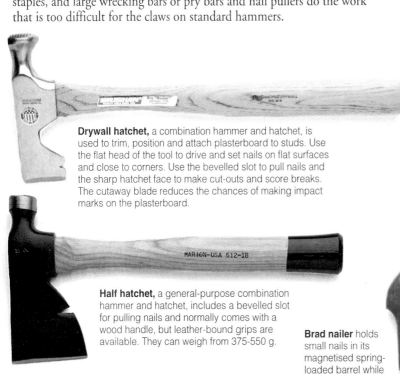

Drywall hatchet, a combination hammer and hatchet, is used to trim, position and attach plasterboard to studs. Use the flat head of the tool to drive and set nails on flat surfaces and close to corners. Use the bevelled slot to pull nails and the sharp hatchet face to make cut-outs and score breaks. The cutaway blade reduces the chances of making impact marks on the plasterboard.

Half hatchet, a general-purpose combination hammer and hatchet, includes a bevelled slot for pulling nails and normally comes with a wood handle, but leather-bound grips are available. They can weigh from 375-550 g.

Brad nailer holds small nails in its magnetised spring-loaded barrel while you drive them in by pushing the handle.

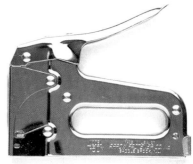

Hand stapler drives staples with a squeeze of the handle. Use it to attach paper-covered insulation, hang plastic sheets, upholster furniture, install screening or for any major stapling job in your home or workshop.

Shingling hatchet is a special tool for installing wooden shingles. The sharp face cuts the shingles and a gauge on the side of the face spaces the shingles evenly; move the screw to the desired depth.

Power brad nailer drives and countersinks brads 25-32 mm (1-1¼ in) long without marking the surface.

Nail puller removes deeply embedded nails. The movable jaws are positioned over the nail and slammed down into the wood under the nailhead. A rocking motion prises the nail out.

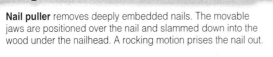

Wrecking (or pry) bar has two angled blades. One blade is used as a nail puller and the other as a prising tool for removing moulding and trim and for separating materials that are nailed together.

Hammer tacker drives in a staple in one motion. Simply strike the tool against the surface to be stapled. Various sizes of staple can be used in a hammer tacker.

Although a number of hand-powered drilling tools are available, every workshop should have at least one electric drill. Equipped with the right bit or attachment, an electric drill can bore holes in almost any material and do the work of other tools as well. The size of a drill is determined by the largest bit shank its chuck accepts. A drill may run at a single speed, two or three set speeds or at variable speeds, which you set to suit the job. Generally, the larger the drill, the slower it runs but the greater its turning power or torque. Before drilling, make sure the work is firmly supported and clamped down. Make a starter hole with a centre punch, awl or nail to keep the bit from wandering.

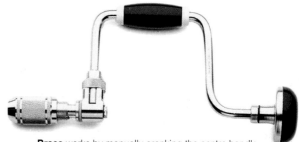

Brace works by manually cranking the centre handle as you apply pressure towards the bit. The brace is suitable for boring large holes in wood and for driving and removing screws. The bits must have a special end that is designed to fit into the brace's chuck jaw.

Hand drill bores holes in wood, soft metal and plastics, using twist or countersink bits with 6 mm (¼ in) shanks. A hand crank turns an interlocking gear to rotate the bit; reverse it to withdraw the bit.

Push drill operates with a repetitive pushing motion that turns a bit and drills a pilot hole. You can use the tool with one hand, leaving the other free to hold the work or guide the tool. The drill accepts very fine (2-17 mm), straight-fluted bits called drill points. The points are stored in the handle; a knurled knob opens the handle.

Miniature hand drill holds very small, high-speed steel bits. This model has a collet on both ends to accept the bits. A miniature drill is especially useful for working on models and jewellery. You can also use it to make pilot holes for small screws.

Standard electric hand drill comes with 6, 10 and 13 mm (¼, ⅜ and ½ in) chucks to hold bits. Select a reversible drill so that you can withdraw bits or loosen screws easily, and get one with variable speeds if you want to use it with the various available accessories. Because of its high speed, the 6mm (¼ in) model is good for boring small holes, but the 10 mm (⅜ in) drill (top, left) can handle most DIY jobs, making it a better choice for the home owner. The 13 mm (½ in) drill (left) can bore larger holes, but because it runs at a slower speed, it is unsuitable for sanding and grinding.

Cordless drill is powered by a battery. One type has a battery built into the drill's handle; recharge it by connecting the transformer to the drill and plugging it into a wall socket. The other type has a removable battery pack that is recharged in a separate unit. Each pack takes 15 min to 3 hr to charge and is designed to be recharged more than 300 times. Buy an extra battery so that you can recharge one while using the other. Don't charge (or store) a tool where the temperature is below 5°C or above 40°C. For longer battery life, always turn the drill off whenever you are not using it.

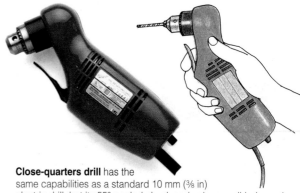

Close-quarters drill has the same capabilities as a standard 10 mm (⅜ in) electric drill, but its 55° angled chuck and unique, well-balanced body shape also allow access to hard-to-reach areas. A finger control allows you to vary the speed up to 1300 rpm. A switch on the bottom of the drill controls forward and reverse directions.

Drill-screwdriver, as the name implies, both drills and drives screws. Its motor has greater torque for driving screws without burning out; it also powers the drill through tough materials quickly. The cordless type, shown here, is easier to manipulate and can be used far from a power outlet without awkward cords.

Drywall driver is designed specifically for driving drywall screws through fibreboard and into wooden studs. The driver tip has a depth stop. Set the torque so that it doesn't overtighten the screw and tear the material or damage the screwhead. Cordless models are available.

Hammer drill can bore into concrete and brick. This tool simultaneously spins a bit and creates a hammering action, which is rated in bpm (blows per minute). The variable-speed feature can turn out up to 40 000 bpm. Most models are reversible and can be quickly switched to a standard rotary-action drill. Some are cordless. A depth stop and a detachable side handle may be included.

D-handle drill is suitable for driving auger bits and for other jobs where high torque is desirable. It comes with a 13 mm (½ in) chuck and with single, double or variable-speed control. The D-shaped spade handle and side handle provide a secure grip for precise control on large jobs.

Right-angle drill has a right-angled head for operating in tight spaces where a standard drill body won't fit. A side handle helps to support the tool. The angled head on this 13 mm (½ in) model can be removed to use the drill straight on; some models do not have this feature. Use high speed for drilling small holes and low speed for large ones.

Drill press combines an electric drill and worktable in one unit. Freestanding and bench-top models are available, but both types must be bolted down. The machine's throat capacity (the space between its rear post and the centre of the bit) determines the maximum size of the workpiece. Secure the work on the machine's table; lower the bit into the work by pulling down on the handle. The permanently positioned drill and adjustable worktable make the drill press the most accurate method of drilling vertical and angled holes. It is also ideal for sanding and shaping attachments.

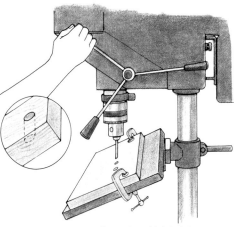

A clamp by the post adjusts the table's height; a clamp under the table adjusts its angle. Clamp smaller work and sheet metal to the table; to guide larger pieces, secure a jig to the table.

DRILL BITS

In order for them to be versatile – so they can make holes of different sizes and in a variety of materials – drills are designed to accept specialised bits. There are bits for wood, ferrous and nonferrous metals, plastic, fibreboard, concrete, masonry, glass and tile. Some bits make extra smooth and accurate entrances and exits, which is desirable in fine woodworking; other, less expensive bits make accurate holes when used properly, but can create rough exits if too much pressure is applied. Most types of bit are available in a wide range of size and quality. For the best results, always use the bit that is recommended for a specific job.

Screw pilot bit comes in several sizes to bore shank and pilot holes for a specific-size wood screw. In the same step you can also create a countersink to recess the screwhead or a counterbore to hide it. The tapered bit (right) creates a snug fit for wood screws.

Twist bit made of carbon steel is designed for wood. For metal, use a bit made of high-speed steel (HSS); lubricate the bit with machine oil when drilling steel or wrought iron, with paraffin when drilling aluminium.

Brad-point bit, the best choice for wood, has a centre point to position it for the exact, clean holes that are required for fine woodworking applications, especially dowelling. Wide flutes eject wood chips to prevent clogging.

Universal countersink, shown here with a drill bit in position, can be adjusted to drill holes from 3 to 7 mm in diameter and counterbores with diameters of 10-15 mm wide. When using the countersink, pass the bit through its centre and position it according to the depth you wish to drill. Align the cutting tips of the counterbore with the cutting edge of the drill bit, and then tighten the screws equally, using the Allen key provided. Take care not to overtighten the screws.

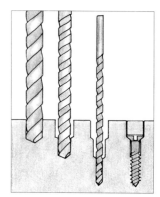

To counterbore a screw without a screw pilot bit, use twist bits slightly narrower than the screw threads and the same width as the head and body. Use a mallet to tap a glued plug into the hole.

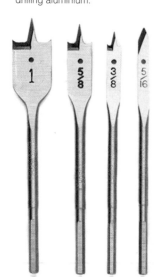

Flat bit has a centre locating point and two sharp flat cutting edges, which work with a scraping action, to bore holes in wood. Start the drill at low speed; as the bit enters the wood, slowly increase the speed. It can leave a rough, splintered exit hole.

Glass/tile bit has carbide tip for boring holes in glass and tile. Drill slowly through pool of turpentine held in by a putty dam.

Countersink bit has an angled tip to form a recess for screwheads in wood, plastic, steel, iron and soft metals. Also use it to deburr and chamfer materials. Lubricate the tip before applying the bit to metal.

Masonry bit is designed for drilling holes at speeds below 400 rpm in masonry, concrete, brick, tile, slate and plaster. The carbide-tipped bit has spiral flutes to channel away dust quickly and efficiently.

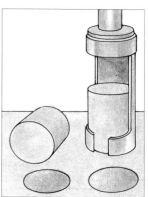

Plug cutter cuts out shapes from hardwood to cover screwheads and nailheads in counterbored holes. The plug should be no less than 3 mm (⅛ in) deep, and no more than 6 mm (½ in) deep. Use the bit with a drill press only.

Auger bit fits into the chuck of a hand brace. The tip of the bit has a point to start holes. The flutes prevent clogging by quickly ejecting wood chips as you drill, an ideal feature for making mortises.

Adjustable bit, or expansion bit, uses adjustable cutters to bore holes of various diameters. It is used to bore holes in wood for installing pipes and wiring and in areas where a rough cut will suffice. To adjust the cutter, release the setscrew; then use the scale on the cutter to determine the hole size and secure the setscrew.

Forstner bit, or centre bit, drills a shallow hole with a sharp outside rim, in wood. It has a small centre spur that enables the bit to create a nearly flat-bottomed hole. To form a mortise, cut overlapping holes. Use the bit in a drill press only.

Fly cutter, or circle cutter, is used on a drill press for cutting circles. A shank holds an arm with a cutter which can be moved to cut different diameters.

Reamer bit is tapered to allow the tip to fit into an already existing hole, whether the material is wood or metal. As the bit moves into the hole, it enlarges the hole. The bit is also useful for removing burrs from metal tubing.

Drill saw bit bores and cuts holes in both wood and metal. After the tip of the bit drills a hole, the teeth on the side of the bit cut the opening. It can also enlarge existing holes. For metal, lubricate the tip before drilling.

Screw point centre bit, a smaller version of the Forstner bit (above) but with a lead screw in the centre, is used for cutting wide, shallow holes in wood. Once the lead screw has 'taken' in the wood, it draws in the rest of the bit with the minimum of effort. It has a square taper shank for fitting into a hand brace.

Step bit incorporates up to 13 diameters in one bit. As the bit penetrates the stock, it drills a larger hole, deburring the hole at the same time. Available in various sizes to cut through wood, plastic and stainless steel up to 13 mm (½ in) thick.

Self-feeding multispur bit bores holes large enough to run conduit or pipes through wood. To provide a fast feeding action, a replaceable threaded screw point pulls the bit to the work. The bit fits ½ in drills only and requires extremely high torque.

Acrylic plastic bit has a tip that can prevent splintering when drilling in plastic. Use scrap plywood or plastic under the work as a backing board. With the work securely clamped to a bench or table, drill slowly with steady pressure. As you near the other side of the work, reduce the amount of pressure on the drill.

Scotch auger is used for heavy-duty boring, especially where power is not available. The eye at the end of the auger takes a strong turning bar. It is about 610 mm (2 ft) long.

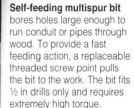

Hole saw with tempered hardened-steel teeth cuts large holes in wood, metal, plastic and fibreboard. The saw is mounted on a hole saw arbor (right) which is inserted into a drill. The bit extends slightly beyond the saw teeth to locate the centre; then the saw is pushed into the stock.

DRILL ACCESSORIES

Although it is not necessary to acquire accessories for your drill, they can make the tool more accurate and easier to use and they can turn the drill into a driver, shaper, sander, grinder or polisher. Some accessories attach to or hold the drill housing, while others fit into the chuck. If you already have a tool such as a sander or grinder, it is best to use that tool for the appropriate job. But if you do not have the additional tools, these attachments are a suitable substitute.

Chuck key comes with an electric drill to lock bits. Hand-tighten bit in chuck; insert key into holes in chuck and turn clockwise. Always remove key before using drill.

Keyless drill chuck operates without a chuck key, by hand-tightening only. You can attach it to a drill that has a standard chuck or purchase one as a replacement part. Some drills are sold with this type of chuck already attached.

Flexible shaft can extend the shaft of an electric drill by about 1 m, making the drill more manageable for intricate detail work and for operations in tight places. One end of the shaft fits into the drill chuck; the other end has its own chuck for small drill bits, rotary rasps and files as well as sanding and buffing attachments.

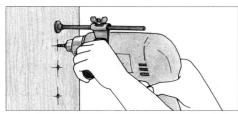

Drill stop and depth stop are guides for drilling holes to a specific depth. A steel drill stop (left) slides onto a bit; a depth stop (right) attaches to the body of an electric hand drill or to a secondary handle and is set to the right position. When either stop contacts the work surface, it stops the penetration of the bit.

Drill gauge is a template for measuring the size of a drill bit. Some have holes from 0.5 to 10 mm, others from 1/32 to 1/2 in. Insert a bit into each hole until you find the one that fits best; the correct dimension is marked near the hole.

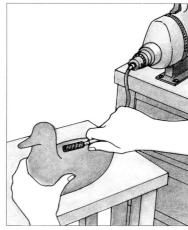

When using a flexible shaft with an electric hand drill, make sure the drill is in a stand secured to a bench. The shaft can also be used with a drill press.

Drill case, available in many styles, organises bits for quick access. Look for a case that indicates bit size near the bit slot. To remove a bit, rotate the lid until the hole in the lid aligns with the desired bit. Tip the case to slide out the bit.

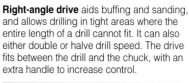

Right-angle drive aids buffing and sanding, and allows drilling in tight areas where the entire length of a drill cannot fit. It can also either double or halve drill speed. The drive fits between the drill and the chuck, with an extra handle to increase control.

Bit extension adds to the length of a hexagonal or flat bit shaft, allowing you to bore deep holes and to make holes in recessed and hard-to-reach places with a spade or auger-type bit. Insert the bit shank into one end of the extension, and secure it with one or two Allen screws. Make sure the bit is seated in a pilot hole before you start drilling. The extension is about 33 cm (13 in) long.

Screwdriver bits let you drive screws with an electric drill; these tempered bits have grooved tips to hold screws more securely.

Screwdriver attachment has a clutch mechanism that stops the drill when the screw is driven in fully or pressure is slackened. Fit the attachment to the chuck of a variable-speed drill and then fix a screwdriver bit into the attachment.

For forward rotation

For reverse rotation

Speed reducer fits on a single-speed electric drill to allow variable-speed operation for screw and nut driving. Hold the reducer's housing when operating. One collar allows forward rotation of the bit; the other collar reverses the direction of rotation.

Rotary files and rasps fit drill presses and flexible shafts. They come in a wide range of shapes; use those with large teeth for wood; with small teeth for metal.

127 mm (5 in) abrasive disc has more than 100 times the life of sandpaper. It is made from tungsten carbide and can be used for sanding and shaping wood, stone, plastic or plaster and for removing rust. Use light pressure and work at an angle of 15°. Make sure it is rotating clockwise before using it.

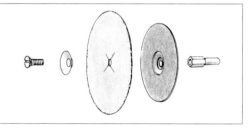

Sandpaper discs convert an electric hand drill to a sander. Some discs are used in conjunction with a backing pad and wheel arbor. Some systems work with self-adhesive sandpaper or have a Velcro backing. Discs are available with garnet and aluminium oxide, in coarse, medium and fine grades.

Drum sander sands curves and irregular shapes in wood, metal, glass fibre and plastic. Lock its shank into the chuck of a portable electric drill or, for better control, in a drill press. The drum is available in various diameters and lengths.

Wire cup brush incorporates wire strands into a circular brush. When mounted in an electric hand drill, it becomes a power scraper for removing paint, rust or stains from wood or metal. Do not exceed maximum speed of 2500 rpm.

Wire wheel, with wires extending from its perimeter, can rotate at a maximum speed of 3000 rpm. You can use it on any size electric drill to remove paint, rust or stains from wood or metal.

Flap wheel sander has a number of sandpaper strips attached to a wheel. The spinning strips conform to the flat or contoured surface of the wood, metal, glass fibre or plastic object you are sanding and buffing. It is available in various sandpaper grits.

Buffing pad is a soft pad for polishing metals. It is usually made of wool or polyester; most pads are washable and reusable.

Fibre disc sands, grinds and cuts paint, rust, metal, tile, brick, concrete and plastic. The disc is made of silicon carbide and attaches to any electric hand drill with a standard backing pad and wheel arbor (right, bottom). Although in some situations it can be used freehand, mounting the drill on a drill stand will allow greater control and safety.

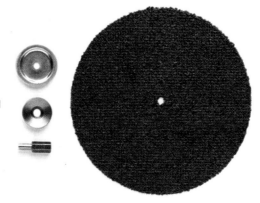

Drilling requires precision boring that is difficult to achieve when holding an electric hand drill, even with steady hands. A variety of drill stands provide the necessary firm support for drilling holes at any angle and when using drill accessories, such as a rotary rasp fixed to a flexible shaft. With buffing, grinding and polishing heads, using a drill stand leaves both hands free to guide the work.

Drill guides ensure the accurate positioning of holes for a variety of drilling applications. The guides on the facing page, with the exception of the mortising attachment, can be used either with an electric hand drill or with a drill press.

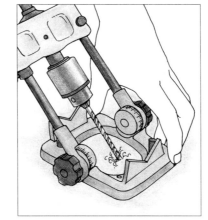

Vertical drill stand is a framework that supports an electric hand drill and turns it into a small bench-top drill press. It has all the basic drill press features: a scaled depth stop, a pull-down handle operation and a worktable. On some models a mounting bracket swivels the drill to a horizontal position for grinding. On other models the worktable can be tilted to make angled cuts. Before using the stand, bolt it securely to a workbench. Some models incorporate a vice.

Precision drill stand attaches to the drill in place of the chuck. Its chuck is mounted on a crosspiece that slides up and down two rods, which are attached to a flat base. The rods can be adjusted and locked into place at 5 degree intervals in order to drill holes at various angles. A collar on one rod acts as a depth stop.

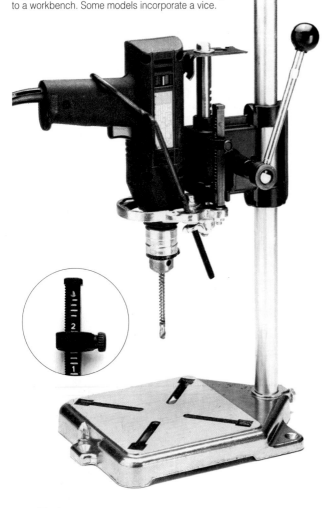

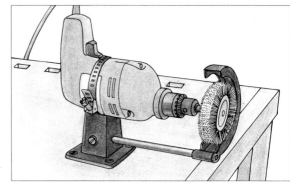

Horizontal drill stand is a base and shield unit that, when bolted to a workbench, holds an electric hand drill in a horizontal position. A metal strap holds the drill securely in place on the stand so that, with various attachments, the drill can be used for sanding, grinding, wire-brushing or polishing. The stand also allows the drill to be operated with a flexible shaft (p.30).

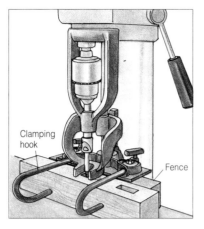

Clamping
hook

Fence

Dowelling jig centres holes in ends or edges of wooden workpieces of almost any thickness. The jig clamps to the workpiece and a centred hole-guide shows where to bore the hole. The holes accommodate standard-diameter dowels.

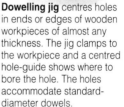

Mortising attachment is bolted on a collar above the chuck of a drill press. A bit removes waste; a chisel shapes the mortise. The attachment includes a fence for guiding the work and clamping hooks to support it. When using the attachment, run the drill press at normal speed and work down to final depth in 3 mm (⅛ in) increments. As the chisel finishes each cut, move the workpiece to continue the mortise.

Dowel centres align corresponding dowel holes in wood workpieces that are to be joined. Drill holes in one workpiece; push dowel centres into the holes, align with the second workpiece and push. The points on the dowel centres leave marks to show where to bore holes in the second workpiece.

Bench sander is used for shaping wood and creating bevelled edges. This model has a mitre gauge which can be set to give angles from 45 to 90 degrees. In addition, the working surface can be tilted downwards to an angle of 45 degrees, giving a wide choice of profiles. The sander is fixed to a bench with sturdy clamps, and is driven by an electric power tool. A metal collar holds the drill in place and protects the chuck. The sander comes with fine, medium and coarse self-adhesive discs.

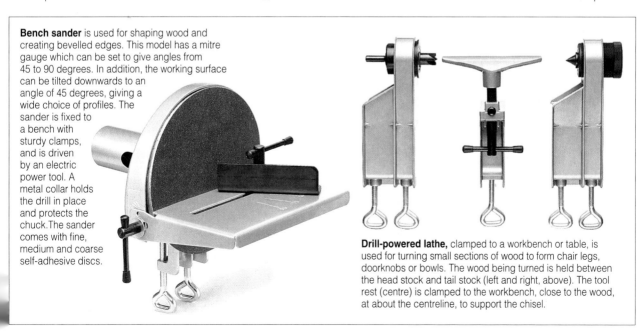

Drill-powered lathe, clamped to a workbench or table, is used for turning small sections of wood to form chair legs, doorknobs or bowls. The wood being turned is held between the head stock and tail stock (left and right, above). The tool rest (centre) is clamped to the workbench, close to the wood, at about the centreline, to support the chisel.

SCREWDRIVERS

Used to insert, remove, loosen and tighten screws, screwdrivers come in many widths and lengths, with different-shaped shanks and with a variety of tips. Screws are driven by torque, or turning power, not by downward pressure. The larger the diameter of the handle, the more torque per turn. Always match the screwdriver tip to the size and type of screw. To drive a screw, hold it and the screwdriver in a straight line. Used normally, a screwdriver will operate without damaging its tip or the screwhead. Never use a screwdriver as a lever, punch or chisel; doing so can damage the tool and the object you are working on.

Round-shank screwdriver has a cylindrical shank, **which is** the steel rod between the tip and handle. The round shape lets you turn the screwdriver quickly by supporting the shank with one hand while rotating the handle with the other.

Stubby screwdriver, designed to be used in restricted areas, has a very short shank. Its large handle permits a firm grip to improve torque.

Square-shank screwdriver is used to drive screws that require a great deal of torque. With an adjustable wrench, grip the square shank and turn the screwdriver; but be careful not to apply too much torque or the screwhead may be stripped or broken. A rubber sleeve over a plastic fluted handle on some screwdrivers also increases torque by enlarging the grip.

Cabinet-handled screwdriver has a fat oval handle that is preferred for woodworking because it fits neatly into the palm of the hand. The parallel-sided tip fits into recessed holes to turn slotted flat-head screws without damaging the wood.

Standard (slotted) screwdriver, the most common type, fits slotted screws. The flared, or winged, tip (left) is best for round or oval-head screws; parallel-sided tip (see cabinet-handled) is best for flat-head screws.

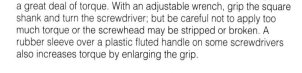

Electrician's screwdriver, designed for working on electrical appliances and equipment, is made with a long shank to reach into deep electrical boxes. It has a plastic tube round the shank to protect the user from electric shock. Before starting work, unplug appliance or turn off power.

Phillips screwdriver fits snugly into a Phillips-head screw. Once the most common cross-head screwdriver, it has been overtaken by Supadriv. It cannot be used successfully on Supadriv screws.

Torx screwdriver, widely used in car repair work, has a star-shaped tip that can be useful for replacing such parts as tail-light lenses. Torx screws are found in household appliances as well as in gardening equipment.

Hex-drive screwdriver for screws that can also be operated with hex keys or Allen keys. Suitable for socket-head screws that are recessed, the screwdriver is available in imperial and metric sizes.

Supadriv screwdriver, the most common cross-head screwdriver, has a square end instead of a pointed tip, like the Phillips. However, in an emergency, it can be used on a Phillips screwhead.

Ball-end hex-drive screwdriver, for socket-head screws, has a round tip that can be angled up to 25 degrees from the surface. This makes it helpful for reaching screws in tight spots. The screwdriver can drive the screw without stripping it.

Security screwdriver is unusual because its tip has three flutes and is flattened. It conforms to a type of screw which is sometimes found in electrical appliances and which is almost impossible to loosen without the correct screwdriver.

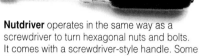

Nutdriver operates in the same way as a screwdriver to turn hexagonal nuts and bolts. It comes with a screwdriver-style handle. Some models come in colour-coded or marked sets to make it easy to identify the size.

Robertson screwdriver, usually colour-coded according to size, can reach screws that are sunk below the surface in furniture and in mobile homes, caravans and boats. The square drive in this screwdriver provides high torque power.

Expansion-tip screwdriver holds a slotted screw as you start to drive it. To use this tool, insert the tip into the screw slot and slide the collar over the split blade, forcing the halves to wedge against each other and to lock into and hold the screw.

Offset screwdriver, useful for driving screws in hard-to-reach spots, is operated with a cranking action. The tips are set at 45 or 90 degrees to the shank; they may be slotted or Phillips – or the screwdriver may have one of each. A ratchet model (far left) lets you drive the screw with a back-and-forth motion without removing the screwdriver.

Cordless power screwdriver, with interchangeable tips, lets you drive a large number of screws without the fatigue of hand-driving. To drive or remove screws, a switch allows you to change the direction of rotation. This model has a locking shaft to permit hand operation as a standard screwdriver for extra torque. To recharge the screwdriver, plug it into a charging unit or place a battery in the unit. Power screwdrivers also come with electrical cords.

Adjustable power screwdriver has a hinge in the middle of its body, which can be snapped into two positions: the conventional straight line of a screwdriver or an angled pistol-grip hold. The torque can also be adjusted on this cordless tool.

Jeweller's screwdriver is ideal for small screws in items like eyeglasses. To use it, apply pressure to the screwdriver's head with your index fingertip; turn the tools' body with your other fingers.

Magnetic screwdriver takes interchangeable tips, which come in popular types and sizes. A magnetic end holds the tips in place. Some models have a ratchet operation for fast work at high torque, as well as a switch for reversing the direction of the drive. The handle may be hollow to store the tips.

Spiral ratchet screwdriver lets you turn a screw by repeatedly pushing the handle. A ratchet switch changes the direction of the shank rotation to allow for both driving and removing screws. The knurled collar just below the switch will lock the shank in the retracted position for use as a conventional screwdriver. In some models the handle provides storage for extra tips.

Screw holder, an attachment that snaps onto most round-shank screwdrivers, allows the positioning of screws where fingers cannot reach. To start a screw, slip it between the holder jaws. Before driving the screw in all the way, slide the holder up the shank, out of the way. It comes in several sizes.

Bradawl (top) and **gimlet** (bottom) are tools for boring pilot holes in wood, making it easier to drive a screw. To use either tool, turn it clockwise. The pilot hole should be narrower and shorter than the screw, leaving enough material for the screw threads to grasp. Gimlets are available in various screw sizes.

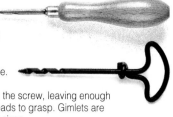

Whether they grip a hard-to-hold workpiece or cut wire or other objects, all pliers have the same design: handles on one side of a pivot joint, for a scissor-type action, and jaws on the other side. Always use a pair of pliers for the job they were intended to do. The smaller long-nose pliers are delicate; forcing them to do work beyond their capacity can render them useless. Use pliers to turn nuts only in an emergency; pliers can strip the nut, making it difficult to remove with the proper tool. Unless explicitly stated, do not assume that pliers designed for electrical work are insulated, even if the handles have a plastic, rubber or similar coating.

Slip-joint pliers have both serrated teeth and coarse contoured teeth to grip objects of different shapes. They can be set in two positions to vary the jaw size.

Curved thin-nose slip-joint pliers are made with a specially shaped nose to let you see the work. As with most slip-joint pliers, they have wire cutters in the jaws.

Angle-nose pliers, slip-joint pliers with three adjustable settings, have an offset head for hard-to-reach areas where added leverage is needed.

Groove-joint pliers grip flat, square, round or hexagonal objects with serrated teeth. The jaws can be set in five positions by slipping the curved ridge into the desired groove.

Straight-jaw locking pliers, also called mole grips, clamp firmly onto objects. A knob in one handle controls the jaws' width and tension. Close handles to lock the pliers; release a lever to open.

Large groove-joint pliers, often used for holding pipes, give increased leverage because of long handles. The jaws stay parallel at all settings, giving them a better grip than slip-joint pliers.

Long-nose pliers, or snipe-nose pliers, hold small objects, especially in electrical work. Narrow, flat jaws may have serrated teeth. They can fit into confined areas and can grip parts. Some models have a wire cutter.

Needle-nose pliers, a smaller version of long-nose pliers, may have smooth, thin, tapered jaws that won't mark or scratch. They are ideal for working with soft metals, especially in jewellery. Some models have serrated teeth, and some have spring-loaded handles.

Bent-nose pliers are also ideal for working on jewellery or small electrical items. The bent nose holds the workpiece away from the pliers and in the user's line of vision.

Round-nose pliers are favoured by electricians and jewellers. They have smooth, tapered, round jaws for bending thin wire and sheet metal into loops of different sizes.

Needle-nose end-cutting pliers work best for cutting thin wire. The cutting area is at the tip of the jaws for cutting items flush or in tight areas.

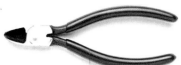  

Diagonal-cutting pliers, also called side-cutting nippers, are designed for cutting wire and thin metal. The cutting area is positioned on the side edge of the jaws to cut precise wire lengths and for cutting flush against a surface or in cramped spaces where larger tools cannot fit.

End-cutting nippers are a larger oval-head version of the needle-nose end-cutting pliers, for heavier wire. Their design keeps knuckles out of the way while cutting the wire flush. They also come with angled jaws.

Fence pliers combine several features in one tool for working on high-tensile wire. The head has wire-cutting slots on each side; the jaws are for straining wire; the hammer head is suitable for driving in staples and the claw pulls them out.

Tile nippers chip, shape and trim irregular contours in ceramic tile up to 13 mm (½ in) thick. They are ideal for shaping tiles to fit round plumbing fixtures.

Bolt cutters are heavy-duty metal-cutting pliers that cut soft to medium-hard materials such as rods, bolts and wire. The handles can be 36-60 cm (14-24 in) long. The length of the handles along with a well-designed pivot mechanism provide the leverage needed to cut through metals.

Wire stripper removes insulation from wire. To stop the blades from cutting into the wire, adjust a screw in a handle; it blocks the handles and the jaws. A band holds the handles closed when not in use.

Wire stripper and cutter removes insulation from a wire and cuts it. To strip a section of wire, place it in a hole, squeeze the handles and pull off the insulation. To cut the wire, set it between the jaws' sharp flat edges.

Pincers are for removing nails from wood. Position the curved jaws over the head of the nail, squeeze the handles and rock the tool to lever out the nail.

Automatic wire stripper cuts and strips wire in one squeeze of the handles, unlike other strippers that require you to pull off the insulation after cutting it. This stripper has two sets of jaws: one pair holds the wire; the other pair cuts and pulls off the insulation, exposing enough bare wire for a connection.

Electrician's pliers are a combination of flat-jaw pliers and wire cutters. The outer portion of the jaws is flat and serrated for a solid grip when pulling and twisting wire. The inner portion of the jaws is a basic cable and wire cutter.

Multipurpose electrician's pliers can measure, strip and cut wire. They also crimp wire connectors and cut machine screws. Models vary in functions, so buy one that suits your needs. As with other wire strippers, the handles do not insulate against electricity.

Tweezers and tongs

While not technically pliers, these holding tools are necessary for delicate work as well as for protecting hands from heat and chemicals.

Tweezers are used for holding small objects. They are ideal for miniature work and making jewellery, and they can help to remove wood or metal splinters. They can have straight or curved blades, with sharp, rounded or flat points that are either smooth or serrated.

Soldering tweezers are fireproof fine-point tools for holding small pieces of metal during soldering. These cross-locking models can double as clamps. To push the ends apart, apply pressure to the centre part of the tool, at the point where the arms overlap.

SPANNERS

Spanners are turning tools that fit around nuts and bolts to provide the needed leverage to loosen and tighten them. A spanner may be fixed, so that it fits only one size of nut or bolt, or adjustable to fit different sizes. Fixed spanners come in both metric and imperial sizes and each is used on the exactly corresponding size nut or bolt. No matter how close the size might seem, using a spanner that is 'almost right' can damage the hardware. One side of the head on some fixed spanners is open to allow the spanner slide into place – useful in cramped working spaces. Ring spanners are stronger, however, and less likely to slip as they engage the nut from the top. They come with 8 points to fit square nuts or with 6 or 12 points to fit hexagonal nuts.

Obstruction spanner is a double open-ended spanner that has one standard open head on one end and a head of the same size on the other end with the opening angled up to 90 degrees. The angled head allows the user to reach nuts or bolts that are otherwise hard to reach.

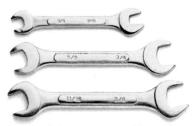

Open-ended spanner has a different-sized opening at each end. They are close in size and in some sets each end will match one on the previous or next size of spanner, providing two same-sized heads – one to turn the nut, the other to hold the bolt. Extra-thin spanners are available too.

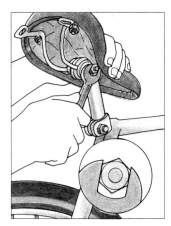

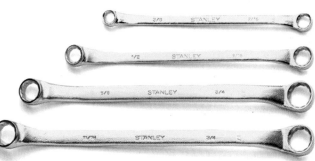

Combination spanner gives you a choice of two different ends of the same size to loosen or tighten a nut or bolt. Use the ring end when the job calls for strength and the speedier open end when less torque is needed.

Crow's-foot spanner, an open-ended head without a handle, is quite rare and has a square hole that accepts either a socket handle or an extension. Depending on the type of handle you choose, the head can be used in line with the handle or at an angle, making it exceptionally useful for tightening or loosening nuts in odd positions.

Torque wrench turns nuts and bolts to an exact tightness. It is ideal for tightening a number of fasteners to the same degree to avoid warping. A scale is attached to the handle of some models; the torque (turning force) is indicated by a pointer that remains stationary as the handle bends under stress. All models accept standard square-drive sockets and adapters; but measuring devices and the amount of torque may vary.

Flare-nut spanner for copper and brass fittings slides over tubing, then down to the fitting. It has a better grip than an open-ended spanner.

Offset double ring spanner is designed for hexagonal or square nuts and bolts. Its handle curves away from the work surface, leaving room for gripping. The rings fit more securely round the fastener than the open-end type. After each turn, lift the wrench and reposition it before continuing.

Multiple ring spanner has five different openings on each head. The handle gives very little leverage, making it suitable only for light work. Its compactness means it is ideal as an extra spanner on bicycle trips.

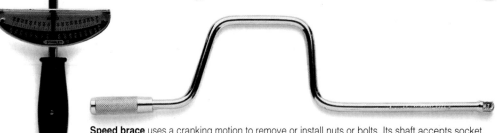

Speed brace uses a cranking motion to remove or install nuts or bolts. Its shaft accepts socket heads, adapters and extensions. The grip remains stationary while the shaft is turned clockwise for tightening fasteners, anticlockwise for loosening.

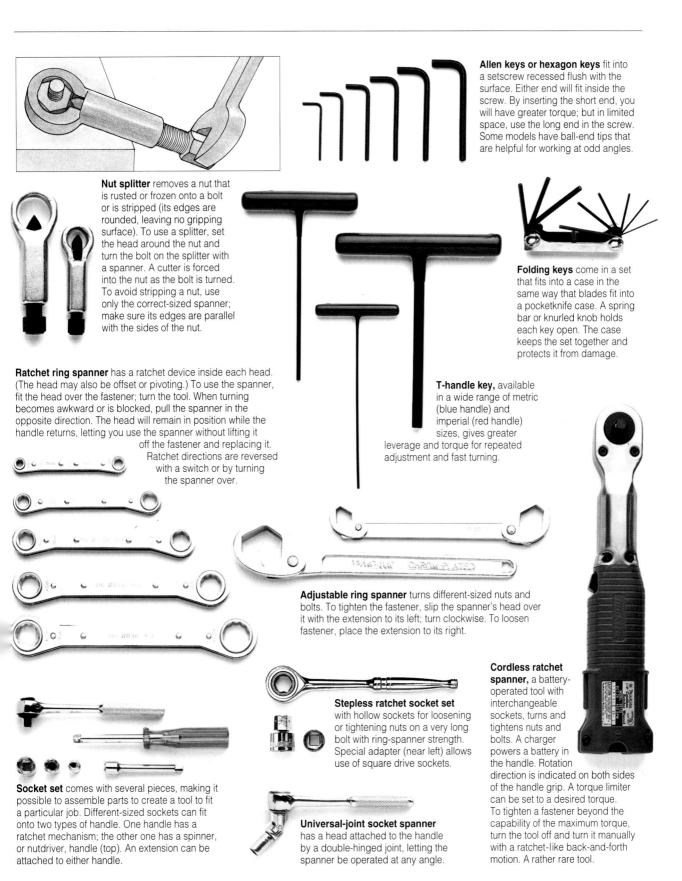

Allen keys or hexagon keys fit into a setscrew recessed flush with the surface. Either end will fit inside the screw. By inserting the short end, you will have greater torque; but in limited space, use the long end in the screw. Some models have ball-end tips that are helpful for working at odd angles.

Nut splitter removes a nut that is rusted or frozen onto a bolt or is stripped (its edges are rounded, leaving no gripping surface). To use a splitter, set the head around the nut and turn the bolt on the splitter with a spanner. A cutter is forced into the nut as the bolt is turned. To avoid stripping a nut, use only the correct-sized spanner; make sure its edges are parallel with the sides of the nut.

Folding keys come in a set that fits into a case in the same way that blades fit into a pocketknife case. A spring bar or knurled knob holds each key open. The case keeps the set together and protects it from damage.

Ratchet ring spanner has a ratchet device inside each head. (The head may also be offset or pivoting.) To use the spanner, fit the head over the fastener; turn the tool. When turning becomes awkward or is blocked, pull the spanner in the opposite direction. The head will remain in position while the handle returns, letting you use the spanner without lifting it off the fastener and replacing it. Ratchet directions are reversed with a switch or by turning the spanner over.

T-handle key, available in a wide range of metric (blue handle) and imperial (red handle) sizes, gives greater leverage and torque for repeated adjustment and fast turning.

Adjustable ring spanner turns different-sized nuts and bolts. To tighten the fastener, slip the spanner's head over it with the extension to its left; turn clockwise. To loosen fastener, place the extension to its right.

Stepless ratchet socket set with hollow sockets for loosening or tightening nuts on a very long bolt with ring-spanner strength. Special adapter (near left) allows use of square drive sockets.

Cordless ratchet spanner, a battery-operated tool with interchangeable sockets, turns and tightens nuts and bolts. A charger powers a battery in the handle. Rotation direction is indicated on both sides of the handle grip. A torque limiter can be set to a desired torque. To tighten a fastener beyond the capability of the maximum torque, turn the tool off and turn it manually with a ratchet-like back-and-forth motion. A rather rare tool.

Socket set comes with several pieces, making it possible to assemble parts to create a tool to fit a particular job. Different-sized sockets can fit onto two types of handle. One handle has a ratchet mechanism; the other one has a spinner, or nutdriver, handle (top). An extension can be attached to either handle.

Universal-joint socket spanner has a head attached to the handle by a double-hinged joint, letting the spanner be operated at any angle.

ADJUSTABLE WRENCHES

Designed to accept pipes, pipe fittings, bolts and nuts, the adjustable wrench may have two jaws – one fixed, the other movable – or a strap or chain that grips the object to loosen or tighten it. Use one of these wrenches when the right-sized fixed wrench is not available or for special tasks such as reaching under a basin. An adjustable wrench usually works best with pressure put on the stationary jaw, not the movable one.

Adjustable wrench is a versatile smooth-jawed wrench for turning nuts, bolts, chrome-faced pipe fittings and small pipe fittings. The movable jaw is adjusted with a worm gear, accessible on both sides of the head. Some models have a measurement scale on the fixed jaw.

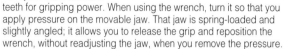

Stillson wrench
turns threaded pipes.
The upper jaw is
adjusted by turning
the knurled knob.
Both jaws have serrated
teeth for gripping power. When using the wrench, turn it so that you apply pressure on the movable jaw. That jaw is spring-loaded and slightly angled; it allows you to release the grip and reposition the wrench, without readjusting the jaw, when you remove the pressure.

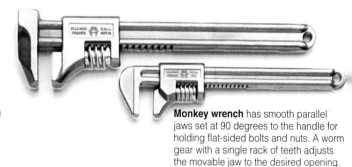

Monkey wrench has smooth parallel jaws set at 90 degrees to the handle for holding flat-sided bolts and nuts. A worm gear with a single rack of teeth adjusts the movable jaw to the desired opening.

Footprint pipe wrench is a traditional, all-purpose plumber's tool that grips the workpiece more tightly as more pressure is exerted.

Vice-grip chain clamp and pipe wrench turns irregularly shaped items and can also clamp together objects of up to a 150 mm (6 in) diameter. Wrap the chain round the object and slide it under the tool's hook. Adjust the thumbscrew to tighten or loosen the chain. Lock the chain in position by squeezing the handles; unlock it by squeezing the lever inside one of the handles.

Chain wrench fits around any large pipe or oddly shaped object. Wrap the chain round the object and secure it on the other side of the jaw. Pull the wrench downwards (with the hook on top).

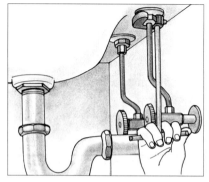

Basin wrench, a plumbing tool for removing and installing taps, has a long handle to reach up under a basin or sink to turn nuts on copper and polythene pipe fittings and taps. The hinged jaw repositions itself after each turn. Buy one with a reversible jaw.

Strap wrench has a canvas webbing that wraps around pipes without marking their finish. Hold the wrench with the claw pointing down; loop the strap around the pipe, then into the opening. Pull the wrench towards the strap's free end.

A clamping tool that holds work steady, the vice is attached, permanently or temporarily, to a work surface. Specialised woodworking vices have smooth wood or metal jaws; metalworking vices have serrated teeth on their steel jaws. Be sure to match the vice to the job; improper use can damage the vice or the workpiece. To protect the workpiece, fasten a jaw face between it and the jaws of the vice. For woodworking, use wood or hardboard jaw faces; if the work is metal, bend smooth sheet metal (at least as wide as the jaws) to a right angle over the jaws or use fibre-faced magnetic jaws.

Mechanic's vice is permanently bolted to a bench top for metalworking. Many models incorporate a small anvil and have a swivel base that locks in place. Some vices can hold round pipe with round serrated pipe jaws located under the flat jaws.

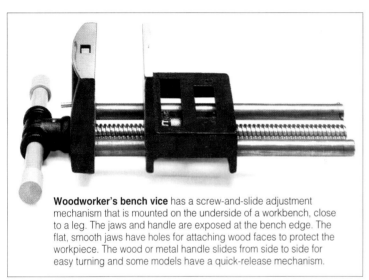

Woodworker's bench vice has a screw-and-slide adjustment mechanism that is mounted on the underside of a workbench, close to a leg. The jaws and handle are exposed at the bench edge. The flat, smooth jaws have holes for attaching wood faces to protect the workpiece. The wood or metal handle slides from side to side for easy turning and some models have a quick-release mechanism.

Drill press vice is bolted onto a drill press worktable to hold metal tubing securely for drilling. Some models tilt for drilling angled holes. Jaws are grooved for a better grip.

Corner cramp is used for holding mitred joints together under pressure. Apply glue to the meeting faces, align them and then gently adjust the pressure on each half of the joint until it is held firmly. Mounting holes in the body of the cramp can be used to fix it to the workbench. Some models of corner cramp have a saw slot which bisects the angle. It is used to guide the blade of a tenon saw to cut an accurate 45 degree angle.

Bench holdfast has a long shaft that slides through a metal collar, which is countersunk in the bench. A lever arm is attached to the notched shaft by a pivot. Turning the screw forces the lever, and the swivel shoe at the end of it, down onto the work. Set a few collars along the edges of the bench to vary your working position.

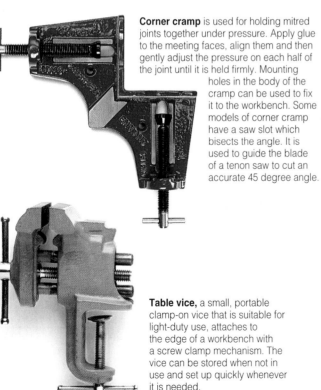

Table vice, a small, portable clamp-on vice that is suitable for light-duty use, attaches to the edge of a workbench with a screw clamp mechanism. The vice can be stored when not in use and set up quickly whenever it is needed.

Vice pegs, whether metal or wood, clamp work in a bench vice. One peg fits into a hole in the bench (you may have to make it); the other peg fits in the movable vice jaw or it may be part of the vice.

Whenever you need extra hands to hold pieces together temporarily, use clamps – which are sometimes called cramps. Use them to grip meeting parts while driving nails or drilling holes for screws, to test-fit pieces before gluing them or to hold a freshly glued assembly until the glue dries.

They come in many sizes and styles. Some have specific applications, while others are used in a variety of situations. Every workshop should have a range of top-quality clamps; buy them in pairs as you need them. The more clamps you have, the better; according to one traditional rule of thumb, too many clamps are just enough. When using clamps, be sure to apply pressure evenly from two sides to avoid twisting the work.

Edge cramp
has three screws extending from the frame to exert right-angled pressure on the edge or side of a workpiece. A three-way edge clamp is also used for positioning a workpiece. The right-angle, or centre, screw can be positioned on or off centre on workpieces of varying thicknesses.

Set of three G-cramps is useful to have for projects where space is limited. Their slim but strong forged steel construction makes them ideal for many small tasks.

Deep-throated G-cramps are shaped for clamping towards the centre of a workpiece, distributing pressure evenly. The deep throat is particularly useful for holding wide pieces where the shallow-throat frame of a standard G-cramp are inadequate. As with most clamps, attach a piece of scrap wood to each jaw with double-sided tape to keep the jaws from marking the work.

G-cramps get their name from their G-shaped frame. A shoe at one end of the screw holds the work against the frame; at the other end is a T-bar. To tighten the screw against the work or change the size of the opening, adjust the screw by turning the T-bar. These cramps are sometimes called C-cramps.

Small parallel clamp operates in a similar way to the hand-screw clamp (far left and below), but its jaws are set parallel. It is ideal for working with small or thin pieces without taking up too much workspace.

Hand-screw clamp can spread pressure over a broad surface area. The jaws work independently, allowing them to angle towards or away from each other or to remain parallel. Set the jaws slightly wider than desired by holding the spindles and rotating the clamp. Slip the jaws over the work and tighten the rear spindle.

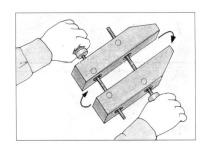

Quick grip spreader is useful when outward pressure needs to be exerted to force two surfaces apart. It is both strong and lightweight and the fast action of the pistol grip and trigger add to its ease of handling. It is designed for one-handed use, freeing the other hand to position the workpiece.

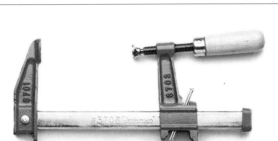

Fast-action bar clamp consists of a bar with a fixed jaw and a sliding jaw. A spring locking device fixes the sliding jaw in place. Set the workpiece against the fixed jaw and slide the other jaw to the work (with the screw set away from the work). Once the clamp is positioned, tighten the screw to hold the work securely.

Solo clamp, as its name implies, is designed for single-handed use. The jaws of the clamp have nylon pads to protect easily marked workpieces. Some models have swivelling metal shoes fitted to the ends of the jaws. The quick-release handle speeds up repetitive work.

Spring clamp operates with hand pressure to open the jaws. Spring pressure forces the jaws closed when the handles are released, allowing the jaws to grip the work. Some models have plastic-coated handles for easier opening and coated tips to protect the workpiece.

Cam-action clamp has a sliding jaw that adjusts quickly to the size of the work. A handle in the movable jaw is set in a perpendicular position to lock both the jaw and the work in place. The jaws are padded with cork to prevent damaging the work surface. Its light weight makes this clamp suitable for most delicate work.

Cramp heads are used in conjunction with a sturdy piece of timber 25 mm thick to create your own sash cramp (see overleaf). Drill a series of holes in the timber at regular intervals to take the fastening pin attached to the head and slide. Once the head and slide are in position, make final adjustments by turning the T-bar. The cast-iron head and slide offer a large thrust surface or clamping area.

Sash cramp is used to hold large boards or frames together while they are being glued. It consists of a steel bar, drilled at intervals to take the fixing peg of a tail slide. The fixing peg is attached by a chain to the tail slide and fits into a hole behind the slide to act as a stop. To hold the workpiece in place, tighten the adjustable jaw which is fixed at the other end of the bar by turning a steel screw with a sliding bar.

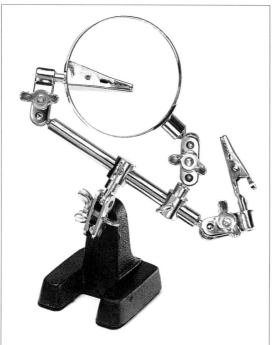

Locking pliers clamp has a sliding jaw that is held in place when pressure is applied from the workpiece. The other jaw is attached to locking handles. Squeezing the handles together applies pressure to the attached jaw – and to the work. A lever in one handle releases the pressure. The frame comes in different shapes to hold pipes and wide workpieces. There are other styles of jaw-locking pliers available.

Third hand is indispensable for making delicate repairs, jewellery or models. Two small crocodile clips on universal joints hold light objects, freeing both hands. An adjustable magnifying glass gives close-up view. Lock crocodile clips and magnifying glass in desired position with wing nuts.

Bench stop is set into a rectangular hole in the surface of a workbench and fixed with three screws. Turning the control which is set into the stop raises the toothed edge to prevent the movement of a workpiece when you are planing it. When the toothed edge is lowered, it is flush with the bench.

Quick-Grip bar clamp has a movable jaw with a pistol-shaped handle. To slide the jaw, pull the trigger near the handle; squeeze the grip to apply jaw pressure. The jaws have removable rubber pads to protect surfaces. An additional corner pad helps when clamping right-angle joints. The lightweight nylon body is resistant to paints, solvents and lubricants.

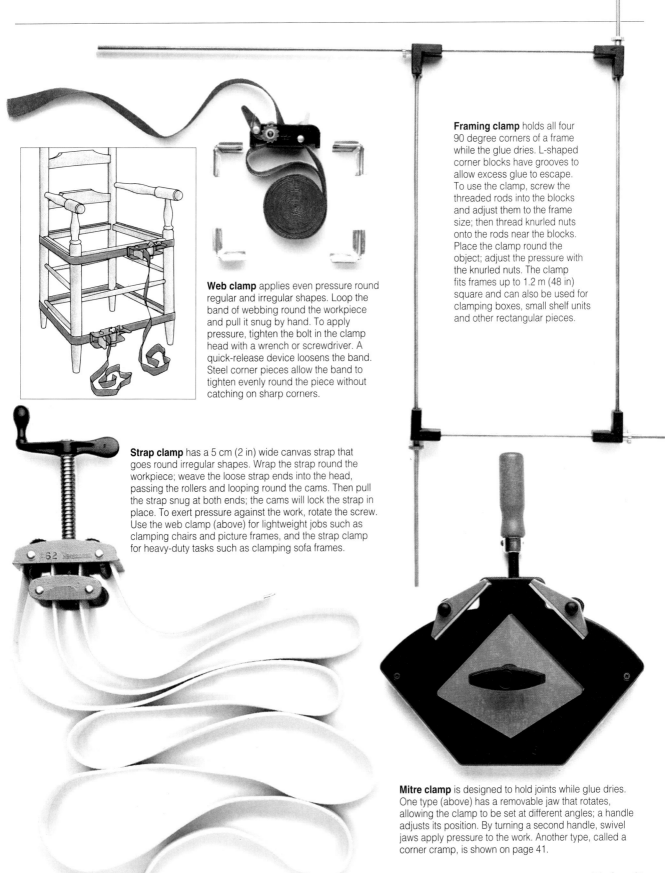

Framing clamp holds all four 90 degree corners of a frame while the glue dries. L-shaped corner blocks have grooves to allow excess glue to escape. To use the clamp, screw the threaded rods into the blocks and adjust them to the frame size; then thread knurled nuts onto the rods near the blocks. Place the clamp round the object; adjust the pressure with the knurled nuts. The clamp fits frames up to 1.2 m (48 in) square and can also be used for clamping boxes, small shelf units and other rectangular pieces.

Web clamp applies even pressure round regular and irregular shapes. Loop the band of webbing round the workpiece and pull it snug by hand. To apply pressure, tighten the bolt in the clamp head with a wrench or screwdriver. A quick-release device loosens the band. Steel corner pieces allow the band to tighten evenly round the piece without catching on sharp corners.

Strap clamp has a 5 cm (2 in) wide canvas strap that goes round irregular shapes. Wrap the strap round the workpiece; weave the loose strap ends into the head, passing the rollers and looping round the cams. Then pull the strap snug at both ends; the cams will lock the strap in place. To exert pressure against the work, rotate the screw. Use the web clamp (above) for lightweight jobs such as clamping chairs and picture frames, and the strap clamp for heavy-duty tasks such as clamping sofa frames.

Mitre clamp is designed to hold joints while glue dries. One type (above) has a removable jaw that rotates, allowing the clamp to be set at different angles; a handle adjusts its position. By turning a second handle, swivel jaws apply pressure to the work. Another type, called a corner cramp, is shown on page 41.

KNIVES, SNIPS AND SCRAPERS

Cutting and scraping tools are necessities for everything from opening taped boxes to removing chipped paint from walls. There are two basic types of knives: one has a sharp blade for cutting materials; the other type has a larger, duller blade for applying compounds to walls and ceilings. Scrapers also have sharp blades; they are used to remove material from a surface. When using a cutting tool, always make sure that the blade is sharp; a dull blade can damage the material it's used on and even cause injury to the user.

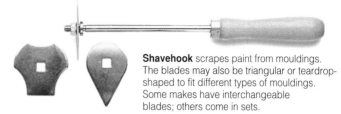

Shavehook scrapes paint from mouldings. The blades may also be triangular or teardrop-shaped to fit different types of mouldings. Some makes have interchangeable blades; others come in sets.

Window scraper removes paint from windowpane without damaging the putty. Hold the scraper so that the wheels glide against the window trim; blade scrapes off paint.

Four-edge blade scraper (above) is for quick paint and varnish removal. Use the knob to apply extra pressure. Two blade edges scrape at once; turn blade over or replace it when dull.

Razor-blade scraper uses a single-edged razor blade to scrape paint and stickers off windowpanes. One model (left) has a retractable blade. The blade on the other model (far left) can be locked in several different positions.

Utility-blade scraper (left) has a guide to help to remove paint from window panes and other flat surfaces.

Craft knife has numerous blades for various tasks and the handle comes in different sizes. A large handle helps cut hard materials; a small handle is better for precision cuts. Craft knives come in various styles and weights. Depending on the blade and handle, the knife can cut paper, plastic, wood, cloth and metal.

Vinyl knife has a blade ideal for scoring hard and soft vinyl and other similar floor coverings.

Trimming knife can be used to cut wood, vinyl and other materials. Some models have a button to adjust the length of the blade and retract the blade into the handle for safety. Spare blades are stored in the handle. Other models have fixed blades. A wide range of blades is available. Large, curved blade (top) is for linoleum and leather; straight blade (centre) cuts paper, card, leather and sheet materials; hooked blade (bottom) penetrates and cuts floor covering and plastic sheeting.

Plastic cutter has angled blade edges for scoring acrylic and other brittle materials. Turn the tool over to use it in an offset position.

Snap-off blade knife has blades that can be snapped off when dull. In this model, the end cap pulls off to allow insertion of the blade cartridge. To snap off a blade, use a slot in the end cap. A locking button adjusts blade position and retracts it into handle.

Razor knife holds a replaceable, standard double-edged razor blade to trim and cut wall coverings, paper and similar materials. Loosen the nut and turn the blade through 90 degrees to give a side-edge cutting surface.

Shoe knife is a general purpose knife, usually with a 102 mm (4 in) blade made of high-carbon steel.

Chisel knife (left) and **filling knife** (right) can be used to spread and smooth wood putty, filler or sealant, and to patch plaster and other similar materials. A chisel knife can also be used to scrape away paint, glue, vinyl and paper wall coverings.

Painter's five-in-one tool has a blade that functions as a paint scraper, putty remover and spreader, gouger and paint roller cleaner. Useful when making repairs, installing window glass, painting and hanging wall coverings.

Joint knife, with a large blade for spreading and smoothing wide areas of joint compound over plasterboard tape, can also be used to patch and smooth wall coverings.

Right-angle joint knife lets you apply wall plaster or joint compound smoothly to corners where walls meet. The handle is offset to allow clearance for fingers.

Putty knife has a Clipt point blade – that is, with one side curved and the other cut at an oblique angle. Press the putty into place with your thumb. Then use the curved edge of the knife to 'rough' it into position. Finally, drag the oblique-angled tip of the knife along the putty to create a bevel edge.

Hacking knife, for chipping away old putty from a window, has a blade that is thicker on one side for use with a hammer. Hold the slightly angled blade tip with the point against the putty. Drive a hammer against the thicker edge of the blade to remove the putty.

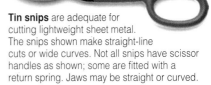

Tin snips are adequate for cutting lightweight sheet metal. The snips shown make straight-line cuts or wide curves. Not all snips have scissor handles as shown; some are fitted with a return spring. Jaws may be straight or curved.

Compound action snips (also known as aviation snips) cut sheet metal with less effort than tin snips. Their compound lever action provides greater control with less hand pressure. The serrated jaws prevent slippage and withstand heavy use. All compound action snips cut straight lines. Specific heads also cut left curves, right curves and a combination of all three cuts. The grips are colour-coded: yellow for combination cuts, red for left-hand curves and green for right-hand curves.

Metal nibblers use a replaceable die and punch combination to cut stainless steel and corrugated sheet metal. They are excellent in hard-to-reach areas and the cutting action ensures that metal is not distorted. They can make straight and curved cuts. To make an internal cut, first drill a starter hole.

Metal shears are cutters for making burr-free straight lines; tight right and left curves; and round, square and irregularly shaped holes. Use them to cut sheet metal, laminates, rigid plastic, vinyl, carpeting, foam rubber and chipboard. The shears can cut up to 5 m (16 ft) per minute. A trigger-operated control allows variable-speed operation. Some models have a head that can swivel 360 degrees.

Tools   47

HANDSAWS

The best handsaws are made of fine-tempered steel and have well-shaped wooden handles. The main difference among handsaws is the shape, number and pitch of their teeth, which make them suitable for cutting wood across the grain or with it, along curved lines or through metal, plastic or wallboard. To prevent binding, saw teeth are usually set or angled away from the blade so that the path or kerf that they cut is slightly wider than the blade's thickness. Generally the more points or teeth per inch (ppi and tpi) a saw has, the smoother and more slowly it cuts. (The number of teeth per inch is always one fewer than the points per inch.) Blades are usually measured in inches.

Plasterboard saw, or drywall saw, makes cutouts in plasterboard for electrical outlets or appliances. The average blade is 6 to 9½ in long with about 11 ppi. The sharp point lets you make plunge cuts without first drilling a hole to accept the blade.

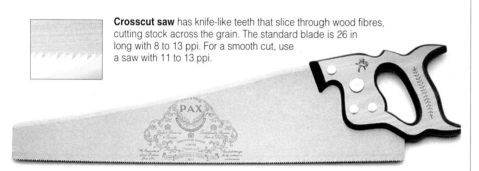

Crosscut saw has knife-like teeth that slice through wood fibres, cutting stock across the grain. The standard blade is 26 in long with 8 to 13 ppi. For a smooth cut, use a saw with 11 to 13 ppi.

Saw set can be used to bend the teeth of a handsaw to the angle needed to effect the desired cut. Sharpen the saw first. Then turn the wheel-like anvil of the saw set to the proper angle, position the jaws of the saw set over a saw tooth, and squeeze the tool's handles together; a plunger will push the saw tooth against the anvil.

Tenon saw is a crosscutting saw for making joints, especially mitres and tenons. The squared end and stiffened rib along its back keep the blade rigid while cutting. Standard blades are 8 to 14 in long with 12 to 15 ppi.

Floorboard or veneer saw has a blade that can be resharpened and has curved teeth in the nose section. Use it for cutting thinner section plywood, chipboard and laminates. Another version has an extra-wide blade with fine, hardened teeth suited for cutting floorboards. Blade length is about 12 in in both versions.

Ripsaw cuts parallel with wood grain by gouging a groove in the wood with coarse teeth shaped like miniature chisels. The standard blade is 26 in long and has 5-8 ppi. A ripsaw with 6½ ppi gives a smooth, fast cut.

General-purpose saw makes both crosscuts and rip cuts in wood and is ideal if you can have only one saw. Its teeth have three bevelled sides, which provide razor-sharp cutting, and deep gullets (spaces between the teeth), which make it easier to clear chips away fast. The blade is 26 in long with 10 ppi, and gives a fast, smooth cut.

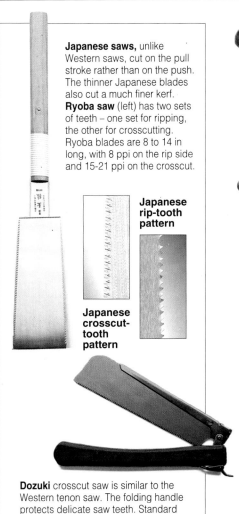

Japanese saws, unlike Western saws, cut on the pull stroke rather than on the push. The thinner Japanese blades also cut a much finer kerf.

Ryoba saw (left) has two sets of teeth – one set for ripping, the other for crosscutting. Ryoba blades are 8 to 14 in long, with 8 ppi on the rip side and 15-21 ppi on the crosscut.

Japanese rip-tooth pattern

Japanese crosscut-tooth pattern

Veneer saw is a small double-edged tool for cutting thin hardwood veneers. Its narrow curved blade facilitates precision work and its elevated offset handle makes it possible to cut flush with a surface. The blade is 3 in long and has 14 ppi.

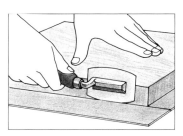

French flush-cut saw is designed for trimming the ends of dowels, tenons and other protrusions flush with a surface. Its 6 in blade is double-edged, with 12 ppi on one side and 21 ppi on the other. To avoid marking the surface adjacent to the cut, the saw teeth have no downward set, but are angled upwards slightly to help the blade to clear the cut.

Dozuki crosscut saw is similar to the Western tenon saw. The folding handle protects delicate saw teeth. Standard blades are 9 in long with 19 ppi.

Carpenter's bow saw is used for cutting curved edges. The twisted cord at the top of the frame supplies tension to keep the blade from wobbling during cutting. By rotating the handles, you can turn the blade to cut at any angle. Blades range from 8 to 12 in long with 9 to 17 ppi.

Folding pocket saw is a handle that accepts saw blades that cut wood, metal, plastic and other materials. It folds to protect the blade's edge and has storage space for extra blades.

Gents saw is a small tenon saw with a straight handle and fine teeth set to cut a very narrow kerf, making it ideal for fine joints. The blade is 10 in long with 17 to 21 ppi.

Bow saw is a heavy-duty tool for cutting logs or for coarse sawing of green wood, dry or seasoned wood or other building materials. The tubular steel frame holds the blade under tension, which can be controlled with the quick-release lever. The replaceable blades are made up of pegged teeth and gullets to allow cutting in both directions.

Compass saw cuts curves quickly in wood, plywood or wallboard. Because the saw has no frame, only a blade and handle, it cuts multiple curves fairly easily, but the thickness of the blade limits the sharpness of the curves it can cut. The blade is 12 in long with 8 ppi.

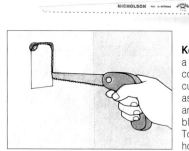

Keyhole saw, a fine-toothed compass saw, cuts light metal as well as wood and wallboard. The average blade is 10 in long with 10 ppi. To start an inside cut, bore a hole and insert the blade.

Nest of saws consists of a handle and a set of compass and keyhole saw blades of different sizes. Rather than acquiring several saws, you can buy one set of nested saws and change the blade to suit each job. Generally the notch in the base of the blade is pushed into the handle and a bolt is slid through it and secured with a washer and wing nut.

Jeweller's saw is a 6 in long saw with fine teeth (26 ppi) for cutting very narrow grooves. It is especially useful for creating delicate dovetails and for model work.

Pad saw can cut curves in awkward places and is more suitable than a compass or keyhole saw for cutting tight curves. Blades for different tasks can be from 4 to 10 in long with 9 ppi. The blade can be inserted into the handle at an angle, and so that it cuts on the pull stroke (like a Japanese saw) for greater control.

General purpose saw can be used to cut wood, metal or plastic. Some have blades that are capable of cutting through nails. The blade is held in place by a large locknut. When it is loosened, the blade can be moved to seven different angles. Some makes will allow as many as nine.

Pruning saw has a blade of specially hardened and tempered steel for cutting branches. Blades are usually about 12-14 in long with 8 ppi. Some models can cut on both forward and reverse strokes; others have double-edged blades.

Curved pruning saw, a knifelike pruning tool, can be folded up to protect the blade when not in use. The tempered steel blade is 10 in long, with long slender reverse teeth (6 ppi) set for cutting on the pull stroke.

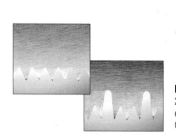

Board saw, a heavy-duty tool for crosscutting timber, has an average blade length of 28 in and 8 ppi. The forward teeth of the blade (far left) are designed to make starting easier. The main teeth (near left) are filed to cut on both the push and pull strokes. Gaps between the groups of teeth make the removal of sawdust easier.

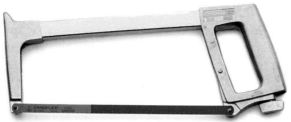

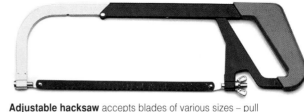

Hacksaw, the traditional handsaw for cutting metal, has extra-hard teeth, a sturdy frame with a pistol-grip handle and a narrow blade, from 10-12 in long with 19-33 ppi. When installing a new blade, apply tension to it by turning the wing nut in the handle. In this model you can store extra blades in the hollow top of the frame.

Adjustable hacksaw accepts blades of various sizes – pull the front part of the frame out as on a trombone. When using a hacksaw, steady the front of the frame with your free hand.

Coping saw has a narrow, flexible blade that can be rotated at any angle to cut small curves, slots and intricate shapes in wood, plastic, glass fibre and mild steel. The blade is pulled taut by turning the wooden handle. To make an inside cut, drill a starting hole and slip the blade through it before attaching it to the saw frame.

Mini-hacksaw consists only of a handle that holds whole or broken hacksaw blades. Use it to cut metal in awkward places where a full-size saw will not fit. The blade is held steady by a screw on the handle.

Rod saw is a wire with carbide chips permanently affixed. It can be attached to a hacksaw frame for cutting glass, ceramic, plastic, masonry, marble, glass fibre and metal. Because it can cut in any direction, it is ideal for curves and for shaping tiles to fit around door frames or plumbing fixtures.

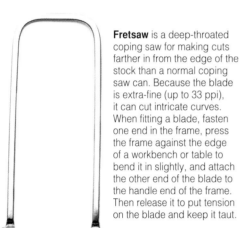

Fretsaw is a deep-throated coping saw for making cuts farther in from the edge of the stock than a normal coping saw can. Because the blade is extra-fine (up to 33 ppi), it can cut intricate curves. When fitting a blade, fasten one end in the frame, press the frame against the edge of a workbench or table to bend it in slightly, and attach the other end of the blade to the handle end of the frame. Then release it to put tension on the blade and keep it taut.

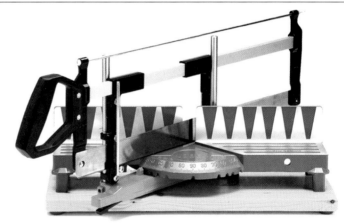

Mitre box holds a backsaw blade in the proper position to make cuts at precise angles. It is often used to cut mitres in moulding. The simplest mitre box is merely a U-shaped wooden structure with a slot through its sides at a 90° angle. The more precise unit shown here comes with its own saw and with clamps to hold work of various sizes and shapes. A dial lets you set the angle of the saw.

Piercing saw cuts lightweight sheet metal, such as silver. Its thin, flexible blade is 5-6 in long with up to 81 ppi. Install a new blade as shown at left for a fretsaw.

Flexible pocket saw is a cutting wire with a handle on each end. It cuts in any direction and can be used on wood, plastic, rubber and plastic piping. To use it, loop round the tree or pipe or other object to be cut and pull first on one handle and then on the other, while applying constant pressure.

In general, a power saw gives a quicker and more precise cut than a handsaw. A jigsaw cuts with a blade that moves up and down; a reciprocating saw cuts with an additional front-to-back motion. A variety of blades allows both saws to cut different materials. After making a cut with any type of portable power saw, wait for the blade to stop moving before laying the saw down.

To cut very tight convex or concave curves, first saw straight lines in the waste material, then cut along the curved line. The pieces of waste material will drop off as the blade makes the cut, giving extra clearance for the saw blade to continue.

Jigsaw can cut straight lines, but it excels at making curved cuts. With the proper blade, it can cut wood, metal, plastic and other materials. Desirable features include adjustable orbital action (to clear away chips and allow faster cutting speed), variable-speed control from 0 to 3200 strokes per minute (spm) for working on different materials, a baseplate that can be tilted for bevel cuts and an antichip device.

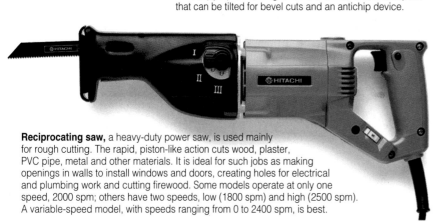

Reciprocating saw, a heavy-duty power saw, is used mainly for rough cutting. The rapid, piston-like action cuts wood, plaster, PVC pipe, metal and other materials. It is ideal for such jobs as making openings in walls to install windows and doors, creating holes for electrical and plumbing work and cutting firewood. Some models operate at only one speed, 2000 spm; others have two speeds, low (1800 spm) and high (2500 spm). A variable-speed model, with speeds ranging from 0 to 2400 spm, is best.

Scrolling jigsaw is a variation on the jigsaw. Its blade holder pivots for cutting intricate curves and contours without the operator turning the body of the saw. There is an automatic scrolling mode, in which the blade turns in the direction the saw is guided and a manual scrolling setting that lets you control the blade with the top-mounted knob, plus settings for normal blade positions.

Jigsaw blades are gauged by the number of teeth per inch (tpi). The more tpi, the smoother the cut; blades with fewer tpi make a rougher but quicker cut. The narrower the blade, the tighter the turning radius. Select the blade to fit the job. At top (from left to right) are blades for wood: crosscut, rough-cut, extra-fine, scrolling (also for plastic) and rough-cut for timber and logs. At bottom (from left to right) are a flush-cut blade for wood and medium, fine and extra-fine blades for cutting metal. Other blades are available for cutting ceramic tile, glass fibre, leather and plaster.

Reciprocating saw blades range in length from 60 to 300 mm (2½ -12 in). Some can cut wood as thick as 300 mm, others metal up to 20 mm thick. Use the shortest blade that will do the job. From top to bottom, the first three blades are for cutting steel pipe of different thicknesses and diameters. The next two are for cutting wood of various thicknesses, then a blade for cutting curves in iron, another blade for cutting curves in wood and a blade for cutting vinyl pipe.

The tool to use for making intricate and accurate curved and piercing cuts is the scroll saw. It is indispensable for creating inlay and marquetry pieces and for making miniatures and fretwork. The saw cuts with a blade suspended between two chucks mounted in arms that move up and down. To reduce teeth marks and blade breakage, look for a saw that holds the blade with a constant-tension arm. Single-speed models are available, but multiple-speed and variable-speed scroll saws are more versatile. Mount the saw on a bench top if it doesn't have its own stand.

Scroll saw blades have ends designed to fit into chucks. Pin-end blades are easier to mount than the smooth ones, but not all saw chucks accept them. All blades can cut very tight curves. Basic blades cut solid wood, plywood, veneer, plastic and some fibrous materials. Very fine blades cut thin nonferrous metals. A spiral-shaped blade allows you to saw in any direction without turning the work.

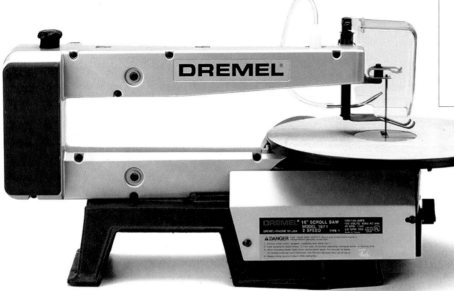

Sawdust blower keeps workpiece clear of debris, allowing a clear view of the cut. The lock knob holds the drop foot in place. The foot can be raised, but it must rest on the work when the saw is running.

Tension control sets tautness of the blade; turn it to tighten or loosen the blade tension. To convert a smooth-end blade to fit a pin-end chuck, use the blade gauge (right of knob) to attach adapters.

To change a blade, first loosen the blade tension by releasing the tension control. The top end of the blade fits into the upper chuck (top). On some models, you can cut pieces longer than the saw's throat depth by rotating the pin-end blade 90° and feeding the wood away from the throat. (Chuck systems differ.) The bottom end of the blade fits into the lower chuck (right). To reach the lower chuck, remove the table insert (replace it before using the saw).

Table adjustment control lets you tilt the saw's table to make bevel cuts up to a 45° angle. Some models can be adjusted up to 45° in the opposite direction.

Ideal for curve cutting and for resawing (making a board thinner), the band saw can also be used to make straight cuts in wood, plastic and metal. Its blade is looped around a set of wheels; the bottom wheel drives the blade into the work. Before buying a band saw, think about how you will use it. It should have adequate throat capacity (the distance from the blade to the left vertical support); this determines the widest board it can cut. The saw should also have suitable cutting depth (the distance from the worktable to the upper blade guard set at its highest position). Cutting depth in smaller band saws runs up to 10 cm (4 in); in larger models, it can be greater than 19 cm (7½ in). A variable-speed saw allows better cutting control.

If the blade is too wide to make a curved cut, first cut several passes to remove waste material. If the cut doesn't finish at another edge of the work, turn the saw off at the end of the cut and back the blade out; otherwise, the blade may be pulled off the wheels.

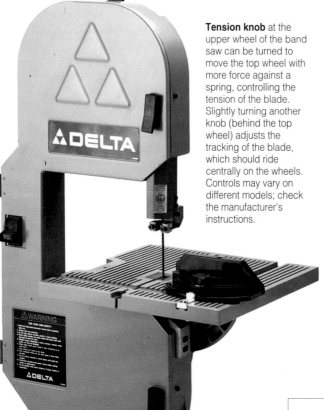

Tension knob at the upper wheel of the band saw can be turned to move the top wheel with more force against a spring, controlling the tension of the blade. Slightly turning another knob (behind the top wheel) adjusts the tracking of the blade, which should ride centrally on the wheels. Controls may vary on different models; check the manufacturer's instructions.

Upper blade guide and guard move up and down to accommodate work of various thicknesses. The guide should be positioned about 3 mm (⅛ in) above the work. The upper blade guide and another one under the table help to keep the blade aligned.

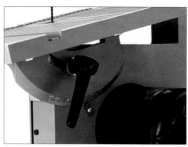

Table-tilting lock holds the table at various angles up to 45°. A scale below the table shows the angle. When you readjust the table for a 90° cut, use a square to make sure the table is set at 90° to the blade.

Access to blade is through a door or panel on the side of the saw. Blades come in various widths with different numbers of teeth. The more teeth on the blade, the smoother the cut; fewer teeth allow a faster but coarser cut. As a general rule, use the widest blade possible.

Portable band saw can be used on a workpiece that is too large to fit on a standard band saw's worktable; it is also easier to move to a work site. When using it, hold the saw with two hands; clamp the work securely, leaving clearance for the saw. Using it with a stand frees your hands. Portable versions are not readily available, but worth seeking out.

The circular saw is used for fast straight cuts in wood or other materials, depending on the blade chosen (pp.58-59). The saw has one of two types of gear: the standard helical gear or the powerful worm-drive gear (not shown) which is used mainly in construction. The size of the saw is identified by the diameter of the largest blade it accepts. Blades range from 125 mm to 300 mm (about 5-12 in). Select a saw that you can handle comfortably and still accomplish your work; a heavy saw can be tiring and hard to control.

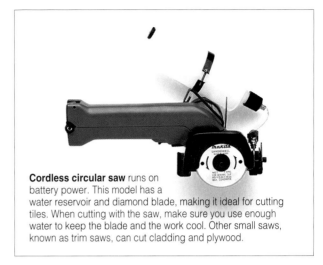

Cordless circular saw runs on battery power. This model has a water reservoir and diamond blade, making it ideal for cutting tiles. When cutting with the saw, make sure you use enough water to keep the blade and the work cool. Other small saws, known as trim saws, can cut cladding and plywood.

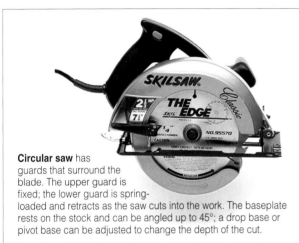

Circular saw has guards that surround the blade. The upper guard is fixed; the lower guard is spring-loaded and retracts as the saw cuts into the work. The baseplate rests on the stock and can be angled up to 45°; a drop base or pivot base can be adjusted to change the depth of the cut.

Sliding compound mitre saw has a blade assembly that slides along a rod, allowing you to cut wide stock by pulling the assembly towards you. The saw can make mitre cuts up to 45°, and it tilts to one side to make compound cuts, also at up to 45° angles. Some models handle stock up to 30 cm (12 in) wide.

Mitre saw combines a portable mitre table and a circular saw to crosscut, mitre cut, bevel and compound cut. Maximum cutting height is 65 mm. Cutting width decreases as the angle increases: maximum cutting width at 45° is 305 mm. At 90° it decreases to 220 mm. The saw is usally fitted with a blade guard, a lock switch, debris guard and dust collector.

Ideal for making precise straight and angled cuts, the table saw can rip and crosscut long boards and wide panels. A circular blade (pp.58-59) protrudes through a slot in the table; the work is pushed into the blade. The diameter of the largest blade the saw can use establishes its size – a 10 in blade is the most common. The blade can be tilted from 0 to 45 degrees. A bench-top model (shown) is portable and requires less space, but a free-standing model makes smoother, more accurate cuts.

Blade guard shields the user's hands from the blade and prevents flying chips. The riving knife, suspended from the blade guard assembly, keeps the kerf (the cut in the workpiece) open behind the blade. If the kerf is allowed to close, the blade will be pinched by the workpiece and will jam and cause the work to kick back and injure the operator.

Mitre gauge can be adjusted to use as a guide for making crosscuts and angled cuts of up to 45°. For a long board, support the weight of the work with one hand; while the saw is running, push the mitre gauge with the work into the blade with the other hand.

Rip fence (above) guides workpiece for rip cuts (cutting with the grain). Move the fence to the width desired for the work and fix it in place. Hold work against the fence while making the cut; push work past blade with a push stick (below). The mitre gauge must be removed to make a rip cut.

Depth of cut is adjusted by moving the blade up or down. On this model, you turn a knob to move the blade; some table saws use cranks. You can also tilt the blade to make bevelled cuts of up to 45°. A scale indicates the degree of the angle.

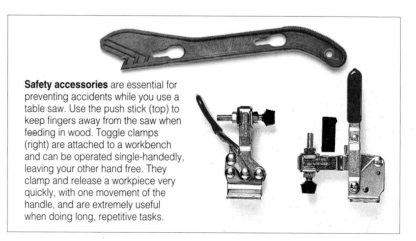

Safety accessories are essential for preventing accidents while you use a table saw. Use the push stick (top) to keep fingers away from the saw when feeding in wood. Toggle clamps (right) are attached to a workbench and can be operated single-handedly, leaving your other hand free. They clamp and release a workpiece very quickly, with one movement of the handle, and are extremely useful when doing long, repetitive tasks.

RADIAL ARM SAWS

The blade assembly of a radial arm saw is suspended from an arm and can be rotated, angled and tilted to make a variety of cuts. The saw is ideal for making crosscuts – especially in long boards – and you can turn the blade housing and use it horizontally. With the proper attachments, you can turn a radial arm saw into a sander, router and drill press. Use only those designed for your model. The size of the saw is based on the diameter of the largest blade (pp.58-59) it will accept; 10 in is a versatile size for a home workshop. Before operating the saw, make any adjustments suggested in the manufacturer's manual.

Riving knife   Pawl

Saw guard covers a blade to prevent injury to the user – a safety feature found on all radial arm saws. This guard is made of clear plastic; others are made of steel. Attached to the guard is an antikickback pawl for making rip cuts. If the work starts to move backwards, the pawl grips it. A riving knife behind the blade keeps the cut open during rip cuts, preventing the blade from jamming in the work.

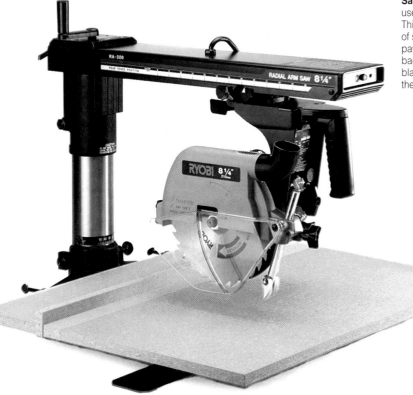

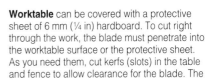

Worktable can be covered with a protective sheet of 6 mm (¼ in) hardboard. To cut right through the work, the blade must penetrate into the worktable surface or the protective sheet. As you need them, cut kerfs (slots) in the table and fence to allow clearance for the blade. The radial arm saw shown is a portable model. It is easy to store and transport to the work site. A heavy-duty floor model, however, will make more accurate cuts.

Arm lock and gauge allow the arm to be set in preset stops for making mitre cuts up to 22.5° left and 45° right (models vary). The arm can also be locked at other angles between stops.

Yoke controls are used to turn blade assembly to position it for rip sawing. The carriage lock knob fixes the carriage in place along the arm, setting the width of the cut.

Bevel controls allow you to tilt blade assembly up to 90° in either direction for making a bevelled crosscut or rip cut. Adjust arm and bevel controls to make compound cuts.

Having a variety of blades will expand the capabilities of your circular saw, table saw or radial arm saw. Blades fall into two categories: standard steel, which must be sharpened often, and carbide tipped. The latter stay sharp longer, but they are more brittle and can be damaged if improperly handled. The number of teeth on a blade, the grind of each tooth and the gullet depth (the space between teeth) determine the smoothness and speed of the cut. Large flat-ground teeth make a fast, rough rip cut; small pointed teeth that alternate left and right cut slowly and smoothly across the grain. To avoid kickback, some blades have a hump behind each tooth. Most blades come in different sizes; match their diameters and arbor holes to your tool.

Rip has large square chisel teeth for making clean cuts parallel with the grain of hardwood and softwood.

Crosscut has small pointed teeth for making smooth cuts at right angles to the grain in hardwood, softwood and plywood.

Combination, with alternating large pointed teeth, can make rip cuts, cross cuts and mitre cuts in all wood materials without your having to change blades.

Chisel-tooth combination has large teeth for making fast, rough rip cuts.

Hollow-ground planer provides clearance for cut because blade body is thinner than cutting edge; its combination-ground teeth make smooth crosscuts and mitre cuts.

Hollow-ground plywood has alternating fine bevel-ground teeth for splinter-free cuts in plywood and panelling.

Plywood/panelling, with small alternating top-bevel-ground teeth, makes smooth cuts in plywood and panelling.

Nonferrous metal/plastic cutter has alternating top-bevel-ground teeth for cutting brass, aluminium, copper and plastics. Oil or wax before using.

Thin kerf with carbide-tipped teeth minimises waste by making fine cuts in wood less than 20 mm (¾ in) thick. This one has vents to prevent overheating.

Combination thin kerf has large carbide-tipped alternating bevel-ground teeth with antikickback humps. Use it for smooth rip cuts and crosscuts in most woods.

Framing thin kerf is for smooth rip cuts in most woods. It has large carbide-tipped square chisel teeth and antikickback humps.

Finishing thin kerf has small carbide-tipped alternating bevel-ground teeth with antikickback humps for making fine crosscuts in most woods.

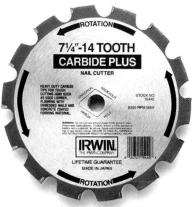

Nail cutter, with large carbide-tipped teeth, can make rough cuts through nails that may be embedded in wood. It's ideal for remodelling and construction work.

Nonferrous metal cutter has carbide-tipped teeth for cutting aluminium, copper, lead and brass. Oil or wax before using.

Nonstick coating is added to hooked carbide-tipped teeth for fine cuts in solid wood, plywood veneers and plastic.

Dado set includes saw blades and chippers, which are assembled to cut housings, rebates and grooves in solid wood and plastic laminate. An adjustable dado head comes assembled; it can be reset for various groove widths. Use dado blades on radial arm saws only.

A woodworking tool that is basically a blade or iron in a holder, the plane can trim and smooth wood, bevel and round off wood edges and straighten irregular edges. Special-purpose planes can cut grooves for joints and shave wood into decorative shapes.

Choose a plane that will accomplish the particular job. Make sure the plane has a readily accessible and easy-to-use depth adjusting nut or wheel; look for a frog – the underlying plate – that fully supports the iron. For planing surfaces, pick a plane with a grooved sole; to plane edges, select one with a flat sole.

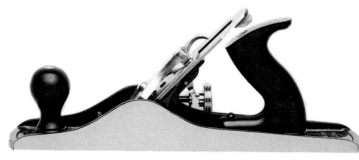

Jack plane has a 355-380 mm (14-15 in) long body for fast roughing jobs and wide boards. To use it on freshly cut wood, set the cap iron back 2mm (1/16 in); for final smoothing, move the cap iron until it's 1 mm (1/32 in) from the cutting edge of the iron. Adjust the iron with the lateral lever and adjusting nut. To remove the iron for sharpening, release the lever cap; then remove the lever cap and cap iron.

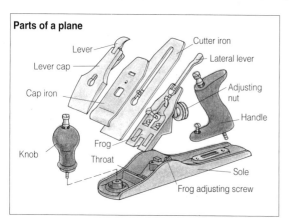

Steel jointer plane, or try plane, is used for accurate edge joining and the initial levelling of wide boards. It has a 560 mm (22 in) sole to prevent the tool from following bumps and dips. To change the depth of cut, move the iron by adjusting the lateral lever and the adjusting nut.

Parts of a plane

Lever
Lever cap
Cap iron
Knob
Frog
Throat
Cutter iron
Lateral lever
Adjusting nut
Handle
Sole
Frog adjusting screw

Wood jointer plane has a fence to guide the tool for squaring and truing wood edges for tight fits. It's ideal for preparing wood for edge-to-edge gluing. To turn the tool into a smoothing plane, unscrew the fence and remove it.

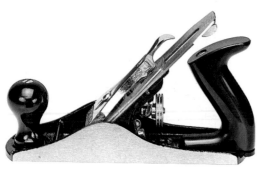

Smoothing plane, also known as a Bailey plane, finishes a surface after rough planing. The corrugated sole reduces friction when used on timbers that contain resin.

Raised panel plane is quite rare and creates a panelled look with an angled sole and iron. It cuts 5 cm (2 in) wide strips and comes in right and left-handed models. A wedge holds the iron in place. To adjust it, tap it with a wood or rawhide mallet.

RB10 plane has a razor-sharp blade which is quickly and easily replaced. Six spare blades are stored in the handle. Use it for stock removal, smoothing and rebating wood. With the RB109 blade fitted you can use it on plastic laminates.

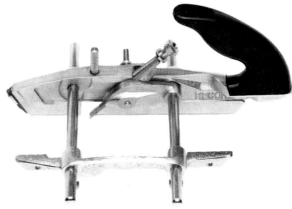

Plough combination plane uses an adjustable fence to guide it across the work edge while cutting grooves or rebates. Some models come with as many as 18 blades, which include blades for cutting beading and tongues, in addition to rebates.

Block plane Designed for single-handed use on end grain.

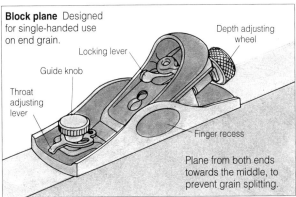

Depth adjusting wheel

Locking lever

Guide knob

Throat adjusting lever

Finger recess

Plane from both ends towards the middle, to prevent grain splitting.

Block plane cuts and trims the end grain of wood and makes fine finishing cuts. An adjusting wheel under the palm rest controls positioning of the iron. Because of its smaller size, the block plane can be used with one hand.

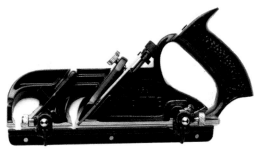

Bullnose plane makes stopped rebates and housings in fine woodworking. The short nose in front of the iron allows cutting at close quarters.

Low-angle block plane, one of several variations of the block plane, is used for shaping fine trim work and end grain. The blade rests at a 12 degree angle for finer cuts on cross grains and end grains. The plane is adjustable for making rougher cuts.

Palm plane fits into places where a standard-sized plane will not. It is very useful for intricate detail work. Another model has a raised handle.

Violin plane, for fine detail work, may have a straight iron or come in a set with matching convex and concave-shaped irons.

Edge plane is fairly rare. Its L-shaped body works like a fence to form true square edges in wood. The blade is skewed for a smooth cut, to prevent wood tearout.

Side rebate plane is designed to enlarge the width of grooves and can work from left to right and vice versa, which is useful if you can work from only one end of a groove.

Rebate plane shapes a rebate in wood. There are two blade positions: centre for general use and forward for bullnose operations. Spurs permit work on cross grain. Some models feature an adjustable, detachable fence.

Shoulder plane has sole and body sides at perfect right angles. As the name implies, it trims and squares the shoulders of tenon and rebate joints.

PLANES, SPOKESHAVES AND SCRAPERS

Although all these woodworking tools perform the same basic functions, smoothing, shaving and shaping wood, each specialises in creating a flat, concave or convex surface. In general, planes and spokeshaves are for finishing workpieces, drawknives for roughing out stock. Most of these tools are held in two hands; the worker pushes or pulls the instrument against the work. To create smooth cuts and prevent injury, keep the cutting edges sharp. When using the tools, make sure you follow the grain of the wood.

Three-in-one plane is a shoulder rebate, bullnose and chisel plane in one tool and it is used to produce a fine, accurate finish on cabinet work. The bullnose head (left) makes it easier to control the depth of cut in tight areas. To convert the plane, unscrew one head and attach the other; the screw is located inside the head. To increase the mouth width, add the shims (centre).

Circular plane, also called a compass plane, has a flexible sole for planing concave and convex surfaces. Place the plane on the work; then, using the adjusting knut to turn the threaded rod, position the sole to fit the contour desired for the work. Once the sole is set, adjust the iron to the correct setting.

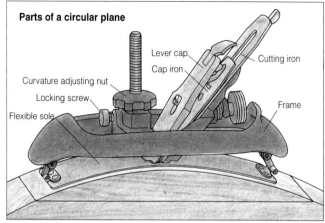

Parts of a circular plane

Lever cap
Cap iron
Cutting iron
Curvature adjusting nut
Locking screw
Frame
Flexible sole

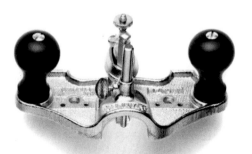

Router plane cuts grooves, housings and other flat-bottomed depressions to a precise depth. It also surfaces the bottom of grooves and housings, parallel with the top surface. Some models have an adjustable, detachable guide fence for general or bullnose (close-quarters) work on straight and curved grooves. 6 mm (¼ in), 13 mm (½ in) and V-shaped cutters are supplied.

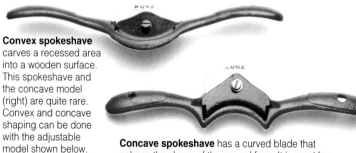

Convex spokeshave carves a recessed area into a wooden surface. This spokeshave and the concave model (right) are quite rare. Convex and concave shaping can be done with the adjustable model shown below.

Concave spokeshave has a curved blade that echoes the shape of the curved face. It is used for smoothing and shaving curved woodwork, such as the rounded rails, posts and legs of chairs.

Miniature router has a single 6 mm (¼ in) cutter blade and is ideal for very fine, narrow work such as inlaying and cutting small stopped or through housings. It can also be used for normal routing and for bullnose work. Set the depth against a marked line on the work; then tighten the cutter by turning the knurled screw.

Adjustable straight spokeshave has two thumbscrews to change the blade depth. A third screw holds the lever cap, which applies pressure to the blade. Loosen it before adjusting the blade depth. Adjustable spokeshaves are available for flat, concave or convex surfaces. With practice, you need to do little sanding after using a spokeshave.

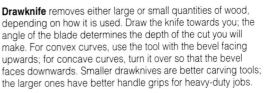

Drawknife removes either large or small quantities of wood, depending on how it is used. Draw the knife towards you; the angle of the blade determines the depth of the cut you will make. For convex curves, use the tool with the bevel facing upwards; for concave curves, turn it over so that the bevel faces downwards. Smaller drawknives are better carving tools; the larger ones have better handle grips for heavy-duty jobs.

Hook scrapers, with their curved, Swedish steel blades, are used for a variety of finishing work. From left to right: the largest scraper is 37 cm (14 in) long and is used for heavy-duty work. The angled handle of the next size gives access to awkward places. The cabinet scraper is used to put a fine finish on all types of wood before polishing, staining or repainting. The finishing scraper puts the finest finish on softwood and hardwoods; the blade goes right to the edge to give access to corners.

Carbide-tipped scrapers have very long-lasting, replaceable, double-edged blades. They can be used for smoothing wood and for scraping off paint, varnish, glue and rust. The blades have convex ground edges to prevent them from damaging surfaces.

Cabinet scraper holds a reversible blade in a body that resembles a spokeshave. The large handles give maximum control and a thumbscrew adjusts the blade. The tool smoothes knots and removes dried glue and paper-thin layers of wood. Use it with the blade angled away from you. Push the tool away, keeping the base flat on the wood.

Cabinet scraper blades come in various shapes. Most have two cutting edges, but the curved scraper has a cutting edge all round. Properly used, a cabinet scraper will produce very fine shavings and give a cleaner finish than an abrasive paper – which always leaves some dust. Use it to smooth small, rough patches on a surface, too.

Small spokeshave is useful for working in areas where bigger tools won't fit and for creating fine detail. It comes with a flat, round or spoon-shaped sole. The blade may be flat or convex. To adjust the blade or to remove it for sharpening, remove the screw and washer.

The portable power plane is great for jobs such as shaving down door edges. But if your projects call for perfect-fitting joinery and workpieces, a power jointer and a thickness planer should also be part of your workshop. Both tools require accurate adjustments to be effective. With them you can cut boards to less than standard thickness and you can also buy less expensive rough-sawn timber and smooth its surface yourself. On a jointer, first flatten and straighten a surface, then straighten and square its edges. Finally give the piece an overall equal thickness with the planer. If the work calls for strong joints, a biscuit joiner is necessary.

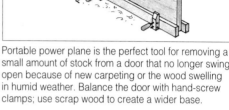

Portable power plane is the perfect tool for removing a small amount of stock from a door that no longer swings open because of new carpeting or the wood swelling in humid weather. Balance the door with hand-screw clamps; use scrap wood to create a wider base.

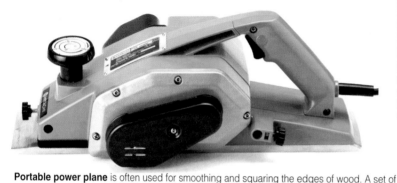

Portable power plane is often used for smoothing and squaring the edges of wood. A set of two rotating blades removes up to 3 mm (⅛ in) of wood per pass; make a series of passes to remove more wood. Planes are sized according to the width of cut they can make. Average cutting width is 82 mm (just less than 3¼ in), but it may vary. As you plane a workpiece, apply even pressure throughout the pass. At the end of the pass let up slightly on the plane's front end to avoid digging into the work. Besides straightening edges, the plane can also make chamfers and tapers. A fence can be attached to the plane to cut specific angles.

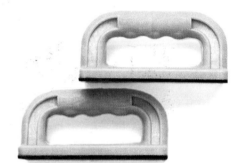

Jointer (sometimes called a planer/thicknesser) flattens, straightens and squares boards 100-200 mm (4-8 in) wide. The machine consists of an infeed table, cutter head, outfeed table and fence. The height of the infeed table is adjustable to change the depth of cut up to 3 mm. A guard (open here to show cutter) protects your hands as you feed the work across the cutter; but if the top edge of a board is lower than the fence top, use push blocks. The fence adjusts up to 45 degrees left and right for bevelling and chamfering.

Push blocks are absolutely essential safety tools when working with the jointer. They can also be used with a table saw or radial arm saw. The blocks shown have foam pads to grip the work securely and their handles are angled to keep your hands away from the fence.

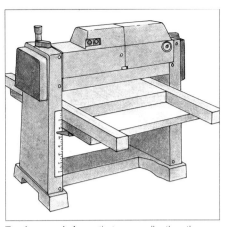

To plane workpieces that are smaller than the manufacturer's recommendations, hot-glue scrap wood to the sides of the work. Make sure the assembly isn't too wide to fit through the planer. After passing the work through the planer, tap on the scrap wood to break it off the workpiece.

Biscuit joiner

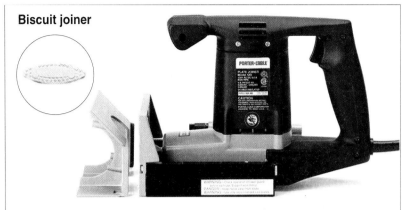

Also called a plate joiner, the biscuit joiner is a unique tool for strengthening the butt, mitre and edge joints in wood. A blade cuts corresponding grooves into each of two workpieces; oval-shaped 'biscuits' of wood (inset) or plastic fit into the grooves and, with a little glue, create a strong joint. (Glue causes the biscuit to expand for a tight fit.) Biscuit joints can be aligned before the glue dries by shifting the pieces laterally. Biscuits are available in several sizes; use the largest one that fits the joint.

Thickness planer sizes wood to a desired thickness after one surface has been straightened or flattened on a jointer. The wood is placed on the table and automatically fed by rollers past rotating blades. It is best to make several passes, removing a small amount of wood each time. The type of wood, its width and the feed rate determine the amount of wood that can be removed. A slower feed means more cuts are made. The more cuts, the smoother the surface. The thickness planer is available in bench-top models that accept wood 100-300 mm (4-12 in) wide and 2-150 mm ($\frac{3}{32}$-6 in) thick. Floor models can accept larger sections up to 910 mm (36 in) wide and 200 mm (8 in) thick. The planer may operate on single-speed, two-speed or variable-speed feed rates. Some thickness planers have blades with a cutting edge on both sides. When one side becomes dull, remove any debris and reinstall the blade with the sharp side in the cutting position. Before changing a blade, make sure that you unplug the machine.

An adaptable woodworking tool, the router can be used to make decorative edges or surfaces, top-quality joinery and freehand or pattern-assisted carvings. It has a ¼, ⅜ or ½ in diameter collet that accepts matching bit shanks. For light woodworking, a ¼ in router is adequate, but a larger collet gives greater versatility. The motor sizes range from ¼ to 3¼ horsepower. The greater the horsepower, the more work the router can handle. Before buying a router, check that the handles feel comfortable and that the on-off switch is within easy reach.

Router bits can be used singly or several can be used in succession to create different shapes. High-speed steel bits require more frequent sharpening than carbide-tipped bits, which last longer but are more expensive. If the bit has a solid or ball-bearing pilot, it serves as a guide that follows the edge of the work.

Standard router with ⅞ hp and ¼ in collet has a motor that adjusts up and down. To change the depth of the cut, loosen the knob and reposition the motor in the base. When the motor is on, keep your fingers clear of the sharp, high-speed bits.

Plunge router, ideal for making interior cuts, is supported with two posts extending up from the base. After setting the depth stop, set the router over the work at the starting point and start the motor; release the plunge locking lever and lower the bit into the work. Some models have variable-speed control.

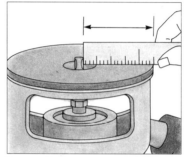

Because bit sizes vary, measure from bit to edge of base before setting a fence or guide. Mark the same distance from the cutting edge.

The router bit spins clockwise and must feed into the work. For cuts on an edge, move the router from left to right; guide it anticlockwise around a continuous piece. For inside cuts, move it clockwise.

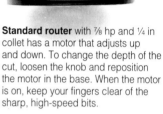

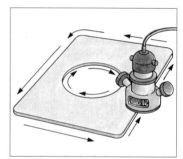

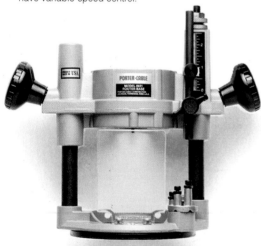

Retrofit plunge base replaces the base on a standard router with a 3½ in diameter motor. It accommodates a standard router converting it into a plunge router. The plunge base also has a locking lever and a multiposition depth stop.

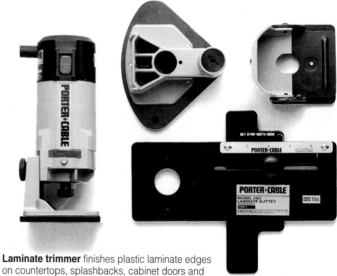

Laminate trimmer finishes plastic laminate edges on countertops, splashbacks, cabinet doors and shelves. Attachments include an offset base (top, centre) to reach into corners, an adjustable base (top, right) to set trimmer at 0° to 45° angles and a slitter (bottom, right) to cut laminate sheets.

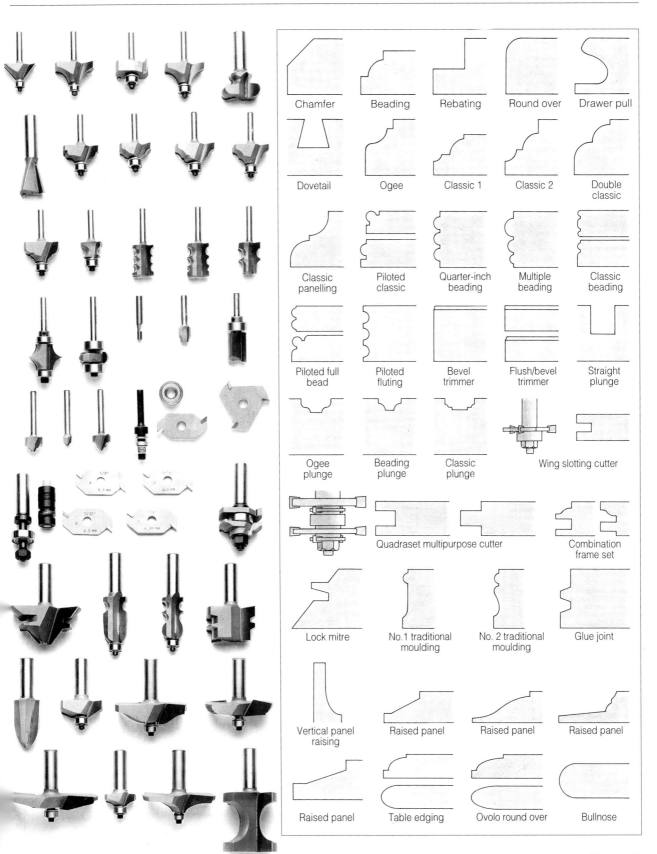

Chamfer

Beading

Rebating

Round over

Drawer pull

Dovetail

Ogee

Classic 1

Classic 2

Double classic

Classic panelling

Piloted classic

Quarter-inch beading

Multiple beading

Classic beading

Piloted full bead

Piloted fluting

Bevel trimmer

Flush/bevel trimmer

Straight plunge

Ogee plunge

Beading plunge

Classic plunge

Wing slotting cutter

Quadraset multipurpose cutter

Combination frame set

Lock mitre

No.1 traditional moulding

No. 2 traditional moulding

Glue joint

Vertical panel raising

Raised panel

Raised panel

Raised panel

Raised panel

Table edging

Ovolo round over

Bullnose

To make perfect cuts and shapes, a router is often used with a template or guide. Models vary from make to make. Before routing with one of these accessories on the actual workpiece, practise on scrap wood until you feel comfortable with it. Because bits vary in width, when setting up a guide or template, always calculate the distance with the bit in place in the collet (p.66).

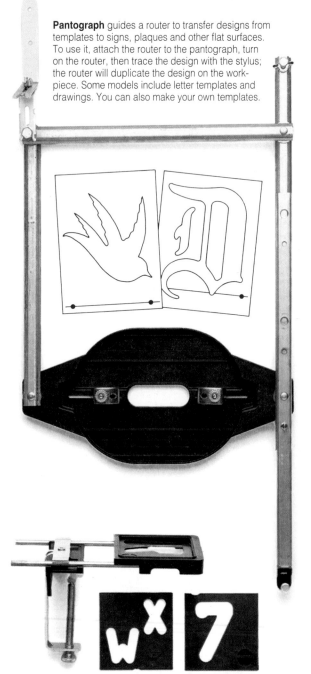

Pantograph guides a router to transfer designs from templates to signs, plaques and other flat surfaces. To use it, attach the router to the pantograph, turn on the router, then trace the design with the stylus; the router will duplicate the design on the workpiece. Some models include letter templates and drawings. You can also make your own templates.

Roller edge guide and guide bushes come in a kit. The roller edge guide, attached to a special baseplate (right), has a bearing that lets you shape decorative profiles when using unpiloted bits. It's also useful for trimming laminate and for edging irregular shapes. Guide bushes (left) and retainer (top) protect precision dovetail, letter and butt-hinge templates. Never use the roller edge guide and a guide bush together.

Straight-and-circular guide directs the router for making cuts parallel with the edge of the work. Use it to make straight or circular plunge cuts. The guide has an adjustable fence for straight cuts; an adjustable trammel point holds the guide in place to make circular cuts. Wing nuts are used to make the adjustments. This model also has a micrometer adjustment for accuracy.

Router table transforms a router into a stationary shaper for precise work. Invert the router and mount it underneath the table; make sure the cutter protrudes up through the hole in the centre of the table. To rout the work surface or edge, place its good face down on the table and push it into the bit. The table includes a cutter safety guard, a guide fence for edging and slotting and a mitre gauge for angles and crosscuts.

Letter templates are used with a guide bush and a straight, V-groove or cove router bit to engrave letters and numbers in wooden signs. A bracket clamps the template and work to a workbench. Letter styles and sizes vary.

Dust extraction hood, for use with a router, gives greater comfort and better vision. Fix it to the router base with thumbscrews. Dust hood sets are available in various styles; there is also a vented base plate with two suction points. Vacuum cleaners for use with a router include a wall-mounted model. Hoses are available in four sizes, with different types of bayonet fitting. Stepped bayonets are useful when a custom-made connection is necessary. Wall-venting bayonets enable dust to be extracted from guards, shields and screen tables.

Mortise-and-tenon jig makes perfectly fitting, round mortise-and-tenon joints for use in constructing furniture and door frames. The jig can create up to three consecutive mortises and tenons without being moved. The joints can also be angled or mitred. A piloted mortise-and-tenon bit is included. This is a rare accessory, but worth seeking out if you have a large project in mind.

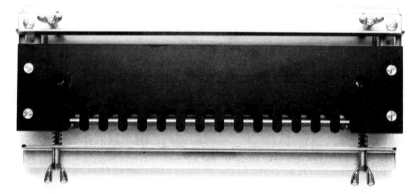

Dovetail template guides router to make strong dovetail joints for fine furniture, cabinet and drawer construction. It is used in conjunction with a guide bush and a dovetail router bit. The guide bush follows the template as the router bit cuts a series of evenly spaced fan-shaped pins and matching recesses simultaneously in the two workpieces. It makes both flush and rebate dovetails.

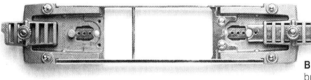

Butt-hinge template fits on door edges and jambs to rout mortises for butt hinges. Before using a router with the templates, attach a butt-hinge guide to its base. A rather rare accessory, for a specialist job.

Postform jig, made of solid laminate, is used with a heavy duty plunge router when making worktops for a kitchen, bathroom or caravan. It will cut butt and scribed joints with great exactness from board up to 40 mm thick. It cuts left and right hand corner joints, the round corners of peninsular joints and the mitred joints that are necessary when fitting a hob across the corner of an L-shaped worktop area. It has the facility to join boards from 400 to 1000 mm wide. The jig is supplied with a width-setting clamp (left).

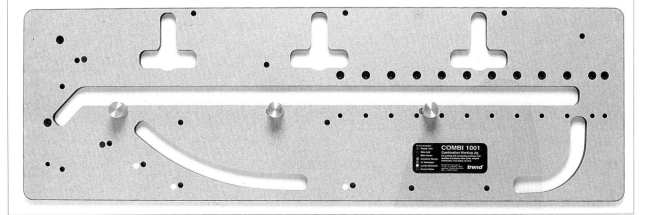

CHISELS, GOUGES AND LATHES

When kept sharp and free of corrosion, a chisel or gouge will last a lifetime. Chisels come in a variety of sizes for working on wood, metal and stone. They are hand-driven or driven with a mallet. The steel blades may have straight or bevelled sides. Straight sides are stronger than bevelled, but a bevelled blade can reach into tight places. The blade shape may be square, round or skewed for specific tasks. Gouge blades are curved to make concave or convex cuts. Store chisels and gouges where their blades cannot be damaged by hitting each other or other tools. Never place one where it can be knocked to the floor; the sharp blade can cause a cut.

Butt chisel has a short blade that makes it easier to work with than a standard chisel. It is hand or lightly mallet-driven. The bevelled sides and straight cutting edge make it ideal for undercutting to create dovetail joints.

Mortise chisel has a thick rigid blade, straight cutting edge and square sides to make mortises and similar joints. The sturdy reinforced handle is struck with a mallet to remove waste.

Skew chisel uses a slicing motion to finish cuts in tight spaces and to trim close to adjacent surfaces. The angled cutting edge (about 60 degrees) gives the chisel its name; the skew on the blade may be right or left-handed or both. The blade sides are straight for strength. This chisel is only hand-driven.

Bevel edge chisel has bevelled sides and a straight cutting edge. You strike the hoop-reinforced handle with a mallet to remove waste when cutting mortises, dovetails and similar joints. It is a good choice for beginners, as it is easy to control.

Spoon bit chisel or gouge has a blade shaped to clean out grooves and small mortises. Using a chisel slightly smaller than the mortise, set the blade's cutting edge along the mortise's bottom edge. The tool can be used in mortises up to 15 cm deep.

Corner chisel, resembling a punch, is used primarily with a mallet. Another model has a handle for striking and for handwork. The L-shaped cutting edge cleans out square holes and corners with angles of 90 degrees and more; also trims and fine-tunes mortises.

Skew chisel with a straight, right skew or left skew cutting edge works like a small paring or carving chisel. Uses include fine-tuning joints and adding detail to fine woodwork.

Concrete point chisel used for breaking out concrete and brickwork. If you are making a channel in a concrete floor, mark out the channel first with a flat, flooring chisel then use the point chisel to remove the unwanted concrete.

Scutch comb chisel is used for roughening and preparing flat surfaces for rendering. The replaceable comb fits into the holder. To use the tool, hold it at 45 degrees to the surface and drive it with a wooden mallet to make a series of shallow, overlapping cuts.

Paring chisel is ideal for cleaning grooves and slicing away small amounts of stock. The straight cutting edge has bevelled sides to allow access to tight spaces. It is made for hand use only; do not strike it with a mallet.

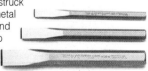

Cold chisel for metalwork is struck with a hammer to cut sheet metal and to chop off rivets, bolts and nails. You can also use one to reach a plumbing fixture by chipping away ceramic tile.

Crank-necked paring chisel has an offset blade to allow you to hold the tool flat against the work surface, even in the middle of the work and still have clearance to hold the handle.

Blind-nail chisel lifts up a small sliver of wood. Hammer a nail in place and then glue the sliver over the nailhead.

Flooring chisel cuts and lifts flooring materials for removal or repair; it is ideal for tongue-and-groove flooring. The wide blade distributes pressure evenly in order to prevent damage to adjacent boards.

Carving chisels, sold separately or in sets, are used for cutting intricate designs into wood and for sculpting. Some carving chisels are designed to be struck. Their cutting edges include gouge, parting, skew, straight, paring and V-groove.

Chip-carving knives have blades in a variety of designs for creating low-relief carvings. Often sold in sets of up to ten knives, they can be stored in a canvas pouch.

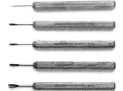

Miniature carving chisel is for extra-fine detail work. It comes with the same variety of blades as standard carving chisels.

Cabinetmaker's carving chisel has a handle that fits into the palm of your hand.

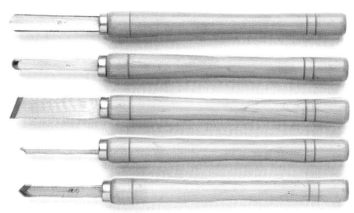

Lathe chisels are used with a lathe to create turned woodwork such as chair legs and rails. A basic set of chisels includes, from top to bottom: gouge for rounding and cutting concave curves; round-nose chisel to form curves and hollows; skew chisel to cut convex curves and to smooth straight or tapered cylinders; diamond-point chisel to cut V-grooves and square shoulders; and parting tool for sizing cuts and to separate the turned work from the waste stock.

Adze is a sculptor's tool for shaping large pieces of wood quickly. One end of the head has an axe-like blade; the other end is shaped like a gouge. The adze is available in several sizes; you can also buy a head with only the axe or only the gouge blade.

Deep-throat gouge is for bowl work on a lathe. If it is handled properly, it leaves a smooth finish that needs no sanding.

Cutting scraper is used for inside finishing of work turned on a lathe. It may have a round or square blade.

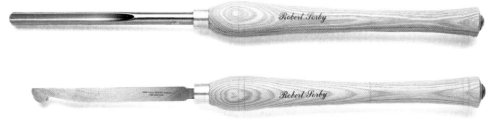

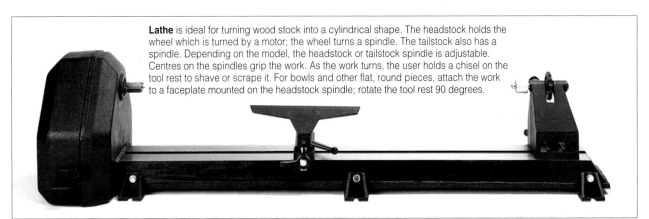

Lathe is ideal for turning wood stock into a cylindrical shape. The headstock holds the wheel which is turned by a motor; the wheel turns a spindle. The tailstock also has a spindle. Depending on the model, the headstock or tailstock spindle is adjustable. Centres on the spindles grip the work. As the work turns, the user holds a chisel on the tool rest to shave or scrape it. For bowls and other flat, round pieces, attach the work to a faceplate mounted on the headstock spindle; rotate the tool rest 90 degrees.

Tools   71

FILES AND RASPS

Depending on the individual tool, a file or rasp can sharpen, shape or smooth while removing metal or wood. Cut, coarseness, length and shape determine the tool's use. The cut refers to the pattern of the teeth. A single-cut file has parallel diagonal rows of ridgelike teeth for smoothing and sharpening metal; a double-cut file has a second set of rows that cross the first for rapid removal of metal stock. The rasp has straight or random rows of individual teeth for fast rough removal of wood or soft metal stock. Single (smooth) cut, second (medium) cut and bastard (rough) cut indicate the coarseness of a file or rasp and generally the longer the tool, the coarser its cut. The shape or profile of a file or rasp can make it useful for specific jobs.

Flat file (near right), a general-purpose file for fast removal of metal, has a slightly tapered shape and a rectangular profile. It has double-cut faces (above) with a single cut along the edges.

Hand file (near centre) is similar to flat file, but it has parallel edges; one edge is safe or uncut to keep it from marring the work.

Pillar file (far centre), a thin file, fits into narrow grooves and slots.

Square file (far right) is shaped to fit into recesses, angles and square mortises and holes for filing. Like the flat file, it tapers towards the end.

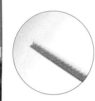

Half-round file (top, far left) has a round and a flat side to file large concave and flat surfaces.

Round file (top, near left) shapes small curves and enlarges and smoothes holes. A tapered one is called a mousetail file.

Triangle file (left) has three sides. Each side is flat and has a single cut.

Saw files sharpen saw blade teeth. From left to right are a chain-saw file, veneer knife file, crosscut file, cant-saw file for saw blades with teeth at an angle of less than 60° and taper file for blades with teeth at an angle of 60°.

Cabinet file (above) has ridge-like teeth that are staggered in parallel rows. Carvers and cabinet-makers use it for sculpting wood.

Wood file (above, right), a half-round file, has teeth that are slightly coarser than those of the cabinet file.

Long-angle lathe file (far left) has a single cut (above) that can leave a smooth finish on lathe metalwork.

Mill file (left, centre) is used to sharpen circular saws, as well as knives, lawnmower blades, shears and axes; also for polishing and deburring.

Double-ended saw file (near left) is for sharpening saw teeth; can be used in both directions.

Three-square (triangular) file (far left) is tapered and has three flat sides for filing metal at angles under 90°.

Knife file (left, centre) is for working on metal pieces with acute angles.

Warding file (left) has a narrow tip to fit into tight areas.

Rifflers are files and rasps used for wood carving and metal crafts. They shape and remove stock in irregular and tight spaces. They vary in size and they come in the same shapes, cuts and coarsenesses as standard files and rasps. Some rifflers have handles and some are double-ended, with a file at one end and a rasp at the other.

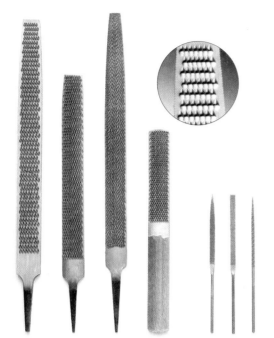

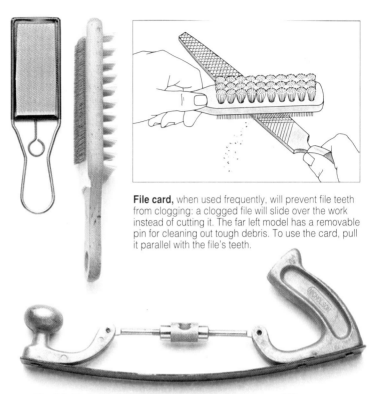

File card, when used frequently, will prevent file teeth from clogging: a clogged file will slide over the work instead of cutting it. The far left model has a removable pin for cleaning out tough debris. To use the card, pull it parallel with the file's teeth.

Rasps have individual teeth, instead of ridges, to rough out shapes and remove stock quickly. They work best on wood but can also be used on leather and soft metals. From left to right are a wood rasp with a rectangular profile and coarse teeth, a cabinet rasp with a half-round profile and medium teeth, a patternmaker's cabinet rasp that also has a half-round profile but fine teeth and a four-in-one rasp, which combines a half-round and a flat profile – each side has a file end and a rasp end. Small rasps are ideal for working in restricted spaces.

Flexible file holder provides easy two-handed gripping and filing power. Secure a file in the holder, then adjust the holder to bend outwards or inwards to suit the stock surface. It can hold files that are 300-360 mm (12-14 in) long.

File handle fits on the file's tang, the pointed end of the file, allowing a better hold on the file and protecting the user from the sharp tang. Handles are usually bought separately from the file. This model has a screw on one end that controls jaws on the other end.

Surform file, like the rasp, has individual teeth punched into metal for cutting wood. The resulting hole near each of the teeth allows shavings to pass through, preventing clogging. The tool can also be used to cut, shave and shape hardboard, some roofing tiles, rigid plastics, glass fibre, aluminium, copper and brass.

Surform plane shapes, planes and removes stock with a two-handed pushing action. The blades cannot be sharpened but are replaceable; remove the screw usually found beside the handle. Blades come in fine, regular and medium cuts and in grits from coarse to fine. Use the plane on wood, plywood, chipboard, plaster, vinyl and linoleum. The regular-cut blade has a feature on one edge for cutting inside corners; the other edge does not cut.

Surform shaving tool works with a pull stroke. Change the depth of cut by adjusting hand pressure. Unlike the other Surforms, the blade simply clips into place.

Surform block plane fits into the palm of your hand. Use it to trim narrow surfaces and to get into tight corners. Blade is reversible.

Surform round file is useful for enlarging holes and shaping curved surfaces.

Surform Planerfile has a handle that unscrews and moves, allowing the tool to be held and used like a file or a plane.

SANDING TOOLS

Hand and power sanders fitted with abrasive papers can shape and remove imperfections in wood and create smooth surfaces prior to finishing. They can also help to remove unwanted paint, rust and finishes from wood, metal and other surfaces. Hand-sanding is made easier with blocks and pads that hold the abrasive. Power-assisted sanding takes less time but sometimes requires extra skill. You can hire large power sanders, especially floor models.

Always wear a dust mask and protective glasses when power-sanding, even if the sander has a dust-collection system. Start a power sander before the abrasive touches the work surface; when you finish, wait until the sander stops moving before setting it down. Empty the dust bag often, particularly when changing from a wood to a metal surface; sparks from the metal can ignite wood dust.

Sanding block holds abrasive sheets. It pulls apart to anchor the sheet ends between the two sections.

Flexible block can be adjusted to the contour of the workpiece. To change its shape, pull the two ends of the block apart or push one end under the other.

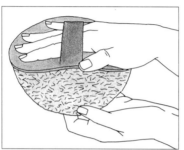

Sanding pad is secured to your hand with a strap, making it convenient for sanding large surfaces. Abrasive discs are attached to the pad with Velcro. The flexibility of the pad allows you to bend it to the shape of the work.

Stick-it block is designed to hold self-adhesive abrasive sheets that grip onto a felt backing. Replacing the sheet is as easy as pulling off the old one and sticking on the new one. The block itself has a large handle with a comfortable grip. Use the straight end of the base to sand into tight corners. The rounded end fits into a concave surface.

Palm orbital sander, for preparing a wood surface before applying a finish, works with an orbital motion. A soft pad covered with an abrasive sheet moves in quick, tight circles while the housing remains stationary. The sander's small size allows for one-handed use; hold the base flush to the work. The sander may come with a dust bag.

Pole sander, when attached to an extension pole, is used for reaching ceilings and upper parts of walls. Abrasive sheets are held in place with metal clips.

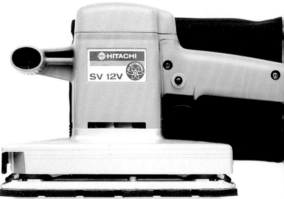

Random orbital sander, available in single and variable-speed models, with second handle, quickly removes stock with coarse abrasive paper. Its random action creates a swirl-free finish when using fine abrasive paper.

Finishing sander (also an orbital sander) has a second handle for two-handed operation. It's available in one, two and variable-speed models. Apply light pressure when sanding; too much can overload the motor. Clamp one-third sheet of an abrasive paper to the pad.

Belt-disc sander (left), which should be bolted to a workbench, lets you sand, buff and sharpen narrow pieces of straight, curved or odd-shaped wood. The belt sander can be raised to fit a job. Attach a buffing belt to polish metals and other materials. The disc sander, with an adjustable worktable, smoothes ends and convex edges of workpieces. Use the mitre gauge for precise sanding. Grinding attachments are available.

Portable belt sander uses a continuous-loop abrasive sheet for fast removal of large, flat areas of wood, for trimming off excess wood and for stripping old paint and finish. Two drum-like rollers control the belt. The back roller is powered by the motor; the front roller is spring-loaded to correct the belt tension. The longer and wider the belt, the heavier and more powerful the tool. Look for a model with a dust-collection bag. Before buying a belt sander, hold it to check if it feels comfortable. Make sure the sander doesn't twist in your hands when you start it. When using the sander, keep the tool level as you move it across the work.

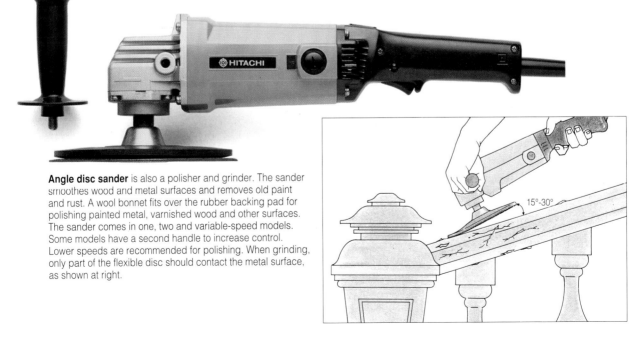

Angle disc sander is also a polisher and grinder. The sander smoothes wood and metal surfaces and removes old paint and rust. A wool bonnet fits over the rubber backing pad for polishing painted metal, varnished wood and other surfaces. The sander comes in one, two and variable-speed models. Some models have a second handle to increase control. Lower speeds are recommended for polishing. When grinding, only part of the flexible disc should contact the metal surface, as shown at right.

15°-30°

ABRASIVES

Although it is often called sandpaper, abrasive paper comes with aluminium oxide, emery, garnet, crushed glass or silicon carbide particles or grit, glued to a paper, cloth or a laminate backing (which is graded by weight). The paper comes in precut sizes or in sheets that can be folded and torn to size; it's graded by numbers that reflect the size of the grit. The finer the grit, the higher the number. Grits vary from 16, which is the coarsest, to 400 for the finest. Lighter backings usually carry finer grits. Other abrasives include metal wools and polishing powders, such as pumice and rottenstone (not shown, but available from specialist suppliers).

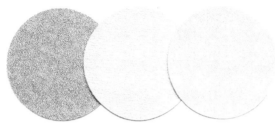

Disc-shaped papers, like other abrasive papers, come in coarse, medium and fine grits. Use coarse-grit papers for fast stock removal; fine-grit papers are best for sanding finishes on wood, metal and plastic surfaces.

Precut abrasive papers come in the same grits as the standard large sheets, but they are cut to fit specific sanders (pp.74-75). Clockwise, the papers fit a sanding block, finishing sander, orbital palm sander with a square pad, portable belt sander and workbench belt sander. The papers may be attached by clamping, an adhesive backing or with Velcro. Most papers have a closed coat – it is completely covered with grains. But to prevent the paper from being clogged with fibres when working on softwoods, choose an open-coat paper with only 70 per cent surface coverage.

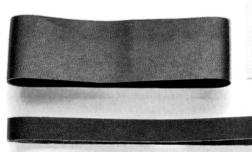

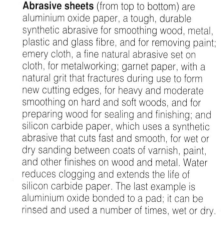

Abrasive sheets (from top to bottom) are aluminium oxide paper, a tough, durable synthetic abrasive for smoothing wood, metal, plastic and glass fibre, and for removing paint; emery cloth, a fine natural abrasive set on cloth, for metalworking; garnet paper, with a natural grit that fractures during use to form new cutting edges, for heavy and moderate smoothing on hard and soft woods, and for preparing wood for sealing and finishing; and silicon carbide paper, which uses a synthetic abrasive that cuts fast and smooth, for wet or dry sanding between coats of varnish, paint, and other finishes on wood and metal. Water reduces clogging and extends the life of silicon carbide paper. The last example is aluminium oxide bonded to a pad; it can be rinsed and used a number of times, wet or dry.

Steel wool can clean, strip and buff metal, wood and other surfaces. It is graded by number: 4 is extra-coarse, 0 is fine and 0000 is superfine. Steel wool can cause rust marks on work that will be exposed to water; use a copper pot scourer instead.

Tile file trims, shapes and cuts narrow strips of tile.

WALLPAPERING TOOLS

To hang wall coverings with professional results, you will find that the tools shown on this page will be helpful. A clean flat surface is necessary to lay the wall covering down on for pasting. If you don't have a large 150 × 90 cm (5 × 3 ft) table, make a temporary one by setting plywood on trestles and covering it with a large plastic dustsheet. Alternatively, if you plan to do a substantial amount of wall covering, buy a pasting table that folds up for storage. For prepasted wall coverings, you will need an inexpensive plastic water tray or trough.

Smoothing brush flattens the wall covering to create a uniform surface without wrinkles and air pockets. The long-bristle brush works best on paper, cloth and delicate coverings such as cork, silk and grass cloth; the gentle bristles won't tear them. The short-bristle model is appropriate for the sturdier vinyl wall coverings. Both are 300 mm (12 in) wide.

Paste brush with 75 mm (3 in) bristles for applying paste and adhesives to wall coverings that are not prepasted. The brush is 150 mm (6 in) wide.

Touching-up kit has a tapered-tip syringe (far left) to repair curled corners on wall covering. To remove an air bubble, slit it with a knife; then inject paste behind the bubble with the needle-tip syringe (left). Smooth down the repair with a seam roller or smoother. Wash area if wall covering is washable.

Wallpaper trimmer has a hardened steel blade and is used for trimming wallpaper to the required length.

Smoother is used on vinyl wall coverings to produce a uniformly smooth surface and to remove air bubbles. It can also serve as a spreader for sealing compound or as a trim guide. Rounded corners will not damage the work.

Casing knife trims wall coverings round outlets, vents, skirting boards and window and door frames.

Seam roller smoothes edges of wall coverings (except embossed). Use rollers with oval barrels for seams, tapered barrels for corners and flat barrels for door and window frames.

Wall-covering shears have sharp blades to cut wall coverings with great accuracy. The handles are designed to provide a comfortable grip.

STEAMWORKS

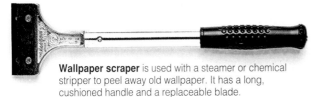

Wallpaper scraper is used with a steamer or chemical stripper to peel away old wallpaper. It has a long, cushioned handle and a replaceable blade.

Wallpaper steamer speeds up the task of removing old wallpaper. Hold the unit against the wallpaper, letting the steam saturate the paper just enough to soften the paste. Then use a scraper to remove the paper.

PAINTING TOOLS

By taking the time to select the right tools and use the correct techniques, an amateur painter can produce outstanding results. Choose the appropriate paint applicators from among the various bristle and foam brushes, rollers, pads and power sprayers. Each applicator has its own benefits, depending on the type of finish being applied, the size of the area being covered and the quality and speed of application desired. Special accessories, including tools for preparing the surface and cleaning up afterwards, also help to make painting tasks easier and to produce professional-looking results.

Trim brush, available with natural or synthetic bristles for oil-based or emulsion finishes, comes in several widths up to 50 mm (2 in). The brush can apply paint to such detail work as skirting boards, door and window trim, and mouldings. It also 'cuts in' paint where rollers cannot reach – such as in corners and where the walls and ceiling meet.

Chisel-edge brush has angled bristles for painting clean edges. Hold the brush so that the ends of the bristles apply the paint. With a steady hand, pull the brush with the shorter bristles leading the way.

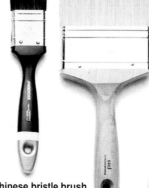

Chinese bristle brush is made with natural animal hairs, which are ideal for applying oil-based paint, varnish and stain. A good brush will provide long service if treated and cleaned properly.

Edger pad has compact fibres to disperse paint quickly and evenly along trim areas. It spreads paint faster than a brush but slower than a roller. One model (right) has guide wheels and a removable pad for cleaning.

Angled pad is especially designed for painting awkward areas such as the inside corners of walls and between walls and ceilings. Pads come in various shapes, some flat and others curved (left).

Wall brush is at least 100 mm (4 in) wide to cover broad areas. To speed the job, use the widest brush possible without using one wider than the work. This brush, with synthetic polyester bristles (others may be nylon), can apply emulsion or gloss paint, varnish and stain.

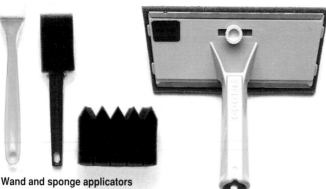

Wand and sponge applicators come in a variety of shapes and sizes for painting neatly in restricted areas. Most come with spare pads. Sash wand applicators are available for painting window frames.

Wall pad is 150-250 mm (6-10 in) wide for large expanses of walls, ceilings and floors. An extension pole can be fitted into the handle.

Pad paint tray can be hung over the rungs of a stepladder or extension ladder. To avoid overloading pad with paint, roll the pad over the revolving wheel in the tray before using it.

Trim rollers have specialised uses. The small roller (below) comes with its own paint tray for touch-ups and hard-to-reach areas. Another roller (centre) applies paint in corners. The third roller (right) is for narrow surface areas. In addition, but not shown, you can get flexible rollers for smaller, irregularly shaped features.

Pipe roller has an indented centre groove in the cover to conform to the contour of heating pipes. Make sure you apply only heat-resistant paint to the pipe.

Roller and paint tray make it possible to apply paint and other finishes quickly and economically to broad surfaces. The roller uses less paint than a brush, requires less effort to spread a smooth, even coat and leaves no brush marks. With the paint tray set on a flat surface, pour paint into the deeper well section. Slip a roller cover onto the roller frame. Place the roller in the well; pull it up to the grooved area, applying slight pressure and rolling it to squeeze out excess paint.

Splatter-shield roller reduces splatters. End caps hold the roller cover in a handle and housing unit. To remove the cover, you may have to prise out tight-fitting end caps. The handle can be connected to an extension pole.

Texture roller has a cover made from pieces of leather. Only the edges of the leather come in contact with the surface and create a pattern. The cover fits only onto a special frame; roller and frame are usually bought as a unit.

Trim guard keeps paint off adjoining straight surfaces. Hold it at right angles to the work with the long edge touching it; the roller cover should fit into its curved shape to let you apply paint to the edge of the work.

Roller covers slide onto a frame or the end caps of a splatter-shield roller. If cleaned properly, most roller covers can be used several times. Roller covers come in various naps for use with emulsion and gloss paints and for special applications.

Extension pole screws into a threaded roller or pad handle, allowing you to reach ceilings and upper wall areas without using a ladder. It also eliminates bending or kneeling when painting floors and sealing driveways. Extension poles can be up to 2 m (6 ft) long. Some models extend even farther.

Self-feeding roller is quite rare and comes with a lid and filler tube that fits on a paint tin. Attach the extension pole (assembled with roller cover and splatter shield) to the lid. Pull pole sections apart to siphon paint into handle. Detach pole from lid; push pole section in to send paint to roller.

Electric paint roller uses an electric pump to apply paint. It is also quite rare but worth looking for as it is even easier to use than a self-feeding roller. The pump feeds paint directly from the tin to the roller through a hose. A push button on the roller handle starts and stops the flow of paint. It is ideal for large projects such as painting several rooms or the exterior of a house.

Pouring spout fits on a standard paint tin. It allows you to pour the paint into a tray without spilling or dripping.

Lid opening tool makes it easier to open standard plastic containers of paint and similar materials without damaging the lipped lid.

Paint mixer fits into the chuck of almost any standard power drill. The plastic blades can be used to stir and blend paint, driveway and roofing sealers and joint compound in the tin, with less mess and more consistency.

Paint sprayer applies paint, stain, varnish and other liquids with a fine mist for fast, even and run-free covering. It is helpful for hard-to-paint projects such as louvred doors and wickerwork.

Paint mitten, for applying paint to unusually shaped items, is worn over a rubber glove. Dip the mitten into paint, then spread the paint over the work.

Paint sponges come in various shapes to apply paints and stains to surfaces. Depending on the sponge, it will leave a smooth or textured pattern.

Stippling brush is dabbed over a stencil to leave a decorative pattern on walls, furniture and other surfaces. Be careful not to overload the bristles with paint.

Varnish brushes with natural bristles are used for applying varnish, lacquer and other finishes. One brush (right) has bristles with an oval profile to hold varnish and to provide best edge control. The badger-hair brush (far right) can hold more varnish with its 'split-end' bristles.

Rubber grainer has concentric circles imprinted on a rubber base. Experiment with dragging and rolling it in wet stain or glaze to create your own effect.

Striping brush utilises natural camel bristles that are cut and set in the ferrule to come to a point. Drag the brush through wet stain or glaze to create a wood-grain or marbling effect. The brush can also be used with a steady hand to create delicate line work.

Graining comb creates a pattern in wet stain or paint to simulate wood grain. The comb comes in different sizes; the steel teeth vary in width.

Wire brush prepares wood, metal and other surfaces for painting by removing loose paint, rust, corrosion and other hardened matter. This model has a built-in scraper on the back of the handle.

Spiked cleaner helps to separate bristles when cleaning a brush. For proper maintenance, always clean out a brush before paint hardens.

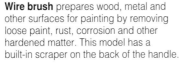

Dustsheets to protect floors and carpets. Lay polythene sheet first, to prevent seepage; then cover it with an absorbent cotton sheet.

Heat gun focuses a controlled amount of heat, usually between 120°C and 590°C, to soften paint so that you can remove it with a scraper. Also use the heat gun to remove glued-down tile and to bend plastic. Temperature can be adjusted to different settings. Start with a low temperature and increase it gradually.

LADDERS AND SAWHORSES

To reach high places or to create extra surfaces for holding your work, a few ladders and sawhorses – and perhaps a portable work centre – are a great help. A 6 m (20 ft) ladder is usually long enough for most domestic needs. Aluminium ladders are lighter and easier to handle than wooden ones.

Caution: Fully open a stepladder and lock its braces before using it. Make sure the ladder is secure and steady. Always face a ladder and hold on when climbing or descending. Move the ladder to a new position rather than stretch sideways. Never use a broken or damaged ladder. Never work on a ladder outdoors during windy or inclement weather. Keep the ladder far away from electrical or other wires. Never work with two people on a ladder, or underneath someone on a ladder. Climb only as high on a ladder as the third rung from the top – a grab rail at the top increases safety. Always store ladders securely – preferably indoors.

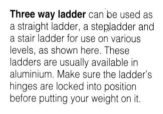

Stepladder can be used indoors and out, available in various heights ranging from about 1.2-4.9 m (4-16 ft). Some have a flat platform at the top which is useful for holding tools. Choose a stepladder with a grab rail, if possible, for added safety. It is possible to get a hook-on platform which covers a step, making standing on it for any length of time more comfortable.

Three way ladder can be used as a straight ladder, a stepladder and a stair ladder for use on various levels, as shown here. These ladders are usually available in aluminium. Make sure the ladder's hinges are locked into position before putting your weight on it.

Sawhorses come ready-made, or you can make your own with 2 x 4s and the brackets shown above. I look-on hardware bins and tool hangers are also available. Use two sawhorses to support a large workpiece, or lay a sheet of plywood across them to make a temporary workbench.

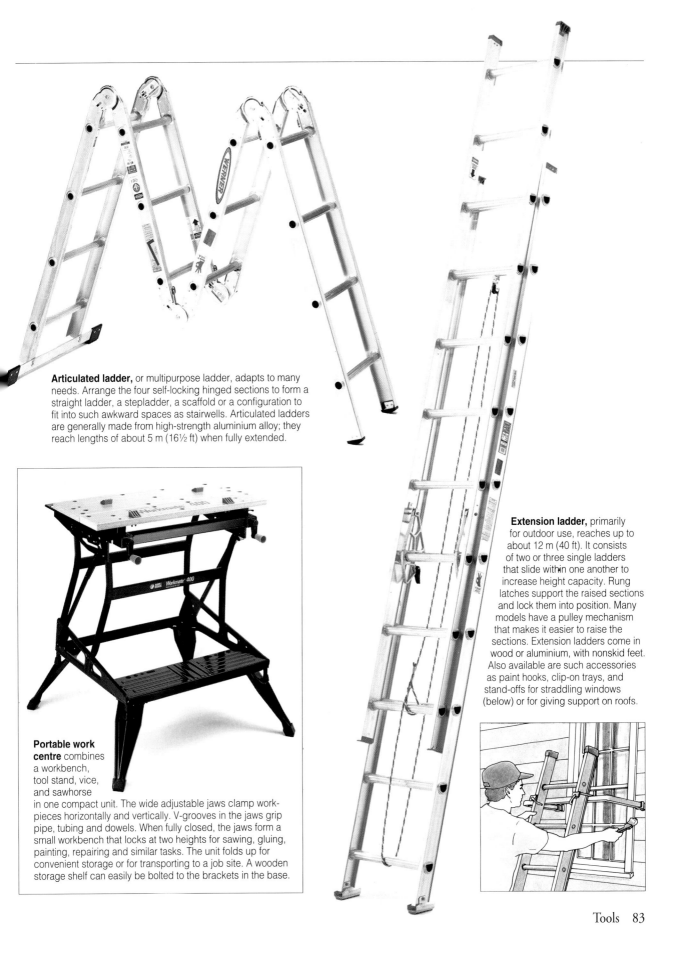

Articulated ladder, or multipurpose ladder, adapts to many needs. Arrange the four self-locking hinged sections to form a straight ladder, a stepladder, a scaffold or a configuration to fit into such awkward spaces as stairwells. Articulated ladders are generally made from high-strength aluminium alloy; they reach lengths of about 5 m (16½ ft) when fully extended.

Extension ladder, primarily for outdoor use, reaches up to about 12 m (40 ft). It consists of two or three single ladders that slide within one another to increase height capacity. Rung latches support the raised sections and lock them into position. Many models have a pulley mechanism that makes it easier to raise the sections. Extension ladders come in wood or aluminium, with nonskid feet. Also available are such accessories as paint hooks, clip-on trays, and stand-offs for straddling windows (below) or for giving support on roofs.

Portable work centre combines a workbench, tool stand, vice, and sawhorse in one compact unit. The wide adjustable jaws clamp workpieces horizontally and vertically. V-grooves in the jaws grip pipe, tubing and dowels. When fully closed, the jaws form a small workbench that locks at two heights for sawing, gluing, painting, repairing and similar tasks. The unit folds up for convenient storage or for transporting to a job site. A wooden storage shelf can easily be bolted to the brackets in the base.

TOOLS FOR SHARPENING

You can sharpen dulled tools on a variety of sharpening stones and grinding wheels and polish metalwork with buffing wheels and a buffing compound. Grinding and buffing wheels are made to fit the chucks of electric drills (for light jobs) or the arbors of a bench grinder (most grinders have two arbors). Before using a wheel, check it by rapping it with a screwdriver handle and listening for a ringing sound. If it makes a buzzing sound, the wheel is chipped or cracked; replace it. Although the grinder has guards, it is wise to wear a face shield for extra protection. When turning on the power, stand to one side of the wheel just in case it shatters. To prevent overheating, use light pressure and cool the work often in water. Keep your grinding wheels true and even by dressing them with the appropriate tool. After cleaning a stone, store it in a closed box. Reapply oil to an oilstone before storing it.

Combination benchstone has coarse or medium grit on one side, fine on the other. The coarse face is for sharpening dull tools; the fine face for a keen, lasting edge. It may be used dry or with oil.

Japanese waterstone sharpens quickly because worn particles on the stone break away and expose new, sharp particles. Before using a medium or coarse-grit stone, soak it in water for about 6 hours; soak a fine-grit stone, for only 5 minutes. Continue to apply water as you work.

Slipstone, with its wedge-shaped profile, has a flat surface for honing straight edges and a round side  for irregular shapes; it is ideal for the inside edge of lathe tools and gouges. To use the stone, move it against the stationary tool. A storage box is available.

Arkansas oilstone, a high-quality natural stone, comes in three grades: soft, hard and black hard. Lubricate the stone with oil.

Gouge stone is shaped to fit the round edge of a gouge chisel. Depending on your stone, apply water or a light mineral oil to the stone. To use it, rub the stone against the gouge.

Lubricating oil is applied to oilstones to increase grinding speed and to prevent the pores in the stones from clogging. When the stone becomes sticky, clean off the oil with paraffin or ammonia.

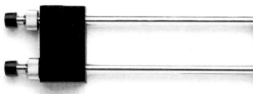

Stone holder keeps stone in place when honing. Grooved rubber soles prevent the holder from skidding. Set the stone in the holder; turn the two knurled wheels to secure it.

Bevel setter and guide sets blades of chisels, planes and spokeshaves to 25 different angles. Place the guide on the setter with the work edge under the angle block. When it's parallel, secure the work.

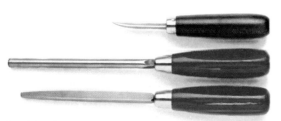

Burnisher forms burr or hooked edge on scraper. Use round (centre) or triangular (bottom) type for general burnishing; round type only with curved scrapers. Dresser (top) is for touch-ups.

Honing guide holds a chisel or plane blade at a set angle for honing. Turn the top knob to hold the blade in place; set the angle of the guide by adjusting the side knob. Wheels let you slide the tool along the stone.

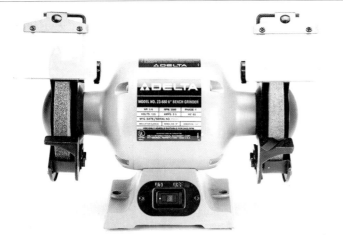

Bench grinder mounts on a workbench or pedestal stand. It has a tool rest for each of the two wheels, spark guards and protective shields. Grinders come in different sizes; always check that the wheel is correct for the grinder you have.

Tapered spindle, or pigtail, fits into a bench grinder to hold accessories. The cone-shaped buffer comes in different grades of coarseness and in various shapes. To buff intricate details in metals, use irregularly shaped buffers, and to polish rings, use narrow ones.

Bench grinder wheels are available in various materials. The stone wheel (top) comes in different grits for sharpening. The wire wheel (centre) can turn the grinder into a stripper to remove rust and paint from small objects. The buffing wheel (bottom) is suitable for applying a polished finish to metal surfaces.

Buffing compounds, when applied to their own buffing wheels, create final finishes. From top to bottom are emery cake, to remove rust from metals; tripoli, to buff brass, steel, aluminium and pewter; white rouge, to add lustre to chrome, steel and nickel; and red rouge, to polish silver and other precious metals.

Strop, a two or four-sided tool covered with leather and slate, gives the finishing touch to a honed blade or tool. It is used in conjunction with strop paste. On the four-sided version, three of the sides are covered with different grades of leather.

Wheel dressers come in a number of styles to resurface a grinding wheel. The silicon carbide stick (above) cleans and restores a clogged wheel. When the wheel has worn unevenly, hold a hooded star wheel dresser (far left) against it. To true a grinding wheel, use the hardy diamond wheel dresser (left), holding it against the bench grinder's tool rest or a homemade jig.

Drill bit sharpener, powered by a standard electric drill (not a cordless drill), sharpens steel twist bits and masonry bits. Set drill in holder, fitting the spindle of sharpener into its chuck; use the collet to hold the bit.

SOLDERING TOOLS

Soldering uses heat to melt a bonding material (solder) and join metal pieces to one another. Soldering irons, guns and pencils are electric heat-generating tools. Acetylene and propane gas-powered torches produce a flame with significantly more heat. When working with any of these heat-producing tools, be extremely careful. Keep a fire extinguisher handy, wear eye protection and other protective clothing, avoid explosive atmospheres and keep the flame away from flammable materials and surfaces. Never leave them unattended, especially near children.

Soldering gun heats small areas electrically, making it ideal for soldering electronic circuits. The interchangeable tip heats quickly when the trigger is squeezed and cools when it is released.

Electric soldering iron has interchangeable tips that come in a variety of shapes to fit the job. The iron shown is for heavy jobs, such as leaded-glass work. Smaller soldering pencils are available for electrical work and light metalworking jobs.

Soft solder comes as solid wire or wire with flux at its centre. Use acid-core solder (top, left) to join pieces that can be washed to get rid of the corrosive flux; rosin-core solder (bottom, left) for electronic work; and lead-free solid-core solder (right) for water pipes.

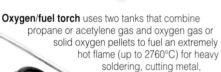

Hard solder flows (melts) at higher temperatures than soft solder. Cut strips, wire or sheets into tiny chips before using.

Cordless soldering iron holds enough butane gas for up to 4 hours of work. Ignite it by pushing a button and use it as a soldering iron or as a hot-air tool. Keep the cover on the tool when not in use.

Flux is brushed onto metal before soldering to prevent oxidation and help solder to flow. Use a noncorrosive rosin flux for electronic work, a zinc chloride flux for all other soft soldering and a floride or borax-based flux for hard soldering.

Oxygen/fuel torch uses two tanks that combine propane or acetylene gas and oxygen gas or solid oxygen pellets to fuel an extremely hot flame (up to 2760°C) for heavy soldering, cutting metal, brazing and welding.

Soldering iron rest can be attached to the edge of the workbench to provide a safe base for the hot iron. Always place the iron on the stand when not using it. Some irons come with small stands of their own.

Torch lighter eliminates dangerous match lighting. Squeezing the trigger causes a small spark that ignites the gas.

Propane torch uses propane gas that mixes with the surrounding air to produce a hot flame (about 1370°C). Different tips are available for soldering, removing paint from metal and other jobs requiring localised heat.

Binding wire of black iron can be tied around pieces being soldered to hold them in place. Select 26 gauge wire for general use.

SHEET-METAL TOOLS

Because of sheet metal's strength, malleability and versatility, a number of specialised tools are available to cut, bend, shape, join and stretch it. In addition to those illustrated below, you will need a number of the tools shown on the preceding pages, including a punch or metal scriber and a micrometer to mark and measure the metal; snips, power nibblers and saws to cut it; drills to make holes in it; various hammers, mallets, stakes and an anvil to pound and shape it; and a machinist's vice to hold it steady while cutting and bending it.

Hand groover flattens and locks a grooved seam when joining sheets of metal. Choose one to fit the seam, place it over the seam and tap the tool with a ball-pein hammer or mallet along the entire seam.

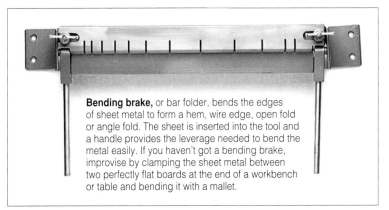

Bending brake, or bar folder, bends the edges of sheet metal to form a hem, wire edge, open fold or angle fold. The sheet is inserted into the tool and a handle provides the leverage needed to bend the metal easily. If you haven't got a bending brake, improvise by clamping the sheet metal between two perfectly flat boards at the end of a workbench or table and bending it with a mallet.

Hand seamer bends and flattens sheet-metal edges. Use it to bend sheets into boxes or similar shapes, to fold over sharp edges to form a hem or add rigidity and to fold over interlocking seams to join multiple sheets.

Hand notcher makes a clean V-shaped cut in sheet metal without slipping. The compound-action handles produce the necessary leverage for fast and easy cutting.

Pitch bowl filled with pitch (below) is used for chasing or repoussé work. Filled with charcoal chips, it can be used for annealing metal or holding small pieces while soldering. Some are available with a stepped support (left) that holds bowls of different sizes.

Hand punch (or lever punch) applies great pressure to cut holes in sheet metal, plastic or leather. The powerful jaws push small metal punches into matching dies which can create different-sized holes.

Chasing and repoussé tools are small blunt punches and chisels that etch decorative designs into metal.

Circle cutter consists of cylindrical pins and a slotted metal base with holes of different sizes. Insert the sheet metal into the slot in the base and punch a hole with the pin and a hammer.

Pop riveter fastens metal to metal, plastic to metal or heavy-gauge fabric to itself or to metal by inserting metal fasteners, called rivets, into predrilled holes.

Sandbag can be used as a malleable backing when pounding dents out of metal. Simply hold the damaged section against the bag and gently pound out the dent with a mallet.

OTHER METALWORKING TOOLS

If you work with metal pipes and tubing, you'll need specialised tools for bending, cutting and joining the sections. If you need to cut threads into any metal rods or plates, you will also need a set of taps and dies. These tools are made of hardened steel and can cut neatly into any softer metal; they can also be used to restore damaged threads in appliance and car parts. Special large dies and diestocks are available for threading brass or steel pipes. Finally, if you are working on metal jewellery, you will find specialised tools to help you to do the job; in addition to the ones shown here, you may need smooth-jaw pliers for handling delicate pieces.

Tubing bender provides leverage to bend rigid copper and steel tubing to a maximum of 180°. Push a length of pipe into top of bender to form handle. Insert tubing into curved channel, step on tread and pull handle until spirit levels in bender indicate the degree of bend you want.

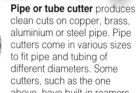
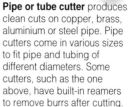

Pipe or tube cutter produces clean cuts on copper, brass, aluminium or steel pipe. Pipe cutters come in various sizes to fit pipe and tubing of different diameters. Some cutters, such as the one above, have built-in reamers to remove burrs after cutting.

Pipe-bending spring aids in bending thin-wall piping, such as copper and aluminium, without flattening or creasing it. The bender is a tightly wound wire coil and is available in standard piping diameters. Both internal and external (shown above) pipe-bending springs are available. With a twisting motion, slide the bender over or inside the pipe; then bend it slowly with your hands or over your knee.

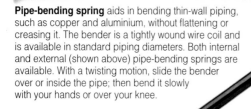

Pipe reamer shaves away rough edges and burrs left inside ends of pipes or tubing after cutting. Turn the reamer as you push it into the pipe. Reamer bits for electric drills are also available.

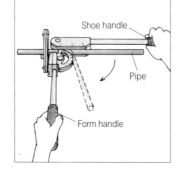

Shoe handle

Pipe

Form handle

Lever bender is operated with two hands to bend pipe. Grasp the tool by its form handle and swing the shoe handle out. Slide piping into groove of curved bending form and slowly pull the shoe handle back until the pipe is bent to the desired angle.

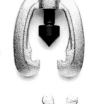

Flaring tool widens ends of flexible tubing to take flare fittings. A double bar type clamp (below) holds tubing while a cone-shaped ram (right) is driven into the tubing to flare it.

Plumber's die and diestock are used to thread brass and steel pipe. Secure the pipe in a vice; fix the die (left) in the diestock (above) and slide it over the pipe. Pressing into the pipe, turn the diestock clockwise until the die begins to cut. Add cutting oil to the end of the pipe and continue turning the diestock without applying pressure. Add more oil from time to time.

Taps cut or restore internal threads in holes in metal so that threaded fasteners can be used.

 Tap wrenches turn the taps in the metal. T-handled wrench (left) gives less leverage than larger model (above).

Diestock (above) holds the dies (below, left) that cut external threads on metal rods. Fit the die into the hole in the diestock with the slit in the die facing the central screw. Tighten the central screw first, then the side screws. Place the die over the end of the rod, press down and turn. Once the die bites, no further pressure is necessary. Keep turning the diestock a half turn forwards, then a quarter turn back, to break the swarf. When the thread is complete, wind the die back to the beginning.

Thread-restoring file renews damaged right or left-handed external threads on screws, pipes or rods of any diameter.

Draw plate is clamped in a vice and wire is drawn through the holes with pliers to change its shape or make it thinner. You can pull the wire through successively smaller holes until the desired gauge is reached.

 Doming punch comes in various sizes for use in chasing or repoussé or to shape thin metal on a doming die (below). Strike the punch with a ball-pein hammer.

Three-in-one tap tree cuts and cleans threads in thin metal or plastic. It is rare, but very useful for threading electrical boxes. Replaceable taps are available in various sizes.

Drill guide

Stud extractor is slipped over the stud to be removed, and a square drive sliding T-bar fitted. The offset knurled washer grips the stud as pressure is exerted, allowing you to unscrew it.

 Doming die has dents of various sizes along its polished steel faces for shaping silver or other metal for jewellery. Tap the metal into the recess with a doming punch.

Bolt extractor removes broken bolts or screws. Drill hole in top of fastener, insert and turn bolt extractor with wrench. You may need a drill guide to help you with hard-to-reach fasteners.

Bolt

 **Wire design block** lets you shape wire or metal strips into square, rectangular, triangular or curved shapes. Lay the metal in the appropriate groove and gently hammer it into shape.

 Bending jig holds bar metal firmly in place while you hammer it into curves. Secure the jig in a vice and arrange the pins for the curve you want.

 **Bracelet bender,** an alternative to the mandrel (below), holds a strip of metal in its upturned end as you bend it round the curve of the tool to shape an open-end bracelet.

Bench pin, a wooden brace used in jewellery making, is clamped to the workbench and used as a surface for sawing or filing small metal pieces.

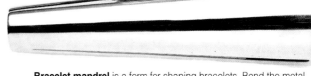 **Bracelet mandrel** is a form for shaping bracelets. Bend the metal round the mandrel with your hands and finish by pounding it with a mallet. Turn the bracelet upside-down for final pounding.

Mandrel cradle holds a bracelet or a ring mandrel in a horizontal position. To use the cradle for a ring mandrel, insert the narrow end of the mandrel into the hole in one end of the cradle.

 **Ring mandrel** works in same way as the bracelet mandrel, but it is graduated to help you to shape a ring into the proper size. Turn the ring upside-down occasionally to compensate for the mandrel's taper.

CONCRETE-WORKING TOOLS

To work with concrete you'll need a number of general-purpose tools, including measuring and levelling tools, a steel square, a hammer and a saw for building forms, and buckets for measuring cement and adding it to the mix. In addition, you will need the specialised tools shown below. If you are sinking a pier footing or a post base, you will need a shovel holer; and if you are mixing your own concrete, a mortar box. Plastic or metal mortar boxes resembling children's sandboxes are available commercially or you can make one by nailing together a frame of boards and adding a marine plywood bottom. For larger jobs, hire a rotating-drum mixer or have ready-mixed concrete delivered.

Screed, feather edge or strike-off board, is the first tool used to level freshly poured concrete. When using one, rest its ends on the tops of the forms. Lightweight aluminium feather edges (like the one shown here) are sold in 4-12 ft lengths, but a long, straight wood batten will also do the job.

Float smoothes concrete after screeding by drawing sand and cement to the surface and pushing aggregate below. Use a magnesium float (top) for air-entrained concrete (concrete with tiny bubbles); otherwise use a wood float (bottom). Floats also come with round edges for curved surfaces.

Edger finishes and rounds the sharp edges of concrete slabs and walkways. The ends of the blade are straight, curved or a combination of straight and curved for various applications.

Groover a form of float that cuts grooves in driveways, paths and patio floors to control the cracking that is caused by expansion and contraction (p.212).

Square-mouth shovel scoops up the maximum amount of concrete. To eliminate air pockets when filling forms, pull the shovel blade up and down in the concrete, then press the concrete against the forms with the back of the shovel.

Mortar hoe can be used to mix concrete and mortar. The large holes in the blade aerate the mixture for a better consistency.

Shovel holer digs deep, narrow holes for posts without disturbing the surrounding area.

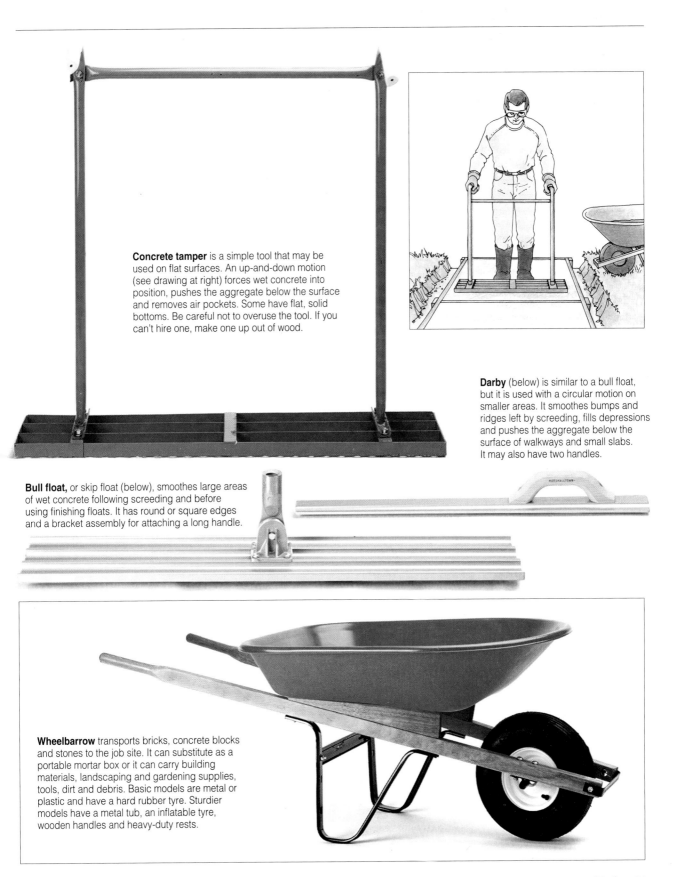

Concrete tamper is a simple tool that may be used on flat surfaces. An up-and-down motion (see drawing at right) forces wet concrete into position, pushes the aggregate below the surface and removes air pockets. Some have flat, solid bottoms. Be careful not to overuse the tool. If you can't hire one, make one up out of wood.

Darby (below) is similar to a bull float, but it is used with a circular motion on smaller areas. It smoothes bumps and ridges left by screeding, fills depressions and pushes the aggregate below the surface of walkways and small slabs. It may also have two handles.

Bull float, or skip float (below), smoothes large areas of wet concrete following screeding and before using finishing floats. It has round or square edges and a bracket assembly for attaching a long handle.

Wheelbarrow transports bricks, concrete blocks and stones to the job site. It can substitute as a portable mortar box or it can carry building materials, landscaping and gardening supplies, tools, dirt and debris. Basic models are metal or plastic and have a hard rubber tyre. Sturdier models have a metal tub, an inflatable tyre, wooden handles and heavy-duty rests.

MASONRY TROWELS

The best trowels have blades and tangs cast from a single piece of carbon steel and handles made of wood, plastic or leather. Trowels with welded blades are less expensive, but they warp and break easily. When buying a trowel, check the quality of the blade by striking it against a hard object and listening for a ringing sound. A long ring indicates a good blade. Also consider the tool's weight, size, balance, flexibility and the angle of its handle. After using a trowel, scrape off any mortar with another trowel or a wire brush and thoroughly rinse and dry the tool. Rub wooden or leather handles with linseed oil.

Concrete finishing trowel is used to smooth a surface after the concrete has begun to set. Hold the trowel nearly level and move it in sweeping arcs across the surface. Make two passes for an extra-smooth surface.

Gauging trowel mixes mortar and applies small amounts in confined areas. It is used mainly to replace crumbled mortar and to patch concrete. In addition, its rounded nose makes it useful for tucking and pushing insulation into tight areas.

Bucket trowel is used for scooping mortar out of a bucket or mortar box. It is also good for buttering bricks and for small smoothing jobs.

Pool trowel or round trowel is a special variation of the concrete finishing trowel. The blade is rounded to prevent it from accidentally digging into the wet concrete, making it ideal for smoothing.

Corner trowels are available for shaping concrete around internal and external corners. The handle is located at the centre of the 90 degree bend in the blade to balance the tool and allow you to apply equal pressure to both sides of the corner.

Step trowel shapes the inside angles on concrete steps. The gentle bend in the blade allows for rounded edges. Trowels for outside angles are also available.

Brick trowel spreads mortar onto bricks or concrete blocks with a technique call buttering. The shape of the blade also makes it ideal for smoothing small patches in concrete.

Pointing trowel applies mortar to joints in brick and concrete block work. This smaller version of the brick trowel is also useful for filling small cavities and repairing old crumbling mortar joints.

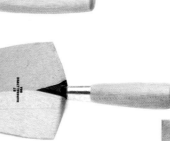

Tile setter is a brick trowel with an extra-wide blade; it holds a greater amount of mortar and smoothes more easily than the standard brick trowel. It is the best tool for buttering large bricks and blocks.

Margin trowel, or window trowel, works mortar into tight spaces and corners where a larger pointed trowel will not fit.

BRICKLAYING TOOLS

When working with bricks, concrete blocks or even stones, you will need a number of specialised tools including some of the trowels on the facing page and a number of the hammers, levels and measuring and squaring tools covered earlier in this section. You will also need tools for carrying, cutting, aligning and cleaning the bricks, and tools for working with mortar, as shown on this page. Finally, you will need a hawk – a flat board with a handle for holding mortar as you work. You can buy a hawk (not shown) or easily make one by cutting a square of plywood and screwing a section of thick dowel or broomstick under its centre. You will also need a plastic or wooden box for mixing mortar – or else a large wooden board.

Tuck pointer is used to pack mortar between concrete blocks or bricks when repointing (restoring crumbling mortar in masonry walls).

Joint raker with skate wheels rakes out mortar from a joint. The length of the nail that scrapes out the mortar can be adjusted to change the appearance of the joint. After raking it, smooth and compress the joint with a narrow jointer.

Jointer shapes mortar in a joint just before it dries, removing excess mortar and adding durability. Standard convex jointer (above, top) leaves a rounded groove. Grapevine jointer (above) patterns mortar. Sledge-runner jointer (left, top) is used for long horizontal joints. V jointer (left, bottom) leaves a V-shaped groove; it also comes without a handle.

Line blocks are attached to outside corners of walls. A string stretched between two blocks creates a guide for laying each level course of bricks, concrete blocks or stones. If you can't use line blocks, use metal line pins (not shown here).

Brick tongs make transporting bricks from supply pile to work area easy and fast. The handle quickly adjusts to hold 6 to 10 bricks. There are also tongs (not shown) that pick up a single concrete block.

Brick chisel or brick bolster cuts brick, stone or concrete block to size and shape when struck with a hammer. Blades range from 75-100 mm (3-4 in) wide. A wider blade helps to make straighter cuts. Always wear gloves and goggles when cutting bricks.

Mason's brush finishes off rough spots in wet joints and cleans brick and concrete block surfaces before you apply mortar. Joints can be weakened if dust and debris are not removed.

Plugging chisel cleans out hardened mortar. Hold chisel in a gloved hand and strike with a club hammer. The direction of the taper in the blade determines whether chisel will cut deep or run shallow along joint.

Rubbing stone is a grooved silicon-carbide stone mounted on a base and handle. Use it to smooth rough areas and to remove marks from dried concrete.

MISCELLANEOUS TOOLS

Although this section has covered hundreds of tools, there are still many more available for working with specific materials. On this and the facing page you will find just a few of the less common tools that make a job easier. Whether it's gluing, veneering, tiling or working with glass or plastic, these tools are worth the money if you will be putting them to a lot of use. Because some tools are such great timesavers, they can be worth buying even if they are used only once or twice; but you may find it more cost-effective to hire one. Buy tools selectively, only as you need them; with time, you will find that your workshop will be well stocked.

Glue brushes are made with natural hog bristles for spreading hot glue. Long handles make it easier to reach into restricted areas. Unlike brushes that use metal ferrules, the bristles are attached to the handles with glue and string so that rust stains cannot spoil the piece; this is especially useful when working on fine woodwork. Brushes are available in various sizes.

Glass glue pot has a removable brush for applying glue to the work. A weight on the handle holds the brush in place and seals the opening in the lid. The handle is spring-loaded; push the brush down to dip the bristles into the glue.

Glue roller applies glue quickly and evenly to flat surfaces and edges. Remove the stopper before applying glue. Holding the bottle in your hand, squeeze it as you roll the tool over the work. The harder you squeeze, the more glue will come out of the tool. Wash the roller in hot soapy water after each use. Dried glue can be removed with a dull-bladed tool.

Hot-melt glue gun heats a glue stick that is inserted into an opening at the rear of the gun; by squeezing the trigger, melted glue is applied to the work. This model is powered by a charger, which also serves as a resting stand. Different glue sticks are available for gluing different materials, including wood, ceramic and plastic.

Three-tip glue applicator has exchangeable nozzles for general-purpose, pinpoint, and dowel hole applications. To prevent glue from drying when not in use, seal bulb opening with Cling Film held in place with a rubber band.

Glue injector has a thin nozzle to apply any type of glue in restricted areas without making a mess. The body holds about 15 ml of glue.

Veneer roller applies pressure evenly as it is rolled over veneer that is being glued to a surface. Use a narrow roller for joining seams.

Toothing blade with serrations is used to scrape a surface before applying glue. The rough surface helps to give a stronger bond.

Scratch brushes are useful for removing rust, surface dirt or flaking paint, or for finishing a surface in a restricted area. The bristles can be made of stainless steel or brass for metals, and nylon or horsehair for gentle abrasiveness. Some come with a metal scraper fitted to the end (not shown).

Veneer block roller fits into your hand comfortably for applying even pressure to veneer. Hold the tool with the heel of your hand against the flat surface.

Veneer punch is used to cut out an irregular-shaped piece of damaged veneer. Then it cuts the same shape from new veneer. Glue the new piece in place. The punch is available with different shapes (right).

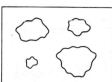

Miniature rotary tool accepts attachments to carve, grind, polish, sand, cut and drill wood, metal, glass and tile. Hold it in your hand or hang it from its hook and attach a flexible shaft. A cordless model is also available.

Woodburning iron has a 25 watt element to create designs in wood by darkening the wood colour. The tool is available with four double-ended tips; pointed tips for fine outlining and blunt tips for 'blocking-in' the design. Always use the rest provided.

Tile cutter scores and cuts ceramic tiles. The long throat accepts tiles up to 300 mm wide. A replaceable wheel under the handle scores the tile as the handle is pulled along a bar. A breaker bar ensures a clean break.

Glass fibre roller has spiral grooves in the roller to work out air bubbles that may form when applying resin to glass fibre cloth.

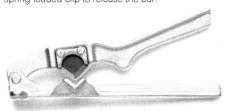

Skeleton gun holds a tube of mastic or sealant. To apply the material to the work, squeeze the trigger; the bar will exert pressure on a disc, pushing material out of the tube. Use the spring-loaded clip to release the bar.

Glass-cutter wheel scores a line in glass. Separate the glass by holding it on each side of the score with your thumbs and index fingers and bending it until it snaps. The notches can be used to snap off thin strips.

Screen installing tool has two wheels to set a gauze window screen and spline into a frame. Use the wheel with a round edge to push the gauze into the channel in the frame, and the wheel with a concave edge for pushing the spline into the channel over the screen.

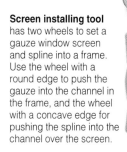

Laminate roller has a smooth rubber roller to apply pressure to sheet laminate while gluing it, creating a strong bond.

Plastic tube cutter is bolted onto a workbench or other flat surface to cut plastic tubing or rubber hoses. Place the work in the V-shaped rest on the bottom arm of the tool. As the top arm is moved down, the blade cuts the tubing or hose.

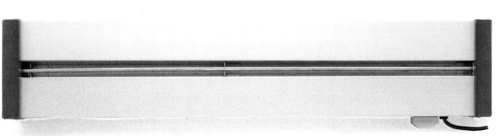

Strip heater is used to heat a sheet of acrylic until it is pliable enough to be formed into any desired shape. It is most often used to make bends or folds in the material. This model can soften acrylic up to 914 mm (36 in) wide and 10 mm (⅜ in) thick. Heating time varies from 30 seconds to 4 minutes, depending on the thickness of the material.

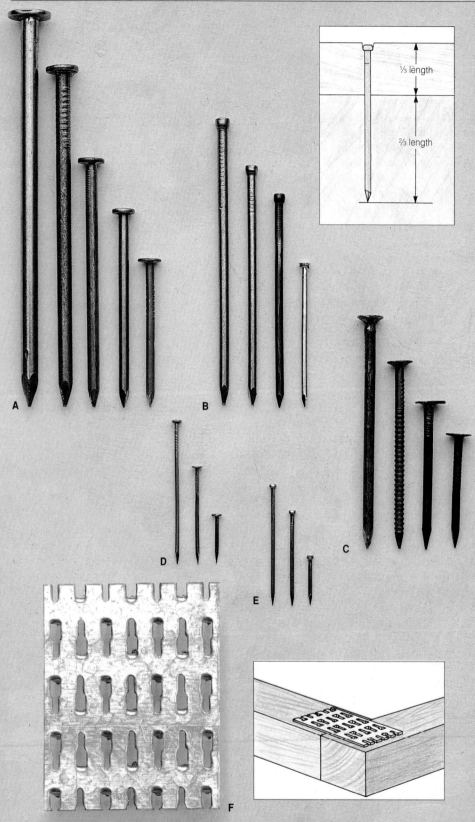

Fasteners are the most common items of hardware, and a nail is the most common fastener. Nails, used primarily to join items permanently, are available in a number of metals, styles and sizes for driving into a variety of materials.

When nailing a thinner piece of material to a thicker one (left), use nails whose length is 3 times the thickness of the thinner piece. If both pieces are of the same thickness, use two or more nails the length of the combined thickness minus 6 mm (¼ in).

Round wire nails (A), heavy-duty nails with a flat head that won't pull through the work, are used in carpentry and building. However, they may split the wood. They are available in a number of sizes and are sold by weight. For further information about how nails are sold see page 347.

Panel pins (B) are thin, small-headed nails for cabinetmaking and attaching trim. The nailhead is usually driven below the surface and the hole filled. Oval wire nails and lost-head nails (not shown) have more holding power than panel pins, are less likely to split wood and are used for door and window frames, flooring or installing trim.

Plasterboard nails (C), for installing all forms of wallboard, have jagged shanks to increase their holding power, as well as sharp points and broad heads. In ceilings and other areas under pressure, use the ringed type, which has more holding power.

Wire nails (D), smaller versions of the round nail, are perfect for light jobs.

Veneer pins (E), or moulding pins, are small finishing nails that are used for fine work with mouldings or veneers.

Timber connector (F) is used for holding together rough butt or mitre joints, such as when making garden sheds and fencing, workbenches and gates. The 'nails' are cut out of a single piece of metal and bent at right angles. To use it, position it across the joint, place a piece of scrap wood over the connector, and drive it in with a heavy, wide-headed hammer or mallet. For best results, fit a connector to both sides of a joint.

Masonry nail (A) is made of hardened steel that resists bending. The nail is used mostly for nailing timber to concrete or masonry walls. The shank may be plain, or it may be fluted to help the nail to grip more tightly.

Boat nail (B) is a ringed, or annular, fastener made of rust-resistant metal. It is ideal for outdoor use where a strong, rust-free bond is needed.

Felt nails (C), or clout nails, have large flat heads that keep them from working through soft materials, such as roofing felt. They are generally galvanised to prevent rusting.

Breeze block nail (D) is designed with helical twist in the shank to allow it to twist its way into breeze blocks without crumbling or shattering them. Breeze blocks are less dense than solid concrete and may be damaged by ordinary masonry nails.

Twisted shank nails (E) turn like screws when driven into flooring and sheet materials, gripping tightly to eliminate squeaking.

Annular ringed nails (F) have shanks that are ringed with deep, closely spaced grooves. The wood's fibre wedges itself into these grooves, resulting in maximum holding power in soft or medium woods. Use when installing subflooring, because the increased holding power keeps it from squeaking or pulling loose.

Escutcheon nails (G) are used for attaching keyhole plates and other backplates or escutcheons. Usually coated with yellow zinc.

Cut floor brads (H) come in either steel or iron and are used for installing tongue-and-groove floorboards. Their flat sides and blunt tips minimise the splitting of hardwood flooring.

Big-headed masonry nails (I) are used with washers to spread the gripping area of the nail and give a more secure fixing. They are zinc-coated to increase their resistance to weather. Use them when fixing down felt roofing or plastic sheet materials which could tear away under pressure. Other uses include fixing downpipe and guttering brackets to masonry and nailing soft material to a concrete floor.

Galvanised nails (J) are coated with zinc to prevent rusting. Use them when exposure to weather is inevitable.

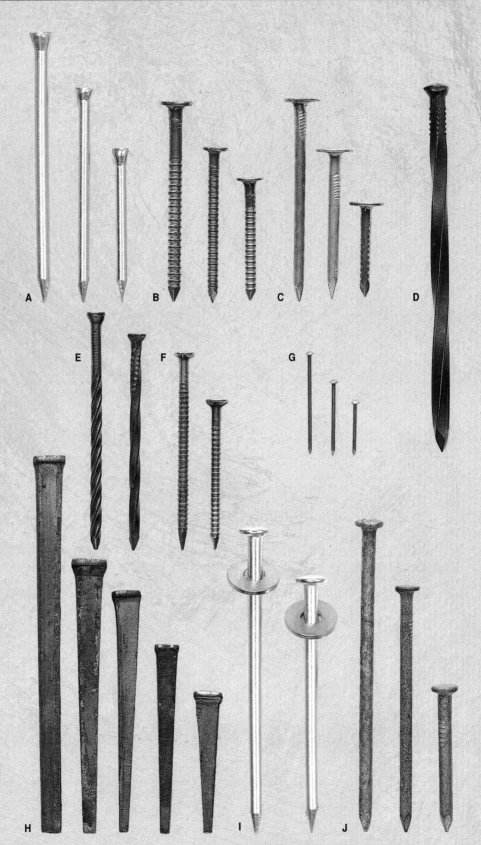

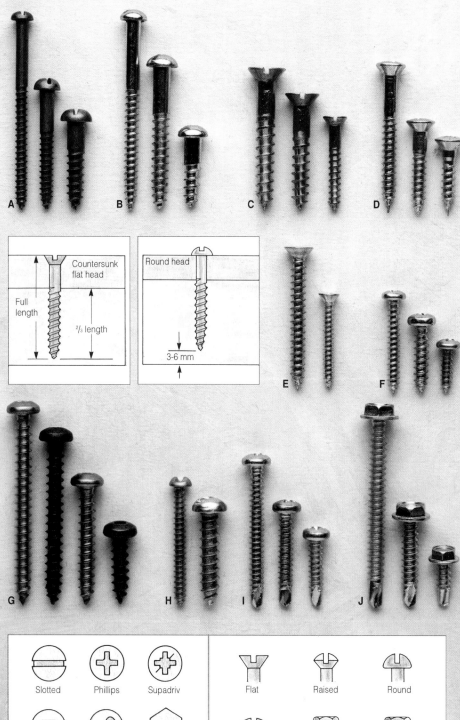

Countersunk flat head

Full length

²/₃ length

Round head

3-6 mm

There are five considerations when choosing a screw: the type and thickness of the material to be fastened, the size of the screw, the material it is made of, the shape of its head and the type of drive. Screws are available for use in wood, wallboard, sheet metal and masonry. They are usually described by their length and diameter. Length may be given in millimetres or inches; their diameter or gauge is a number from 1 to 20. The higher the number, the bigger the gauge. They come in brass and stainless steel to resist corrosion, in hardened steel for heavy work and some are coated with chromium, brass or zinc. There are various types of head and drive (see below). Phillips and Supadriv are both cross-headed, but Supadriv gives a more secure drive. They are not interchangeable, but in an emergency, a Supadriv can be used on a Phillips screwhead. One-way screws are used for security because they cannot be unscrewed easily. Square and hexagon heads are not common.

Wood screws hold two pieces of wood together, providing a strong joint that can be dismantled. Shown are brass and zinc-plated round-head screws with slotted drives **(A, B)**, flat-head screws with slotted drives **(C)** and raised-head screws with Supadriv drives **(D).** When deciding on screw size, take into account the combined thickness of the woods being fastened. Two-thirds of the screw should enter the second piece and the screw should be 3-6 mm (¹/₈ to ¹/₄ in) shorter than the total thickness.

Self-tapping screws fasten two pieces of metal together. Shown are flat-head **(E)** and pan-head **(F)** screws with cross-head drives, pan-head screws with square **(G)** and one-way **(H)** drives and self-tapping screws with Phillips-drive pan heads **(I)** and hexagon washer heads **(J)**. Self-tapping screws have winged tips that cut threaded holes in metal as they are driven, pulling the two pieces tight.

Slotted	Phillips	Supadriv
Square	One-way	Hexagon

Screw drives shown in the top row are the most common. Use a screwdriver with the correct tip to drive them. Use a spanner to drive a hexagon drive screw.

Flat	Raised	Round
Pan	Hexagon	Hexagon washer

Screw heads come in various shapes. Flat head is flush with the surface when countersunk; raised is partly countersunk; the others rest on top. Hexagon heads come with or without attached washers.

Drywall screws (A), thin, sharp screws with bugle-shaped heads, cut through wallboard and anchor themselves in wood or metal battens, holding the wallboard tighter than a nail can. Their cross-head drive allows you to countersink screws without damaging the wallboard's surface.

Coach screws (B) are heavy-duty wood screws that come up to 150 mm (6 in) long, in diameters up to 12 mm ($\frac{1}{2}$ in). Generally, use a coach screw for heavy-duty work such as building a workbench. They are available with hexagon heads (shown) or square heads. Drive them with a spanner.

Masonry screws have sharp, widely spaced threads that are driven directly into concrete without an anchor. The screws shown have hexagon washer heads **(C)** and flat heads **(D).**

Post and screw (E) is used to join case units, such as kitchen cabinets, or to put together frames that may later need to be taken apart and reassembled. The screw is driven through the two pieces, and the cap is pushed into a recess in the second piece and screwed on. A light plastic version of this fastening is used on acrylic plastic.

Thumbscrew (F) is a machine screw (p.102) with a wide, thin head that can be grasped with thumb and forefinger and turned into a threaded plate or bracket. It is used in areas that require frequent adjustment by hand.

Vine eye screw (G) is a fastener used when installing suspended ceilings. Screw the threaded end into a joist and hook the wire that supports the metal grid of the suspended ceiling into the hole in the unthreaded end.

Hanger bolt (H) has machine-screw threads on one end and normal screw threads on the other. To install one, drill a pilot hole in the wood and thread two nuts side by side onto the machine-screw end of the hanger bolt, locking them together. Grasp the nuts with a wrench and drive the screw in.

Dowel screws (I) are used mainly for attaching table legs and other furniture work. Predrill holes, grasp the screw with locking pliers with taped jaws, and screw it into the top of a table leg; then screw the leg into the tabletop.

Screw cup washers (J) supply a hard surface against which to tighten screws without damaging wood.

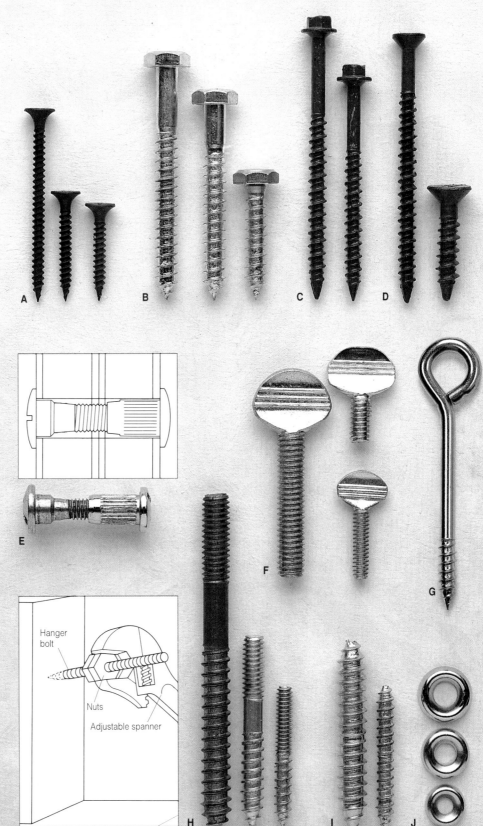

Hanger bolt

Nuts

Adjustable spanner

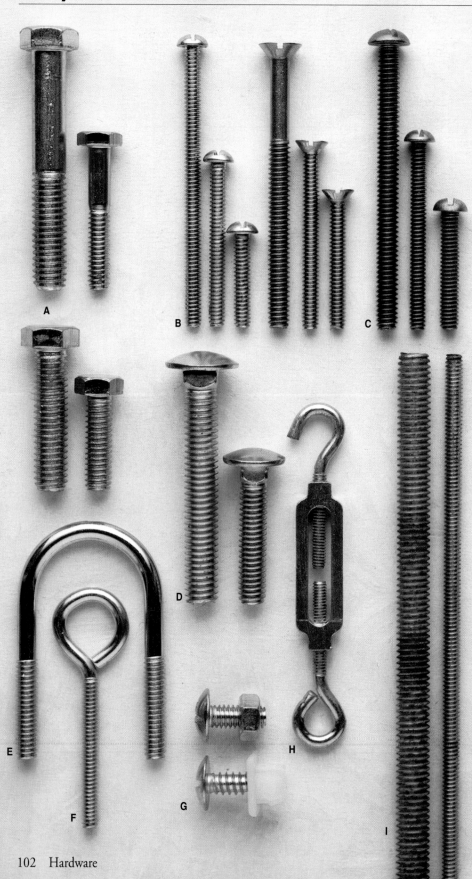

A bolt used with one or two washers and a nut or piece of threaded metal makes the strongest bond and is also easy to take apart without damaging the materials. A bolt should be long enough to protrude through the outside of the nut when assembled, letting at least one of the bolt's threads show. A bolt's size is generally given as the diameter in millimetres, inches or gauge, followed by the type of thread, which is usually metric. However, on older machines and installations you may find BSW (British Standard Whitworth) or UNF/C (United National Fine/Coarse) or BA (British Association). After the type of thread, comes the length of the bolt, in either metric or imperial measurements.

Machine bolt (A) is a strong bolt with a hex or square head.

Machine screws (B) and **(C)** have round or flat slotted heads that can be countersunk. Although they look like bolts, they are called screws because they are often screwed into threaded metal instead of a nut.

Carriage bolt (D) is used in woodwork and sheet-metal work. It has a smooth round head and square shoulders that sink into the wood or fit in a hole, to keep the bolt from turning.

U-bolt (E) holds pipes and other objects snug against a wall or ceiling.

Eyebolt (F) holds wires, ropes and other objects in place.

Licence-plate fastener (G) is a short machine screw with a nut or plastic backplate for attaching licence plates.

Turnbuckle or straining eyebolt (H) has threaded hooks or eyes that move in or out when the sleeve is turned, exerting diagonal pull to keep a gate or screen straight.

Threaded rod or studding (I) is commonly used to join objects over a span of up to 1 m (more than 3 ft).

Flat washer (A) is used under a bolt head or nut to to spread the load and protect the surface. A large flat washer with a small hole is a mudguard washer. It can cover a hole that is larger than the bolt being used in it, eliminating the need to fill the hole.

Lock washer (B) also known as a split-ring or spring washer, exerts a slight spring-like pressure because of its near-spiral shape; this keeps a nut from loosening. When bolting pieces of wood together, it is best to use a flat washer under a lock washer.

Toothed washer (C) has external or internal teeth (or both), which give additional gripping power to a bolt. The washer can also be shaped for use with a flat-head machine screw.

Hex nut (D) screws onto the threaded end of a bolt to tighten the bolt against the pieces being fastened. It may be screwed on over a washer.

Square nut (E) is basically the same as a hex nut, except that it has only four sides instead of six.

Dome nut (F) is a decorative nut that covers the end of the bolt and conceals any exposed threads.

Knurled nut (G) can be turned by hand for fast assembly and disassembly. Its coarse outer design makes it easy to grip between thumb and forefinger. Two styles are shown.

Lock nut (H) has a fibrous lining next to the threads that prevents the nut from coming loose when subject to vibration or stress.

Push nut (I), or axle nut, is used to cover the end of a rod or to hold a small wheel on an axle. It has no threads, but is simply pushed on. Plastic push nuts with steel spring inserts are also available.

T-nut (J) permits the easy driving of machine screws in wood. Drill a hole and hammer the T-nut into place, with its prongs penetrating the wood.

Wing nut (K) is used to fasten units that will be repeatedly disassembled and reassembled. Always drive a wing nut with your fingers; using pliers may damage the nut.

Threaded insert (L) screws into the wood and becomes a receptacle for a bolt to screw into. It is easier to conceal than a T-nut.

T-nut

Threaded insert

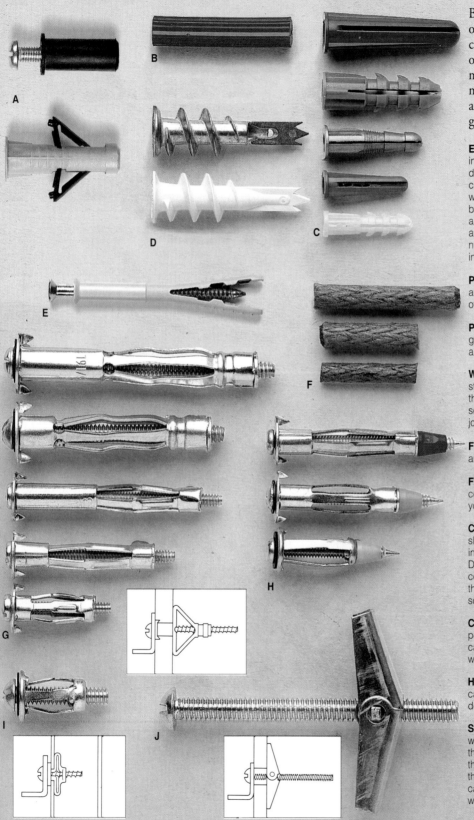

Because fittings sometimes pull out of masonry or wallboard, crumbling the material instead of holding fast inside it, you may need to use some of the many wall plugs and toggles that are available in various sizes to give a firm grip.

Expanding fixings (A) are inserted into walls and expand when a screw is driven in. The multipurpose fixing (top) can be used in both cavity and solid walls. As its screw is tightened, the black rubber sleeve compresses into a strong 'rivet'. Super toggle cavity anchor (bottom) is inserted with its nylon arms held back; on release inside the cavity they spring open.

Plastic plug (B), a type of plastic anchor, has straight sides and is made of strong plastic for heavier jobs.

Plastic wall plugs (C) expand and grip the sides of the starter hole when a screw is driven in.

Wallboard anchors (D) need no starter holes. Simply push one into the wallboard and drive it in with a screwdriver. Use them for lightweight jobs or for repetitive work.

Frame fixing (E) is used for fixing door and window frames to solid masonry.

Fibre plugs (F) will hold screws in concrete or masonry. Install them as you would plastic wall plugs.

Cavity fixings (G) are screws in sleeves. Push the sleeve and screw into a predrilled hole in a hollow wall. Drive in the screw, and the sleeve will collapse, drawing its shoulders against the inside surface of the wall. Remove screw and use it to secure the item.

Cavity wall drive anchors (H) have pointed screws in their sleeves. They can be hammered directly into wallboard without drilling a starter hole.

Hollow-door anchor (I) is a small cavity-wall plug for use on hollow-core doors or similar surfaces.

Spring toggle (J) has spring-loaded wings. Push the screw and the wings through a predrilled hole, then tighten the screw. The wings will open against the inner surface of the wall. Unlike the cavity fixing, the wings of this toggle will fall off if you remove the screw.

Hollow-door hook (A) can be used on partitions as well as doors. Drill a hole, taking care not to drill right through the other side, insert the plug and tighten the screw. The plug expands to hold the hook firmly in place.

Expanding bolt fixings (B) come in various styles. Projecting bolt (top) allows a fixture to be hung on the bolt before the nut and washer are fitted. Loose bolt (bottom) is used when a neat finish is required.

Rawlbolt hook and eye (C) Based on the same principle, the hook is for attaching chain barriers or lighting fixtures; the eye is used for guy ropes and suspended ceilings.

Plastic toggle (D) works in the same way as a metal spring toggle, but comes with a pointed screw and does not require a large entrance hole. Unlike the metal version, it remains in place if the screw is removed.

Wood joiners (E) with four widely spaced prongs are driven straight in to strengthen woodworking joints.

Corrugated fasteners (F) hold together lightweight butt and mitre joints, such as those on screens and picture frames. Drive them in across the joint.

Blind rivets (G) join sheet metal to sheet metal. They are installed through predrilled holes with a riveting tool which applies pressure to the head of the rivet and then cuts off the unwanted mandrel.

Cotter pin (H) or split pin holds thin rods or shafts. Push it through a hole in the shaft, fold the legs out on the other side of the hole, and wrap them round the shaft. It can also be used for attaching ornate drawer pulls.

Tacks (I) are used to attach carpet or fabric to wood and for other light jobs.

Upholstery tacks (J) come with a variety of decorative heads to complement the style of the furniture.

Staples (K) in various forms are used on fabrics, insulation or picture frames or for holding wiring flat. Make sure the appliance is disconnected at the wall socket before hammering in staples over electric wiring.

Glazier's points (L) are driven into a window frame to hold in the glass.

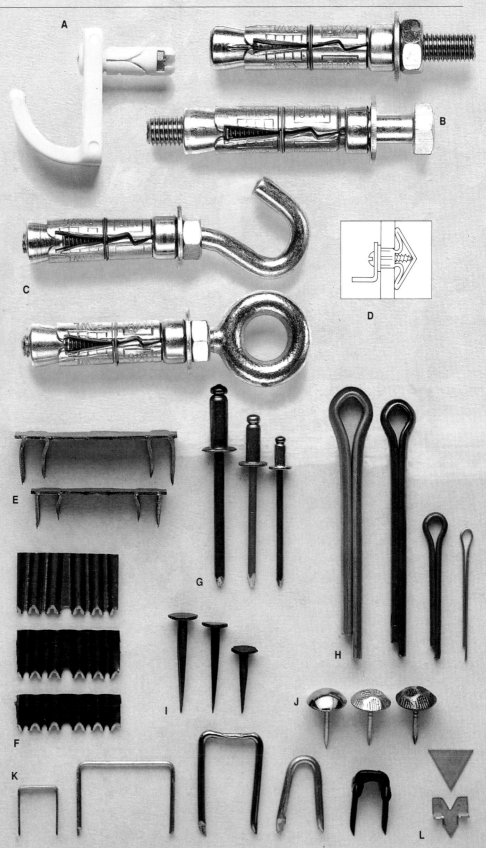

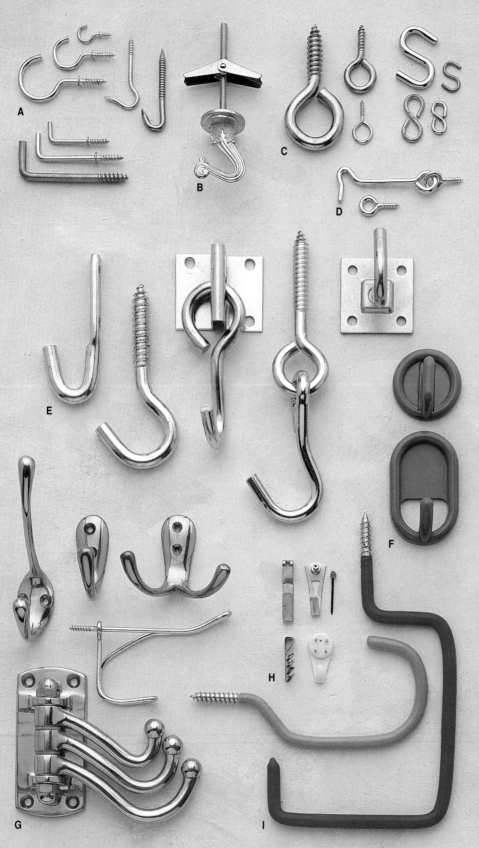

Whether you want to support a clothes line or hang up a coffee cup, you'll be able to find a hook of the right shape and size to do the job. Use large hooks for heavy objects; a small hook may pull away from the surface when it is supporting a heavy load. Before installing a hook that screws into place, make a pilot hole with a nail or drill.

Screw hook (A) has a threaded end that screws into ceilings, wood or walls, The open end supports various items. The rounded-tip hook is for household uses; the pointed-tip hook is for suspended ceilings and the L-shaped hook supports wide objects.

Ceiling hook (B) combines a hook with a toggle bolt for hanging a plant from a ceiling. It can also be used to relocate a hanging ceiling lamp with a long flex, without having to remove and refix the ceiling rose.

Screw eye (C) has a ring-shaped end. Use it alone by fitting objects through the ring. Or link an S hook or 8 hook to it; the linking hook can hold the object.

Hook and eye (D) has a hook which is attached to a screw eye that screws into a gate or door. The hook fits into another screw eye to close the gate.

Rope hook (E) comes in various designs. From the left: a general-purpose hook with two holes in the flat stem for screws, a porch-swing hook, a hammock hook with a plate to secure it to a flat surface, a hammock hook with a screw eye for a round surface, and a clothes-line hook that is screwed to a flat surface.

Self-adhesive hook (F) for lightweight objects. To install it, wipe the surface clean, remove the lining paper and press hook in place.

Coat hook (G) may have one, two or more hooks in various directions for hanging coats and hats. The three-hook model has pivoting hooks.

Picture hook (H) is nailed into a wall. Attach a wire to the back of a picture frame to hang it on the hook.

Heavy-duty hook (I) is for hanging objects in a garage or workshop. For items like bicycles, use them in pairs.

BRACKETS

Sets of two or more brackets are useful for supporting a variety of items. Before mounting them, measure accurately and make sure they are level.

Curtain and shade brackets come in pairs. To install a cafe rod, screw the first brackets shown **(A)** above a window for an outside mount, or attach socket brackets **(B)** to window jambs for an inside mount. Nail roller blind brackets **(C)** inside the jambs (or on other models, outside the jambs or on the wall). A U-shaped curtain rod fits onto outside-mount brackets **(D)**; slip the opening in the rod over the bracket hook and push the rod into place.

Rail brackets support handrails (screwed into wall studs), footrails and gallery rails. A flat rail rests on top of a flat-rail bracket **(E)**; a round rail slips through a post-rail bracket **(F)** or its end fits into a flange bracket **(G)**.

Shelf brackets (H) are attached to a wall to support a horizontal storage or display shelf. Screw in a bracket every 75-100 cm for a light load and even closer for a heavy load. The almond-coloured bracket has a decorative cover that slips over the metal support after it has been screwed into place.

Shelf studs (I) slip into holes drilled in a cabinet's sides, two at each end of a shelf. Make sure that all four holes align horizontally.

Bookcase clips (J) are shown fitted in a side-mounted standard (near right). They support shelves in cabinets or bookcases – use two clips at each end of a shelf. Screw four standards in place (you can recess them); use a level to check plumb. Fit clips into slots at same height on each standard, which can be cut to size.

Adjustable shelving brackets (K) slide into slots in a wall-mounted standard (far right) to support shelves. Screw the standards into wall studs, using a level to check plumb. When the bracket is in place, turn the thumbscrew to secure it. The hook on the tip of the bracket prevents the shelf from slipping off.

Spring-loaded folding bracket (L) can be raised and locked in placed to create an extra work surface where space is limited. Light pressure on the release lever allows you to fold the surface out of the way.

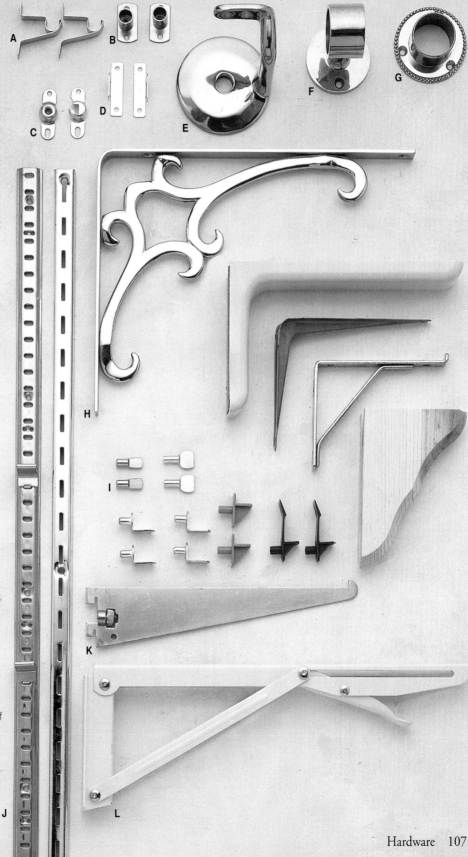

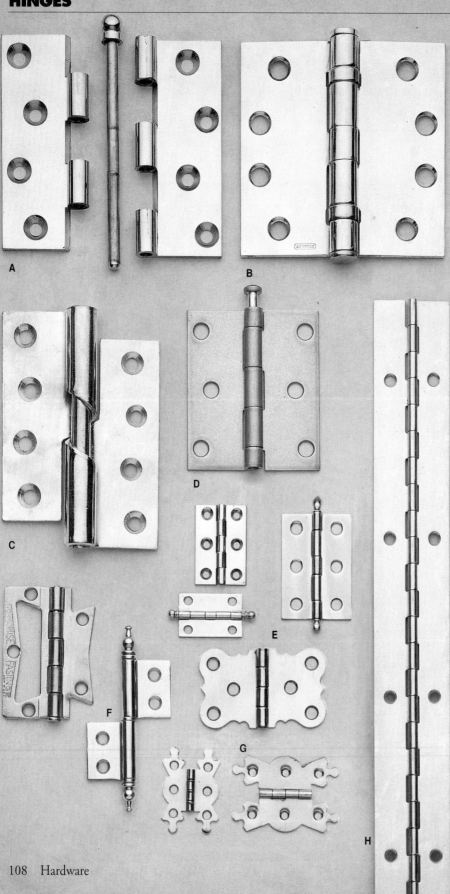

A B C D E F G H

A hinge usually has two leaves held together with a pivot pin inside knuckles or a barrel. Most cabinet hinges can be used on either left or right-handed doors; but rising butt and lift-off hinges must be correctly 'handed'. Hinges can be surface-mounted, known as overlaid or laid on, but the leaves create a slight gap between the door and frame when the door is closed. Recessed leaves are set in, flush with the surface.

Loose-pin butt hinge (A) has a detachable pin to allow for door removal without unscrewing the hinge. The head of the hinge pin must always be on top. Some butt hinges have a fixed pin. They are suitable for an exterior door where the barrel is exposed outside; to remove the door, you must unscrew the hinge.

Ball-bearing hinge (B), for heavy doors, has a ball-bearing assembly that is permanently lubricated.

Rising butt hinge (C), used on an interior door, has a barrel that is split diagonally. As you open the door, one leaf rides up the other, lifting the door clear of the carpet. The door's weight pulls it closed.

Cabinet butt hinge (D) is attached to flush-mounted cabinet doors. It comes with a removable button-top pin.

Small butt hinge (E) may have a fixed or a loose pin. It is often used on small boxes. Attach it with nails or screws.

Flush hinge (F), for a lightweight door, is surface-mounted but doesn't create a gap. To install the type shown on the left, screw the small leaf to the door, the large leaf to the frame; when closed, the small leaf fits into the large one. On the other type, the bottom leaf swings under the top one.

Decorative hinge (G) comes in a variety of ornamental designs for fine wood furniture, cabinets and boxes. Choose suitable decorative hinges.

Piano hinge (H), also known as a continuous hinge, is used for table flaps and chest tops where extra strength is important. Supplied in 2 m lengths, the hinge may be cut to the exact size required. It can be surface-mounted or recessed.

Desk hinge (A), a straight strap hinge, is most often found recessed into writing desks and other wooden flaps.

Card-table hinge (B) looks similar to the desk hinge but has a 180 degree stop, making it suitable for small table flaps that fold out of the way.

Single strap hinge (C) comes in large, heavy-duty sizes for doors, gates, boxes and chests. The steel one shown here is sometimes called a T-hinge. The small decorative hinge can be used on jewellery boxes.

H-and-L hinge (D) is surface-mounted on a cabinet door. A larger version is available for standard-weight house doors; another variation of the hinge allows you to mortise the jamb leaf.

Snake hinge (E) is a decorative form of the plainer H-hinges below it. They are generally used on small chests, on furniture and on cabinet doors, and can be mounted either vertically or horizontally, as desired.

Doll's house hinge (F) is small enough to use on doll's house and delicate jewellery-box lids.

Gravity hinges (G) come in various forms. The café door hinge set (top) has a lower section which rides up as the door is pushed open, raising the pin in the upper section through its plastic stay. Gravity pulls it down again when the door is released. The metal lift-off hinge (bottom) is used to hold mirrors on dressing tables.

Drop-leaf hinge (H), similar to the backflap hinge, is used on fold-down table flaps made with a rule joint. The hinge's longer leaf should be screwed to the table flap.

Backflap hinge (I) is a fixed-pin butt hinge with wide leaves that provide better support for flaps and lids. It can be recessed into wood.

Butler's-tray hinge (J) comes with rounded or square corners. It's a small, sturdy hinge for trays and other small tables with leaves that fold up. The hinge surface is flat when open, with no protruding barrel; in the up position, a steel spring holds the leaf at 90°.

Easy-clean hinge (K) makes cleaning casement windows easier because it allows you to put your hand through the gap between frame and window to reach the outside of the glass.

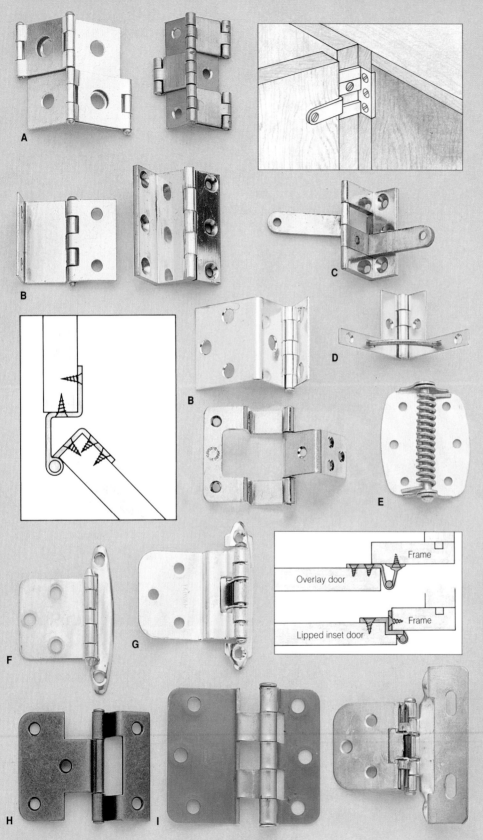

Double-acting hinge (A) is mounted along the side edges of a folding door or screen. The two linked sets of leaves and barrels permit the panels to swing open from both directions. To avoid binding, the leaves of the hinge (less the barrels) must be equal to or less than the thickness of the wood.

Cranked hinge (B) is used on flush inset cabinet doors. The size of the hinge must match the door thickness. For extra support, the right-angle leaf attaches to both the edge and the back of the door. Only the barrel shows when the door is closed. The double cranked pivot hinge (bottom) has two right-angle leaves for even greater strength. One leaf is attached to the door, the other leaf to the frame. Extra support is given to the door in that the fixing screws enter the door from two directions.

Double-flap cranked hinge (C) is mounted on a cabinet's centre stile, or partition, to hold two doors. Each door, which overlays half the stile, can be opened independently 180°.

Quadrant hinge (D) is recessed in mortises made in the edges of a small box. It holds the lid open at 100°.

Spring hinge (E) has a coiled spring that returns a door to its closed position. Surface-mount it on a cabinet door and on other places where self-closing doors are needed.

Overlay hinge (F), for a cabinet door, has a short leaf that is mounted on the exterior surface of the cabinet frame. The long leaf is attached to the back of the door. The hinge allows the door to overlay the frame.

Inset cabinet hinge (G) is similar to the overlay hinge, but the long leaf is offset so that it can be used on a lipped cabinet door. Concealed under a barrel is a spring that, when activated, snaps the door shut.

Semiconcealed overlay hinge (H), for a cabinet door, is almost hidden when the door is closed. A short leaf is offset so that the leaf can be mounted inside the cabinet frame. When the door is closed, only the barrel shows. Use it on overlay doors.

Semiconcealed inset hinge (I), when mounted on a lipped cabinet door, is hidden except for the barrel. The spring-loaded hinge (near left) snaps the door shut when you release it.

Pivot hinge (A) is mounted at top and bottom of an overlay cabinet door and against the cabinet frame. Elongated screw holes permit easy adjustment. When the door is closed, only the pivot pin is visible. Mount the hinge at top as shown; mount both halves of the hinge at bottom horizontally.

Centre hinge (B) comes in a variety of sizes for use on doors that cannot be fastened at the butt edge. The hinge is recessed into two mortises at the top or bottom of the door, making it almost invisible. With the offset knife hinge (bottom), only the pivot point shows.

Double spring-action hinge (C) is a self-closing hinge that allows the door to swing in both directions. It comes in numerous sizes for a variety of doors. Some types must be mounted to a strip that you hang from the doorjamb.

Glass-door hinge (D) for laid-on glass doors is spring loaded to prevent the door from swinging open. No other sort of catch should be necessary to keep doors closed. It will be necessary to drill 30 mm diameter holes in the glass door to accept the hinges.

Flush-fitting flap hinge (E) provides a gap-free joint on cabinets and other furniture with down-swinging flaps. Recess one side of the hinge into the bottom surface of the cabinet frame and the other into the flap. Small adjustments can be made after fitting to ensure a perfectly flush fit.

Invisible hinge (F) comes in a variety of styles for small cabinet doors and other lightweight applications. You mount it in a recess made with a drill or router. When the hinge is closed, the leaves lie flat together; the knuckles slide out of sight into gaps in the leaves. Select the hinge size that is close to but less than the thickness of the cabinet stock.

Counter hinge (G), with its pleasingly solid appearance, is used for counters or tables with lift-up sections. Its double-throw action allows it to lie flat along the table or counter top and, as it is usually recessed into the surface, it makes cleaning very easy.

Concealed cabinet hinge (H), a face-frame hinge that swings open to 170°, is for inset and overlaid cabinet doors. A cup is recessed into the door, and the baseplate is attached to the cabinet side. Loosen the screws to adjust alignment of the door.

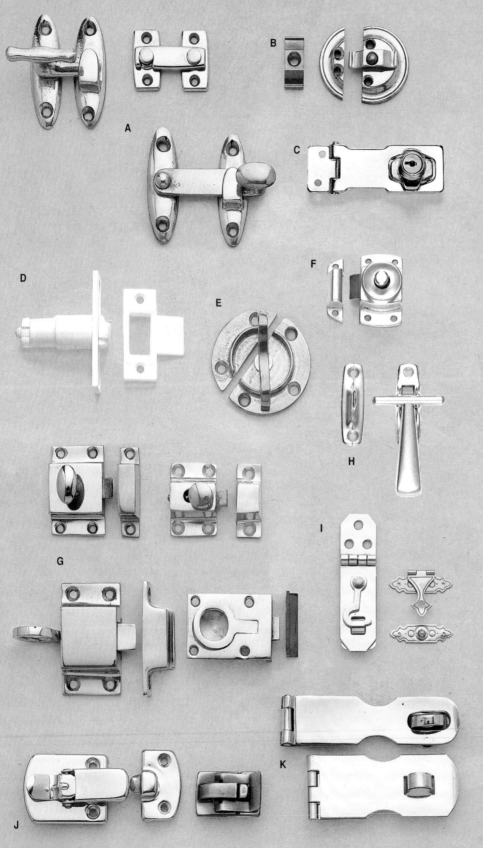

To keep a door or lid closed, latches and catches are mounted on furniture, cabinets and boxes. They come in a variety of sizes and functions for different needs. Small locks add a degree of privacy, but not security.

Turn catch (A) holds cupboard, cabinet and other small doors closed. Space the plates so that the arm fits the matching plate. When using the catch on a pair of doors, secure one door with a small interior bolt, mounted at the top or bottom of the door.

Button catch (B) can be turned to hold a light-duty door in place. The simpler form (left) is screwed on near the edge of the door. It is also available attached to a plate (right). The two parts of the plate must be fitted to the door and frame so that they meet exactly when the door is closed.

Cylinder hasp lock (C) gives double security: the hasp folds over to cover its retaining screws, and the cylinder turns and is then locked, to hold the hasp in place securely.

Adjustable door catch (D) is used on communicating doors and walk-in cupboards. It pushes open easily.

Table catch (E) is screwed to the underside of a table that accepts extensions. The catch pulls sections tightly together and holds them level.

Push-button catch (F) is surface-mounted. Press button to release.

Cupboard latch (G) has a spring latch that slides into a strike plate. Draw the latch back by turning the knob (top) or pulling out the catch (bottom, left) or the flush ring lever (bottom, right).

Slam catch (H) has a hook mounted on one surface and a T-shaped handle on the other. Lowering the handle locks the catch; raising it releases it.

Hasp (I) is ideal for holding lids closed on small boxes. The arm is held in place with a snap or hook.

Case clip (J), for suitcases, holds the lid in place with an arm that snaps over the opposite plate.

Security hasp (K) has an arm that swings over the screw plate, to stop an intruder from removing screws. A padlock slips through the keeper.

Bullet catch (A), with a spring-loaded ball in a cylindrical case, fits into a recess cut into the edge of a flush cabinet door. When the door is closed, the ball fits through the strike plate into a small hole in the cabinet wall.

Double-ball catch (B) can be used on flush, overlay and inset cabinet doors. Two balls snap over the strike from the front or side (inset). To adjust the amount of tension on the balls, tighten the screws.

Roller catch (C) operates on the same principle as the double-ball catch. The rollers are spring-loaded.

Spring-pressure catch (D), for a cabinet door, has a roller that fits into the strike's hook. Attach the catch shown at top to the door's bottom edge, the strike to the frame's base. Mount the other catch on the cabinet's vertical frame, the strike on the door. To open the door, push against it.

Magnetic catch (E) holds a cabinet door closed by magnetically pulling in a metal strike plate. Screw the catch to the inside of the cabinet and the strike plate to the inside of the door. Use a pull to open the door.

Magnetic pressure catch (F) is a magnetic and spring-pressure catch in one. No handles are needed; simply push the door to open it. Attach metal strike plate to a wood door.

Glass-door catch (G) works just like the magnetic pressure catch, but the strike plate is designed to slide onto the glass door, eliminating the need to drill through the glass.

Cupboard lock (H) has a bolt that operates left and right. Surface-mount the lock; cut a recess to take the bolt.

Drawer lock (I) has a double keyhole, letting you set the lock in a vertical or horizontal position. Mount it in a recess in a desk, cabinet or other furniture.

Mortise lock (J) is ideal for sliding doors, rolltop desks and other furniture. The model at far right has a spring-loaded dust cover.

Cylinder locks (K) come in different designs for drawers and cabinet doors. Surface-mount a lock by drilling a hole through the surface or fit it into a mortise. The lower lock (far right) is designed to be fitted to glass cabinet doors; to install one, you will need to cut a hole through the glass.

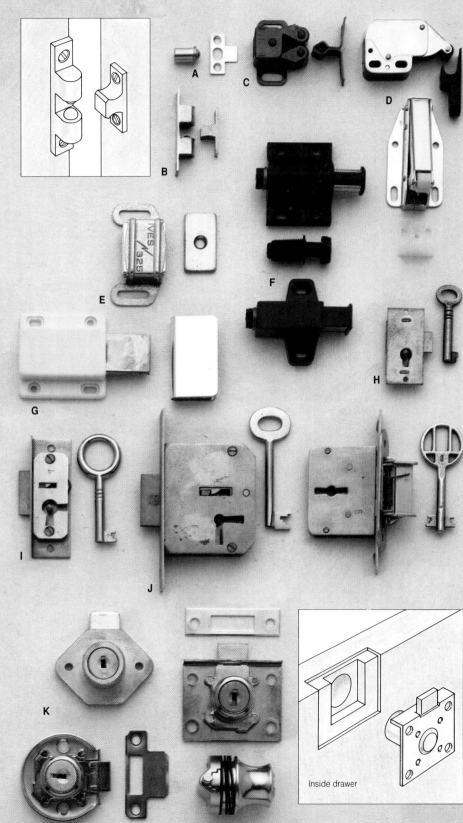

Inside drawer

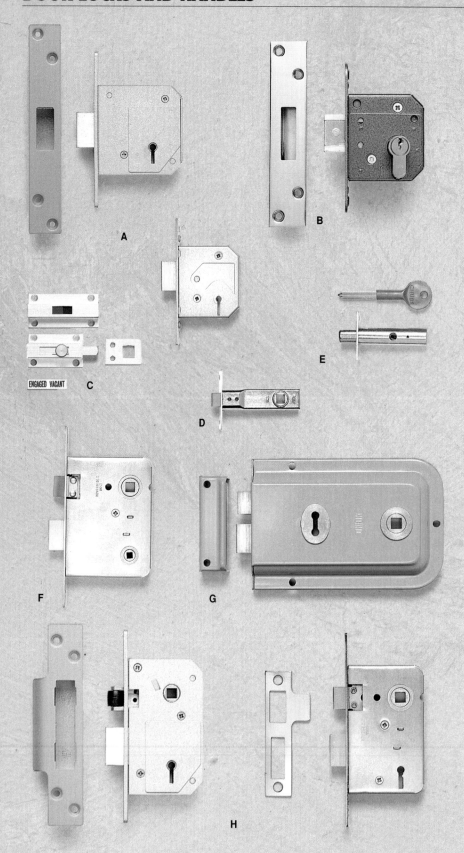

The installation of door locks and handles usually involves boring one or two holes into the door and making a mortise in the door jamb. Designs vary, so follow the maker's instructions. Most insurance companies will recommend fitting a mortise deadlock in addition to a latch.

Mortise deadlocks (A), for use on final exit doors, are operated by a key only. The more levers a lock has, the more secure it is. The lock on the far left has five levers, and to its right, a three-lever lock. The lock is set into the door; the strike plate into the jamb, making them virtually tamperproof.

Cylinder deadlock (B) is set into the door, in the same way as a mortise deadlock. The lock is activated by a Yale-type key alone, and can be locked and opened from both sides.

Lavatory door bolt (C) is a simple sliding bolt which reveals a message when activated.

Mortise latch (D) keeps a door closed but does not lock it. It is best used for interior doors which are unlikely to need locking. It is operated by a mortise latch handle (facing page, B).

Door rack bolt (E) can be used on doors and French windows. Bolt is fitted, mortise-style, to top and bottom of opening edge and is operated by the key only, from the inside.

Bathroom mortise lock (F) works in conjunction with a bathroom handle (facing page, C). A thumb-turn on the inside of the door locks the door, but there is an emergency release device on the outside. They are either left or right opening, so buy the correct set.

Rim lock (G) is screwed to the inside face of a door and is easy to install but does not offer great security. It should not be used as the only means of security on external doors.

Mortise sashlocks (H) are used in conjunction with a mortise handle (facing page, A). The latch is operated by a handle and the lock is activated only by a key. A 5-lever lock (far left) offers more security than the 2-lever lock (left). Both models shown are suitable for doors with narrow stiles; wider models are also available with the handle beside the keyhole.

Mortise-lock handle (A) is used on a back door, or on interior doors which may require locking from time to time. It can be locked from both sides.

Mortise-latch handle (B) has no keyhole, because it is used on interior doors where no privacy or security is required. Downward pressure on the handle draws back the latch inside. It can also be used on a bathroom or lavatory door with a lavatory door bolt (facing page, C).

Bathroom handle (C) is locked by turning the thumb-screw just below the handle. However, in emergencies, it can be unlocked by removing the release device on the outside of the door. If you have one fitted, make sure every member of the family knows how to activate the release mechanism.

Doorknobs (D) can be used to work the latch on either a mortise latch or a mortise sashlock. When fitting one, make sure it is far enough from the edge of the door to let you open the door without scraping your knuckles.

10-lever rim automatic deadlock (E) is opened from the outside by a key with a unique number. From the inside, the latch can be opened by means of the handle. For greater security, the inside handle can be locked by giving a complete clockwise turn of the key. When locked from the inside, the door cannot be opened from the outside and can be opened only with the key on the inside. This lock is not suitable for emergency exit doors.

Automatic deadlock (F) suitable for an inward opening front door. This lock deadlocks automatically when the door is shut. To keep the bolt in the withdrawn position, turn the black knob clockwise and press the lock button. To lock the door from the inside, turn the key and depress the entire knob, holding it in while you turn the key back again and remove it. To unlock it, repeat the action and the knob will spring out. When going out, lock the knob from the inside and pull the door closed behind you. It will unlock from the outside with a turn of the key. Make sure that anyone left inside has access to a key, if you lock the door on going out.

Cylinder nightlatch (G) does not offer enough security on its own. It should be used in conjunction with a mortise deadlock. The latch has a button to lock it open or closed.

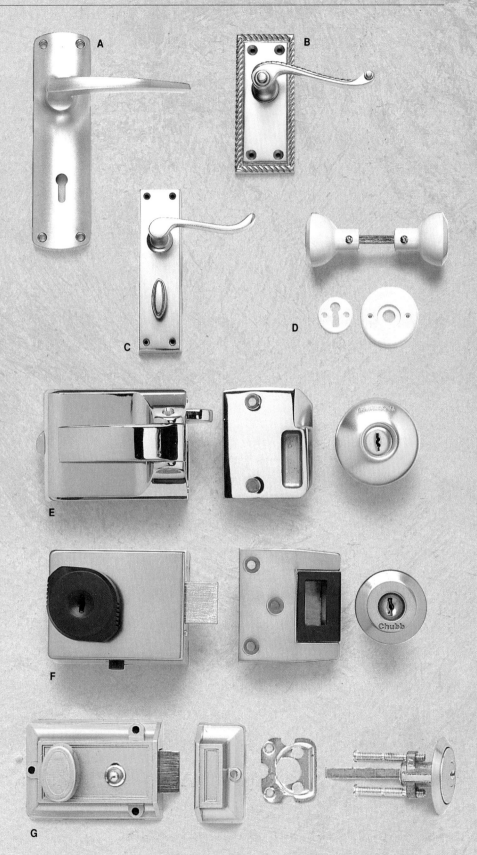

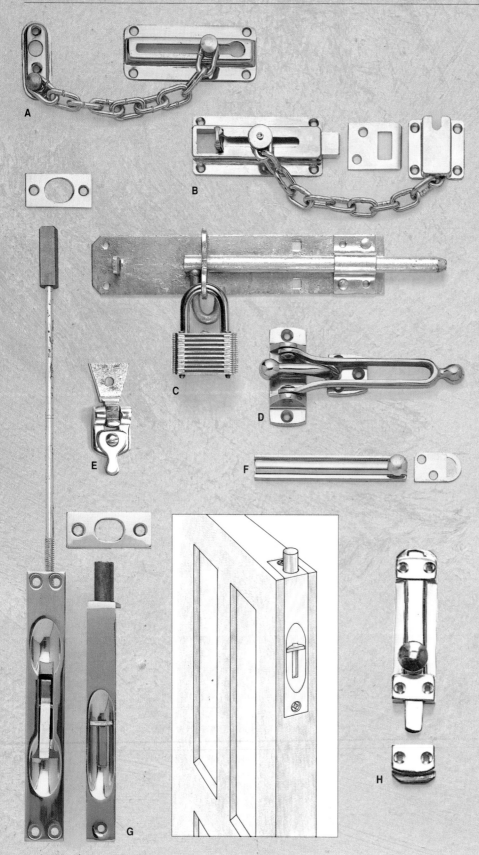

The bolts on this page are for doors that require additional security. The accessories on the facing page add convenience to standard door use.

Door chain guard (A) lets you open a door slightly to view visitors or for ventilation. Attach the slide piece to the door; screw the chain piece to the doorjamb or frame. Make sure you use 75 mm (3 in) long screws.

Deadbolt and chain guard (B) gives added security with a deadbolt. Attach the long slide plate in a horizontal position on the surface of the door, flush with the edge. Screw the chain plate to the door frame, opposite the slide plate. Position the strike plate on the doorjamb so the bolt can slide into it; the plate may have to be mortised.

Brenton pad bolt (C) is fixed to doors and gates with carriage bolts. The pad bolt is designed to take a padlock and is galvanised for better weathering.

Swing bar guard (D) is stronger than a door chain guard. Fix the long arm piece to the door frame, and the smaller piece to the front surface at the edge of the door, about 2 cm (¾ in) away from the long arm piece. They should be level, their edges parallel.

Citadel bolt (E) is recessed into the doorjamb and folds back until it is needed. To activate it, close the door and swing the rounded end of the bolt forward. Raise the lever to lock the bolt at 90 degrees. The door cannot be opened from outside.

Surface bolt (F) can be used in a vertical or horizontal position on doors and cabinets. Position it with the slide bolt on the door and the strike on the jamb, making sure the bolt will pass easily through the strike.

Extension flush bolts (G) are used to hold the inactive door of a pair of doors in place. The bolt is installed in a recess cut into the door's edge. The door must be at least 3.5 cm (1⅜ in) thick. The shorter bolt (left) is for wooden doors; the other (far left) has a longer bolt for metal doors. Their strike plates, which must be recessed in the receiving surface, are also shown.

Brass bolt (H) can be used vertically or horizontally. The combination can also be used to hold the two parts of a stable door together.

Door viewer (A) allows a normal or wide-angle view through a door. Bore a hole through the door; insert the tube and screw it into the threaded ring.

Door knocker (B) is installed on an outer door. Centre it 1.5 m (about 5 ft) from the bottom of the door.

Kickdown doorstop (C), attached near the bottom of a door, holds the door open in any position. To use it, kick down the tip so that it rests flat on the floor. When the stop is not in use, the tip should point up.

Foot-operated doorstop (D) is fitted near the base of a door. Press down on the circular plunger to activate the rubber-covered stopper; to raise it, press on the release bar.

Letter plate (E) is installed over a slot cut in the door. Attach the outside cover plate, then the inside plate.

Skirting-board bumper (F) stops an opening door before its handle hits the wall. When installing the rigid bumper (top) allow clearance for a vacuum cleaner. The flexible bumper (below) bends to make it easier for you to vacuum under it.

Floor doorstop (G) screws into the floor to stop a door from opening any farther. Position stop with the rubber pad flat against the door. Make sure door handle does not touch wall.

Spring door closer (H) is installed on the hinged side of the doorjamb. The roller arm fits into a central boss. It moves as the door is opened, then the boss forces the door to close.

Wall-mounted bumper (I) stops a doorknob from marking a wall. Screw the bumper onto the wall; make sure it aligns with the knob.

Concealed closer (J) automatically closes doors up to 50 kg. Embed the cylinder in the door; fix the anchor plates to door and jamb. When the door is opened, the chain is exposed.

Door spring (K) comes in several styles. It is designed to shut a light door. Fix one end to the jamb and the other to the door.

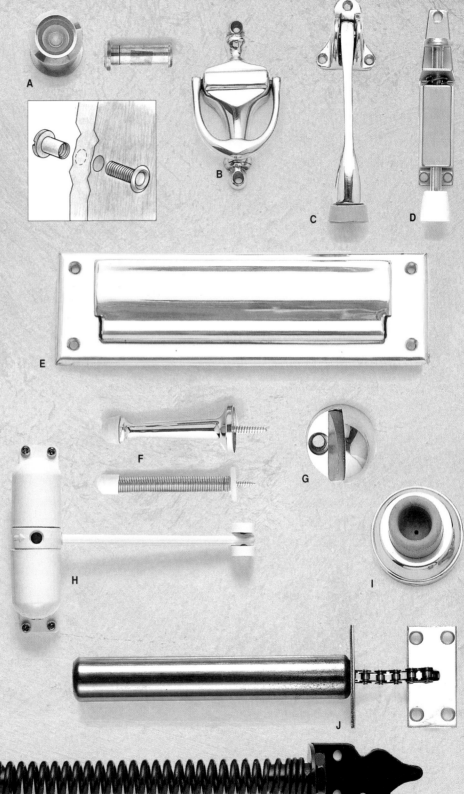

WINDOW HARDWARE

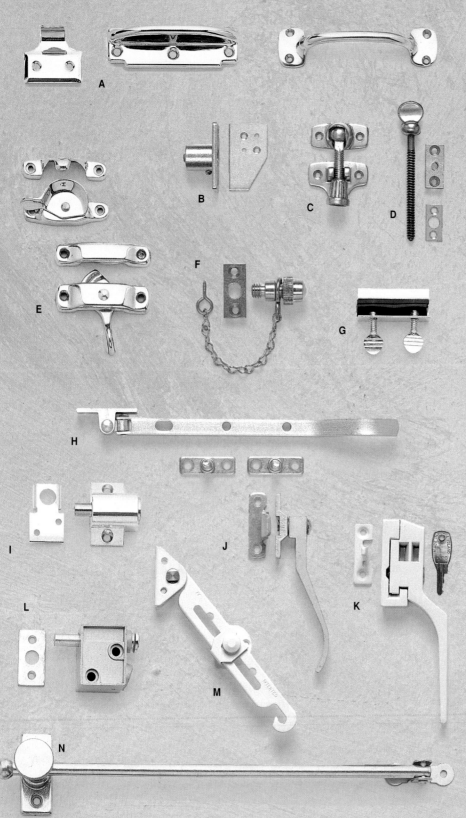

Opening, closing and securing a window are easy when it is fitted with the proper hardware. Some items here are accessories, others are replacement parts.

Sash lifts (A) are screwed into the face of the lower sash's bottom rail. Grasp the lift to pull the sash up.

Window bolt (B) for wooden sash windows. Fit the plate to the top of the lower sash and the key-operated bolt to the lower rail of the top window. You can position the bolt to allow a small opening for ventilation.

Sash fast (C) has one half fixed to the top sash and the other to the lower sash to hold both together.

Sash screw (D) goes right through the inner frame into the outer one.

Sash latches (E) draw the two sashes together to reduce draughts and rattling. The strike plate is attached to the upper sash's bottom rail. Attach the other piece to the top edge of the lower sash's top rail.

Acorn (F), fixed to one sash, screws into the plate on the other.

Thumbscrew lock (G) keeps a metal double-hung or sash window from opening beyond a desired point.

Casement stay (H) holds a window open but does not provide much security when closed.

Double-hung sash lock (I) has two strike plates to lock the sash closed or slightly open for ventilation. Use a key to open the bolt; to lock it, push in bolt.

Casement handle (J) offers no security when used on its own.

Lockable window handle (K) is a key-operated lock for a casement window.

Sash window lock (L), also for patio doors, is attached to window's side edge. To lock window, push in bolt.

Securistay (M) for pivot or hinged windows can prevent an upstairs window from opening fully.

Sliding rod (N) operates a casement window. The rod, attached to the rail, slides through a holder installed on the windowsill. Tighten the knurled knob to secure the rod in place.

BATHROOM HARDWARE

The easiest way to give your bathroom a new look is to replace the existing accessories. Remember that surface-mounted fixtures cannot be installed where you have removed recessed ones. Brass items may have a protective finish; to clean, wipe them with a soft dry or damp cloth, then buff with a dry cloth.

Towel rail (A) has a rod that is held in place with two endpieces, or bases, which are secured with toggle bolts or wall anchors. To install it, measure and mark the placement of the bases on the wall. Attach one base; slide the rod into the indentation in its side. Slip the second base over the other end of the rod; secure it to the wall. The porcelain and brass bar has bases that are screwed into the wall. The bases of the white rail slide onto brackets; first screw the brackets into the wall.

Double towel rail (B) has two rods spaced apart, allowing clearance for towels to dry. Brackets hold the rail in place; make sure they are level, correctly spaced and installed very securely. Slip the bases onto the brackets; secure them with screws and wall plugs.

Towel ring (C) needs less space than a towel rail; it's installed with only one bracket. Screw the bracket to the wall; slip the base onto the bracket; tighten the screw in the bottom of the base.

Grab bar (D) provides support above a bath or in shower cubicle. Fix it to wall vertically or diagonally with expanding bolts or with wall plugs provided.

Toothbrush and glass holder (E) can be screwed in place on the wall above a basin or it may slide onto a bracket attached to the wall. Secure the glass holder to the bracket with a setscrew; the brass holder has a dome-shaped knob that screws into the bracket.

Soap dish (F) is placed above a basin, using a bracket. The blue porcelain dish is permanently attached to the wall with tile adhesive. Hold it in place with masking tape until the adhesive has set enough to take the weight. Recessed soap dishes are available too.

Paper holder (G) can be screwed in place, attached like the double towel rail (above) or recessed into a ceramic tile wall as it is installed.

FURNITURE PULLS AND KNOBS

A

B

C

A

D

Drill

Hole saw

Chisel

Pull

E

The pulls and knobs needed to open drawers and cabinet doors come in a wide variety of styles, shapes and materials. Nylon, chrome, marble, plastic and glass pulls and knobs are ideal in kitchens and bathrooms, and they can give other rooms a modern, functional look. Wood, brass and ceramics lend elegance to living room and bedroom furniture, and are available in many modern designs (this page) as well as antique styles (facing page).

Simple pull (A) can be installed vertically on a door or horizontally on a drawer. Position the pull, mark the door or drawer where the ends of the pull touch it, and drill screw holes at these marks. Then hold the pull in position and drive the screws into it from the other side.

Semicircular nylon pull (B) can be used singly or paired with a matching pull to make a single circular pull. You can also mount one semicircular pull on each door of a cabinet to form a full circle when the doors are closed.

Furniture knob (C) is installed like a pull but with only one screw. If the knob has a plate, slide it onto the screw between furniture and knob.

Drop pull (D) is more complicated to install. Drill a screw hole for each post, slide on the backplate and screw one of the small posts into place with the hole in its surface facing in the direction of the other screw hole. Slide one of the pins in the drop, or bale, into the hole in the installed post, slide the other pin into the hole in the second post, and screw the second post to the drawer. If the bale is already attached to the pull, install the pull as you would a standard pull.

Recessed pull (E) is used mainly on sliding doors. To install a recessed pull, chisel out a mortise or hollow just large enough to accept the pull. If the pull is circular, use an electric drill with a hole saw to start the mortise, then finish it with a chisel. Sand the edges of the opening smooth, and firmly wedge the pull into place. On some recessed pulls you must glue the pull into place or fasten it with tiny screws, which are supplied.

William and Mary period drop pulls (right) use split pins in place of screws. Position the pull and drill a hole for the pin. Force the bale (drop) over one leg of the pin and push it down into the pin's bend. Then slide the backing plate over the pin behind the bale, thread the pin through the hole in the door or drawer, and bend its legs open, using pliers with the jaws taped to prevent scratching. Gently hammer the ends of the pin against the inside of the furniture.

Other antique styles (right and below) include Queen Anne, Sheraton, Chippendale and Hepplewhite. If a pull uses decorative bolts and nuts in place of split pins or screws, countersink the nut on the inside of the drawer or door and saw off the protruding end of the bolt to give a smooth, snag-free surface. If you are replacing a pull and the original bolt holes are up to 3 mm (⅛ in) too far apart or close together, stretch or push together the arms of the new bale to make it fit. If this doesn't work, install a new pull with a plate that will cover the old holes.

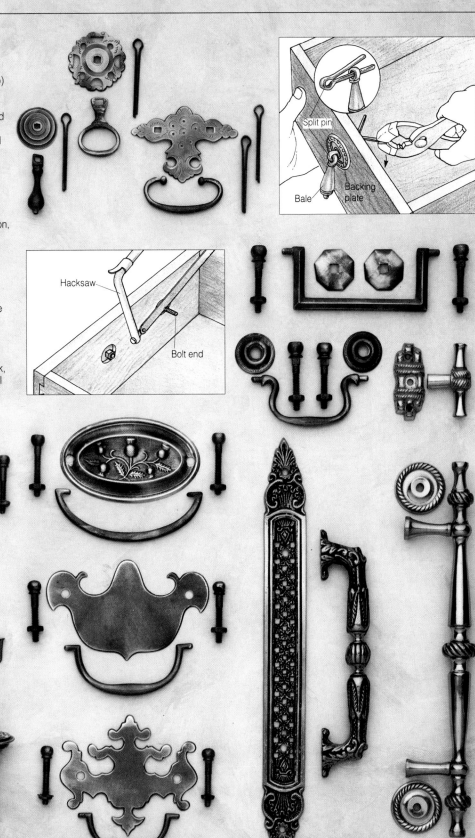

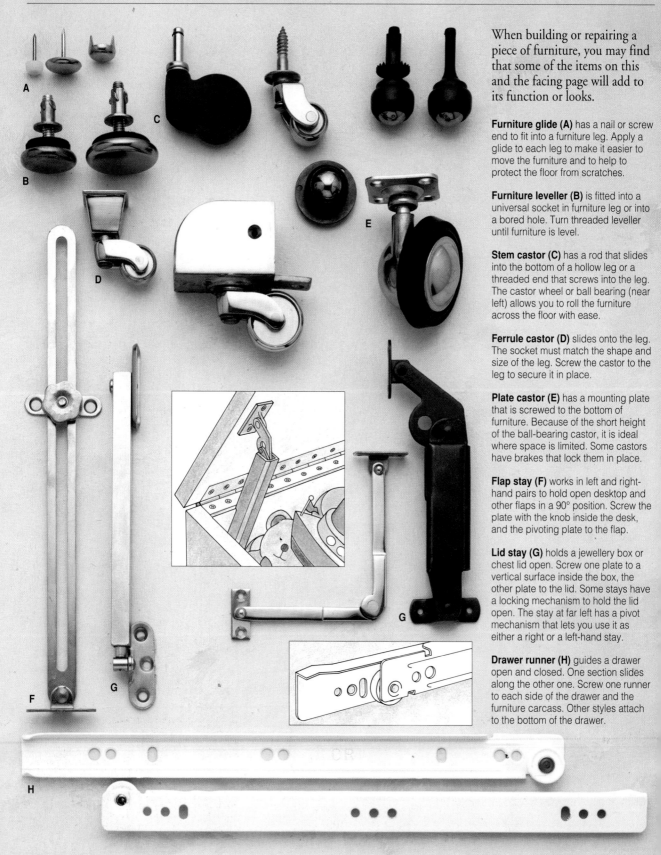

When building or repairing a piece of furniture, you may find that some of the items on this and the facing page will add to its function or looks.

Furniture glide (A) has a nail or screw end to fit into a furniture leg. Apply a glide to each leg to make it easier to move the furniture and to help to protect the floor from scratches.

Furniture leveller (B) is fitted into a universal socket in furniture leg or into a bored hole. Turn threaded leveller until furniture is level.

Stem castor (C) has a rod that slides into the bottom of a hollow leg or a threaded end that screws into the leg. The castor wheel or ball bearing (near left) allows you to roll the furniture across the floor with ease.

Ferrule castor (D) slides onto the leg. The socket must match the shape and size of the leg. Screw the castor to the leg to secure it in place.

Plate castor (E) has a mounting plate that is screwed to the bottom of furniture. Because of the short height of the ball-bearing castor, it is ideal where space is limited. Some castors have brakes that lock them in place.

Flap stay (F) works in left and right-hand pairs to hold open desktop and other flaps in a 90° position. Screw the plate with the knob inside the desk, and the pivoting plate to the flap.

Lid stay (G) holds a jewellery box or chest lid open. Screw one plate to a vertical surface inside the box, the other plate to the lid. Some stays have a locking mechanism to hold the lid open. The stay at far left has a pivot mechanism that lets you use it as either a right or a left-hand stay.

Drawer runner (H) guides a drawer open and closed. One section slides along the other one. Screw one runner to each side of the drawer and the furniture carcass. Other styles attach to the bottom of the drawer.

Decorative plates (A) come in an unlimited number of shapes, sizes and styles. They can embellish both bought furniture and pieces that you make yourself. They work especially well on antique reproductions. To install a plate, screw or nail it in place through the small holes in the plate. Some plates have larger holes to accept drawer or door pulls.

Keyhole escutcheon (B), a type of decorative plate, fits over a small keyhole. If you install the lock yourself, place the escutcheon over the hole last. The escutcheon can also serve as a dummy, giving the appearance of a lock where none is installed.

Decorative angle plates (C) come in a variety of shapes and sizes. Wrap the L-shaped plate and the Y-shaped plate (near right) round a piece where two sides meet; fit the corner plate and the Y-shaped plate (far right) over corners where three sides meet. Nail the plates in place.

Leg plate (D) firmly holds a chair or table leg in place. Attach the plate to the top of the leg with a bolt; screw the plate to the underside of a chair seat or table surface. Choose plates that will set the legs straight or angled.

Brace and plate (E) provide extra support on wood joints. Fix them to a piece as it's assembled or when you mend a break. The straight plate joins two butt pieces, the T-plate joins opposing pieces. The L-shaped and flat corner braces support right-angle pieces; the three-sided corner brace is for heavy-duty use.

Knockdown fitting (F) joins pieces temporarily, allowing you to take apart and reassemble them when necessary – for instance, when moving heavy furniture. They come in many styles.

Shrinkage brace (G) has one plate with a vertical or horizontal slot, allowing wood to move as it shrinks or expands with humidity changes.

Table fork (H), for extending table, has two plates and a U-shaped fork. Mount one plate under stationary section, the other plate on the leaf; slide the fork into the plates to hold the two sections together. Use two table fork latches for each leaf.

Glass door pull (I) slides over the edge of a glass cabinet door. An inside pad prevents damage to glass.

WOODWORKING

WOODS

A primary building and crafts material, wood offers strength, beauty or a combination of both. Sizes range from thick beams for houses to paper-thin strips of veneer for furniture.

Of the hundreds of wood species, only a few softwoods are used in the building trade. Hardwood and softwood is sold in DIY centres and timber yards as sawn timber, planed boards and manufactured products such as mouldings and doors. A well-stocked timber yard will have a good collection of sizes, qualities and lengths, mainly in imported softwoods

but also in popular species of hardwood from sustainable sources and forests that qualify as well managed. Because of the need to conserve rare hardwoods, many people buy softwoods and stain them to look like hardwood.

On the pages that follow, woods are identified as durable or nondurable. Durable woods will last for more than 15 years outdoors, in contact with the ground. Nondurable woods are best kept for interior use and would last no more than ten years outdoors unless they are pressure-treated.

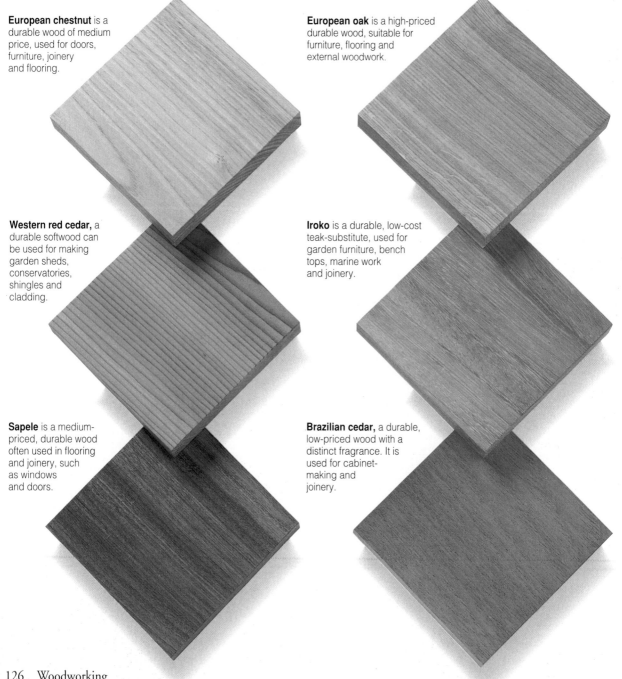

European chestnut is a durable wood of medium price, used for doors, furniture, joinery and flooring.

European oak is a high-priced durable wood, suitable for furniture, flooring and external woodwork.

Western red cedar, a durable softwood can be used for making garden sheds, conservatories, shingles and cladding.

Iroko is a durable, low-cost teak-substitute, used for garden furniture, bench tops, marine work and joinery.

Sapele is a medium-priced, durable wood often used in flooring and joinery, such as windows and doors.

Brazilian cedar, a durable, low-priced wood with a distinct fragrance. It is used for cabinet-making and joinery.

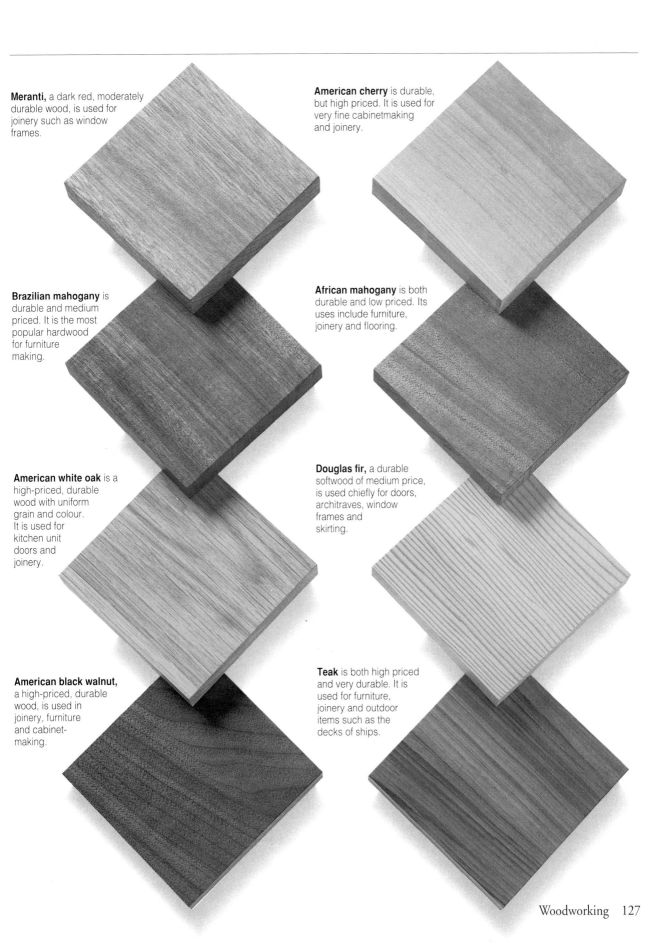

Meranti, a dark red, moderately durable wood, is used for joinery such as window frames.

American cherry is durable, but high priced. It is used for very fine cabinetmaking and joinery.

Brazilian mahogany is durable and medium priced. It is the most popular hardwood for furniture making.

African mahogany is both durable and low priced. Its uses include furniture, joinery and flooring.

American white oak is a high-priced, durable wood with uniform grain and colour. It is used for kitchen unit doors and joinery.

Douglas fir, a durable softwood of medium price, is used chiefly for doors, architraves, window frames and skirting.

American black walnut, a high-priced, durable wood, is used in joinery, furniture and cabinet-making.

Teak is both high priced and very durable. It is used for furniture, joinery and outdoor items such as the decks of ships.

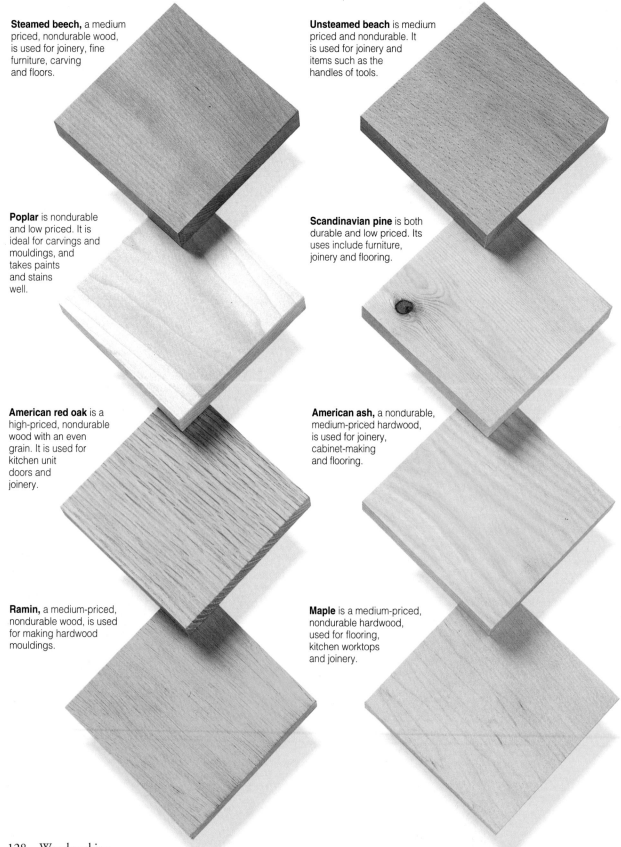

Steamed beech, a medium priced, nondurable wood, is used for joinery, fine furniture, carving and floors.

Unsteamed beach is medium priced and nondurable. It is used for joinery and items such as the handles of tools.

Poplar is nondurable and low priced. It is ideal for carvings and mouldings, and takes paints and stains well.

Scandinavian pine is both durable and low priced. Its uses include furniture, joinery and flooring.

American red oak is a high-priced, nondurable wood with an even grain. It is used for kitchen unit doors and joinery.

American ash, a nondurable, medium-priced hardwood, is used for joinery, cabinet-making and flooring.

Ramin, a medium-priced, nondurable wood, is used for making hardwood mouldings.

Maple is a medium-priced, nondurable hardwood, used for flooring, kitchen worktops and joinery.

MANUFACTURED BOARDS

An alternative to solid wood, manufactured boards are made by laminating or compressing layers of wood or wood fibres to form panels. The most common types are plywood, blockboard, chipboard, hardboard and medium-density fibreboard (MDF).

Hardwood-veneer plywood is sold according to the veneer species, the cut (p.170) and the core type (MDF, chipboard or plywood). Softwood plywood is made up of laminated layers of veneer, and graded for interior or exterior use, strength and the quality of its outer veneers. Another form of plywood is oriented strand board, made in cross-oriented layers of Scots pine for maximum strength.

Hardboard has a smooth face and canvas-textured back; it can also be perforated and oil-tempered. Blockboard is faced with birch or poplar and is usually 5-ply. Chipboard is often used for internal subflooring. For more details, see page 345.

Plywood core thickness can vary from 6-38 mm (¼-1½ in) and even thicker. Some specialist birch plywoods go down to 0.4 mm. From left to right are a hardwood-veneer panel; two plywoods (the number of layers is referred to, for example, as 3-ply or 5-ply); chipboard, which can be layered; and oriented strand board (the long fibres are visibly layered).

Tongue-and-groove panels are used as subflooring material. The panels can be made from plywood, oriented strand board or chipboard; the ends are tongued and grooved for a tighter fit.

Hardwood-veneer plywood (below, top) is presanded and ready for finishing; the superior quality outer veneers come in 'paint' and 'stain' grades. Use it where the final look is important. Birch is cross-grained and oak veneer is long-grained. They are the most common; other veneers can be ordered.

CDX plywood (below, bottom) has softwood outer veneers that may be knotty. They should be treated or covered if they are to be used outdoors permanently.

Chipboard (below, top) may be tongued and grooved, for flooring; C1 is standard; and C4 is moisture resistant. A presealed grade of chipboard is used for roofing rough sheds and barns.

Oriented strand board (below, centre) has exterior gluing and is a cheaper alternative to construction ply. Used for sheathing and for flat roofs.

MDF (below, bottom) is stable and machines well. Use it for painted cabinet doors and also as a veneer substrate.

All trees belong in one of two broad divisions, hardwoods or softwoods, depending on whether they are broad-leaved or coniferous. But in their actual characteristics, distinctions between the two types tend to blur. Certain softwoods are harder than some soft hardwoods, but because hardness and strength go hand in hand, the strongest woods are also more difficult to work and require the sharpest tools. These dense woods are also less forgiving of careless joinery.

All woods have grain, a term that describes the direction of fibres. Relative cell size, which can determine whether a wood needs a filler before finishing, is called texture. The patterns of various timbers are caused by either the natural fibre patterns or deviations from a tree's normal growth.

Freshly sawn timber has a high moisture content and should be seasoned or dried before working. Timber yards usually sell kiln-dried wood with a moisture content of about 20 per cent. Wood that has less than 10 per cent moisture content is recommended for furniture-making; the range above 10 per cent is suitable for structural uses.

After seasoning, wood continues to shrink during dry spells and swell with humidity. This tendency is critical to the woodworker because it can cause warped boards, splits, loose joints or swollen-shut drawers. To combat this, choose a stable type of wood. Buy kiln-dried boards in advance and store them indoors for about a month to condition them to the humidity of your home. After working, apply a sealing finish on all surfaces to retard further moisture exchange.

Wood comes in various grades. For softwood projects, choose a joinery grade timber for fine finishing and other grades for construction. In hardwood, first and second (FAS) boards are about 85 per cent defect free. The use of hardwoods is a sensitive area because of the destruction of hardwood forests. Many reputable timber suppliers are committed to the Environmental Policy for Wood Products, which supports the forestry principles adopted by the United Nations and the International Tropical Timber Association to ensure that all forests within their jurisdiction are managed sustainably by the year 2000. This may limit your choice of hardwoods, but it is possible to use a softwood that is in plentiful supply and stain it to look like hardwood. Most stains produce a very realistic result (pp.166-9).

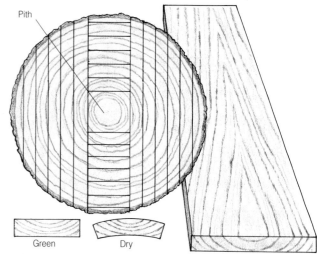

Plain-sawing, or flat-sawing, yields boards whose growth rings intersect the surface at less than 45°. Boards containing the pith (the soft core at the trunk's centre) will cup severely or split, and thus are usually ripped into two narrower boards. Plain-sawn boards warp as they dry.

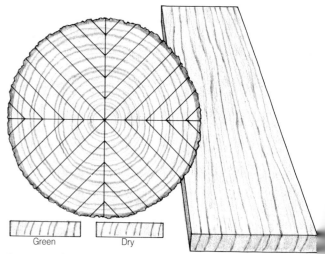

Quarter-sawing produces wood with a close, even grain pattern because the growth rings form an angle of 45° to 90° to the board surface. Quarter-sawing results in more waste than plain-sawing; thus boards milled this way are more expensive. While quarter-sawn wood may check or crack (facing page), it is less prone to warp.

Types of grain

Straight grain is strong and runs parallel with the edges of the board.

Irregular grain occurs when normal growth pattern is altered by defects in the wood.

Wavy grain, weaker than straight, has attractive figure but is difficult to work.

Spiral grain is a natural growth pattern ascending a trunk. Wood may twist.

Interlocked grain results from successive layers of wood spiralling in opposite directions. These boards, sliced from one block, show how the wood fibres changed course.

Defects in wood

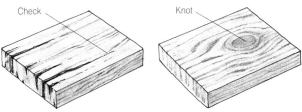

Check

Knot

Wood dries more quickly along the grain than across it. The resulting uneven moisture loss causes cracks, called checks or shakes, on the ends. Knots occur when a tree branch dies and the trunk grows round it. They can vary from 5 to 40 mm (about ¼-1½ in) in diameter.

Stacking timber

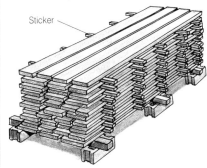

Sticker

To ensure good air circulation and to minimise warp, the layers of board are separated with small dry strips of wood, called stickers. They are positioned at each end of the stack and about every 40 cm (16 in) along the length of the boards.

Types of warp

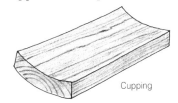

Cupping

Bowing

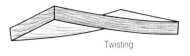

Twisting

Wood distorts when it shrinks or swells unevenly. The stress thus produced in the fibres causes a deviation from the board's flatness. The less stable a wood, the more it will warp.

Wood types

Wood	Characteristics	Texture	Ease of working	Ease of finishing
Ash, American	Strong and stable	Coarse	Moderate	Sands and stains well
Beech	Strong but unstable	Fine	Fairly difficult	Easy to oil or varnish, but stains unevenly
Cedar, Brazilian	Fairly stable	Fine	Easy	Easy to oil or varnish; stains and polishes well
Cedar, Western red	Stable	Coarse	Easy	Corrosive to iron, so avoid using iron nails
Cherry, American	Strong, stable	Fine	Easy	Very easy to oil or varnish
Chestnut, European	Strong, stable	Coarse	Easier than oak	Corrosive to iron. Easy to oil or varnish
Fir, Douglas	Stable	Coarse	Easy	Take care not to 'pick up' or catch the grain
Iroko	Strong	Coarse	Difficult	Finishes well when filled. Dust can be an irritant
Mahogany, Brazilian	Stable	Fine	Easy	Best of all mahoganies; stains and polishes well
Maple	Very strong	Fine	Difficult	Polishes well
Meranti, dark red	Fairly stable	Coarse	Easy	Finishes satisfactorily when filled
Oak, American red	Fairly strong	Coarse	Moderate	Corrosive to iron; unsuitable for exterior use
Oak, American white	Strong, fairly stable	Coarse	Moderate	Corrosive; stains and polishes well
Pine, Scandinavian	Fairly stable	Coarse	Very easy	Very easy to paint or varnish; stains unevenly
Poplar (sometimes called Tulipwood)	Fairly stable	Fine	Very easy, but dents easily	Easy to paint or stain
Ramin	Strong but unstable	Fine	Moderate	Paints and stains well
Sapele	Strong, fairly stable	Coarse	Difficult	Difficult to stain; polishes well
Teak	Very strong, very stable	Coarse to medium	Very difficult; hard to glue	Oils well; don't paint or varnish it
Walnut, American black	Strong, stable	Fine	Moderate	Easy to oil or varnish

Squaring: getting it straight

The first step in any woodworking project is to choose the best board face of each member and make it exactly flat. In addition, each piece must have one level edge that is squared to the first face. These two surfaces will become the reference for all measuring, marking and cutting operations on the opposite surface and edge, and at each end.

If you have access to a jointer and a thickness planer, you can buy timber rough-sawn in nominal dimensions (the least expensive kind) and then mill one face and each edge on the jointer and the other face on the planer. If you have only hand planes, you can buy more expensive boards that are surfaced or dressed to a nominal thickness and width. Even more costly are those cut to exact length, thickness and width, as from a cutting list. When planing by hand, use a jack plane, followed by a smoothing plane; then square the edge with a jointer or jack plane (p.134).

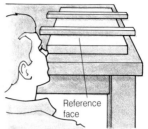

Check flatness on best face with straightedge along dotted lines (right). Light will show at low spots. Mark high spots with pencil; plane smooth.

Check for twisting by placing a straight piece of wood at each end of the board and sighting down their top edges. Mark and plane the high spots.

On best edge, check for high spots and squareness of corner, using planed face as reference. Mark spots to be planed both across edge and along it.

Measuring and marking

To reduce the length of rough-sawn timber to manageable dimensions, mark the boards about 2.5 cm (1 in) oversize before cutting. Dressed timber with accurate reference surfaces can be cut to the finished lengths. But mark and cut them 1-2 mm (1/32-1/16 in) wider to allow for smoothing with a jointer plane. Once you have squared the face and edge of a board, mark the reference face with a loop and the reference edge

with a V. These marks will help you to orient the pieces in the right direction. Then measure and mark the cuts for the rest of your project.

A sharp scribing tool is the most accurate for marking, but if you are using a pencil, choose one with a hard lead, sharpened to a chisel point. Use the same tools for the entire project, and avoid changing the marking-gauge setting until you have marked all parts

having the same measurement. Pencil a cross to mark centres of holes, with a circle round the cross for extra clarity. Heavily marked wood can be confusing to interpret, so make pencil notes beside the marks on the waste side of the wood to avoid cutting errors.

Finally, remeasure everything before sawing; finding a mistake after you have made the cut may mean having to start again with a new piece of wood.

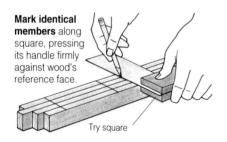

Mark identical members along square, pressing its handle firmly against wood's reference face.

Try square

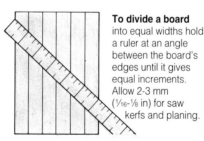

To divide a board into equal widths hold a ruler at an angle between the board's edges until it gives equal increments. Allow 2-3 mm (1/16-1/8 in) for saw kerfs and planing.

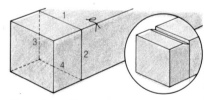

To mark cutoff line, hold try square handle on reference surface; mark lines in sequence. Chisel recess in waste to guide saw.

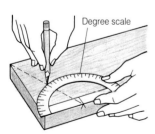

Degree scale

Setting an angle Align index line of protractor with starting point on board edge; mark. Join the two points with straightedge.

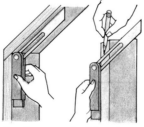

Copying an angle Adjust the bevel-gauge blade to the angle you want to copy; transfer this angle to new piece.

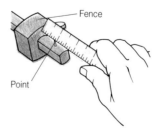

Fence

Point

Setting marking gauge Loosen thumbscrew; push fence away from point with ruler. Tighten screw; check setting.

Drawing a gauged line Grasp the handle tightly, tilt gauge and pull toward you (shown here) or push away, trailing pin on line.

Most sawing involves cutting a straight line along the grain (ripping), across the grain (crosscutting) or at an angle to it (mitre or bevel cut). The following are the most common woodworking saws: panel saw, with teeth designed for both ripping (with the grain) and crosscutting (across the grain); tenon saw for joint cutting; dovetail saw for fine work; keyhole saw for cutting out small areas; circular saw, with blades for rip or crosscutting, for straight cuts; jigsaw for shaped work; and band saw for intricate work.

Wood should not move or vibrate while being cut. When handsawing, support the wood on a saw bench. Hold the saw at about a 60° angle to the wood surface for ripping; at about 45° for crosscutting. Because wood can splinter where the saw teeth exit, place the good side up when cutting with a handsaw or saw bench; put the good side down when using a circular saw or when using a jigsaw. To avoid making the board short by the width of the saw kerf (the groove cut by the blade) saw on the waste side of the lines. Allow 3 mm (⅛ in) for the kerf on a saw bench.

When you are ripping, the saw may bind (the kerf closes, pinching the blade). A circular saw tends to bind if it twists off a straight line or exposes too much blade. When a circular saw blade binds, the saw will kick back, or jump dangerously towards you. To prevent handsaws and circular saws binding, drive wedges into the kerf. On a saw bench, a splitter is part of the guard or is mounted as an accessory. Boards that are not held securely on a saw bench may shoot back at you. To prevent kickback when ripping on a saw bench, press the board against the fence with a clamped guide or feather board. Buy one from a supplier or cut kerfs at 6 mm (¼ in) intervals in an angled board to make 'fingers'. Another safety tool is a push stick, a notched stick that guides narrow pieces.

Start panel saw against wooden straightedge guide. Pull saw towards you to mark kerf in waste. Keep blade straight. Extend index finger along handle to keep saw near cut line.

To rip with circular saw, run baseplate against a batten clamped to work. (If clamped on waste side, saw could be pulled away from straightedge, making the work smaller than measured.) Guide narrower cuts by using saw's adjustable rip fence.

Ripping accurately on a saw bench depends on fence being parallel with blade. To check, measure between blade and fence at both front and rear of blade (inset). To keep hands away from blade, use feather board as a brace to control work and a push stick to move it.

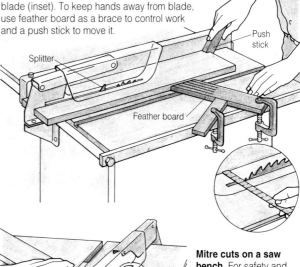

Splitter Push stick Feather board

Mitre cuts on a saw bench For safety and accuracy, screw auxiliary fence, made from straight piece of hardwood or plywood, to mitre gauge; sandpaper glued to the fence will prevent wood from shifting as you slide it into the blade.

Auxiliary fence

▶ **SAFE PRACTICES** ◀

General rules
▷ Let saw reach full speed before cutting; keep work clear of blade until you are ready to cut.
▷ Keep locks and clamps tight. Support work firmly.

Saw bench
▷ Make sure guard and splitter, which holds cut stock open after cut, are in place and properly adjusted. Set blade to protrude 3 mm (⅛ in) above work.
▷ Use a push stick when ripping stock less than 7.5 cm (3 in) wide. Clamp a feather board behind saw blade and brace it from the side.
▷ Keep widest part of board between blade and fence. Hold on to work until completely clear of blade. If work is narrow, use a push stick.
▷ Hold stock against fence or mitre

gauge. Never cut freehand.
▷ To guard against kickback, never stand in area directly behind saw blade and fence.
▷ Make deep cuts in two or more passes; adjust blade each time.

Circular saw
▷ Clamp work firmly so it won't shift. Make sure the blade is sharp and clean.
▷ Never remove or wedge up the retractable blade guard.
▷ Support waste for a long cut.
▷ Stand to one side of the saw, out of the way of kickback.
▷ Stand with weight firmly on both feet; don't reach too far with the saw. Don't let saw drop at end.
▷ Always adjust the blade to the height needed for a particular job. Before adjusting, unplug the saw. (More safety tips, pages 12-13.)

Two types of hand tool shape wood: cutting and scraping. Cutting tools (chisels, drawknives, spokeshaves and planes) carve the wood, leaving a smooth surface. And because they tear out end grain, they are most efficiently used to work along the grain of straight-grained woods. Scraping tools (files, rasps and Surform tools) pull the fibres off wood rather than cut them, leaving a fuzzy surface. Use the tools in any direction, regardless of grain.

Precise planing depends on a keen blade, correct adjustment and a flat sole. Set the plane mouth according to the work: with the opening widest on a jack plane, medium on a jointer plane and narrow on a smoothing plane. In addition, you may have to file smooth the cap iron, which keeps the blade from tearing the wood, to make it fit snugly to the plane blade. Move the cap iron about 1 mm ($\frac{1}{32}$ in) away from the blade edge – set it closer for fine work, farther away for rough.

Because taking too thick an initial cut can jam the blade in the wood, adjust the plane for a fine shaving and test the cut; then gradually increase the shaving thickness. For the smoothest results on a surface, finish planing with progressively finer cuts. To prevent end grain from chipping, support it by clamping or gluing a piece of scrap wood to the work before you begin planing, or plane end grain from the ends of the wood towards the middle.

Although it's sometimes necessary to work directly across the grain, chisels are best used along the grain, so that the blade doesn't catch or split off chunks of wood. When chiselling a groove, use a chisel that is slightly narrower, or it will chip the groove sides. Use a bevelled edge chisel for general shaping work and light tapping with a mallet. Use a firmer chisel, or mortise chisel, which is much sturdier, for mallet work, such as cutting mortises. To control the depth of the cut, work with the chisel's bevel down; raise the handle to go deeper, lower it to cut parallel with the surface. Make a width stop cut across the grain to prevent splitting the grain. Secure the work so it can't move, and always keep your hands behind the cutting edge. Never cut towards yourself.

Drawknives and spokeshaves are useful for curved work. A drawknife resembles a chisel in that it can remove both large and small amounts of wood depending on how you manipulate it. A spokeshave is closer to a plane, with its blade enclosed by a sole. Choose cylindrical handles for an easy grip and ball-shaped handles for carving wood. When drawknifing, keep both hands on the handles. For safety and accuracy, keep your body balanced as you pull the blade towards you, so you can stop cutting at any moment if the grain splits. Store all cutting tools on a rack because leaving them lying on a work surface is asking for an accident.

Files, rasps and Surform tools are primarily used to shape curved work rapidly. All cut on the push stroke and leave surfaces that must be smoothed with a plane, cabinet scraper or sandpaper. For greatest versatility, choose a half-round tool. Work a rasp or file diagonally, with one hand pushing the handle while the heel of the other hand guides the tool toe. A Surform, which is useful for rounding off square corners, is used similarly, but because it is shaped like a plane, it is easier to hold. Clean the teeth of files and rasps with a special brush called a file card, pulling it in the direction of the file's lines or teeth. To clean a Surform, pull the shavings out.

Using a plane

Begin a pass with pressure on the plane's toe, equalise pressure in mid pass, and end with pressure on the heel. Keep the plane sole flat on the wood. Supplement the force of your arms with back and shoulder power, and shift your weight from rear foot to front foot as you finish each stroke.

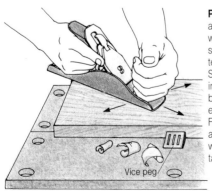

Plane diagonally across wide board with overlapping strokes; this avoids tearing the grain. Stretch your rear index finger along blade edge for extra control. Finish planing along the grain, with blade set to take a fine shaving.

Vice peg

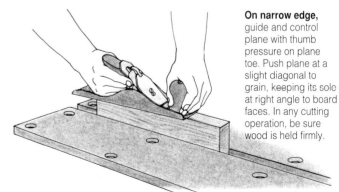

On narrow edge, guide and control plane with thumb pressure on plane toe. Push plane at a slight diagonal to grain, keeping its sole at right angle to board faces. In any cutting operation, be sure wood is held firmly.

Using a chisel

Chisel across grain with bevel up (first make side cuts with tenon saw or dovetail saw). Cut in halfway from one side, reverse board, and cut in from opposite direction. For heavier work, use a firmer chisel.

Saw cut

To cut recess, first outline ends using a chisel held vertically, with bevel inward. Score waste every 6 mm (¼ in); then cut waste out from centre to ends, holding chisel bevel-down at a shallow angle.

Shape a curve from side to end grain by overlapping cuts. Drive chisel with mallet to remove large amounts of wood; fine-tune the curve with chisel and body weight, as shown.

Grain direction

Grain direction

Chisel a hollow a little at a time from ends to centre to avoid lifting the grain. Saw centre of hollow to desired depth beforehand.

Saw cut

Grain direction

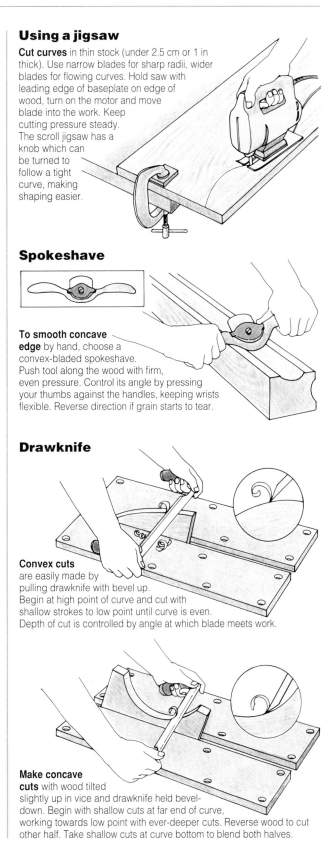

Using a jigsaw

Cut curves in thin stock (under 2.5 cm or 1 in thick). Use narrow blades for sharp radii, wider blades for flowing curves. Hold saw with leading edge of baseplate on edge of wood, turn on the motor and move blade into the work. Keep cutting pressure steady. The scroll jigsaw has a knob which can be turned to follow a tight curve, making shaping easier.

Spokeshave

To smooth concave edge by hand, choose a convex-bladed spokeshave. Push tool along the wood with firm, even pressure. Control its angle by pressing your thumbs against the handles, keeping wrists flexible. Reverse direction if grain starts to tear.

Drawknife

Convex cuts are easily made by pulling drawknife with bevel up. Begin at high point of curve and cut with shallow strokes to low point until curve is even. Depth of cut is controlled by angle at which blade meets work.

Make concave cuts with wood tilted slightly up in vice and drawknife held bevel-down. Begin with shallow cuts at far end of curve, working towards low point with ever-deeper cuts. Reverse wood to cut other half. Take shallow cuts at curve bottom to blend both halves.

SHAPING WOOD ON A LATHE

In spindle turning (centre work), the wood, held between the headstock and tailstock of a lathe, is shaped into chair or table legs, stair balusters and other cylindrical objects. Knot-free, straight-grained hardwood with fine to medium texture is easiest to turn; coarse-textured wood may splinter. Softwood is usable, but it is hard to turn crisp details. Wood may be seasoned or (green) wet, but green wood may split or shrink unevenly as it dries. Large or very thin pieces take more skill to turn; start with a blank 50-75 mm (2-3 in) square.

To set up, check that the cup centre of the tailstock is tight to the wood, but not so tight that the wood doesn't turn freely. Adjust the tool-rest position so that the scraping tool will be just above the wood's centre line (raise it a bit higher for a cutting tool) and close to the wood (without hitting it). Move the tool rest inwards as you reduce the wood's diameter.

Caution: Wear a face shield, and turn off the lathe before you adjust the tool rest or measure your progress.

Scraping tools – round-nose scrapers and diamond-points – are easier for beginners to handle. These tools can carve many shapes, but they leave a rough surface that must be sanded. Experienced turners cut or slice work with cutting tools: gouges, skew chisels and parting tools. Cutting tools shave the work, leaving a clean finish that needs little or no sanding. All tools must be sharp (pp.198-9).

First, with the lathe running at slow speed, rough out or remove corners of the blank in small sections; as the wood becomes round, increase the speed. Begin the first section 2.5 cm (1 in) from one end, and make a series of passes from alternating directions. To avoid splits when starting the next section, move your tool toward the turned section. Rough

Mounting the wood

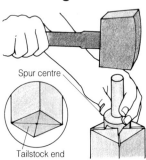

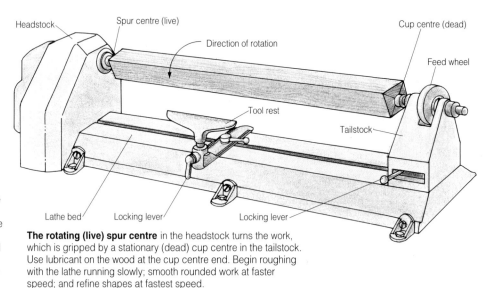

Preparing the blank Draw two diagonal lines on each end of piece to find exact centre. With handsaw on headstock end, score lines; drive spur centre into saw cuts. Mark centre of X with awl on tailstock end (inset). If wood is more than 50 mm (2 in) square, plane or saw off each corner so blank is octagonal.

The rotating (live) spur centre in the headstock turns the work, which is gripped by a stationary (dead) cup centre in the tailstock. Use lubricant on the wood at the cup centre end. Begin roughing with the lathe running slowly; smooth rounded work at faster speed; and refine shapes at fastest speed.

How to hold the tool

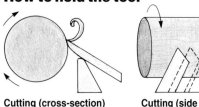

Cutting (cross-section)   Cutting (side view)

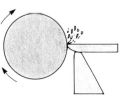

Scraping (cross-section)   Scraping (top view)

To cut a shape, rub bevel of skew chisel on wood, then lift handle to angle bottom half of cutting edge into wood; move in direction of work.

To scrape, hold round-nose tool horizontal (or slightly down) and flat on rest, ease edge into work, and scrape lightly along the blank.

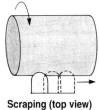

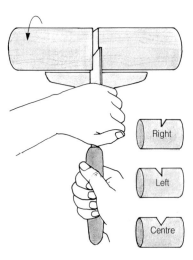

V-cutting Score centre line of V-cut with point of skew. Then, holding tool 90° to the work, cut V-bottom with heel of skew cutting edge. To make a right or left V-shape (keeping one side of V at 90°), cut right or left side of centre line at 45° or desired angle with bevel edge of skew. For centred V-cut, cut each side to bottom, widening the shape as necessary.

out the end sections with repeated passes moving from the ends towards the middle. To scrape, move a round-nose scraper along the tool rest parallel with the floor. To cut, place the centre edge of a square-end gouge against the revolving wood; then roll it slightly in the direction of travel with your lower hand and move it along the rest with your upper hand. To avoid catches, grasp the tool firmly and use gentle, steady pressure – never force it into the wood.

To sand your work as it rotates on the lathe, remove the tool rest and press a small pad of garnet paper (backed with a scrap of leather to protect you from heat build-up) against the work, or hold both ends of a garnet paper strip under (not over) it. Start with 180-220 grit aluminium-oxide abrasive on smooth work, 80 grit on rough. Remove work from the lathe with a dovetail saw.

From rough to final shape

Grip gouge overhand to begin rounding. Cup fingers to steady tool; brace handle against body.

Finish truing diameter with round-nose scraper held underhand and horizontal.

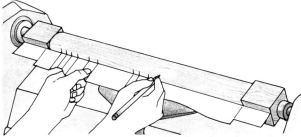

To lay out a design, hold uncut edge of hardboard template against cylinder; mark lines where cuts will be made (shown). Next, hold pencil on rest, its point on marks; hand-rotate wood to sketch lines on cylinder.

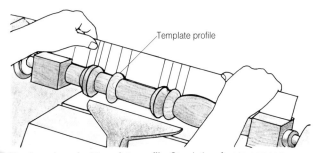

Template profile

Check work against template profile Stop lathe often to compare your work with a cut profile of your design. For small jobs, measure diameters with outside calipers.

Turned shapes

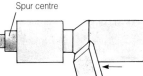

Spur centre

Square shoulder Score shoulder line with point of skew. With lower half of edge (but not heel), cut away wood leading to shoulder. Then smooth vertical wall of shoulder. Repeat until shoulder cut is correct depth.

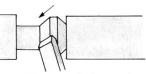

Bead Make V-cut (facing page) on both sides of bead. Round one side of bead by rolling skew down-hill from bead centre toward V-cut in one smooth, flowing motion. End with blade edge vertical. Repeat rounding motion on other side.

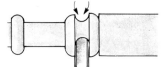

Cove Start cut with gouge rolled on side. Raise handle to engage wood, and roll tool, rubbing bevel on wood, through cut from a shoulder to cove centre. At end of cut, gouge top faces up. Cut in from other shoulder.

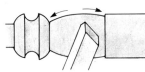

Urn shape Beginning at widest and narrowest diameters, rough out shape with skew to within 2 mm (¹⁄₁₆ in) of final size. Roll skew from high to low points. Cut small concave shapes with gouge, similar to motion for coves.

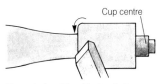

Cup centre

Round shoulder Start cut at highest point of shoulder, engage edge of skew near heel, and roll skew downhill so heel drops into valley. Finish with blade vertical.

TURNING HOLLOW SHAPES ON A FACEPLATE

In faceplate work, a block of wood, mounted first on a faceplate and then screwed onto the headstock, can be sculpted, as for a bowl. You can remove wood across and along its grain. It is best to use finely textured hardwoods because they will produce smoother turnings than softwoods and coarse-grained hardwoods, which tear out. Irregular grain patterns show well, but you should avoid wood with knots or splits. If you are still learning, work on blocks that are 150-200 mm (6-8 in) in diameter and 50 mm (2 in) thick. Use scraping tools; round-nose and diamond-point scrapers are easier to handle than gouges and chisels, and are less likely to catch in the wood.

Before mounting a blank on the lathe, true the base and round off the edges – square corners are dangerous. If a backer is needed, make it from hardwood; softwood and plywood won't hold the screws. Wood up to 300 mm (12 in) in diameter and 50 mm (2 in) thick can be mounted to the backer with hot-melt glue from a glue gun. Screw a faceplate to the backer and then trace the outline onto the blank. Working quickly, run a bead of glue round the edge of the backer and inside the matching line on the blank. Hold the pieces together for a minute, then mount them.

To turn a bowl in one mounting, shape the exterior first. True the outer edge with the lathe running slowly. Then change to medium speed and begin shaping. During the final shaping, switch to higher speed. Keep the tool flat on the rest, and work with a light touch. Before hollowing the inside, measure the stock's thickness and decide the desired bowl depth. Never go below 6 mm (¼ in) thick. To sand the piece, remove the tool rest and use 60, 80, 120 and finally 180 or 220 grit aluminium-oxide paper. To sand large-diameter work, run the lathe at slow speed; for small-diameter work, run it at faster speed. Separate the work and sand the glue off the foot. Shape a base or foot with a chisel, if desired.

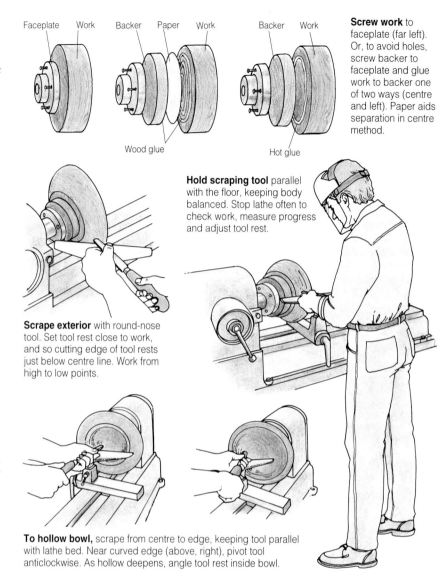

Screw work to faceplate (far left). Or, to avoid holes, screw backer to faceplate and glue work to backer one of two ways (centre and left). Paper aids separation in centre method.

Hold scraping tool parallel with the floor, keeping body balanced. Stop lathe often to check work, measure progress and adjust tool rest.

Scrape exterior with round-nose tool. Set tool rest close to work, and so cutting edge of tool rests just below centre line. Work from high to low points.

To hollow bowl, scrape from centre to edge, keeping tool parallel with lathe bed. Near curved edge (above, right), pivot tool anticlockwise. As hollow deepens, angle tool rest inside bowl.

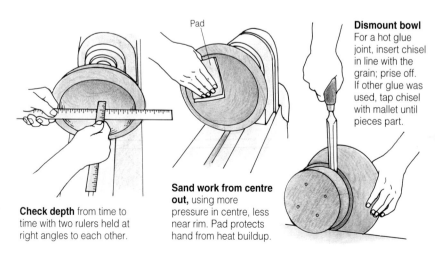

Check depth from time to time with two rulers held at right angles to each other.

Sand work from centre out, using more pressure in centre, less near rim. Pad protects hand from heat buildup.

Dismount bowl For a hot glue joint, insert chisel in line with the grain; prise off. If other glue was used, tap chisel with mallet until pieces part.

JOINTS: AN INTRODUCTION

A woodworking project is only as strong as the joints used in it. Hundreds of joints have been developed, most derived from six groups (see chart). The dovetail, for example, can be made with visible pins and tails (through dovetail) or varied so that the pins and tails are half visible (half lapped) or fully hidden (secret mitre). Tenons may be mitred when they meet in a mortise, as in a table leg, or are wedged for strength.

How do you pick the best joint for the job? Strength is a major consideration, but appearance, your expertise and the tools you own are important factors as well. Cutting a joint without the right tools and skills is risky – loose-fitting joints will have a poor glue bond; overtight joints will have to be forced together, which can damage the wood fibres and split one of the pieces of the joint. As a general rule, always select the least complex joint that will work for the project.

The strength of a joint depends on the amount of gluing surface the joint provides and on whether that surface is long grain (parallel with the wood fibres) or end grain (across the fibres). Long grain holds the glue on the surface for a strong bond; end grain absorbs it, resulting in poor adhesion. The strongest joints interlock, such as dovetail pins and tails, or have maximum long-grain to long-grain gluing surfaces and minimum end-grain surfaces, such as edge joints. Joints that mate end-grain surfaces, such as butt joints, are usually reinforced with nails, screws, splines or wooden biscuits. These devices can be used to reinforce other joints as well.

Common joints

Type		Tools to use	Uses	Strength	Ease of making
Butt and edge	Butt Edge	Tenon saw or panel saw; table saw or circular saw. Finish edge joints with plane or jointer	Butt: for rough carpentry	Butt: weak; reinforce with fasteners	Butt: very easy
			Edge: for large surfaces	Edge: strong	Edge: fairly easy but must be smooth and accurate
Face and edge mitres	Edge mitre Face mitre	Mitre box, tenon saw and plane; power mitre saw; table saw	Frames and mouldings	Weak; strengthen with dowels, keys, or splines or tongues	Difficult to cut accurately with hand tools; easier with power saw
Halving joints	Cross halving Corner halving	Tenon saw and chisel; router; band saw	Frames, frame-and-panel doors, and interlocking grid construction	Fairly strong	Easy
Interlocking joints: dovetail, finger	Dovetail	Dovetail saw and chisel; router with template. Dovetail jigs available	Drawers, cabinets and boxes	Extremely strong when cut by hand; strong when cut by machine	Difficult with hand tools; easier with power tools
Grooved joints: rebate, housing, tongue-and-groove	Double rebate Rebate Housing	Tenon saw and chisel; router	Drawers, cabinets, boxes, and shelves	Rebate: fairly strong	Rebate: fairly easy
				Housing: strong	Housing: fairly easy
				Tongue-and-groove: strong	Tongue-and-groove: fairly easy
Mortise-and-tenon	Through tenon Through mortise Bridle	Hand drill and firmer chisel; router; drill press; band saw; mortiser	Frames and legs for tables and chairs, frame-and-panel cabinets	Strong	Fairly difficult with hand tools; easier with power tools

Although wide surfaces in carpentry are often veneer-covered plywood, some fine table or desktop projects may call for solid boards joined edge to edge. Because edge joints have plenty of gluing surface and no porous end grain, they may be bonded with glue. To help to align the boards, use dowels, biscuits or splines (tongues). For a precise joint – critical to strength – the mating edges must be smooth, straight and squared to the faces. Before gluing, dry-clamp the assembly to find any gaps. Examine the joints with a lamp shining behind the work; mark high spots (where no light shows through), plane them and recheck.

When gluing, tighten the clamps enough so that the glue oozes beads, but don't overtighten – this will squeeze out too much glue. To keep excess glue from sticking to the straightedges or reacting with the metal clamps, put a layer of waxed paper or Cling Film wherever they touch.

Butt and mitre joints, even when precisely cut, are inherently weak because of the minimal gluing surface and the presence of end grain, which does not accept glue well. These joints will need to be reinforced with metal

fasteners (nails or screws), dowels, wooden biscuits, keys, splines, tongues or glue blocks (blocks glued and nailed or screwed to the inside corners of joints). Although visible nails and screws are acceptable on utility cabinets and shelves, more refined work calls for countersunk or counterbored screws and filled nail holes (p.150).

Dowels can be either blind (hidden) or through (ends exposed). A dowelling jig aids in drilling perfectly aligned holes to the proper depth, or you can use a homemade guide.

Oval-shaped biscuits are an easy alternative. To install them, you need a machine known as a biscuit or plate joiner. Biscuits, made from textured compressed wood, absorb the glue and expand, creating a very strong joint. They come in three sizes – choose the largest that will work with your wood. Biscuits are not recommended for joining warped or bowed plywood panels; instead use dowels or tongues.

Caution: Never use a biscuit joiner freehand. Clamp the work, and butt the machine against the work or a stop block. Watch for kickback and keep your fingers away. For more on mitre joints, see pages 133, 149 and 158-9.

Blind-dowel butt joint

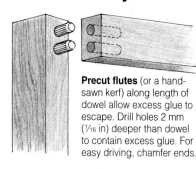

Precut flutes (or a hand-sawn kerf) along length of dowel allow excess glue to escape. Drill holes 2 mm (1/16 in) deeper than dowel to contain excess glue. For easy driving, chamfer ends.

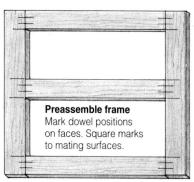

Preassemble frame
Mark dowel positions on faces. Square marks to mating surfaces.

Drill holes so that they are aligned and same depth in each piece. Jig increases accuracy; without one, check drill straightness often with a try square. Masking tape on bit marks depth at which to stop drill.

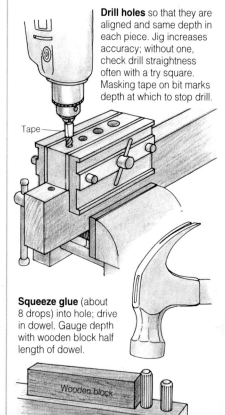

Tape

Squeeze glue (about 8 drops) into hole; drive in dowel. Gauge depth with wooden block half length of dowel.

Wooden block

Making an edge joint

V- mark

To prevent warp, lay out boards with growth rings in alternating direction. If grain is matched instead, attach frame to work when glue is dry. V-mark aids reassembly.

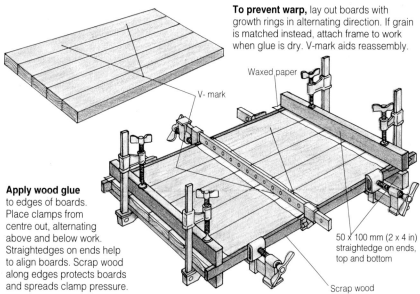

Waxed paper

Apply wood glue to edges of boards. Place clamps from centre out, alternating above and below work. Straightedges on ends help to align boards. Scrap wood along edges protects boards and spreads clamp pressure.

50 x 100 mm (2 x 4 in) straightedge on ends, top and bottom

Scrap wood

Making biscuit joints

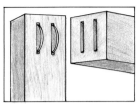
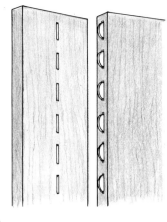

Wood biscuits can substitute for nails, screws or dowels in butt joints (right). In frame work (above), biscuits can be used instead of mortise-and-tenon joints (although they are not as strong) or tongues. Wood must be wider than 48 mm (1⅞ in), the length of smallest biscuit slot.

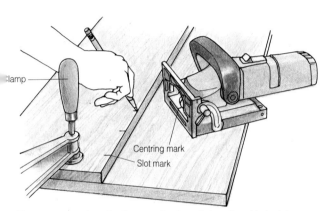

Clamp

Centring mark
Slot mark

To measure and mark, clamp mating boards together. Mark slots for biscuits in both pieces, using centring mark on biscuit joiner. In butt joints, the closer the slots, the stronger the joint (strengthen frame construction by using two biscuits equally spaced on centre).

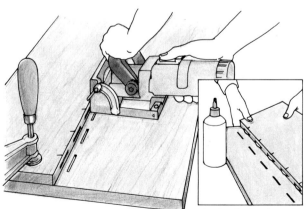

To cut, align centring mark on joiner base with pencil mark, and plunge in the blade; when it springs back, go to next mark. For slots in bottom piece, position joiner vertically with its base against edge of mating board.

Apply glue in slots with split-nozzle applicator or thin wood scrap; insert biscuits. Clamp joint until glue swells the biscuits, at least 10 minutes.

Strengthening mitre joints

Caution: Guard must be used over blade. (Removed here to show angle of blade)

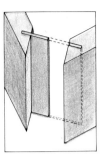

Edge mitre joint (p.159) is stronger with tongue placed closer to inner corner. Cut tongue from plywood or hardwood scrap.

To cut spline slots, tilt the table saw blade 45°. Hold the work securely against the mitre gauge with one hand; press it against rip fence with the other.

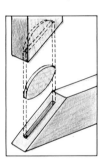

Front fence

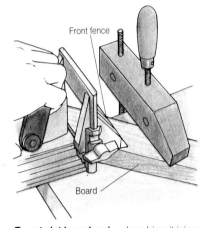

Board

Face mitre has biscuit located at 90° angle to mitre cut.

To cut slot in end grain, place biscuit joiner against mitre cut on board, and lock front fence into place. Clamp the work securely so that it will not shift.

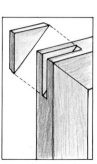
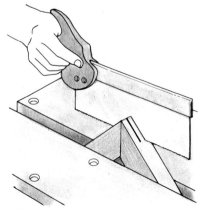

Mitre key (triangle of wood) is one-third thickness of joint but may be as thin as 2.5 mm (³⁄₃₂ in).

After glued mitre joint has dried, cut two parallel slots into corner with dovetail saw. Chisel out waste and test-fit key. Apply glue to key and tap in with hammer. Let dry, saw key flush and plane smooth.

HALVING JOINTS

Halving joints connect two boards at an angle, usually at 90 degrees. Corner-halving joints, at the ends of boards, are made with wide, flat cuts; cross-halving joints, formed by two notches, join boards at any point between the ends. A T-halving has an end-halving and an intersecting cross-halving and forms a T-shape. T-halvings that have to tolerate tensile (pulling) stress are best dovetailed.

You can make a halving joint with boards of equal or of unequal thickness. With equally thick boards, cut half their thickness; otherwise, cut no more than half the thickness of the thinner piece. Because the grains of the pieces cross, keep the halving width under 10 cm (4 in) or the wood may split as its moisture content changes. Mark the cutting lines on the board edges with a square or a marking gauge.

Mark the shoulders of the dovetail halving with a square; use a marking gauge on the cheek. With a sliding bevel, mark the dovetail angle between 8 degrees and 12 degrees (a 1:5 to 1:8 ratio of flare to length).

Although corner halvings are most easily cut with a radial arm saw fitted with a dado head, you can make repeated cuts with a standard blade. Or use hand tools: after marking the joint on the wood, saw the shoulder (cross-grain cut) with a tenon saw; then remove the waste by turning the piece on end and sawing along the grain with the same saw. To cut accurate cross halvings, first score the shoulder lines on the waste side with a wide chisel held vertically. Then, with the chisel held bevel-up at an angle, remove a sliver on the waste side of the line to form a groove in which to start the saw cut.

Corner halving joint

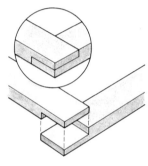
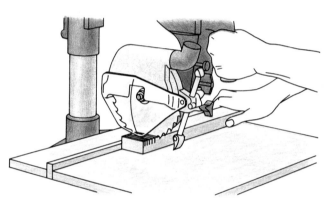

Set height of standard blade using mark on board edge as reference. Fine-tune depth of cut on scrap. Start at end and work towards shoulder, overlapping passes. Pare rough cut with chisel. You can also use a dado head (p.144), or use a band saw, as in cutting a tenon (p.147).

Cross halving joint

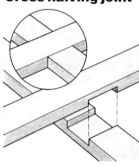
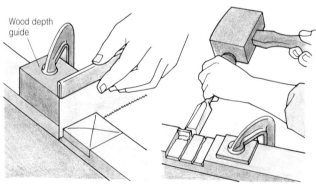

Wood depth guide

For straight cut when cutting sides of halving, press saw against wood depth guide, which should be just thick enough so that the rib on top of the saw hits the guide when cut is right depth. Make a cut at each side, then score the waste at 2.5 cm (1 in) intervals with tenon saw. Remove waste with a mallet and chisel, held bevel-up, and working from edges towards centre. Trim corners with chisel held bevel-down.

Dovetail halving joint

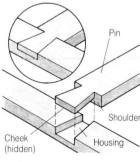

Pin

Shoulder

Cheek
(hidden)

Housing

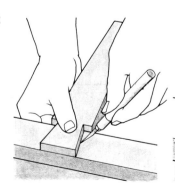
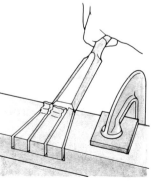

Mark pin's shoulders, cheek and dovetail angle. Saw dovetail shoulders, cheek and angle, in that order, with dovetail saw. For an accurate fit, use the finished dovetail as the template to mark the housing on mating piece. Saw and chisel the housing as you did for the cross halving joint.

DOVETAILS WITH A TEMPLATE

These decorative joints are fairly easy to cut with a router and a dovetail fixture. The fixture holds a template and has bar clamps and stop screws to hold both sides of the joint in proper alignment. The router, fitted with a dovetail bit and a guide bushing, follows the template, cutting the tails and the sockets simultaneously.

Make a few test cuts in scrap wood of the same width and thickness as the workpieces. Place each board in the fixture so that it butts against its stop screw and is flush with the mating piece (see illustration below). Make the initial shoulder cut in the tail board, guiding the bit along the tips of the template fingers. Advance the router from left to right with slow, steady pressure. Next, guide the bit in and out of the template's fingers, cutting deep into the recesses of the template. Make a second pass from right to left.

Test-fit the joint. If the fit is loose, increase the bit's depth of cut. If it is too tight, decrease the depth of cut. If the tails do not fit all the way into the sockets, move the template back slightly. If the tails are too deep in the sockets, slide the template forward.

Once the test joint fits perfectly, you are ready to cut the actual workpieces. If you are making a drawer or box, mark a

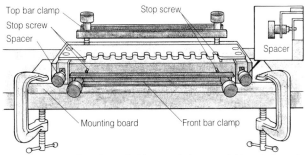

Dovetail fixture Bar clamps hold two workpieces at right angle to each other. Stop screws establish the proper offset. Spacers hold template; adjust them up and down, forward and back, to correct depth of cut.

letter on the inside surface of all four pieces; mark each bottom edge. Cut the grooves for the bottom panel before routing the dovetails. When clamping the pieces in the fixture, always place the boards with the same edge (either bottom or top) butted against the stop screws, lettered surface facing out. Note that two joints must be cut on the right side of the fixture and two on the left side (see chart). The socket pieces (front part A and back part C) are always clamped to the top of the fixture, the tail pieces (side pieces B and D) to the front.

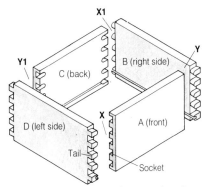

Mark inside surfaces near bottom edge. Cut grooves for bottom piece before routing X and Y joints. Front and back pieces have blind dovetail sockets; sides have through tails.

Setting up the workpieces

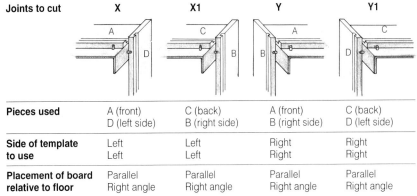

Joints to cut	X	X1	Y	Y1
Pieces used	A (front) D (left side)	C (back) B (right side)	A (front) B (right side)	C (back) D (left side)
Side of template to use	Left Left	Left Left	Right Right	Right Right
Placement of board relative to floor	Parallel Right angle	Parallel Right angle	Parallel Right angle	Parallel Right angle

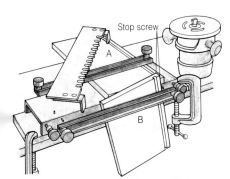

Set up joint Y Clamp side B as a guide for front piece A. Butt A against side B and top right stop screw. Reposition B flush with top edge of A and bottom right stop screw.

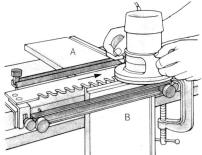

Make the first pass from left to right across tips of template's fingers. This shallow groove helps to prevent splintering when the tails and sockets are cut.

Rout tails and sockets, advancing the router from left to right. Keep the bushing that guides the bit in contact with template at all times. Make another final pass from right to left.

A channel cut across the grain, called a housing, or an L-shaped cut along the edge or end of a board, called a rebate, allow you to join wide boards at right angles. The mating piece fits into the housing or rebate.

Rebating both pieces, called a double rebate, adds a little more shoulder strength. When combined as a rebate-and-housing joint, the two lock together to resist twisting. The depth of a housing is typically one-third the thickness of the cut board, while a rebate's depth is between one-half and three-quarters of the thickness of the board.

Assemble all four types of joint with glue and nails or screws. Strengthen the joint, if necessary, by fastening a hardwood cleat or wooden batten at each end of the entering board. Glue and screw the cleats to the entering pieces and to the vertical sides or back of the support pieces.

Housing can be made by hand with a router plane or with a tenon saw and chisel. Alternatively, you can use a router with a straight bit or a radial arm saw equipped with a standard blade or a dado head.

A dado head consists of two outer cutting blades and usually four inner chipper blades (p.59); it cuts a housing in one pass, whereas a standard blade takes several passes.

To set up a dado head, stack as many chippers as needed between the two blades to obtain the desired width of cut.

Caution: Never use the chippers by themselves without the outer blades, because they will splinter the wood.

Through housing joint

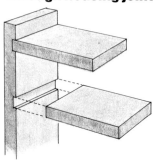

Stopped housing joint

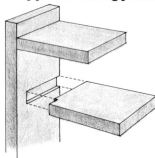

Dovetail housing

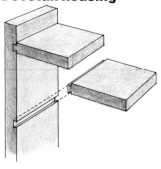

Cutting housing on a radial arm saw

Through housing Mark housing width on work (inset). Set dado cutter to the width of the housing. Set blade to depth of housing. Position housing directly in front of the dado cutter and pull arm across.

Stopped housing Position work so that stopped end is nearest to you. Pull radial arm across and stop at the shoulder line.

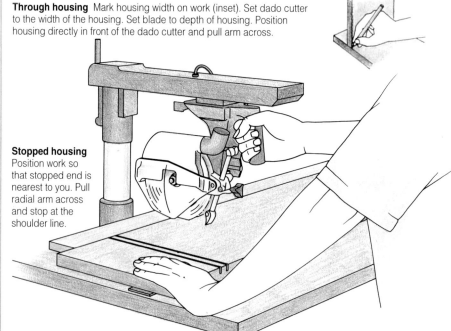

Dovetail housing with a router

Cutting housing Guide router against T-square. Remove most of waste with straight bit equal in size to narrowest part of correct dovetail bit. Install dovetail bit; finish housing in one pass.

T-square

Fence

Direction of travel

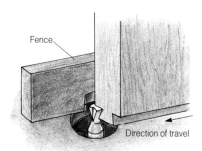

Mating dovetail Mount router in table. Make a wood fence with slot for dovetail bit. Clamp fence to router table. Practise on scrap. Start router, push stock against fence and move it from right to left. Reverse wood and repeat.

Test-cut all housing in scrap wood. To prevent the saw blade, housing head or router bit from splintering the wood as it completes and exits the cut, support the edge with scrap wood. For best results, cut routed housing in two or three passes by increasing the depth of cut with each pass. This reduces vibration and chatter of the router bit and produces a much cleaner cut.

A blind, or stopped, housing stops short of the board's edge and is hidden from view when assembled. To cut a stopped housing with a router, clamp a stop block to the work and guide the router along the straightedge. Square the stopped corners with a chisel. Notch the front corners of the entering piece to fit the stopped end of the housing.

Dovetail housings are strong, decorative interlocking joints. This housing, with its angled sides, can be cut with a tenon saw or a router fitted with a dovetail bit. When routing a dovetail housing, make the initial cuts with a straight bit. On the last pass, cut the angled shape with a dovetail bit.

To rout the mating dovetail ends of the shelves, mount the router in a router table or use a router jig. Practise on scrap wood, test-fit the board, and readjust the bit height or fence.

Rebate joints can be cut with a router or with a radial arm saw and a dado head. (If you prefer hand tools, use a rebating plane or a tenon saw and chisel.) Rout rebates with either a straight bit or a guided bit. With a straight bit, you must use either an edge guide or a straightedge to control the cut.

Rebate joints

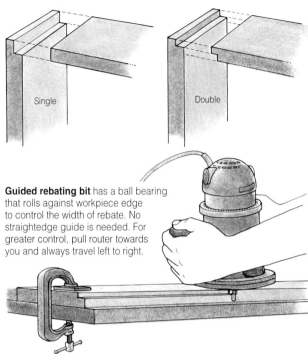

Single

Double

Guided rebating bit has a ball bearing that rolls against workpiece edge to control the width of rebate. No straightedge guide is needed. For greater control, pull router towards you and always travel left to right.

Edge guide attachment allows you to rout rebates with straight bit. Guide fastens to router's base and rides against edge of workpiece.

Tongue-and-groove joints

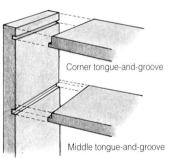

Corner tongue-and-groove

Middle tongue-and-groove

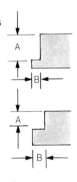

Corner tongue-and-groove and middle tongue-and-groove joints differ in the thickness of the tongue and width of the groove. In a corner tongue-and-groove joint (top), A is three-quarters of the thickness of tongued board; B is a quarter of the thickness of grooved board. In a middle tongue-and-groove joint, A can equal half to two-thirds of the thickness of the tongued board, and B can be one-third of the grooved board.

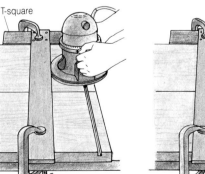

T-square

Rout multiple joints side by side for maximum accuracy. Clamp squared boards and wooden T-square securely to work surface. Test cut on scrap first.

Shoulder rebate plane can be used to trim rebate if fit is too tight.

MORTISE-AND-TENON JOINTS

Through mortise-and-tenon

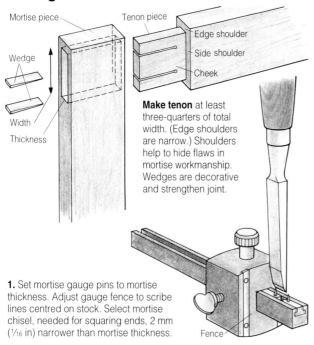

Mortise piece

Tenon piece

Edge shoulder

Side shoulder

Cheek

Wedge

Width

Thickness

Make tenon at least three-quarters of total width. (Edge shoulders are narrow.) Shoulders help to hide flaws in mortise workmanship. Wedges are decorative and strengthen joint.

In these strong framework joints, the projecting piece, or tenon, should fit snugly into the opening or mortise. A tight fit allows the large amount of long-grain glue surface on both pieces to adhere well. On wide stock, you can make the most of the long-grain glue surface by spacing multiple mortise-and-tenons evenly across the board (facing page).

Mortise-and-tenon joints may be through or blind (hidden), and each kind can have one to four shoulders. Rounding the tenon profile with a file, a rasp or a router makes a more decorative but slightly weaker through joint. On wide boards you can make multiple rounded joints by using a jig and a router.

The size of the stock determines the dimensions of the joint. On pieces of similar thickness, the mortise and each side shoulder of the tenon usually equal one-third the thickness of the stock. A larger mortise piece (as in a table leg) can take a thicker tenon. The edge shoulders of a three or four-shouldered tenon can vary from a sliver to a quarter of the width of the tenon piece. When marking several mortise-and-tenon joints, always orient the mortise gauge fence against the equivalent stock face. If a piece is to have a tenon on both ends, calculate the distance between the two joints by measuring between the length lines (step 5).

1. Set mortise gauge pins to mortise thickness. Adjust gauge fence to scribe lines centred on stock. Select mortise chisel, needed for squaring ends, 2 mm (1/16 in) narrower than mortise thickness.

Fence

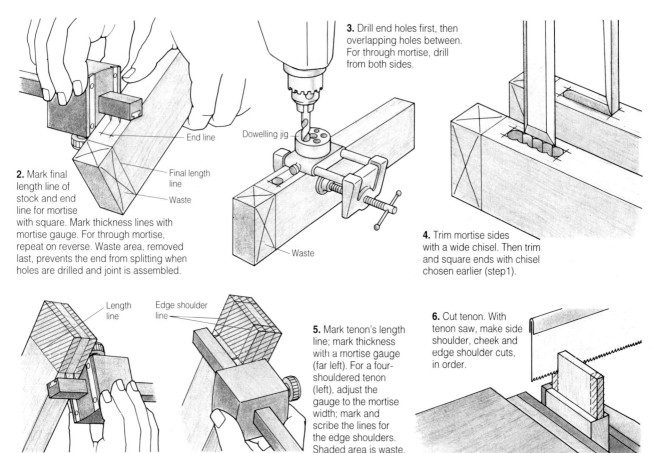

2. Mark final length line of stock and end line for mortise with square. Mark thickness lines with mortise gauge. For through mortise, repeat on reverse. Waste area, removed last, prevents the end from splitting when holes are drilled and joint is assembled.

End line

Final length line

Waste

3. Drill end holes first, then overlapping holes between. For through mortise, drill from both sides.

Dowelling jig

Waste

4. Trim mortise sides with a wide chisel. Then trim and square ends with chisel chosen earlier (step 1).

Length line

Edge shoulder line

5. Mark tenon's length line; mark thickness with a mortise gauge (far left). For a four-shouldered tenon (left), adjust the gauge to the mortise width; mark and scribe the lines for the edge shoulders. Shaded area is waste.

6. Cut tenon. With tenon saw, make side shoulder, cheek and edge shoulder cuts, in order.

First, cut the mortise. Set the mortise gauge pins and mark the thickness of the mortise. Cut a blind mortise 2 mm (1⁄16 in) deeper than the tenon length to allow for the glue. Drill the mortise holes on a drill press, or use a dowelling jig and a hand drill fitted with a twist bit whose diameter is the same as the mortise thickness. Drill a through mortise from both sides to prevent tearout. Mortises can also be made with a plunge router (below) or with a standard router and jig. For a standard router, clamp the mortise piece and jig to a workbench. Tilt the router; begin cutting slightly short of the end of the mortise; remove 3-6 mm (1⁄8-1⁄4 in) of stock on each pass. Cut the tenon to fit with a handsaw or band saw.

Wedges inserted into a through tenon (facing page) strengthen the joint. Before gluing, mark two cuts in the tenon's end, drill a 3 mm (1⁄8 in) hole at the base of each cut to prevent splitting, and saw the cuts. Assemble the joint, and tap the wedges into the cuts with a mallet.

The number, width and thickness of multiple mortise-and-tenons are determined by the size of the tenon piece. To find equal spacing between tenons, as well as the width of the two edge shoulders, measure the width of the tenon piece and decide the number and width of the tenons you want. Add the total tenon width and subtract it from the tenon piece width. Divide the remaining space by the number of tenons plus one. For example: four 20 mm wide tenons will be needed on a 140 mm wide board. The space between tenons: 4×20 mm = 80 mm; 140 mm – 80 mm = 60 mm; 60 mm ÷ 5 = 12 mm between tenons.

Tools that speed the work

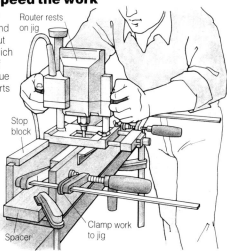

Use plunge router with a straight bit and homemade jig to cut mortise. The jig, which is a trough made of 18 mm plywood, glue and screws, supports router base. Front and back stops on one side of jig set the mortise width. Spacer blocks bring stock to top of jig. Make repeated passes, removing no more than 3 mm with each pass. Square rounded ends with a chisel.

Router rests on jig

Stop block

Spacer

Clamp work to jig

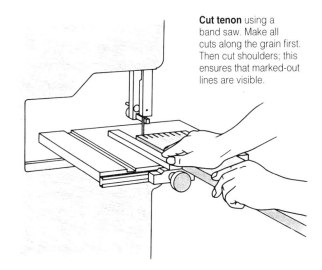

Cut tenon using a band saw. Make all cuts along the grain first. Then cut shoulders; this ensures that marked-out lines are visible.

Multiple mortise-and-tenons

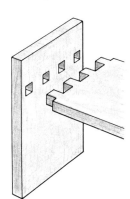

Tenon 'fingers' are shaped to fit into the gaps formed by matching mortises in wide piece of stock. The joint may be blind or through.

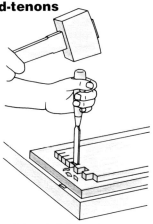

Cut waste between tenons with a band saw. Then remove the waste and finish off the shoulders by vertical paring with a bevel edge chisel.

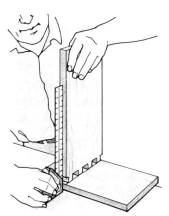

Position and mark mortises using a square and the prepared tenon piece as a template. Scribe and mark the waste areas with an X, to avoid mistakes.

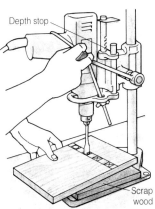

Depth stop

Scrap wood

Drill waste with a drill press and spur bit or brad point bit. Lock depth stop. Clean and square mortises with a chisel slightly narrower than mortise.

GLUING AND CLAMPING

When selecting a glue for a job, ask yourself these questions: What type of materials am I gluing? Will the piece be indoors or outdoors? Does the glue need to be water-resistant or water-proof? Are the joints loose? How much stress will be placed on the glue and the joint? For a repair job, what glue was used before? Use the product label and the chart below to help you to choose.

Whatever your choice, follow these basic rules. Apply the glue evenly and smoothly on both surfaces. If the end grain of wood is part of the joint, apply two coats; allow the first to dry before applying the second. Put the project together within the glue's assembly time (how long the glue can be worked and the pieces adjusted). Drying time may be longer if a wood's moisture content is above 10 per cent or the air temperature is below 21°C. Always allow a way for excess glue to escape (for example, the bottom of a blind mortise is deeper than its tenon).

Caution: When using a toxic glue, follow safety precautions on the label carefully. Work in a well-ventilated area, and avoid getting glue in your eyes or on your skin. Keep glue well away from any open flame. When using epoxy or contact cement, extinguish pilot lights.

Before applying glue, dry-fit (test-assemble) all joints to make sure they fit properly. This allows you to make

Gluing

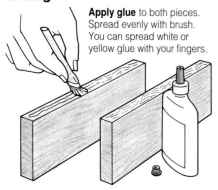

Apply glue to both pieces. Spread evenly with brush. You can spread white or yellow glue with your fingers.

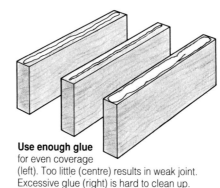

Use enough glue for even coverage (left). Too little (centre) results in weak joint. Excessive glue (right) is hard to clean up.

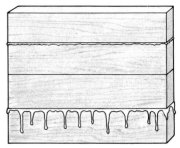

Glue line squeeze-out (top) shows strong joint. No excess (middle) means a weak joint; too much is messy (bottom).

A glossary of glues

Type of adhesive	Assembly time	Uses	Characteristics	Solvent
(PVA, polyvinyl acetate)	7-10 minutes	Interior woodwork, card, ceramics	Nonstaining, dries clear	Warm water
PVA waterproof	7-10 minutes	Exterior woodwork, masonry	Nonstaining, dries clear	Warm water
Scotch glue	Few minutes	Indoor furniture, antiques	Needs to be melted in a special pot	Warm water
Pearl glue	Few minutes	Indoor furniture, antiques	In pellet form. Melt as Scotch glue	Warm water
Urea formaldehyde	20-30 minutes	Indoor and outdoor furniture, marquetry	Powder mixed with water	Soap and warm water
Resorcinal resin	Varies	Woodwork, indoors and out	Liquid resin and catalyst	Cool water
Aliphatic resin	5-10 minutes	General woodwork	Heat-resistant; sets faster than PVA	Warm water
Rubber resin (Impact)	15-20 minutes	Fixing sheet materials and laminates	Both surfaces coated	Special solvents available
Epoxy resin	Varies	Timber, metal, ceramics	Fills holes, sets hard	Acetone
Clear resin	Varies	Fixing thin sheet and edging strips	Similar to rubber resin but not as strong	Special solvents available
Superglue (cyanoacrylate)	Seconds	Small repairs, modelling, jewellery-making	Not waterproof Not gap-filling	Soapy water
Glue gun & glue sticks	Varies	For holding work such as tiles and for repairs which won't get hot	No great strength but fast-working	None

adjustments for a better fit, to decide on the number and type of clamps needed and to establish the assembly sequence – gluing a piece in place too early can cause others to fit badly or not at all. For example, to assemble a bookcase with housed sides, place one side with the housings facing up. Next insert the shelves in the housings, check for fit and adjust as needed. Then align the housings of the other side piece, and readjust if needed.

Disassemble, noting the order. Follow the same sequence when gluing the pieces together.

When clamping, work on a level surface such as a workbench or, for a large project, the floor. Unless your clamps have covers, their jaws should never touch the work. (Unprotected metal clamps may react with the glue and stain the piece.) Insert Cling Film or waxed paper between the jaws and the work. This stops the pieces from

adhering to the clamp or to the scrap wood used to spread the pressure.

When workpieces are clamped with the right amount of glue, a small bead of glue will be forced from the joint. Wipe it off immediately with the correct solvent because wood stains and finishes won't penetrate dried glue. Clamping pressure should never be so tight that it forces out most of the glue (which is called starving the joint) or deforms the project.

Clamping

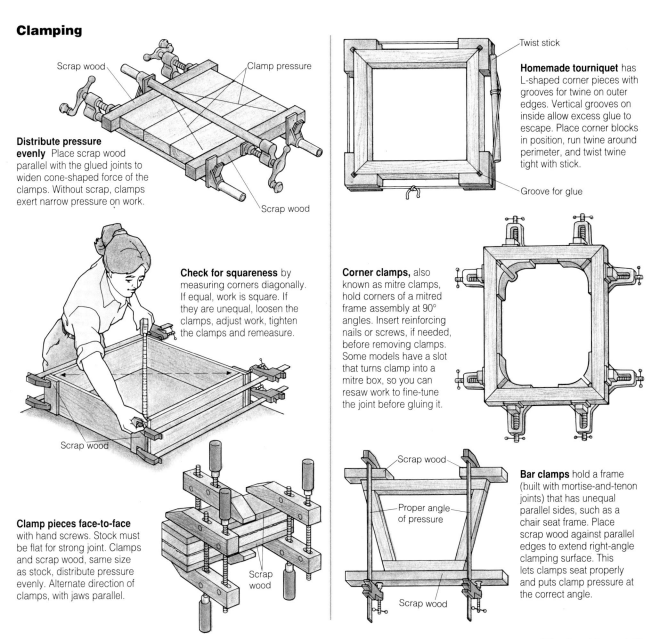

Distribute pressure evenly Place scrap wood parallel with the glued joints to widen cone-shaped force of the clamps. Without scrap, clamps exert narrow pressure on work.

Scrap wood

Clamp pressure

Scrap wood

Twist stick

Homemade tourniquet has L-shaped corner pieces with grooves for twine on outer edges. Vertical grooves on inside allow excess glue to escape. Place corner blocks in position, run twine around perimeter, and twist twine tight with stick.

Groove for glue

Check for squareness by measuring corners diagonally. If equal, work is square. If they are unequal, loosen the clamps, adjust work, tighten the clamps and remeasure.

Scrap wood

Corner clamps, also known as mitre clamps, hold corners of a mitred frame assembly at 90° angles. Insert reinforcing nails or screws, if needed, before removing clamps. Some models have a slot that turns clamp into a mitre box, so you can resaw work to fine-tune the joint before gluing it.

Clamp pieces face-to-face with hand screws. Stock must be flat for strong joint. Clamps and scrap wood, same size as stock, distribute pressure evenly. Alternate direction of clamps, with jaws parallel.

Scrap wood

Scrap wood

Proper angle of pressure

Scrap wood

Bar clamps hold a frame (built with mortise-and-tenon joints) that has unequal parallel sides, such as a chair seat frame. Place scrap wood against parallel edges to extend right-angle clamping surface. This lets clamps seat properly and puts clamp pressure at the correct angle.

Screw holes are usually perpendicular to the wood. Use a vertical drill stand, provided its table is level; with a hand or electric drill, use a drill guide or a predrilled hardwood block clamped to the wood to keep the bit straight. When drilling at an angle, mark the starting point with a centre punch and start the hole with a smaller bit to keep the final bit from drifting.

Pilot holes, drilled slightly narrower than the diameter of the threads, allow screws and bolts to enter straight and easily. Control the hole depth with a drill stop, a depth gauge or a piece of tape wrapped round the bit. To prevent tearout on through holes, drill from both sides or drill into a scrap block clamped to the back of the wood.

Screws and bolt heads may be flush with a surface or they may be recessed; if desired, fill the recess with a plug or with wood filler.

Drive a screw with a screwdriver tip the same width as the screw's slot; one too wide gouges the stock, too narrow damages the screwhead. To drive a nail into hardwood, first drill a pilot hole slightly narrower and shorter than the nail. Strike the nail squarely; at the end of the blow, slide the hammer forward or backward to emphasise the level position of the hammer. This lessens the chance of bending the nail.

To remove a bent nail, use a claw hammer or pincers. You can avoid marking the surface by placing a small piece of scrap wood or metal between the tool and the wood.

Hold headless and panel pins with pincers and pull them straight out, wiggling them a little if necessary.

Installing screws and bolts

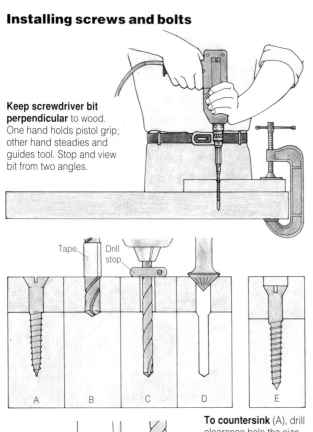

Keep screwdriver bit perpendicular to wood. One hand holds pistol grip; other hand steadies and guides tool. Stop and view bit from two angles.

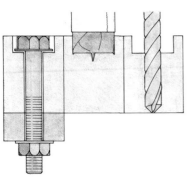

To countersink (A), drill clearance hole the size of unthreaded shank (B), then pilot hole the diameter of shank minus threads (C). Finish with countersink bit (D). To drill a counterbored hole (E), first drill recess, then follow countersink steps. To save time, use a combination bit. For bolts (left), first drill recess the diameter of the bolt head.

Nailing techniques

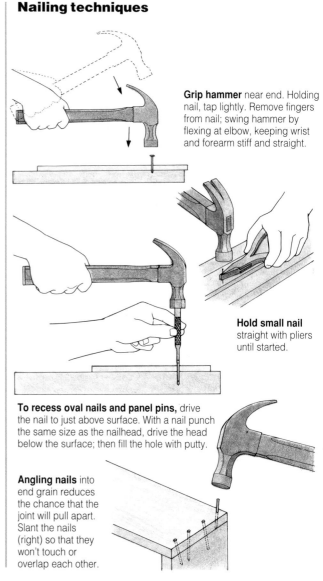

Grip hammer near end. Holding nail, tap lightly. Remove fingers from nail; swing hammer by flexing at elbow, keeping wrist and forearm stiff and straight.

Hold small nail straight with pliers until started.

To recess oval nails and panel pins, drive the nail to just above surface. With a nail punch the same size as the nailhead, drive the head below the surface; then fill the hole with putty.

Angling nails into end grain reduces the chance that the joint will pull apart. Slant the nails (right) so that they won't touch or overlap each other.

HINGES

The style and positioning of the hinge knuckle determines the swing action of a hinge. For a simple hinge with two equal leaves, place the knuckle at the intersection of the two pieces. To mark for a mortise, measure the width of the leaf to the centre of the hinge knuckle with a marking gauge. If you are making many mortises of the same size, consider buying or making a jig that you can use with a router.

A drop-leaf table, hinged with one long and one short hinge leaf, has a recess chiselled into the mortise on the tabletop. This recess holds the hinge knuckle. Before mounting a drop-leaf hinge, make a rule joint by routing the mating tabletop and leaf edges with matching cove and rounding-over bits.

On typical house doors, hinges spaced unevenly look even at eye level. Put the lower hinge farther from the bottom of the door than the upper hinge is from the top; place the middle hinge, if any, slightly above the halfway point between the others.

Mortising with a router

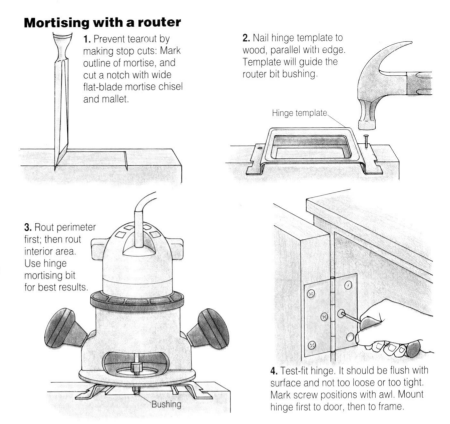

1. Prevent tearout by making stop cuts: Mark outline of mortise, and cut a notch with wide flat-blade mortise chisel and mallet.

2. Nail hinge template to wood, parallel with edge. Template will guide the router bit bushing.

Hinge template

3. Rout perimeter first; then rout interior area. Use hinge mortising bit for best results.

Bushing

4. Test-fit hinge. It should be flush with surface and not too loose or too tight. Mark screw positions with awl. Mount hinge first to door, then to frame.

Setting a drop-leaf hinge

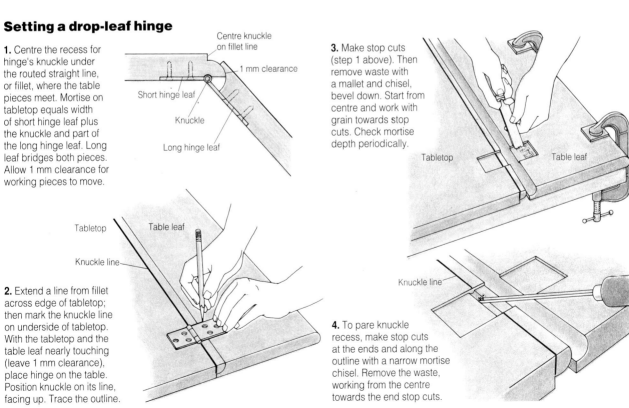

1. Centre the recess for hinge's knuckle under the routed straight line, or fillet, where the table pieces meet. Mortise on tabletop equals width of short hinge leaf plus the knuckle and part of the long hinge leaf. Long leaf bridges both pieces. Allow 1 mm clearance for working pieces to move.

Centre knuckle on fillet line
1 mm clearance
Short hinge leaf
Knuckle
Long hinge leaf

2. Extend a line from fillet across edge of tabletop; then mark the knuckle line on underside of tabletop. With the tabletop and the table leaf nearly touching (leave 1 mm clearance), place hinge on the table. Position knuckle on its line, facing up. Trace the outline.

Tabletop
Table leaf
Knuckle line

3. Make stop cuts (step 1 above). Then remove waste with a mallet and chisel, bevel down. Start from centre and work with grain towards stop cuts. Check mortise depth periodically.

Tabletop
Table leaf

4. To pare knuckle recess, make stop cuts at the ends and along the outline with a narrow mortise chisel. Remove the waste, working from the centre towards the end stop cuts.

Knuckle line

Layers of real wood, called plies, are glued together to make the sheet material known as plywood. Softwood plywood is suitable for construction; hardwood-veneer plywood often substitutes for solid wood in frame-and-panel construction and in furniture. The type of glue that joins the plies determines whether the plywood is for interior or exterior use.

Plywood's 1220 × 2440 mm (4 × 8 ft) sheets have some advantages over solid wood. The sheets are strong and relatively stable; you can get pieces large enough for a door or a tabletop, without edge joints. However, its size makes it awkward to transport, handle and store. Have someone help you with large sheets. When storing, avoid damp areas that will damage plywood fibres and cause it to warp.

The secret of plywood's strength and stability lies in the crisscross layering of the plies. The thickness of the centre

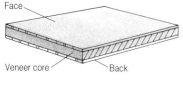

Face · Veneer core · Back

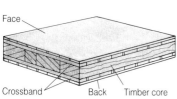

Face · Crossband · Back · Timber core

ply, or core, varies according to the type of plywood and may be sandwiched between crossband layers. The outer plies are the faces, or if not of equal quality, the face and the back. If the outer layers are thin and you must hand-sand them, use very fine grit paper.

When sawed, plywood splinters where the saw exits. To avoid splintering the good face, place it facing upwards when cutting with a table saw and downwards when using a circular saw. If you are using a handsaw, use a fine-tooth one and work with the good face upwards.

When joining plywood, choose joints that cover the edge. Tongue-and-groove (facing page), multiple mortise-and-tenon (p.147), router dovetail (p.143), biscuit and spline joints (pp.140-1) work well.

Use nails and screws to fasten plywood to solid wood or to another piece of plywood. In some cases a combination of nails or screws and glue is necessary. Plywood resists splitting, so nails and screws can be placed close together and 3 mm (⅛ in) from the edges of sheets on the face and back. Screws driven into plywood edges will split the layers apart.

However, knock-down fittings, such as scan fittings (facing page), create a strong interlocking joint and allow for easy disassembly (and reassembly) of a project. For hinges, choose a wraparound style that allows screws in the edge and the face of the plywood piece.

Cover exposed plywood edges with moulding or with veneer tape that matches the plywood's face. Depending on the type of tape you buy, you will apply it with glue, iron it on or peel and stick it on. For edges that will get hard use, such as a tabletop, choose solid wood moulding.

2nd cut

1st cut

Lay out project pieces on plywood sheet, being careful to avoid odd grain patterns and awkward, unnecessary cuts. Allow for power saw-blade kerf of about 3 mm (⅛ in). Make all lengthwise cuts first for easier handling of large sheet. Measure again after each cut.

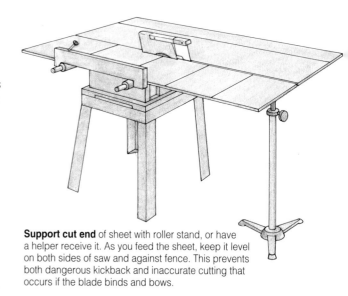

Support cut end of sheet with roller stand, or have a helper receive it. As you feed the sheet, keep it level on both sides of saw and against fence. This prevents both dangerous kickback and inaccurate cutting that occurs if the blade binds and bows.

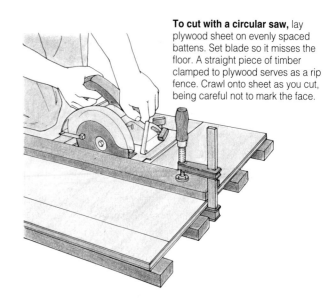

To cut with a circular saw, lay plywood sheet on evenly spaced battens. Set blade so it misses the floor. A straight piece of timber clamped to plywood serves as a rip fence. Crawl onto sheet as you cut, being careful not to mark the face.

Plywood joints

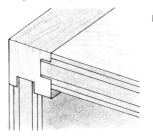 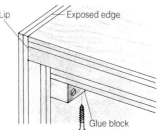 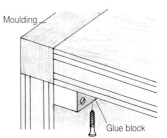 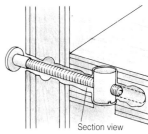

Tongue-and-groove joint is strong. Tongue is one-third of the wood's thickness and should fit snugly into the groove. Corner piece hides plywood ends.

Double rebate joint A lip of face veneer and crossband in side piece covers mating piece's edge. Add glue blocks; cover exposed edge with veneer tape.

Hide edges with moulding. Align moulding and plywood with wood biscuits or splines (pp.140-1) and glue pieces. Glue blocks add more strength.

Scan fitting Drill countersink and shank holes for bolt. Drill intersecting dowel hole. Insert dowel; align its opening with screwdriver. Slide bolt into hole through dowel.

Edge treatments

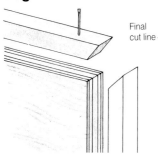 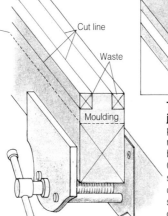

Cover edges with decorative or plain moulding. Measure and mitre corners carefully. Attach with glue and finishing nails. To prevent hardwood moulding from splitting, drill pilot holes for nails.

Tongue-and-groove joint Cut groove in plywood edge, using router and straight bit or slotting cutter. On table saw use a standard blade or dado head. Next rout, saw or plane tongue on moulding.

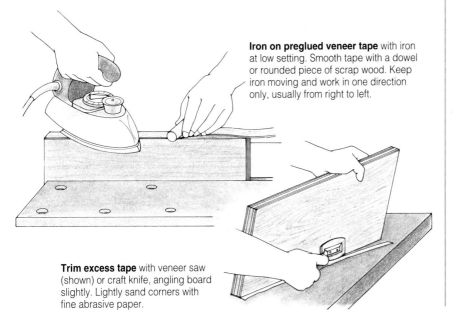

Iron on preglued veneer tape with iron at low setting. Smooth tape with a dowel or rounded piece of scrap wood. Keep iron moving and work in one direction only, usually from right to left.

Trim excess tape with veneer saw (shown) or craft knife, angling board slightly. Lightly sand corners with fine abrasive paper.

Frame and panel

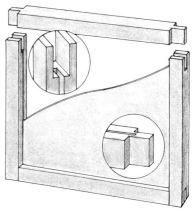

Bridle joint is U-shaped mortise and two-shouldered tenon. In each frame piece, cut panel groove same thickness as plywood – about 6 mm (¼ in). Extend groove into tenon to accept panel corners. Cut mortise (below); then cut tenon to fit (pp.146-7).

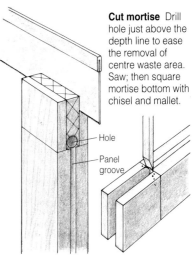

Cut mortise Drill hole just above the depth line to ease the removal of centre waste area. Saw; then square mortise bottom with chisel and mallet.

BASIC CABINET FORMS

A cabinet is basically a box. Large cabinets often consist of a solid wood frame supporting either manufactured or solid wood panels. Smaller boxes don't require the support of a frame.

The easiest drawer to fit in a cabinet is an overlay drawer, which has a front face that covers part of the cabinet frame. More challenging to build is the flush drawer, which fits within its opening. Options for cabinet door styles are similar to those for drawers. If the piece has both doors and drawers, make them the same style.

To make a drawer, rout grooves along the bottom edges of the drawer front and sides to accept a thin plywood, hardboard or MDF bottom panel. The back is narrow and rests on top of the bottom panel; so it needs no groove. Cut recesses for the back in the side pieces, and construct two dovetail halving, finger or rebate-and-housing joints for the front corners. Next assemble the front, sides and back. Slide the bottom panel into its grooves from the back (this helps to square the box) and nail or screw the bottom to the back.

Shelves, if they are adjustable, rest on clips inserted into the holes of a metal track (above, right) or on wood dowels or metal pins inserted into holes drilled in the cabinet sides. Fixed shelves are often housed in place.

Doors may be of solid plywood or frame-and-panel construction – a solid wood frame around a panel of plywood or solid wood. The frame is joined with mortise-and-tenon, mitred spline, or stile joints (facing page).

Tables, chairs, beds and the bases of some cabinets use leg-and-rail construction, made usually with dowel or mortise-and-tenon joints. Tenons can be either stub (at least 2.5 cm long) or mitred to avoid meeting within the leg. To reinforce leg-and-rail joints, fasten blocks with screws (right). For more on joints, see pages 139-47; on hinges, page 151; on frames and panels, page 153; on plywood, pages 152-3; on building boxes, pages 143 and 149.

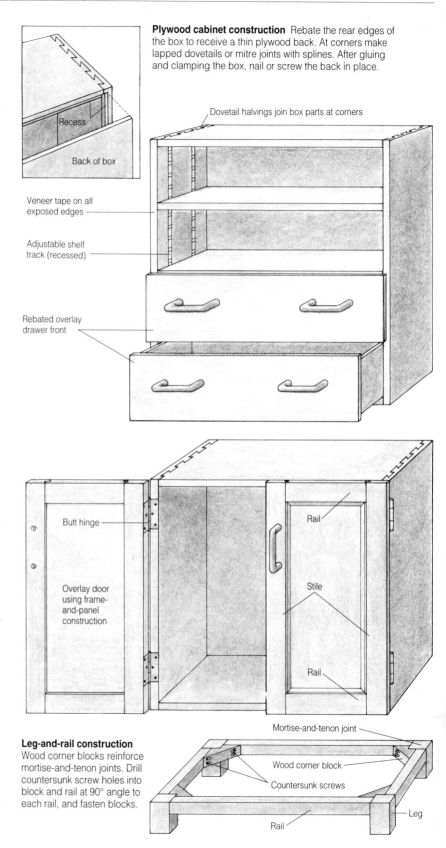

Plywood cabinet construction Rebate the rear edges of the box to receive a thin plywood back. At corners make lapped dovetails or mitre joints with splines. After gluing and clamping the box, nail or screw the back in place.

Recess

Back of box

Dovetail halvings join box parts at corners

Veneer tape on all exposed edges

Adjustable shelf track (recessed)

Rebated overlay drawer front

Butt hinge

Overlay door using frame-and-panel construction

Rail

Stile

Rail

Leg-and-rail construction
Wood corner blocks reinforce mortise-and-tenon joints. Drill countersunk screw holes into block and rail at 90° angle to each rail, and fasten blocks.

Mortise-and-tenon joint

Wood corner block

Countersunk screws

Leg

Rail

Drawers and supports

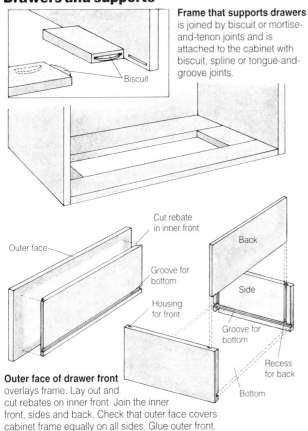

Frame that supports drawers is joined by biscuit or mortise-and-tenon joints and is attached to the cabinet with biscuit, spline or tongue-and-groove joints.

Biscuit

Outer face

Cut rebate in inner front

Back

Groove for bottom

Housing for front

Side

Groove for bottom

Recess for back

Bottom

Outer face of drawer front overlays frame. Lay out and cut rebates on inner front. Join the inner front, sides and back. Check that outer face covers cabinet frame equally on all sides. Glue outer front.

Side-hung drawers ride on matching wood glides screwed inside the case. Before assembling drawer, rout side grooves. If the grooves are stopped at the front, they function as a drawer stop.

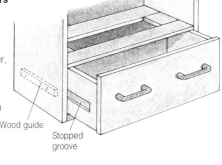

Wood guide

Stopped groove

Wood slide

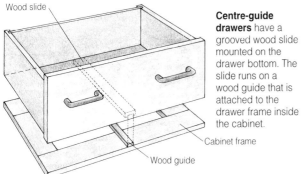

Centre-guide drawers have a grooved wood slide mounted on the drawer bottom. The slide runs on a wood guide that is attached to the drawer frame inside the cabinet.

Cabinet frame

Wood guide

Frame-and-panel construction

Rout stile joints with a matched pair of bits called stile and rail cutters. Mount the router upside-down in a router table. On the four inner frame edges, cut grooves for the panel with a beading (moulding) stile bit (A); change to a beading rail bit; then cut rail ends (B) to fit stile moulding.

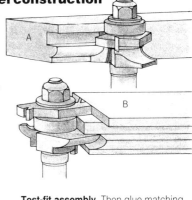

A

B

Rail

Stile

Panel

Rail

Test-fit assembly Then glue matching rail and stile; insert panel edges into grooves. Glue second stile, then second rail. Clamp stile joints.

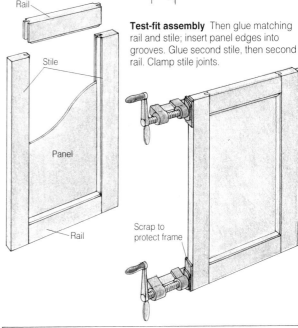

Scrap to protect frame

Building a table

Support solid wood top with slotted metal brackets, which let screws move with wood. For maximum length and strength, mitre tenon ends (inset); allow 2 mm (1/16 in) gap for glue pocket.

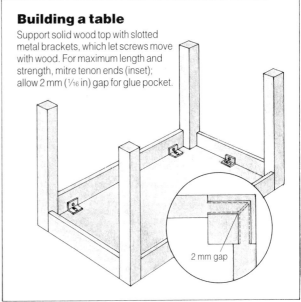

2 mm gap

Moulding creates an attractive finished look and hides flawed joints where walls meet floors, ceilings and door and window frames. Moulding also protects vulnerable edges, stops the swing of a door in its frame, holds window sashes in place and keeps water away from the top of a window.

Always take great care when selecting mouldings that are to be joined. Each mill makes different profiles, and slight variances occur even in the same profile from the same mill. Ensure that each piece you buy is consistent from end to end and that the profiles of all pieces to be used in the same project are very well matched.

Mouldings generally come in lengths ranging from 1.8 m to 4.8 m (6-16 ft), rising in 300 mm (12 in) increments. You can buy mouldings with standard profiles in knot-free grades of softwood without having to order them specially; or you can order them to be made up in other species of wood. Custom mouldings can be ordered from a timber yard or you can make your own with a router.

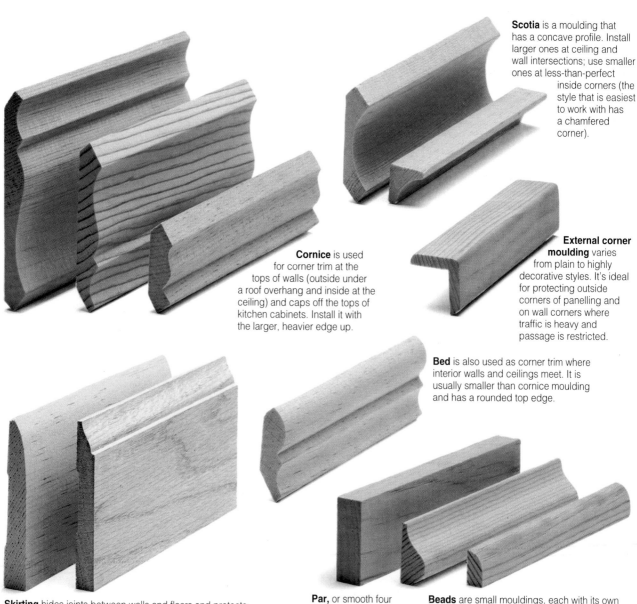

Scotia is a moulding that has a concave profile. Install larger ones at ceiling and wall intersections; use smaller ones at less-than-perfect inside corners (the style that is easiest to work with has a chamfered corner).

Cornice is used for corner trim at the tops of walls (outside under a roof overhang and inside at the ceiling) and caps off the tops of kitchen cabinets. Install it with the larger, heavier edge up.

External corner moulding varies from plain to highly decorative styles. It's ideal for protecting outside corners of panelling and on wall corners where traffic is heavy and passage is restricted.

Bed is also used as corner trim where interior walls and ceilings meet. It is usually smaller than cornice moulding and has a rounded top edge.

Skirting hides joints between walls and floors and protects wall surfaces from damage by vacuum cleaners, brooms, furniture and feet. In general, skirting has an unmoulded lower edge, allowing you to add a bead. The top is often decorative, making an extra beading unnecessary.

Par, or smooth four sides, is a square-edged moulding. Use it alone or combine it with other mouldings to create a decorative look.

Beads are small mouldings, each with its own reference number. It fits on top of par when it is used as a skirting; or it can be applied to panelling as a finishing touch. It may also fit flush against the lower edge of skirting or par. It hides edges of carpeting and other flooring.

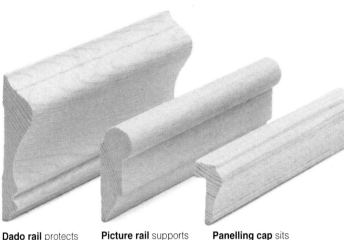

Quadrant, an easy-to-find moulding, fits into corners. You can also combine it with other mouldings to build up a profile.

Half round is used for finishing shelf edges and also adds a decorative element to furniture. It can be part of a built-up moulding profile such as one that surrounds a fireplace.

Dado rail protects walls from damage by chair backs. It visually reduces wall height and serves as a horizontal dividing line between two different surfaces, such as wall covering and paint.

Picture rail supports framed pictures and paintings, which are suspended from it with hooks. The rail should continue all the way round the room's circumference, fairly close to the ceiling.

Panelling cap sits on top of wainscot (wood panelling on the lower portion of a wall). It protects the wood end grains and enhances the overall appearance.

Small moulding adds a finished look to shelves, screens, furniture and frames; also use it to create your own moulding profiles.

Door weather mould is fitted to the base of an external door. A groove on the underside prevents rain from entering. This design is reversible.

Architraves for windows and doors cover the gaps between the frames (jambs) and the wall. They stiffen the frame and anchor it in the opening. It comes in plain and moulded profiles, such as colonial (far left) and clamshell (centre), and in several widths. Apron moulding (left) can also be applied under windowsills.

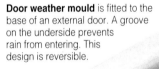

Handrail is an integral part of a staircase, fitted direct to the wall or in conjunction with spindles. It must be securely fixed to the wall, because it may have to take the weight of someone who stumbles.

Door stop is added to door or window frames to stop the swing of a door or window and to hold a sliding or hung unit in place. It also serves to hide the joint and, to a degree, seals against air infiltration and sound transmission.

WORKING WITH WOODEN MOULDINGS

Decorative moulding can be used as a finish on walls and on furniture and built-in cupboards. It can be used as skirting to cover the join of floor and wall. Inside corners have coped joints, outside corners have edge mitres.

Angled ceiling moulding, called coving, is similarly mitred and coped, except that the outside corners are compound mitred – the end of each board has both a face and an edge mitre cut (p.141). To saw a compound mitre by hand, place the coving in a mitre box with the ceiling edge down. On a radial arm saw or

a table saw, adjust the blade and the mitre gauge to cut a compound mitre.

If installing moulding on a cavity wall, locate the studs with a stud finder or by knocking on the wall (listen for a solid sound), and then mark their positions. Nail the moulding to the studs with oval nails.

For solid walls, you will need to drill and plug the wall, then screw the moulding in place. To avoid splitting hardwood moulding, predrill all nail or screw holes 1 cm (about ½ in) from the edges and 2.5 cm (1 in) from each end. For a tight fit against butt ends,

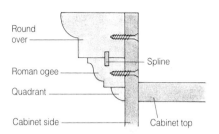

taper both ends of the coped piece by slightly undercutting the back edge.

With a router and various bits, you can create your own mouldings. Or use homemade and stock mouldings (above) to create more complex profiles.

Installing coving

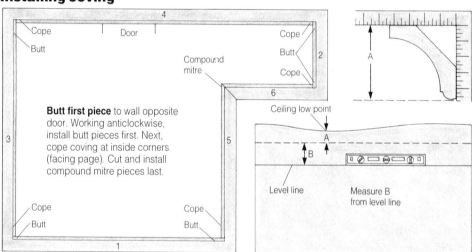

Butt first piece to wall opposite door. Working anticlockwise, install butt pieces first. Next, cope coving at inside corners (facing page). Cut and install compound mitre pieces last.

Ceiling low point

Level line

Measure B from level line

To find A, the distance from top edge (ceiling) to bottom edge (wall) of a coving, hold it against a try square (near left).

Draw a level line around room at a convenient height. Measure up from line at intervals to find ceiling's low point. From this low point, measure down distance A and mark. Then find B by measuring from level line up to A mark. On each wall, transfer same distance (B) from level line for bottom edge of coving.

Install coving with finishing nails anchored in studs and ceiling joists; then recess nails. On solid walls, drill and plug holes, then screw coving to wall. Fill holes and gaps; sand smooth when dry.

Making a compound mitre

Exploded view of coving shows how it angles away from the corner of a wall. To cut the correct angle automatically, place coving in a mitre box with the ceiling edge down.

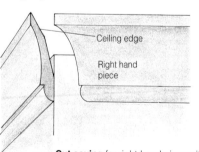

Cut coving for right-hand piece with ceiling edge down and wall edge against fence; waste is to right of saw. For left-hand coving, saw on opposite diagonal, with waste to left of saw.

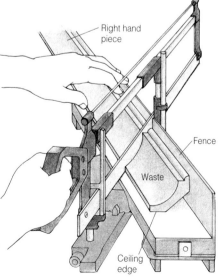

Right hand piece

Fence

Waste

Ceiling edge

Test fit If necessary, trim back edge of mitre on right-hand piece with block plane. Keep blade away from front moulded edge.

Installing skirting board

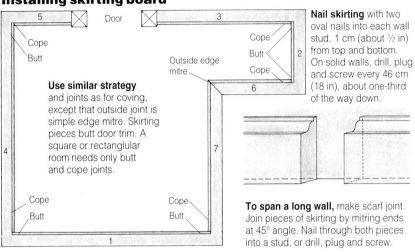

Use similar strategy and joints as for coving, except that outside joint is simple edge mitre. Skirting pieces butt door trim. A square or rectanglular room needs only butt and cope joints.

Nail skirting with two oval nails into each wall stud, 1 cm (about ½ in) from top and bottom. On solid walls, drill, plug and screw every 46 cm (18 in), about one-third of the way down.

To span a long wall, make scarf joint. Join pieces of skirting by mitring ends at 45° angle. Nail through both pieces into a stud, or drill, plug and screw.

Making an outside edge mitre

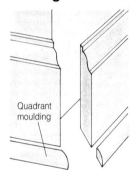
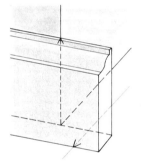
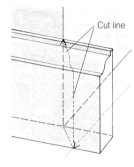

Skirting edge mitres must match exactly for a good join. Nail quadrant moulding to skirting to close gap between skirting and bare floor (not with fitted carpets).

1. Place uncut skirting in turn against wall. Draw the lines on the floor where they intersect and V-marks on each piece at wall corner and floor intersection.

2. Draw perpendicular lines from V-marks on front and back of each piece. Connect these lines across top and bottom edges to mark exact cut line (about 45°).

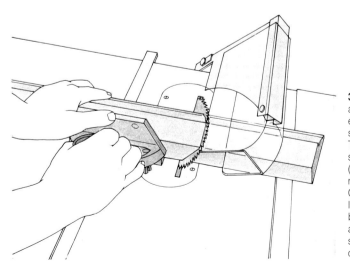

3. On table saw, angle blade for edge mitre; place skirting face up. Test-cut on scrap side of lines 1 cm (about ½ in) from marked mitre. Compare cut to lines; adjust the blade. When the angle matches, saw mitre cut in one pass.

Coped joints

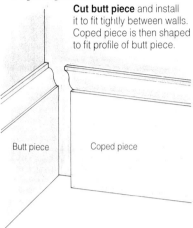

Cut butt piece and install it to fit tightly between walls. Coped piece is then shaped to fit profile of butt piece.

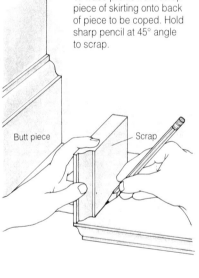

1. Trace profile from scrap piece of skirting onto back of piece to be coped. Hold sharp pencil at 45° angle to scrap.

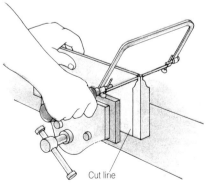

2. With coping saw at 90° to back of skirting and with blade angled, saw curved part of profile. Turn piece upside down; cut straight part with dovetail or tenon saw. Test fit. Use file to adjust profile, then to undercut (bevel) back.

STAINS, FILLERS AND FINISHES

A wide range of wood finishing products is available in timber yards and DIY centres. To choose the right one, first decide exactly what you want it to do.

Stains, fillers and finishes can enhance wood's natural grain, they can cause it to reflect or absorb light and some will enrich or change its colour or texture. On an unsightly surface, fillers and finishes can obscure some of the problem. Most fillers and finishes offer a degree of protection from sunlight, abrasion, water and chemicals.

The skills and tools needed to create and apply or lay down a finish vary with the product, the surface involved and technique you decide to use.

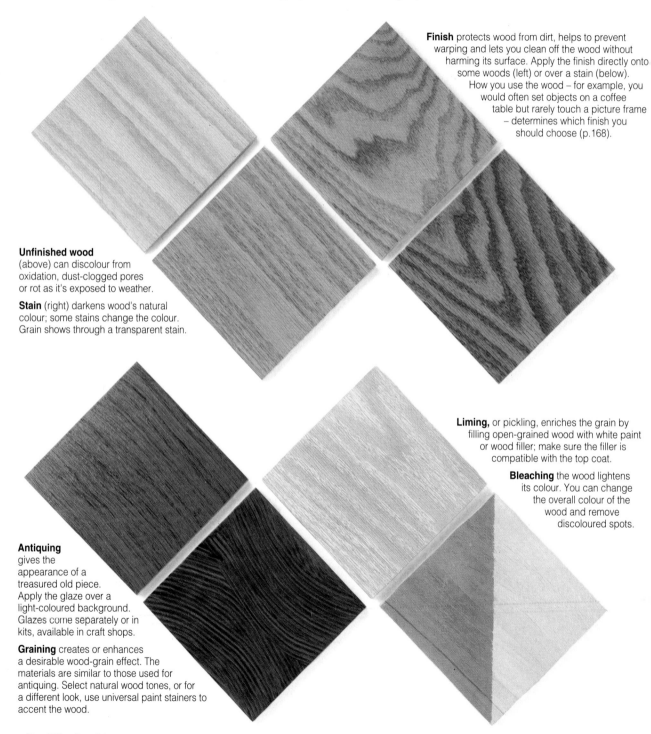

Finish protects wood from dirt, helps to prevent warping and lets you clean off the wood without harming its surface. Apply the finish directly onto some woods (left) or over a stain (below). How you use the wood – for example, you would often set objects on a coffee table but rarely touch a picture frame – determines which finish you should choose (p.168).

Unfinished wood (above) can discolour from oxidation, dust-clogged pores or rot as it's exposed to weather.

Stain (right) darkens wood's natural colour; some stains change the colour. Grain shows through a transparent stain.

Liming, or pickling, enriches the grain by filling open-grained wood with white paint or wood filler; make sure the filler is compatible with the top coat.

Bleaching the wood lightens its colour. You can change the overall colour of the wood and remove discoloured spots.

Antiquing gives the appearance of a treasured old piece. Apply the glaze over a light-coloured background. Glazes come separately or in kits, available in craft shops.

Graining creates or enhances a desirable wood-grain effect. The materials are similar to those used for antiquing. Select natural wood tones, or for a different look, use universal paint stainers to accent the wood.

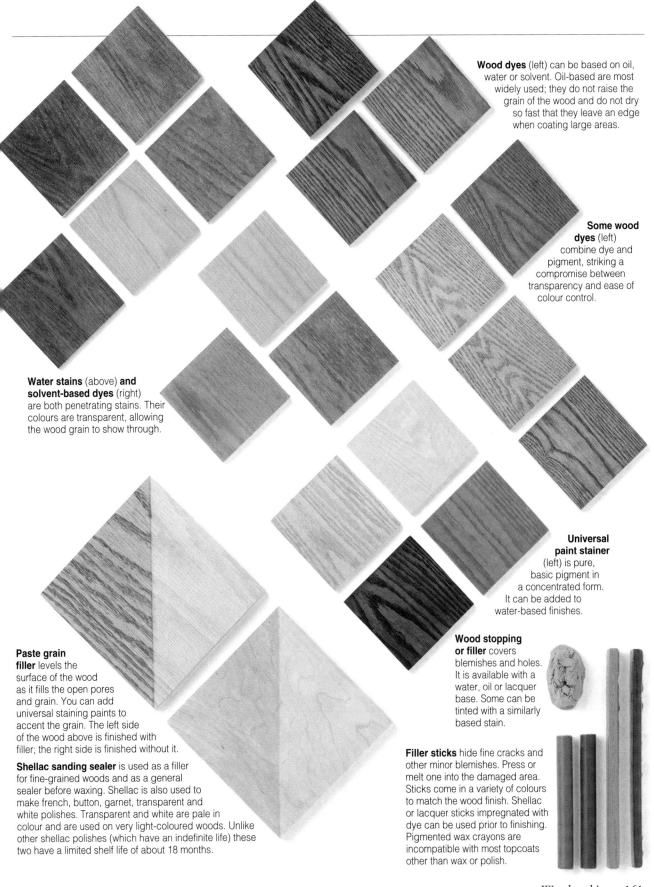

Wood dyes (left) can be based on oil, water or solvent. Oil-based are most widely used; they do not raise the grain of the wood and do not dry so fast that they leave an edge when coating large areas.

Some wood dyes (left) combine dye and pigment, striking a compromise between transparency and ease of colour control.

Water stains (above) **and solvent-based dyes** (right) are both penetrating stains. Their colours are transparent, allowing the wood grain to show through.

Universal paint stainer (left) is pure, basic pigment in a concentrated form. It can be added to water-based finishes.

Wood stopping or filler covers blemishes and holes. It is available with a water, oil or lacquer base. Some can be tinted with a similarly based stain.

Paste grain filler levels the surface of the wood as it fills the open pores and grain. You can add universal staining paints to accent the grain. The left side of the wood above is finished with filler; the right side is finished without it.

Shellac sanding sealer is used as a filler for fine-grained woods and as a general sealer before waxing. Shellac is also used to make french, button, garnet, transparent and white polishes. Transparent and white are pale in colour and are used on very light-coloured woods. Unlike other shellac polishes (which have an indefinite life) these two have a limited shelf life of about 18 months.

Filler sticks hide fine cracks and other minor blemishes. Press or melt one into the damaged area. Sticks come in a variety of colours to match the wood finish. Shellac or lacquer sticks impregnated with dye can be used prior to finishing. Pigmented wax crayons are incompatible with most topcoats other than wax or polish.

VENEERS

When you are hiding imperfections in solid wood or covering a manufactured wood such as particleboard, veneer adds an attractive look to any project. You can apply it to shelves, to furniture, to an inexpensive door and to almost any object where a decorative finish is desired. Veneers offer access to a variety of woods that would otherwise be unavailable because of their expense or inappropriateness as a solid wood.

Suppliers store and sell veneer sheets in consecutive order, primarily to facilitate matching procedures (p.170) but also to ensure uniform patterns, colour and texture in a finished piece. Veneer is shipped flat or rolled, according to the size of the sheet. Be sure to order about 20-30 per cent more than you think you will need, to allow for cutting and matching.

Handle veneer with great care; it is very fragile.

Veneer sheets (right) are usually identified according to the wood species, the cutting method used to produce the veneer, the part of the tree from which it was cut (it may have a burl or knot) and its pattern. These variables give an endless selection for your project.

Edge trim (right) comes in strips. It may have a heat-sensitive adhesive backing or be applied with glue. Cover the exposed edges of plywood or veneered chipboard with it.

Inlay strips (right) create a decorative band round or near the edge of a workpiece. Thin strips of natural wood are preassembled in geometric designs, greatly simplifying the amount of work that goes into a project. They are easily inlaid into shallow grooves that are routed into the workpiece. Order strips from woodworking catalogues or look for them in specialist shops. They are available in 1 m lengths and are from 2-22 mm wide.

Decorative inlays come in a wide variety of designs. A combination of naturally or artificially coloured woods can be used to create patterns. Recess the veneer into the workpiece, or glue it as an overlay on top of the surface.

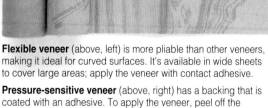

Flexible veneer (above, left) is more pliable than other veneers, making it ideal for curved surfaces. It's available in wide sheets to cover large areas; apply the veneer with contact adhesive.

Pressure-sensitive veneer (above, right) has a backing that is coated with an adhesive. To apply the veneer, peel off the protective paper, position the veneer and press it in place.

ORNAMENTAL WOOD TRIM

As the last touch before staining and finishing a surface, create an impressive look by adding one or more ornamental trims. Or add made-to-order reproduction trim to replace pieces when restoring an old piece of wood furniture. Most of these trims are available in walnut, oak, cherry and other hardwoods. They can enhance a cabinet, chest, headboard, bookcase, door, window, staircase, wall or gazebo.

Ornamental trims arc casy to apply, requiring only a little adhesive or a few small brads, and they will accept any type of finish to match the other materials you are working with.

Preshaped pieces come in a variety of configurations and sizes to use on a piece of furniture, such as a chair or a baby's cot, and for creating architectural details. Some items, such as the galley railing (left), are preassembled.

Decorative carvings have embossed (not carved) patterns in beech, birch and other hardwoods. They can be found in mail-order catalogues.

Decorative half-round mouldings are suitable for cabinetwork, picture framing and trim or borders for walls, ceilings, doors or windows.

Wood filigree, often seen on antique furniture (especially around glass cabinet doors), comes in a variety of intricate designs. You can apply it to fancy boxes, storage chests and picture frames. It is available through certain woodworking mail-order catalogues.

The finish you put on a piece will magnify any imperfections in the wood, so prepare all surfaces carefully. On new construction prepare the pieces before assembly.

Although some hand-sanding is always necessary, the amount you have to do can be greatly reduced by using a cabinet scraper. Proper scraping leaves lacy shavings. When you find yourself creating dust instead of shavings, sharpen the blade (pp.198-9).

Power tools speed the sanding process. For rough work use a belt sander, follow with a finishing sander (orbital or oscillating) and end with light hand-sanding. Always work through a sequence of grits. For rough work, use 80 grit. On smooth surfaces, start with 120 grit (fine), then 180 (very fine) and finally 220 or 240.

Sand parallel with the grain or scratches will show. Clean the wood between grits with a tack rag. Make your own tack rag by dampening a piece of cheesecloth with white spirit, then kneading a little varnish into it. If your finish is water-based, dampen the cloth with water.

Caution: Wear a dust mask. When power-sanding, connect your sander to a vacuum cleaner if possible.

For a high-shine finish in open-grain woods such as oak or walnut, fill the pores with paste grain filler. This comes in wood tones or neutral; you can tint neutral paste grain filler with universal tinting colours (p.167).

Filling is unnecessary for a natural look or for wood with small pores. Follow the maker's suggestions as to whether to fill before or after staining.

Before staining, prime any porous end grain with a sanding sealer so that it will absorb the stain uniformly (especially important with softwoods). Apply two liberal coats to the end grain. It will not need sanding.

Scraping

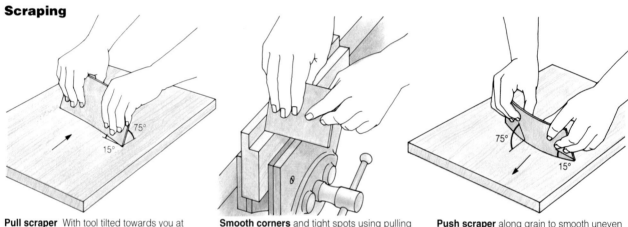

Pull scraper With tool tilted towards you at 75° and skewed at 15° angle to the grain, pull along grain. Bow the scraper slightly so convex shape cuts and corners don't mark work.

Smooth corners and tight spots using pulling motion (tilted towards you at 75°); keep fingers clear of cutting edge. Be careful not to gouge wood with scraper corner.

Push scraper along grain to smooth uneven surfaces and irregular grain. Angle tool as for pulling, but tilt it to opposite 75° angle. Bow blade so convex part faces direction of cut.

Filling

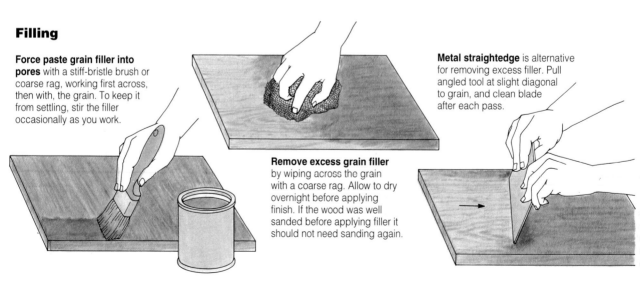

Force paste grain filler into pores with a stiff-bristle brush or coarse rag, working first across, then with, the grain. To keep it from settling, stir the filler occasionally as you work.

Remove excess grain filler by wiping across the grain with a coarse rag. Allow to dry overnight before applying finish. If the wood was well sanded before applying filler it should not need sanding again.

Metal straightedge is alternative for removing excess filler. Pull angled tool at slight diagonal to grain, and clean blade after each pass.

Sanding

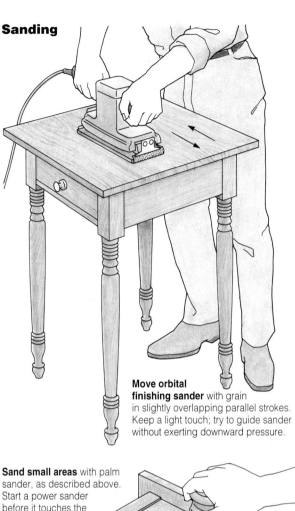

Move orbital finishing sander with grain in slightly overlapping parallel strokes. Keep a light touch; try to guide sander without exerting downward pressure.

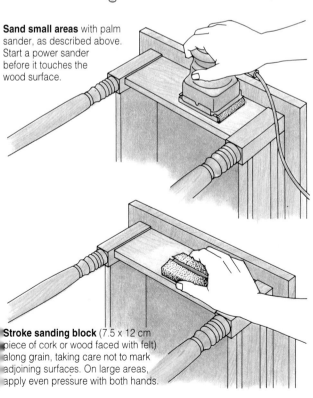

Sand small areas with palm sander, as described above. Start a power sander before it touches the wood surface.

Stroke sanding block (7.5 x 12 cm piece of cork or wood faced with felt) along grain, taking care not to mark adjoining surfaces. On large areas, apply even pressure with both hands.

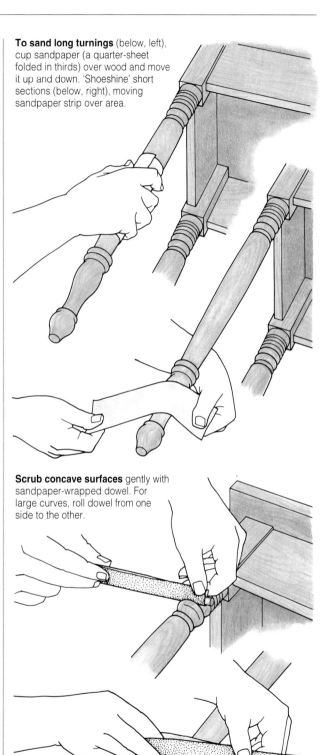

To sand long turnings (below, left), cup sandpaper (a quarter-sheet folded in thirds) over wood and move it up and down. 'Shoeshine' short sections (below, right), moving sandpaper strip over area.

Scrub concave surfaces gently with sandpaper-wrapped dowel. For large curves, roll dowel from one side to the other.

For tight grooves, work folded sandpaper with back-and-forth motion. Alternate pressure on each side of V-cut.

In the past, staining meant changing the colour of wood to another natural shade, and dyeing meant giving it an exotic colour, such as red, green or blue. As the number of available stains and dyes grew, the distinction became blurred and now the terms are almost interchangeable.

Unlike a finish or a varnish, which leave a fine coat on the surface of the wood, stains and dyes penetrate the wood, leaving nothing on the surface, but needing to be sealed afterwards.

There are various types of stain: the most popular is oil-based. In addition, there are water, solvent and spirit-based stains as well as chemical stains.

Oil based stains are widely used because they are quick-drying, light fast, and penetrate the wood without raising the grain. The stain sinks in quickly, so use a cloth to wipe it on and not a brush, as the starting point of the brushmarks will be too visible. Have a second, clean cloth ready to wipe off any excess stain.

You may need to use a brush if you are staining an intricately carved piece, but keep a clean cloth at hand to soak up any excess, otherwise the result will be darker where the stain pools. The solvent is usually white spirit.

Water based stains are usually Vandyke or Mahogany crystals which are dissolved in boiling water and applied when cool. They do not withstand light well, and they raise the grain of the wood, so the wood must be sanded before varnish can be applied. Apply the stain with a damp cloth, not a brush, and unless you apply two coats, the result may be patchy. Dilute the stain to make the result lighter.

Spirit-based stains consist of aniline dyes dissolved in methylated spirit. They dry quickly and are difficult to apply evenly. They also raise the grain.

Chemical stains are colourless and change the colour of the wood by a chemical reaction. They are applied with a brush, and when the wood has become the colour you want, you can stop the reaction by neutralising them with methylated spirit.

There are exterior wood stains which combine colour and finish in one coat, changing the colour of the wood as well as leaving a film on the surface.

Application Stains will not cover a defect, so make sure the wood you intend to stain is in good condition. Remove any traces of glue from round joints, as it will prevent the stain from penetrating and it will leave the area paler than the rest of the surface.

When staining a piece of wood with exposed end grain, remember that it is very absorbent, so the stain will come up darker than you expect. You can prevent this by applying a coat of sealer to the end grain before staining it. Use a white or transparent french polish, or a thinned application of teak oil or clear polyurethane.

Remove disfiguring stains with oxalic acid from a chemist, but as it is poisonous it must be labelled and kept out of the reach of children.

Bleaching You cannot stain wood a lighter colour; it must be bleached. First remove any existing finish and then apply a proprietary two-part wood bleach. The first part makes the wood look darker, but it is actually the catalyst that aids the second part, which actually bleaches the wood. Wear rubber gloves and protect your eyes.

Basic techniques

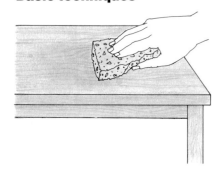

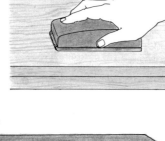

1. Before using a water-based stain, dampen the surface of the wood first, in order to raise the grain. Then allow it to dry.

2. Whisk off raised fibres with fine sandpaper (pp.164-5); then vacuum all sanding dust from surface. Don't use a tack rag because it may leave a residue on the wood that will interfere with staining.

Wipe wood stain onto the prepared surface following direction of grain. Use a clean lint-free cloth to rub until colour is uniform. Rub hard for a light colour, lightly for a darker one. When applying a stain to a vertical surface, work from the bottom upwards to catch runs.

SPECIAL EFFECTS

Liming (pickling) and antiquing are two ways to artificially age a piece of furniture. Liming involves filling the wood pores with white paint or with a paste wood filler before finishing, creating a two-tone effect. Antiquing consists of top-coating enamelled or painted wood with a contrasting glaze, then wiping it off to create the illusion of wear. Graining, the art of producing imitation wood grain on bland surfaces, uses the same two-step procedure as antiquing. Because none of these decorative finishes protects wood surfaces (pp.168-9), finish the piece with the surface finish recommended on the label of the products you buy.

Liming

Brush on paste grain filler; then scrub off excess across grain with a coarse rag, leaving filler in pores. Let it dry for 24 hours before sealing.

Graining

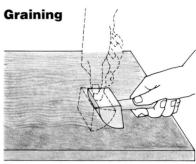

Simulate grain patterns by dragging the coarse side of the graining comb through the glaze with a twisting and rocking motion. Or use a stiff brush or whisk broom.

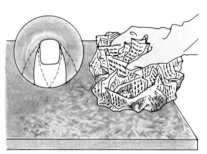

Create texture by pressing a piece of crumpled newsprint into glaze (experiment on scrap first). To make knots, twist thumb, leaving some 'grain' in the knot.

Antiquing

Brush base coat in direction of grain, and allow to dry for 24 hours. If the old finish is in good condition, paint right over it, but carefully sand new wood (pp.164-5). Antiquing kits contain everything needed, or you can buy the components separately.

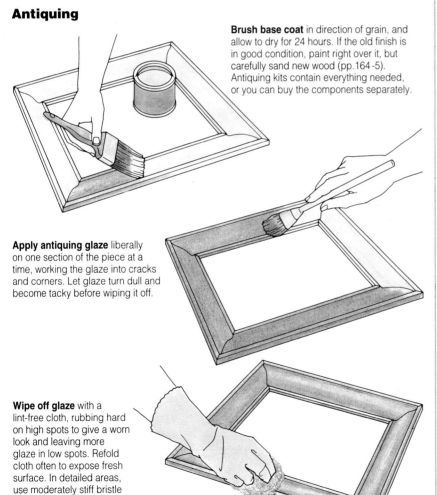

Apply antiquing glaze liberally on one section of the piece at a time, working the glaze into cracks and corners. Let glaze turn dull and become tacky before wiping it off.

Wipe off glaze with a lint-free cloth, rubbing hard on high spots to give a worn look and leaving more glaze in low spots. Refold cloth often to expose fresh surface. In detailed areas, use moderately stiff bristle dry brush to remove glaze, wiping brush often on a cloth to clean it.

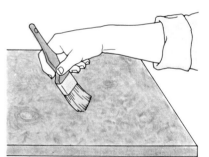

For added realism, brush over completed grain with dry brush. Angle brush as shown, and feather out grain lines with a light stroke.

Unify look of grain by overgraining. Allow first coat of glaze to dry, and then with a pad of coarse cloth, apply a second grain pattern in straight, parallel lines.

The type of finish you choose depends on how the object will be used and the final appearance you hope to achieve. Surface finishes (varnish, polyurethane, lacquer) build up a protective film on the surface of the wood. Penetrating finishes (oils) sink into the wood, hardening within its fibres.

Surface finishes resist stains and abrasion better than penetrating finishes, but they are more difficult to spot-repair. They may also look too shiny unless they are rubbed along the grain using 000 steel wool; penetrating finishes usually produce a soft sheen – rather than a shine – that emphasises the wood's colour and grain.

Consider, too, the composition of the finishing material. While all penetrating finishes have a solvent base, varnish, lacquer and polyurethane are also available with a water base.

Water-based types are nontoxic and nonflammable, but sometimes they can be difficult to apply correctly and may raise the wood grain. In addition, these finishes may not be compatible with oil-based stains and fillers. If there is any doubt about compatibility, contact the maker first.

All finishes magnify imperfections in the wood, so you must sand with a very fine grit – at least 220 – before finishing. Treat all parts of the object the same – back, front, underside, and top – so that they will react evenly to moisture changes and won't warp. If working with softwood, seal the wood first (p.164). For best results, the air temperature should be moderate and the humidity low. Consult the label for specific instructions. Allow the finish to dry between coats as recommended on the product label.

Minimise dust in the area before applying a finish, or unwanted specks could settle in. To avoid creating air bubbles, stir a surface finish slowly, gently and thoroughly, and never drag a brush against the can rim to remove excess; instead, tap the brush lightly against the inside edge of the can. Dip a third of the brush into the finish and flow it on gently.

For a lustrous sheen, polish a dried surface finish as follows: apply a liberal amount of light lubricating oil to a cloth or felt pad; sprinkle some fine pumice onto the cloth. Rub the oil on the surface, stroking along the wood grain. When the surface is satiny smooth, wipe off the oil with a clean soft cloth, and apply two coats of paste wax. For a glossier look, repeat the process using fine pumice powder and oil before waxing.

Type	Surface effect	Application	Solvent	Considerations
Alkyd varnish	Durable built-up finish, matt or gloss. Darkens wood slightly	Brush on liquid type; non-drip type. Apply 2–3 coats	White spirit or turpentine	General-purpose protection. Spar (marine) varnish good for exterior work
Acrylic water-based varnish	Same as above, but may darken wood less	Brush on. Apply 2–3 coats	Water	Environmentally safe. May raise the wood grain. Dries faster than solvent varnishes
Polyurethane	Extremely durable finish, matt or gloss; can look plastic. Darkens wood slightly	Brush on liquid type, non-drip type. Apply 2–3 coats	White spirit or turpentine	Extremely durable; good for objects subject to heavy wear
Cellulose lacquer	Matt or glossy, accents grain of wood. Darkens wood less than other finishes, but may appear yellow	Brush or spray on; apply at least 3 coats. Brushing types may leave lap marks	Lacquer thinner	More protection than oils but less than varnishes. Highly flammable; apply in explosion-proof spray booth
French polish (includes button, garnet, white and transparent)	High gloss. Should be used indoors only, for furniture, panelling and flooring	Use a 'rubber' made by wrapping cotton wool in cotton or linen cloth	Alcohol	Can be applied over other finishes but requires some skill. Damaged by water, alcohol and heat. Can be scratched easily
Danish oil	Natural-looking matt finish that enhances wood grain. Clear or colours available; all darken wood	Wipe on. Apply 3 coats; apply 4 coats for objects receiving heavy use	White spirit or turpentine	Good for interior objects. May be used on external objects but needs to be reapplied at regular intervals
Tung oil	Natural-looking matt sheen. Enhances colour and grain of wood	Brush or wipe on. Apply 2–3 coats; rub in vigorously	White spirit or turpentine	Suitable for all interior objects, especially carvings. Little protection against abrasion; somewhat resistant to staining
Yacht and marine varnish	Durable finish. Darkens wood slightly	Brush on. Apply three coats	White spirit or turpentine	High gloss finish. Greater durability than polyurethane varnishes. Do not normally peel or flake from surface

Brushing techniques

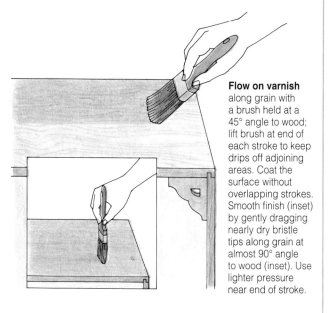

Flow on varnish along grain with a brush held at a 45° angle to wood; lift brush at end of each stroke to keep drips off adjoining areas. Coat the surface without overlapping strokes. Smooth finish (inset) by gently dragging nearly dry bristle tips along grain at almost 90° angle to wood (inset). Use lighter pressure near end of stroke.

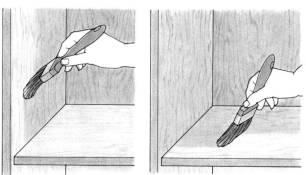

On inside corners, apply varnish first to the vertical surface, from bottom up. Then coat the horizontal surface. Work from the back corner toward front edge, brushing out any drips from the vertical face.

On outside corners, work horizontally, lifting brush at end of each stroke. To keep varnish from sagging, begin vertical stroke from bottom, catching any drips from horizontal face as you work.

Stripping

Paint strippers dissolve the old finish so it can be lifted off the surface. Those containing methylene chloride, which is a suspected carcinogen, work quickly (usually within 15 minutes) and effectively, but must be used with great caution. Nontoxic water-based strippers work more slowly, and because they may raise the grain, necessitating light sanding after stripping, they may not be the right choice for valuable or veneered pieces. Apply all strippers the same way. Pat on a thick coat with a cheap paintbrush, wait for the recommended time and then scrape off the old finish. If necessary, reapply stripper to any stubborn patches.

Caution: Use methylene chloride stripper outdoors or in a very well ventilated workspace. Wear a respirator that will protect you from harmful vapours (some filters will screen out only solid particles). Always wear safety goggles and nitrile rubber or PVC gloves, not the thin latex type. Protect the floor with newspaper, rather than a plastic dust sheet.

Keep fresh water and clean rags nearby, in case some of the stripper splashes onto your skin or into your eyes.

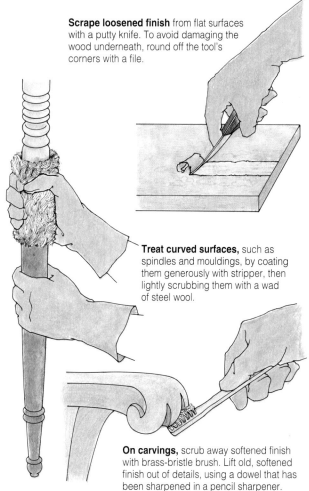

Scrape loosened finish from flat surfaces with a putty knife. To avoid damaging the wood underneath, round off the tool's corners with a file.

Treat curved surfaces, such as spindles and mouldings, by coating them generously with stripper, then lightly scrubbing them with a wad of steel wool.

On carvings, scrub away softened finish with brass-bristle brush. Lift old, softened finish out of details, using a dowel that has been sharpened in a pencil sharpener.

WORKING WITH VENEER

Veneering is the process of gluing a thin layer of decorative wood over a thicker plain base. Most veneers are a nominal 0.6 mm thick for cabinet-making; thinner, flexible veneers are available for curved surfaces. Veneer is sold by the square foot in pieces of various lengths, in sheets or rolls. Flatten pieces of veneer before use by spraying them lightly with water and then stacking them in a pile; separate the layers with brown paper. Lay a plywood panel on top of the stack, and weight it with bricks. When the veneer is flat, let it dry for five days in the stack, changing the paper daily.

Veneer may be either sliced or rotary cut. Sliced veneer is normal and is cut across the log, giving it the lively grain of sawn wood. Rotary cutting is less common; the veneer is peeled off a log, much like unwinding a roll of paper towels. The grain of rotary-cut veneer looks stretched out – the

  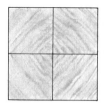

Edge matching   Book matching   Diamond pattern

growth rings are more widely spaced than in the uncut log.

Veneer is packed in the order it is cut. To keep the slices in sequence, number each one with chalk as you unpack it. The veneers may be arranged in different ways. In edge matching, you slip consecutive veneers off the pile, lay them next to each other, and join them edge-to-edge, creating a repetitive pattern. In book matching, you remove sheets

Edge-joining veneer

1. Overlap the two veneer sheets by about 1 cm (½ in). Clamp straightedge along centre of overlap. Cut with veneer saw, using multiple light strokes. Remove waste veneer.

2. On good face, tape across joint every 15 cm (6 in) with veneer tape. Tape along joint. Carefully lift panel to light to check for fit. Light shows through if joint is not tight.

3. Place veneer, tape side down, at edge of work surface; open joint so that one piece hangs down. Apply thin coat of PVA glue to edges. Close, wipe off excess glue and cover with a sheet of polythene and weights.

Gluing to substrate

Brush PVA glue evenly onto substrate. Apply veneer to both sides. Protect lower veneered side with plain paper. Then weight or clamp.

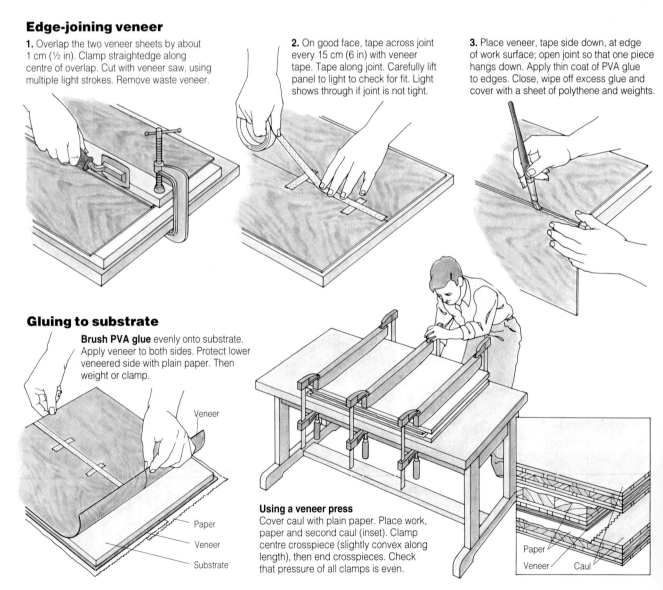

Veneer

Paper
Veneer
Substrate

Using a veneer press
Cover caul with plain paper. Place work, paper and second caul (inset). Clamp centre crosspiece (slightly convex along length), then end crosspieces. Check that pressure of all clamps is even.

Paper
Veneer   Caul

from the pile as you would turn the pages of a book, giving a mirror-image effect. To create a diamond pattern, cut four identical squares or rectangles of veneer so that the grain is diagonal. Then position the squares to form a pattern of either concentric diamonds or radiating lines.

Most materials can be veneered, if they are clean and smooth (bumps can be transmitted through the veneer). Apply veneer with its grain perpendicular to the grain of manufactured wood. To prevent warping, veneer both sides.

Cut veneer with a craft knife or veneer saw held at 90°. Whenever possible, cut with the back face up. Veneer should overhang the surface being covered (the substrate) by about 1 cm (½ in) on all sides. Trim the waste with a veneer saw after the veneer has been glued but before scraping off the veneer tape. When both sides have been veneered, cut the

work to size and cover the edges with veneer edging tape, which is usually ironed on (pp.152-3).

To form a strong glue bond between veneer and its substrate, place even pressure on the work, adding slightly more force on the centre. Weight down small areas of veneer with bricks or concrete blocks; if clamping, set one clamp every 23 cm (9 in). When using a veneer press, the plywood cauls (protective panels) should be larger than the work on all sides and the crosspieces should have convex bottoms. Weight hard-to-clamp areas with a sand-filled plastic bag.

Veneered surfaces break fairly easily, especially on their edges. Before patching, smooth the broken edges of the old veneer and square them with a craft knife so that they are at a right angle to the substrate. Before repairing veneer, make sure that the substrate is smooth and free of old adhesive.

Edge border

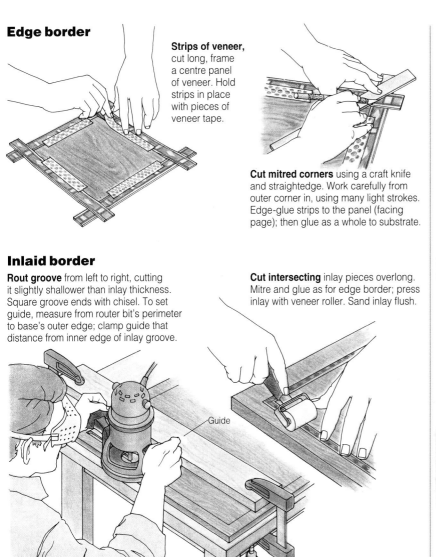

Strips of veneer, cut long, frame a centre panel of veneer. Hold strips in place with pieces of veneer tape.

Cut mitred corners using a craft knife and straightedge. Work carefully from outer corner in, using many light strokes. Edge-glue strips to the panel (facing page); then glue as a whole to substrate.

Inlaid border

Rout groove from left to right, cutting it slightly shallower than inlay thickness. Square groove ends with chisel. To set guide, measure from router bit's perimeter to base's outer edge; clamp guide that distance from inner edge of inlay groove.

Cut intersecting inlay pieces overlong. Mitre and glue as for edge border; press inlay with veneer roller. Sand inlay flush.

Guide

Repairs

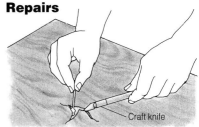

Craft knife

Blister Slice in line with grain and gently lift veneer. Push in PVA glue with toothpick or glue injector. Press with flat roller; cover with polythene and weight with a heavy object.

Raised veneer Remove dried glue with craft knife or pin. Apply fresh glue with small brush or toothpick, and weight as above.

Hole Lay white paper over hole, rub patch pattern with pencil. Lightly glue template to face side of patching material. Cut patch with many light strokes on waste side of cut line. Test-fit patch; trim to fit; then glue and clamp.

Gluing and clamping repairs

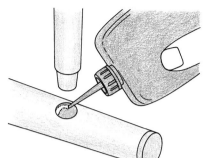

Regluing a joint Always tap a joint apart where possible. Clean off old glue, then apply new glue to the rim of the hole, so that glue is taken in.

Force angled joint together with a tourniquet. Wrap rope in a figure-of-eight pattern. Tighten rope with a twist stick.

Twist stick

Try the gentlest approach first when reviving a worn furniture piece. If the finish is sound but lifeless, a thorough cleaning with a mild detergent or a dewaxer may add enough brightness. If not, a finish restorer, which dissolves a thin layer of existing finish and replaces it with a film of fresh finish, may be sufficient. For grubby surfaces, try a restorer and cleaner. A light application will remove surface dirt, oil or wax, leaving a varnish coat both intact and clean.

Disguise small scratches with dye-impregnated wood markers, stick shellac or even crayons. Deeply scratched pieces may require sanding and a complete refinishing.

To remove water rings, dampen a soft cotton cloth (old towelling is fine) with mineral oil, dip the cloth into fine pumice stone or rottenstone, and gently rub the ring until it disappears.

To raise a dent, prick it several times with a pin, cover it with a damp cloth and press with an iron on the steam setting for a few seconds. Allow the area to dry and repeat if needed.

Disassemble a piece carefully when many joints need repairing, when a part needs replacing or if repairing one part will damage another part. Begin by reviewing the overall assembly. Invert tables to see how the apron and top are attached to the legs. Look inside frame-and-panel cabinets to

locate glue blocks and screws. To aid reassembly, note the order of disassembly and mark mating pieces.

Loose joints can be tapped apart with a rubber mallet, but forcing tight joints can break the pieces. Try to soften the glue. Drill or prick several small holes into the joint. Then, with an artist's brush, apply a 1:1 mixture of white vinegar and water; wait 1 to 2 hours and tap the joint apart.

Breaks along the wood grain usually reglue well, but cross-grain breaks do not; strengthen the latter with dowels or splines. Try to tighten a loose dowel joint by gluing string or a layer of cheesecloth round the dowel to increase its diameter. You can widen the end of a dowel on a disassembled piece by splitting the end and inserting a hardwood wedge. Tighten a loose tenon by gluing wood shims to it; then trim them to fit. Build up a loose finger or dovetail joint with veneer pieces. For a good bond, clean old glue out of all joints before regluing.

Troublesome doors often respond to one of several repairs. Check for high spots by rubbing chalk on the door's edge and then closing the door; plane the spots where the chalk was removed. Plug a stripped screw hole with glue and toothpicks, and redrill. Check hinge mortises. Chisel shallow ones deeper, and pack those that are too deep with pieces of veneer.

Repairing a split

Gently prise apart the pieces of a lengthwise break with a putty knife or an old screwdriver.

Wedge pieces far enough apart to allow insertion of a small glue brush. Coat both surfaces of split with glue. Remove wedge.

Clamp repair tightly. Scrap wood on both sides equalises clamp pressure and protects wood surface.

Scrap wood

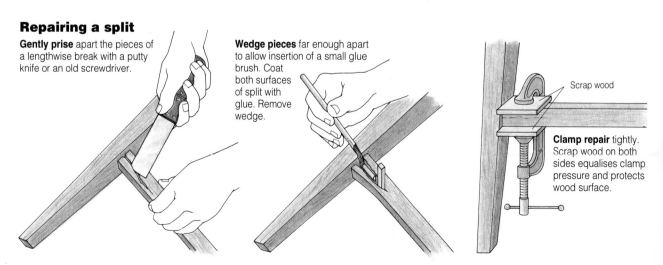

Broken dowelled rail

Saw off broken wood on rail. Drill dowel hole. Make hole half the width of rail and 3 mm (⅛ in) deeper than necessary (for excess glue); use tape on bit to guide depth. Test-fit new grooved dowel in rail.

In mating leg, fill all gaps by gluing a dowel in old hole; let dry. Saw off excess dowel filler and drill a hole in leg to accept new dowel. Test-fit pieces. Coat dowel with glue; insert into rail. Lightly tap rail into leg with mallet.

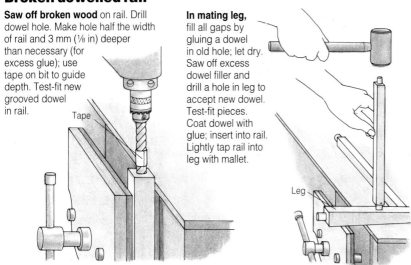

Broken mortise-and-tenon

Saw off remains of broken tenon. Within outline of tenon, drill holes for mortise at least 2.5 cm (1 in) deep plus 3 mm (⅛ in) for excess glue. Trim mortise with chisel (p.146). Drill or chisel out remains of tenon in old mortise.

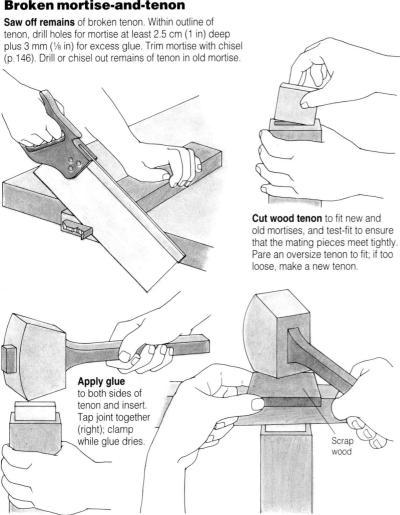

Cut wood tenon to fit new and old mortises, and test-fit to ensure that the mating pieces meet tightly. Pare an oversize tenon to fit; if too loose, make a new tenon.

Apply glue to both sides of tenon and insert. Tap joint together (right); clamp while glue dries.

Drawer repairs

Remove bottom Pull nails with pincers and slide out panel. Replace, if needed, with 3-6 mm (⅛-¼ in) thick hardboard or plywood. Use 10 mm (⅜ in) for larger drawers.

Replace piece First, knock apart corner joints. Examine joints to determine direction of mallet blows. Soften glue (facing page). Wood block protects wood during blows. Insert new part, glue and clamp.

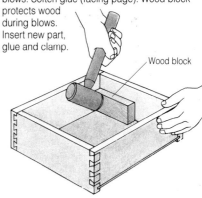

Wood block

Replace uneven or worn runners Plane down high spots. Shave front corner area with chisel. Cut hardwood strips (maple or birch is best) to fit.

Runner

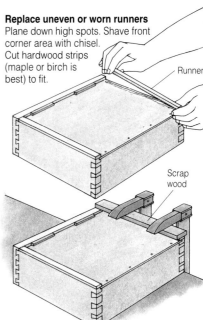

Scrap wood

Glue and align hardwood strips along drawer edges. Place clamps every 15 cm (6 in); protect wood with scrap. When dry, test-fit drawer; plane or sand high spots on new strips.

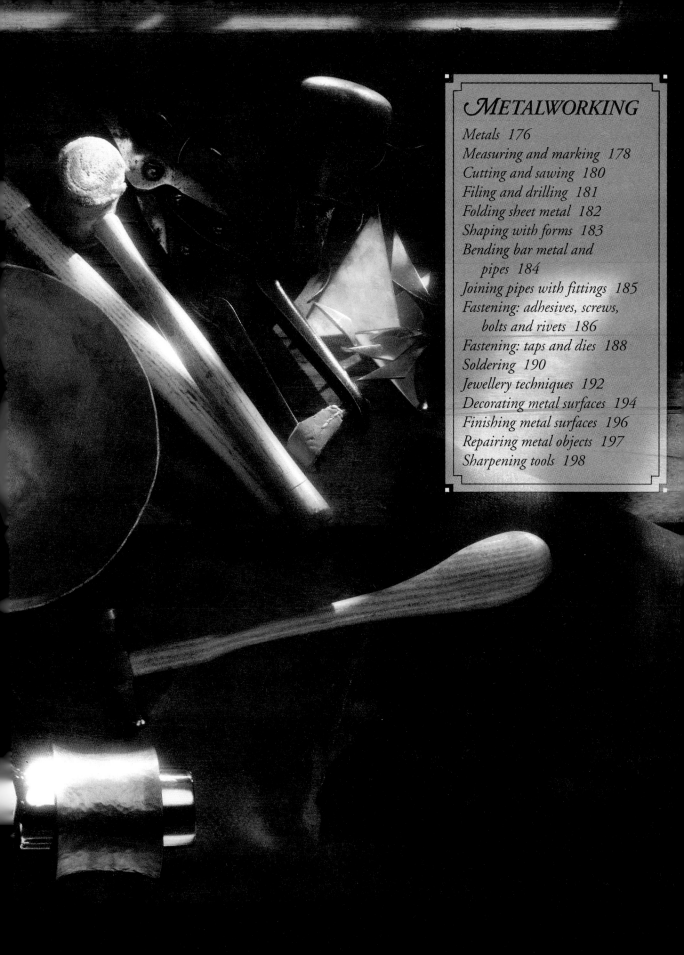

METALWORKING

Although replaced to a degree by plastics, metals are still put to a wide variety of uses around the home, as in flashing, cladding, window frames, cabinets, pipes and ducts. Metals can be soft or hard, beautiful or nondescript, malleable or rigid, thick or paper-thin. They are divided into two broad categories: ferrous (containing iron) and nonferrous, which includes all the other base metals (such as copper, aluminium, nickel and zinc) and the precious metals (gold, silver and platinum). Often two or more elemental metals are combined (alloyed) to alter their visual properties or working and performance characteristics, such as hardness, strength, corrosion resistance and melting points. The metals you are most likely to work with are sterling silver, copper, brass, steel and aluminium alloys. Metals are sold in sheets less than 5 mm (³⁄₁₆ in) thick, in plates 6 mm (¼ in) thick or more and in bars, which include strips and flats (narrow sheets and plates), round, square and hexagonal rods and tubing, angles and channels and various other shapes.

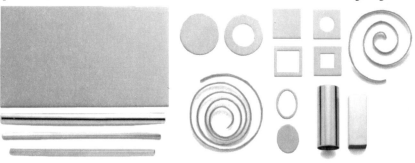

Silver and the other precious metals (gold and platinum) are highly stable chemically and resist oxidation and corrosion from acids. Silver and gold are also pliable and easy to work. They are available in preformed or standard sheets, plates, standard wire, flat bezel wire, tubing and rods. Also available are foil, leaf and shot (granules) for casting and alloying as well as prefabricated chains, clasps, earring posts and jump rings that simplify jewellery making.

Copper is often used in both rigid and flexible water supply piping and fittings. It also comes in sheets of different gauges, including thin foil, rolls of tapelike foil for stained-glass work, wire, tubes, flats and bars. Circular sheets are ideal for shaping bowls, and small preshaped pieces of sheet copper can be used in jewellery making or other decorative items. Copper is also the chief component in brass and bronze alloys.

Brass, an alloy of copper and zinc, is sold in sheets, plates, tubes, rods, angles and wire. It is stronger and harder than copper and resists corrosion, although decorative items are usually coated to prevent tarnish. Thin brass-plated steel pipe is also available. Solid brass is widely used for plumbing pipe and fittings, including nipples and unions and flare, compression and threaded fittings (below). Banding (bottom) is used for decorating furniture, boxes, lamps and bowls. Bronze, a copper-tin alloy, has properties and uses similar to those of brass.

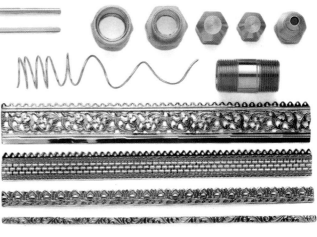

Plain carbon steels, alloys of iron and carbon only, are the steels used in home workshops.They come in three varieties: low, medium and high-carbon. The most widely used is low-carbon or mild steel, which is easily drilled, cut and bent. It is available in a vast array of shapes including rods, tubing, angles and flats, as shown at right, and is ideally suited for threaded heating and gas pipes and fittings (below). Medium-carbon steel, a harder alloy, is found in castings and in many shop tools. High-carbon steel is extremely hard, making it ideal for cutting tools.

Aluminium is either cold-rolled or alloyed in order to give it strength. It is lightweight and easily drilled and cut, but it can only be soldered and welded using special techniques and fluxes. Although aluminium resists atmospheric corrosion, anodising (an electrochemical coating process) dramatically improves its performance. It comes in sheets, preshaped flashing and rods, and in many other forms, including angles, preformed thresholds, TV antennae and framework for windows, screens and greenhouses.

Working with metal, whether forming original work or making repairs, requires careful preparation and good materials. Sources for metal and supplies are diverse. For nonferrous metals (copper, brass or aluminium) try hardware, building or plumbing supply stores. For ferrous metals (iron or steel) visit a sheet-metal or welding shop or a scrapyard. Craft shops and jewellery suppliers carry metals, other materials and special tools for jewellery making.

The thickness of sheet metal and wire is sometimes expressed in gauge numbers; the lower the gauge number, the thicker the metal. A gauge plate can measure metal thickness roughly, but

a micrometer or a vernier caliper is more precise, measuring any piece to hundredths of a millimetre. Mark the measurement on any leftover metal for future use. Check angles or find centre

points with a combination set. Mark straight lines on sheet metal with an indelible pen or a scriber and a steel rule, curves and circles with dividers, and points with a centre punch.

British Imperial Standard Wire Gauge

No	in	mm	No	in	mm	No	in	mm
1	0.300	7.62	11	0.116	2.95	21	0.032	0.81
2	0.276	7.01	12	0.104	2.64	22	0.028	0.71
3	0.252	6.40	13	0.092	2.34	23	0.024	0.61
4	0.232	5.89	14	0.080	2.03	24	0.022	0.56
5	0.212	5.38	15	0.072	1.83	25	0.020	0.51
6	0.192	4.88	16	0.064	1.63	26	0.018	0.46
7	0.176	4.47	17	0.056	1.42	27	0.016	0.41
8	0.160	4.06	18	0.048	1.22	28	0.015	0.38
9	0.144	3.66	19	0.040	1.02	29	0.014	0.35
10	0.128	3.25	20	0.036	0.91	30	0.012	0.30

Measuring metal thickness

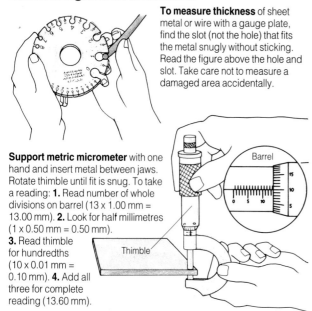

To measure thickness of sheet metal or wire with a gauge plate, find the slot (not the hole) that fits the metal snugly without sticking. Read the figure above the hole and slot. Take care not to measure a damaged area accidentally.

Support metric micrometer with one hand and insert metal between jaws. Rotate thimble until fit is snug. To take a reading: **1.** Read number of whole divisions on barrel (13 x 1.00 mm = 13.00 mm). **2.** Look for half millimetres (1 x 0.50 mm = 0.50 mm). **3.** Read thimble for hundredths (10 x 0.01 mm = 0.10 mm). **4.** Add all three for complete reading (13.60 mm).

Barrel

Thimble

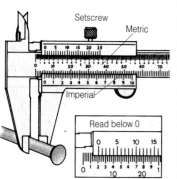

Setscrew
Metric
Imperial
Read below 0

Vernier caliper has both imperial and metric scales. On the metric scale, the main measurement is in millimetres; the sliding scale is in 0.02 mm divisions. To take a reading: **1.** Read whole number of mm on main scale to the left of 0 mark on sliding scale (8.00 mm). **2.** Look for a line on the sliding scale that coincides with a line on the main scale and multiply by 0.02 (12 x 0.02 = 0.24 mm). **3.** Add them for the complete reading (8.24 mm).

Marking metal

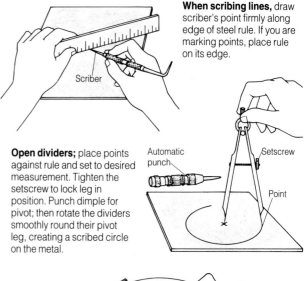

Scriber

When scribing lines, draw scriber's point firmly along edge of steel rule. If you are marking points, place rule on its edge.

Open dividers; place points against rule and set to desired measurement. Tighten the setscrew to lock leg in position. Punch dimple for pivot; then rotate the dividers smoothly round their pivot leg, creating a scribed circle on the metal.

Automatic punch
Setscrew
Point

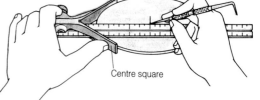

Centre square

Automatic punch

Marking a centre point:
1. Press round metal against centre square of combination set; scribe along rule. Rotate metal 90 degrees; repeat. Centre point is where lines intersect.

2. Place tip of automatic punch on centre point. With one hand, press down on sleeve until punch recoils, forming a slight dimple.

Making a pattern

When creating any metal object, start by making a full-sized pattern, or template, on heavyweight paper or thin cardboard. Original designs for two-dimensional items, such as plaques or pieces of jewellery, can be drawn on graph paper first, then transferred to pattern paper by tracing over carbon paper. Cut out the pattern and fasten it to the metal with rubber cement. Then cut the metal directly round the pattern. For larger objects – or for such three-dimensional objects as ducts, decorative pieces or the box shown on this page – make a pattern called a development, which shows all parts of the object unfolded and flattened.

Draw a development with a sharp pencil and an accurate straightedge. Check all measurements twice, using one line as a baseline from which to measure; this avoids compounding any errors. Distinguish cut lines from fold lines and calculate allowances for seams and edges. When you have finished, cut along the cut lines with scissors or a utility knife (use a steel rule to guide the blade); then assemble the pattern to test the design and to establish a logical sequence of work steps to follow when creating the actual object. (For folds, refer to the work sequence on page 182.) If the project is complicated, make a list of these steps so that you can refer to them.

Holding work securely

Accidents happen quickly in metal-working. Avoid them by securing the work with clamps or in an engineer's vice so that it cannot move during an operation. In a home workshop, fasten an engineer's vice at one corner of the workbench, near or over a leg. The vice's fixed jaw should project about 1.3 cm (½ in) beyond the bench's edge. Read the safety precautions on pages 10-13. In particular, protect your eyes to prevent injury from metal splinters, and wear heavy gloves and long sleeves to protect you against sharp edges.

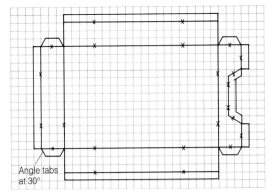

Angle tabs at 30°

Making a development 1. For a three-dimensional object, begin by drawing the bottom or base. Extend all dimensions to form the sides, adding the appropriate amounts for seam and edge tabs. Angle the ends of the tabs towards each other at about 30 degrees to make them easier to fold. Mark lines indicating folds with Xs. Cut out the pattern and test it by folding it to its final shape, holding the seams temporarily closed with masking tape.

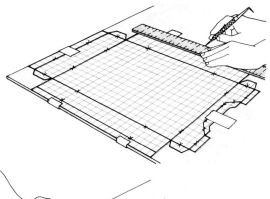

2. To scribe the pattern onto sheet metal, fasten it securely to the metal with masking tape. Using a steel rule as a straightedge, lightly trace the pattern's outline onto the metal with a scriber. Align rule carefully with the pattern's edges, and always keep scriber's point against the rule's bottom edge.

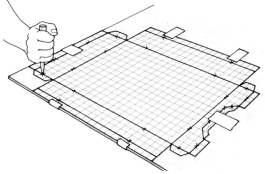

3. With an awl or a punch, mark fold lines and any internal cut lines by punching gently through the pattern in at least two places along each line. Remove the pattern. Using the scriber and rule, scribe along fold lines lightly to avoid weakening the metal, then scribe over the outline and any other cut lines more firmly, making these lines deeper.

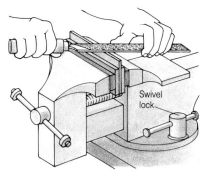

For safety and control, tighten swivel and vice jaws firmly. Working close to jaws lessens chattering and movement of metal and reduces strain on vice.

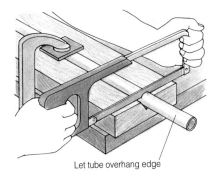

Let tube overhang edge

Wooden V-block holds a round tube or rod securely for drilling, sawing or shaping. Clamp tube in single V-block or use two V-blocks in an engineer's vice.

There are many ways to cut metal, depending on the type, size and amount of stock to be cut. Very thin metal, such as aluminium siding, can be cut by scoring with a trimming knife several times along the cut line, using a steel straightedge. Most wire can be cut with side-cutting pliers. For sheet metal thinner than 18 gauge, use snips. Compound action snips, with their compact size and compound leverage, handle well; ordinary tinsnips leave a smoother edge. If you have long or multiple cuts to make, choose electric shears or a nibbler. Both make curved and straight cuts quickly, but a nibbler cuts a channel through the metal, leaving a smoother edge. Before cutting, lubricate along the cut line with light machine oil.

A circle cutter, available through jewellery suppliers, forms small discs and other shapes (such as half-moons or semicircles) for jewellery work. For thick metal plate and round stock, cut with a hacksaw or – for soft or thinner metals – an electric jigsaw fitted with a metal-cutting blade. A cold chisel struck with a hammer will cut rough openings in metal too thick for snips, and can shear through solid stock such as bolt shafts.

Caution: Read the precautions on pages 12-13; in particular, protect your hands and eyes against flying metal chips and sharp edges. Always clamp or grip workpieces securely and file rough edges smooth immediately after they have been cut.

Cutting techniques

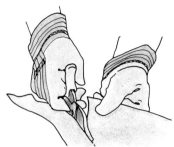

Snips Grip work with your free hand; slightly angle straight-cutting snips above surface. Work on waste side of cut line; don't close blades completely. Curl waste aside.

Circle cutter
To make shapes from sheet metal, first remove all pins. Slide metal into groove under hole (for varied shapes, position metal partially under hole). Insert pin in hole; strike with hammer to punch piece out.

Pin

Groove

Power shears Let waste overhang work surface. Cut slowly for thick metal or tight cuts, faster for thin sheets or long cuts. Curl waste aside. Wear safety goggles.

For inside curves, first drill or punch a starter hole. Using compound action snips, make first cut close to line, then trim remaining metal.

Cold chisel For inside shapes, grip chisel loosely and tilt. Strike chisel with ball-pein hammer, slicing metal with chisel blade.

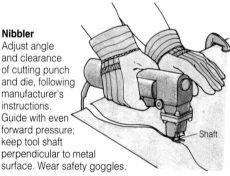

Nibbler
Adjust angle and clearance of cutting punch and die, following manufacturer's instructions. Guide with even forward pressure; keep tool shaft perpendicular to metal surface. Wear safety goggles.

Shaft

Sawing metal

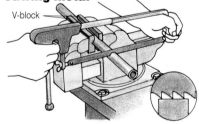

V-block

Hacksaw For efficient cutting, blade should have at least three teeth touching edge of metal. Hold saw at both ends. Cut on forward stroke; rotate round stock to complete cut.

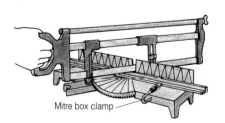

Mitre box clamp

Angled cuts Cut soft metal to specific angles in a mitre box. Clamp or hold metal in box; use metal-cutting blade with mitre box saw, or use hacksaw, as at left.

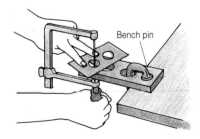

Bench pin

Piercing saw Install blade through drilled hole in metal. Hold work against bench pin and keep it centred in bench pin slot. Keep blade vertical to work; cut on downstroke only.

FILING AND DRILLING

For shaping and smoothing metal edges, mill files are usually the best choice; but for soft metal, particularly aluminium, choose a curved-tooth file with deeply cut teeth. Single-cut files, having a single series of parallel teeth, cut more slowly than double-cut files; the latter have a second row of teeth overlapping the first at an angle. Most files come in three grades – smooth cut, second cut and bastard (coarsest) – but longer files, regardless of grade, leave a coarser surface than shorter files. Choose a file shape that matches the work, whether round, square, triangular or flat.

Always put a handle on a file before working; it is safer and gives better leverage. Place the handle on the file's tang, and strike the handle against a hard surface until it is tight.

Hold the file at both ends and push it with long, slow strokes. (Draw-filing, shown on this page, is an exception.) Using your arms and shoulders as well as hands, apply even pressure. Maintain a steady rhythm, but lift the file on the return stroke to avoid dulling its teeth.

Prevent clogged teeth by rubbing chalk over a file before use, and regularly clean files by brushing with a file card.

Cross-file to remove burrs from a cut edge. Lay file diagonally across workpiece edge, square to sides. Push file forwards and sideways.

Draw-file to produce smooth, finished edge. Hold file flat against surface, square to work's sides. Pull tool towards you; use fresh teeth for each stroke.

Round file smoothes tight curves. Push file forwards and sideways along curve (as in cross-filing) while rotating blade.

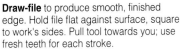

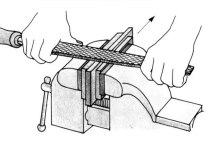

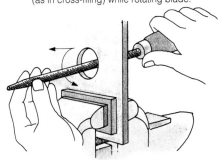

Drilling holes in metal

Drill holes in metal for fasteners, decoration or instead of sawing when making large holes. A drill press provides stability, accuracy and control, but a portable electric drill mounted in a stand can also drill through sheet metal and small stock. Make holes in thinner metal and stationary pieces with a variable-speed portable drill.

Choose sharp high-speed twist bits. Mark the location of the hole by denting the centre of it with a punch (p.178), and back the metal with scrap wood. Apply several drops of light household oil to the bit and the hole as you work. When drilling thick metal or steel, make a well with modelling clay to contain the oil. Drill slowly and exert firm but not undue pressure, slowing the drill speed if the bit squeaks, and pausing if it turns bluish or if smoke appears. Raise the bit frequently to clear waste and to add oil.

Caution: Wear safety goggles to protect your eyes from metal chips, and clamp all workpieces firmly unless they are stationary.

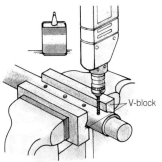

V-block

To drill holes in tubing, clamp tubing in V-blocks or vice. Insert dowel to reinforce thin walls and to guide bit straight through other side; be sure bit can exit freely.

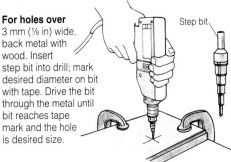

For holes over 3 mm (⅛ in) wide, back metal with wood. Insert step bit into drill; mark desired diameter on bit with tape. Drive the bit through the metal until bit reaches tape mark and the hole is desired size.

Step bit

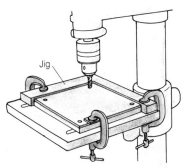

Jig

Drill press For uniformly placed holes, make a two-sided jig. Back metal with wood. Clamp the jig firmly on drill press table; rotate metal for each hole.

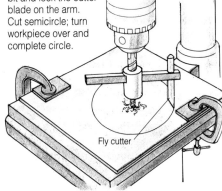

Fly cutter makes large holes in thin-gauge metal. Punch centre point for drill bit; clamp work. Insert fly cutter in drill press, centre the bit and lock the cutter blade on the arm. Cut semicircle; turn workpiece over and complete circle.

Fly cutter

FOLDING SHEET METAL

When working with sheet metal, first bend it with gloved hands before moving on to bending and striking tools. Fold gradually by working along the entire fold line in stages, starting in the middle and working towards the ends. A bending brake, available at metalworking suppliers, provides greatest accuracy. A homemade brake can consist of two pieces of hardwood clamped together; align the metal's fold line between them and bend along it.

Complete bends and folds with a flat-faced mallet, and finish edges with a setting hammer. Never use a damaged wooden, plastic or rawhide mallet; polish steel hammer faces (p.196) to remove nicks and scratches.

Plan the work sequence beforehand by assembling the development (p.179). File rough edges smooth and complete any decorative surface work (p.194-5); then form the edges and seams. Complete the object by making inside folds.

Folding sequence for a box begins with top edges, then each side and the seam tabs. For final inside folds, or when box will no longer fit in bending brake, use a hatchet stake.

Hand seamer makes edges and narrow folds. Align edge of tool with fold line; tighten jaws with screws. Bend in stages along fold line by lifting tool upwards; close seam with mallet.

Hatchet stake can be made of hardwood with a bevelled top edge. Align fold line over edge of stake. First make fold with hands; then make a crisp crease with wooden mallet.

Hatchet stake

Bending brake folds sheet metal that is thinner than 14 gauge. Adjust brake jaw for metal thickness. Clamp metal so fold line aligns with edge of plate; push plate up to fold sheet to desired angle.

Edges

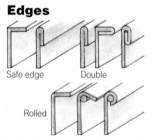

Safe edge   Double

Rolled

Edge treatment strengthens and smoothes edges, and provides neat appearance. Rolled, or wired, edge (right) is strongest.

Rolled edge 1. Width of fold should be 3½ times diameter of wire. Bend edge upward along fold line with hand seamer or brake. Hold wire in place; close fold with mallet.

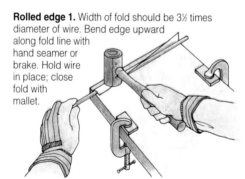

2. Support seam with block of wood; curl edge round wire with wedge-faced setting hammer. Snip off excess wire with diagonal-cutting pliers.

Seams

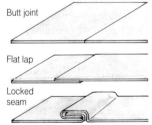

Butt joint

Flat lap

Locked seam

Seams are metal joints that can be soldered or fastened with rivets or screws. Locked seam (right) needs no fasteners or solder.

Locked seam 1. Bend folds of equal width on both edges, one opposite the other. Lay scrap wood inside each fold; hammer down until almost closed; then remove wood and interlock edges (inset). Place seam over clamped pipe and flatten with mallet.

2. Fit channel of appropriate-sized hand groover over seam. Strike handle of groover with ball-pein hammer as you move channel along the seam.

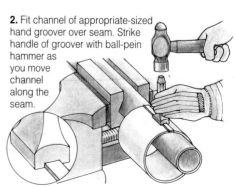

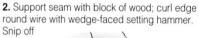

SHAPING WITH FORMS

Because metal is ductile – it flows, rather like modelling clay – it can be shaped by striking it against a form with a hammer or a mallet. You can create such objects as vases, bowls and trays using two basic forming techniques: raising and sinking.

Deep objects are raised by striking their outer surface against solid forms called stakes. Various stakes are available at metalworking suppliers, but you can improvise with pieces of metal or hardwood. Jewellers use tapered stakes called mandrels for shaping rings and bracelets (p.193).

When sinking a shallow object, strike its inner surface against a hollow form, such as a sandbag or a mould made by gouging a bowl-shaped depression in the end grain of a hardwood block. Strike the metal squarely with the tool's face, not its edge, and use gentle, even blows. Keep steel hammer faces free of nicks (p.196).

Prolonged beating hardens most metal and it ceases to flow, becoming brittle and likely to crack. Annealing or heating the metal will restore its malleability. (Do not anneal aluminium, lead or pewter.) After annealing, remove any oxide residue by cleaning the object in pickle (p.190-1).

To finish a formed piece, you can decorate or planish it (p.194-5), then polish and buff it (p.196).

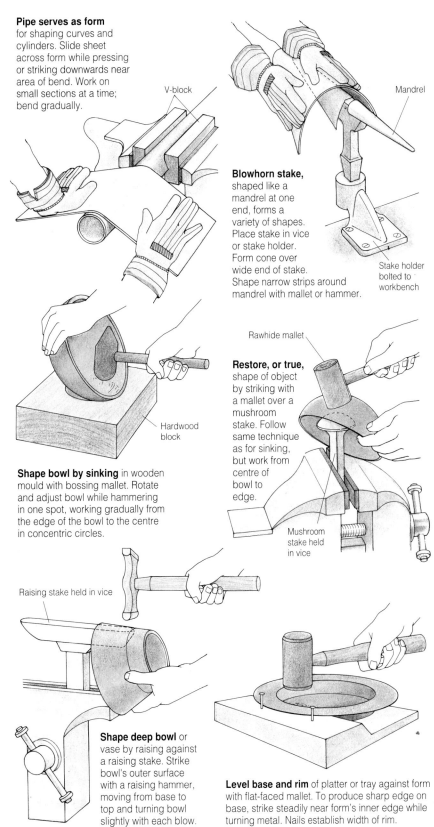

Pipe serves as form for shaping curves and cylinders. Slide sheet across form while pressing or striking downwards near area of bend. Work on small sections at a time; bend gradually.

V-block

Mandrel

Blowhorn stake, shaped like a mandrel at one end, forms a variety of shapes. Place stake in vice or stake holder. Form cone over wide end of stake. Shape narrow strips around mandrel with mallet or hammer.

Stake holder bolted to workbench

Hardwood block

Shape bowl by sinking in wooden mould with bossing mallet. Rotate and adjust bowl while hammering in one spot, working gradually from the edge of the bowl to the centre in concentric circles.

Rawhide mallet

Restore, or true, shape of object by striking with a mallet over a mushroom stake. Follow same technique as for sinking, but work from centre of bowl to edge.

Mushroom stake held in vice

Raising stake held in vice

Shape deep bowl or vase by raising against a raising stake. Strike bowl's outer surface with a raising hammer, moving from base to top and turning bowl slightly with each blow.

Annealing Set piece on firebrick; heat all over with bushy torch flame until metal glows dull red. Allow to cool; then quench in water. Wear gloves and handle metal with tongs.

Level base and rim of platter or tray against form with flat-faced mallet. To produce sharp edge on base, strike steadily near form's inner edge while turning metal. Nails establish width of rim.

BENDING BAR METAL AND PIPES

Bar metal is classified as strips and flats as well as shaped rods (pp.176-7). Bending and twisting techniques apply to all types of bar metal; in general, ferrous metals are harder to bend than nonferrous. For tubing, use special bending tools.

Most bar metal up to 6 mm (¼ in) thick and 13 mm (½ in) wide can be bent cold. However, tight curves can overstretch metal, so make allowances when laying out. A bend of 90° will lengthen the outside of the curve by half the metal's thickness and shorten the inside of the curve by the same amount. Align the workpiece exactly perpendicular or parallel to the vice jaws, protecting soft metal with V-blocks

or scrap wood. Bend gradually and smoothly, checking the angle of the bend several times with a template or T-bevel. Use hand pressure first; then strike the metal with a hammer or mallet. For an exact shape bend round a stationary form, such as a pipe clamped parallel with the vice jaws.

Heating metal makes it easier to bend and increases the amount it will stretch. Heat the area of the bend with a propane torch until you can bend the metal smoothly.

Caution: Remove any nearby flammable objects and direct the torch flame only towards the area of bend. Wear gloves and protective clothing. Do not heat aluminium.

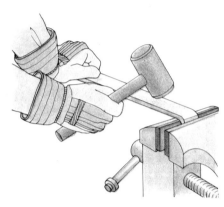

Cold-bending Mark point of bend on metal strip; clamp metal in vice. Bend by hand for looser curve; for extra leverage, slip a length of pipe over the strip's free end. For tight curve, strike metal just beyond edge of vice.

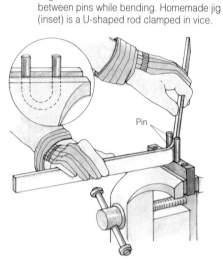

Bending jig makes scrolls and other complex bends. Set distance between pins slightly larger than the metal's thickness; feed metal between pins while bending. Homemade jig (inset) is a U-shaped rod clamped in vice.

Pin

Twisting strips Clamp one end of strip in vice. Grip other end with adjustable wrench or locking pliers. Twist with steady pressure to produce spiral.

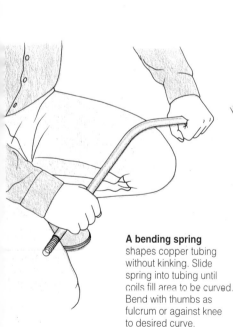

A bending spring shapes copper tubing without kinking. Slide spring into tubing until coils fill area to be curved. Bend with thumbs as fulcrum or against knee to desired curve.

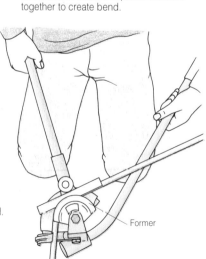

For heavy tubing and electrical conduit, use a pipe bender. Clamp pipe against former and place guide block between pipe and movable handle. Squeeze handles together to create bend.

Former

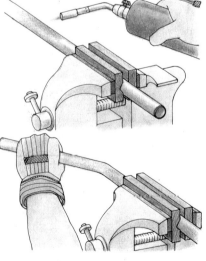

Bend flats, strips and rods secured in vice by heating area of bend with torch until metal glows red. Extinguish torch; grasp free end of metal with gloved hand and bend sideways.

JOINING PIPES WITH FITTINGS

Steel pipes are joined with threaded fittings. Flexible copper tubing is joined with compression or flare fittings, and both flexible and rigid copper tubing can be soldered (pp.190-1). Certain fittings require threaded pipe; for these, pipe can be purchased prethreaded or threaded to order at hardware, building or plumbing suppliers. Special fittings join incompatible materials. When buying fittings, specify the pipe's inside diameter, the material and whether it forms part of a water supply system or a drainage system.

Make careful calculations before cutting pipe to length – with rigid pipe, adjustments are seldom possible. Calculate both the width of the fitting and the amount it will overlap the pipe. Cut the ends of pipes exactly square, using a tubing cutter or, for steel pipe, a hacksaw (p.180). To prevent disturbed water flow inside pipes, remove burrs – the rough edges produced by cutting – by reaming the ends.

Tighten and loosen threaded fittings with two pipe wrenches; holding the pipe stationary with one wrench prevents damage to other joints. Hold a pipe wrench so that its jaws face the direction in which force is applied.

Caution: Before making modifications to a plumbing system, check with your local building inspector; building and plumbing codes prohibit some repairs and installations unless done by a licensed professional. Shut off the water supply and drain a plumbing pipe before working on it.

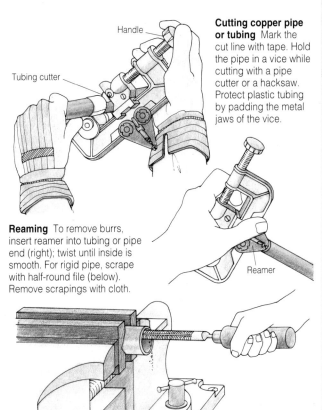

Cutting copper pipe or tubing Mark the cut line with tape. Hold the pipe in a vice while cutting with a pipe cutter or a hacksaw. Protect plastic tubing by padding the metal jaws of the vice.

Handle

Tubing cutter

Reaming To remove burrs, insert reamer into tubing or pipe end (right); twist until inside is smooth. For rigid pipe, scrape with half-round file (below). Remove scrapings with cloth.

Reamer

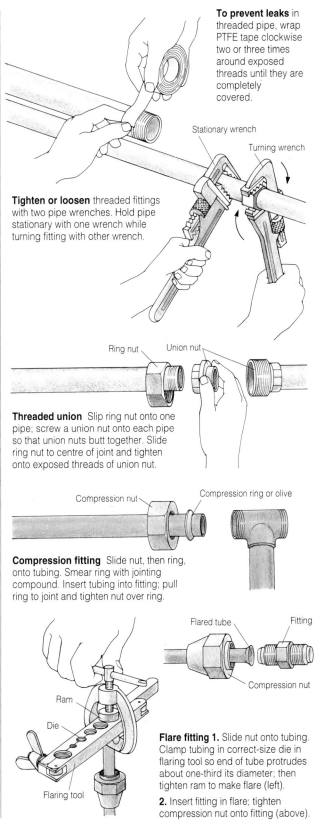

To prevent leaks in threaded pipe, wrap PTFE tape clockwise two or three times around exposed threads until they are completely covered.

Stationary wrench

Turning wrench

Tighten or loosen threaded fittings with two pipe wrenches. Hold pipe stationary with one wrench while turning fitting with other wrench.

Ring nut   Union nut

Threaded union Slip ring nut onto one pipe; screw a union nut onto each pipe so that union nuts butt together. Slide ring nut to centre of joint and tighten onto exposed threads of union nut.

Compression nut   Compression ring or olive

Compression fitting Slide nut, then ring, onto tubing. Smear ring with jointing compound. Insert tubing into fitting; pull ring to joint and tighten nut over ring.

Flared tube   Fitting

Compression nut

Ram

Die

Flaring tool

Flare fitting 1. Slide nut onto tubing. Clamp tubing in correct-size die in flaring tool so end of tube protrudes about one-third its diameter; then tighten ram to make flare (left).

2. Insert fitting in flare; tighten compression nut onto fitting (above).

Adhesives

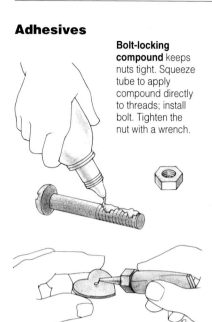

Bolt-locking compound keeps nuts tight. Squeeze tube to apply compound directly to threads; install bolt. Tighten the nut with a wrench.

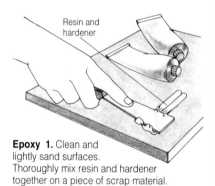

Cyanoacrylate adhesive forms a quick bond between nonporous materials. Apply a drop to one surface; press parts together firmly for 30 seconds.

Resin and hardener

Epoxy 1. Clean and lightly sand surfaces. Thoroughly mix resin and hardener together on a piece of scrap material.

Scrap wood distributes pressure of clamps

2. Spread thin mixture over both pieces; clamp together until adhesive sets. Wipe away excess adhesive immediately.

Adhesives can create a strong bond for metal, but it is important to use the correct high-quality adhesive and to clean the surfaces thoroughly (degrease metal by wiping with methylated spirit or a commercial degreasing agent). Follow the manufacturer's instructions for application and drying time.

To prevent threaded fasteners from loosening (particularly fasteners installed in engines, appliances and other vibrating machinery), coat them with bolt-locking compound, available at hardware and car accessory shops. Small metal objects that receive little stress, such as costume jewellery and appliance trim, can be bonded with cyanoacrylate adhesive, also known as superglue. Select the right viscosity: liquid cyanoacrylate for tight-fitting flat surfaces; a thicker gel formula for loose-fitting pieces. Use epoxy where moderate stress is likely, when bonding metal to a nonporous material, or where rough-textured metals fit loosely. Resin and hardener must be in exactly equal proportions: too much hardener causes a weak joint, too little slows drying.

Caution: Work in a well-ventilated area when using adhesives; don't smoke, eat or drink. If cyanoacrylate or epoxy adhesive contacts your skin, remove it promptly with acetone (found in nail polish remover).

Threaded fasteners and rivets are stronger than most adhesives. Fasteners are available in a variety of metals; if possible, match the fastener to the metal being joined. But if rusting is likely, use nonferrous fasteners, such as aluminium or brass.

Screws

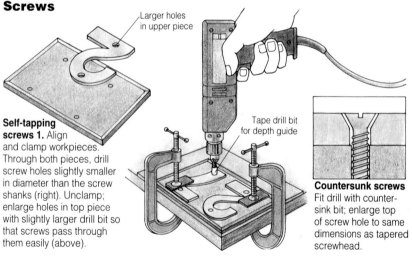

Larger holes in upper piece

Tape drill bit for depth guide

Self-tapping screws 1. Align and clamp workpieces. Through both pieces, drill screw holes slightly smaller in diameter than the screw shanks (right). Unclamp; enlarge holes in top piece with slightly larger drill bit so that screws pass through them easily (above).

Countersunk screws Fit drill with countersink bit; enlarge top of screw hole to same dimensions as tapered screwhead.

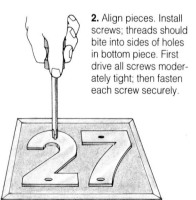

2. Align pieces. Install screws; threads should bite into sides of holes in bottom piece. First drive all screws moderately tight; then fasten each screw securely.

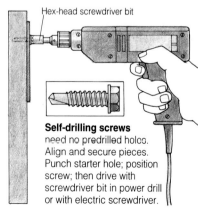

Hex-head screwdriver bit

Self-drilling screws need no predrilled holes. Align and secure pieces. Punch starter hole; position screw; then drive with screwdriver bit in power drill or with electric screwdriver.

Screws for joining sheet metal are usually self-tapping; they are driven with a screwdriver or a nutdriver, and cut threads inside a predrilled hole.

Self-drilling screws will create both a pilot hole and the threads inside; ask the manufacturer for information on the maximum thickness of pieces that can be joined. (To remove threaded fasteners that have become stuck, try the methods shown on page 189.)

For thicker pieces accessible from both sides, use bolts. Coach screws or carriage bolts can be used to attach metal to wood. A tightened bolt should extend beyond the nut by two or three threads. Allow for the additional thickness of washers, which distribute pressure under the bolt head and the nut. A variety of specialised nuts are available; use cap nuts when fastening children's equipment, or wherever safety is a concern, and use wing nuts on bolts that will need to be unfastened. If needed, you can thread bolt holes yourself (p.188).

Blind rivets are strong enough only for light sheet metal work like gutters and aluminium cladding or for car body repairs, but they are easy to install with a blind-rivet tool and are more versatile than ordinary rivets. The work can be accessible from only one side, but there must be enough room for the rivet to be able to form on the other side.

Bolts

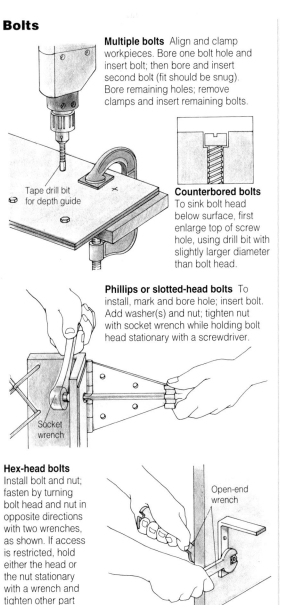

Multiple bolts Align and clamp workpieces. Bore one bolt hole and insert bolt; then bore and insert second bolt (fit should be snug). Bore remaining holes; remove clamps and insert remaining bolts.

Tape drill bit for depth guide

Counterbored bolts To sink bolt head below surface, first enlarge top of screw hole, using drill bit with slightly larger diameter than bolt head.

Phillips or slotted-head bolts To install, mark and bore hole; insert bolt. Add washer(s) and nut; tighten nut with socket wrench while holding bolt head stationary with a screwdriver.

Socket wrench

Hex-head bolts Install bolt and nut; fasten by turning bolt head and nut in opposite directions with two wrenches, as shown. If access is restricted, hold either the head or the nut stationary with a wrench and tighten other part with a socket wrench.

Open-end wrench

Rivets

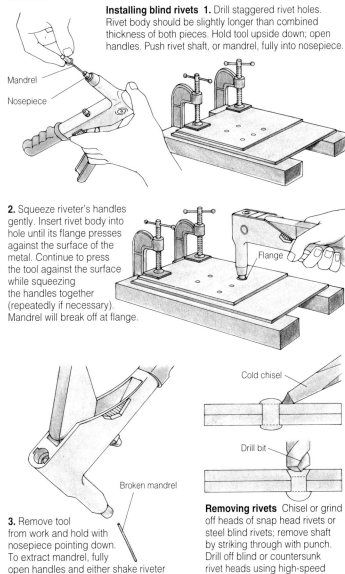

Installing blind rivets 1. Drill staggered rivet holes. Rivet body should be slightly longer than combined thickness of both pieces. Hold tool upside down; open handles. Push rivet shaft, or mandrel, fully into nosepiece.

Mandrel

Nosepiece

2. Squeeze riveter's handles gently. Insert rivet body into hole until its flange presses against the surface of the metal. Continue to press the tool against the surface while squeezing the handles together (repeatedly if necessary). Mandrel will break off at flange.

Flange

3. Remove tool from work and hold with nosepiece pointing down. To extract mandrel, fully open handles and either shake riveter or withdraw mandrel with fingers.

Broken mandrel

Cold chisel

Drill bit

Removing rivets Chisel or grind off heads of snap head rivets or steel blind rivets; remove shaft by striking through with punch. Drill off blind or countersunk rivet heads using high-speed electric drill; punch out shaft.

Taps are used for cutting threads in holes; dies for threading rods. Both tools are often used for renewing damaged threads when repairing car parts, small-engine machinery (lawn mowers, garden tractors, chain saws) and household appliances.

The ISO metric system has been adopted as the standard screw thread in the UK but other thread forms are still available.

British Standard Whitworth (BSW) has a coarse pitch and is used for general engineering and threads in soft material.

British Standard Fine (BSF) has a fine pitch and is used for parts that are subject to vibration, and Unified Fine (UNF) and Unified Coarse (UNC) are commonly used in automotive engineering.

Fully tapped hole goes through workpiece.

Blind hole ends inside workpiece.

Metric taps and dies are stamped with their diameter and the pitch of the screw thread in millimetres. Others are usually stamped with their diameter in inches and the number of threads per inch (tpi).

Drill the hole to be tapped using the drill bit size indicated by a chart (often provided with tap and die sets) or by reading the markings directly on the taps. Complete blind holes with a bottoming tap, which cuts threads to the base of the hole.

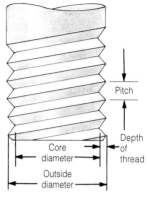

Thread anatomy The outside diameter of threads determines size of tap or die to use for cutting. Drill bit for pilot hole is slightly larger than core diameter.

Drilling tap holes

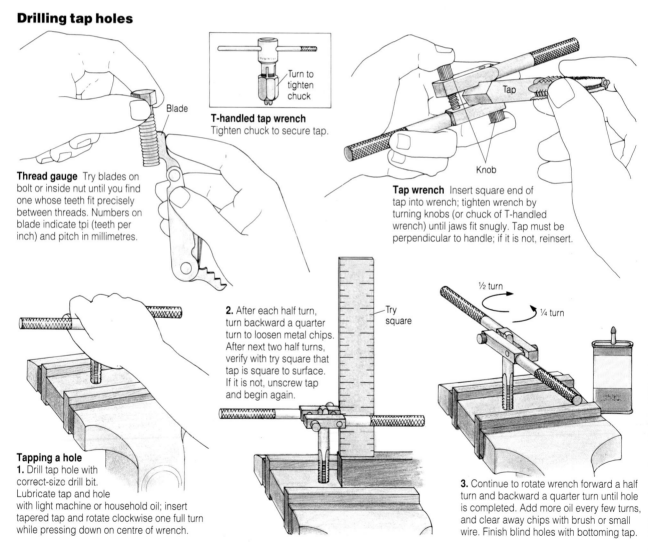

Thread gauge Try blades on bolt or inside nut until you find one whose teeth fit precisely between threads. Numbers on blade indicate tpi (teeth per inch) and pitch in millimetres.

T-handled tap wrench Tighten chuck to secure tap.

Tap wrench Insert square end of tap into wrench; tighten wrench by turning knobs (or chuck of T-handled wrench) until jaws fit snugly. Tap must be perpendicular to handle; if it is not, reinsert.

Tapping a hole
1. Drill tap hole with correct-size drill bit. Lubricate tap and hole with light machine or household oil; insert tapered tap and rotate clockwise one full turn while pressing down on centre of wrench.

2. After each half turn, turn backward a quarter turn to loosen metal chips. After next two half turns, verify with try square that tap is square to surface. If it is not, unscrew tap and begin again.

3. Continue to rotate wrench forward a half turn and backward a quarter turn until hole is completed. Add more oil every few turns, and clear away chips with brush or small wire. Finish blind holes with bottoming tap.

Extracting broken fasteners

A broken or rusted bolt or screw can often be removed by soaking it with penetrating oil for 15 minutes. Then, if the head is accessible, twist out the fastener with locking pliers.

Another method is to strike a centre punch with a ball-pein hammer against one edge of the fastener head, turning the fastener anticlockwise.

For fasteners broken off below the surface, use a screw extractor. Most have left-hand threads; some have straight flutes along the shank. Both are turned anticlockwise with a wrench to extract the broken fastener.

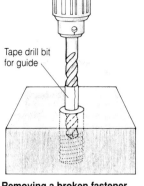

Tape drill bit for guide

Removing a broken fastener
1. Punch starting point in centre of broken fastener. With a drill bit smaller than the fastener, drill at least 10 mm (⅜ in) into broken shaft.

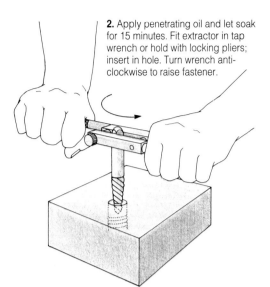

2. Apply penetrating oil and let soak for 15 minutes. Fit extractor in tap wrench or hold with locking pliers; insert in hole. Turn wrench anticlockwise to raise fastener.

Threading rods with dies

Dies are held in a special wrench called a diestock. Some diestocks have an adjustable collar called a diestock guide that fits snugly around the rod to keep the die perpendicular to the handle.

Most tap and die sets include several dies; choose a die whose diameter corresponds to the size of the rod to be threaded. Adjustable dies can be made larger or smaller with a centre screw on one side. To test the fit of an adjustable die, cut the threads first with the die fully open. Screw a nut onto the rod. If the fit is too tight, adjust the die so it is smaller and recut the threads.

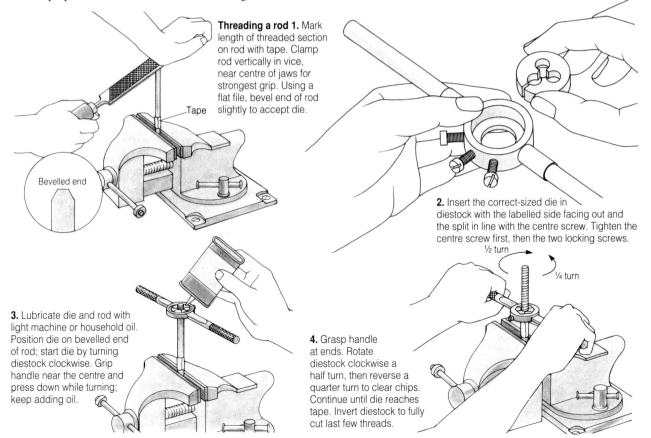

Threading a rod 1. Mark length of threaded section on rod with tape. Clamp rod vertically in vice, near centre of jaws for strongest grip. Using a flat file, bevel end of rod slightly to accept die.

Tape

Bevelled end

2. Insert the correct-sized die in diestock with the labelled side facing out and the split in line with the centre screw. Tighten the centre screw first, then the two locking screws.

½ turn

¼ turn

3. Lubricate die and rod with light machine or household oil. Position die on bevelled end of rod; start die by turning diestock clockwise. Grip handle near the centre and press down while turning; keep adding oil.

4. Grasp handle at ends. Rotate diestock clockwise a half turn, then reverse a quarter turn to clear chips. Continue until die reaches tape. Invert diestock to fully cut last few threads.

SOLDERING

Soldering joins metals by melting between them an alloy, called solder, that acts as a glue. For soft-soldering, the usual method for joining sheet metals and electronic parts, the solder is made chiefly of tin and lead; copper plumbing pipes should be joined with lead-free solder. These solders melt at 371°C or under – too low a temperature to cause changes in the metals being joined. Hard-soldering creates stronger joints and is needed to join silver or for fine craft work. Silver solder contains silver, copper and zinc, with melting points between 593°C and 788°C. Heating a metal to accept hard solder creates microscopic spaces into which the solder can flow; so hard-soldered joints have more strength than soft-soldered joints and can be filed flush without weakening.

Brazing is a type of hard-soldering generally used to join steel or dissimilar metals; it requires a brass solder with a melting point between 982°C and 1649°C. It requires skill and the high heat created by an air/fuel torch.

An electric soldering pencil or gun provides sufficient heat for soft-soldering stained-glass joints or small electronic components. To soft-solder metal objects, use an electric soldering iron. A propane torch produces a flame suitable both for soldering copper pipes and for hard-soldering.

Before soldering, cover the surfaces with the appropriate flux to avoid the formation of oxides, a dark scaly film that prevents solder from adhering. For soft-soldering all except electronic items, use a zinc chloride flux, wiping away any excess with a cloth after soldering. Delicate electronic work requires a resin flux, which is less messy to work with. For hard-soldering use fluxes containing borax.

After hard-soldering, remove oxides with pickle, which is a cleaning solution. Use a pickle that does not contain sulphuric acid – available from craft and jewellery suppliers.

Soft-soldering with an iron

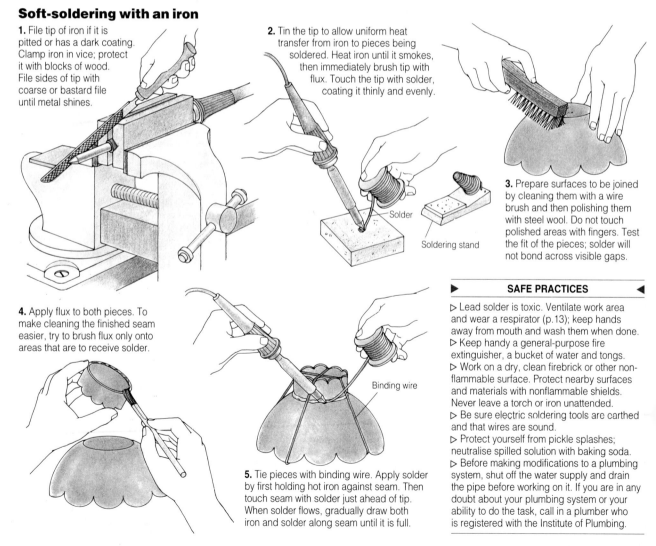

1. File tip of iron if it is pitted or has a dark coating. Clamp iron in vice; protect it with blocks of wood. File sides of tip with coarse or bastard file until metal shines.

2. Tin the tip to allow uniform heat transfer from iron to pieces being soldered. Heat iron until it smokes, then immediately brush tip with flux. Touch the tip with solder, coating it thinly and evenly.

Solder

Soldering stand

3. Prepare surfaces to be joined by cleaning them with a wire brush and then polishing them with steel wool. Do not touch polished areas with fingers. Test the fit of the pieces; solder will not bond across visible gaps.

4. Apply flux to both pieces. To make cleaning the finished seam easier, try to brush flux only onto areas that are to receive solder.

Binding wire

5. Tie pieces with binding wire. Apply solder by first holding hot iron against seam. Then touch seam with solder just ahead of tip. When solder flows, gradually draw both iron and solder along seam until it is full.

SAFE PRACTICES

▷ Lead solder is toxic. Ventilate work area and wear a respirator (p.13); keep hands away from mouth and wash them when done.
▷ Keep handy a general-purpose fire extinguisher, a bucket of water and tongs.
▷ Work on a dry, clean firebrick or other non-flammable surface. Protect nearby surfaces and materials with nonflammable shields. Never leave a torch or iron unattended.
▷ Be sure electric soldering tools are earthed and that wires are sound.
▷ Protect yourself from pickle splashes; neutralise spilled solution with baking soda.
▷ Before making modifications to a plumbing system, shut off the water supply and drain the pipe before working on it. If you are in any doubt about your plumbing system or your ability to do the task, call in a plumber who is registered with the Institute of Plumbing.

Soldering copper pipes

1. Clean fitting and pipe. Ream inside pipe to remove burrs (p.185). With steel wool (above) or a wire brush, polish pieces until they shine; then apply a thin coat of flux to both pieces (below).

2. Heat joint area. Tack a piece of non-flammable material to nearby surfaces. Brush entire joint with torch flame to heat it thoroughly, concentrating more heat on heavier part of fitting.

3. Apply solder to joint. When flux bubbles, touch solder to side of fitting opposite flame. At correct temperature, solder will melt instantly and flow around seam. Hold flame away from seam as solder flows. Wipe off excess solder with damp cloth.

Hard-soldering with a torch

Flame is hottest above inner core

Spark maker

1. Prepare and flux surfaces as for soft-soldering, using appropriate flux. Light torch by holding tank upright, opening valve about half a turn, then igniting gas with spark maker held beside nozzle. Adjust flame to produce pointed inner cone.

2. Heat metal near seam until the flux bubbles. Hold solder with tweezers and apply to seam while holding flame to one side as solder flows.

For delicate work, cut solder sheet into small squares; place them where pieces will join. Apply flame evenly to both pieces; as metal heats, solder will melt into joint.

3. Clean oxidised pieces by dipping into pickle. Do not boil heating solution – follow manufacturer's instructions. Hold piece with brass tongs only; steel or iron will affect metal. Rinse pieces under running water.

Welding and blacksmithing

Welding joins metals – usually steel – by melting them so that they fuse together. The high heat required can come from a torch that mixes fuel with pure oxygen or from a powerful electric transformer called an arc welder. Strong welded joints are required for repairs to machinery, metal furniture and outdoor equipment, as well as to tools and to metal used for structural purposes. Though fairly simple in theory, welding requires expert instruction and much practice. Secondary schools and vocational schools may offer courses in welding, and hire shops carry welding equipment.

Blacksmithing has seen a revival in interest in recent years. Ample space and equipment is needed, including a forge for heating metal and a selection of hammers and stakes for pounding it into shape. Craft items like fireplace tools, decorative hardware and wrought-iron gates are the stock-in-trade of most modern-day smiths.

Local colleges may offer courses in blacksmithing. Equipment can be homemade or bought at car boot sales and auctions. A smith who shoes horses is known as a farrier; for instruction consult an agricultural college.

Wire – round, half-round, square and rectangular – serves as a basis for many jewellery and metalworking projects. Wire can be pulled through a metal drawplate (a process called drawing) to change its shape and thickness; it can be decoratively twisted by itself or with other wires; and it can be fashioned into jump rings, then used to form a chain or create findings – the elements that hold together many jewellery pieces.

Finger rings are made with wire or with strips cut from sheet metal. Use a graduated ring mandrel, which has standard ring sizes marked at intervals along its length, to form new rings or to reshape damaged ones. Calculate the length of metal needed to form a given ring size by using the linear scale provided on some mandrels, or by forming a template from a strip of paper. First wrap the paper around the desired ring size on the mandrel, then add twice the thickness of the metal stock for the template's total length.

The metal found in commercial chain is sometimes filled with solder, which lowers its melting point and makes it difficult to repair by soldering. Homemade solid wire jump rings, however, make durable links and chains. Making circular jump rings is shown; you can also create oval and square jump rings by winding the wire around a form with the desired shape.

Buy commercial findings – such as settings for stones, clasps for necklaces and bracelets and posts for earrings and cufflinks – at craft or jewellery suppliers, and use them to replace broken findings or to form new pieces. Unless you are experienced, don't try to repair or set valuable stones; it is easy to lose or damage them.

Hard-soldering with the technique for delicate work shown on page 191 is the best way to join metal jewellery pieces. For a project with many joints, use silver solder designated hard, medium and easy-flo in succession to avoid melting completed joints while heating others. Glue together any pieces that can't be heated (p.186).

Working with wire

Drawing wire File wire tip to a 2.5 cm (1 in) long point; then lubricate it with beeswax or light household oil. Clamp drawplate in vice; insert wire from plate's unnumbered side into smallest possible hole of desired shape. Hold tip; pull wire through hole. Pull through successively smaller holes until wire reaches desired gauge. Anneal frequently (below).

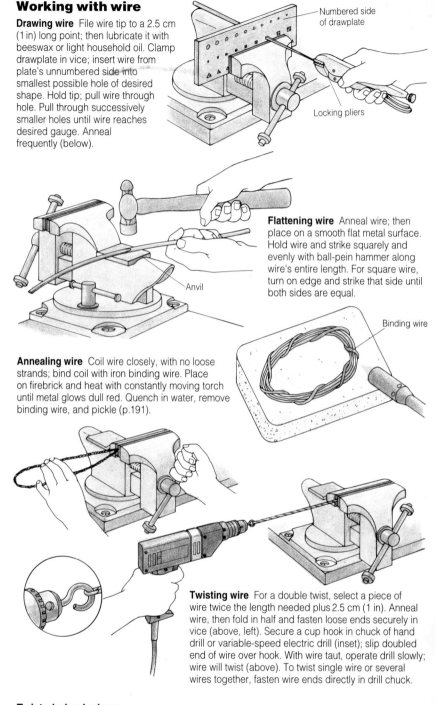

Flattening wire Anneal wire; then place on a smooth flat metal surface. Hold wire and strike squarely and evenly with ball-pein hammer along wire's entire length. For square wire, turn on edge and strike that side until both sides are equal.

Annealing wire Coil wire closely, with no loose strands; bind coil with iron binding wire. Place on firebrick and heat with constantly moving torch until metal glows dull red. Quench in water, remove binding wire, and pickle (p.191).

Twisting wire For a double twist, select a piece of wire twice the length needed plus 2.5 cm (1 in). Anneal wire, then fold in half and fasten loose ends securely in vice (above, left). Secure a cup hook in chuck of hand drill or variable-speed electric drill (inset); slip doubled end of wire over hook. With wire taut, operate drill slowly; wire will twist (above). To twist single wire or several wires together, fasten wire ends directly in drill chuck.

Twisted wire designs

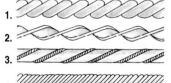

1.
2.
3.
4.

Twisted wire can form rings, patterns on flat brooches, earrings or bracelets. To make a bracelet, loop wire to desired diameter and solder ends together.
1. Double-twist round wire, then flatten.
2. Twist single strand of flat wire.
3. First twist single square wire, then double-twist round wire and wind together by hand.
4. Twist together several strands of round wire.

Forming a ring

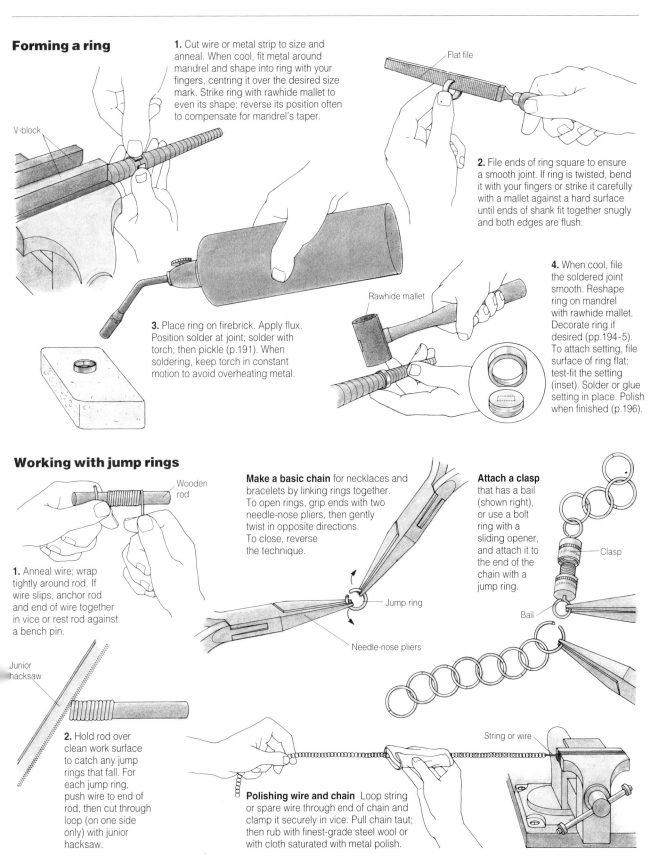

1. Cut wire or metal strip to size and anneal. When cool, fit metal around mandrel and shape into ring with your fingers, centring it over the desired size mark. Strike ring with rawhide mallet to even its shape; reverse its position often to compensate for mandrel's taper.

V-block

Flat file

2. File ends of ring square to ensure a smooth joint. If ring is twisted, bend it with your fingers or strike it carefully with a mallet against a hard surface until ends of shank fit together snugly and both edges are flush.

4. When cool, file the soldered joint smooth. Reshape ring on mandrel with rawhide mallet. Decorate ring if desired (pp.194-5). To attach setting, file surface of ring flat; test-fit the setting (inset). Solder or glue setting in place. Polish when finished (p.196).

Rawhide mallet

3. Place ring on firebrick. Apply flux. Position solder at joint; solder with torch; then pickle (p.191). When soldering, keep torch in constant motion to avoid overheating metal.

Working with jump rings

Wooden rod

1. Anneal wire; wrap tightly around rod. If wire slips, anchor rod and end of wire together in vice or rest rod against a bench pin.

Junior hacksaw

2. Hold rod over clean work surface to catch any jump rings that fall. For each jump ring, push wire to end of rod, then cut through loop (on one side only) with junior hacksaw.

Make a basic chain for necklaces and bracelets by linking rings together. To open rings, grip ends with two needle-nose pliers, then gently twist in opposite directions. To close, reverse the technique.

Jump ring

Needle-nose pliers

Attach a clasp that has a bail (shown right), or use a bolt ring with a sliding opener, and attach it to the end of the chain with a jump ring.

Clasp

Bail

String or wire

Polishing wire and chain Loop string or spare wire through end of chain and clamp it securely in vice. Pull chain taut; then rub with finest-grade steel wool or with cloth saturated with metal polish.

Metal objects can be decorated by a variety of techniques; among them are hammering, and etching and colouring with chemicals. Decoration must be applied at the appropriate point during construction. For example, items like bowls or vases that are shaped by raising or sinking cannot be decorated until after they are formed. But an item with flat sides can be decorated before it is folded or attached to other pieces. Practise decorative techniques on pieces of scrap metal before attempting them on the actual piece.

Planishing is the technique of hardening and smoothing metal by hammering. A skilfully planished surface has many small indentations that add texture and sparkle to the piece. Polished hammers are reserved for planishing; keep their faces smooth (p.196). A ball-pein hammer can also be used to create patterned surfaces – reflecting the various contours of either the face of the hammer or the surface it strikes. Always wear safety goggles when striking metal with hammers.

Cutting holes to form a pattern in the metal is called piercing. Holes are started with a fine drill and cut out with a piercing saw.

In chasing, blunt punches, struck with a hammer, are used to create a pattern in shallow relief. When the pattern is also raised in relief by hammering it from behind, the

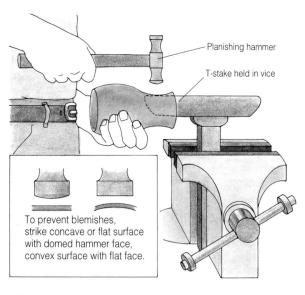

Planishing hammer

T-stake held in vice

To prevent blemishes, strike concave or flat surface with domed hammer face, convex surface with flat face.

Planishing Hold piece on stake or against other hard surface. Work with light in front of you. Strike squarely and evenly with planishing hammer, working in a spiral from base to rim (for a bowl, work from centre outwards). Deliver blows from wrist; overlap points of impact.

Chasing and repoussé

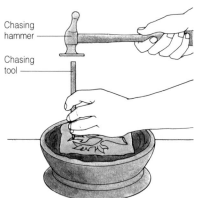

Chasing hammer

Chasing tool

1. Heat pitch and mount work face-up in pitch bowl so that metal is supported at all points. Trace outline and details with chasing tool by striking tool end lightly with hammer. Hold tools firmly to avoid slips; deliver blows from wrist.

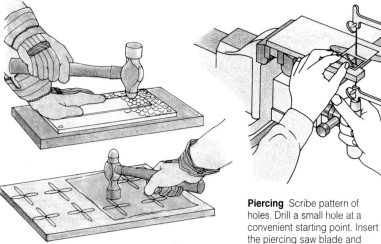

Impact and hammer textures For a dimpled pattern, hold work against a hard surface; strike work with a round hammer face (top). To reproduce a surface texture, hold workpiece against surface; strike workpiece all over with flat face until design is imprinted (bottom).

Piercing Scribe pattern of holes. Drill a small hole at a convenient starting point. Insert the piercing saw blade and then fasten it to the saw frame. Holding the work on a V-board which is clamped in a vice, cut round the pattern, keeping the saw vertical and cutting only on the downward stroke.

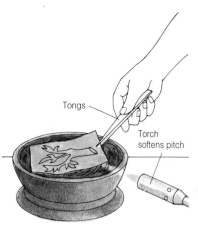

Tongs

Torch softens pitch

2. Warm pitch to remove chased work. For repoussé work, anneal (p.183); then mount work face-down in pitch and emboss with repoussé tools, using the same hammer technique as for chasing. Proceed alternately on front and back until design is defined.

technique is called repoussé. Strike both chasing and repoussé tools with a lightweight chasing hammer on a surface that yields slightly. Pitch set in a special bowl is ideal (it is available at metalworking suppliers), but softwood or a sandbag can serve equally well as a work surface. Heat pitch with a torch to soften it before positioning or removing an object, but do not ignite it. To remove excess pitch, soak the metal in lacquer thinner.

In etching, a design is created on metal by dissolving part of the surface with a corrosive mordant. This is usually nitric acid and its use is best left to professionals. However, copper, zinc and brass can be etched with ferric chloride, a safer solution available at electronics, printmakers and crafts suppliers. The parts of the design to be protected from the mordant are coated with a resist, which can be a wax solution called liquid etching ground.

Exposing metals to some chemicals creates a thin layer of corrosion that changes their patina, or texture and colour. After treatment, polish the metal if desired (pp.196-7), then protect it from further coloration by giving it a coat of lacquer or wax.

Caution: Wear safety goggles and rubber gloves when working with chemicals, and follow any other precautions for handling, storage and disposal listed by the manufacturer.

Etching

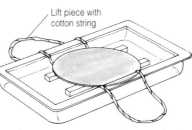

Metal scriber

1. Degrease surface first, with a weak ammonia solution. Paint on liquid etching ground, front and back, and scribe the design onto it (above). Or cover clean metal with a stencil and paint on liquid etching ground into uncovered areas (below). Remove stencil; tidy edges with a sharp tool.

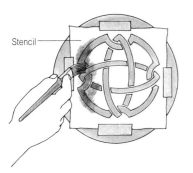

Stencil

Lift piece with cotton string

2. Submerge piece upside-down on plastic supports in the mordant in a glass or plastic container. Rock the container gently to encourage solid deposits to fall out of the line.

3. After 30 minutes, rinse piece with water and check progress. Repeat every 15 minutes until metal has dissolved to desired depth. Remove resist with soft cloth soaked in white spirit.

Protecting finished surfaces

Lacquer creates a hard film that resists marking and scratches. Brush or spray on two thin coats; allow to dry in between. For small items, substitute clear nail polish.

Wax seals out air and moisture where hard finish is not desired. Select a fine-quality furniture wax that contains no silicone. Apply, allow to harden and then buff with clean soft cloth. Repeat until desired sheen is achieved.

Creating a patina

When treating metal objects to create a surface patina, adjust the recipes below proportionally if greater or smaller amounts are needed for the size of the object. The effect of the treatment will vary depending on the type of metal and the surrounding conditions; try recipes on scrap metal first. Before treatment, wash metal thoroughly in a bucket of water mixed with detergent and a tablespoon of ammonia; when the metal is clean, water will no longer form beads on the surface. Dry the metal with a clean soft cloth, and from then on handle it only by the edges. Mix chemicals in a glass or porcelain container and use only distilled water. Check the object frequently to gauge its progress. Follow the manufacturer's instructions for storage and handling of chemicals.

To darken silver or copper, mix 15 ml potassium sulphide (available from jewellery and crafts suppliers) in 200 ml warm water. Hold the piece with tongs and dip it into the solution. Rinse under running water.

To darken steel, aluminium or bronze, apply gun blueing, available at gun shops. Rub the blueing over the metal with fine-grade steel wool until you achieve the desired effect.

To give copper a variegated blue pattern, wet the piece, then sprinkle it with table salt. Place the object beside an open bowl of ammonia and cover both with a plastic bucket or small plastic tent. Leave until the desired effect is achieved (sometimes several days).

To colour copper, brass or bronze green, mix 15 ml ammonium chloride (sal ammoniac, available from jewellery and crafts suppliers), 15 ml table salt and 30 ml ammonia in about 1 litre warm water. Pour solution into a plastic spray bottle and spray the piece all over. Allow to dry; keep on repeating the process until the desired effect is achieved.

To turn copper dark brown, coat your fingers with a thin film of linseed oil, then rub the piece all over, applying just enough oil to cover the surface. Warm the piece evenly with a propane torch until the oil starts to smoke. Wipe off excess oil with a clean cloth.

The final stages of many metalworking projects are sanding, which smoothes the surface, and buffing, which creates sheen or lustre. (For filing, which removes rough edges and burrs, see page 181.)

Complete polishing consists of rubbing with successively finer grades of abrasive, beginning by hand with abrasive paper (or by using an attachment on a portable power drill), and then buffing with an electric polishing machine, such as a bench grinder.

Start with a medium (120 grit) or very fine (240 grit) abrasive – silicon carbide is a good choice. When the surface is uniform, switch to an extra-fine (320 grit) abrasive. For a fine polish, work up to at least a 400 grit abrasive, then buff.

Buff on a bench grinder fitted with a cloth disc called a buffing wheel. Hold large items in your hands, but brace smaller or flat items against a board. The wheel should always rotate downwards towards you.

To buff rings and other extremely small objects, slip them onto a tapered mandrel or shaped dowel. Working slightly lower than the centre of the wheel, present the item to the wheel, turning it slowly to expose every part of it. Wear safety goggles, and allow no one to stand where they might be hit by an item accidentally pulled from your grasp by the wheel.

Apply buffing compounds directly to the wheel; start with either tripoli or white diamond and proceed to rouge. Install a separate wheel for each compound. After using each one, clean the metal by washing it with a mixture of household detergent, water and a few drops of ammonia. Rubber gloves will prevent compounds from soiling your hands.

A portable power drill fitted with a buffing pad attachment and clamped into a horizontal drill stand can substitute for buffing with a bench grinder. Fit the drill into the stand, and run it with the trigger locked. Apply the polishing compound and buff as you would with a grinder.

Preliminary polishing
Secure piece; rub metal with abrasive paper wrapped round stick, file or dowel. Use two or more grades of abrasive; alternate direction of strokes with each successive grade.

Sanding block

Polishing hammer face Clamp hammer in vice; polish as described above but with abrasive paper wrapped round wood block or secured in sanding block. To buff, coat leather-covered block with white diamond compound; rub hammer face with circular motion.

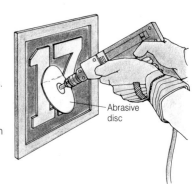

Portable drill speeds polishing. Fit abrasive disc (shown) or buffing pad on a drill arbor according to manufacturer's instructions. If object is not stationary, clamp it securely. Running tool at high speed, move disc across surface at even rate; exert light pressure. Wear goggles and gloves.

Abrasive disc

Buffing with a bench grinder

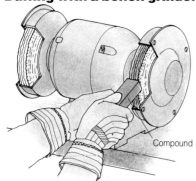

Preparing wheel Wear goggles and gloves. Touch end of compound stick to moving wheel below centre-line. Coat wheel evenly with compound every 5 minutes during use. When surface becomes shiny, hold buff rake (or an old fork) against surface of pad until the cloth is no longer compacted; then reapply compound.

Compound

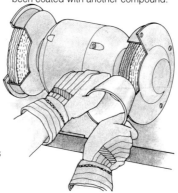

Buffing Grip work tightly with fingers; hold below wheel's centreline. Turn piece constantly to expose whole surface. Clean work before changing to a wheel that has been coated with another compound.

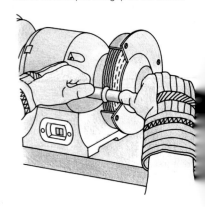

Buffing small items Fit the item over a shaped dowel (shown below) or a tapered mandrel. Present it to the buffing wheel, turning slowly. Wear gloves to protect your hands and keep a firm grip on the dowel.

REPAIRING METAL OBJECTS

Metal objects with minor rust and damage can usually be repaired. But rust destroys metal quickly; prevent it by painting outdoor tools, toys and other items with rust-resistant paint and storing them in a dry place, and by using galvanised metal for outdoor fasteners, railings and fencing.

Clean metal with mild detergent and water, and brighten tarnished metal by rubbing it with commercial polish. Careful malleting on a sandbag, stake or with the aid of a dolly block (a polished steel block available at car accessory shops) flattens dents. Solder small cracks (p.190) or patch cracks and holes with a two-part glass fibre repair kit, available at hardware and car accessory shops. Read the kit maker's instructions before use: some of these compounds are not suitable for making structural repairs or repairs to containers of liquid or gas.

An alternative to sanding away rust is a rust-inhibiting fluid. Scrape off any loose rust, then apply the fluid. It hardens and seals the remaining rust, creating a rustproof surface that can be primed and painted.

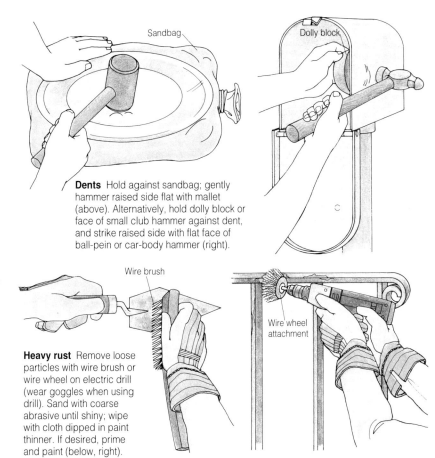

Dents Hold against sandbag; gently hammer raised side flat with mallet (above). Alternatively, hold dolly block or face of small club hammer against dent, and strike raised side with flat face of ball-pein or car-body hammer (right).

Heavy rust Remove loose particles with wire brush or wire wheel on electric drill (wear goggles when using drill). Sand with coarse abrasive until shiny; wipe with cloth dipped in paint thinner. If desired, prime and paint (below, right).

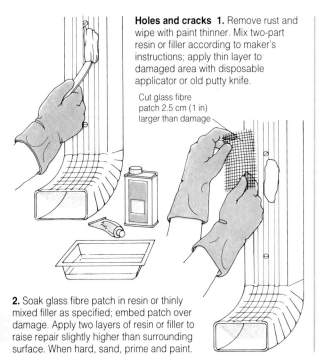

Holes and cracks 1. Remove rust and wipe with paint thinner. Mix two-part resin or filler according to maker's instructions; apply thin layer to damaged area with disposable applicator or old putty knife.

Cut glass fibre patch 2.5 cm (1 in) larger than damage

2. Soak glass fibre patch in resin or thinly mixed filler as specified; embed patch over damage. Apply two layers of resin or filler to raise repair slightly higher than surrounding surface. When hard, sand, prime and paint.

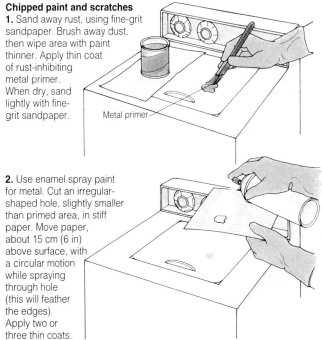

Chipped paint and scratches
1. Sand away rust, using fine-grit sandpaper. Brush away dust, then wipe area with paint thinner. Apply thin coat of rust-inhibiting metal primer. When dry, sand lightly with fine-grit sandpaper.

Metal primer

2. Use enamel spray paint for metal. Cut an irregular-shaped hole, slightly smaller than primed area, in stiff paper. Move paper, about 15 cm (6 in) above surface, with a circular motion while spraying through hole (this will feather the edges). Apply two or three thin coats.

Inspect tools before each use; a dull tool is neither efficient nor safe. With practice and good equipment, you can sharpen most straightedged tools. But saw blades, carbide-tipped tools and other hardened or contoured edges are best sharpened professionally.

Sharpening causes the sides of a blade to meet at an angle, called a bevel, the steepness of which is crucial to the blade's performance.

In general, resharpen a blade to its original bevel. Chisel and plane blades come with bevels ranging from 15° to 30°. Add a narrow secondary bevel 5°

degrees greater; this speeds honing by reducing the cutting area. Hollow-grinding (grinding the primary bevel against the edge of the bench grinder wheel until the blade is slightly concave) produces a similar result.

Primary bevel

Secondary bevel

Hollow ground

A bench grinder speeds sharpening and is very useful for reshaping damaged edges. Buy new grinding wheels as needed; install a medium and a fine-grit wheel to use as a pair.

When grinding, follow the safety precautions listed below and on pages 12-13. Improper use of a bench grinder is not only highly dangerous, it can destroy the tool's temper, that is, its hardness and resiliency.

Hand-sharpen and hone blades with flat sharpening stones and curved slipstones. A good selection includes either a combination coarse/fine India or silicon carbide stone and two waterstones, one of 1000 grit and a second that is 6000 grit. Keep the stones well lubricated. For a keen edge, finish up with a leather strop.

Sharpening with a bench grinder

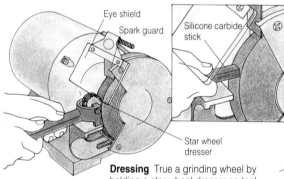

Eye shield
Spark guard
Silicone carbide stick
Star wheel dresser

Dressing True a grinding wheel by holding a star wheel dresser on tool rest; while running the grinder, slide dresser lightly from side to side against wheel's edge (above). To restore clogged wheel, use same technique, but with silicon carbide stick (inset).

Hollow grinding Set tool rest to desired bevel angle. Hold tool with both hands; place on rest and slide from side to side against edge of wheel. Keep forefinger against bottom edge of rest to steady tool.

Tool rest

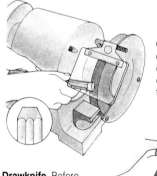

Cold chisel Grind away mushroomed or split head of cold chisel to reduce chances of splintering, which can cause injury. Taper ground end (inset) to reduce chance of future damage.

Drawknife Before grinding, ensure that blade can move freely across grinder wheel. Bevel blade by sliding it across the wheel, supported on the tool rest. To hone, clamp one handle of tool in vice; start at opposite end and slide sharpening stone along blade's bevelled side. To remove burr, reverse tool and repeat on other side.

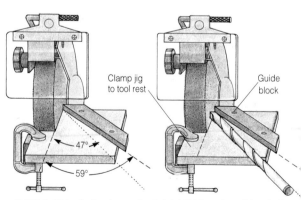

Clamp jig to tool rest
Guide block
47°
59°

Drill bit Make jig for sharpening twist drill bit against side-grinding wheel. Clamp jig to level tool rest; place bit on jig against guide block. Press one side of tip against wheel; roll bit clockwise while slowly pivoting it to guideline at 47°. Repeat for other side.

Honing a sharp edge

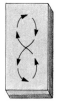 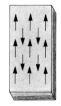

To prevent uneven wear on stone, move blade in figure 8 pattern. Simpler technique is back-and-forth motion.

Hone primary bevel on chisels, plane irons and spokeshaves by rubbing blade over medium stone (above, right) until you can feel a burr on blade's flat side. To create secondary bevel, raise blade 5° (inset) and rub over fine stone until burr forms. Remove burr both times (right) by gently rubbing blade's flat side on stone until blade is smooth.

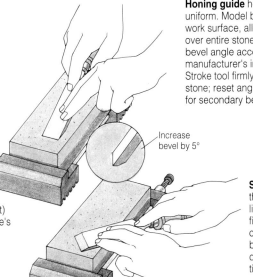

Increase bevel by 5°

Stone holder

Honing guide helps to keep angles uniform. Model below rolls along flat work surface, allowing blade to travel over entire stone. Fit tool and set bevel angle according to manufacturer's instructions. Stroke tool firmly along stone; reset angle for secondary bevel.

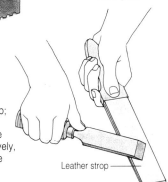

Angle gauge

Roller guide

Strop on leather that has been lightly coated with fine polishing compound. Hold blade against strop; draw back several times on each side of blade. Alternatively, hone on a very fine stone (6000 grit).

Leather strop

Special techniques

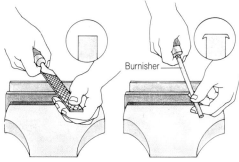

Burnisher

Scraper Clamp in vice; protect with scrap wood. Make edge perfectly square with file or stone (left). For bevelled cabinet scrapers, file bevel to original angle. Create burr (hooked edge) by pushing burnisher along edge while pressing down firmly (right). On final strokes, tilt tool downwards slightly to make burr curl over.

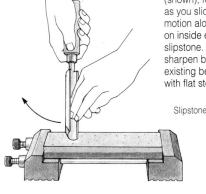

Gouges On gouge with outside bevel (shown), follow the existing bevel angle as you slide the edge with a rotating motion along a flat stone. Remove burr on inside edge by stroking with a slipstone. On gouge with inside bevel, sharpen by stroking with slipstone at existing bevel angle; remove burr with flat stone.

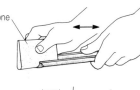

Slipstone

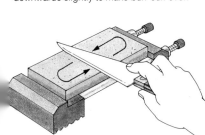

Knife With cutting edge leading, draw blade across stone from handle to tip. Maintain bevel angle. Turn blade over and repeat. Use same number of strokes for each side. Strop for razor edge.

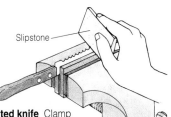

Slipstone

Serrated knife Clamp knife in vice with bevelled side of serrations facing. Sharpen each serration by stroking lightly with curved edge of slipstone held at bevel angle. Remove burrs by rubbing unbevelled side of blade on flat stone.

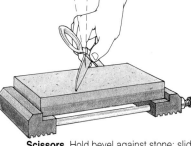

10°

Scissors Hold bevel against stone; slide blade forwards diagonally along stone, moving from point to pivot. Repeat for other blade. Remove burrs by opening and closing scissors several times.

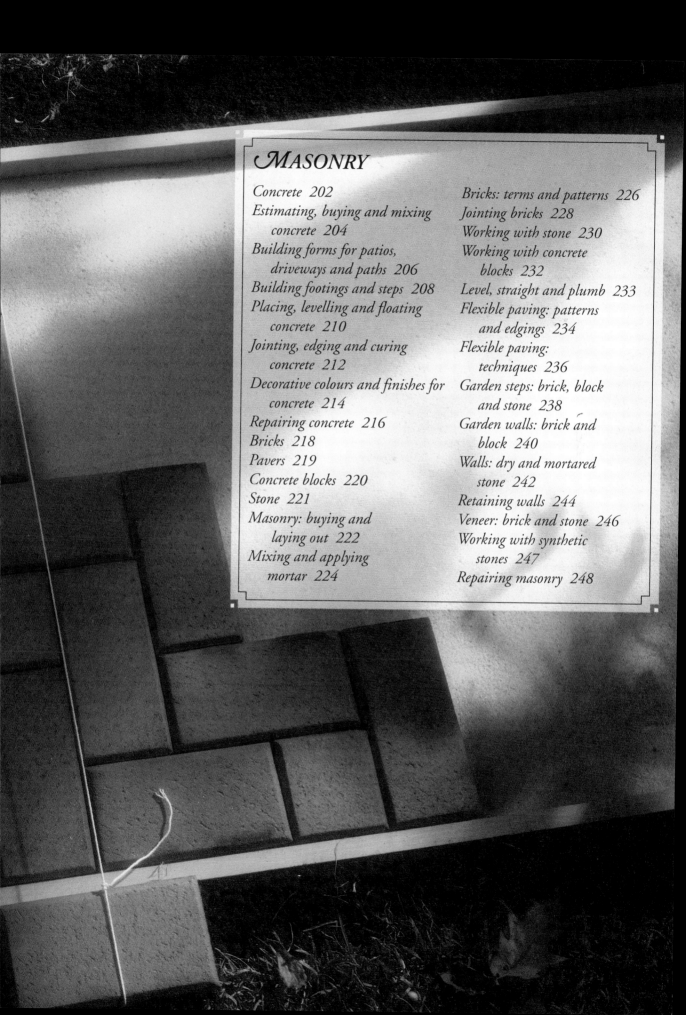

MASONRY

Concrete is a mixture of sand and coarse aggregates – either gravel or crushed stone – held together by cement. When mixed with water, the cement hardens by chemically reacting with the water (not by drying out) and adheres to particles of aggregate in the mixture – and to anything else it touches, so keep clean all the tools you use with fresh concrete.

For the vast majority of concrete work, the cheapest cement is best. Sulphate-resisting cement may be required for critical foundations in certain clay soils. High alumina cement should be used if the concrete is to be exposed to intense heat or strong acids.

If in any doubt about a project, seek professional advice.

Metallic-oxide permanent pigments can be added for colour. Brighter colours can be obtained by using a more expensive, white cement.

You can also liven up a concrete surface before it sets by roughening it, carving designs into it, adding exposed aggregate or imprinting or rolling it with a pattern.

Aggregate can vary widely in colour and shape – even pieces within the same type may vary. For the best results, make sure the pieces are as uniform as possible and choose a shape and size suitable to the project. Standard sizes are 5 mm (concreting sand), 10 mm, 20 mm and 40 mm. Builder's sand is too soft for use in concrete.

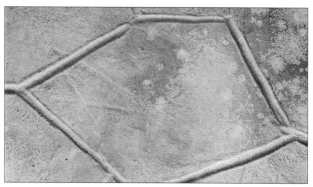

False flagstone effect can be hand-tooled easily into concrete before it sets. If you wish, add a colour pigment to the concrete mix. Strike off the poured concrete, smooth it with a float, cut the outlines of flagstones into the surface with a brick jointing tool and smooth the surface again. Spray on a colour sealer when the concrete is hard.

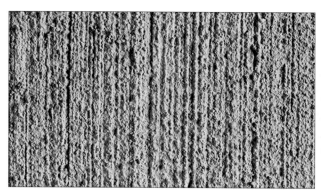

Brooming, achieved by dragging the bristles of a yard broom over wet concrete, yields a rough-textured, nonslip surface. The 'grain' usually runs straight, either along the length of the surface or across it, but there are many decorative variations, including wavy grain, diagonals and alternating diagonals. Colour can be added to the concrete.

Pebbled surface, or exposed aggregate finish, offers a more variable type of rough-textured surface than brooming. Sprinkle decorative aggregate randomly or in a pattern over the surface of poured concrete (coloured or not) before it sets. When the concrete is firm, wash and brush the surface to expose the tops of the aggregate.

Decorative aggregates used in textured concrete vary widely in colour and shape according to the rock. You can use any kind, but rounds and cubes cover best and rough textures bond better than smooth ones; flat stones tend to dislodge. Do not use a flaky aggregate as shown in the top left sample.

Basket weave

Herringbone

Square

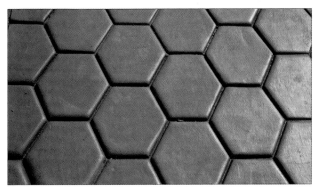

Hexagon

Charcoal cobblestone

Yellow-ochre cobblestone

Imprinting offers a quick method of creating a false finish with a repeat pattern. By pressing an imprinting tool into wet concrete (which is usually coloured), you can create any number of designs to make a driveway, path or patio floor look as though it is paved with bricks, cobblestones, slate, granite, concrete paving stones or tiles. A few of the patterns available in commercially made imprinting tools are shown here. You can use a single pattern for an entire area, or combine two or more to create a more creative design or to add a border or separate a section. Seal the imprinted concrete after it has hardened.

Compared with hand-laid paving stones, imprinted concrete does not tilt out of level so easily because of frost, and there are no spaces between units for grass and weeds to grow through. However, if the surface is damaged, you must replace the entire slab, or at least a large section of it, rather than only one or two individual paving stones.

Running bond brick

A successful concrete project requires careful planning and preparation. First, determine the composition of your concrete. Choose aggregate that is no larger in diameter than one-third of the slab's thickness. Aggregate larger than 2 cm (¾ in) is hard to spread and to compact with hand tools. Select a mix from the table below.

Outdoor projects, especially those that must withstand freezing and thawing without surface scaling, require air-entrained concrete. Tiny air bubbles in the mixture act as pressure-relief chambers to absorb ice as it expands when the concrete freezes. These bubbles also make this type of concrete easy to work with. An air-entraining agent can be bought from builders' merchants in the form of one sachet to be mixed with one bag of cement. The sand content should then be reduced to 60 litres (2.1 cu ft) or two level boxes.

To blend the ingredients properly, always mix air-entrained concrete in a mechanical cement mixer. To estimate how much concrete you need, use mathematical formulas (p.344) or graph paper (below). Add 5-10 per cent for wastage.

Paths, patios and driveways must be 10 cm (4 in) thick – 15 cm (6 in) for any areas of heavy traffic.

Measuring based on weight is more accurate than that based on volume because sand increases in volume when wet. The water content is not shown in the table because it varies so much with aggregate shape, grading and moisture content and the workability required. It will be about 20 litres (0.7 cu ft), but use only half of this to start with and add more to give the minimum workability required to achieve full compaction. Too much water reduces strength and durability and increases drying shrinkage.

If a project needs 1 m³ (1.3 cu yd) or more, consider using ready-mixed concrete. Franchise operations are available in many areas, and the ingredients are mixed to your orders at the site. Have the site prepared and helpers on hand when the concrete arrives. Advice on quantities and mixes is also available. Look in *Yellow Pages* under 'Concrete products' and 'Concrete – ready mixed'.

For small jobs, it is possible to buy premixed bagged concrete with all the dry ingredients in correct proportions. Just add clean water and blend with a hoe, spade or trowel. Or you can buy the dry ingredients in separate bags from builders' merchants.

Caution: Wet concrete can cause serious burns. Wear long sleeves, long trousers, rubber boots and gloves as well as goggles. Wash concrete splashes off your skin with water, and off any tools, before it hardens.

Estimating concrete quantities

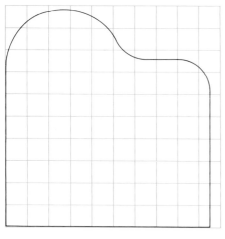

To find the volume of an irregular shape Lay out the design on the ground, staking it at its widest points. Measure; then draw the shape to scale on graph paper with one square equalling 1m² (1.2 sq yd). Count all the filled squares and those that are one-third or more filled. Then multiply the area by the thickness to find cubic metres.

Determine moisture content of sand by squeezing. Damp sand won't stick together. Properly wet sand (above) forms ball but leaves no noticeable moisture on palm. Overly wet sand forms ball and leaves palm moist.

To measure by volume, build a bottomless gauge box with inner volume of 30 litres (310 x 310 x 310 mm). Place box on flat surface. Fill, then lift box away. Take measured ingredients to mixing site. Alternatively, use three 10 litre (2.2 gallon) buckets.

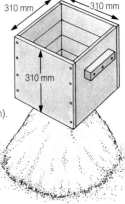

310 mm · 310 mm · 310 mm

Table of mix proportions to give 113 litres or 0.113 m³ (4 cu ft) of compacted concrete			
	Weight (kg)	Bulk volume (litres)	Batch
Cement	50	35	One 50 kg bag
5 mm sand	106	64	Two heaped boxes
10 mm aggregate	100	60	Two boxes

The amount of water varies with different coarse aggregates and types of sand. Add only enough water for minimum workability.

Working with concrete

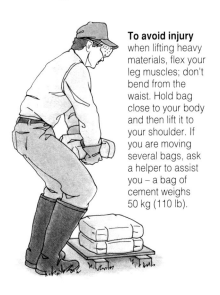

To avoid injury when lifting heavy materials, flex your leg muscles; don't bend from the waist. Hold bag close to your body and then lift it to your shoulder. If you are moving several bags, ask a helper to assist you – a bag of cement weighs 50 kg (110 lb).

Cement mixer

Anchor mixer with sandbags and mix a trial batch. Before starting the mixer, load the coarse aggregate and half the water. Start mixer. Add the sand, cement and remaining water, in that order. Mix for at least 3 minutes or until all ingredients are blended and uniform in colour. Shovel a portion onto a flat surface and test the consistency (below).
Caution: To avoid injury, keep your head, hands and shovel away from the blades when the mixer is on. Don't wear loose clothing that might get caught in outer moving parts.

Mixing concrete by hand 1. Spread coarse aggregate (measured in the gauge box or by the bucket) onto a mixing board or into large container. Add the measured quantity of sand, follwed by the cement. Turn with a spade, from one side of the mixing board to the other, then back again. Do this three times to mix dry ingredients thoroughly.

2. Heap up dry ingredients and form depression in centre. Add half the water. Mix by pulling dry ingredients little by little into the centre and pushing wet mixture to the sides. Gradually add more water until the workability is the minimum required. Turn three times, as above.

3. Test mix for proper consistency by smoothing surface with hoe or a shovel, then making a row of narrow troughs. Correctly mixed concrete will hold peaks. Aggregate should be barely discernible throughout the mix. If the mixture is too lumpy, add more sand, cement and water, and then use less aggregate in subsequent mixes.

Site preparation

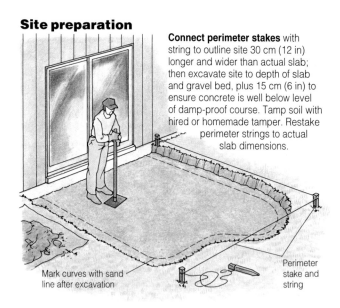

Connect perimeter stakes with string to outline site 30 cm (12 in) longer and wider than actual slab; then excavate site to depth of slab and gravel bed, plus 15 cm (6 in) to ensure concrete is well below level of damp-proof course. Tamp soil with hired or homemade tamper. Restake perimeter strings to actual slab dimensions.

Mark curves with sand line after excavation

Perimeter stake and string

Grading the stakes

String guideline

Mark high point of slab surface: Drive stakes on both sides 4 cm (1½ in) outside final slab location (space is allowed for forms to be nailed to stakes). Stretch and level chalked string; then snap it against the wall. Drive the tops of stakes level with snapped line. Stretch new perimeter string guidelines to mark placement of graded stakes for the slab.

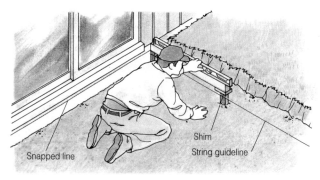

Snapped line

Shim

String guideline

Drive stake 1 m (3 ft) away from wall with inner face of stake resting against string guideline. Nail 20 mm (¾ in) thick shim beneath one end of 1 m (3 ft) long straight batten. Place level and batten across stakes, with shim down and away from wall; drive stake until batten is level. Carry on to end; repeat on other side. Nail the forms flush to tops of stakes.

Formwork or shuttering helps to shape concrete while it is wet. Because of the pressure wet concrete exerts, forms must be sturdy and well braced, usually with stakes driven into the ground and nailed to the form. The tops of the forms serve as guides when pouring and as bearing surfaces when smoothing the concrete (pp.210-11).

Most formwork is temporary, designed to be removed after the concrete has hardened sufficiently. Leave nails slightly proud to make dismantling easy. To make wooden forms easier to remove, wet them thoroughly, then wipe them with oil or a chemical release agent before starting to pour. When constructing forms for a slab to be poured in stages, place and stake temporary partition forms called stopboards.

Straight forms are made of shuttering ply, a cheaper type of plywood designed for this purpose, or from 50×100 mm boards. (A planed 50×100 mm board is actually 95 mm wide, so take this into account when exact measurements are required.) Make gradual curves by shaping 25×100 mm softwood boards, and sharper curves with plywood or hardboard. Green timber is easier to bend than kiln-dried timber, and it draws less moisture away from the concrete (which can weaken it) during curing.

Sometimes forms are left in place permanently for decoration, in which case they also serve as control joints, reducing cracking in large slabs (pp.212-13). Select a naturally decay-resistant species or use pressure-treated wood. Before use, coat nonpressure-treated timber with a clear wood preservative. Cover the exposed edges of all permanent forms with masking tape to prevent staining.

To drain properly, slabs should have a 1 in 50 slope in one direction. Good drainage makes walks and drives less slippery when wet and keeps water on an uncovered patio away from the house. If drainage for a level patio that is separate from the house is not essential, stake the forms 2.5 cm (1 in) above ground. To create a slope, drive stakes to a graded height and fasten forms flush with their tops. To grade from the middle to both sides of a wider slab, as for a driveway, set the central divider boards the required distance higher than the forms along the sides. When screeding the concrete, place the screed across the central form and a side form to grade the slab to the correct pitch.

Prepare the site by excavating an area deep enough for the slab, plus a gravel layer and allowance of 15 cm deeper than the damp-proof course, and 30 cm (12 in) wider on all sides to provide room for nailing. Gravel supports the slab and drains water that collects under it. Drainage is important in all climates, especially in areas where the ground freezes. In low-lying areas or where there is heavy clay, compact a 10 cm (4 in) thick layer of 20 mm (¾ in) gravel beneath a slab.

Note: Slabs should be kept at least 15 cm (6 in) below the level of the damp-proof course, to reduce the chance of rain splashing back off the concrete onto any absorbent surfaces above the damp-proof course.

Contraction and expansion joints

Contraction joints Concrete shrinks as it dries out, which means that it will crack if contraction joints are not inserted at 5 m (15 ft) intervals or less, in 150 mm (6 in) thick slabs or at 4 m (12 ft) intervals in 100 mm (4 in) slabs.

A simple contraction joint can be formed by folding a 100 mm (4 in) wide strip of polythene round a 50 mm (2 in) wide flat metal bar and pressing it into the concrete at the joint position. Withdraw the bar immediately, using pliers, leaving the edge of the polythene just below the surface of the concrete. The surface can then be given the desired finish. When the concrete shrinks it will crack at this position, and the ragged joint below the fold will interlock the slabs to prevent differential settlement.

Alternatively, you can insert a 50 mm (2 in) wide strip of 3 mm (⅛ in) hardboard, and leave it in place.

Always try to have the joints meeting the edges at right angles, and when tamping, tamp towards the joint.

Expansion joints Compressible expansion joints are needed against a structure like a wall, a column or a manhole which may be damaged by the high forces generated on such rare occasions as when heat causes concrete to expand more than it has shrunk in drying or, more commonly, when contraction joints have filled with sand and cannot close. A 10 mm (about ½ in) joint is usually adequate in an expansion joint. Fill it with a compressible material such as bituminous felt or expanded polystyrene.

For more information about joints, see pages 212-13.

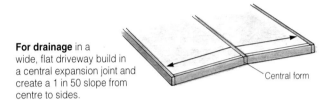

For drainage in a wide, flat driveway build in a central expansion joint and create a 1 in 50 slope from centre to sides.

Central form

Building a temporary form

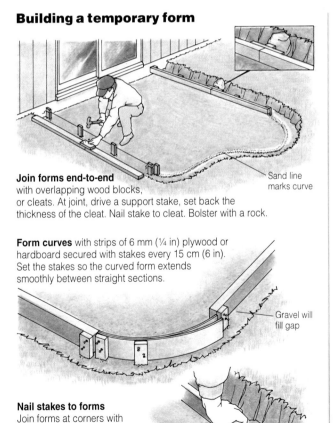

Sand line marks curve

Join forms end-to-end with overlapping wood blocks, or cleats. At joint, drive a support stake, set back the thickness of the cleat. Nail stake to cleat. Bolster with a rock.

Form curves with strips of 6 mm (¼ in) plywood or hardboard secured with stakes every 15 cm (6 in). Set the stakes so the curved form extends smoothly between straight sections.

Gravel will fill gap

Nail stakes to forms Join forms at corners with butt joint. Brace sides of joint with support stakes.

Gravel will fill gap

Nails left protruding

Making a permanent form

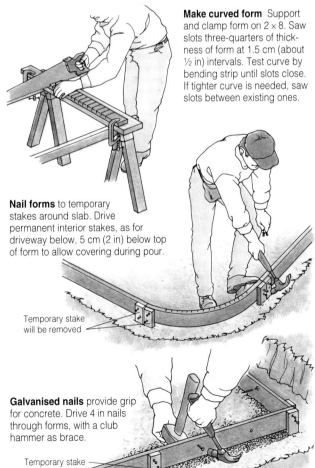

Make curved form Support and clamp form on 2 × 8. Saw slots three-quarters of thickness of form at 1.5 cm (about ½ in) intervals. Test curve by bending strip until slots close. If tighter curve is needed, saw slots between existing ones.

Nail forms to temporary stakes around slab. Drive permanent interior stakes, as for driveway below, 5 cm (2 in) below top of form to allow covering during pour.

Temporary stake will be removed

Galvanised nails provide grip for concrete. Drive 4 in nails through forms, with a club hammer as brace.

Temporary stake

BUILDING FOOTINGS AND STEPS

Laying out a footing

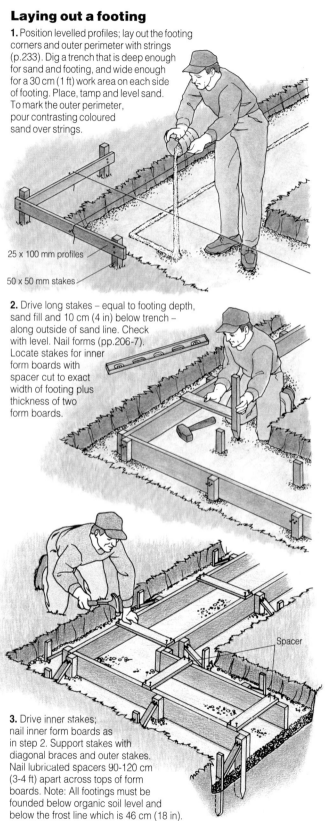

1. Position levelled profiles; lay out the footing corners and outer perimeter with strings (p.233). Dig a trench that is deep enough for sand and footing, and wide enough for a 30 cm (1 ft) work area on each side of footing. Place, tamp and level sand. To mark the outer perimeter, pour contrasting coloured sand over strings.

25 x 100 mm profiles

50 x 50 mm stakes

2. Drive long stakes – equal to footing depth, sand fill and 10 cm (4 in) below trench – along outside of sand line. Check with level. Nail forms (pp.206-7). Locate stakes for inner form boards with spacer cut to exact width of footing plus thickness of two form boards.

Spacer

3. Drive inner stakes; nail inner form boards as in step 2. Support stakes with diagonal braces and outer stakes. Nail lubricated spacers 90-120 cm (3-4 ft) apart across tops of form boards. Note: All footings must be founded below organic soil level and below the frost line which is 46 cm (18 in).

Concrete footings support the weight of vertical structures and hold them in place. In planning a project involving footings, local building regulations may apply.

Pier footings, which usually consist of concrete columns sunk into the ground, are used as spot supports for fence posts and storage sheds. Use pier footings for a concrete landing and steps up to 76 cm (30 in) high (facing page) and pier-and-panel walls (pp.240-1). They should give enough support and will require less excavation than a continuous footing. (Steps higher than 76 cm are usually supported by a continuous footing.)

A continuous footing, as for a garden wall, has a depth equal to the thickness of the wall above it. The width of the footing is usually twice its depth. A deep, narrow footing is preferable to a shallow, wide one. It is critical that the footing surface be smooth to ensure a level base and that the sides are straight and plumb (p.233).

When excavating for footings, dig a trench that is deep enough to hold a layer of tamped sharp sand 10 cm (4 in) thick. The sand provides a stable support for the footing. The base of the footing should rest below the frost line. In hard, compacted soil, wooden forms may not be needed for continuous footings; a straight-sided trench with a layer of sand in the bottom may do. This is sometimes called a trench-fill foundation. The trench is dug at least 46 cm deep and filled almost to ground level with concrete.

Concrete steps If the steps are to be tied to the house, this must be done below the damp-proof course to avoid ground water bridging it by capillary attraction. The alternative is for the steps to avoid contact with the house at and below the damp-proof course. The concrete itself is sufficiently watertight to avoid capillary attraction.

When planning, keep safety and ease in mind. The risers and treads must be uniform; 15 cm (6 in) risers are the easiest to climb; 18 cm (7 in) is the maximum height. Treads should be deep enough to stand on easily – at least 28 cm (11 in) and preferably 30-35 cm (12-14 in). To increase the depth of the treads, angle the risers inward 15° from top to bottom. For drainage, concrete treads must have a 1 in 50 slope from back to front. Extend the landing at least 15 cm (6 in) beyond the door on each side.

Side forms for steps up to 76 cm (30 in) high can be made of 20 mm (¾ in) plywood; riser forms can be plywood or nominal 25 mm (1 in) thick timber.

To allow for smoothing the treads prior to removing the forms, bevel the bottom edges of the riser forms. Brace all forms well and lubricate the insides (p.210).

The grain of the wood forms will show on the concrete. When you remove the forms (about 3 days after the pour), smooth the step sides by brushing on grout made of 1 part cement to 1½ to 2 parts sand and diluted with enough water to resemble thick paint. Let it dry for 1 to 2 hours; then rub off any excess with dry hessian or sacking.

Building steps

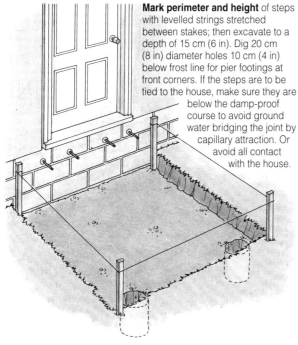

Mark perimeter and height of steps with levelled strings stretched between stakes; then excavate to a depth of 15 cm (6 in). Dig 20 cm (8 in) diameter holes 10 cm (4 in) below frost line for pier footings at front corners. If the steps are to be tied to the house, make sure they are below the damp-proof course to avoid ground water bridging the joint by capillary attraction. Or avoid all contact with the house.

Layout for landing, treads and risers Allow enough space on landing for door to open. To decide number of steps, divide height of steps by the riser height. Build riser form with 15° forward tilt, tread with a 1 in 50 slope for drainage.

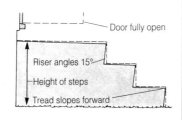

Door fully open

Riser angles 15°

Height of steps

Tread slopes forward

Cut two step profiles, including 15 cm (6 in) below grade and riser forms. Stake and brace profiles, then riser forms. Pour concrete into lowest tread first. Allow it to stiffen for about 30 minutes (time varies with temperature and stiffness of mixture when poured), so that it will resist pressure when successive treads are poured.

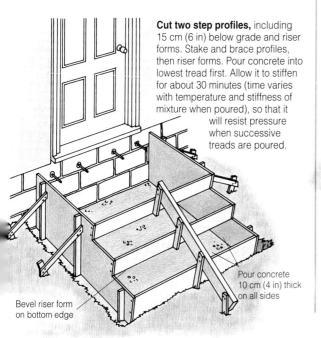

Bevel riser form on bottom edge

Pour concrete 10 cm (4 in) thick on all sides

Setting a post

1. Dig post hole. With handles parallel, raise shovel holer and thrust it into ground. Open handles, and rock or rotate tool as you remove it to excavate soil. Only one-quarter of the post should be buried, so that, under pressure, it leans instead of breaking. If you need to make a large number of holes or are working in rocky soil, consider hiring a professional with a power auger. A hand auger is also available.

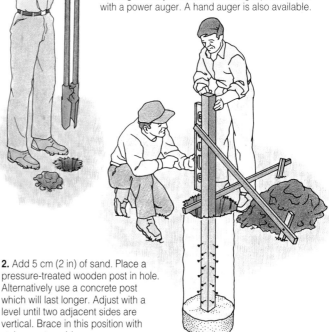

2. Add 5 cm (2 in) of sand. Place a pressure-treated wooden post in hole. Alternatively use a concrete post which will last longer. Adjust with a level until two adjacent sides are vertical. Brace in this position with stakes on two sides.

3. Put second post in its hole; align posts. Hang taut line level between posts; adjust height of second post, if needed, so heights are uniform; adjust second post's vertical position (step 2).

4. Tamp sand round post until hole is three-quarters full. Sand fill is better than concrete because the post will lean under pressure rather than break, and can be realigned. Top up with tamped soil, sloped at the surface to shed water. Remove the braces.

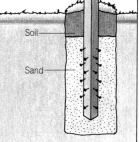

Soil

Sand

Preparation

1. Prepare forms and gravel bed (pp.206-9). Then wet down all interior surfaces to minimise settling and to keep moisture from being drawn away from concrete as it dries.

2. To prevent concrete from sticking, coat the inside of wet wooden forms with oil or a chemical release-agent.

Whether you mix concrete by hand, in a portable mixer or have ready-mixed concrete delivered by lorry, you must plan ahead. To prepare for on-site mixing, erect platforms large enough to hold the ingredients and function as the mixing site. Then lay boards for transporting concrete by wheelbarrow from there to the pouring location.

To prepare for delivery of ready-mixed, plan a route for the lorry. If the lorry must travel over unpaved ground or manoeuvre in tight quarters, ask the company to inspect the site beforehand and help you to devise the best route. Usually lorries are equipped with 3 m (10 ft) chutes for pouring concrete directly into forms. Often suppliers also have supplementary chutes that can be used. These chutes must be level or inclined downwards for the concrete to flow properly. With a franchise operation, you will have to move the concrete from the lorry to the site with wheelbarrows on boards.

Several helpers will be needed for spreading and levelling the concrete. Everyone should wear protective clothing, including goggles, a long-sleeved shirt, long trousers, thick work gloves, and knee-high heavy rubber boots, preferably without buckles.

Caution: Concrete is caustic and can cause chemical burns on skin; it will corrode leather, cloth and other material unless promptly washed off.

Concrete poured in hot weather stiffens rapidly, shortening the time available for finishing. Surface drying is a problem on days when humidity is low or when there is a wind.

In cold weather the concrete you intend to pour must be air-entrained (p.204); don't pour concrete into forms containing snow or ice or onto frozen ground. Regardless of the weather conditions, avoid overworking poured concrete; doing so weakens it. A sheen of water will appear as you level or strike off the concrete and float it. Delay further smoothing until the sheen has evaporated.

Pouring

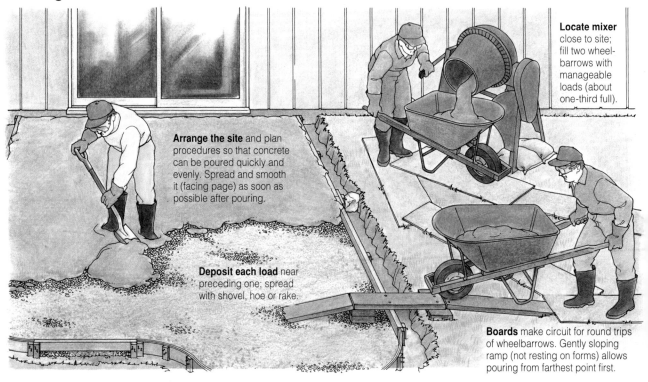

Locate mixer close to site; fill two wheelbarrows with manageable loads (about one-third full).

Arrange the site and plan procedures so that concrete can be poured quickly and evenly. Spread and smooth it (facing page) as soon as possible after pouring.

Deposit each load near preceding one; spread with shovel, hoe or rake.

Boards make circuit for round trips of wheelbarrows. Gently sloping ramp (not resting on forms) allows pouring from farthest point first.

Spreading

Tamp concrete with a straight batten on edge. Start at far end of pour; deliver vertical blows, moving board half its thickness with each blow.

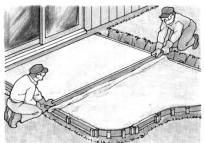

Strike off or screed top by sawing back and forth with board used for tamping. Raise the board's leading edge slightly on forward stroke. Excess concrete ahead of board fills hollows.

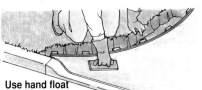

Use hand float to screed odd-shaped areas. Tamp, then smooth surface with tool. Fill any hollows with spare concrete.

Handling ready-mixed concrete

Be ready when lorry arrives. Make sure you have enough helpers, as the concrete comes down the chute fast and must be mixed and tamped rapidly, before it begins to harden. Start with chute at farthest point of pour. Dampen chute and forms with hose; then signal driver to pour the concrete. Reposition chute as form fills. If crew falls behind, ask driver to pour the concrete more slowly. Signal driver to stop when concrete in the chute will complete the job. .

Plunge spade into the mix to fill corners thoroughly, get rid of voids and settle the mix.

Tamp to push aggregate below surface; then level by screeding (see left).

Floating

Smooth screeded surface with bull float after surface water has evaporated. Push tool at right angle to screed marks, with front edge slightly raised. Pull tool back with blade flat.

Use Darby for smaller areas. Sweep tool in wide arcs, pressing lightly on blade's trailing edge. Work from centre to edges. On wide slabs, support yourself on kneeboards.

Move hand float in circles to smooth bull float or Darby marks. Lean on second float for support. Keep floating to a minimum. For a skid-resistant surface, finish with broom texture (p.215).

Contraction and expansion joints

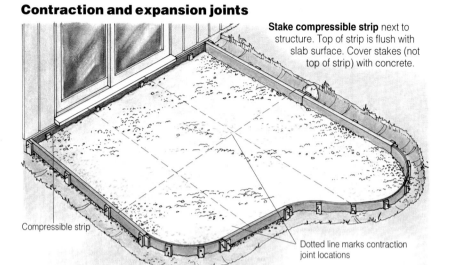

Stake compressible strip next to structure. Top of strip is flush with slab surface. Cover stakes (not top of strip) with concrete.

Compressible strip

Dotted line marks contraction joint locations

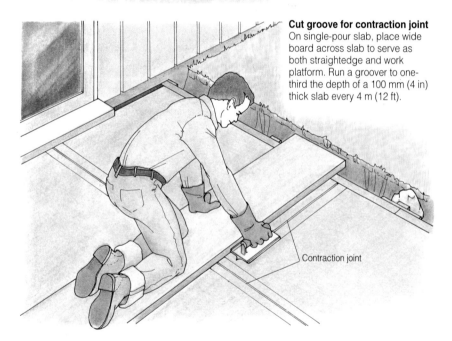

Cut groove for contraction joint On single-pour slab, place wide board across slab to serve as both straightedge and work platform. Run a groover to one-third the depth of a 100 mm (4 in) thick slab every 4 m (12 ft).

Contraction joint

Construction joints

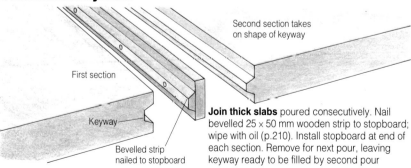

Second section takes on shape of keyway

First section

Keyway

Bevelled strip nailed to stopboard

Join thick slabs poured consecutively. Nail bevelled 25 x 50 mm wooden strip to stopboard; wipe with oil (p.210). Install stopboard at end of each section. Remove for next pour, leaving keyway ready to be filled by second pour

Concrete should be cured for seven days after casting – the first day being most important. This means it must be protected from drying or freezing.

A 4 m (12 ft) long slab shrinks by about 2 mm (1/16 in) as it dries. But after curing, a massive 40°C heating or cooling is required to produce a 2 mm contraction or expansion in a 4 m long slab. This is the reason why concrete very rarely expands to more than its cast size.

Predetermined contraction joints are needed to prevent random cracks caused by shrinkage. These joints should be sealed with an elastomer at the surface to prevent the joint filling with debris. If a joint is allowed to fill so that it cannot close on the next heating cycle, the slabs will push themselves apart.

Compressible expansion joints will be needed to absorb the movement where the slabs butt up against walls, columns or manholes. They contain compressible material such as asphalt-impregnated fibre, soft board or expanded polystyrene.

Construction joints happen where the first lot of concrete is allowed to harden for at least 16 hours before the next lot is cast against it. They will automatically become contraction joints because the concrete cracks naturally at that point. They can be made into expansion joints by placing compressible material against the old before casting the new. If the two pours are required to work together, they must be tied together with reinforcing rods laid before the first pour – direct bonding rarely works when the second pour is more than 4 cm (1½ in) thick.

In unreinforced slabs, contraction joints should be formed every 5 m (15 ft) at most; for 100 mm (4 in) thick slabs, reduce this to 4 m (12 ft). These joints can be induced to crack by inserting a strip of polythene to a third of the slab's depth (p.207).

If a contraction joint is formed at a construction joint, a keyway needs to be made, as shown on the left.

Edging and curing

Edging 1. Immediately after smoothing with a bull float or a Darby (p.211), separate concrete from the form by slicing along form with a mason's trowel inserted at least 2.5 cm (1 in) deep.

2. When concrete stiffens enough to hold an impression, round edges with an arrising or edging tool. Repeat after each finishing step if necessary.

Curing 1. When concrete is hard enough to withstand surface abrasion, cover it with wet hessian. Keep hessian moist for entire curing period, or spray water on slab and cover with plastic sheeting.

Edging and sealing joints

The edges of joints are often rounded with an arrising or edging tool to reduce the danger of breaking up into chips or fragments (which is known as spalling) when a stone gets trapped in a joint. If you do not have a professional arrising tool you can make one by bending the lip of a piece of sheet metal 90 degrees round a wooden dowel. Then fix a block of scrap wood to the metal to act as a handle. However, you may prefer to create sharp, square edges to minimise the size of the pieces of debris that are able to get into the joint.

It is desirable, but not essential, to seal the joint to keep out all debris. If the joint is to be sealed, a groove 10 mm (⅜ in) wide should be formed at the surface. The sides of the groove must be clean and a 10 mm (⅜ in) strip of paper should be placed in the bottom to prevent bonding.

An elastomer, such as a two-part polysulphide or a silicone rubber sealant, is placed in the groove, about 6 mm (¼ in) deep. As the joint opens, the elastomer stretches across the gap. The elastomer may pull away from the sides after about five years and should then be replaced.

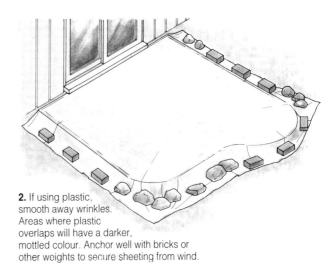

2. If using plastic, smooth away wrinkles. Areas where plastic overlaps will have a darker, mottled colour. Anchor well with bricks or other weights to secure sheeting from wind.

Anchoring wood posts to concrete

Metal bases embedded in concrete piers (right) or foundation walls secure wooden sills and posts used in house framing. Embed base according to maker's instructions. Bases should be held in position temporarily until concrete has hardened. To position base A, place a wood brace in U of base, and screw. Position a waxed cardboard tube in the hole; then pour concrete. Place base and brace in wet concrete across top of the tube (inset). To position elevated post base B in wet concrete, place it across 50 x 50 mm spacer boards. Let concrete cure seven days before attaching post.

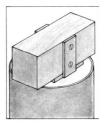

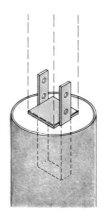

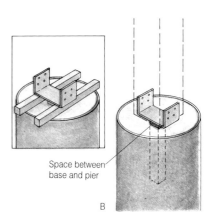

A

B

Space between base and pier

DECORATIVE COLOURS AND FINISHES FOR CONCRETE

Colouring the top layer

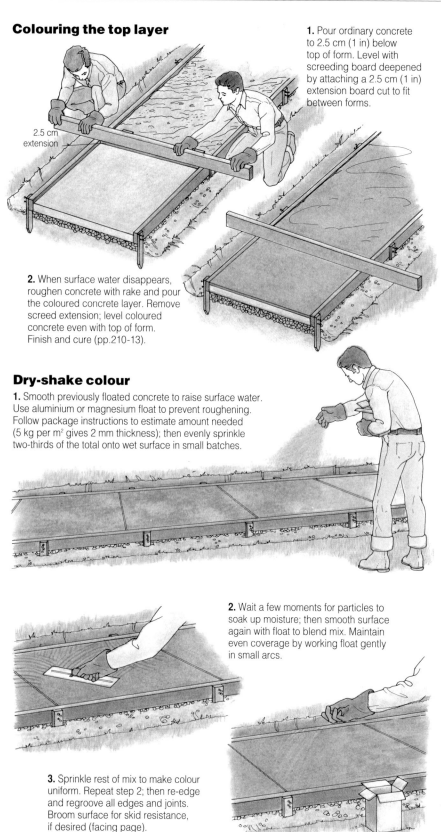

1. Pour ordinary concrete to 2.5 cm (1 in) below top of form. Level with screeding board deepened by attaching a 2.5 cm (1 in) extension board cut to fit between forms.

2.5 cm extension

2. When surface water disappears, roughen concrete with rake and pour the coloured concrete layer. Remove screed extension; level coloured concrete even with top of form. Finish and cure (pp.210-13).

Dry-shake colour

1. Smooth previously floated concrete to raise surface water. Use aluminium or magnesium float to prevent roughening. Follow package instructions to estimate amount needed (5 kg per m² gives 2 mm thickness); then evenly sprinkle two-thirds of the total onto wet surface in small batches.

2. Wait a few moments for particles to soak up moisture; then smooth surface again with float to blend mix. Maintain even coverage by working float gently in small arcs.

3. Sprinkle rest of mix to make colour uniform. Repeat step 2; then re-edge and regroove all edges and joints. Broom surface for skid resistance, if desired (facing page).

It is easy to add colour or texture while finishing concrete. Textured surfaces also make slabs and paths less slippery.

There are two main ways to colour concrete: by blending powdered mineral pigment (which is available from concrete suppliers) with the mix, and by sprinkling poured concrete with a pigmented sprinkle finish after the concrete has been smoothed with a float (p.211). The sprinkle finish is a rich mixture of pigment, cement and sand which draws water from the body of the concrete and increases its strength.

Concrete can also be painted or stained with purpose-made products; however, the results vary and are not as long-lasting as the other two methods.

Pigments for concrete consist of mineral oxides and are added at the rate of up to 10 per cent of the weight of the cement. Any more is wasteful and weakening. Read the instructions on the container and consult the supplier for specific advice.

For good results with pigment, use white cement instead of the usual grey variety. Using white sand instead of the ordinary type, while not necessary, will further improve the colour.

To save money on pigment and expensive ingredients, use concrete made with standard ingredients (without pigment) for the bulk of the pour. Screed the bottom layer; then immediately mix the concrete for the coloured layer, using pigment and the white cement and sand. Be careful not to add too much water. Pour, screed and finish the coloured layer.

When finishing the concrete, do not overwork it by smoothing the surface too much. This weakens the slab and can cause powdering. At the curing stage, use damp hessian rather than plastic sheeting. Seal the slab according to the pigment maker's instructions.

To create a textured finish before the surface hardens, roughen it with a broom, embed pebbles in it, carve it with masonry tools or imprint it with brick design tools. For complex finishes, pour and finish small sections at a time.

Brooming

Hold broom at low angle and drag bristles across concrete to produce ridged nonslip surface. Don't let brush strokes overlap or cross each other at angles. Use soft bristles to create fine lines, stiff bristles to make a deeper design.

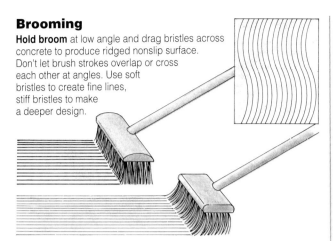

Imprinting a brick design

Place two imprinting tools across width of floated concrete; third begins new row. Step on each one. Move first two to finish new row and begin next. Pour and stamp small areas so design imprints well. Easiest slabs to fill have 90° angles. Hand tools (provided by maker) fill in other shapes and gaps between forms. Polythene can be used under the tool to give a rounded, cobbled effect.

Pebbled texture

1. Wet clean, round pebbles or other smooth stones 2-4 cm (¾-1½ in) in diameter. Add 1 part cement to 5 parts pebbles. Pour and screed small section of concrete. Sprinkle pebbles evenly (as shown), or create a mosaic pattern on surface.

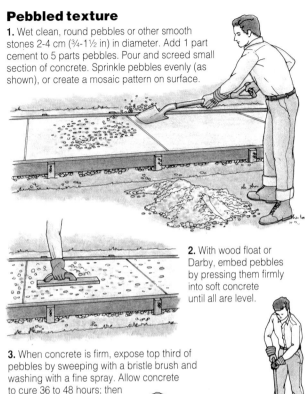

2. With wood float or Darby, embed pebbles by pressing them firmly into soft concrete until all are level.

3. When concrete is firm, expose top third of pebbles by sweeping with a bristle brush and washing with a fine spray. Allow concrete to cure 36 to 48 hours; then remove cloudy residue by washing stones with solution of 1 part hydrochloric acid to 20 parts water. Rinse the slab with water immediately.

Caution: Add acid to water, never the other way around; use non-metallic container. Wear rubber gloves and safety goggles.

False flagstone

1. After smoothing concrete with float, carve outlines of design with a brick jointing tool or bent copper tube.

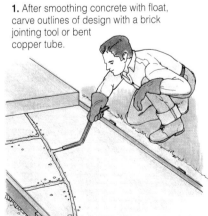

2. Smooth and retool the concrete to finish the flat surfaces and to deepen the outlines.

3. Brush outlines carefully with a dry paintbrush to smooth their edges and remove particles.

REPAIRING CONCRETE

Despite its sturdiness, concrete can deteriorate with age and exposure to severe weather, and it can also suffer damage from settling or from rough treatment. Using concrete that is not air-entrained, and overworking it, can also weaken a slab. To repair concrete successfully, clean the area well and create a good bond between the surface and the patching compound.

To fill cracks and holes make up a patching compound of 1 part cement, 2½ parts sand and enough water to make a stiff paste for vertical surfaces.

Alternatively, it may be easier to buy a proprietary patching compound containing latex, epoxy or other polymers. These usually bond well,

even when filling small cracks and resurfacing surfaces that are scaling.

As another alternative, add SBR (Styrene Butadiene Rubber) building adhesive to the mixing water (1 part adhesive to 4 parts water) and coat the crack with neat SBR.

To reduce a dusty or powdery condition, sweep and vacuum the slab, then wash it with soapy water and a wire brush (use strong powdered detergent). Scrub the surface again with more soapy water and a fibre brush; then rinse it with clean water.

For a lasting repair, all unsound concrete must be removed. The surface must have a grout vigorously scrubbed into it to pick up any remaining dust.

Make the grout with of 1 part of water to 1 part of SBR to 6 parts of cement. The 1-to-2½ repair mortar must follow within about 10 minutes, before a skin forms on the SBR.

Repairs thicker than 3 cm should contain the concrete mix described on page 204. Repairs thicker than 4 cm should be done in layers.

Each layer should cure for three days and dry for at least four days before preparing the next layer. Drying allows microscopic cracking and the relief of debonding stresses to occur before adding another layer.

Caution: Protect yourself from concrete compounds by wearing safety goggles, long sleeves and gloves.

Filling cracks with repair mortar

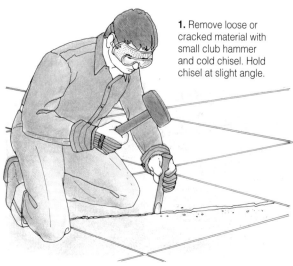

1. Remove loose or cracked material with small club hammer and cold chisel. Hold chisel at slight angle.

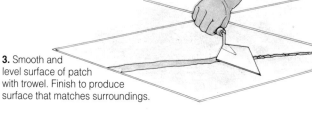

2. Clean crack with brush; dampen if the compound directions specify. Force compound into crack with edge of trowel.

3. Smooth and level surface of patch with trowel. Finish to produce surface that matches surroundings.

Patching large holes in layers

1. Chisel sides of hole until vertical; prepare hole as for cracks. Brush with grout (mix 1 part cement and 1 part sand; add water and SBR building adhesive to consistency of house paint).

2. Fill hole to within 6 mm (¼ in) of surface with homemade compound (see above). Avoid overwetting mix; this weakens it.

3. Apply finish layer of commercial patching compound, following package directions. Feather edges of patch. Finish to match surrounding concrete.

Rebuilding edges and corners

1. Chisel away loose particles, and brush damaged area well. Mix patching material according to maker's directions. Dampen concrete before applying if maker's directions specify.

Plan to square up edges of repair to make it look neater – however, it is impossible to disguise it totally.

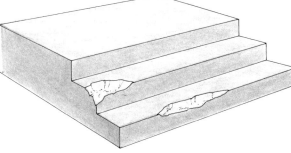

2. Erect, lubricate and brace form to contain and shape patch. Apply compound. Smooth surface with trowel and edger (pp.206-13).

Replacing a broken slab

Break up damaged slab with sledgehammer. Slab will crack along contraction joint. Remove broken pieces, and cover with layer of sand as for new slab (pp.206-7).
Caution: Bend knees as you lift and lower hammer. Straighten knees a little at top of swing. Let the hammer fall of its own weight. Check the hammer's head often for looseness. Wear goggles and heavy work gloves.

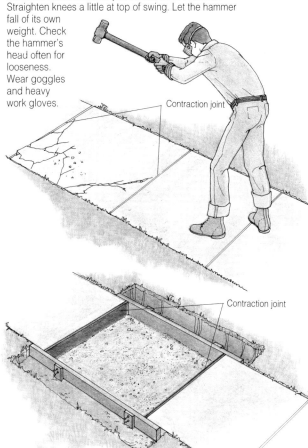

Contraction joint

Contraction joint

Erect forms level with existing path. Repair damaged edges of adjacent slabs to give them a sharp, square edge. Wait at least a day for concrete to harden sufficiently. Then pour concrete and finish as for new slab (pp.206-13.)

Resurfacing

1. Remove damaged surface by chiselling at an angle or by striking with a 1.5 kg (3¼ lb) club hammer. Avoid heavy blows that might crack slab. Clean slab thoroughly with wire brush and broom.

2. Wet slab and allow moisture to soak in if patching compound directions specify. Apply compound; smooth with float. Finish surface with broom to roughen finish, if desired (p.215).

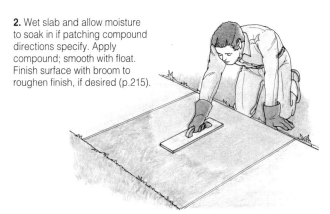

BRICKS

Most bricks are made from some type of clay, fired in a kiln. Softer clays are used in moulds; stiffer clays may be moulded under pressure as solid bricks or with an indentation, called a frog, pressed into them. Another method forces a column of clay through an opening which forms the length and width of the brick; the column is then wire-cut to form the height of the bricks. The type of clay and method of firing will determine the variety of colours and textures, but the body colour may also be changed by additives and the faces by the application of coloured sands before firing.

Calcium silicate bricks, known as 'sandlime' or 'flintlime', are made from a mixture of lime and either sand or crushed flint. They have a pleasingly sharp, regular form and may be coloured by the addition of pigments. Concrete bricks are moulded from a mixture of sand and cement and can also be coloured. All types come in a variety of shapes and sizes.

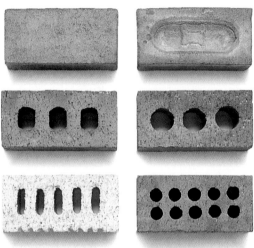

Facing bricks are used for exposed work. They may be plain or frogged (top row) or perforated (above). They come in a variety of colours and some are glazed (below, right). Most bricks are modular – they relate in size to each other. Metric modular bricks (top right) were introduced to ease the change to metrication and look best in a long stretch of wall.

Special bricks are made specifically to form unusual features. Variations on dog-leg (top left) and curved or radial (bottom left) can be used for either convex or concave shapes. Universal joint bricks (centre) form interesting angles and corners. Saddleback capping (top right) encourages water to run off the top of a wall.

Rounded edges or ends on bricks, known as bullnoses, were originally designed to reduce water penetration, but are also used by architects and designers to add interest to otherwise flat walls and to create decorative details. These bricks can also be used to frame doors or windows or to form cornices.

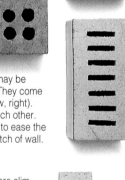

Slip bricks are slim, lightweight, real clay bricks, often used to create a veneer of brick over an existing wall of a less attractive finish. The bricks are quick to apply and are available in a variety of colours and textures.

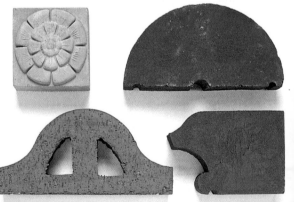

Other decorative bricks include plaques (top left), cornices (bottom right) and copings. Plaques may be formed in one piece, as shown here, or depending on their size, be made up of a number of sections. Cornices are used largely in renovation and refurbishment and ensure that original design elements are faithfully restored. Copings are formed with a drip channel or groove, to encourage water to drip off, away from the bricks below. Holes, as shown in the wave coping (bottom left), serve to reduce cracking in the firing process.

Shelf angle brick can be placed to form a hidden horizontal expansion joint that accepts flashing or to create a drainage channel for moisture trapped behind a brick wall. Shelf angle bricks can also be used to form lintels above window and door openings. The extended lip may run along the length of the brick, as shown, or along the end.

Although bricks and flat-cut stones (p.221) can be used as pavers, bricks are probably more versatile, as they can be laid in a number of attractive patterns or be set on end at an angle to form a sawtooth edging (p.235).

However, concrete pavers that are pressed in a mould under extreme pressure are equally versatile. They are usually laid on a prepared bed of sand and then the joints are filled with fine sand. The sand enables the pavers to move slightly, allowing them to transmit and spread the load of the traffic they carry. To compact the pavers and lock them together, you will need to hire a plate vibrator, and work systematically over the entire surface. Pavers are relatively quick to lay and can be walked or driven on almost immediately.

Both brick and concrete pavers are sufficiently durable to withstand exposure to rain and frost and stand up to heavy domestic traffic and, in some cases, commercial traffic.

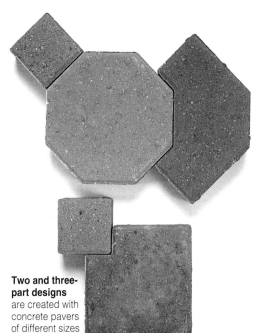

Concrete cobbles in two or three sizes make it possible to create both random and intricate patterns. They are usually sold in shrink-wrapped pallets, each containing blocks of one size only. No two blocks are exactly the same colour, which helps to create a traditional, aged look.

Two and three-part designs are created with concrete pavers of different sizes and, sometimes, different colours. Because the shapes are complementary, they can be used in a variety of patterns and combinations without needing to be cut.

Concrete block paver with a 3 to 1 size ratio makes it possible to lay a number of pleasing, symmetrical patterns. Chamfered edges and variegated shading add texture and colour.

Clay pavers and cobbles have the rich, natural colour of bricks. Pavers are suitable for reasonably heavy traffic and domestic driveways, but cobbles are not as tough – they should be kept for domestic and landscape uses. Cobbles arrive grouped in a 'brick' of eight, and can be split apart quite easily with a brick bolster and club hammer.

Interlocking pavers in concrete create a more uniform pattern, and the use of different colours adds interest. Some patterns combine two distinctive shapes in a single unit, giving an attractive result but simplifying the laying out of the pavers.

Edge blocks can be used to finish off a paved area without the need to cut special blocks and can be useful in starting off a paved area with a good, strong edge. Some blocks are designed to be used flat, others can be stood on end to give a decorative edge to flowerbeds and lawns. Specially formed corner pieces are available too.

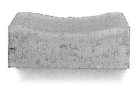

Feature blocks such as channel or drainage shapes (shown in profile, above) and kerb edges are useful and practical when laying driveways and patios. It is possible to buy grates and access covers to match the style you choose.

CONCRETE BLOCKS

Concrete blocks are used primarily in both foundation and retaining walls, and in walls above damp-proof courses. They are durable and resist harmful penetration of moisture.

Lightweight aggregate (LWA) blocks are used mainly for insulation and dense aggregate blocks are used for strength. In addition to the traditional rough grey rectangles, blocks are available in a variety of colours, textures and shapes for almost any application. Blocks are heavier than bricks, more utilitarian than either bricks or stones and fairly inexpensive.

Because blocks come in a variety of sizes that fit one another, there is no need to cut them into smaller sizes, as must be done with stones. Hollow blocks are available either with through-going cores which can carry vertical reinforcement, or blind – with hollows that hold insulation.

Solid plain block is 100 mm thick with a face size of 440 x 215 mm. This dense concrete building block is very strong and can be used for load-bearing walls. Its density enables it to store daytime heat, yielding it up at night.

Plain concrete block, the basic wall unit, has plain ends and two or more hollows or holes. Some makers include a cutting slot in a proportion of their plain blocks.

Four-cavity block in dense concrete, with blind hollows that can hold insulation. It is 100 mm thick and its work size is 225 x 450 mm. The shape of the cavities and the thickness of the block's wall may vary from one manufacturer to another.

Twin-core hollow block in dense limestone concrete measures 140 x 215 x 440 mm which gives a work size of 225 x 450 mm – the most commonly used face. It is suitable for direct decoration.

Four-cavity splitter block, in lightweight aggregate concrete, can be split with a brick bolster and a club hammer to create units of different lengths.

Split stone block is used as a feature for external walls of houses or laid flat for patio walls. It adds character to a wall and if it contains quartz aggregates, it will sparkle attractively.

Partition blocks are narrow units designed for partition walls inside a house, garage or other building. The ground-down surfaces of the blocks shown make them aesthetically pleasing for indoor use. The red block has a single score in its face. The white one is a semisolid block.

Screen block creates decorative designs in walls and fences and allows for privacy without cutting out all light. Screen blocks are ideal for closing in patios or swimming pools. An almost unlimited number of patterns is available, ranging from simple to intricate.

For a combination of strength, diversity, durability and natural beauty, there is no building material equal to stone. Stone can be roughly shaped, cut to precise dimensions or used as it is found in nature. Its surface can be rough and irregular, smooth and flat or polished to a high gloss that is impervious to stain. Because of its versatility, it is used for interior and exterior walls and floors, fireplaces and chimneys, countertops, roofing, paths and driveways and countless other landscaping and architectural applications.

Stones for walls or facing work are generally sold by the tonne; paving flags, slate and tiles, by the square metre. In rubble masonry, rough uncut stones of various shapes and sizes are fitted together. In ashlar masonry, cut stones with squared-off surfaces are tightly fitted. In either case, the stones may be coursed (layered in rows) or random. Stone walls may be laid dry (without mortar) or with or without the mortar showing. Ashlar mortar joints are usually 3-6 mm (⅛-¼ in) wide; never more than 13 mm (½ in).

River fieldstone (right) is most commonly used in mortarless construction. The section of wall shown here is made up entirely of flat stones, called strips.

Slate (far right) is available in dozens of earthy colours ranging from greys and greens to purples and reds. It is shown here in a section of floor that has been laid in a geometric pattern.

Corinthian granite (right), with its flat surface and irregular shapes, can be laid in a mosaic pattern with 13 mm (½ in) mortar joints, as demonstrated in the segment of wall shown here.

Salt-and-pepper granite (far right), cut into large squared blocks and strips, is ideal for walls. The section of wall shown here has 13 mm (½ in) pointed mortar joints.

Cotswold/Derbyshire millstone (right), a variety of limestone and sandstones, can be arranged in random strips to form a mortarless wall. The variety of sizes keeps spaces between the stones to a minimum.

Rough-textured marble (far right), like all marble, is very difficult to cut; buy it precut. Pink marble, shown here in a section of ashlar wall, has tight 3-6 mm (⅛-¼ in) joints.

When planning a masonry project, choose the material that best suits your skill level and the finished look you have in mind.

Bricks and concrete blocks are uniform in size and lend themselves to formal designs. Although both are available in many sizes, the dimensions of individual units are proportionally related in most cases. This makes them easy to fit together in patterns, lessens the amount of skill and time required to build with them and simplifies estimating materials. These projects are relatively easy to design because their dimensions can be based on the size of the individual units. Also, their uniform shape, texture and colour allow you to predict the appearance of a finished project.

Stones that are uniformly shaped, or dressed, can be treated like brick or block. Roughly dressed stones (with protrusions cut off, but not squared) and undressed stones vary in size, shape and surface features. They tend to create less structured designs that emphasise texture and colour more than precise or geometric patterns.

Working with undressed and roughly dressed stones requires much more creativity, skill and time than working with bricks, blocks or dressed stones. Each piece must be chosen or cut to fit its neighbours like pieces of a jigsaw puzzle. Thus it is necessary to have many stones on hand to choose from. (As a rule, the more irregular the stones, the more stones you will need.) Also, it is difficult to predict precisely the appearance of the finished project. Nevertheless, these types of stones have considerable aesthetic appeal, and the extra effort associated with this work is well rewarded.

Bricks are rated for their resistance to weathering, particularly the effects of freeze-thaw cycles. (Moisture inside the bricks expands when it freezes, causing them to break.)

Clay bricks are classified as F for frost resistant, M for moderately frost resistant and O for not frost resistant.

Grades of undressed stones

Suitable

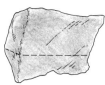

Irregular; needs shaping

Poor (unusable)

They are also classified by soluble salt content as L for low and N for normal. Brickwork which is very exposed and liable to freezing while saturated should be built from FL or even FN bricks.

Where protected by eaves or overhangs, ML and MN bricks are satisfactory. OL and ON should be used indoors only and protected from saturation and frost during building.

The most frequently used brick sizes are to BS 3921. These bricks are customarily sold by their nominal or coordinating dimensions, which include a nominal allowance of 10 mm for mortar joints; this simplifies the estimating of quantities of bricks needed and allows for slight variances in actual dimensions that occur during manufacturing.

The nominal size for a standard brick is $225 \times 112.5 \times 75$ mm; the manufacturer aims at 'worksize' dimensions of $215 \times 102.5 \times 65$ mm. It is standard practice in the UK to give brick dimensions in the order of length, width and height.

To determine the number of bricks needed for a project, calculate the size of the area (p.344) and subtract the areas of openings or unpaved sections.

When estimating quantities of bricks for projects involving mortar, use the nominal size. The rule of thumb is that 60 standard bricks are needed per square metre including mortar joints. Add 5 to 10 per cent to the total to allow for waste.

In practice, the number of bricks will vary considerably, depending both on whether the bricks are solid or have frogs (or large perforations) and on the skill of the person laying them.

For large jobs you can use a special slide rule called a brick masonry estimator, available from suppliers. (This estimator will also help you gauge the amount of mortar and, specifically, how much sand, cement and lime you will need for a given job. See page 224.)

A simple, approximate guide is that one 50 kg bag of ready-mixed mortar – the standard size – makes enough mortar to lay 60 bricks or about $1m^2$ in stretcher half-bond (p.227).

For a wall more than one brick thick, multiply the result by the number of bricks making up the structure's thickness.

Where bricks are to be laid close together without mortar (as in a patio or path with sand in the joints), use the actual dimensions; allow about 45 to 50 bricks per square metre.

Bricks are usually sold in strapped packs of about one cubic metre, which contain 400 or more bricks. The cube will weigh up to a tonne. Other quantities can be supplied loose.

When ordering bricks, find out whether delivery will be made to the work site or to the roadside. Before delivery, prepare a sturdy wooden storage platform, and if the bricks are to be stored for a long time before being used, protect them from rain.

Blocks are made of concrete and contain a variety of aggregates for different uses. Quantities are estimated in the same way as for bricks. Most concrete blocks are 440 mm long and 215 mm high. The length and height allow for a nominal joint of 10 mm, which gives a nominal face size of 450×225 mm – the equivalent of six normal bricks.

A single course is as high as three courses of standard bricks laid in mortar. This relationship is useful when laying brick and block together, such as when constructing a brick-faced retaining wall (p.246).

Blocks may have other nominal widths; they are 100 mm (4 in) and 140 mm (5½ in). These are usually laid with the width side down. Sometimes, solid blocks may be laid so that the width faces out, consequently building a course height other than 225 mm into the wall. This gives a greater degree of flexibility to a large module.

Block weight depends on the block's concrete density, thickness and whether hollow or solid. Blocks can weigh from 10 kg to 25 kg and quantities larger than 10 m² can be delivered on a crane-fitted vehicle for easier handling.

They can be cut, but to avoid having to cut them, you can buy half sizes and special shapes for use around door and window frames – however, they can be expensive. If blocks are stored outside, cover them with plastic to keep them clean and dry.

Smaller concrete block units, called pavers or paving stones, are laid without mortar on beds of sand and make durable and decorative paths, patios, steps and driveways (pp.234-9).

Stones that are dressed, roughly dressed, and undressed can be bought at a stone yard and delivered. Granites are the hardest and often the most expensive; limestones and sandstones range from soft to nearly as hard as some granites; slates are split along their layers to form paving flagstones.

Undressed stone can often be obtained more cheaply from local quarries, construction sites and farms; but hauling stones yourself is heavy, sometimes dangerous, work. (If you do haul your own stones, be careful not to overload your vehicle.)

When selecting undressed stones, choose pieces with clearly defined surfaces that will sit level in a wall and will support the stones above with a minimum of shaping or shimming.

Bricks

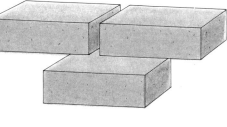

Place standard bricks with 10 mm mortar joints to form horizontal increments of 112.5 mm or 225 mm. Mortar joints are staggered for strength.

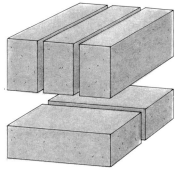

Thickness of three standard bricks plus mortar joints equals the length of a similar brick.

Turn a simple corner by alternating position of whole bricks. Width of two standard bricks plus mortar joint equals length of one brick.

Concrete blocks

Webs and face shells taper slightly so blocks can be unmoulded at the factory. Others flare, providing a little more mortar surface. Place blocks with thicker side up.

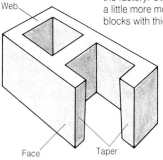

Web

Face Taper

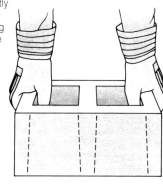

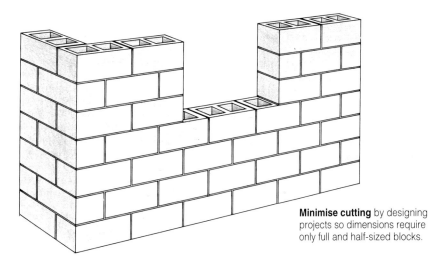

Minimise cutting by designing projects so dimensions require only full and half-sized blocks.

Mixing mortar

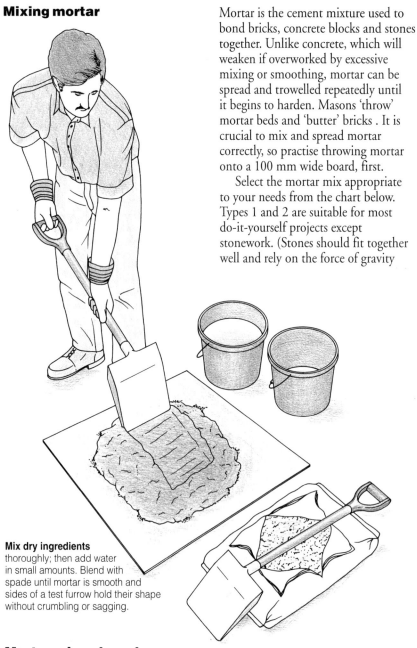

Mix dry ingredients
thoroughly; then add water
in small amounts. Blend with
spade until mortar is smooth and
sides of a test furrow hold their shape
without crumbling or sagging.

Mortar is the cement mixture used to bond bricks, concrete blocks and stones together. Unlike concrete, which will weaken if overworked by excessive mixing or smoothing, mortar can be spread and trowelled repeatedly until it begins to harden. Masons 'throw' mortar beds and 'butter' bricks . It is crucial to mix and spread mortar correctly, so practise throwing mortar onto a 100 mm wide board, first.

Select the mortar mix appropriate to your needs from the chart below. Types 1 and 2 are suitable for most do-it-yourself projects except stonework. (Stones should fit together well and rely on the force of gravity rather than the strength of the mortar.) Use type 4 for interior walls only because it cannot withstand any weathering or freezing. Before restoring brickwork more than 100 years old, consult an experienced mason about the proper mortar mix; mortar that is too strong may cause bricks in such masonry to crack.

There are three ways to mix mortar. The first is from scratch using Portland cement, hydrated lime and sand; or from masonry cement (Portland cement premixed with admixtures) plus sand; or, most easily, from bags containing all the dry ingredients.

Buy materials for mortar from a DIY centre or builder's merchant to be sure of getting the right kinds. Use only building sand (not 'sharp' or 'screeding' sand) which is clean, finely graded and salt-free. Water should be clean tap water. Use a separate bucket and spade to measure and add the cement, to avoid spoiling it.

Mix the dry ingredients on a clean mixing board, using a second spade. Add just enough water to achieve the right consistency – a stiff mix that falls off the spade cleanly. Mortar that is too wet will run out between the joints; if it is too dry, the bond will be weak.

To use a power mixer, add three-quarters of the water, half the sand and all the masonry cement (or Portland cement and lime) required. Mix briefly, then add the remaining water and sand; mix again for at least 3 minutes.

Caution: Wear waterproof gloves when working with mortar.

Mortar mixes by volume

Type	Use	Strength	Portland cement	Lime	Sand	Masonry cement	Sand
1	Load-bearing, freeze-thaw weathering, below-ground walls and garden brickwork	Strongest	1	¼	3¾	1	3
2	General use and below ground level, where engineering quality bricks are used	About 75% of Type 1	1	½	4½	1	4
3	For all walls and buildings above damp-proof course level	About 33% of Type 1	1	1	6	1	5
4	Interior work only	About 14% of Type 1	1	2	9	Not applicable	

Loading the trowel

1. Chop a slice of mortar from the mound on the board – a 600 mm (2 ft) square piece of 18 mm (¾ in) plywood) – enough to cover three or four bricks. When chopping, hold trowel perpendicular to board with thumb extended along top of handle; relax forearm and let blade drop.

2. Without changing your grip, use the blade of the trowel to shape slice into rounded loaf or wedge, whose length approximately equals that of the blade.

3. Rotate wrist to scoop up the mortar by sliding trowel underneath it. Forearm and palm of gripping hand should face up. Lift loaded trowel and flick it down and up rapidly to settle mortar firmly on blade.

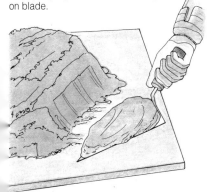

Throwing the mortar bed

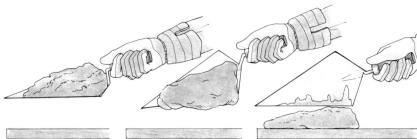

1. Hold tip of loaded trowel at starting point, parallel with ground, with palm of gripping hand facing up.

2. Throw the mortar by rotating your wrist and flicking trowel downward while pulling tool towards you in a straight line.

3. End with trowel perpendicular to surface and mortar along centreline of bricks or practice board. If it is not, return mortar to board, remove bricks. Try again using fresh bricks.

4. Furrow the wet mortar by drawing the pointed end of the blade along the centre of the mortar. Spread it to cover entire surface of bricks.

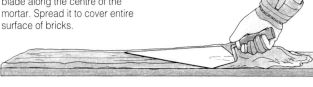

Buttering a brick

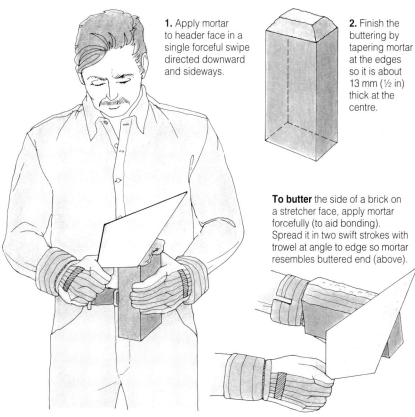

1. Apply mortar to header face in a single forceful swipe directed downward and sideways.

2. Finish the buttering by tapering mortar at the edges so it is about 13 mm (½ in) thick at the centre.

To butter the side of a brick on a stretcher face, apply mortar forcefully (to aid bonding). Spread it in two swift strokes with trowel at angle to edge so mortar resembles buttered end (above).

Brick positions

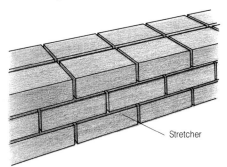

Stretcher is placed horizontally with its long narrow side exposed. This is the most common position for bricks and forms the basis of running, stack and open bonds.

Stretcher

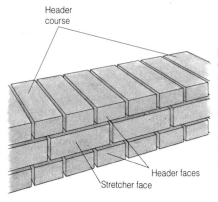

Header course

Header shows end of brick with wider surface on horizontal. Headers are common in one-brick walls (215 mm thick) and are combined with stretchers to make the decorative feature of many pattern bonds.

Header faces

Stretcher face

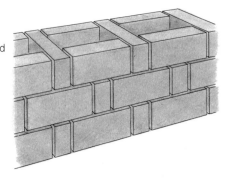

Rat-trap bond is laid with long narrow sides down and reveals a brick's long, wide bed surface, between headers, bedded on edge.

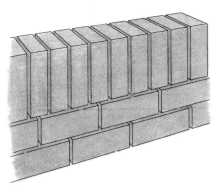

Soldier stands on end with long narrow side exposed. Soldiers are commonly used within pattern bonds to simulate arches over doorways and windows.

Bricklaying is an intricate skill that has many aspects of an art. Over the centuries, bricklayers have developed colourful yet precise terms to describe every feature of bricks and the ways they are used.

In a wall or any other structure, bricks are identified by their position when installed (see left). The exposed surface of an installed brick is called its face. The horizontal layer of mortar on which bricks are laid is called a bed. A layer of bricks in a structure is called a course. A vertical section of brick masonry walling may be half a brick thick (102 mm) or one brick thick (215 mm). A row or course of bricks overlapping across a one-brick wall width acts as an important bond course, tying in a wall from front to back, and is commonly known as a header course.

Any piece that is less than a whole brick is called a bat. A half bat is a brick split to divide its length in half. The nominal dimensions of a standard modular half bat are $102 \times 65 \times 102$ mm ($4 \times 2\frac{5}{8} \times 4$ in); a three-fourths bat and a one-fourth bat are three-quarters and one-quarter of the length, respectively. Quarter bats that are used at corners to maintain joint spacings are called closers.

The term bond describes three different ways that bricks are tied together in a structure: a pattern bond implies the arrangement of the bricks; a mortar bond refers to the adhesion of that material with the masonry units; and a structural bond refers to metal ties or anchors used in masonry construction, and to the overlapping of masonry units to stagger and thereby strengthen their vertical joints.

Pattern bonds are named to reflect their appearance; they also may or may not have important structural qualities. Some are suitable only for veneer work (p.246). Before selecting a bond, check with your local planning office to make sure it is appropriate for your project.

Decorative design

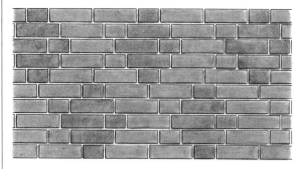

Monk bond pattern places a header after every two stretchers in each course. Use a brick of contrasting colour to outline diamond shape. To create a larger diamond pattern, place the header after every three stretchers. Before building, draw your project and its pattern on graph paper.

Forming patterns in walls 102 mm thick

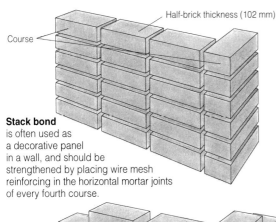

Course — Half-brick thickness (102 mm)

Stack bond
is often used as
a decorative panel
in a wall, and should be
strengthened by placing wire mesh
reinforcing in the horizontal mortar joints
of every fourth course.

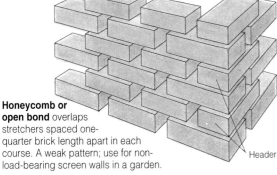

**Honeycomb or
open bond** overlaps
stretchers spaced one-
quarter brick length apart in each
course. A weak pattern; use for non-
load-bearing screen walls in a garden.

Header

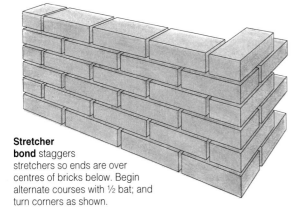

**Stretcher
bond** staggers
stretchers so ends are over
centres of bricks below. Begin
alternate courses with ½ bat; and
turn corners as shown.

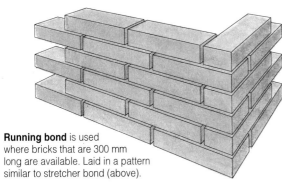

Running bond is used
where bricks that are 300 mm
long are available. Laid in a pattern
similar to stretcher bond (above).

Forming patterns in walls 215 mm thick

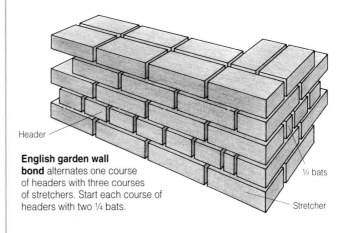

Header — ¼ bats

Stretcher

**English garden wall
bond** alternates one course
of headers with three courses
of stretchers. Start each course of
headers with two ¼ bats.

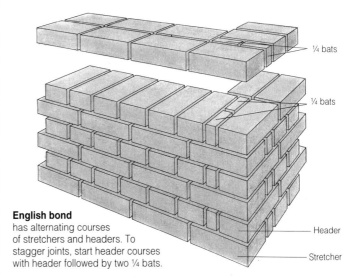

¼ bats

¼ bats

English bond
has alternating courses
of stretchers and headers. To
stagger joints, start header courses
with header followed by two ¼ bats.

Header

Stretcher

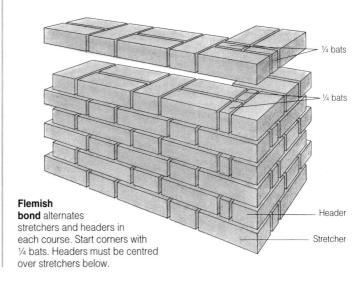

¼ bats

¼ bats

**Flemish
bond** alternates
stretchers and headers in
each course. Start corners with
¼ bats. Headers must be centred
over stretchers below.

Header

Stretcher

JOINTING BRICKS

Joints are the layers of mortar between bricks. They are named for their position in the structure: horizontal joints are called bed joints; vertical joints between bricks in a course are cross joints. If a wall is more than one brick thick, the vertical joint between the stretchers is called a collar joint.

When laying bricks, apply the mortar forcefully to aid its adhesion (p.225). Then push the bricks into place with one motion; don't move them further except to tap them gently immediately afterward, using the handle of a brick trowel, to settle and level them. Repositioning them breaks the seal between the mortar and the bricks, interfering with the bond and causing cracks in the mortar. If a brick is too low or is misaligned, remove it together with the mortar in the joint; then clean and replace the brick, using fresh mortar. Check your work often with a level and stretched string to make sure bricks and courses are placed properly (p.233).

The mortar is ready to be surface-finished when it is hard enough to retain a thumbprint without leaving any residue on your thumb. Finishing shapes and compresses the joints, strengthening and sealing them against moisture. Using a trowel to finish joints is called striking; using a special jointing tool is called tooling. It is best to work from bottom to top.

Many styles of mortar joints have been developed. Some are purely decorative and only for indoor use; others are designed to shed water and are best for outdoor work. After the initial shaping and trimming, clean all joints by brushing them with a medium-soft bristle brush or sacking. After brushing, rework the joints if necessary to sharpen their details and remove any imperfections.

While mortar joints form the main structural bond for masonry, expansion joint material inserted at certain points (facing page) allows the bricks and the mortar to expand and contract with changes in temperature and humidity. These expansion joints are placed at 8-10 m (26-32 ft) intervals in brick walls and at strategic points in solid brick patios and paths. Generally, you do not need to use expansion joints in a project, vertical or flat, that is less than 8 m (26 ft) long or in any type of sand-bedded brick paving.

Laying bricks

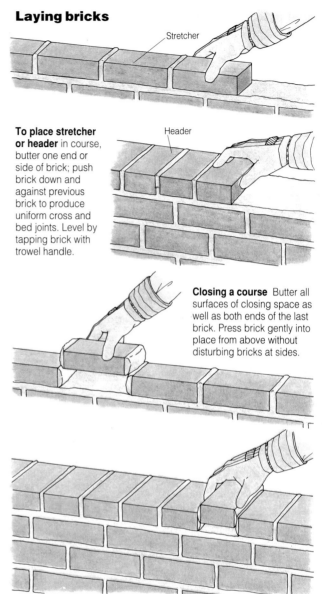

Stretcher

To place stretcher or header in course, butter one end or side of brick; push brick down and against previous brick to produce uniform cross and bed joints. Level by tapping brick with trowel handle.

Header

Closing a course Butter all surfaces of closing space as well as both ends of the last brick. Press brick gently into place from above without disturbing bricks at sides.

Tooling head and bed joints

Trim away excess mortar by slicing upward with edge of trowel as each brick is bedded, and after tooling head and bed joints.

Shape cross joints first. Press and slide the jointing tool over vertical surfaces to smooth and compact the mortar before it hardens.

Smooth bed joints next, using the same tool, to create continuous horizontal lines. Avoid gouging joints with tool or knuckles.

Mortar joints and shapes

Weathered Sheds water well. Form by running trowel tip against under side of upper course while pressing tip inwards at 10° angle. Shape of cross joints is the vertical equivalent, all indented on left-hand side.

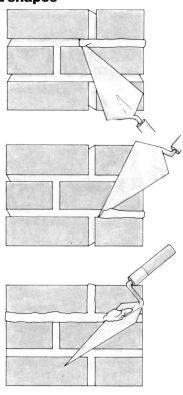

Reverse struck Opposite of weathered; sheds water poorly, so use for internal walls only. Work from above; recess lower edge of mortar by pressing trowel tip inward against top of lower brick course. Cross joints as weathered.

Flush Moderately water-resistant but not strong because mortar is not compressed. Slice away excess mortar with trowel to leave flat surface. May be compacted with small piece of wood to improve weather resistance.

Half round This is the most common joint finish. Sheds water well. To form, see facing page. Use a short length of suitably bent pipe or rod of 15-18 mm diameter. Or buy a purpose-made brick jointer.

Birdsmouth Dramatic appearance. Sheds water well. Form with V-jointing tool. Practise first to avoid unevenness; the centre line of the joint must be spaced evenly between bricks.

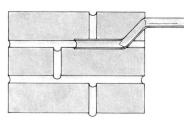

Recessed Forms strong shadow lines. Create by removing 6-10 mm of mortar from joints with raking tool. Afterwards, clean exposed surfaces thoroughly. Bricks must be frost-resistant quality if this is used externally.

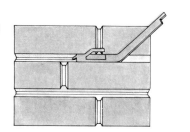

Expansion joints in solid brick paving

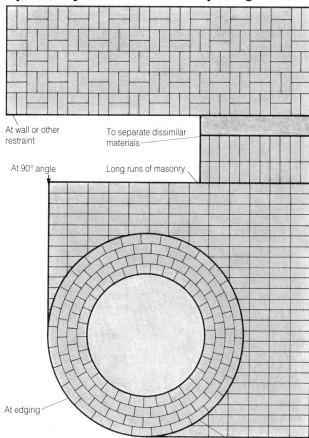

At wall or other restraint

To separate dissimilar materials

At 90° angle

Long runs of masonry

At edging

To separate bond patterns

Neoprene or foam backer rod and sealant expansion joints allow for differing expansion and contraction of bricks and mortar. Pour concrete slab (pp.204–13) prior to laying solid brick paving.

How to cut a brick

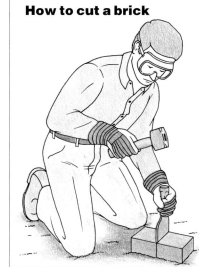

Mark cutting line round brick with pencil and straightedge. Place stretcher face of brick on a heap of sand or soft soil. Hold bolster on cutting line and strike firmly with club hammer. Turn brick onto opposite face and repeat. Finally, place brick flat and, with bolster on pencil line, strike again. Repeat these steps in rotation until brick breaks on cutting line. **Caution:** Wear heavy-duty gloves and goggles.

WORKING WITH STONE

Lifting stones

To lift a stone safely, bring it close to your body. When rising, 'hug' the stone, using your thigh muscles to stand. Keep your back straight. Avoid carrying stones more than a few steps; a stone 30 cm (1 ft) square and 15 cm (6 in) thick can weigh about 35 kg (77 lb) or more.

Long digging bar levers stone from ground

Prise stone from ground with levers. Start with long steel digging bar; then insert a sturdy plank and prise alternately with these until one plank can serve as a ramp on which to slide the stone. Place wood blocks beneath planks to keep them from sinking into sides of hole. Do not reach beneath the stone when rolling it free.

Because stone is heavy and working with it requires physical fitness, a novice should start a project gradually. Have a medical examination, and warm up before working by doing stretching exercises that include touching your toes, and spend no more than 4 to 6 hours daily lifting and moving stones until your muscles are developed. Always wear protective clothing, including heavy leather work gloves, sturdy boots with steel toes and safety goggles (when cutting).

Rely on mechanical aids to save physical effort and to avoid possible injury. To lift stones, use digging bars, ramps and hand or power winches. When using a winch, wrap a chain – not the winch cable – around the stone, and attach the winch cable to the chain. A winch cable can break if it is looped around an object and then hooked to itself.

For hauling stones over short distances, get a sturdy wheelbarrow with solid arms and a pneumatic tyre. (For maximum manoeuvrability, load stones so most of the weight is in the rear.) Or place stones on a wooden plank and roll the plank along on logs or pipes. When carrying stones long distances, use a pickup truck with heavy-duty suspension, or a flatbed trailer or a stoneboat attached to a similar powerful vehicle. To avoid losing control, drive cautiously when hauling stones. Inspect the brakes beforehand and upgrade them if necessary so that they are in excellent condition. When carrying flat or thin stones, place them on edge and wedge them to keep them from falling; if laid flat, they can break when bounced.

Dry-stone (mortarless) masonry is the best type for novices because it requires fitting stones together and relies on gravity to hold them in place – the key to all stonework. Shaping the stones is an important part of dry-stonework; for best results use a 0.9 kg (2 lb) or a 1.8 kg (4 lb) club hammer and at least two chisels: a broad-bladed stone chisel or a pitching tool for scoring and for splitting grained stones; and a point, tapered on all sides like a sharpened pencil, for focusing blows over small areas. When shaping stones, support them on a firm but resilient surface (p.236). Professional stonemasons use a sturdy homemade wooden table, padded with sawdust or several layers of carpet; the height of such a table should be about 15 cm (6 in) below the user's waist.

The properties of stone

Type	Physical characteristics	Workability	Durability*	Use
Granite	Hard, dense; coarse-grained or speckled; grey, blue, pinkish	Difficult; hard to cut	Excellent	Walls, foundations, chimneys (not cut to fit)
Limestone	Medium-soft; light to dark grey	Easy; cuts well	Medium to poor	Walls, foundations, chimneys
Sandstone	Soft to medium-hard; brown, grey, reddish	Easy to medium (there are soft and hard sandstones)	Medium	Hard types: walls, foundations, chimneys. Soft types: interior veneer
Slate	Soft; dark grey or black	Medium; splits easily with grain; cut across grain with masonry saw	Medium to poor	Patios, paths, roof shingle

*Includes resistance to weather

Moving stones

Roll stone onto a plank resting
on logs or pipes. Push plank forward,
or lever it from behind with a 2 x 4, while removing
rollers from rear and setting them in pathway ahead.
On soft ground, place boards beneath rollers for support.

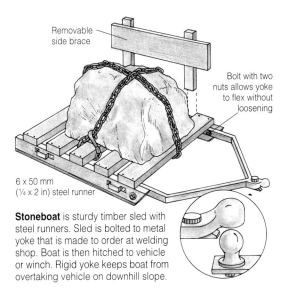

Removable
side brace

Bolt with two
nuts allows yoke
to flex without
loosening

6 x 50 mm
(¼ x 2 in) steel runner

Stoneboat is sturdy timber sled with
steel runners. Sled is bolted to metal
yoke that is made to order at welding
shop. Boat is then hitched to vehicle
or winch. Rigid yoke keeps boat from
overtaking vehicle on downhill slope.

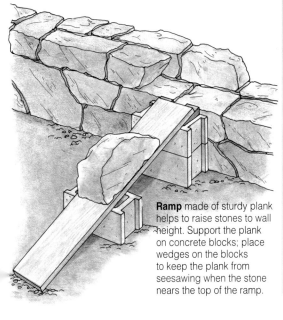

Ramp made of sturdy plank
helps to raise stones to wall
height. Support the plank
on concrete blocks; place
wedges on the blocks
to keep the plank from
seesawing when the stone
nears the top of the ramp.

Splitting stones

To split stone along the grain,
mark line around the stone with soft
pencil; then drive metal wedges or
series of chisels along grain. Strike
in succession, one blow each
with a club hammer, until
crack widens and stone
splits apart.

Cutting and fitting stones

Choose stones by studying space that
needs filling; select the stone with closest
shape. Stones in a wall should tilt towards
the centre and exert chiefly
vertical pressure. Successive
courses should cover vertical
joints between stones below.

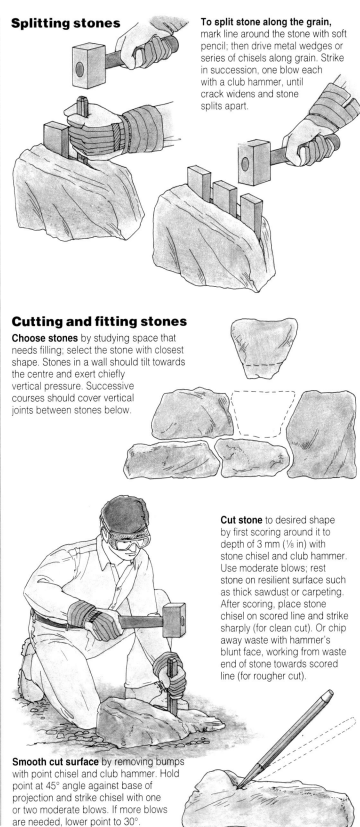

Cut stone to desired shape
by first scoring around it to
depth of 3 mm (⅛ in) with
stone chisel and club hammer.
Use moderate blows; rest
stone on resilient surface such
as thick sawdust or carpeting.
After scoring, place stone
chisel on scored line and strike
sharply (for clean cut). Or chip
away waste with hammer's
blunt face, working from waste
end of stone towards scored
line (for rougher cut).

Smooth cut surface by removing bumps
with point chisel and club hammer. Hold
point at 45° angle against base of
projection and strike chisel with one
or two moderate blows. If more blows
are needed, lower point to 30°.

Laying blocks in courses

Some hollow concrete blocks have inset end webs to ease handling and laying.

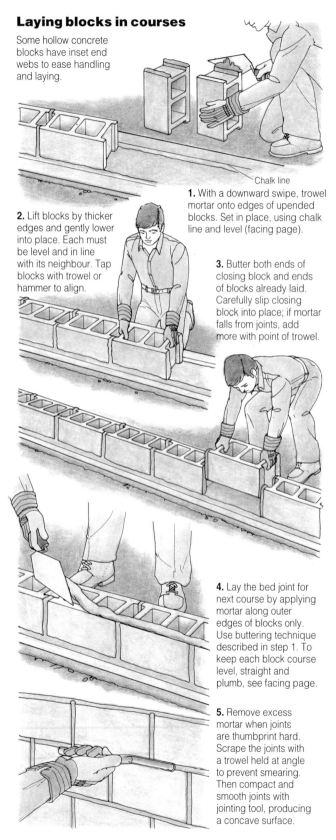

Chalk line

1. With a downward swipe, trowel mortar onto edges of upended blocks. Set in place, using chalk line and level (facing page).

2. Lift blocks by thicker edges and gently lower into place. Each must be level and in line with its neighbour. Tap blocks with trowel or hammer to align.

3. Butter both ends of closing block and ends of blocks already laid. Carefully slip closing block into place; if mortar falls from joints, add more with point of trowel.

4. Lay the bed joint for next course by applying mortar along outer edges of blocks only. Use buttering technique described in step 1. To keep each block course level, straight and plumb, see facing page.

5. Remove excess mortar when joints are thumbprint hard. Scrape the joints with a trowel held at angle to prevent smearing. Then compact and smooth joints with jointing tool, producing a concave surface.

Many people find that laying concrete blocks is faster and easier than laying bricks. You can butter several blocks at one time; in addition, because of their weight, you set the blocks in place without pushing them. Their larger size means that levelling and aligning require less time.

Concrete blocks take the same type of mortar as bricks, and the joints are a standard 1 cm ($\frac{3}{8}$ in). The mortar bed beneath the first concrete block course must cover the entire area; you apply mortar for subsequent block courses only to the blocks' outer edges. Lay blocks with their thicker edges uppermost; the wider surfaces hold more mortar (p.223). Cover stored concrete blocks on dry, firm, level ground, under a sturdy plastic sheet to keep out moisture and dirt.

Control joints (deliberately weakened vertical seams) are necessary in certain walls to reduce cracking caused by the movement of the masonry. These walls have large openings, intersect other block walls, are restrained at each end or have varying heights or thicknesses. In addition, concrete blocks that are joined to other structural materials require control joints. Locate control joints where the greatest stresses occur and at intervals along the wall's length equal to its height or up to 1¼ times its height. Weak mortar – a 1:1:6 mixture (p.224) – allows movement to occur in every joint rather than being concentrated at control joints.

Because control joints act as a focus for cracking and, therefore, occasionally crack themselves, gasket material keeps the wall in alignment as it shifts. Choose gaskets that are designed for the shape of the blocks you are using.

Control joints

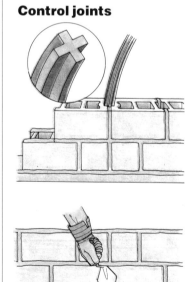

Neoprene gasket strip (inset) maintains alignment of blocks in a control joint; it fits channel in specially formed blocks. Tubular and rectangular gaskets are available for use with flat-ended blocks. Install gasket strip in lowest course; build wall using whole and half-size special blocks to make vertical joint within overall bond pattern.

Mortar in control joint acts as backer for caulking compound sealer. Rake out mortar to a depth of 2 cm (¾ in), then fill the joint with caulking compound. But first brush primer into the joint if caulking instructions specify.

LEVEL, STRAIGHT AND PLUMB

In all types of masonry, aligning the building units accurately is crucial to success. To build straight walls that do not lean or bulge, each brick or concrete block must be checked three ways – lengthwise, across its width and vertically – as it is set in place and, if necessary, adjusted before proceeding.

To ensure straightness, snap a chalk line on the footing, the length of a wall. So that the chalk line won't be covered with mortar, snap it at a uniform distance – say, 5 cm (2 in) – from the footing's edge. Each time you lay a brick in place, measure between it and the line at both ends to make sure the unit and the line are exactly parallel.

Masons build or raise the ends of a wall first; then they fill in the centre of the wall by steps in the courses, which is known as racking back. Stretch a mason's line between the raised ends of a wall, as a guide.

A homemade storey rod allows you to check that your mortar joint is the proper thickness as you build each course. To make a storey rod, mark squared lines on a board at intervals equal to the thickness of your masonry unit plus a mortar joint. Make as many marks as there are courses in the wall. Hold the rod next to the construction to check the mortar joint for each course.

Building a raised corner

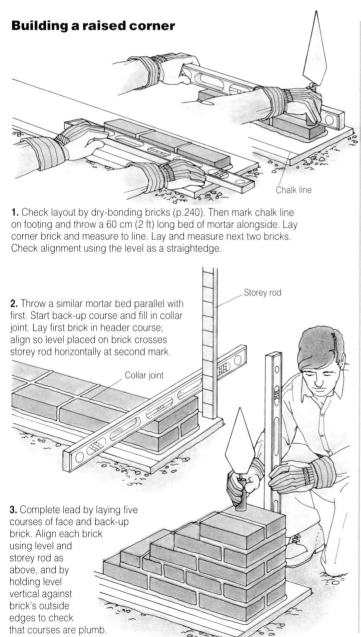

1. Check layout by dry-bonding bricks (p.240). Then mark chalk line on footing and throw a 60 cm (2 ft) long bed of mortar alongside. Lay corner brick and measure to line. Lay and measure next two bricks. Check alignment using the level as a straightedge.

Chalk line

2. Throw a similar mortar bed parallel with first. Start back-up course and fill in collar joint. Lay first brick in header course; align so level placed on brick crosses storey rod horizontally at second mark.

Storey rod

Collar joint

3. Complete lead by laying five courses of face and back-up brick. Align each brick using level and storey rod as above, and by holding level vertical against brick's outside edges to check that courses are plumb.

Creating a true corner

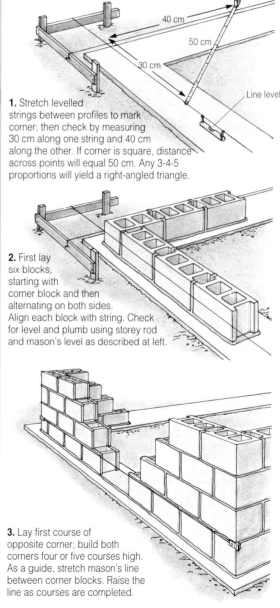

40 cm

50 cm

30 cm

Line level

1. Stretch levelled strings between profiles to mark corner; then check by measuring 30 cm along one string and 40 cm along the other. If corner is square, distance across points will equal 50 cm. Any 3-4-5 proportions will yield a right-angled triangle.

2. First lay six blocks, starting with corner block and then alternating on both sides. Align each block with string. Check for level and plumb using storey rod and mason's level as described at left.

3. Lay first course of opposite corner; build both corners four or five courses high. As a guide, stretch mason's line between corner blocks. Raise the line as courses are completed.

When used as paving, bricks and concrete pavers are often laid in sand (without mortar) on a flat, firm base and restrained with an edging of wood or PVC. This method, called flexible paving, is easy to install and repair.

Brick paving is usually laid in classic patterns: running bond, stack bond, basket weave and herringbone. Of these, herringbone (shown below) is the most durable and stable because the bricks interlock at right angles.

Concrete pavers are available in many shapes; the more intricate ones come with installation instructions.

Paving flags are also popular for flexible paving. Because no edging is required, it is easier to lay out an area for paving flags than for bricks or concrete pavers. In addition, you can space the sand joints irregularly. But

make sure the flags are well supported underneath; otherwise there is a danger that they will break when stepped on. (For further details on how to lay paving flags, see pages 236-7.)

With sandy, well-drained soil and for light-duty areas such as patios, excavate the site to the depth of the paving plus 5 cm (2 in) for a bed of tamped sand.

With other soils and for heavy-duty areas, but not driveways, excavate 10 cm (4 in) deeper to allow for the addition of a layer of well-compacted crushed stone beneath the sand.

For driveways, excavate enough to allow for a 20 cm (8 in) layer of crushed stone beneath the sand.

When laying out a project, base its shape on the dimensions of the paving units in order to minimise cutting.

You can cut bricks fairly easily by hand (p.229), but you will need to rent a guillotine-type splitter to cut pavers. Pavers that create special patterns usually come with half blocks for filling in outside edges.

Edging can be made from pressure-treated timber strips or heavier landscaping ties, anchored with stakes or spikes. Alternatively, you can anchor proprietary PVC edging strips (such as Marshalls' Keyform) with 300 mm (12 in) metal spikes. Or you can dig a narrow trench and add a brick edging (facing page).

To reduce the chance of tripping over wood or PVC edging strips, place the top surface of the edging about 5 mm (¼ in) below the paving. The paving will settle more with time and the two will eventually be level.

Patterns

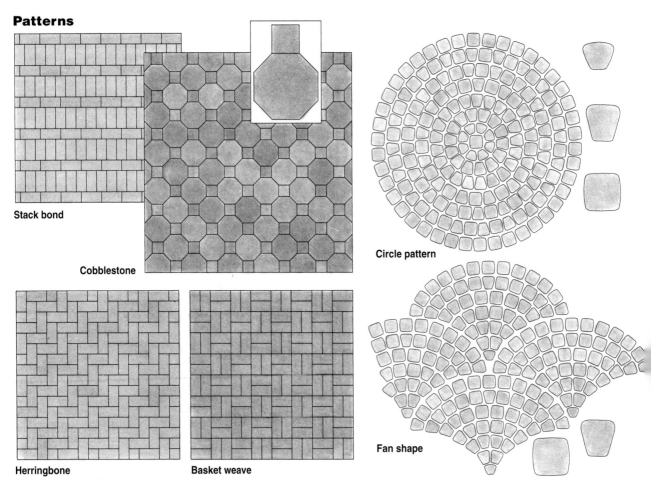

Stack bond

Cobblestone

Circle pattern

Herringbone

Basket weave

Fan shape

Brick edging

Lay out project. Position corner stakes so that connecting strings outline edges of project. Mark edges with a sand line (p.208). Dig a trench equal to length of bricks plus 5 cm (2 in) for crushed stone, if used. Keep outer sides vertical.

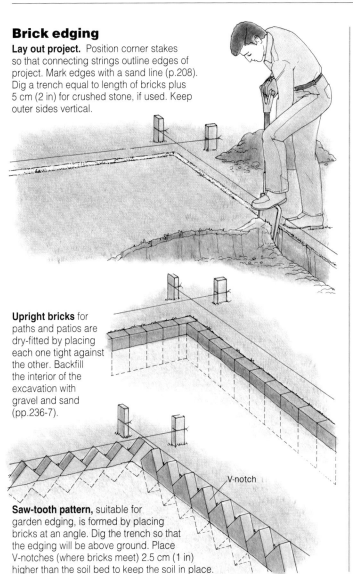

Upright bricks for paths and patios are dry-fitted by placing each one tight against the other. Backfill the interior of the excavation with gravel and sand (pp.236-7).

Saw-tooth pattern, suitable for garden edging, is formed by placing bricks at an angle. Dig the trench so that the edging will be above ground. Place V-notches (where bricks meet) 2.5 cm (1 in) higher than the soil bed to keep the soil in place.

V-notch

Wood strip edging

Dig level trench that is wide enough to allow work area outside perimeter. Place edging. Drive stakes at 1 m (3 ft) intervals and where boards join. Recess stakes 2.5 cm (1 in) below top of edging. Fasten with nails or screws.

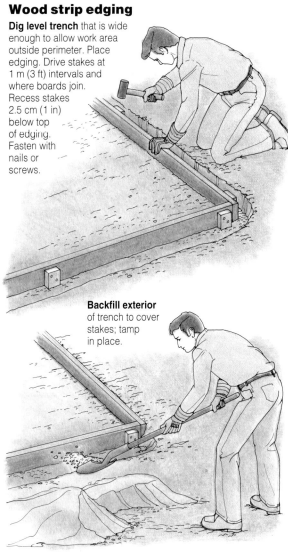

Backfill exterior of trench to cover stakes; tamp in place.

Two ways to set landscaping ties

Set timber flush with ground. Butt-join them with 25 cm (10 in) nails driven at an angle and staggered. To hide nails, drive them into sides of strips. Add crushed stone, sand and paving. Backfill exterior.

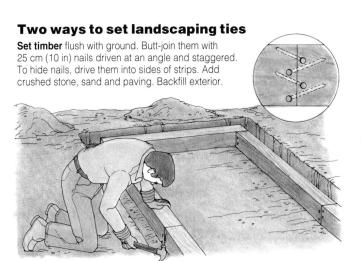

At each end and in centre, drill 15 mm (⅝ in) holes. Insert 13 x 460 mm (½ × 18 in) mild-steel rods. With club hammer, drive rods into holes until flush with edging. Lay paving; backfill exterior.

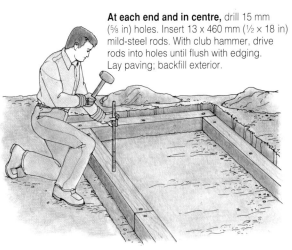

Paving with bricks

1. Spread and tamp rubble over excavated site; then level with a screeding board and extension (the thickness of the sand plus the pavers). Fill low areas. Add sand; spread with extension equal to the thickness of the pavers.

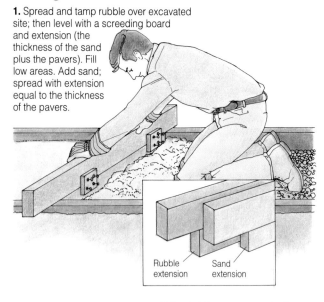

Rubble extension   Sand extension

2. Lay bricks one course at a time. Align them so that they nearly touch – with a 3 mm (⅛ in) gap. Drop bricks in place; do not slide them on the sand; level by tapping with a mallet.

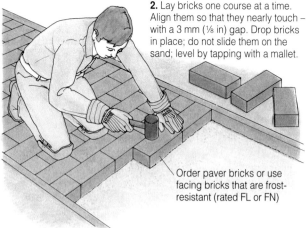

Order paver bricks or use facing bricks that are frost-resistant (rated FL or FN)

3. Spread coarse sand over bricks after all are laid; then sweep sand into cracks. Spray site with garden hose to moisten and settle sand. Do not tamp bricks. Repeat two or three times, until joints are filled.

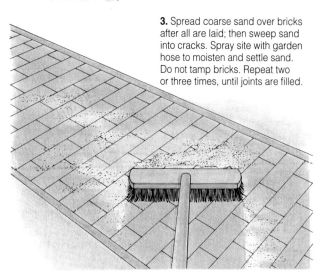

To lay out areas for sand-laid paving, tie strings to stakes as for poured concrete and mortared masonry projects (pp.206-8, 233). The strings determine the perimeter and establish a height from which to measure downwards when excavating the site. To outline curved areas, lay a garden hose or rope on the ground. Drive stakes along the hose or rope outline and stretch strings between them. The strings need not follow the exact shape of the curve.

If the paved surface is to be flat, use a spirit level to adjust each string. If the surface must slope to promote drainage away from a building, the strings that are stretched in the direction of the slope should be angled downwards 2.5 cm for every 3 m (2 in for every 10 ft) of their length.

The most crucial step in building with flexible paving is site preparation; a firm and flat site minimises the settling of the paving. As a rule, it is easier to excavate the entire site to the depth required and then install the edging and paving. If you install anchored wood edging (pp.234-5) before laying the pavers, you can use it as a guide when levelling the sand and rubble beds on which the paving will rest.

To use the edging as a levelling guide, rest the ends of a screeding board (pp.211, 214) on it and drag the extension over the rubble, then the sand. If the area is wider than the board, or if you prefer to install the edging last, as you might for vertical or angled brick edging, place temporary strips of wood equal to the height of the edging on the ground before adding the first layer of fill. Use these to support the ends of the board. After levelling the beds, remove the strips and fill the areas by adding material with a trowel.

Take extra time to make sure that the rubble bed (or the excavation, if rubble is not used) is tamped and level. You can tamp small areas with a hand tamper (p.206), but for best results, tamp large areas with a plate vibrator, a motor-powered tool that can be hired.

Caution: Plate vibrators are noisy; wear ear protectors.

Don't tamp a sand bed. Until the paving is laid, protect the bed from rain either by covering the sand with plastic sheeting when you have finished for the day or by spreading the sand in 1 m² (10 sq ft) areas just before installing the paving. Stay off the sand bed by working from outside the perimeter or by kneeling on previously laid sections.

When paving with paving flags, first fit as many uncut flags together as possible to minimise the amount of shaping you have to do.

To cut flags, support them on sand-covered ground. If you will be cutting a number of flags, raise the work to a more comfortable height and reduce back strain by building a sturdy sand table to rest them on. Make the table surface out of 20 mm (¾ in) plywood, use 2 × 4s to support the table, and add a rim of 1 × 2s to contain the layer of sand.

Place paving flags with their more level and attractive side up. Avoid using small flags; they tend to sink into the ground or to tip when stepped on.

A patio of concrete pavers

1. Prepare 10 cm deep rubble base with screeding board (facing page). To tamp large area, move hired plate vibrator across base several times. Spread and smooth coarse sand 5 cm deep; do not tamp.

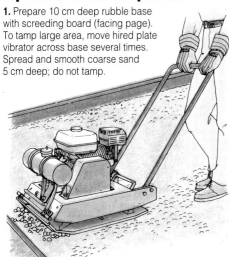

2. Lay pavers starting at 90° corner. Align edge units precisely; set all pavers in place without disturbing sand. Follow manufacturer's suggested sequence when using irregularly shaped units.

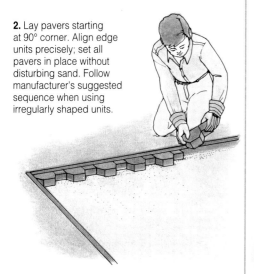

3. Keep pavers aligned by following string stretched parallel with courses. Complete patio; then tamp pavers with plate vibrator. Sweep sand into joints and tamp pavers again with vibrator. Do not wet. Repeat until joints are full.

Shaping paving flags

Place flag so that the edge to be cut overlaps edging of previously laid stone. Judge cut line by eye and mark both sides with chinagraph pencil. Or use a piece of roof slate.

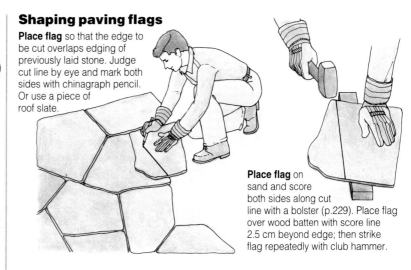

Place flag on sand and score both sides along cut line with a bolster (p.229). Place flag over wood batten with score line 2.5 cm beyond edge; then strike flag repeatedly with club hammer.

Laying paving flags

1. Lay paving flags 1.5 cm (about ½ in) apart. Arrange largest flags round perimeter of site to help to keep the rest from shifting. Place flag on ground and test fit; then lift it and regrade area underneath by removing or adding sand to accommodate flag's uneven surface.

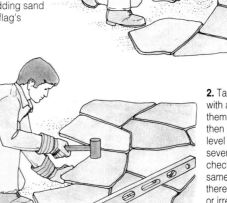

2. Tap flags lightly with a mallet to settle them. Lay several flags; then place a mason's level across them in several directions to check that all are the same height and that there are no high edges or irregularities that can cause tripping.

3. Finish project by filling joints with sand and wetting it as for flexible brick walk (facing page). Use scrap wood to tamp sand between flags after each application.

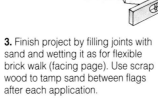

For more permanent bedding, lay paving flags on a dryish mortar, rather than direct onto sand.

Scrap wood

Masonry 237

Above-ground steps generally require a concrete footing to prevent settling and cracking, and often a railing for safety. Steps leading into a building should be wider than the doorway and, if the door opens out, should have a landing that is deeper than the door. Steps that are built into a steep slope may also need retaining walls at the sides (pp.244-5). Before you begin, consult your local authority to find out what codes apply.

To design above-ground steps that are safe and easy to climb, look at the suggested measurements on page 208. Along gently sloping paths, consider a series of long landings of about 2 m (6 ft) divided by low risers, or a series of landings interrupted by pairs of identical steps. They are often more comfortable and more appealing than a single compact flight. These designs are safer too, especially if the steps tend to be slippery.

Lay out steps by measuring the slope's rise, or height, and its run, or horizontal distance. Often the rise is fixed by the physical constraints of the site. For example, the relationship between the door and the ground level determines the rise of above-ground steps. When this is the case, the run can usually be adjusted as necessary to fit the steps. With in-ground steps, both rise and run measurements may be more flexible.

To calculate the number of steps, divide the overall rise by 15. If it does not divide equally, divide by the nearest number that does. Determine the number of treads by dividing the run measurement by a tread depth – at least 30 cm – that goes into the run equally. If the rise or the run of the steps happens to divide awkwardly, spread the remainder evenly among the treads or risers, or adjust the overall measurement. For example, take a 90 cm rise with a 1.8 m run. The run divides into six 30 cm treads, requiring six risers. The rise divides into six risers that are each 15 cm high.

Alternatively, transfer the run and rise measurements to graph paper and sketch uniform combinations of riser and tread (to scale) so that they fill the space comfortably and safely.

Above-ground steps using concrete blocks

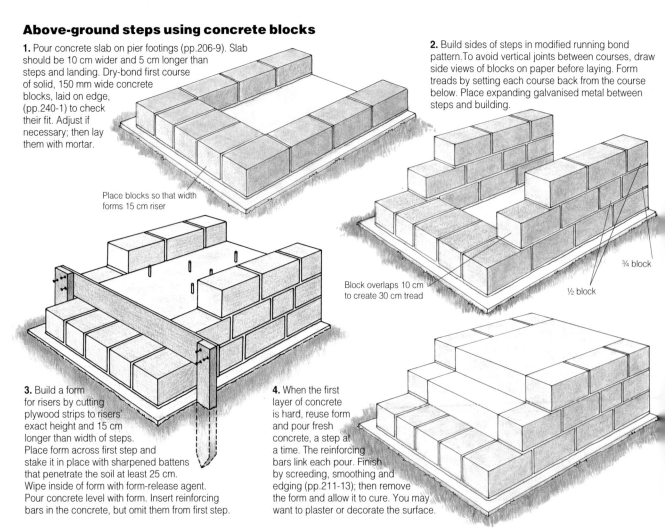

1. Pour concrete slab on pier footings (pp.206-9). Slab should be 10 cm wider and 5 cm longer than steps and landing. Dry-bond first course of solid, 150 mm wide concrete blocks, laid on edge, (pp.240-1) to check their fit. Adjust if necessary; then lay them with mortar.

Place blocks so that width forms 15 cm riser

2. Build sides of steps in modified running bond pattern. To avoid vertical joints between courses, draw side views of blocks on paper before laying. Form treads by setting each course back from the course below. Place expanding galvanised metal between steps and building.

Block overlaps 10 cm to create 30 cm tread

¾ block

½ block

3. Build a form for risers by cutting plywood strips to risers' exact height and 15 cm longer than width of steps. Place form across first step and stake it in place with sharpened battens that penetrate the soil at least 25 cm. Wipe inside of form with form-release agent. Pour concrete level with form. Insert reinforcing bars in the concrete, but omit them from first step.

4. When the first layer of concrete is hard, reuse form and pour fresh concrete, a step at a time. The reinforcing bars link each pour. Finish by screeding, smoothing and edging (pp.211-13); then remove the form and allow it to cure. You may want to plaster or decorate the surface.

In-ground steps with bricks and pavers

Garden steps can be built of any combination of materials; the method shown below, incorporating bricks and pavers, can be adapted if you substitute heavy wooden beams or railway sleepers for the bricks. To avoid having to cut bricks, pavers or sleepers, adjust the dimensions of the steps.

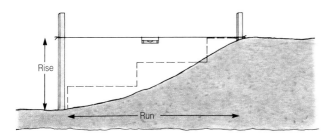

1. Drive in stakes at both top and bottom of the slope. Using string and a line level, measure between the stakes to find the run. On the taller stake, measure the distance from the ground to the string in order to find the rise. Calculate how many uniform steps you can fit into the rise. The formula is given on the facing page.

Flagstone steps

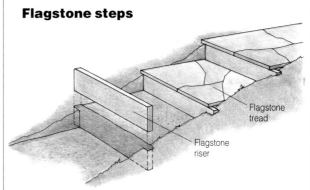

Excavate, allowing for stone tread and a 5 cm (2 in) layer of sand above a 10 cm (4 in) bed of well-rammed hardcore. Then dig narrow, straight trenches right across for flagstone risers. Extend the trenches beyond the width of the steps, to accommodate risers snugly. Install risers; then add hardcore fill and sand. Lay flagstone treads so they overlap risers. Trim edges if necessary. Check treads often with a level, and reposition them as needed to ensure flat surfaces (pp.236-7).

7. When positioning the paving slabs, allow a slight fall (5 mm in 30 cm) towards the front of the slab, to encourage water to run off. Repeat for subsequent steps, allowing drying time of half a day between steps.

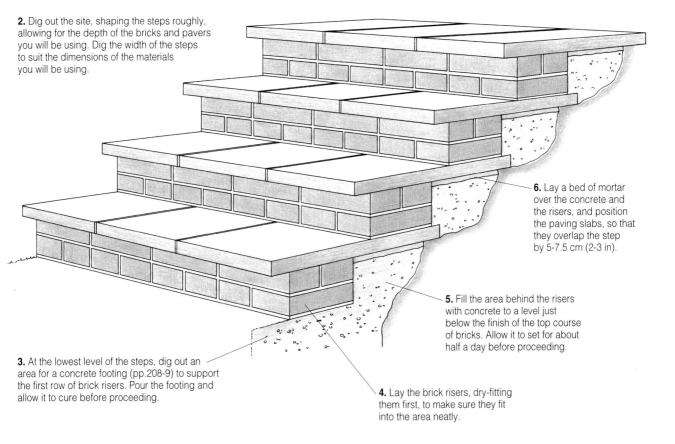

2. Dig out the site, shaping the steps roughly, allowing for the depth of the bricks and pavers you will be using. Dig the width of the steps to suit the dimensions of the materials you will be using.

6. Lay a bed of mortar over the concrete and the risers, and position the paving slabs, so that they overlap the step by 5-7.5 cm (2-3 in).

5. Fill the area behind the risers with concrete to a level just below the finish of the top course of bricks. Allow it to set for about half a day before proceeding.

3. At the lowest level of the steps, dig out an area for a concrete footing (pp.208-9) to support the first row of brick risers. Pour the footing and allow it to cure before proceeding.

4. Lay the brick risers, dry-fitting them first, to make sure they fit into the area neatly.

Freestanding masonry walls are quite safe if properly designed and built. Consult your local building control officer as well as the local planning officer before beginning a wall project. You can often obtain sample plans.

As a rule, support a wall with a continuous foundation that is at least 500 mm below final ground level. However, if the ground is not firm, or the foundation will be standing on clay – which may shrink in hot weather – you should seek expert advice.

Half brick thick walls should be no higher than 710 mm (28 in) in the most sheltered conditions and less in exposed conditions. For a higher wall, build a 215 mm thick wall or else a 102 mm thick wall with brick piers at intervals. The piers rest on footings

that can be from 460 to 610 mm (1 ft 6 in-2 ft) square. (The size of the piers and the panels must be designed to suit the site and conditions.)

Pier-and-panel walls derive their strength from steel reinforcing rods, sometimes called rebars, which must be pushed into the foundation at the pier locations after eight courses have been built and while the concrete is still wet. Overlap rods if you need to join them but don't allow rod ends to coincide with the top of a concrete fill.

Most concrete block walls that are non-load-bearing do not require reinforcement, but walls that are made of screen blocks must be reinforced with pilasters, whose function is similar to piers. (Like piers, pilasters contain vertical reinforcing rods.)

In addition, wire joint reinforcing must be embedded horizontally in every other course to compensate for the inherent weakness of the stack bond pattern (pp.226-7) in which screen blocks are usually laid.

All free-standing walls of bricks and blocks are best protected from rain and frost by a precast concrete coping which projects at least 50 mm each side and has drip throating grooves. Bricks set on edge may look attractive but do not throw rainwater clear of the wall faces below, as precast copings do.

Stucco can be applied to masonry for both appearance and protection. A typical formula for stucco is 1 part masonry cement and 3 to 5 parts very fine sand, mixed with clean water to a workable consistency.

One brick thick wall (215 mm)

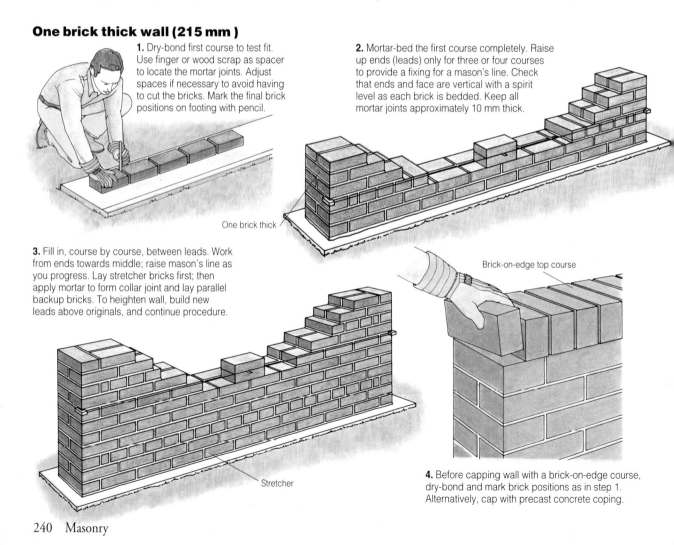

1. Dry-bond first course to test fit. Use finger or wood scrap as spacer to locate the mortar joints. Adjust spaces if necessary to avoid having to cut the bricks. Mark the final brick positions on footing with pencil.

2. Mortar-bed the first course completely. Raise up ends (leads) only for three or four courses to provide a fixing for a mason's line. Check that ends and face are vertical with a spirit level as each brick is bedded. Keep all mortar joints approximately 10 mm thick.

One brick thick

3. Fill in, course by course, between leads. Work from ends towards middle; raise mason's line as you progress. Lay stretcher bricks first; then apply mortar to form collar joint and lay parallel backup bricks. To heighten wall, build new leads above originals, and continue procedure.

Brick-on-edge top course

Stretcher

4. Before capping wall with a brick-on-edge course, dry-bond and mark brick positions as in step 1. Alternatively, cap with precast concrete coping.

Pier-and-panel walling

1. Excavate pier footings at least 500 mm (about 20 in) deep. Fill with concrete and cast a continuous strip footing between piers to support panels. The concrete supporting the panels needs to be only 150 mm (6 in) thick.

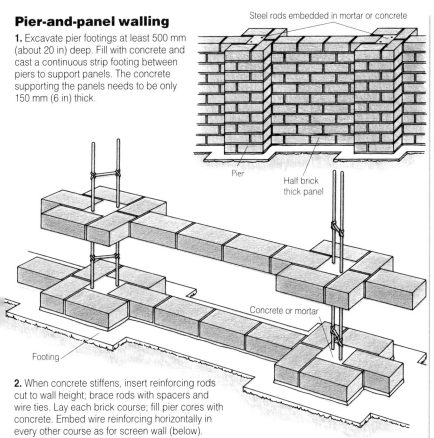

Steel rods embedded in mortar or concrete

Pier

Half brick thick panel

Concrete or mortar

Footing

2. When concrete stiffens, insert reinforcing rods cut to wall height; brace rods with spacers and wire ties. Lay each brick course; fill pier cores with concrete. Embed wire reinforcing horizontally in every other course as for screen wall (below).

Screen wall

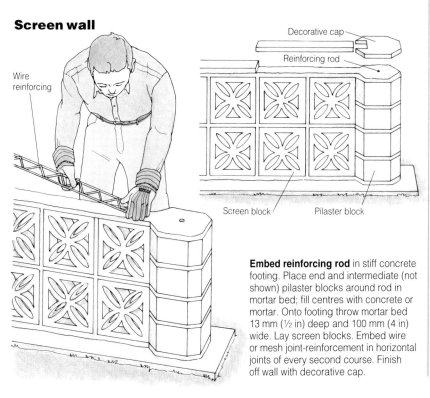

Wire reinforcing

Decorative cap

Reinforcing rod

Screen block

Pilaster block

Embed reinforcing rod in stiff concrete footing. Place end and intermediate (not shown) pilaster blocks around rod in mortar bed; fill centres with concrete or mortar. Onto footing throw mortar bed 13 mm (½ in) deep and 100 mm (4 in) wide. Lay screen blocks. Embed wire or mesh joint-reinforcement in horizontal joints of every second course. Finish off wall with decorative cap.

Rendering a block wall

1. Dampen wall; brush on PVA building adhesive. Apply first coat of stucco 10 mm (⅜ in) thick by spreading it forcefully with plasterer's steel laying-on trowel, then smooth with gentle, circular movement with wooden float.

2. Score first coat with scarifier or other raking tool. Keep surface damp for 48 hours by covering with plastic sheeting.

3. Apply final coat of rendering 6 mm (¼ in) thick with plasterer's trowel. Mix in pigment to add colour. To add texture, pattern your strokes.

WALLS: DRY AND MORTARED STONE

The courses of a stone wall can be random or irregular, using uncut, roughly dressed or dressed stones in no particular pattern, or they can be regular, with the stones fitted tightly in level courses.

Walls can be laid with or without mortar. Novices should begin with a dry stone wall (one built without mortar) that is no more than 1 m (3 ft) high. Dry stone walls move as the temperature changes, so they are more flexible than mortared ones. Dry stone walls need no concrete footing and require excavation to below organic soil – possibly only 15 cm (6 in).

The force of gravity holds well-built walls together and pulls apart poorly laid ones. These guidelines will help you to work effectively with gravity and maximise friction between the stones. Tilt the stones slightly towards the centre of the wall. You can also taper or batter the faces of a wall to a minimum of 1 in 12 – or 1 cm in every 12 cm.

In dry retaining walls you must taper the outer face or slant the inner face (pp.244-5). Fit each stone so that it contacts the adjacent stones in as many places as possible. Place the stones 'stretchered' – staggering vertical joints by laying one stone over the joint between the two below. For stability, make the wall at least two stones thick – a wall 1 m (3 ft) high should be about 60 cm (2 ft) thick. Use a bonding or through stone every 1m² (11 sq ft). These stones, ideally as long as the wall is thick, are laid crossways to hold the stones together.

Coursed dry stone wall with shaped stones

Random mortared wall with undressed stones

A mortared or wet wall can be built with the mortar either visible or recessed so that it is hidden from view. Both ways, mortar improves the bonding between stones, permitting higher walls and vertical faces. But the same principles for working with gravity apply: mortar is not as durable as stone, and when it fails, gravity and friction take over.

A mortared wall is relatively inflexible. Instead of moving slightly to adjust to the forces of heating and cooling or of growing tree roots, a mortared wall cracks. To minimise movement, build a wall on a footing or a trench-fill foundation (p.208) placed just below the frost line. On a slope, install a pipe on the uphill side to drain the water behind the wall (pp.244-5). Never lay more than three courses – or 60 cm (2 ft) of wall height – in a day, so that the mortar can set enough to withstand the weight of the next courses. A mortar mixture for stone is 1 part hydrated lime, 1 part cement and 6 parts building sand, with a plasticiser to make the mortar workable. Add water slowly until the mixture stands in peaks like whipped cream.

Keep the mortar off the stones' faces because the cement will stain the stones. A newly built wall should be kept cool and damp for about a week to extend the curing time and strengthen the mortar. Mist the wall with a hose and cover it with plastic sheeting. If necessary, shade it, too.

Caution: Wear waterproof gloves when working with mortar; protect your eyes with goggles.

Putting gravity to work

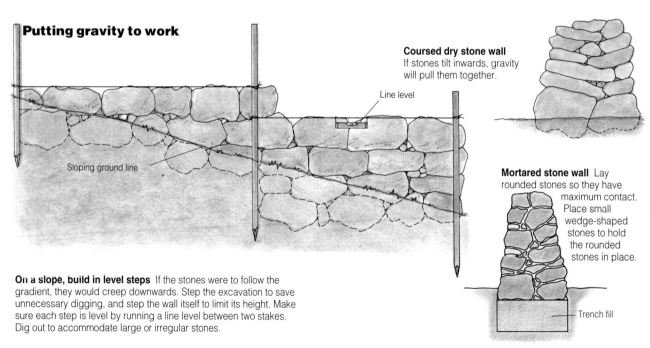

Coursed dry stone wall
If stones tilt inwards, gravity will pull them together.

Line level

Sloping ground line

Mortared stone wall Lay rounded stones so they have maximum contact. Place small wedge-shaped stones to hold the rounded stones in place.

Trench fill

On a slope, build in level steps If the stones were to follow the gradient, they would creep downwards. Step the excavation to save unnecessary digging, and step the wall itself to limit its height. Make sure each step is level by running a line level between two stakes. Dig out to accommodate large or irregular stones.

Laying a dry wall

Place the first course on firm, level ground, using batter frames and nylon lines to guide the construction. Place the larger, more irregular stones on the bottom, digging as needed so they slope down slightly towards the centre of the wall. Fill the centre with smaller stones. As you add courses, stagger the vertical joints.

Turn corners by overlapping long and short stones from each leg in alternating courses. These stones tie the legs together. In a run, they are called tie stones; at a corner, they are called quoins.

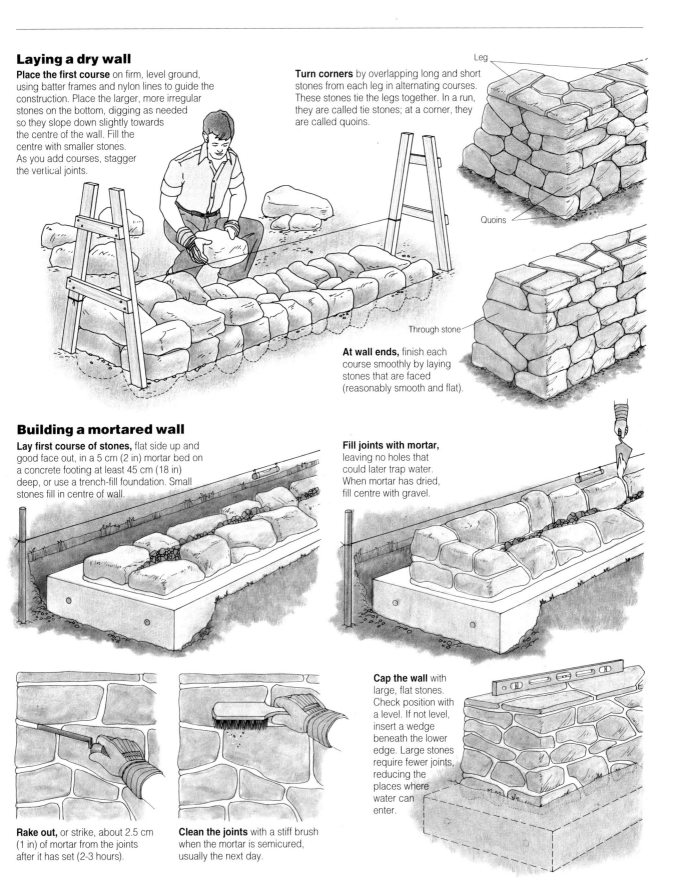

Leg

Quoins

Through stone

At wall ends, finish each course smoothly by laying stones that are faced (reasonably smooth and flat).

Building a mortared wall

Lay first course of stones, flat side up and good face out, in a 5 cm (2 in) mortar bed on a concrete footing at least 45 cm (18 in) deep, or use a trench-fill foundation. Small stones fill in centre of wall.

Fill joints with mortar, leaving no holes that could later trap water. When mortar has dried, fill centre with gravel.

Rake out, or strike, about 2.5 cm (1 in) of mortar from the joints after it has set (2-3 hours).

Clean the joints with a stiff brush when the mortar is semicured, usually the next day.

Cap the wall with large, flat stones. Check position with a level. If not level, insert a wedge beneath the lower edge. Large stones require fewer joints, reducing the places where water can enter.

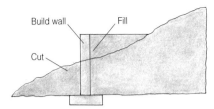

Build wall
Fill
Cut

On sloping land, retaining walls hold back the soil, preventing erosion and creating a more usable landscape. These walls are commonly made of stone or concrete block – either the standard kind or one of the many types of interlocking block that require no mortar. The design of the wall depends on the building material and such technical factors as the soil type, the wall height and the site conditions.

A stone wall, if laid dry, requires no footing and should slope or batter in towards the bank. Whether it is made of stone or concrete block, a gravity wall, which is thick at the bottom and steps up gradually, relies on its mass to hold back the soil.

Soils vary in their ability to absorb or drain water as well as the ways they react when wet or frozen. Water can exert more pressure on a retaining wall than soil, so drainage is very important. If you are in doubt, consult an expert. Generally, soils that drain well and remain stable when wet (such as gravel and sandy gravel) will not put as much pressure on a retaining wall as those that absorb water or lack cohesiveness (such as soft clay and silt). In addition, soils differ in their ability to bear weight – a factor for high walls only. Consult your local authority for advice about local soil conditions. If you learn that the soil conditions are a concern, or if you are unsure, backfill the area behind the retaining wall with gravel rather than the soil found on site.

Site conditions A rainy climate, a high water table (the level of a site's groundwater), or the presence of a nearby lake, stream or spring may affect the design of a wall. When soil becomes wet, its load-bearing capacity is reduced, its weight increases and it tends to move laterally.

In cold climates, wet soil freezes and expands, putting tremendous pressure on the wall. To reduce increased soil pressure, install special drainage for all types of retaining walls over 60 cm (2 ft) high, even dry-stone walls.

Drainage can be provided by weep holes, gravel backfill, a drainage pipe or a combination of these elements. A 2 mm stipple coat prevents water from seeping through the wall itself and prevents the efflorescence water causes (p.248). Make the stipple coat with 6 parts of cement to 9 parts of water and 1 part of SBR (styrene butadiene rubber). Scrub it vigorously into the surface at a rate of 5 kg of the mixture to 1 m^2 (1 lb per sq ft).

Wall height Retaining walls more than 1 m (3 ft) high are governed by local building regulations. Generally, the higher the wall and the steeper the slope of the bank being supported, the stronger the wall – and the footing below it – must be. To hold back a steep bank, a series of low walls giving a terraced effect is an attractive and less demanding alternative to a single high wall. Get a contractor to build walls more than 1.2 m (4 ft) high, and an engineer or architect to design retaining walls more than 2.4m (8 ft) high.

Concrete block retaining walls

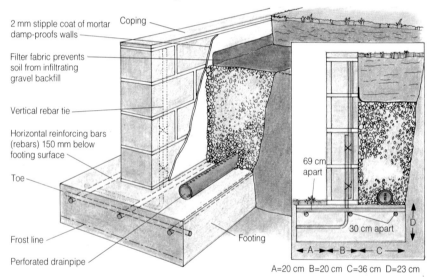

2 mm stipple coat of mortar damp-proofs walls

Coping

Filter fabric prevents soil from infiltrating gravel backfill

Vertical rebar tie

Horizontal reinforcing bars (rebars) 150 mm below footing surface

Toe

Frost line

Perforated drainpipe

Footing

69 cm apart

30 cm apart

A   B   C

D

A=20 cm B=20 cm C=36 cm D=23 cm

Footing for a typical 1 m high retaining concrete block wall (above) extends 360 mm into bank. To tie the wall to the footing, vertical 10 mm rebars run through the block courses every 81 cm and are bent to extend into toe of footing. Place horizontal 10 mm rebars 30 cm apart along the length and 69 cm apart across the width of footing.

Gravity wall (right) has a vertical face and a stepped back profile, with a base equal to at least half the height. This wall depends on its weight and on friction between the wall and the ground for its ability to resist horizontal pressure. Use blocks of 100 mm and 140 mm widths to build stepped wall with staggered mortar joints.

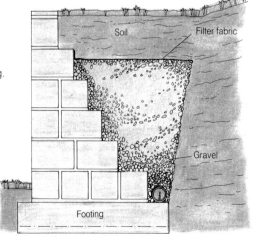

Soil

Filter fabric

Gravel

Footing

Dry-stone retaining wall

Excavate to firm subsoil; lay stone courses. Backfill with gravel as you build, extending large stones into the hill. Excess water will drain through dry wall joints. For clay soil, add a drainpipe behind wall and cover clay with filter fabric to prevent it from penetrating gravel.

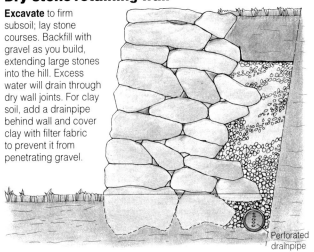

Perforated drainpipe

Vertical-face dry wall

Slant back of wall into slope. Lay a narrow base course; backfill with gravel or soil, and pack it with digging bar (p.230). Repeat, laying gradually thicker courses. The top course of a 90 cm (3 ft) wall should be about 60 cm (2 ft) thick.

Perforated drainpipe

Check angle with batter board of plywood or nailed boards. Build it as tall as the wall's height, with a base 5 cm (2 in) long for each 30 cm (12 in) of height. Add two shims in base to keep it even.

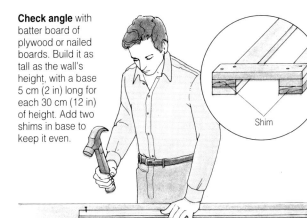

Shim

Mortared retaining wall

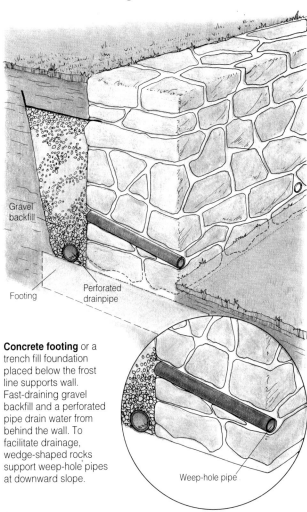

Gravel backfill

Footing

Perforated drainpipe

Weep-hole pipe

Place batter board against the wall as you lay each course. For a long wall you can stake several batter boards about 90-120 cm (3-4 ft) apart and add a levelled line.

Concrete footing or a trench fill foundation placed below the frost line supports wall. Fast-draining gravel backfill and a perforated pipe drain water from behind the wall. To facilitate drainage, wedge-shaped rocks support weep-hole pipes at downward slope.

VENEER: BRICK AND STONE

Veneer masonry is a decorative cladding that enhances the face of a structure. It can be made of brick, natural stone or a synthetic stone that is lighter in weight and easier to install than natural stone. Applying full-size bricks or stones as cladding (bottom of page) requires traditional masonry techniques. These include building a footing to bear the weight of the materials (the footing must be below the frost line if the veneer is outdoors) and arranging and mortaring the individual bricks or stones so that those on the bottom support those on top. In addition, metal ties or wire reinforcing may be needed to fasten the cladding to the wall.

Veneer bricks, also called brick slips, can be 15-25 mm (½-1 in) thick and are lightweight. You can buy packs that contain 30 faces or 10 corners. You will also need building adhesive, spacers and premixed mortar. To cut thin bricks, use a tile cutter or a circular saw with a diamond-tipped blade.

Synthetic veneer masonry These products come as panels or individual pieces resembling various kinds of bricks or building stones. Many are suited for both outdoor and indoor use; some are designed especially for hearths. Synthetic masonry is easy to install almost anywhere. If it will be visible from the side, use corner pieces; these units have a 90 degree angle that allows the 'stones' to turn corners.

When preparing surfaces for installing synthetic masonry, follow the maker's instructions. Set thin bricks in a layer of adhesive, and fill the joints with mortar. For synthetic stones, apply a scratch coat of mortar; then let it dry. (Spread the mortar directly on bare masonry; cover other surfaces with metal lath first.) Next apply mortar to the back of each piece and press it into place; fill the joints with mortar.

Brick slips for interiors

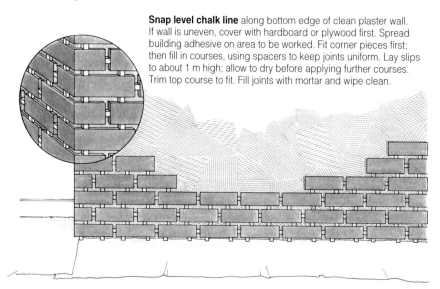

Snap level chalk line along bottom edge of clean plaster wall. If wall is uneven, cover with hardboard or plywood first. Spread building adhesive on area to be worked. Fit corner pieces first; then fill in courses, using spacers to keep joints uniform. Lay slips to about 1 m high; allow to dry before applying further courses. Trim top course to fit. Fill joints with mortar and wipe clean.

Brick-on-block retaining wall

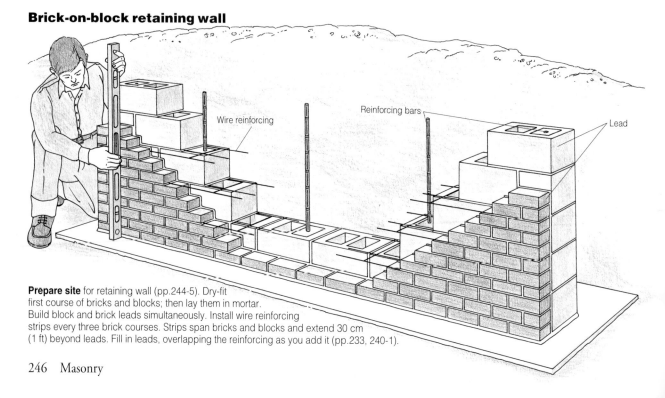

Wire reinforcing

Reinforcing bars

Lead

Prepare site for retaining wall (pp.244-5). Dry-fit first course of bricks and blocks; then lay them in mortar. Build block and brick leads simultaneously. Install wire reinforcing strips every three brick courses. Strips span bricks and blocks and extend 30 cm (1 ft) beyond leads. Fill in leads, overlapping the reinforcing as you add it (pp.233, 240-1).

WORKING WITH SYNTHETIC STONES

Setting the stones

Lay hearth pieces, if any, first (bottom of page); protect them with plastic sheeting. If necessary, staple or nail metal lath to studs in wall at 15 cm (6 in) intervals. Apply mortar scratch coat. Attach units, working from top down.

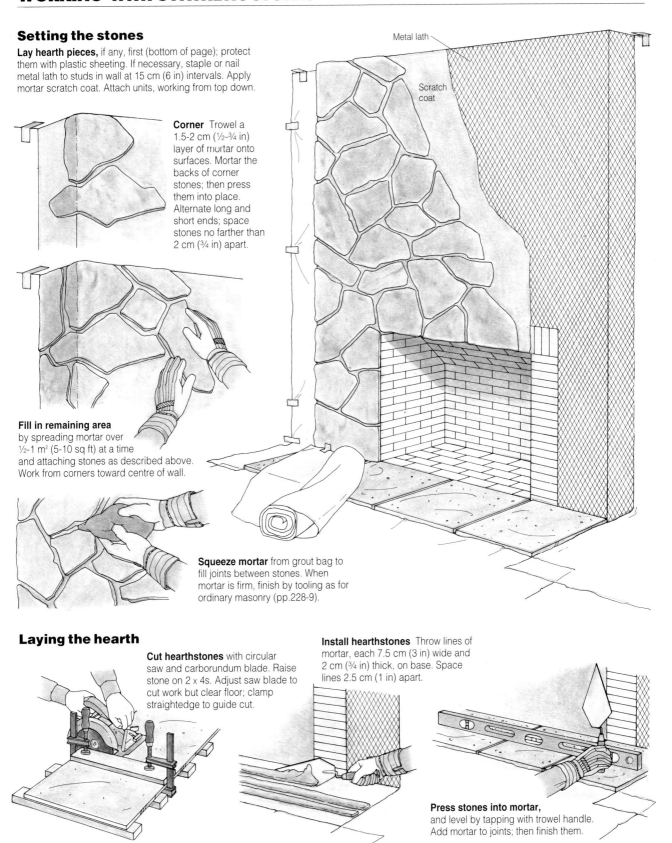

Metal lath

Scratch coat

Corner Trowel a 1.5-2 cm (½-¾ in) layer of mortar onto surfaces. Mortar the backs of corner stones; then press them into place. Alternate long and short ends; space stones no farther than 2 cm (¾ in) apart.

Fill in remaining area by spreading mortar over ½-1 m² (5-10 sq ft) at a time and attaching stones as described above. Work from corners toward centre of wall.

Squeeze mortar from grout bag to fill joints between stones. When mortar is firm, finish by tooling as for ordinary masonry (pp.228-9).

Laying the hearth

Cut hearthstones with circular saw and carborundum blade. Raise stone on 2 x 4s. Adjust saw blade to cut work but clear floor; clamp straightedge to guide cut.

Install hearthstones Throw lines of mortar, each 7.5 cm (3 in) wide and 2 cm (¾ in) thick, on base. Space lines 2.5 cm (1 in) apart.

Press stones into mortar, and level by tapping with trowel handle. Add mortar to joints; then finish them.

Masonry should be repaired as soon as the damage is discovered. If neglected, small problems that are relatively easy to fix can become major ones. Most masonry damage is caused by moisture, settling or impact – the most serious being caused by moisture freezing during cold winter weather.

Efflorescence, a white powder often found on new masonry surfaces, is usually caused by moisture introduced during construction. The moisture should dry in a few months, and rain usually washes away the powder.

If efflorescence continues or if it appears on older masonry, look for an entry point for moisture, such as cracks, crumbling mortar, deterioration around windows, doors and chimneys, and dampness caused by moisture-saturated soil against masonry below

ground. Repairing all but the last usually involves replacing damaged building materials, applying a patch, then repointing. Once you have solved the moisture problem, remove the efflorescence by scrubbing it with a stiff brush and water.

Before repairing cracks in mortar joints, seal off any entry points of moisture. If cracks redevelop, consult a builder. For pointing, use mortar that is 1 part masonry cement, 3 parts sand for brick – or 4 to 5 parts sand for stone – and enough water to make the mix the consistency of soft ice cream.

Dampness in embedded masonry is more difficult to cure; the soil around the masonry must be drained. If the masonry is a foundation wall, first check that gutters are not clogged and that drainpipes are placed beneath

downpipes to carry run-off away. Sometimes you may find it necessary to rearrange the soil so that it slopes away from the masonry.

With foundations and retaining walls, gullies at the footing level can become blocked. Clear them with a Sanisnake drain auger if you can gain access to their openings.

In basements, a high water table can cause dampness. Installing a sump pump beneath the floor, and perhaps land drainpipes in surrounding soil, may solve the problem.

For severe or persistent moisture problems, it is best to consult a builder or surveyor. Often, the solution is to dig along the outside of the wall (or the high side of a retaining wall), and install perforated drainpipes surrounded by a layer of gravel.

Repointing cracked mortar joints

1. With cold chisel and club hammer, drive out old mortar to depth of about 1.3-2 cm (½-¾ in). Wear goggles and thick gloves for protection. Chisel a square-sided groove, exposing bare stone on at least one side of each joint. Brush away chips and dust.

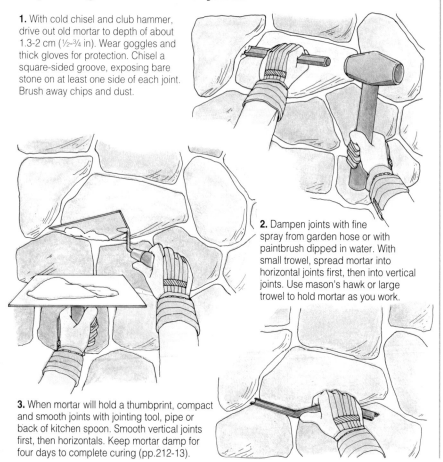

2. Dampen joints with fine spray from garden hose or with paintbrush dipped in water. With small trowel, spread mortar into horizontal joints first, then into vertical joints. Use mason's hawk or large trowel to hold mortar as you work.

3. When mortar will hold a thumbprint, compact and smooth joints with jointing tool, pipe or back of kitchen spoon. Smooth vertical joints first, then horizontals. Keep mortar damp for four days to complete curing (pp.212-13).

Replacing a broken brick

1. Chisel away damaged brick and surrounding mortar. Clean wall cavity and dampen it; spread mortar on bottom surface.

2. Dampen new brick; mortar top and sides; then slide into place from hawk or trowel. Add extra mortar to joints if necessary.

Filling large cracks

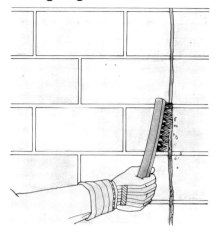

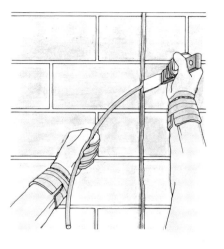

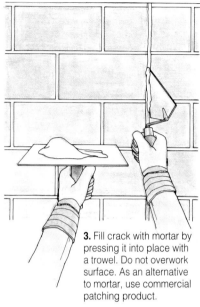

1. Brush out all debris carefully, using a wire brush, or blow it out. In concrete block masonry it is better not to chisel out a crack, as you would for concrete. Mortar will adhere to a clean crack in a block.

2. Pack cracks with strips of expanded polystyrene or foam pipe lag to within 1.3 cm (½ in) of surface. Next, dampen the crack with clean water and brush all surfaces with PVA building adhesive.

3. Fill crack with mortar by pressing it into place with a trowel. Do not overwork surface. As an alternative to mortar, use commercial patching product.

Rebuilding a broken block

1. Carefully chisel off loose or weak sections of damaged face shell. Dampen area, and apply mortar to webs.

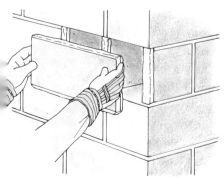

2. Cut face shell from new block. Apply mortar and press block into place. Mortar fills gaps between cut shell and repair area. Finish joints as for whole blocks (p.232).

Repairing rendering

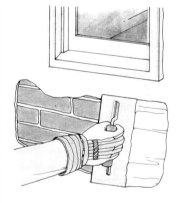

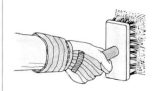

1. Correct any structural or moisture problems. Chisel away loose material; brush repair clean. Dampen area, then trowel on mortar until it is level with surrounding surface.

2. Compact and smooth new mortar with batten or wood float. Add more mortar if necessary. Disguise repair by feathering mortar beyond borders of patch with trowel.

3. Keep mortar damp for five days until cured. Then apply new masonry paint with a large paintbrush. If desired, add texture by using freehand strokes or by spattering with a brush.

CERAMICS, GLASS AND PLASTICS

CERAMIC TILES

In addition to being beautiful, ceramic tiles are durable and easy to clean. They come in various colours and may be plain or hand-painted. Grout, the material placed between tiles, comes in colours to match or contrast with the tiles.

When choosing tiles, consider where they will be used; this will determine what the composition should be (p.254). Then think about appearance – large patterns will look out of place in a small room. Although tiling a whole section with hand-painted tiles may be too expensive for most budgets, you can select a few as accent pieces to combine with more affordable tiles. Because manufacturers make tiles in different thicknesses, whenever you mix tiles be sure that their thicknesses match. When you visit a designer or tile supplier, take along photos, colour swatches and dimensions.

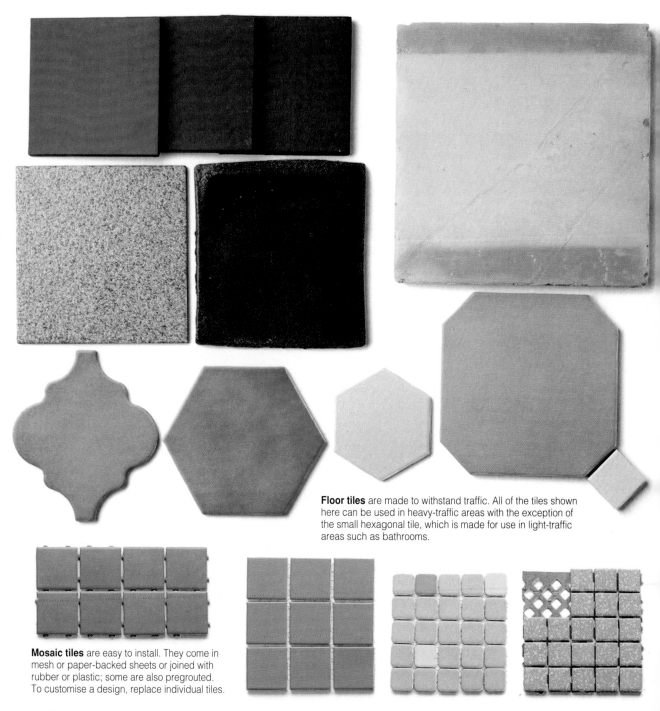

Floor tiles are made to withstand traffic. All of the tiles shown here can be used in heavy-traffic areas with the exception of the small hexagonal tile, which is made for use in light-traffic areas such as bathrooms.

Mosaic tiles are easy to install. They come in mesh or paper-backed sheets or joined with rubber or plastic; some are also pregrouted. To customise a design, replace individual tiles.

Wall tiles are designed specifically for walls; if you install them on a floor they will most likely crack under the weight of people and furniture; they also scratch easily. You can create your own geometric patterns by selecting plain tiles of different colours and arranging them as you want. Tiles may come designed for complementary arrangements, including tiles with matching patterns (far right, top), or repeating patterns (far right, centre). Some manufacturers also make matching border tiles.

Feature tiles come in a variety of shapes and sizes to create a smooth transition between adjacent surfaces or to give a finished look by forming rounded edges or corners. They are usually designed to match standard tiles.

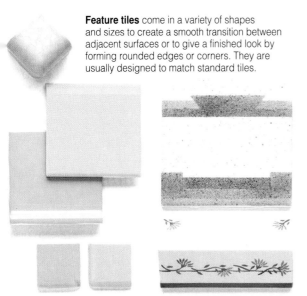

Dual-use tile (above) is suitable for walls and floors. If installed on a floor, make sure dual-use tiles are rated for use in light-traffic areas. These tiles are not suitable for floors exposed to heavy traffic.

Insert tiles (above) accent or border wall tiles. Some are strong enough for floors.

Border tiles come with different patterns and profiles; you can use them in single rows or stack them to create a distinctive look. Use the tiles to accent the tops of tiles that end some way up a wall or to break up a solid block of plain tiles.

Ceramic tile provides an attractive, durable covering for surfaces as diverse as walls, worktops, floors and hearths. Tiling a surface is not difficult, but careful planning and installation will pay off – careless work can result in cracked, uneven or loose tiles.

Before choosing a type of tile, consider the degree of water-resistance, strength, slipperiness and stain resistance necessary for the location. Most tiles are classified for use on either walls or floors. Most wall tiles are not strong enough to be set on floors or high-use areas; many floor tiles are too large for worktops and too heavy for walls.

Glazed tiles are easier to keep clean; unglazed tiles are usually less slippery underfoot but are more easily stained. However, sealing unglazed tiles with a commercial tile sealant will make them stain-resistant but more slippery. The sealer will need renewing every year.

Tiles with a textured surface also wear well and are less slippery than standard tiles.

Glazed tiles generally absorb less water than unglazed tiles, but water resistance is gauged by the amount of water the bisque of a tile absorbs. In descending order of absorption, tiles are classified as nonvitreous (readily absorbs water), semivitreous, vitreous and impervious (absorbs less than 0.05 per cent of its weight).

If your dealer doesn't know the classification, ask to be shown the manufacturer's specifications (usually on the packaging). Tiles may also be designated as standard grade, second grade or decorative thin wall tile. Most tile sold is standard grade; second-grade tile may have imperfections in shape or glaze.

Tiles can be either set on a thick mortar bed (best left to professionals) or laid over a substrate thinly coated with adhesive (known as thinset installation).

The type of substrate may vary, but it must be clean, flat and very stable – movement causes tiles to loosen and crack. (If in doubt about the strength of a worktop, add extra cross braces underneath.)

Plaster in good condition is the ideal surface for tiling. Plasterboard can be tiled over without any special treatment, but should be sealed with two coats of drywall topcoat in wet areas, such as round a shower.

Refer to the chart below when choosing tiles and matching them with the correct substrate and adhesive. Plan the layout and install the tiles following the steps on pages 256-7.

Special techniques for preparing the substrate and installing floor tiles are shown on pages 334-6.

Mosaic tile sheets are commonly set on a mesh backing, and are described on page 258. Pregrouted sheets of larger tiles are laid out and set in much the same way as individual tiles. However, it's easier to snip or tear individual tiles off the backing sheet before cutting them.

It is possible to hire tile-cutting equipment. If you have many tiles to cut, hire a masonry saw or an electric tile saw with a water-cooled diamond blade. A portable, cordless tile saw makes accurate cuts, but make sure the tile is securely held on a stable surface before cutting. Hire a tile breaker for thick floor tiles, up to 32 mm (1¼ in).

Ceramic tile is extremely hard – use carbide-tipped drill bits and fit power saws with blades specified for cutting ceramic tile. To avoid chipping the glaze, drill and cut through the face of the tile, not the back.

Caution: In addition to following the safety precautions shown on pages 12-13, inspect all hired tools for sound cutting edges and proper guards before leaving the shop. When cutting or drilling tiles or mixing powdered adhesive, wear goggles and a dust mask; also wear ear protection when using power tools.

When using adhesives, work in a well-ventilated area and extinguish all open flames (including pilot lights). Water keeps bits and blades cool, but never submerge part of the body of a power tool in water.

Choosing tile

Location	Tiles	Substrate	Adhesive
Indoor floors	Glazed floor tiles, pavers (must be sealed), quarry tile, terracotta, mosaic	Concrete slab, plywood	Thin-bed cement-based; thin-bed epoxy
Outdoor floors	Some glazed floor tiles, mosaic, pavers, quarry tile	Concrete slab	Thin-bed cement based
Wet walls (such as shower surrounds and splashbacks)	Glazed wall tiles, mosaic	Plaster, plasterboard sealed with drywall topcoat	Thin-bed cement based; thin-bed ready-mixed water resistant
Worktops	Glazed heavy-duty tiles, small glazed floor tiles, mosaic	Plywood, MDF or chipboard sealed with PVA/water mix	Thin-bed cement-based; thin-bed ready-mixed water-resistant
Indoor walls	Glazed wall tiles, mosaic, small glazed floor tiles	Plasterboard, wallboard, plaster, plywood	Thin-bed cement-based; thin-bed ready-mixed

Cutting tiles to fit

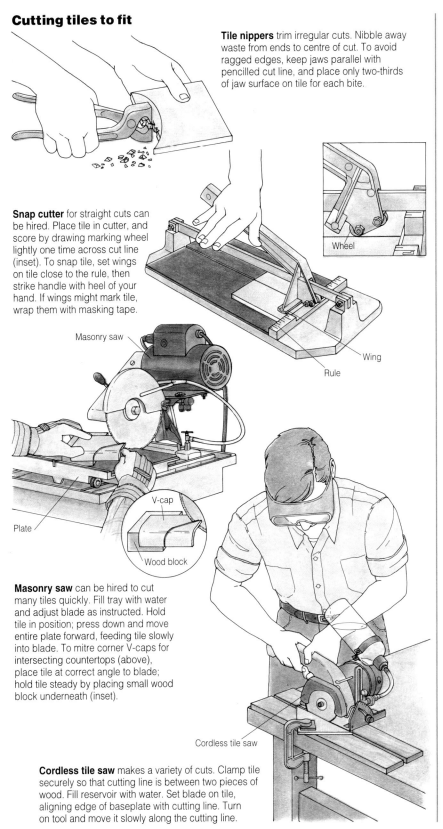

Tile nippers trim irregular cuts. Nibble away waste from ends to centre of cut. To avoid ragged edges, keep jaws parallel with pencilled cut line, and place only two-thirds of jaw surface on tile for each bite.

Snap cutter for straight cuts can be hired. Place tile in cutter, and score by drawing marking wheel lightly one time across cut line (inset). To snap tile, set wings on tile close to the rule, then strike handle with heel of your hand. If wings might mark tile, wrap them with masking tape.

Wheel

Wing

Rule

Masonry saw

V-cap

Plate

Wood block

Masonry saw can be hired to cut many tiles quickly. Fill tray with water and adjust blade as instructed. Hold tile in position; press down and move entire plate forward, feeding tile slowly into blade. To mitre corner V-caps for intersecting countertops (above), place tile at correct angle to blade; hold tile steady by placing small wood block underneath (inset).

Cordless tile saw

Cordless tile saw makes a variety of cuts. Clamp tile securely so that cutting line is between two pieces of wood. Fill reservoir with water. Set blade on tile, aligning edge of baseplate with cutting line. Turn on tool and move it slowly along the cutting line.

Drilling holes

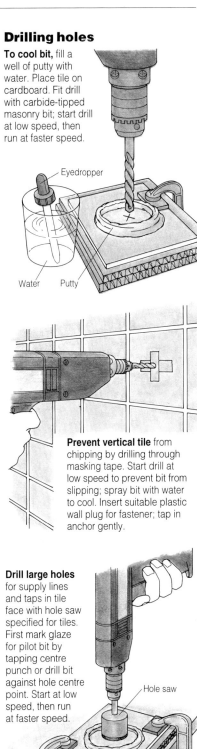

To cool bit, fill a well of putty with water. Place tile on cardboard. Fit drill with carbide-tipped masonry bit; start drill at low speed, then run at faster speed.

Eyedropper

Water   Putty

Prevent vertical tile from chipping by drilling through masking tape. Start drill at low speed to prevent bit from slipping; spray bit with water to cool. Insert suitable plastic wall plug for fastener; tap in anchor gently.

Drill large holes for supply lines and taps in tile face with hole saw specified for tiles. First mark glaze for pilot bit by tapping centre punch or drill bit against hole centre point. Start at low speed, then run at faster speed.

Hole saw

Choose a tile to match the size of your room – large pavers suitable for an impressive entrance would overwhelm a small bathroom. See page 347 to work out the number of tiles you need; buy 15 per cent extra to allow for breakage.

For the best results, lay out the tiles accurately; they must be evenly spaced on the substrate before you set them in adhesive. On a vertical surface, use a layout rod to mark the position of the tiles; for a horizontal surface, you can use the tiles themselves. If it is necessary to cut tiles at the ends of rows, they should be the same size at each end and more than half a tile wide. Tiling round irregular shapes is not easy; a round sink, for example, requires curved cuts in all the surrounding tiles.

Make grout joints 3-6 mm (⅛-¼ in) wide. Some tiles have built-in lugs to ensure consistent joint size; otherwise, place tile spacers between tiles or use preset sheets of tile (check grout joints between sheets with a straightedge). Spacers are most useful when the tiles are uniform, but for all types, check that the tiles are parallel with the layout lines.

If the surface is not square, you can make corrections in the layout, such as cutting end tiles so that they taper gradually. To protect countertop tiles from cracking with any substrate movement, leave a 3-6 mm (⅛-¼ in) silicone sealer-filled gap between the tiles and the wall or splashback, or if the tiles continue on the vertical surface, install cove tiles (p.259). Leave a small silicone sealer-filled gap between the substrate and the splashback, if possible.

Set most tiles with a square-notched trowel – with 10 mm (⅜ in) notches for tiles with lugs or ribs on the back or with 6 mm (¼ in) notches for other tiles. Lift a tile from the setting bed to see if its entire back is covered with adhesive; if not, use a trowel with larger notches.

Grout can sometimes be coloured to match your tile. (Lighter shades are more prone to staining.) A light grout used with dark tiles, and vice versa, can look dramatic but will magnify any mistakes in the installation.

Layout patterns

Jack-on-jack is easier to install than running bond. Turn jack-on-jack 45° for diagonal design.

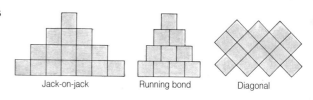

Jack-on-jack   Running bond   Diagonal

Marking the layout

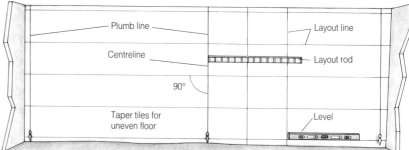

To mark wall layout, first snap a plumb line from ceiling to floor at the wall's centreline or at a focal point (door or window). Then use the layout rod to mark layout lines approximately every 60 cm (2 ft) in all directions, carefully checking horizontal lines for level. Mark corner plumb lines from the last possible joint on the layout rod; then adjust width of cut tiles on ends as needed. Taper end tiles to allow for irregularities at wall edges.

To make layout rod, mark tile and joint widths along a 1.8 m (6 ft) long wooden batten.

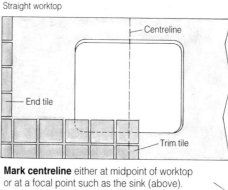

Mark centreline either at midpoint of worktop or at a focal point such as the sink (above). First determine position of trim or end tiles, then main tiles, avoiding narrow cuts along edges. On an L-shaped worktop (above, right) start layout at inside corner and work out in both directions. Mitre trim tiles at corner, if desired. When layout looks right, snap chalk lines to guide installation in 60 cm (2 ft) sections. Mark tiles to fit sink and tap cutouts (right); transfer the cut line to the tile's top for cutting. If possible, install sink and tap on top of the tile; otherwise, fill space between sink or tap and tile with silicone sealer.

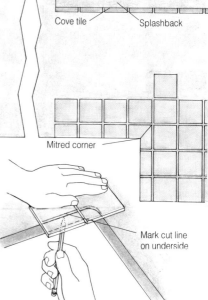

Setting tile

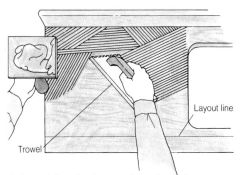

1. Spread tile adhesive onto the wall with the trowel's smooth edges; comb with the notched edges to form ridges, keeping the trowel angle consistently at 30° to the surface. To prevent the adhesive drying before you are ready to use it, work in 60 cm (2 ft) square areas.

Layout line

Trowel

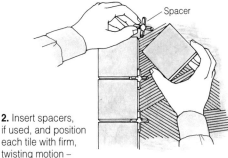

Spacer

2. Insert spacers, if used, and position each tile with firm, twisting motion – don't slide. Clean any excess adhesive off the face of the tiles and at least halfway into the joints. If you don't have specially made spacers, use matchsticks or even small lengths of dry, uncooked spaghetti to create regular spaces between the tiles.

3. To seat the tiles firmly in the adhesive hold a wooden block over each one and tap it with a mallet. After laying several rows, use a spirit level to check that you have installed the tiles level and square. When you have finished, remove spacers with trimming knife. If you used match-sticks or spaghetti, remove them with tweezers or needle-nose pliers.

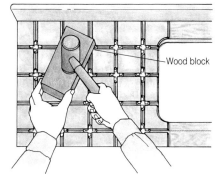

Wood block

Applying grout and sealant

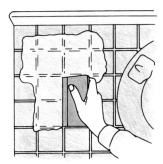

Pack tile grout into joints with a squeegee. Keep the squeegee at an angle of about 45 degrees to the tile surface as you spread the grout. Press firmly and leave the minimum amount of grout on the surface of the tiles.

Clean off any excess grout with a damp sponge, as soon as you have finished. Then, after an hour, remove hazy residue with a clean, damp cloth. When the grout is completely dry, polish with a clean cloth.

Sealing grout and tiles

Foam sponge applicator

Allow grout to cure for 30 days before sealing both grout and tiles with penetrating sealer. Highly porous tiles, such as terracotta, may require specialised sealer. Brush on several light coats of sealer with foam sponge applicator; wipe the sealer off the face of glazed tiles and also tiles that will be exposed to food. Keep joints clean with commercial grout cleaner; reseal grout joints once a year.

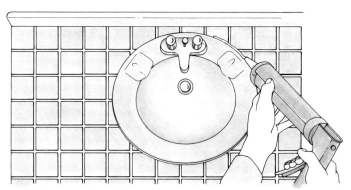

Seal around edges of basin and bath with silicone sealer, shaping the bead with a wet finger. Also seal under rim of basin before installation. Because the weight of the water in some moulded baths can change the shape of the bath, opening up the seam, it is advisable to fill the bath before applying the sealant.

SPECIAL TECHNIQUES

Trimming edges

Set trim tiles first For a V-cap, butter the horizontal edge of substrate with adhesive; then butter back of tile's vertical edge (below).

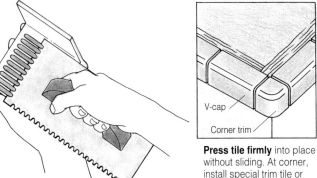

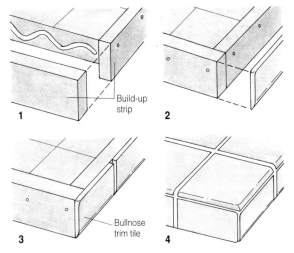

Press tile firmly into place without sliding. At corner, install special trim tile or mitre-cut V-caps (p.255).

Support trim tile on build-up strips where countertop is too thin. Apply solid wood or plywood strips to the edges of counter before laying tile. Secure strips with PVA glue and nails or screws.

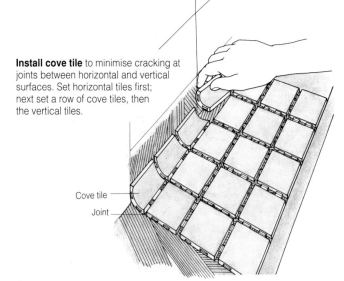

Install cove tile to minimise cracking at joints between horizontal and vertical surfaces. Set horizontal tiles first; next set a row of cove tiles, then the vertical tiles.

Cove tile
Joint

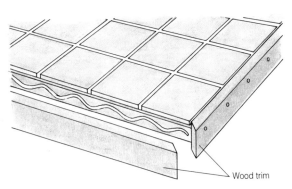

Wood trim

Seal the wood trim with several coats of polyurethane to repel moisture. Secure it with PVA glue and wood screws; for a better finish countersink screwheads. Further information on how to countersink screws appears on page 150.

Installing fixtures

To stick fixtures direct to wall, set them in latex thinset adhesive or in plaster of paris mixed with acrylic latex grout additive. Coat fixture and wall with adhesive, position fixture and hold in place overnight with strips of masking tape. Clean off excess adhesive. Do not use fixture for 24 hours.

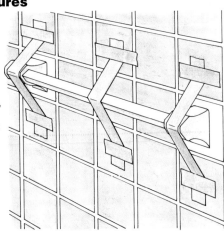

To fit fixtures onto existing tile surface, first drill hole for clip-on fixture in centre of tile (p.255). Install clip; slide fixture over clip; then seal narrow joint between fixture and wall.

Fixture
Clip

Installing mosaic tile

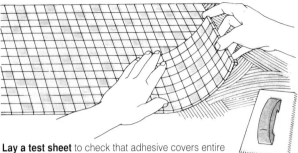

Lay a test sheet to check that adhesive covers entire back of sheet (most mosaics require trowel with triangular, 6 mm notches). To set, roll up sheet loosely, set one edge on layout line and unfurl in place. Check for square every 60 cm (2 ft); grout as shown on page 257. Soak off any mounting paper.

Tiling a curved surface

To lay tiles around a gradual curve, first cut tile into lengthwise pieces. Work in 60 cm (2 ft) square rows across surface. Align pieces carefully, and fully cover back of tiles with adhesive. (Do not use spacers on curved surface.) For 90° corners, buy corner tiles.

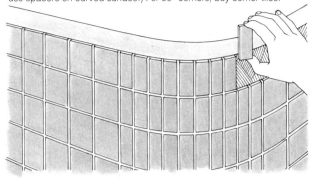

Repairing grout

1. Remove damaged or discoloured grout with a trimming knife with an old, disposable blade in it, working from top of joint. Clean away all debris with a damp sponge. If crumbling or cracking of grout is extensive, consult a professional.

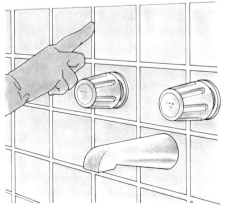

2. Dampen joint, and apply new grout with a gloved finger. Compact grout in joint. For repairs larger than 30 cm (1 ft) square, use a squeegee. Seal grout (p.257).

Replacing tile

1. Remove grout round tile as shown at left. Break up tile with chisel and small club hammer. Wear gloves and safety goggles.

2. Scrape off old adhesive with a chisel knife, without gouging substrate. Clean away all debris; vacuum area around repair thoroughly.

3. Apply new adhesive to substrate and to back of tile. Fit tile in place, twisting it slightly as you position it. Wipe off excess adhesive. Let it dry and then regrout.

Margin trowel

Modern glass has the same humble beginnings as ancient glass – molten silica sand. To create a polished surface, glass is floated on a bath of molten tin. It is then annealed (heated and slowly cooled). When plastic is laminated between two layers of glass, the 'sandwich' can be safely used as a car windscreen; if it is broken, the pieces remain attached to the plastic. Some glass has wire mesh embedded in it; this glass is ideal where security is important, such as in a window next to a front door. Transparent metal coatings on low-emissivity (low-E) glass make it reflect heat while admitting light. Subtle texturing makes glass nonreflective for glazing picture frames; dense patterns produce an obscure finish that gives privacy. You can even change a speciality glass from an obscure to a clear finish (and vice versa) simply by flicking a switch.

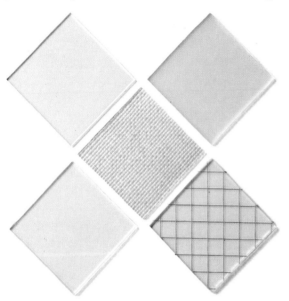

General-purpose glass suits many home uses, including clear glass for windows, light-diffusing ground glass for light fixtures, and patterned glass for bathroom windows. Special glass is laminated with plastic (bottom, left) or has wire set in the glass (bottom, right), this prevents flying shards by holding them in place.

Glass blocks are available in many textures, colours, sizes and shapes – some have angled ends (above). They can be used to make an exterior wall, a floor or a translucent room divider.

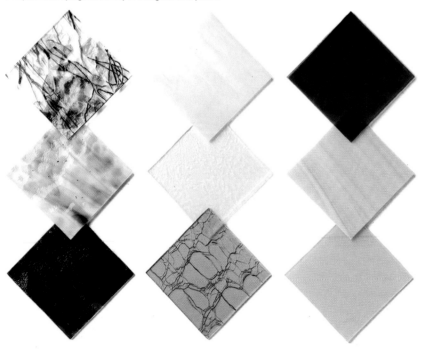

Stained glass is found in the world's most beautiful lampshades and window murals. Speciality houses stock dozens of types of stained glass in a variety of textures and colours, both translucent and opaque. The glass is coloured by adding metal alloys such as copper, iron and cobalt. Antique-style glass is made by hand; other glass is machine-made. The names of the glass are as exciting as their appearance: (top to bottom, far left) fracture streamer, ring mottle, stipple; (top to bottom, centre) iridized, single glue chip, crackle; (top to bottom, left) hand-blown 'antique', opal and flashed.

WORKING WITH GLASS

Thicknesses and types of glass vary, so ask a retailer which glass is best for your application. Always carry and store glass upright; otherwise it may break under its own weight.

Caution: When you handle glass, wear goggles and heavy gloves. Dispose of shards in a closed container, or wrap them with several layers of paper; then discard. Although a supplier will make long cuts, you can make short ones using the techniques shown below and on page 262. First wipe the glass clean with commercial cleaner; then back it with scrap softwood. The cutting, which is really controlled breaking of the glass, is done in two steps: scoring with a glass cutter and then breaking the glass along the score (known as breaking out the score).

Score patterned glass on its smooth side, mirrored glass on its uncoated side. Score curved shapes round a stiff paper template; gentle curves can be broken out in the same way as straight cuts; sharper curves and circles require radial lines.

Lubricate the cutter's wheel with light oil, and grip it comfortably. Score briskly and steadily – a sizzling sound indicates the correct pressure; white flakes mean you have pressed too hard. Never go over an imperfect score; this can damage the cutter. Break out the glass immediately after you have scored it, starting at the score's finished end.

To score, position cutter just short of far edge of glass, aligned against wood or plastic nonskid straight-edge. Keeping wheel perpendicular to glass, draw cutter towards you quickly and smoothly. Run tool off glass at end of score.

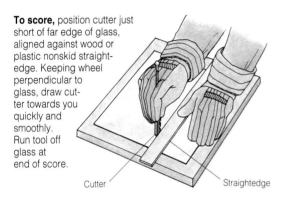

Cutter

Straightedge

Break out glass that is 3 mm (⅛ in) thick or thicker, over a pencil in line with and at end of the score. Gently press down on both sides of the score.

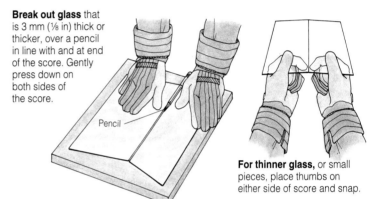

Pencil

For thinner glass, or small pieces, place thumbs on either side of score and snap.

Break out narrow edge strips with glass pliers. If pieces break off unevenly, nibble away any remaining glass with the pliers (left) or the notches on the glass cutter. Running pliers (right) are safe and effective for all types of glass. Slide glass 2.5 cm (1 in) off work surface, align jaws with score and squeeze handles gently.

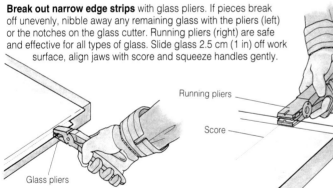

Running pliers

Score

Glass pliers

Smooth rough edges with a carborundum sharpening stone (shown) or silicone carbide abrasive paper. Lubricate cut edge of glass with water or oil. Lightly stroke stone along edge in one direction.

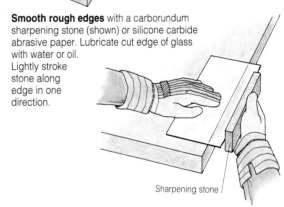

Sharpening stone

Cutting circles and sharp curves

1. For circles, place glass on corrugated cardboard. Position circle cutter on glass with suction cup in centre. Score circle by rotating cutter arm round cup with even pressure. (Score sharp curves against a stiff paper template.) Turn piece over and press down gently along score with thumbs, not quite breaking it out.

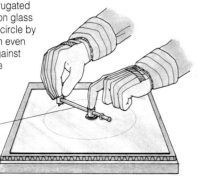

Circle cutter

2. Turn piece over; remove cardboard; then score freehand radial lines from glass edges to just short of (but not touching) the original score. Break out radial lines with glass pliers; circle or curved shape will now break out completely.

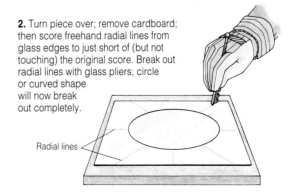

Radial lines

Safety glass is available in three types: laminated, wire (security) and tempered. Although tempered glass cannot be cut, both laminated and wire glass can be scored and broken out (p.261), with an additional step of separating the nonglass material. In the case of laminated glass, this material is a sheet of plastic sandwiched between two layers of glass; wire glass has a layer of wire mesh embedded in it. Score laminated glass on both sides; after breaking out each score, sever the plastic sheet as shown below.

Small 'bull's-eye' breaks in car windscreens can be repaired by using an epoxy solution available as a kit at some car accessory shops. Use it to repair damage up to 2.5 cm (1 in) wide on the outside of a windscreen.

When removing broken panes of glass, wear heavy gloves and goggles and work from the top down to prevent injury from falling shards. If the pane does not have broken pieces that make removal easy, tape the glass with masking tape in a crisscross pattern, then break it with a hammer.

Describe the application of the glass to your dealer to ensure that you buy the correct type and thickness for its replacement. To decide whether you need tempered glass at doorways or elsewhere, check building regulations.

Make a template of cardboard for odd shapes, such as diamonds or ovals. Glazing compound, which is used both to bed the glass in the frame and to cover the glazier's points, is available in cans and in cartridges that fit in a mastic gun.

You can also bed the glass with a self-adhesive foam strip. Install the foam around the inside of the frame's rebate, press the glass into place and insert the points. Then seal the glass with glazing compound, completely covering the points.

Caution: Do not try to replace or repair sealed units or gas-filled high-efficiency windows yourself.

Cutting safety glass

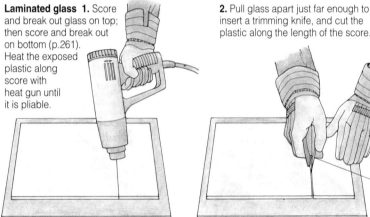

Laminated glass 1. Score and break out glass on top; then score and break out on bottom (p.261). Heat the exposed plastic along score with heat gun until it is pliable.

2. Pull glass apart just far enough to insert a trimming knife, and cut the plastic along the length of the score.

Trimming knife

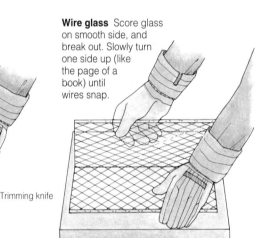

Wire glass Score glass on smooth side, and break out. Slowly turn one side up (like the page of a book) until wires snap.

Installing fasteners

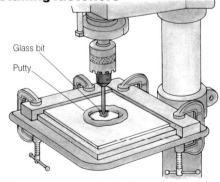

Glass bit

Putty

1. Drill holes up to 1.3 cm (½ in) wide in glass with spade bit in drill press or hand drill. (Have supplier drill larger holes; or use a circle cutter, page 261.) Drill into a well of putty filled with water. Run bit at low speed, feeding it evenly into glass. Drill no closer than 2.5 cm (1 in) to edge.

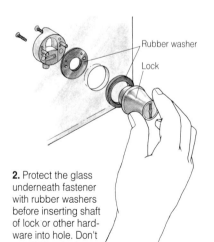

Rubber washer

Lock

2. Protect the glass underneath fastener with rubber washers before inserting shaft of lock or other hardware into hole. Don't overtighten fastener.

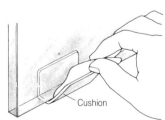

Cushion

Magnetic catch Install self-adhesive cushion of two-part hardware first; then slide catch into place.

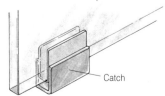

Catch

Replacing glass in a metal frame

Solid frame 1. With pliers, prise out rubber gasket from frame. If damaged, buy new gasket. Remove any glass and clean out frame with wire brush. Measure frame from inner edges; cut or order glass 2 mm (¹⁄₁₆ in) smaller in length and width.

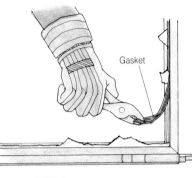

Gasket

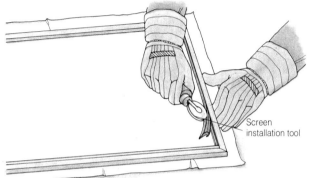

Screen installation tool

2. Coat inside of frame with the adhesive recommended by glass supplier. Position glass in frame. Using screen installation tool or fingers, press gasket under frame lip all round. If gasket is too short, lengthen it by stretching as you insert it.

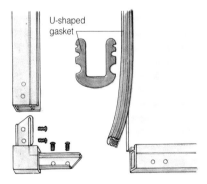

U-shaped gasket

Three-sided frame
To disassemble frame, unscrew two corners (or remove rivets, page 187), releasing one side. Gently slide out U-shaped gasket and glass. Cut or buy new pane; then fit new gasket round it. Slide glass and gasket into sash, position the side piece, and screw or rivet corners together.

Replacing glass in a wood frame

1. Working from outside, remove broken glass; use putty knife to remove old glazing compound and points. Soften hard compound with hot air gun. Newer windows may have foam strip instead of compound.

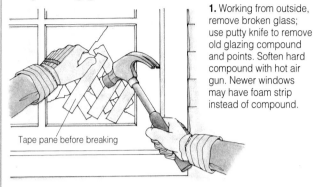

Tape pane before breaking

Putty knife

Glazier's point

2. Clean out rebate with a wire brush; coat with a wood sealer. Measure to inside of rebate; order or cut glass

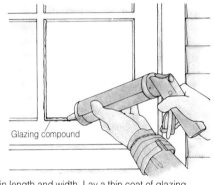

Glazing compound

2 mm (¹⁄₁₆ in) smaller in length and width. Lay a thin coat of glazing compound (or foam strip) inside rebate, then press in glass. Hold pane in place as you press in glazier's points every 10 cm (4 in).

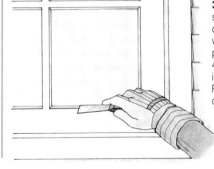

3. Cover points and seal glass with glazing compound. Smooth with wet finger or flexible putty knife, forming 45° bevel so that putty is invisible from inside. Paint when compound dries, in several days.

Minor repairs

Fixing a windscreen 'bull's eye' Align adhesive seal and pedestal over the cleaned damage. Empty the chemicals into injector and shake. Press injector into pedestal; then follow manufacturer's directions to shoot resin into repair. Leave whole assembly in place for 4 hours; then use a craft knife to scrape away excess resin and free the pedestal.

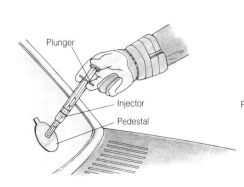

Plunger

Injector

Pedestal

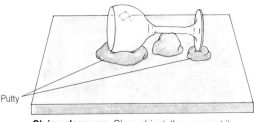

Putty

Gluing glassware Clean object; then support it with putty, or improvise another way to hold it steady. Glue with UV-sensitive adhesive, following safety precautions given with adhesive.

Traditionally, pieces of coloured glass are arranged in a rigid framework of lead 'came' that is soldered only at the joints. Although lead came is suitable for windows and large decorative pieces, it can overpower intricate designs. The copper-foil technique shown here is more appropriate for these. Soldered copper-foil seams look delicate, yet they are strong enough to support sturdy boxes and lamps.

To start, pencil a full-sized drawing or 'cartoon' onto plain paper. Keep your design simple – straight lines are easiest for novices to cut. Then make two copies. Cut one into templates for use when cutting the glass; the other copy is a guide onto which you will place the pieces of glass after edging them with foil. Cut the glass and smooth its edges (p.261); then clean it with commercial glass cleaner.

Adhesive-backed copper foil comes in different sizes; for most work, use foil that is 6 mm (¼ in) wide and 0.025 mm (0.001 in) thick. For the perimeter, you can use slightly wider foil. Wrap outside corners as you would a parcel, folding down one side of the foil, then pressing the second side over the first. To avoid splitting the foil on curved edges, ease it gently around the curve. Immediately after

Joining glass with copper foil

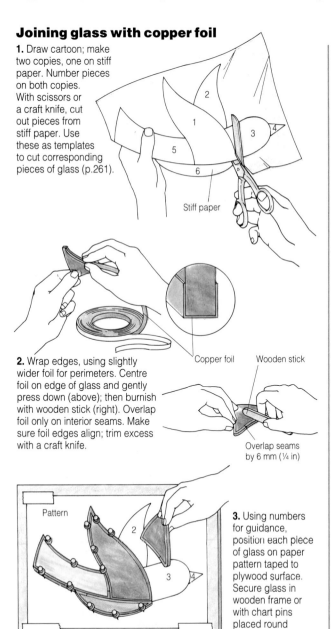

1. Draw cartoon; make two copies, one on stiff paper. Number pieces on both copies. With scissors or a craft knife, cut out pieces from stiff paper. Use these as templates to cut corresponding pieces of glass (p.261).

Stiff paper

2. Wrap edges, using slightly wider foil for perimeters. Centre foil on edge of glass and gently press down (above); then burnish with wooden stick (right). Overlap foil only on interior seams. Make sure foil edges align; trim excess with a craft knife.

Copper foil

Wooden stick

Overlap seams by 6 mm (¼ in)

Pattern

3. Using numbers for guidance, position each piece of glass on paper pattern taped to plywood surface. Secure glass in wooden frame or with chart pins placed round the perimeter.

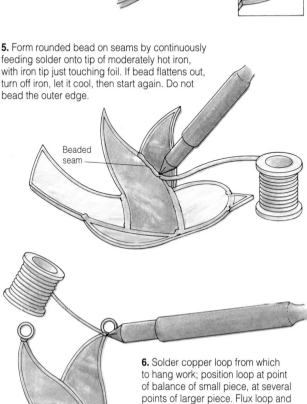

4. Brush oleic acid flux along seams (inset). To tack, hold solder over each seam; lightly touch iron to solder. Next, tin seams by melting dab of solder on foil then quickly drawing tip along foil for flat, thin line. Tin both sides of perimeter; prop object upright to tin outer edge.

Tacked seam

Solder

Tip of iron

5. Form rounded bead on seams by continuously feeding solder onto tip of moderately hot iron, with iron tip just touching foil. If bead flattens out, turn off iron, let it cool, then start again. Do not bead the outer edge.

Beaded seam

6. Solder copper loop from which to hang work; position loop at point of balance of small piece, at several points of larger piece. Flux loop and point on foil; then solder.

wrapping each piece, position it on its corresponding number on the paper.

Follow the soldering instructions on page 190. Tin the tip of the soldering iron with the same 60/40 lead/tin solder you will use for the seams, and flux the seams so the solder adheres. Most copper-foil seams are first tinned, which creates a thin flat surface, and then beaded for a gently rounded finish; the perimeter need only be tinned. Manipulating the iron and spool of solder requires practice; if you are having difficulty, switch them to the opposite hands, work more slowly or change to a more comfortable grip.

Immediately after soldering, dust the work with talcum powder and rub it with a soft cloth. If desired, apply a liquid patina, available at craft shops, to colour the seams either copper or black. Wearing rubber gloves, dip a sponge into the patina and wipe it along a seam. Wait a few seconds, and then rub the seam with a dry cloth. To brighten the patina, rub it with brass polish. Prevent dark corrosion from building up on copper foil by rubbing it periodically with fine steel wool.

Caution: Lead is toxic. Ventilate the work area well. Wash hands after handling lead, solder or patina; dispose of these materials carefully (p.11).

Three-dimensional objects

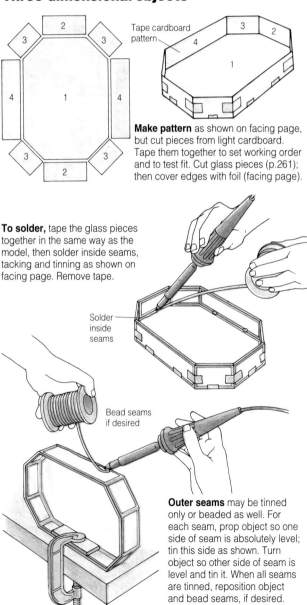

Make pattern as shown on facing page, but cut pieces from light cardboard. Tape them together to set working order and to test fit. Cut glass pieces (p.261); then cover edges with foil (facing page).

To solder, tape the glass pieces together in the same way as the model, then solder inside seams, tacking and tinning as shown on facing page. Remove tape.

Solder inside seams

Bead seams if desired

Outer seams may be tinned only or beaded as well. For each seam, prop object so one side of seam is absolutely level; tin this side as shown. Turn object so other side of seam is level and tin it. When all seams are tinned, reposition object and bead seams, if desired.

Repairing lead-came glass

Glazing knife

Joint

Use glazing knife to cut came at each soldered joint around broken piece (came may be H or U-shaped; see inset). Wearing gloves, prise up came and remove broken glass with glass pliers. Clean debris from came channel with wire brush.

Came

Trace outline of broken piece onto light cardboard. Cut glass to fit outline, insert glass into came, then lightly push came down on glass. Push glazing putty into the opening between glass and came, then push came down fully.

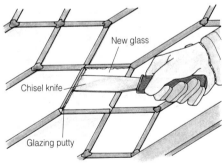

New glass

Chisel knife

Glazing putty

To resolder came at joints, first brush on oleic acid flux. Holding solder to seam, touch iron to both came and solder until solder flows; then quickly move iron away. When soldering is done, colour seams with patina to match rest of piece.

INSTALLING GLASS BLOCKS

Glass blocks make strong, attractive walls and windows that are easy to maintain and keep clean. The blocks are laid in mortar and require some masonry skills to install, but few special tools are needed. Most supplies, including plastic spacers, expansion strips, reinforcing rods and silicone, can be purchased from your glass block supplier. Before incorporating corner and end blocks in your design, find out if they're offered in the pattern and size you wish to use.

Because glass blocks are non-load-bearing (they cannot support building weight from above), you'll need to frame the opening – consult the block supplier for details. Show your design to a structural engineer or other qualified professional to determine whether extra floor joists or supporting structure will be needed to bear the wall's weight. Reinforcing rods secure the glass blocks to the surrounding structure and expansion joints at the head and jambs prevent the wall from cracking with any structural movement.

Use a ready-mixed glass block bedding mortar to lay the blocks. Mix with water as instructed on the bag and mix only what you will use in an hour. Build up a wall two or three courses at a time, raking back the joints as you go. Ensure that the wall is not out of alignment and as each course rises, check that it is level and plumb. If one end of a block wall will be unframed, suspend a plumb bob from the free end of the header and check that the wall is vertical.

To prevent the weight of the upper courses of block from squeezing wet mortar out from between the lower courses before it hardens, insert plastic spacers which keep the blocks evenly spaced. Fit one spacer to each side of each corner, and slip a piece of wire (supplied with the spacers) through the

Preparing the structural opening

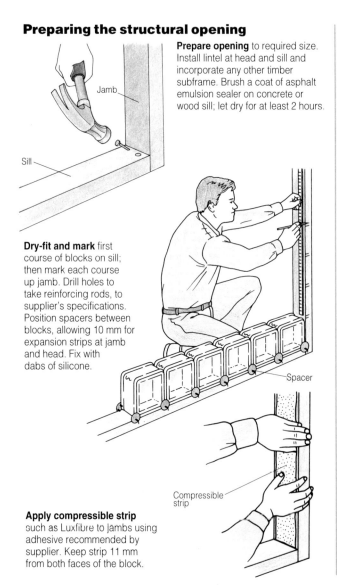

Prepare opening to required size. Install lintel at head and sill and incorporate any other timber subframe. Brush a coat of asphalt emulsion sealer on concrete or wood sill; let dry for at least 2 hours.

Dry-fit and mark first course of blocks on sill; then mark each course up jamb. Drill holes to take reinforcing rods, to supplier's specifications. Position spacers between blocks, allowing 10 mm for expansion strips at jamb and head. Fix with dabs of silicone.

Apply compressible strip such as Luxfibre to jambs using adhesive recommended by supplier. Keep strip 11 mm from both faces of the block.

Laying the first course

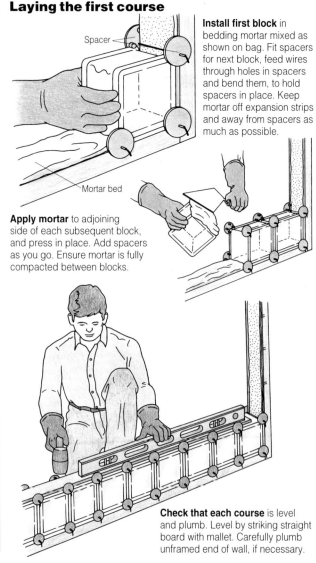

Install first block in bedding mortar mixed as shown on bag. Fit spacers for next block, feed wires through holes in spacers and bend them, to hold spacers in place. Keep mortar off expansion strips and away from spacers as much as possible.

Apply mortar to adjoining side of each subsequent block, and press in place. Add spacers as you go. Ensure mortar is fully compacted between blocks.

Check that each course is level and plumb. Level by striking straight board with mallet. Carefully plumb unframed end of wall, if necessary.

central holes, bending the ends to hold the spacers in place. When the mortar has set, remove the wires and the spacers and use them again for the next courses of block.

Joints should be raked back to a depth of 10 mm and left for two days, then finished with a fine pointing mortar (grey or white). Then use a gun to force mastic into the jambs and head to cover expansion strips and form a weathering seal.

Glass blocks can also be purchased preassembled, but the panels are so heavy you will need help to position them. Panels that are designed to replace windows may come with built-in adjustable louvre vents.

A mortarless system for installing glass blocks is also available. You insert thin plastic strips between the blocks and then seal them with silicone sealant; full instructions are provided by the manufacturer of the system.

Building up the wall

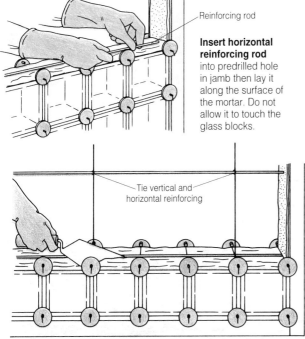

Lay bedding mortar, mixed to maker's recommendations, to a depth of 5 mm (about ¼ in) along the top of the first row of blocks.

Reinforcing rod

Insert horizontal reinforcing rod into predrilled hole in jamb then lay it along the surface of the mortar. Do not allow it to touch the glass blocks.

Tie vertical and horizontal reinforcing

Insert vertical reinforcing where required, tie with wire to horizontal reinforcing. Cover with further 5 mm bed of mortar. Complete the wall, laying no more than three courses at a time.

Finishing the wall

Remove spacers Rake out bedding mortar to a depth of 10 mm (⅜ in). Mix and apply pointing mortar as directed on bag. Wipe panel with clean, damp sponge. Allow to dry and buff residue with clean cloth. Remove any mortar left on glass with dry, non-metallic abrasive pad. Do not use cleaning agents or chemicals – they may mark the glass.

Remove any mortar on expansion strip on head and jambs. Fill with a bead of flexible silicone: with any structural movement, mortar would crack at these locations. Smooth silicone with a wet, gloved finger.

Curves and corners

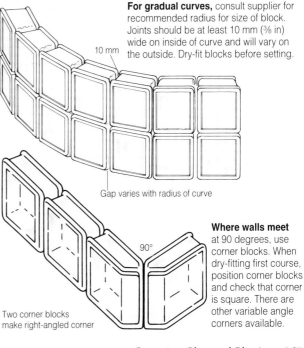

For gradual curves, consult supplier for recommended radius for size of block. Joints should be at least 10 mm (⅜ in) wide on inside of curve and will vary on the outside. Dry-fit blocks before setting.

10 mm

Gap varies with radius of curve

Where walls meet at 90 degrees, use corner blocks. When dry-fitting first course, position corner blocks and check that corner is square. There are other variable angle corners available.

90°

Two corner blocks make right-angled corner

PLASTICS

The variety of plastics on the market makes them among the most versatile of all do-it-yourself materials. For example, chlorinated polyvinyl chloride (cPVC) never corrodes, sweats or allows scale buildup. As clear as glass, sheet acrylic is easy to shape, resists sunlight and doesn't break readily.

Polycarbonate, a virtually unbreakable but lightweight plastic, is simple to install. Glass-fibre patching materials, when layered and saturated with liquid resin, make extremely strong repairs in glass fibre, metal and wood products. Sheet laminate creates an inexpensive worktop that is easy to maintain. Acrylic and polyester resin solid-surface materials are also ideal for worktops. They cost more than sheet laminate, but they can be custom-edged with your choice of router bit and scratches can be sanded away.

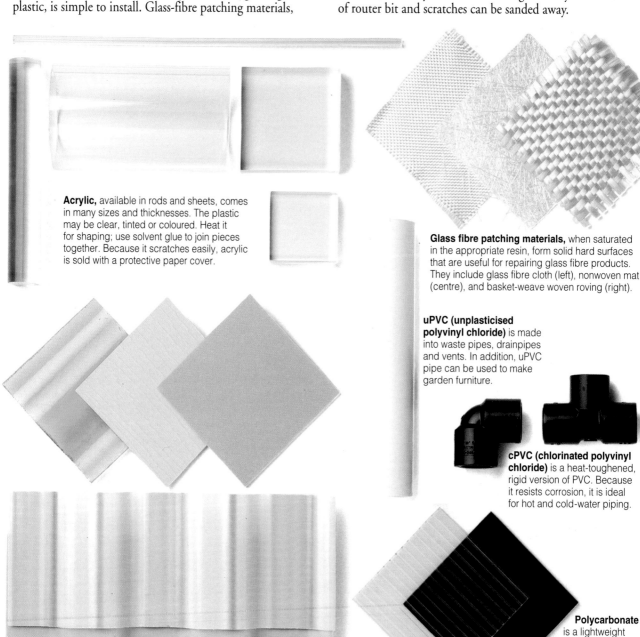

Acrylic, available in rods and sheets, comes in many sizes and thicknesses. The plastic may be clear, tinted or coloured. Heat it for shaping; use solvent glue to join pieces together. Because it scratches easily, acrylic is sold with a protective paper cover.

Glass fibre patching materials, when saturated in the appropriate resin, form solid hard surfaces that are useful for repairing glass fibre products. They include glass fibre cloth (left), nonwoven mat (centre), and basket-weave woven roving (right).

uPVC (unplasticised polyvinyl chloride) is made into waste pipes, drainpipes and vents. In addition, uPVC pipe can be used to make garden furniture.

cPVC (chlorinated polyvinyl chloride) is a heat-toughened, rigid version of PVC. Because it resists corrosion, it is ideal for hot and cold-water piping.

Polycarbonate is a lightweight impact resistant thermoplastic. A twin-walled variety (far left) has insulating air channels. The 1220 x 2440 mm (4 x 8 ft) panels are translucent, so they are ideal for greenhouses and porches.

Preformed glass fibre panel, a durable maintenance-free material, comes in a variety of colours and configurations. Use these panels for a wide range of building projects such as patio covers, carport roofs and greenhouses.

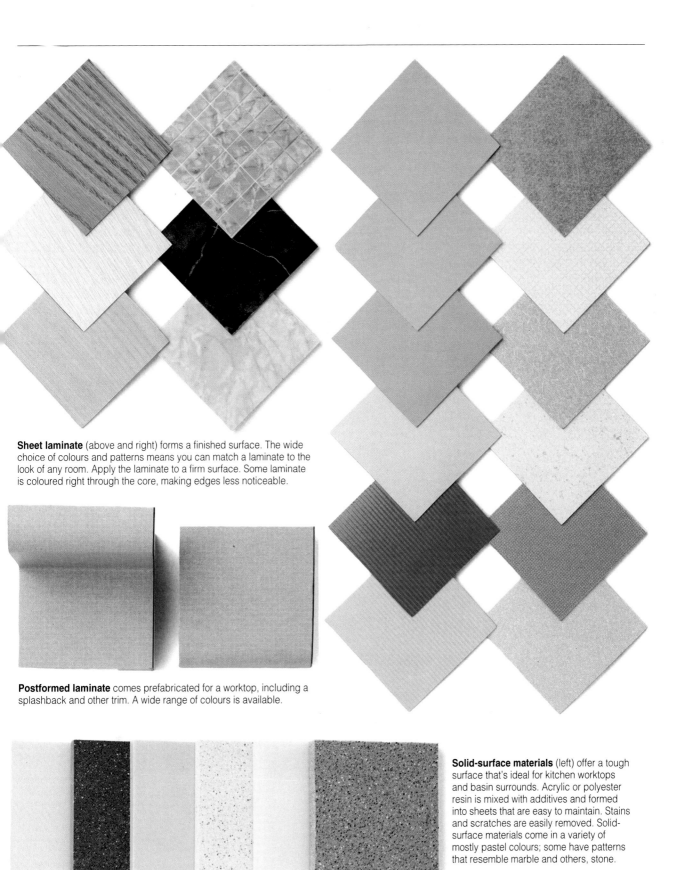

Sheet laminate (above and right) forms a finished surface. The wide choice of colours and patterns means you can match a laminate to the look of any room. Apply the laminate to a firm surface. Some laminate is coloured right through the core, making edges less noticeable.

Postformed laminate comes prefabricated for a worktop, including a splashback and other trim. A wide range of colours is available.

Solid-surface materials (left) offer a tough surface that's ideal for kitchen worktops and basin surrounds. Acrylic or polyester resin is mixed with additives and formed into sheets that are easy to maintain. Stains and scratches are easily removed. Solid-surface materials come in a variety of mostly pastel colours; some have patterns that resemble marble and others, stone.

WORKING WITH PLASTIC SHEET AND TUBING

Clear acrylic sheets and other shapes are used in craft objects, for making furniture and as a substitute for glass. Chlorinated polyvinyl chloride (cPVC) and unplasticised polyvinyl chloride (uPVC) are two types of rigid plastic tubing: cPVC tubing forms hot and cold-water supply lines; the wider uPVC tubing is used for drainpipes, electrical conduit and lightweight or outdoor furniture. To work with any of these plastics, you will need some basic woodworking, metalworking and glazing skills.

There are special tools and supplies for working with plastics. You can avoid damaging ordinary tools by following the maker's instructions for plastics. For example, when cutting acrylic with a jigsaw, running the tool at high speed can melt the plastic behind the blade. The plastic may then fuse together, ruining the cut.

Despite its toughness, acrylic is easily scratched and so comes coated with protective paper. Leave as much of the paper on the plastic as possible until the project is complete. Remove the paper by lifting it at one corner and pulling it off the sheet. Scratches on plastic are best removed with a proprietary scratch remover. To stop them sagging, store acrylic sheets either upright or flat and well supported.

Acrylic sheets can be joined with threaded fasteners, rivets or posts and screws, but pieces are usually cemented with a special solvent. The most common technique is cementing along the seams by capillary action (facing page). If solvent spills on an unprotected piece of acrylic, wipe it quickly with a clean soft cloth.

You can join both cPVC and uPVC with a solvent cement; use only the cleaner, primer and cement specifically recommended for joining each plastic.

Most plastics can be bent if they have been heated first, but for cPVC and uPVC the temperature must be controlled so precisely that doing it

Cutting and drilling

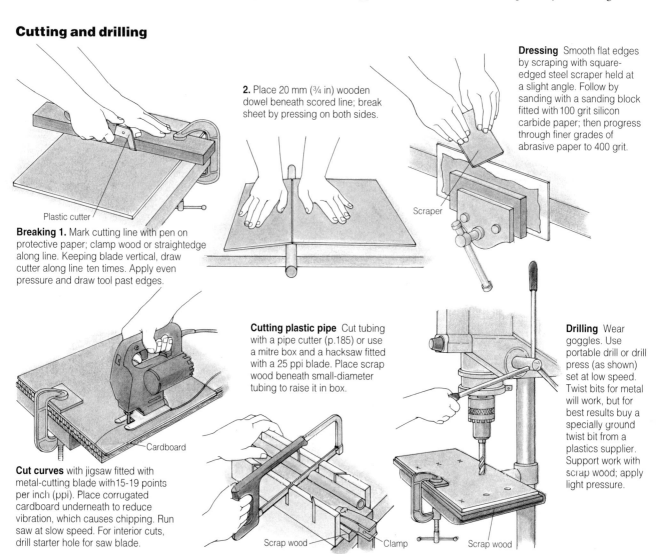

2. Place 20 mm (¾ in) wooden dowel beneath scored line; break sheet by pressing on both sides.

Dressing Smooth flat edges by scraping with square-edged steel scraper held at a slight angle. Follow by sanding with a sanding block fitted with 100 grit silicon carbide paper; then progress through finer grades of abrasive paper to 400 grit.

Scraper

Plastic cutter

Breaking 1. Mark cutting line with pen on protective paper; clamp wood or straightedge along line. Keeping blade vertical, draw cutter along line ten times. Apply even pressure and draw tool past edges.

Cardboard

Cut curves with jigsaw fitted with metal-cutting blade with 15-19 points per inch (ppi). Place corrugated cardboard underneath to reduce vibration, which causes chipping. Run saw at slow speed. For interior cuts, drill starter hole for saw blade.

Cutting plastic pipe Cut tubing with a pipe cutter (p.185) or use a mitre box and a hacksaw fitted with a 25 ppi blade. Place scrap wood beneath small-diameter tubing to raise it in box.

Scrap wood — Clamp

Drilling Wear goggles. Use portable drill or drill press (as shown) set at low speed. Twist bits for metal will work, but for best results buy a specially ground twist bit from a plastics supplier. Support work with scrap wood; apply light pressure.

Scrap wood

yourself is not recommended. It is easy to bend acrylic using a strip heater, available (often as a kit) from a plastics supplier or hardware store.

Caution: When using power tools to cut, sand or drill plastic, wear safety goggles and a dust mask. Wear heatproof gloves while heating and bending plastic.

When cementing, follow all the precautions listed by the manufacturer; work in a well-ventilated area and do not allow solvent to get on your skin.

Before modifying a plumbing system, remember to shut off the main water supply and drain a pipe before working on it.

Smoothing edges

Buff edges with 10 mm (⅜ in) drill fitted with buffing pad; first coat the pad with either tripoli or rouge polishing compound (available at craft suppliers). Finish with a nonstitched disc of clean muslin or flannel. Do not buff seam edges.

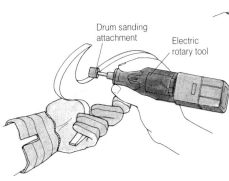

Sand and polish curves and tight spots with an electric drill or a small rotary tool specially for working with acrylic. Sand edges with drum sanding attachment; buff with hard felt and muslin or flannel discs. To avoid overheating plastic, use a light touch and low speed.

Joining plastic tubing

Preparing joints

With a sharp knife or reamer, remove burrs on cut ends; bevel walls slightly. Smooth ends of fitting and tubing with 120 grit garnet paper. Assemble tubing and fitting to test fit; mark a line across both pieces with a pencil. Detach the pieces and clean them by swabbing with the appropriate cleaning fluid, using the applicator supplied. After cleaner dries, apply primer to remove gloss; then apply the cement.

Joining Apply a second coat of cement to tubing and immediately insert in fitting with marks misaligned by a quarter turn; quickly twist until marks align. Hold together for at least 30 seconds then wait 24 hours before applying full pressure. A thin line of cement should be visible right round the new joint.

Bending with heat

Heating Mark area of bend; remove 10 cm (4 in) wide strips of paper from both sides of sheet. Centre uncovered area just above heating element; turn sheet several times for even heating. Hold for 1 to 5 minutes, until the plastic softens.

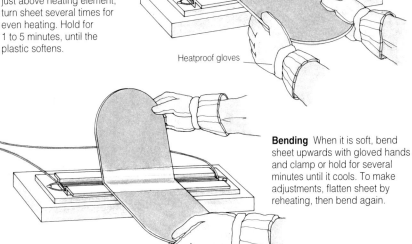

Bending When it is soft, bend sheet upwards with gloved hands and clamp or hold for several minutes until it cools. To make adjustments, flatten sheet by reheating, then bend again.

Joining acrylic sheets

Remove paper near edges; place pieces to be joined so seams are horizontal. Tape, clamp or brace pieces together; edges must be even so pieces fit with no gaps. Then carefully draw needle-nose applicator along seam, squeezing gently to dispense solvent evenly. Don't blot excess solvent; allow capillary action to draw it into joint.

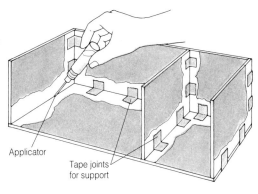

GLASS FIBRE

Glass fibre, a material made from threads or fragments of spun glass, comes in different forms. As a building material, it is moulded into hard panels; for shaped objects, it is matted or woven into a fabric and then bonded with resin.

Preformed glass fibre panels are easy to work with and can be cut with a jigsaw fitted with a fine-tooth blade. For an outdoor project such as a patio roof, heavyweight corrugated or ridged panels are best; for indoor use or where rigidity is not necessary, use lighter flat panels. Supplies for building with the panels, such as sidewall flashing and corrugated closure strips, are also available. To clean the panels, hose them with water; if they discolour, apply a refinisher recommended by the manufacturer. Glass fibre panels will not bear a person's weight; never attempt to walk on them.

Glass fibre laminate is used to make shaped objects such as car bodies, boats, swimming pools and baths. Layers of fabric are bonded together with a liquid resin that cures with the addition of a catalyst, forming a tough, durable shell. Holes up to 1.3 cm (½ in) in diameter in glass fibre laminate can simply be filled with putty – a mixture of resin and filler. Larger areas of damage are repaired by patching with layers of fabric and resin. However, if you suspect that the damage may have affected the structural integrity of an object, consult a professional before attempting the repair.

A repair patch (p.274) usually consists of alternating layers of mat and cloth; in large projects, woven roving (or matting) can be used. A successful repair depends upon choosing the correct fabric and resin; the chart on the facing page will help you to choose the best combination.

Polyester resin – used for most laminate repairs – is easier to work with and less expensive than epoxy. There are two types: air-dry or tack-free contains wax, which floats to the surface of the repair, sealing off the air and allowing the resin to cure with a hard surface. The other type, air-inhibited, cures to a tacky surface unless covered with waxed paper or polyvinyl alcohol spray (PVA release agent) which can be found at marine supply stores and specialist suppliers. Wash the spray off with warm water after the resin cures. Fabric will bond better if you use air-inhibited resin for the inner layers of a repair; if you use air-dry resin for the outer layers, it will harden so that the surface can more easily be sanded.

Epoxy resin cures hard, but slowly. It will bond well with many materials but is more difficult to work with than polyester. If in doubt whether to use epoxy or polyester resin for a repair, contact the manufacturer of the object or try a small test patch on an inconspicuous spot.

The outer finish coat of glass fibre laminate is gel coat, a specially formulated polyester resin. Wash the gel coat often with detergent and water (or wipe it with a solvent such as acetone), and buff with wax to protect it. Scratches that do not penetrate too far beneath the gel coat can easily be repaired with a mixture of gel coat and filler, which is often available in a kit at marine supply stores.

Working with glass fibre panels

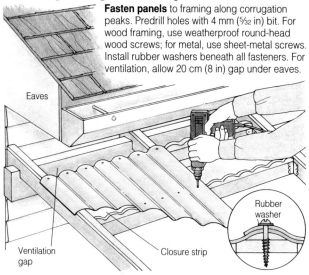

Fasten panels to framing along corrugation peaks. Predrill holes with 4 mm (5/32 in) bit. For wood framing, use weatherproof round-head wood screws; for metal, use sheet-metal screws. Install rubber washers beneath all fasteners. For ventilation, allow 20 cm (8 in) gap under eaves.

Eaves

Rubber washer

Ventilation gap

Closure strip

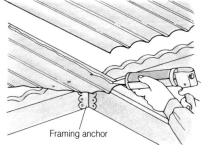

Seal panels by applying permanently flexible (nondrying) mastic or clear silicone sealant to seam area on peaks of corrugations. Also, before installing flashing (below), seal along the length of peaks that will be covered by flashing.

Framing anchor

Install flashing where panels meet side walls; match aluminium flashing corrugations to those in panels. Slide flashing under boarding. These panels are commonly used for carports and conservatories, which do not need to be completely waterproof.

Boarding

Side wall flashing

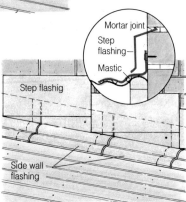

For masonry walls, secure side wall flashing every 20 cm (8 in) with masonry anchors. Cover with step flashing: first grind or chisel a small groove in mortar joint. Fold back top edge of flashing, and insert in groove as shown (inset). Fill joint with mastic or clear silicone.

Mortar joint

Step flashing

Mastic

Step flashig

Side wall flashing

PATCHING GLASS FIBRE LAMINATE

Material	Characteristics	Use	Hints
Glass fibre mat	Fairly thick and stiff; easily moulded to curves; adds adhesion	Alternate with cloth or roving (matting) for general repairs	Use as first and final layers. Most commonly used weight is 45 g (1½ oz) mat
Glass fibre cloth	Thin and strong; leaves a smooth finish	Alternate with mat for small repairs	Make small cuts in cloth when moulding to curved surfaces so fabric lies flat
Woven roving	Thick, silky, heavily textured; provides stiffness, strength and bulk	Alternate with mat for large repairs	Handle carefully as it tends to unravel; do not place directly under gel coat
Polyester resin	Tough, water-resistant, compatible with many laminated objects; easy to work with	General laminating, especially glass fibre boats; do not use on objects that may contain polystyrene foam	Shelf life may be limited; use within 90 days; use air-inhibited for inner layers of repair, air-dry for outer layer; clean equipment with acetone
Epoxy resin	Creates a stronger bond and is more water-resistant than polyester; can be difficult to work with; cures more slowly than polyester	Bonds glass fibre to dissimilar materials, such as wood, metal, and many household plastics	Requires precise mixing and temperature control; clean equipment with acetone
Gel coat	Hard, glossy, waterproof; can be tinted by mixing with pigment; can be mixed with filler to add bulk	Forms waterproof, protective colour coat on finished surface of repair	Air-dry type is best. When mixing, add pigment and test colour before adding catalyst; thin with acetone before spraying
Putty	Depending on filler, adds hardness or bulk	Fills flaws that have penetrated beneath gel coat	Use car-body filler (available in kits) for small flaws; lightweight filler (in rolls, chips or powder) for large areas or where lightness is important. Sand gently after patch dries

Mixing chemicals

Measure ingredients, following maker's instructions carefully. For polyester resins, vary proportions according to temperature: in cool conditions use more catalyst; in warm conditions use less. Do not work in extreme temperatures or direct sunlight. Make several test batches to evaluate curing time and quality of mix. Prepare only as much resin as you can apply in about 20 minutes (once cured, it cannot be used).

Repairing minor damage

1. Clean damaged area by wiping with acetone. Protect surface round repair with tape. Fit a power drill with a drum sanding attachment; make V-shaped groove along the damaged section.

Drum sanding attachment

2. Sand edges of groove, then blow away dust (do not touch). Mix gel coat with catalyst and filler according to manufacturer's instructions. Pack groove with mixture, building it up 2 mm (¹⁄₁₆ in) above surface.

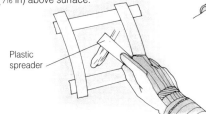

Plastic spreader

3. Spray with PVA, or cover with wax paper and push squeegee across surface to force out air. After 2 hours, wash off PVA with warm water or remove paper. Sand and buff area.

(Continued)

PATCHING GLASS FIBRE LAMINATE

Preparing the damaged area

Grind damaged area with electric drill fitted with sanding attachment. Use coarse abrasive paper; taper edges back 5 cm (2 in) from opening (on front and rear if possible). If damage is inaccessible from rear, grind hole to a roughly oval shape. Wipe with acetone.

If rear is accessible, tape a piece of cardboard over front of damage. From rear, build up three layers of fabric and resin (p.273), as shown below. Remove the cardboard and continue the repair from the front.

If rear is inaccessible, form backing by covering a piece of cardboard with three layers of fabric and resin (p.273), as shown below. Allow it to cure; remove cardboard; edge backing with bonding mixture of resin and fumed silica. Insert it through hole; hold it against rear with screw and pliers. Secure with self-tapping screws; let it cure.

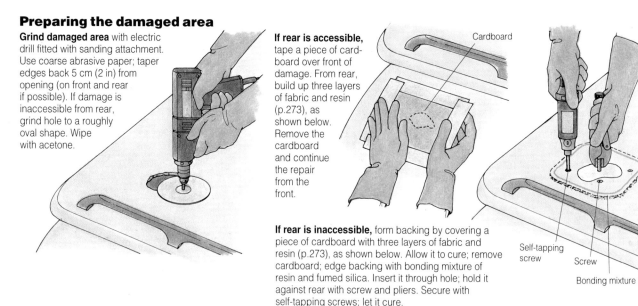

Cardboard

Self-tapping screw
Screw
Bonding mixture

Building up the patch

Protect area around front of damage with tape. Remove screws. Cut a piece of mat slightly larger than the sanded area; then cut progressively larger pieces of alternating fabric. Saturate first piece of mat with resin, and brush resin around sanded edges. Press piece into place over hole.

Add successive layers of fabric and resin, pressing with laminate roller to remove all air bubbles. Do repairs thicker than 3 mm (⅛ in) in two stages, allowing first layers to cure before continuing.

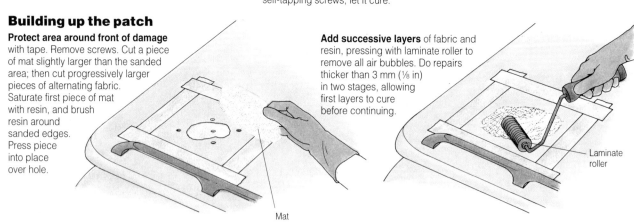

Mat

Laminate roller

Finishing the patch

When patch has cured, sand area with palm sander fitted with medium, then fine, abrasive paper. Wipe area with acetone.

Remove paper and wet-sand with fine abrasive paper, followed by extra-fine. Remove tape. Coat an electric drill buffing attachment with rubbing compound formulated for glass fibre. Buff the patch (below); then apply car polish or liquid wax with a soft cloth.

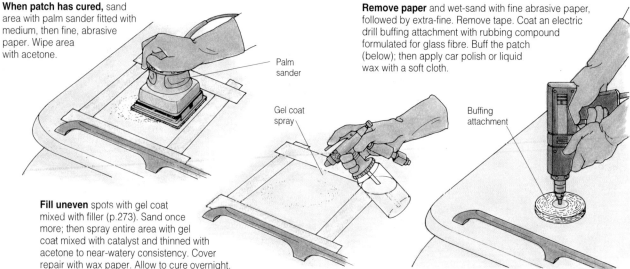

Palm sander

Gel coat spray

Buffing attachment

Fill uneven spots with gel coat mixed with filler (p.273). Sand once more; then spray entire area with gel coat mixed with catalyst and thinned with acetone to near-watery consistency. Cover repair with wax paper. Allow to cure overnight.

Postformed worktops are made of plastic laminate bonded to a core material (generally chipboard). The front edge of the worktop is rounded and sometimes the rear edge curves up to form a splashback. They come in standard widths and lengths.

Buy L and U-shaped worktops in two or three sections with mitred corners. Butt-and-scribe joints are best for the corner joints. Ask a kitchen specialist with a cutting service to cut them for you, as a mitre jig and heavy-duty router are needed.

Strips of laminate for finishing off cut ends are available. Apply these after scribing (see method on page 276).

Before removing an old worktop, shut off the water, gas and electricity supply to any fixtures or appliances; then remove the sink and appliances, noting how they are installed so that you can put them back correctly. Get an electrician to disconnect and remove built-in items such as a hob or a waste disposal unit. Working from inside the base cabinets, remove any fasteners from the worktop; then prise it free with a flat pry bar.

Take the measurements for a new worktop as shown below and make a detailed sketch of the cabinet layout to take with you when ordering.

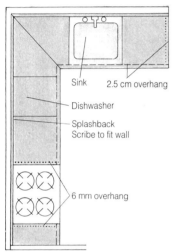

- Sink
- 2.5 cm overhang
- Dishwasher
- Splashback Scribe to fit wall
- 6 mm overhang

Measuring a worktop For L-shaped top (left), measure along rear of each run of base cabinets, from corner to far end. Also measure from the wall to the front of the cabinets. Add 25 mm (1 in) where edges overhang cabinets; add 3 mm (⅛ in) where cabinets butt up against an appliance or a wall. For a new sink or appliance, measure inside base cabinets.

Levelling With the worktop removed (right), check if top edges of cabinets are level. If not, insert shims under or behind cabinets – first loosen the cabinets from the wall if necessary – or tack strips of wood to top edges. If needed, install corner and cross braces to support the new worktop and provide fastening surfaces. Make sure that the corners are square; otherwise the worktop will not fit.

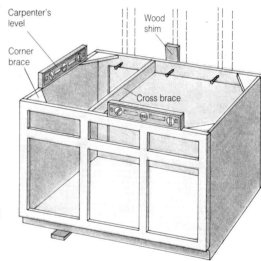

- Carpenter's level
- Wood shim
- Corner brace
- Cross brace

Belt sander

Installing a worktop 1. Place worktop in position. If end section butts up against an uneven wall, scribe the contours of the wall onto the edge. Wearing goggles and a dust mask, sand the edge to match the scribed line. Refit the countertop, and repeat for rear edge of splashback (above) if there is one.

Frame

2. To make sink cut-out, first mark outline for new sink with the instructions or template provided with the sink. For an existing rimless sink, turn sink upside down and trace rim; draw cutting line 10 mm (⅜ in) inside traced line. If sink has metal frame, hold frame in position; mark cutting line round the outside of the vertical edge, as shown.

3. To cut sink opening, first drill starter holes in corners of outline, turn piece over, and redraw guidelines. Wearing a dust mask and goggles, remove waste with jigsaw fitted with fine-tooth blade. File or sand edges smooth.

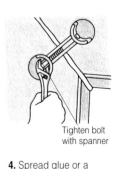

Tighten bolt with spanner

4. Spread glue or a coloured sealant (such as Colorfill which is made for the purpose) along the mitred edges of the worktop. Fit sections together so that surfaces are flush; secure with fasteners (above). Install wood screws in worktop's underside through corner braces. Apply clear silicone sealant to any gaps along the splashback and ends.

Sheets of laminated plastic for use on worktops, and on other flat or curved surfaces, are available in hundreds of patterns and colours. Most have a dark core that is visible at the edges, but a variety called colour-through laminate has a single colour throughout. When choosing laminate, avoid glossy or patterned styles in kitchens – heavy use can dull them. A light-coloured laminate shows wear less readily and is easier to match. Buy vertical-grade laminate for use on walls and cabinets.

Sheet laminate can be applied over almost any smooth, level surface. High-density chipboard is used most often as a substrate for worktops, although more expensive plywood is stronger and less likely to absorb moisture, which causes laminate to lift and buckle. Use medium density fibreboard (MDF) or plywood for cabinets – they hold fasteners more securely and are lighter than chipboard.

Make cut-outs for a sink (p.275) or appliance in the substrate before covering it with laminate. Smooth irregularities in the substrate and fill depressions with spackling compound; then wipe clean.

Cutting laminate

Scoring and breaking
Pencil a cutting line on face of laminate. With metal straightedge as a guide, score along line several times with a plastic cutter; then break by lifting edge of sheet. For small strips, clamp straightedge along cutting line, score and lift sheet.

Plastic cutter

Cutting narrow strips
For strips 10 cm (4 in) wide or less, fit laminate trimmer with slitter attachment and solid carbide straight-cutting bit. Clamp laminate to bench; fit piece between slitter's baseplates with guide on edge. Push tool along cutting line.

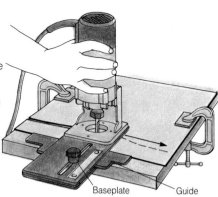

Baseplate   Guide

Laminating a vertical surface

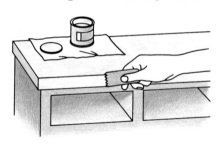

1. Apply contact adhesive with toothed spreader: two thin coats to the substrate, one to the laminate. Allow each coat to dry until adhesive appears hazy and is not sticky.

2. Carefully align individual strip against edge; press into place, and roll with roller or tap with wood block and hammer. (Attach strips to opposite ends of substrate first; trim; then attach any remaining strips.)

Installing preglued laminate
For bendable strips, first ensure that surface is clean and dry. Set hot air gun to medium; hold several inches from strip. As laminate softens; press strip down.

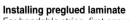

Hot air gun

Bendable laminate

Trimming Make edges of vertical laminate square. Fit router or laminate trimmer with flush-trimming bit; move from left to right along edge.

Edge treatments

Build up an edge
and cover with laminate or a preglued strip. Attach build-up strip of wood with PVA glue and finishing nails.

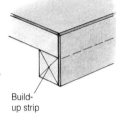

Build-up strip

Solid wood edging
is stronger and more durable than laminate. Flanged edging fits groove routed in the substrate panel. Secure with PVA glue.

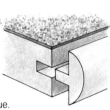

Attach laminate to both sides of the substrate unless (as with a worktop) it is securely fastened to a frame; otherwise it will warp. Laminate vertical surfaces before horizontal ones, and fit pieces to the back and sides of an object first, then to the front.

Glue laminate to the substrate with contact adhesive. Choose an inflammable contact adhesive; it is safer than the flammable variety.

Cut laminate with a laminate trimmer or with a circular saw, jigsaw or table saw fitted with a laminate blade. Keep leftover pieces to use for repairs. Bevel exposed edges with a router or laminate trimmer; then file to prevent chipping, applying pressure on the downward stroke. When trimming with a router or trimmer, use only self-guiding solid carbide bits.

Despite its toughness, sheet laminate is subject to burns, scratches and stains. Try to remove stubborn stains by dabbing with bleach for one minute and then rinsing with water.

Caution: When sanding, cutting or trimming laminate, wear goggles and a dust mask. If using contact adhesive, work in a well-ventilated area.

Laminating a horizontal surface

Applying adhesive Apply contact adhesive to substrate and laminate. Lay dowels or cardboard strips on substrate (these will not stick) and set laminate on top. Do not let laminate touch substrate until it is in position. Then remove dowels individually, starting at end of surface, as you press laminate into place.

Smoothing Roll entire surface with a rolling pin or soft cloth, working from centre of panel toward edges. Exert strong pressure to remove all air bubbles.

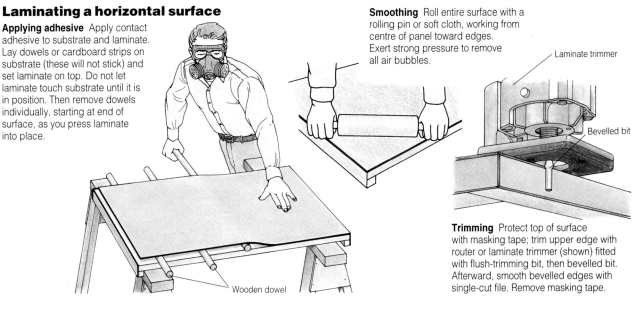

Laminate trimmer

Bevelled bit

Wooden dowel

Trimming Protect top of surface with masking tape; trim upper edge with router or laminate trimmer (shown) fitted with flush-trimming bit, then bevelled bit. Afterward, smooth bevelled edges with single-cut file. Remove masking tape.

Cut-outs and splashbacks

Cutting sink opening If there is no sink cut-out in substrate, cut opening as shown on page 275. If cutout exists, first apply laminate to substrate, then drill starter hole in laminate. Insert router fitted with flush-trimming bit; guide router to edge of cut-out, then clockwise around cut-out.

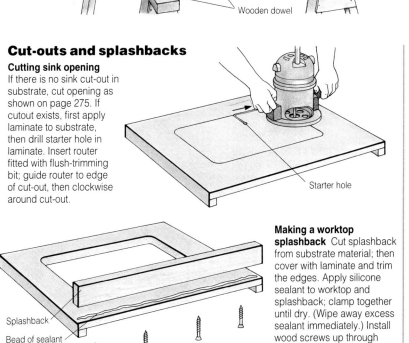

Starter hole

Splashback

Bead of sealant

Making a worktop splashback Cut splashback from substrate material; then cover with laminate and trim the edges. Apply silicone sealant to worktop and splashback; clamp together until dry. (Wipe away excess sealant immediately.) Install wood screws up through worktop into splashback.

Making repairs

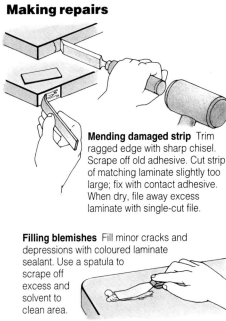

Mending damaged strip Trim ragged edge with sharp chisel. Scrape off old adhesive. Cut strip of matching laminate slightly too large; fix with contact adhesive. When dry, file away excess laminate with single-cut file.

Filling blemishes Fill minor cracks and depressions with coloured laminate sealant. Use a spatula to scrape off excess and solvent to clean area.

Ceramics, Glass and Plastics   277

SOLID-SURFACE MATERIAL

Solid plastic sheets, known as solid-surface material or solid surfacing, have the best features of marble and alabaster, which they resemble, yet they can be worked with power tools and joined with almost invisible seams. Usually formed from a blend of acrylic or polyester resin combined with a mined mineral, these synthetics are heavy, durable and stain-resistant. Round off all inside and outside corners; custom-profiling (shaping the edges with a router) is optional.

Solid-surfacing is more expensive than many other materials, so before selecting a brand, check that its warranty extends to do-it-yourself installation. Study the manufacturer's instructions carefully; if you don't have the carpentry skills necessary to work with the material, consult an installer trained by the manufacturer.

Before beginning to work, check that all sheets have the same batch number and peel off the protective coating. For worktops, measure the base cabinets as described on page 275.

Cutting sheets

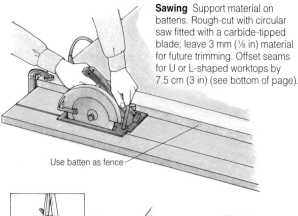

Sawing Support material on battens. Rough-cut with circular saw fitted with a carbide-tipped blade; leave 3 mm (⅛ in) material for future trimming. Offset seams for U or L-shaped worktops by 7.5 cm (3 in) (see bottom of page).

Use batten as fence

Sink cut-out To make a template, first calculate the sink outline (p.275). Enlarge outline by the distance between the router bit and the edge of its base; saw a plywood template to this measurement. Clamp template to piece, drill a starter hole and rout away the cut-out, using a 13 mm single-flute straight-cutting carbide bit. Sand edges smooth with 100 grit paper.

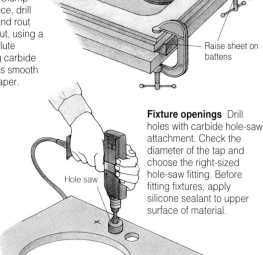

Edge of template
Sink outline
Raise sheet on battens

4 cm

Mark cut line using template

Outside corners First make a template to a radius of 4 cm (1½ in). Mark a 4 cm square at the corner of a small piece of plywood. Place compass point on the inside point of the square and scribe an arc across the corner (inset). Cut template along this arc, mark cut line on material, then rough-cut material to cut line with jigsaw (left). Clamp template to underside of corner; smooth with router fitted with a self-guiding, straight-cutting bit.

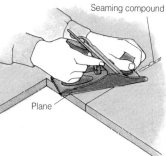

Fixture openings Drill holes with carbide hole-saw attachment. Check the diameter of the tap and choose the right-sized hole-saw fitting. Before fitting fixtures, apply silicone sealant to upper surface of material.

Hole saw

Joining sheets

1. Clamp sheets 6 mm (¼ in) apart and rout along edges with double-flute straight-cutting carbide bit. Guide router with straightedges clamped parallel with gap (inset). Clean edges with methylated spirit, and position sheets 3 mm (⅛ in) apart. Mix seaming compound and fill seam according to maker's instructions; clamp sheets together until compound hardens.

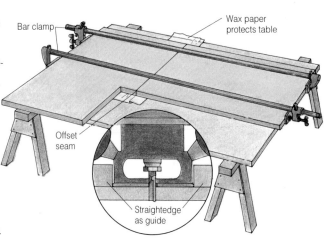

Bar clamp
Wax paper protects table
Offset seam
Straightedge as guide

Seaming compound

Plane

2. Remove excess dried compound with a cabinet scraper or a sharp plane; to avoid gouging material, round corners of plane iron with file. Sand with 100 grit paper. Finish surface (facing page).

Remove the old worktop and, with drywall screws, fix 10 cm (4 in) wide supporting strips of 20 mm (¾ in) plywood over the top edges of the cabinets. Add crossbraces spaced 61 cm (24 in) apart if you are using 20 mm (¾ in) thick surfacing, or at 46 cm (18 in) intervals for 12 mm (½ in) thick surfacing. Also add crossbraces from front to back where sinks, for example, will be located and where worktop seams will lie.

Caution: Wear a dust mask when cutting, routing and sanding solid surfacing. Seaming compound is very flammable; work in a well-ventilated area and follow all safety precautions suggested by the manufacturer.

Finishing

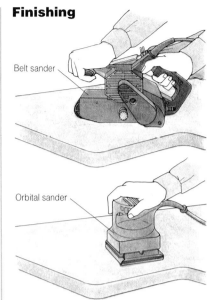
Belt sander

Orbital sander

For matt finish, sand entire surface (top), by hand or with power sander, with 100 grit paper followed by 180 grit; then polish with fine plastic abrasive pad secured to orbital sander.

Adding dropped edges

1. Turn piece over. Cut 40 mm (1½ in) wide strips of surfacing to fit exposed sides. Roughen mating surfaces with 60 grit garnet paper. Test-fit strips; then apply seaming compound to strips. Secure with spring clamps at 10 cm (4 in) intervals until compound hardens.

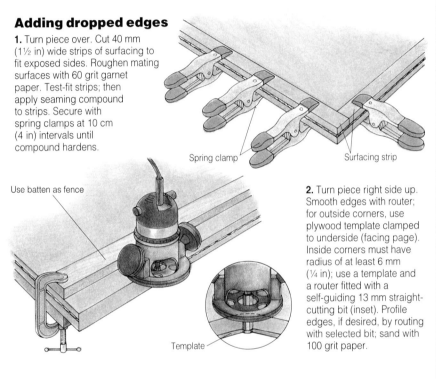
Spring clamp
Surfacing strip
Use batten as fence
Template

2. Turn piece right side up. Smooth edges with router; for outside corners, use plywood template clamped to underside (facing page). Inside corners must have radius of at least 6 mm (¼ in); use a template and a router fitted with a self-guiding 13 mm straight-cutting bit (inset). Profile edges, if desired, by routing with selected bit; sand with 100 grit paper.

Buffing pad

For glossy finish (for low-use surfaces), sand with 220, then 320 grit paper. Fit a drill with a buffing pad; polish until glossy with liquid car-polishing compound.

Adding a splashback

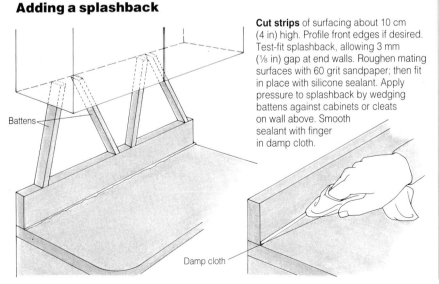
Battens
Damp cloth

Cut strips of surfacing about 10 cm (4 in) high. Profile front edges if desired. Test-fit splashback, allowing 3 mm (⅛ in) gap at end walls. Roughen mating surfaces with 60 grit sandpaper; then fit in place with silicone sealant. Apply pressure to splashback by wedging battens against cabinets or cleats on wall above. Smooth sealant with finger in damp cloth.

To remove blemishes, scrub with abrasive cleanser or sand with 100 grit paper. For deep flaws, grind away damage with an electric rotary tool, then fill depression with seaming compound. Finish surface.

Ceramics, Glass and Plastics 279

PAINT AND WALL COVERINGS

Paint is basically pigment, which provides a particular colour, and a binder in an oil or water-based solvent. As the paint dries, the solvent evaporates, leaving an opaque film.

Some oil-based paints have volatile solvents. Newer alkyd-oil-based paints leave more brush strokes than their old counterparts, but they also dry faster than the old linseed-oil-based paints. There is a move towards water-based paints which are environmentally friendly and allow you to clean paintbrushes with water. Most water-based paints have a latex binder, which may be vinyl, rubber, polyvinyl acetate or acrylic resins. Latex paint offers superior colour retention, easy cleaning and low toxicity.

Textured paint, with granular additives, hides defects as it adds character to a surface. It comes premixed or as a dry powder. You can create special effects with textured paint (below) or with glaze applied over a paint (facing page).

Textured paints

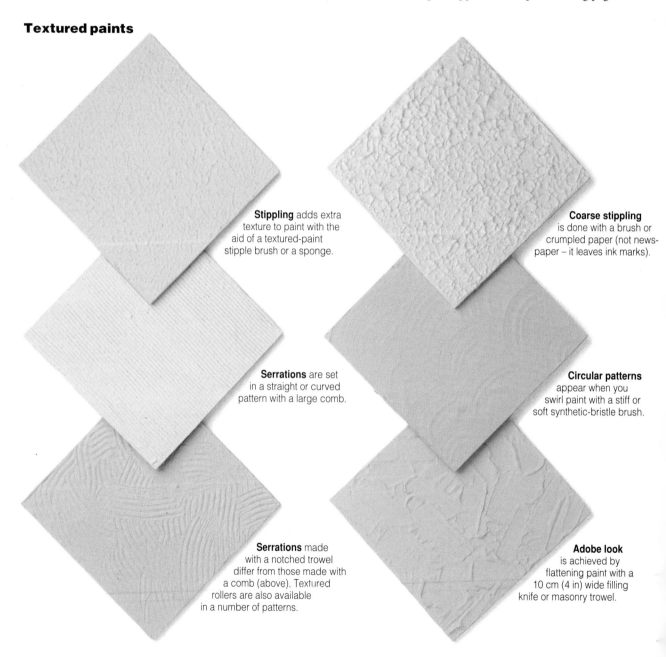

Stippling adds extra texture to paint with the aid of a textured-paint stipple brush or a sponge.

Coarse stippling is done with a brush or crumpled paper (not news-paper – it leaves ink marks).

Serrations are set in a straight or curved pattern with a large comb.

Circular patterns appear when you swirl paint with a stiff or soft synthetic-bristle brush.

Serrations made with a notched trowel differ from those made with a comb (above). Textured rollers are also available in a number of patterns.

Adobe look is achieved by flattening paint with a 10 cm (4 in) wide filling knife or masonry trowel.

Glazed paints for special effects

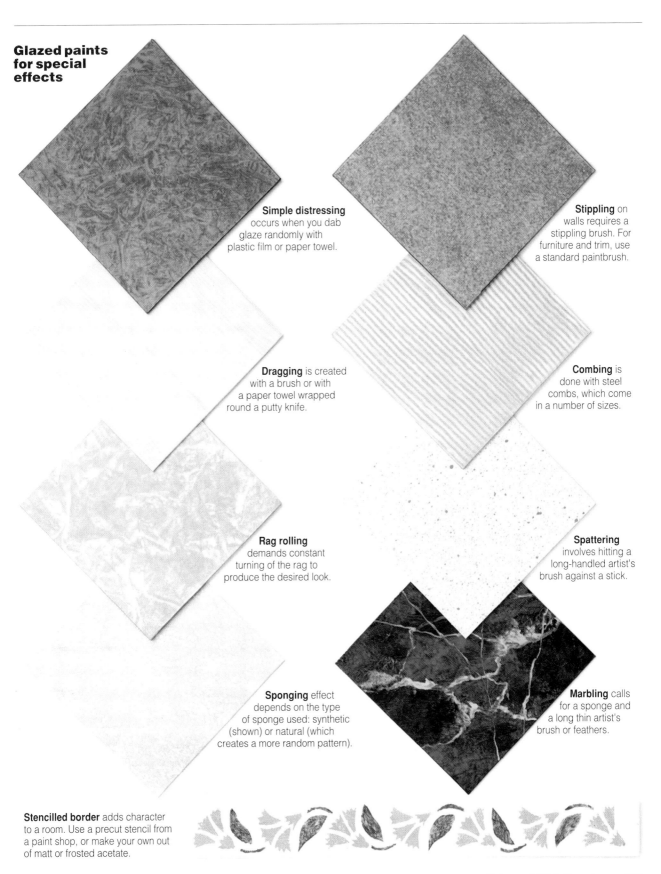

Simple distressing occurs when you dab glaze randomly with plastic film or paper towel.

Stippling on walls requires a stippling brush. For furniture and trim, use a standard paintbrush.

Dragging is created with a brush or with a paper towel wrapped round a putty knife.

Combing is done with steel combs, which come in a number of sizes.

Rag rolling demands constant turning of the rag to produce the desired look.

Spattering involves hitting a long-handled artist's brush against a stick.

Sponging effect depends on the type of sponge used: synthetic (shown) or natural (which creates a more random pattern).

Marbling calls for a sponge and a long thin artist's brush or feathers.

Stencilled border adds character to a room. Use a precut stencil from a paint shop, or make your own out of matt or frosted acetate.

Primer and undercoat Interior and exterior surfaces usually need some preparatory coating. Painted surfaces that will be exposed to the weather need special care. Exposed end grain on wood must be thoroughly soaked with primer to stop rain penetrating, but primer is not waterproof, so don't leave a primed surface exposed to the weather for long. Apply undercoat and topcoat as soon as possible.

Paint For the best results choose well-known brand names and always select primer, undercoat and topcoat made by the same manufacturer. Buy the best quality paint you can afford.

Flat and eggshell finishes are the least shiny and reflective. They are often used on walls and ceilings in living areas and hallways, where they tend not to show surface flaws and brush or roller marks.

Medium sheen (both semigloss and satin) is often used on kitchen and bathroom surfaces, where a soft but rather shiny look is desired.

Glossy finishes are easy to wash and are best for high-wear areas. High-gloss oil-based paints are much glossier than similar vinyl paints, and wash and wear better. Paint containing enamel also has these characteristics, but may become brittle and yellow with age.

The right paint for the surface

Follow the manufacturer's advice shown on the paint tin. This will tell you what surfaces can be coated with the paint, how many coats may be required, as well as the paint's drying time and expected coverage.

Coating	Where used	Description	Advice
Undercoat	Interior and exterior primed surfaces before applying topcoat. Dark surfaces which are to be painted a paler colour	A full-bodied paint with more pigment than topcoat. Has good covering power	Apply a second coat if previous colour shows through the first. Wash tools with white spirit after applying undercoat
Oil-based or synthetic gloss paint (topcoat)	Interior and exterior woodwork and metalwork. Can also be applied to walls and ceilings if desired	Both decorative and protective. A relatively thin coating with little covering power	An undercoat is necessary on wood, but not on metal. Apply two thin coats rather than one thick one. Clean brushes immediately with white spirit
Nondrip or one-coat	Gloss for interior and exterior woodwork and emulsion for ceilings	Combines undercoat and topcoat. Stays on the brush well. Good for beginners	Two coats may be needed when covering a dark colour. Clean tools with white spirit
Interior emulsion paint	Walls and ceilings	Water-based, which makes tools easy to clean. Dries quickly and does not leave brush marks. Acrylic resins can be added to make it more hard-wearing	Does not need an undercoat. Diluted with water, it forms its own primer. Use a roller for fast coverage. Apply two or three coats. Clean tools with soap and water
Exterior emulsion paint	Outside walls	Water-based, but very hard-wearing. Looks clean for longer, as rain washes off some of the surface, taking dirt wth it	Fill any fine cracks before painting. Apply with a wide brush or a shaggy roller. Clean tools with soap and water
Masonry paint	All types of exterior rendering	Most are strenghtened with silica, nylon or sand, which help to form a more durable finish	Use stabilising solution on the surface, and fungicide if necessary, before painting. Clean tools with water
Microporous (acrylic) paint	Exterior, new, untreated timber. Can also be applied to most interior surfaces	Water-based. Some are one-coat, others two. Allows surface to breathe; keeps out damp. Reduces blistering and flaking	Drying time is faster than oil-based paint. Clean tools with water and detergent. Gloss microporous is not as shiny as oil-based gloss
Bituminous paint	Exterior metal pipes and guttering and over concrete	A special paint for waterproofing surfaces	Other paints won't take over it, so once you have applied it, continue to use it. Clean brushes with paraffin, and keep them for bituminous paint only
Textured (plastic) coating	Interior walls and surfaces with unattractive or uneven surfaces	Much thicker than paint. Forms a permanent coating that is difficult to remove	Apply with a shaggy roller unless maker specifies otherwise. Coat with emulsion once dry. Clean tools with white spirit
Anti-condensation paint	Surfaces in bathrooms, kitchens and any area likely to have a steamy atmosphere	Semiporous emulsion which absorbs humidity and allows it to evaporate as the air dries. Prevents droplets forming on the surface. Often contains a fungicide to deter mould	Apply as interior emulsion. Will not cure condensation but will reduce its effect on the painted surface. Clean tools with water and detergent
Enamel paint	Metal and wood, children's toys and furniture	Nontoxic. Contains very finely ground pigment. Sometimes available with a rust inhibitor	No primer or undercoat needed. Best for small jobs. Clean brushes with white spirit

Brushes For fine finishes, choose the best brushes, keeping cheaper brushes for applying wood preservatives or for use as dusting brushes. Pig bristle is best, though a number of synthetic bristles are now included in certain brushes – especially those used with water-based paints. Brushes of a given size may vary considerably in price, according to the amount of bristle packed into them: the more bristle, the better. If you keep good quality brushes for finishing work and take good care of them, they will improve with age. For normal jobs, you should be able to manage with 50 mm (2 in), 25 mm (1 in) and 13 mm (½ in) brushes, plus a 100 mm (4 in) or 150 mm (6 in) brush for wider surfaces such as walls and flush doors.

Rollers Use a foam roller for general-purpose painting on smooth or lightly textured surfaces. Replace the sleeve as soon as it starts to crumble.

A mohair roller has very fine, short pile which creates high finishes on smooth surfaces such as doors and walls. They are not as good on textured surfaces, and are difficult to clean when used with gloss finishes because the sleeve cannot be removed.

Use a shaggy pile roller, made of lambswool, imitation lambswool or nylon pile, for textured surfaces. Special nylon grades are available for exterior use where surfaces may be rough.

Paint pads The pad has a fine layer of mohair, bonded to a foam pad which, in turn, is mounted on a handle. Pads vary in size and are best used with water-based paints. They are suitable for smooth and slightly textured surfaces and will apply thin coats of paint quickly and evenly.

Aerosols Best suited to surfaces like Lloyd Loom basket-weave furniture and wrought-iron railings.

Spray guns Choose an airless gun, where paint is pumped out of the nozzle, because this type creates far less overspray. Not ideal for house painting as so much masking would be needed, and there is the risk of spray drift.

Estimating paint quantity

Calculate area of walls by adding length of room to width and multiplying by 2, then multiplying result by room's height. Compare area with coverage given on paint label; for two coats, double the number of cans.

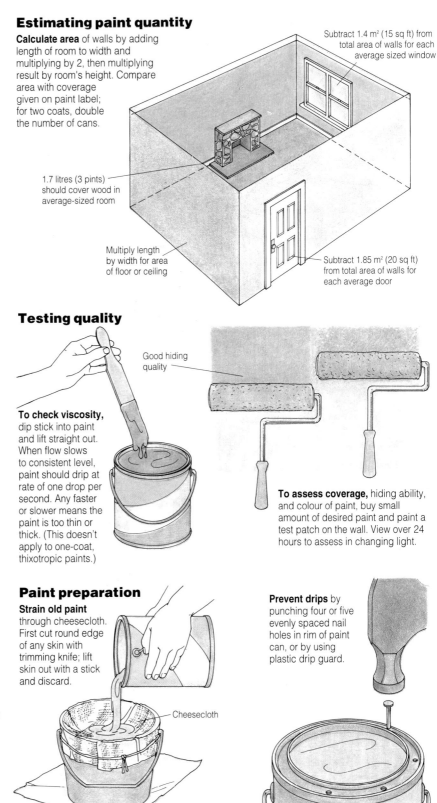

Subtract 1.4 m² (15 sq ft) from total area of walls for each average sized window

1.7 litres (3 pints) should cover wood in average-sized room

Multiply length by width for area of floor or ceiling

Subtract 1.85 m² (20 sq ft) from total area of walls for each average door

Testing quality

To check viscosity, dip stick into paint and lift straight out. When flow slows to consistent level, paint should drip at rate of one drop per second. Any faster or slower means the paint is too thin or thick. (This doesn't apply to one-coat, thixotropic paints.)

Good hiding quality

To assess coverage, hiding ability, and colour of paint, buy small amount of desired paint and paint a test patch on the wall. View over 24 hours to assess in changing light.

Paint preparation

Strain old paint through cheesecloth. First cut round edge of any skin with trimming knife; lift skin out with a stick and discard.

Cheesecloth

Prevent drips by punching four or five evenly spaced nail holes in rim of paint can, or by using plastic drip guard.

When developing a colour scheme, work with the colour wheel as your basic tool. Combine your own colour preferences with the information it provides to achieve the effects you want. Colours that are opposite one another on the wheel are known as complementary colours. They work well together, as do adjacent or related colours (next to each other on the wheel). Using a complementary colour as an accent can enliven a scheme that has different shades of the same colour.

Colour influences people's moods; avoid having too little or too much of it in one place. Combine wall colours with the existing elements in the room – pictures, curtains, upholstery and carpeting; exterior colours should be influenced by what surrounds your home. When decorating from scratch, you can begin with the colour of one element and then build your scheme around it.

Warm or cool Red and yellow and the combinations made from these primary colours are called warm colours – they heat up a room and give it life. In cool climates and in sunny rooms, warm colours create a cosy feeling. The cool colours are blue, green and purple. In hot climates, these colours make a room feel cooler.

By adding white, you lighten the shade of a colour. Lighter shades can brighten rooms that have little natural light. By adding black, you darken a colour's shade. Darker shades create a feeling of intimacy. Light shades appear lighter when placed against a dark background. Against a light background, dark shades seem darker.

Colour can help to improve a room's proportions. Lighter shades reflect light, making walls appear to recede and giving the impression of a larger room; darker shades make a room seem smaller and cosier. For a long, narrow room, paint the end walls a darker shade or a warmer colour than the side walls; this appears to bring in the end walls and widen the room. To make a room seem larger, paint all the walls and any trim the same colour; this will also unify an irregular space. Paint the ceiling a darker shade to

Outer colour wheel has 12 colours. Red, yellow and blue are primaries. Each secondary colour (orange, green and purple) is a combination of two primaries. When you blend colours you change their basic character, creating a wide variety of choices.

Inner colour wheel shows how neutrals may be warm (those on right side) or cool (those on left side). Combine neutrals with brighter colours to create satisfying schemes.

lower it visually and a lighter shade to give the effect of height.

Colour intensity An intense colour is known as highly saturated. Whether it is warm or cool, a saturated colour attracts the eye. Use intense colours as accents and for dramatic effect – on a single wall, for instance. In some spaces, such as hallways, an intense colour can be chosen as a main colour because the room is only for passing through. A gloss paint makes any colour stand out; the same colour in a low gloss or matt is less obtrusive.

To draw attention to a particular wall or to an interesting feature such as moulding, introduce a new colour or a glossier finish. Alternatively, you can minimise an awkward feature, like a badly positioned door or radiator, by painting it the same colour as the background, in a semigloss.

For variety, introduce new colours in different rooms. But maintain unity by featuring a main colour from one room as an accent elsewhere. A wall covering that is multicoloured, mixing some or all of your colours on some walls – for example, in a hallway – can also unify a colour scheme throughout the house.

Choose indoor colours that are one shade lighter than you think you want. Once they have dried on the wall, they will be darker than they appear on the paint chip. Before making a final decision, try the paint-chip test described below, or buy a small can of the desired paint and paint a sample board. Hang the board up for a day, assessing the colour as the paint dries and the light changes.

Shades

Adding white or black changes a colour's shade, permitting many gradations within a single colour. Different colours can also be blended together; brown, for instance, is a mixture of red, yellow and black.

Paint chips

Sample paint chips help you to choose shades. Cut the same shade from four chips and tape them together. Compare with furnishings and accessories, and tape to wall to observe in different lighting.

Interior colours

Semigloss coral walls create a stimulating room. Red walls can also wake up a quiet room and lend a cosy, intimate feeling. Try red for dining areas, rooms with northern exposures and rooms used mainly at night.

Cool colours are serene and relaxing. Here, the soft grey-green of the walls is picked up in accessories such as the cushions, picture and curtain fabric. Use cool colours in rooms that receive morning or afternoon sun.

Shades of the same colour – in this case cream – are used to create a simple look. You can brighten up neutral colours with contrasts (such as the green here). Such a scheme would suit living rooms and conservatories.

Exterior colours

When choosing paint colours, keep in mind these factors. A small house will seem larger if you paint the entire structure, including any trim, the same light colour (below). Any paint with a glossy finish will exaggerate surface flaws.

A three-colour exterior scheme (right) with neutral or mid tone walls, darker trim and a complementary coloured door emphasises architectural features. Change colours only where a surface changes and harmonise colours with brick or any other features whose colour cannot be easily altered. (If masonry needs cleaning, which may alter its colour, clean it before selecting colours.) Sunlight makes any colour seem lighter; so select a slightly darker shade than the one you actually want. Strong colours will fade faster outdoors than light colours. A house's surroundings change with the seasons; choose colours that will be pleasing all year round.

It is essential to clean and repair all surfaces before painting. First remove wallcoverings (p.312), curtains and all hardware except light switch plates and socket outlets. Working from top to bottom, sponge-wash walls and trim with a solution of powder or liquid cleanser, then rinse. Before washing the ceiling, cover the floor with dust sheets. Follow ladder safety precautions shown on pages 290-1.

If paint is thick, remove it with a heat gun or with a chemical stripper. After applying the stripper, let the paint soften, and then scrape and sand as you would when using a heat gun.

Caution: Have a bucket of water handy, in which to drop burning paint. Do not have newspaper on the floor when using a heat gun. Dispose of all debris properly afterwards.

Fill dents and small holes in plasterboard as shown on the facing page. For larger holes, cut a new piece of board to be inserted behind the hole. Coat the edges with plasterboard adhesive and pull it into position using a piece of string knotted on the inside of the patch. When the patch is firmly fixed, cut the string and level the area with one-coat repair plaster.

In a plastered wall, large or widening cracks, or cracks radiating from window or door corners, may indicate structural problems; have these professionally evaluated. Also do this where you discover water damage.

Removing paint

2. Immediately scrape softened paint from flat surfaces with a chisel knife. (Round off corners of knife to avoid gouging wood.) Either heat paint or scrape it – doing both at the same time could damage wood.

Shavehook

3. Scrape mouldings with shavehook or triangular blade scraper. For intricate carving, use pointed object such as an awl. Treat entire surface until bare wood is visible.

4. When most of the paint has gone, let dry; then remove any residue with palm sander or sanding block fitted with successively finer grits of abrasive paper.

Stripping paint:
1. Soften the paint by holding the heat gun 7.5-15 cm (3-6 in) away. Move it back and forth until paint blisters.
Caution: To avoid scorching the wood, keep the tool moving. Wear gloves – and a mask if your lungs are sensitive.

Repairing wood trim

Scrape away loose paint with a stiff chisel knife. Dig away any rotted wood. Brush wood hardener on bare wood and soft areas.

Repair paste

Fill depressions with wood repair paste; let dry. Smooth and feather edges with medium, then fine, abrasive paper.

Exposed nail

Nailset

Exposed nails 1. For doors, windows and other trim, reseat nails with nail set. Fill nail holes with acrylic sealant; fill joints with sealant or paintable filler.

2. Apply a fast-drying primer, or a standard primer. Let it dry; then sand lightly.

Repairing damaged plasterboard

Fill dents with filling compound, using putty knife wide enough to span damaged area. Smooth with wet sponge, let dry for 24 hours, then recoat. Smooth again; sand lightly after a further 24 hours.

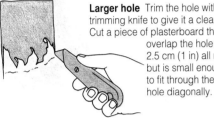

Larger hole Trim the hole with a sharp trimming knife to give it a clean edge. Cut a piece of plasterboard that will overlap the hole by 2.5 cm (1 in) all round, but is small enough to fit through the hole diagonally.

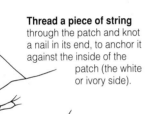

Thread a piece of string through the patch and knot a nail in its end, to anchor it against the inside of the patch (the white or ivory side).

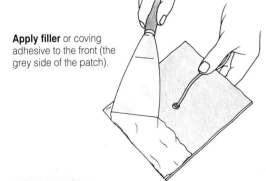

Apply filler or coving adhesive to the front (the grey side of the patch).

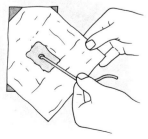

Guide the coated patch through the hole and use the string to pull it firmly against the wall. Hold it taut while you fill the hole with one-coat plaster. When the plaster has almost set, cut the string and touch up the surface.

Filling holes in plaster

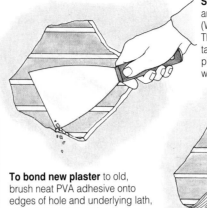

Scrape away loose paint from area around hole, using large putty knife. (Wear goggles and a dust mask.) Then scrape loose plaster from hole, taking care not to remove sound plaster. Undercut hole's inside edge with putty knife.

To bond new plaster to old, brush neat PVA adhesive onto edges of hole and underlying lath, with an old paintbrush.

PVA adhesive

Fill hole with repair plaster, using wide putty knife. For a deep hole, cross-hatch plaster while still wet, let it dry, then apply second coat. A single coat is enough for a shallow hole.

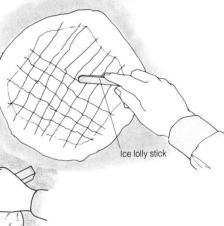

Ice lolly stick

Level the last coat by drawing the edge of a flat, smooth piece of wood across it, with a sawing action. Sand patch lightly after 24 hours.

Repairing cracked plaster

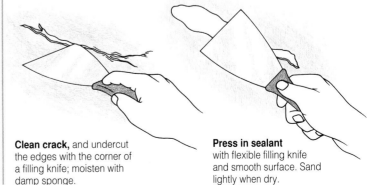

Clean crack, and undercut the edges with the corner of a filling knife; moisten with damp sponge.

Press in sealant with flexible filling knife and smooth surface. Sand lightly when dry.

Reducing clutter from the room and carefully masking your work area will help your project to go smoothly and make cleaning up easier.

Remove curtains, floor covering and any light furniture; move the heavier pieces to the centre of the room. Wash and repair the walls, ceiling and trim (pp.288-9). Then vacuum and dust the area thoroughly. Turn off the radiator.

Remove all exposed hardware such as window locks, curtain rods and picture hooks; tape the fasteners to the hardware so they don't get lost.

Use cotton dustsheets to cover everything that won't be painted – it is not wise to use inexpensive polythene dustsheets as water runs off and wet plastic is slippery. Cotton cloths are also best for floors because they absorb paint splashes. However, if you do use plastic dustsheets on the floor, cover them with newspaper or old sheets to absorb water and paint.

Cover wood trim which is not to be painted with good-quality masking tape. To prevent paint from creeping behind the tape or paper, press its edge down with a flexible putty knife. Remove the masking tape just before the paint dries; it may damage the trim as you pull it off, if left on for too long.

Protect wall switches and sockets with strips of masking tape where they meet the wall. Surface-mounted switches can be eased away from the wall when papering, but the power supply must be switched off before the screws are loosened.

Masking window glass can save time, but if you have only one window and a steady hand, it may be easier to scrape dried paint off the glass with a single-edge razor blade.

Caution: Keep children and pets out of the work area. Before leaving for any length of time, clean up or store your paint and materials.

Preparing to paint

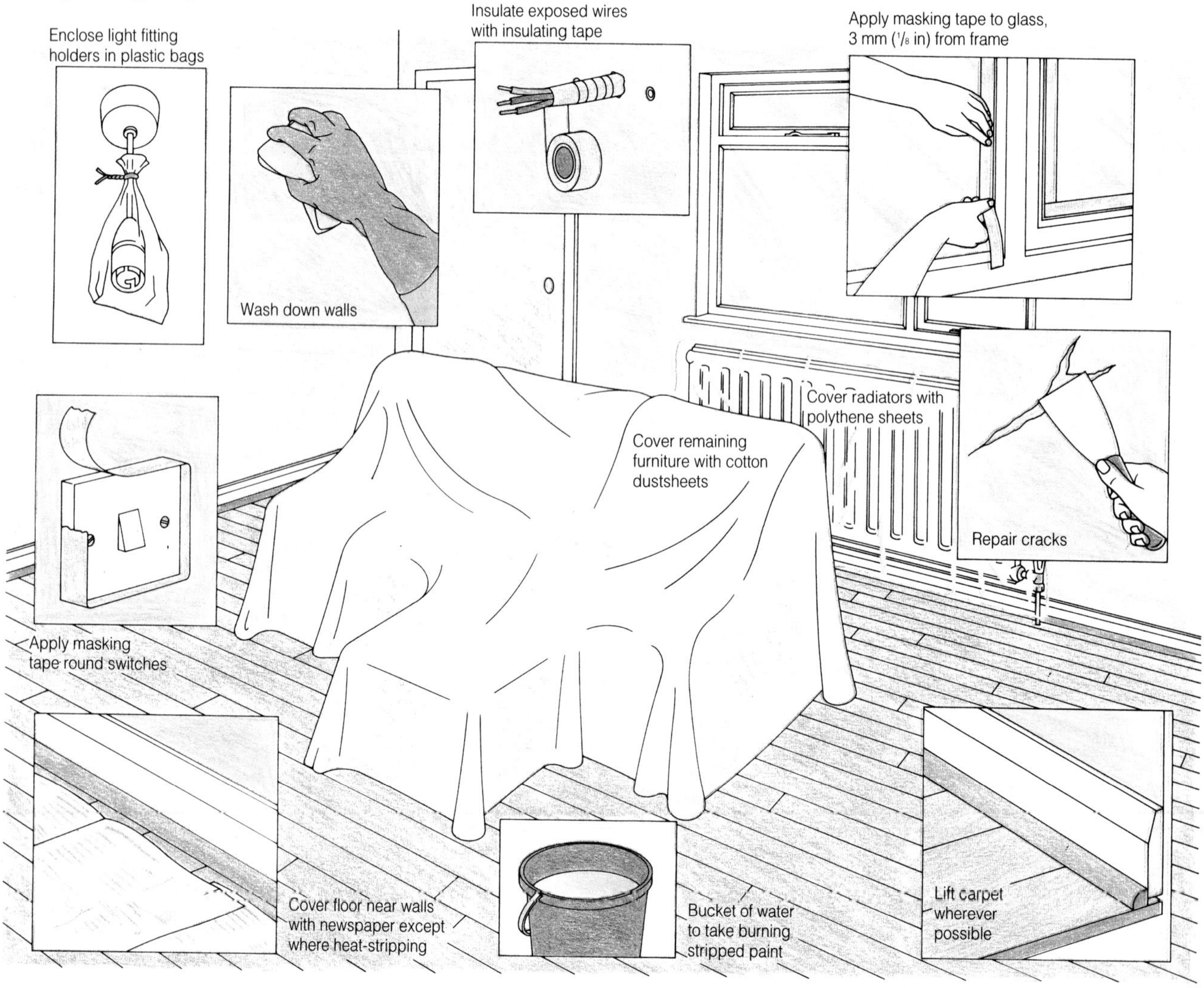

Enclose light fitting holders in plastic bags

Wash down walls

Insulate exposed wires with insulating tape

Apply masking tape to glass, 3 mm ($\frac{1}{8}$ in) from frame

Cover radiators with polythene sheets

Repair cracks

Cover remaining furniture with cotton dustsheets

Apply masking tape round switches

Cover floor near walls with newspaper except where heat-stripping

Bucket of water to take burning stripped paint

Lift carpet wherever possible

WORKING WITH LADDERS AND SCAFFOLDING

Usually one ladder is required when painting a room; for exteriors, you will often need at least two. Stairs call for special set-ups (p.297). Indoors use stepladders; if you use an extension ladder to reach a high ceiling, wrap the tops of its side rails with cloth to protect the wall. Scaffolding can be constructed with ladders and planks; for large set-ups, you can rent more elaborate scaffolding from a hire shop. You need not fall very far to hurt yourself, so always follow the basic safety rules given here.

Stepladder

Position ladder so that feet are level and steady on floor. For balance, lean your body into ladder. When you can no longer comfortably reach work surface, get down and move ladder. Don't over-reach, or the ladder may topple. Ideally, choose steps with a grab rail.

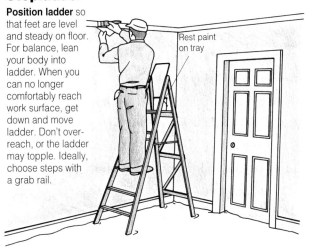

Rest paint on tray

Scaffolding

Construct scaffold from a strong, straight scaffold plank supported by two stepladders. Extend plank at least 30 cm (1 ft) beyond steps. For spans over 1.5 m (5 ft) use two planks for extra strength.

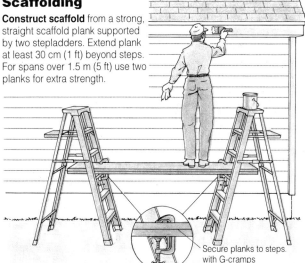

Secure planks to steps with G-cramps

Extension ladder

To raise, set the unextended ladder on the ground with its feet close to the wall, and walk up, under the ladder, hand over hand, working towards the wall. With ladder in position, extend it and pull out base to the correct angle.

Angle ladder so that distance between its feet and wall equals a quarter of the ladder's height. Both feet should be an equal distance from the wall, so that ladder does not rock. On a hard or slippery surface, have a helper hold the ladder steady or place a sandbag at the base.

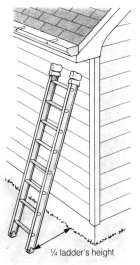

¼ ladder's height

Haul up supplies in a bucket on a rope, or have someone hand them to you. Hang paint cans and supplies from a notched pole that fits through the top rung of an aluminium ladder.

Paint and Wall Coverings   291

PAINTING WITH BRUSHES

Paint woodwork first, then mask it (p.290) and paint the ceiling and walls. Or if you are wary of splashing newly painted trim, begin by painting the ceiling and walls, and do the woodwork last. If you are planning to paper walls, paint the trim first and carry a little paint onto the walls. When painting large surfaces, first use a 50 mm (2 in) brush to outline or cut in round windows, doors and other trim and at the intersections of ceilings and walls, then cover the remaining surface using a wide brush or a roller (pp.294-5).

For an even coat, use the entire tip of the brush to apply the paint. Hold the brush comfortably, with your thumb supporting its underside, but shift your grip now and then to avoid fatigue. When you need to reload the brush with paint, smooth out or feather your strokes by gradually lifting the bristles off the work surface during the stroke. To avoid lap marks, work towards the most recently painted section, overlapping the wet edges. Don't stop work in the middle of an unbroken section; you may end up with colour variations.

Paint windows and exterior doors early in the day so that you can close them at night without the paint sticking.

Using a paintbrush

Load brush, covering one-third of bristle length. To remove excess paint, lift brush straight up and slap it lightly against inside of can. Don't drag brush over rim.

Cut in at ceiling with narrow edge of brush if wall and ceiling colours are different. Keep paint off adjacent surface; remove smudges with a putty knife wrapped in paper towel.

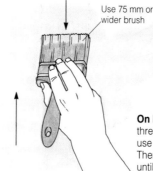

Use 75 mm or wider brush

On large areas, apply paint with two or three overlapping diagonal brush strokes; use largest brush that is comfortable. Then feather paint with vertical strokes until coverage is smooth.

At corners, around woodwork and wherever roller won't reach, cut in using width of brush. Work slowly to prevent splatters.

Caring for a paintbrush

Remove excess paint with a brush comb before washing brush. Alternatively, work brush back and forth across paper towel.

Brush comb

Wash emulsion paint out of brush with warm water, separating bristles with your fingers. For oil-based paint, clean with white spirit or a brush cleaner.

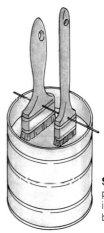

Store brushes overnight in paint thinner by drilling holes in handles and suspending brushes on a piece of stiff wire.

For long-term storage, wrap brushes in their original plastic wrappers or wrap bristles in paper or foil.

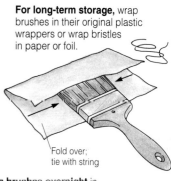

Fold over; tie with string

Painting a window

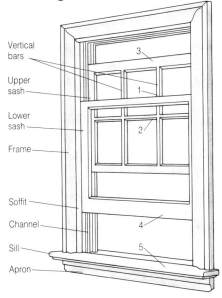

Vertical bars
Upper sash
Lower sash
Frame
Soffit
Channel
Sill
Apron

Work order: First remove locks and handles. Paint vertical bars, then horizontal, then the rest of the sash. For double-hung windows, paint as much of upper sash as possible, reverse the sash positions, and paint lower parts of upper sash. Then paint lower sash. Finally, paint soffit, apron, sill and frame. If you paint sash channels, sand them first. To prevent sashes sticking, move them while paint is still wet.

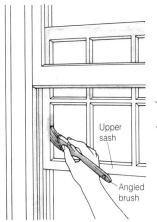

Upper sash
Angled brush

Begin in middle of unpainted area, using 40 mm (1½ in) angled brush. Brush out in both directions, then stroke towards wet areas. Put paint in small container for convenience.

Lower sash

Check sash corners now and then for paint build-up and drips; remove by gently dabbing with dry brush. Remove drips at bar intersections in same way.

Painting a door

Frame
Door stop
Rail
Stile
Wedge

Work order: Before painting, remove or cover doorknob and firmly prop door open with pair of wedges. If door is new, paint bottom edge before hanging, to prevent wood from absorbing moisture and warping. Paint side and top edges of door first. Then paint panel edges. Follow with panel surfaces. Finish with rails, then stiles.

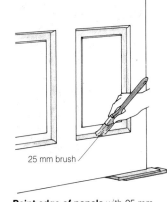

25 mm brush

Paint edge of panels with 25 mm (1 in) angled brush, working from top to bottom. To stop drips, dab paint into corners.

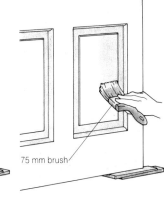

75 mm brush

Paint panel surfaces with 75 mm (3 in) brush, working from centre of panel to edge. Feather strokes to smooth paint.

Painting trim

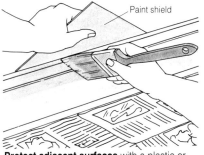

Paint shield

Protect adjacent surfaces with a plastic or metal shield, wiping it frequently with a clean cloth. Paint with the wood grain; use two coats.

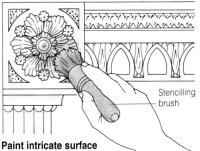

Stencilling brush

Paint intricate surface with stiff-bristle brush, such as a stencilling brush. Force paint into all crevices; remove paint build-ups and drips.

Paint and Wall Coverings   293

PAINTING WITH ROLLERS AND PADS

Match the thickness and type of roller to your job. A foam or standard pile is fine for most flat and semigloss paints on smooth surfaces; for high-gloss paint, choose a mohair roller sleeve. For textured paint (p.299) or concrete, use a shaggy nylon sleeve. Before painting, dampen a roller with water (for emulsion) or white spirit (for alkyd), then blot excess on paper towel.

A power roller requires the same techniques as a manual roller. Even though its speed makes it a tempting investment, the time needed to clean it may cancel out any time saved.

Painting pads are less messy than rollers, but they apply a thinner coat of paint. Certain pads are useful for painting over irregular surfaces and for reaching tight spots (p.298); angled pads are available that make it easy to get clean coverage next to trim.

Apply each coat of paint without stopping so that wet paint won't overlap dry. If you must stop, do so at a natural break in the surface, such as a window or door. When painting new wallboard, wait for the first coat of paint to dry, then fill visible seams and repairs before applying the next coat.

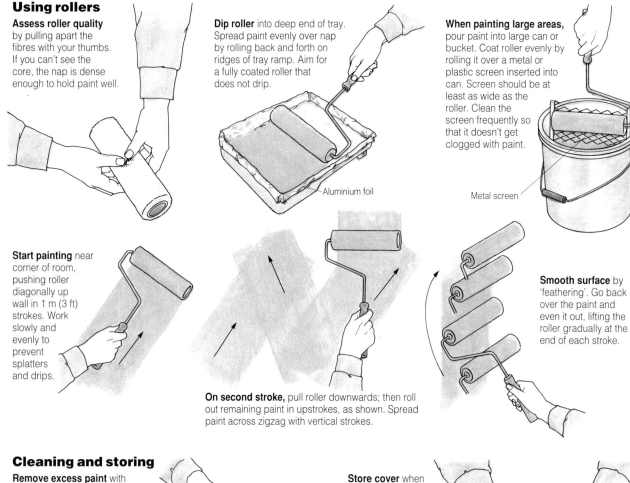

Using rollers

Assess roller quality by pulling apart the fibres with your thumbs. If you can't see the core, the nap is dense enough to hold paint well.

Dip roller into deep end of tray. Spread paint evenly over nap by rolling back and forth on ridges of tray ramp. Aim for a fully coated roller that does not drip.

Aluminium foil

When painting large areas, pour paint into large can or bucket. Coat roller evenly by rolling it over a metal or plastic screen inserted into can. Screen should be at least as wide as the roller. Clean the screen frequently so that it doesn't get clogged with paint.

Metal screen

Start painting near corner of room, pushing roller diagonally up wall in 1 m (3 ft) strokes. Work slowly and evenly to prevent splatters and drips.

On second stroke, pull roller downwards; then roll out remaining paint in upstrokes, as shown. Spread paint across zigzag with vertical strokes.

Smooth surface by 'feathering'. Go back over the paint and even it out, lifting the roller gradually at the end of each stroke.

Cleaning and storing

Remove excess paint with curved side of brush comb. Then wash roller cover with soap and hot running water (for emulsion) or with white spirit (for alkyd paint). Wear rubber gloves while rubbing white spirit into nap.

Brush comb

Store cover when dry, wrapped in paper or aluminium foil. If you use plastic, punch a few air holes in it to prevent staining caused by damp or mildew.

Painting ceilings and walls

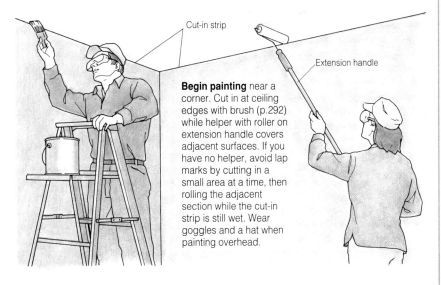

Cut-in strip

Extension handle

Begin painting near a corner. Cut in at ceiling edges with brush (p.292) while helper with roller on extension handle covers adjacent surfaces. If you have no helper, avoid lap marks by cutting in a small area at a time, then rolling the adjacent section while the cut-in strip is still wet. Wear goggles and a hat when painting overhead.

Roll on paint in diagonal strokes, as shown on facing page. Cover only a 1 m (3 ft) section at a time; then feather the surface to even out coverage. Move from a dry section into a wet one, overlapping edges to prevent streaks. Roll slowly to minimise splashing.

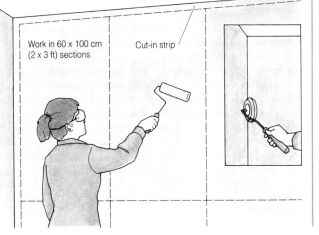

Cut in and paint walls after ceiling. A corner roller works well for 90° or acute angles (inset). Starting in upper corner, work in sections of about 60 x 100 cm (2 x 3 ft), working towards lower corner. Apply and distribute the paint as shown on facing page.

Work in 60 x 100 cm (2 x 3 ft) sections

Cut-in strip

Painting with pads

Before loading pad, dampen it first (with water for emulsion paint, white spirit for oil-based paint). Then press it into paint until fibres are saturated. Blot off excess on tray's ridges or roller.

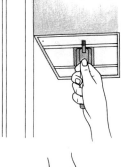

Use an angled paint pad to get paint close to mouldings, and use the edge of the moulding as a guide.

Use an old baking tin if you have no proprietary paint tray. Dab the pad lightly onto the paint.

Dab pad on kitchen towel after cleaning it, to remove excess water or white spirit. Don't use newspaper as print may transfer.

Paint and Wall Coverings   295

PAINTING WITH SPRAYERS

Spray-painting saves time, especially when you need to paint irregular surfaces such as furniture, but it takes some practice before you can produce an even, drip-free coating. Apply two or three thin coats – never one thick one, which could sag and drip.

All sprayers require thorough cleaning after use. Before buying or hiring a sprayer, balance these factors against the reduced painting time.

If you do decide to spray, match the tool to the job. For instance, the airless paint sprayer shown here may not be suitable for painting very large areas. Although most paints can be sprayed, some sprayers can't spray thick paints. Ask your dealer or hire shop to explain how to use the sprayer, and make sure you have an instruction manual in case problems arise.

Before filling the sprayer, strain the paint (p.285) to avoid clogging the nozzle; then thin the paint by about 10 per cent with water or paint thinner, depending on the type of paint. Select the correct nozzle and make sure it is clear. Because spraying produces a lot of overspray, mask all surfaces you want to protect. First, practise your technique on scrap material. If the paint is thin enough, it will cover the surface evenly in an elliptical pattern.

Caution: Never spray-paint out of doors in windy weather. Overspraying can cause considerable damage to finishes such as car bodywork. Also, never point a sprayer at anyone or spray paint directly onto your skin.

Unplug the sprayer before filling, cleaning or servicing it. Always wear the appropriate respirator (p.13).

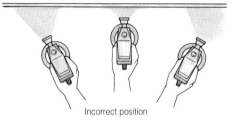

Incorrect position

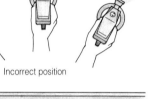

Correct position

Move spray gun parallel with surface, at a distance of about 30 cm (1 ft). To maintain even coverage, keep sprayer upright and bend your wrist; don't swing sprayer in an arc.

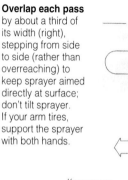

Overlap each pass by about a third of its width (right), stepping from side to side (rather than overreaching) to keep sprayer aimed directly at surface; don't tilt sprayer. If your arm tires, support the sprayer with both hands.

Keep power cord out of your way

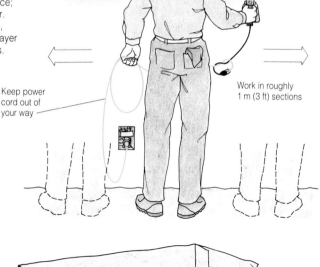

Work in roughly 1 m (3 ft) sections

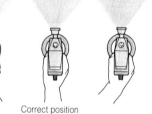

Outside corner

Inside corner

At corners, keep spray gun moving to feather edges of sprayed area. For outside corners, aim directly at intersection of walls; for inside corners, aim at each wall in turn. If ceiling and wall colours differ, cut in at top of wall (p.292).

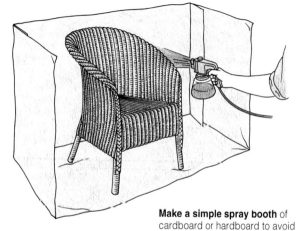

Make a simple spray booth of cardboard or hardboard to avoid overspray. Always work outdoors.

PAINTING STAIRWELLS

Reaching the ceiling and upper walls of a stairwell usually requires scaffolding. You can rent scaffolding or make your own with scaffold boards supported on a combination of sawhorses, extension ladders and stepladders. Get the boards from your local hire shop.

For extra strength on spans longer than 1.5 m (5 ft), double the boards; don't try to span a gap longer than 3 m (10 ft) without extra support from beneath. When erected, the scaffold boards should be level and should extend beyond the end supports by at least 30 cm (1 ft). Clamp the boards to their supports.

For extra safety and to reduce the risk of falling, place the scaffold no farther than your body's width from the wall and, as you work, keep it free of extra paint, tools and materials.

Mask and cover the area under and beyond the edge of the work platform. Paint balusters and railings with paint mittens, and steps with brushes and small rollers. Cut in round ceilings and walls as you would normally (p.292).

Caution: When working at heights, follow the safety information given on page 291, in particular making sure that your platform is secure.

To prevent a ladder from slipping, screw a wooden cleat to the floor to brace its feet (if possible, lift up any carpet to do this). Block access to the stairs, and either leave doors wide open or block them closed to prevent them from being opened into the scaffold.

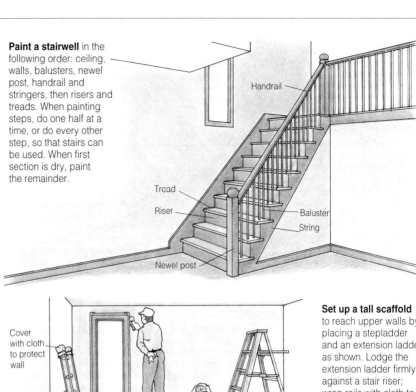

Paint a stairwell in the following order: ceiling, walls, balusters, newel post, handrail and stringers, then risers and treads. When painting steps, do one half at a time, or do every other step, so that stairs can be used. When first section is dry, paint the remainder.

Handrail

Tread

Riser

Baluster

String

Newel post

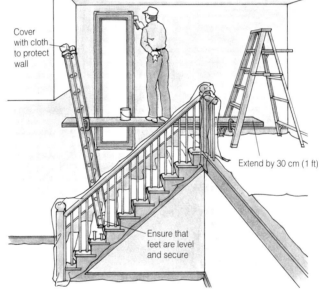

Cover with cloth to protect wall

Extend by 30 cm (1 ft)

Ensure that feet are level and secure

Set up a tall scaffold to reach upper walls by placing a stepladder and an extension ladder as shown. Lodge the extension ladder firmly against a stair riser; wrap rails with cloth to protect walls. Run two scaffold boards between the ladders, securing them to the rungs with clamps. If space is limited at upper part of stairway, use a stepladder or sawhorse propped against the upper wall.

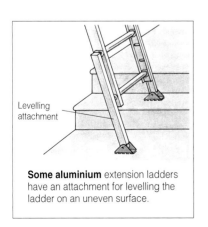

Levelling attachment

Some aluminium extension ladders have an attachment for levelling the ladder on an uneven surface.

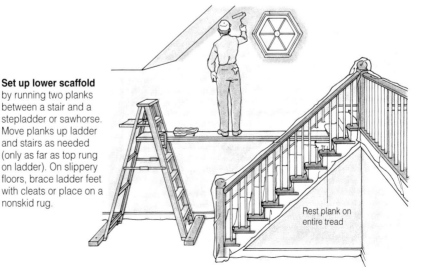

Set up lower scaffold by running two planks between a stair and a stepladder or sawhorse. Move planks up ladder and stairs as needed (only as far as top rung on ladder). On slippery floors, brace ladder feet with cleats or place on a nonskid rug.

Rest plank on entire tread

Paint and Wall Coverings 297

SPECIAL PAINTING TECHNIQUES

Most paint jobs include at least one hard-to-reach area or an irregular surface. While it's possible to paint almost anything with a combination of brushes and rollers, some items require the special techniques or tools shown below.

Reaching all surfaces of kitchen and bathroom cabinets can be difficult; to manoeuvre more easily in tight spaces, try a brush with a short handle. Before painting cabinets,

remove the doors, drawers and hardware, and wash all surfaces. Lightly sand new or previously painted wood. To prevent warping from uneven moisture absorption, use an equal number of coats of paint on all the cabinet's surfaces.

An airless sprayer (p.296) will quickly paint decorative metalwork and louvred shutters, but you can get similar, if slower, results with a paint mitten or a flexible paint pad.

Painting cabinets

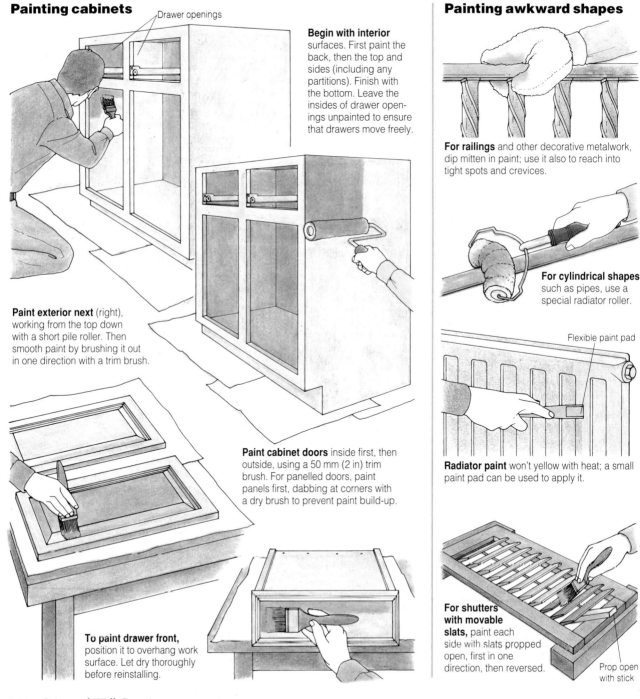

Drawer openings

Begin with interior surfaces. First paint the back, then the top and sides (including any partitions). Finish with the bottom. Leave the insides of drawer openings unpainted to ensure that drawers move freely.

Paint exterior next (right), working from the top down with a short pile roller. Then smooth paint by brushing it out in one direction with a trim brush.

Paint cabinet doors inside first, then outside, using a 50 mm (2 in) trim brush. For panelled doors, paint panels first, dabbing at corners with a dry brush to prevent paint build-up.

To paint drawer front, position it to overhang work surface. Let dry thoroughly before reinstalling.

Painting awkward shapes

For railings and other decorative metalwork, dip mitten in paint; use it also to reach into tight spots and crevices.

For cylindrical shapes such as pipes, use a special radiator roller.

Flexible paint pad

Radiator paint won't yellow with heat; a small paint pad can be used to apply it.

For shutters with movable slats, paint each side with slats propped open, first in one direction, then reversed.

Prop open with stick

PAINTING WITH TEXTURED PAINT

In addition to providing a decorative surface, textured paint hides cracks and other flaws in walls and ceilings. Once applied, it's difficult to remove, but it can be freshened or its colour changed with a coat of paint. Use a textured roller to create patterns. Alternatively, use one of the techniques shown below. Premixed coatings have a thinner texture; water-based emulsion paint provides a heavier coat.

Before applying the textured paint, practise your pattern on heavy cardboard. Fill any large holes or dents in the surface of the wall (pp.288-9); the paint itself will fill minor flaws. Prime the wall with an appropriate primer and apply the textured paint. Let it dry for the time specified on the label; then create the final pattern. Before adding another colour over the top, let the finished pattern dry for 24 hours.

Applying textured paint

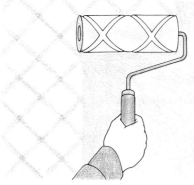

Mix textured paint to desired consistency and apply with a paintbush, 1 m (3 ft) square sections at a time. Use a textured roller to create pattern, then move on to next section.

To colour the texture, paint over it with flat emulsion. First cut in round trim and wall edges with a brush. Dab paint into all crevices, then smooth it outwards.

To colour remaining surfaces, use a roller fitted with a shaggy nylon roller cover. Roll on emulsion paint in W or M shaped strokes; then fill in remaining spaces.

Making your own patterns

Circular pattern Position a slightly damp natural sponge against paint, then rotate.

Ridges Rake notched trowel across paint in curved or straight motion.

Fine ridges Comb paint with large-tooth plastic or metal hair comb.

Adobe look Dab and twist paint slightly with concrete finishing trowel or putty knife.

Swirls Twist stiff-bristled brush against paint; softer bristles create more subtle look.

Stipple Repeatedly place crumpled piece of wax paper or plastic against paint.

With a few improvised tools, glaze that you make yourself and the techniques shown here, you can decorate surfaces in a variety of ways. More subtle than patterned wallpapers and more elaborate than plain painted surfaces, decorative paint finishes can alter the appearance of a room dramatically. You can treat a whole room or, as is more usual, use one effect to accent a single wall, an architectural detail, a piece of furniture or a craft item.

Glaze is the basic material of most decorative painting and is a semitransparent paint – either oil or water-based – that you apply over a base coat. The glaze is distressed in such a way that the base coat shows through the glaze unevenly, creating a pattern. The most common technique is to brush or roll the glaze over the base coat, then distress it (facing page), resulting in a smooth, subtle finish. You can also apply the glaze over the base coat with a distressing tool, which produces a more clearly defined pattern. Or combine these techniques, using paints or glazes of different colours for a multilayered effect.

A simple, effective recipe for glaze that combines oil-based paint, solvent and glazing liquid is given below. As it's difficult to match consecutive batches exactly, always mix a bit extra.

The base coat over which you put the glaze can be either emulsion or oil, but it should have a satin or eggshell lustre. Let a new base coat dry for 24 hours before you apply the glaze. Oil glazes (which were originally known as scumble glazes) dry slowly, giving you more 'open' time in which to work – especially on marbling – whereas emulsion glazes dry fast and are recommended only for small areas.

Once the glaze is dry, you can apply a clear varnish, which provides a protective coating and gives the surface its final sheen. Varnish is almost always used when marbling (p.302), and on furniture or craft objects.

Before choosing a finish, consider the condition of the surface. Combing, stippling and dragging can highlight any imperfections in the surface. Before tackling a project, practise your technique on a test board.

Mask and prepare the room as you would for any painting job (p.290). Always start in an inconspicuous spot such as behind a door or in a corner, doing the most dominant wall last.

Caution: Oil-based products have strong fumes, so wear a respirator if you are sensitive (p.13) and rubber gloves. Work in a well-ventilated area, keep pets and children away, and dispose of materials safely.

Making your own glaze

Stir together 1 part each of oil-based paint and white spirit; then add 1 part scumble glaze. Mix the glaze thoroughly, stirring up from bottom of container. Test on a painted board; glaze should be thin but not runny. To thicken, add more paint; to thin, add white spirit. To increase transparency, add more scumble glaze.

Glazing liquid

Applying glaze

Glaze   Base coat

On walls, roll glaze over base coat in 60-90 cm (2-3 ft) vertical strips; then brush it out in one direction, feathering overlaps (p.292) to avoid dark edges. Have a helper follow behind, distressing the glaze before it dries.

For a linear glazing pattern, such as combing or dragging, smooth glaze over base coat in vertical strokes, then distress.

Short strokes

For random distressing techniques or for marbling (p.302), apply glaze with brush, making short, angled strokes in all directions.

Ways of distressing glaze

Simple distressing
Dab firmly at glaze with paper towel, a clean lint-free cloth or a piece of lightweight plastic. To keep the pattern random, rotate material in your hand often. Periodically expose clean surface of material or change to a fresh piece.

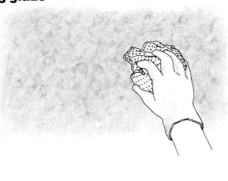

Sponging off Pat a solvent-dampened sea sponge against the surface, changing its position in your hand frequently. Hold the sponge delicately, without squeezing it. Man-made sponge gives a more defined, regular look.

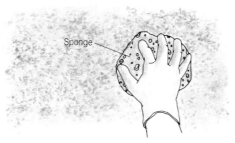

Sponge

Stippling Firmly press stippling brush (or less expensive stainer's brush) into wet glaze; for crisp pattern, avoid sliding. Frequently wipe glaze off brush with clean cloth. Keep bristles at right angle to surface.

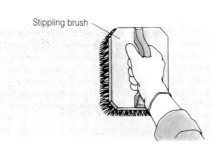

Stippling brush

Rag-rolling For pattern resembling crushed velvet, shape a clean lint-free cloth about 30 cm (1 ft) square into a loose sausage shape and roll it down the surface in vertical strips. Overlap the strips slightly.

Combing Place steel or rubber comb at 45° angle to surface; drag down to etch pattern into glaze, forming straight, wavy or zigzag lines. Don't overlap the rows; clean the comb at the end of each row. Use a comb with narrow teeth for tight spots.

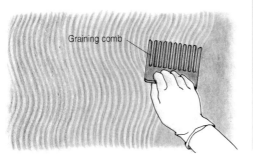

Graining comb

Spattering

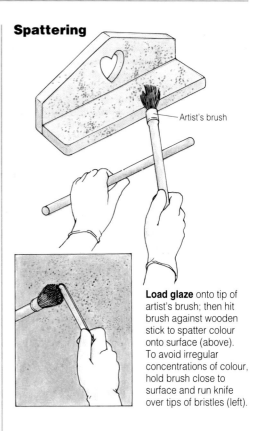

Artist's brush

Load glaze onto tip of artist's brush; then hit brush against wooden stick to spatter colour onto surface (above). To avoid irregular concentrations of colour, hold brush close to surface and run knife over tips of bristles (left).

Dragging

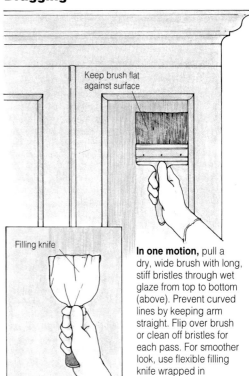

Keep brush flat against surface

Filling knife

In one motion, pull a dry, wide brush with long, stiff bristles through wet glaze from top to bottom (above). Prevent curved lines by keeping arm straight. Flip over brush or clean off bristles for each pass. For smoother look, use flexible filling knife wrapped in paper towel (left).

MARBLING

The easiest way to create the look of marble is gradually to build up a clouded effect over a base coat with one or two colours of oil-based glaze, blending them with distressing tools to create a subtle effect. Let this clouding dry, then use a feather or an artist's brush to paint on the glaze veins.

Two often-reproduced marbles are 'verde' (which is shown here and has a black base with green clouding and grey veins) and 'Carrera' (composed of a white base with light grey clouding and medium grey veins).

Before beginning to work, assemble the tools and glazes (pp.300-1) you will need. Then practise the technique (especially the veins) on a sample board. Refer to a real piece of marble or to a photograph for help in making your 'marble' realistic.

Good projects for beginners are objects that could actually be made of marble, such as mantelpieces or tabletops. With a larger area, such as a wall or a floor, divide it into 30 cm (1 ft) square sections and work on one at a time. For a realistic effect, flow the clouding and veins across the sections.

Almost any paintable surface can be marbled, as long as it is clean and smooth. Remove old paint only if it is thick or flaking. Smooth the surface with fine abrasive paper, and then apply the base coat, which can be either emulsion or oil-based paint (but first make sure that it is compatible with the existing surface and the type of glaze).

Most marbled projects are finished with several coats of clear oil or water-based varnish (p.168), to enhance the deception. All varnishes yellow with age, oil-based ones more than water-based. This can eventually dull a marbling job, so a water-based varnish is preferable. Too glossy a finish will highlight any surface irregularities. Ask your paint dealer about the best type of varnish for your marbling project.

Caution: When you are working with oil-based glazes, follow the safety measures described on page 300.

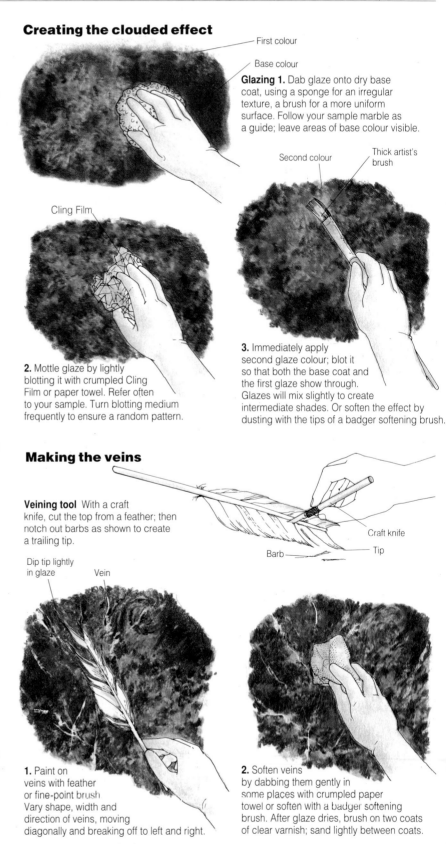

Creating the clouded effect

First colour

Base colour

Glazing 1. Dab glaze onto dry base coat, using a sponge for an irregular texture, a brush for a more uniform surface. Follow your sample marble as a guide; leave areas of base colour visible.

Cling Film

2. Mottle glaze by lightly blotting it with crumpled Cling Film or paper towel. Refer often to your sample. Turn blotting medium frequently to ensure a random pattern.

Second colour

Thick artist's brush

3. Immediately apply second glaze colour; blot it so that both the base coat and the first glaze show through. Glazes will mix slightly to create intermediate shades. Or soften the effect by dusting with the tips of a badger softening brush.

Making the veins

Veining tool With a craft knife, cut the top from a feather; then notch out barbs as shown to create a trailing tip.

Craft knife

Barb

Tip

Dip tip lightly in glaze

Vein

1. Paint on veins with feather or fine-point brush. Vary shape, width and direction of veins, moving diagonally and breaking off to left and right.

2. Soften veins by dabbing them gently in some places with crumpled paper towel or soften with a badger softening brush. After glaze dries, brush on two coats of clear varnish; sand lightly between coats.

STENCILLING

Creating the stencil

Draw design on paper, indicating colours of elements. For symmetrical design, fold paper over, draw half the design and cut. You can also draw the design directly on acetate with lead or wax pencil.

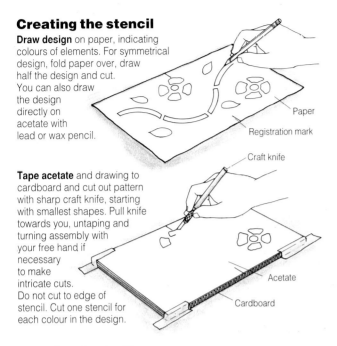

Paper

Registration mark

Craft knife

Tape acetate and drawing to cardboard and cut out pattern with sharp craft knife, starting with smallest shapes. Pull knife towards you, untaping and turning assembly with your free hand if necessary to make intricate cuts. Do not cut to edge of stencil. Cut one stencil for each colour in the design.

Acetate

Cardboard

Marking the wall

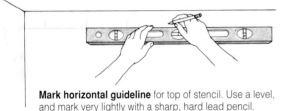

Mark horizontal guideline for top of stencil. Use a level, and mark very lightly with a sharp, hard lead pencil.

Walls, ceilings, floors, furniture and other objects can be made brighter or given a more traditional look by applying a stencilled pattern. It can be a continuous border, a design that completely covers a surface or simply an accent for a focal point. You can purchase stencils ready-made, copy a design from a pattern book (available at paint and art supply stores) or create your own design. Enlarge or reduce the pattern as necessary (p.338).

Stencilling requires few materials. If you're making your own stencil, you'll need acetate or stencil paper. Acetate is easier to cut, and because it's transparent, it's easier to align with registration marks. Protect the work surface with heavy cardboard, and cut out the stencil with a sharp craft knife.

When painting, tape stencils to the surface with masking tape. Paint the stencil with either special stencil paint or artist's acrylics. Thin paint can bleed behind the stencil and smudge, so if necessary, thin the paint only to a creamy consistency with white spirit (for oil-based paint) or water (for emulsion). Apply the paint with a stippling brush, but don't overload it; it's easy to add more. For a more mottled look, use a sponge. You can stencil on most surfaces, but for best results, stencil over flat emulsion or oil-based paint.

Follow the steps at left to measure and make registration marks along a horizontal wall border, fine-tuning the spacing as necessary to compensate for uneven walls or obstacles. Start at the centre and work outwards, completing one colour at a time. Let the paint dry before positioning the stencil sheet for the second colour. If you have a complicated design, you can also avoid smudging by 'leapfrogging' round the room, doing every other stencil repeat. Allow it to dry, then go round the room again to fill in the missing spaces.

Registration mark

Length of stencil

Divide each wall by length of stencil to find number of pattern repeats. Adjust spaces between repeats to avoid awkward pattern breaks at corners and obstacles. Lightly pencil registration marks along horizontal guideline, working out from centre of each wall to both corners.

Painting the stencil

First-colour stencil

Second-colour stencil

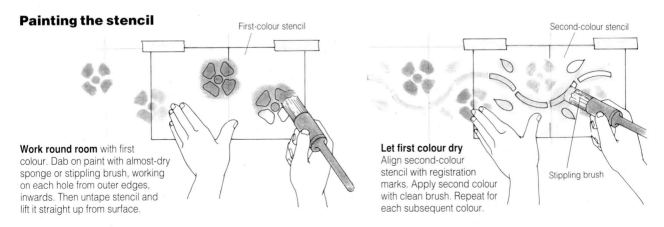

Work round room with first colour. Dab on paint with almost-dry sponge or stippling brush, working on each hole from outer edges, inwards. Then untape stencil and lift it straight up from surface.

Let first colour dry
Align second-colour stencil with registration marks. Apply second colour with clean brush. Repeat for each subsequent colour.

Stippling brush

Paint and Wall Coverings 303

PREPARING THE EXTERIOR

If new exterior decoration is to look good and resist weather, careful preparation is essential. As a general rule, start at the top and work down.

Don't undertake any work at roof level unless you are happy at heights. Before starting, ensure your ladder is in good condition, and anchor it so that it can't move in any direction. A ladder stand-off is useful, to hold the ladder clear of guttering and provide a good grip on the wall. To move on the roof, obtain a roof ladder from your local hire shop. It hooks over the ridge, giving you safe access.

Roof repairs Ridge tiles can work loose through the action of frost. Set loose ones in new mortar. Check tiles or slates; loose ones can be set in place with expanding foam filler or with an epoxy-based repair paste.

Destroy moss growing on roofs with a proprietary moss killer available from garden centres. Allow the moss to blacken and then remove with a stiff brush. Wear a face mask.

Clean out gutters and check all the downpipes for blockages. Always pull a blockage upwards; never push it down. Get a Sanisnake tool from a hire shop to clear difficult blockages.

Working on walls Wash down rendered walls with warm water and detergent, starting at the top and working down, so that you don't dirty what has already been cleaned.

Kill off moulds with a proprietary fungicide, following the instructions.

Wash brickwork with plain water – cleaning powders will stain. Check that pointing is sound. If it is very soft and crumbly, rake out about 1.3 cm (½ in) and replace it with new mortar.

Make the new mortar with the minimum of water because a dry mix won't stain brickwork (p.224). Remove any mortar stains on brickwork with Disclean – which is acidic, so be sure to protect your eyes and hands.

Fill cracks round windows and doors with an exterior-grade sealant to prevent rain getting in and rotting the frames. Check all exterior paintwork for damage. Paint in good condition can be washed with a sugar soap solution. Paint in poor condition should be stripped.

Preparing to paint

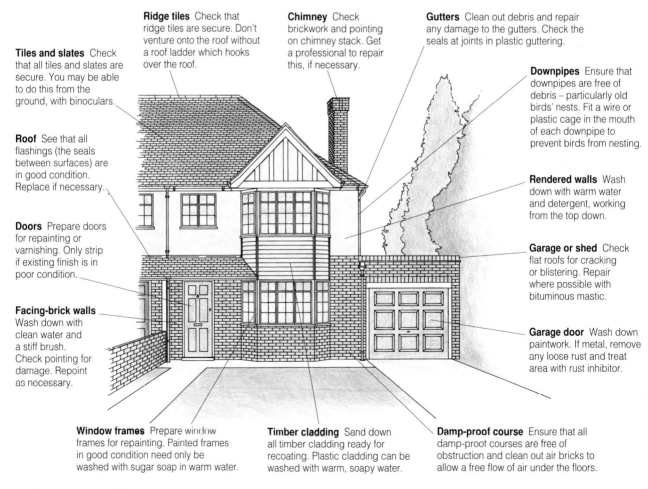

Ridge tiles Check that ridge tiles are secure. Don't venture onto the roof without a roof ladder which hooks over the roof.

Chimney Check brickwork and pointing on chimney stack. Get a professional to repair this, if necessary.

Gutters Clean out debris and repair any damage to the gutters. Check the seals at joints in plastic guttering.

Tiles and slates Check that all tiles and slates are secure. You may be able to do this from the ground, with binoculars.

Roof See that all flashings (the seals between surfaces) are in good condition. Replace if necessary.

Doors Prepare doors for repainting or varnishing. Only strip if existing finish is in poor condition.

Facing-brick walls Wash down with clean water and a stiff brush. Check pointing for damage. Repoint as necessary.

Downpipes Ensure that downpipes are free of debris – particularly old birds' nests. Fit a wire or plastic cage in the mouth of each downpipe to prevent birds from nesting.

Rendered walls Wash down with warm water and detergent, working from the top down.

Garage or shed Check flat roofs for cracking or blistering. Repair where possible with bituminous mastic.

Garage door Wash down paintwork. If metal, remove any loose rust and treat area with rust inhibitor.

Window frames Prepare window frames for repainting. Painted frames in good condition need only be washed with sugar soap in warm water.

Timber cladding Sand down all timber cladding ready for recoating. Plastic cladding can be washed with warm, soapy water.

Damp-proof course Ensure that all damp-proof courses are free of obstruction and clean out air bricks to allow a free flow of air under the floors.

Cleaning and preparing exterior surfaces

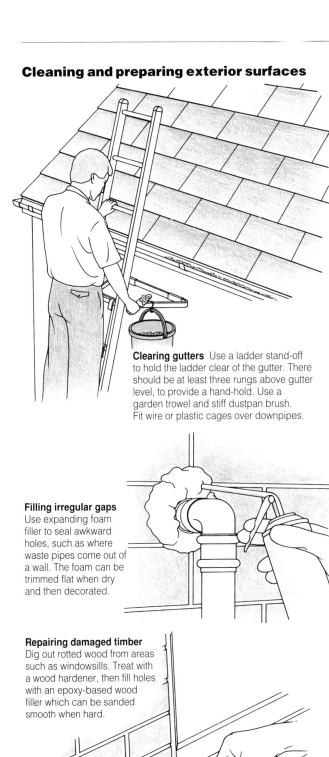

Clearing gutters Use a ladder stand-off to hold the ladder clear of the gutter. There should be at least three rungs above gutter level, to provide a hand-hold. Use a garden trowel and stiff dustpan brush. Fit wire or plastic cages over downpipes.

Repairs to flashings If flashings have deteriorated or have cracked, clean off debris, treat with flashing primer, then coat with self-adhesive flashing tape, pressing down well with an old wallpaper seam roller.

Filling irregular gaps
Use expanding foam filler to seal awkward holes, such as where waste pipes come out of a wall. The foam can be trimmed flat when dry and then decorated.

Sealing gaps Clean out old mortar and putty from gaps round doors and window frames. Fill with outdoor sealant, which will remain flexible to accommodate expansion and contraction. It will surface-harden to allow painting.

Repairing damaged timber
Dig out rotted wood from areas such as windowsills. Treat with a wood hardener, then fill holes with an epoxy-based wood filler which can be sanded smooth when hard.

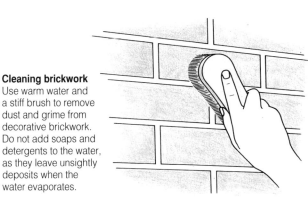

Cleaning brickwork
Use warm water and a stiff brush to remove dust and grime from decorative brickwork. Do not add soaps and detergents to the water, as they leave unsightly deposits when the water evaporates.

For all exterior painting work, choose the best quality primers, undercoats and topcoats that you can afford and buy them from the same maker, to ensure that all are compatible. Finish all the preparation of all surfaces before starting to do any painting – you don't want dust, dirt and flakes of old paint to spoil a newly decorated surface.

Treat all bare wood and metal with a suitable primer, followed by an undercoat. Undercoat is also necessary when you want to cover a strong base colour, as a topcoat has little or no hiding power. Paintwork that is in good condition, and which is to be decorated with the same colour, doesn't need an undercoat.

As a rule, once all preparatory work is complete (pp.304-5) start at the top and work downwards.

Fascias and soffits Fascia boards are usually the same colour as gutters and downpipes, so it may make sense to paint the gutters straight after the fascias. Soffits usually match the walls or windows of a house. Apply knotting to cover any defects and then a coat of undercoat. If there is to be a change of colour, you may need a second coat.

Sand lightly to remove any rough areas and then apply a coat of gloss with a wide brush, finishing with the grain. Allow it to dry completely and apply a second coat of gloss.

Gutters and downpipes If you have plastic guttering, unclip it to make painting easier. Metal guttering may have to stay in place and it may be easier to paint it before starting the fascia. Clean out all debris before starting. Paint inside the guttering with leftovers of good quality paint – it doesn't matter if the colours don't match, because they won't be seen. Then paint the outside of the gutters and the downpipes.

Pipes treated with bituminous paint are best recoated with similar paint. If you wish to switch to oil-based paint, first prime the old paint with an aluminium primer-sealer so that the bitumen doesn't bleed through.

It isn't necessary to paint plastic gutters and downpipes, but if you want them to match a particular colour scheme, give them two coats of exterior grade gloss.

New plastic gutters and downpipes are quite difficult to paint, because the paint does not adhere to the surface very well. Manufacturers advise that you allow them to weather for at least a year before attempting to paint them.

Doors Paint the sections of exterior doors in the same order as you would for interior doors (p.293). Remove all doorknobs, handles, knockers and other door furniture before you start working on the surface.

If you are going to replace paint with varnish, strip off the paint with a proprietary brand of paint stripper and try to follow the manufacturer's instructions closely.

Fill any scratches and holes in the wood with an exterior grade wood stopping that matches the natural colour of the door. When it is dry, smooth it with fine abrasive paper and then wipe it throughly with a damp cloth before applying the finish.

You may want to stain the wood before varnishing it (pp.160-1, 166-9). Choose a varnish specially formulated for outdoor use which contains both a fungicide to prevent mould growth and a UV filter to reduce bleaching by the sun. It is possible to buy a varnish that is microporous – it allows the wood to

Exterior trim

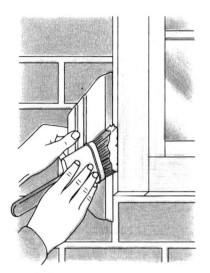

Hold trim guard over areas adjacent to trim to protect them from paint. This is important when painting beside bricks. Alternatively, cover these areas with masking tape.

Downpipes

Protect brickwork from splashes of paint by holding a piece of stiff board or cardboard behind downpipes and any other pipes when you are painting them.

Concrete

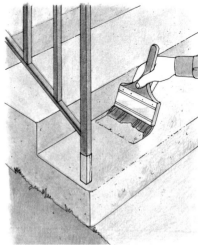

Apply masonry paint with a 10-15 cm (4-6 in) coarse-bristle brush, first in one direction, then the other. Force paint into angles and surface irregularities. Mask base of railings with tape.

'breathe'– which cuts down on the amount of blistering and flaking which will occur in time.

Windows and windowsills Do all preparation of surfaces before starting to paint, and then paint window frames before windowsills. It is best to paint window frames early in the day, so that they are dry by nightfall and can be closed without sticking.

For sash windows, reverse the sashes and paint exposed horizontal surfaces before painting the verticals. Then restore the sashes to their normal position and paint remaining surfaces, this time, verticals first.

Brighten tiled windowsills with red tile paint. No undercoat is necessary, but for best results apply two coats with a 50 mm (2 in) brush. Red tile doorstep paint is also available for thresholds and unglazed tiles.

The open grain of oak sills can present a problem. Seal the wood with an epoxy-based wood filler and sand it smooth before painting. Alternatively, decorate with a microporous paint.

Timber cladding Paint or varnish timber cladding – stain preservative finishes are available which enhance the appearance of the timber and do not crack or peel with age as a number of varnishes are liable to do. This is another area where microporous paint is useful.

Work from the top downwards and paint sections about 1 m (1 yd) long at a time. Use a brush that is just a bit narrower than the width of one board. Paint the edge of the timber first, and then the face, finishing with strokes that follow the grain.

Painting walls For treating walls that have been rendered, there are special masonry paints, some of which contain additives, such as sand, that are designed to fill hairline cracks and provide a subtle texture.

Before painting walls, protect areas such as porch roofs, the tiling above bay windows and on tiled sills, and also the adjacent flower borders with cotton dustsheets or newspaper fixed in place with masking tape.

Rendering which has been cleaned but still feels chalky should be sealed with a stabilising solution before you apply paint. This will bind any loose material to the wall, providing the new paint with a sound surface.

Do not try to paint the whole width of a wall at once. Instead, divide the wall into sections and complete a section at a time. If you cannot complete a whole section in one work session, stop at a corner or a door, so that joins will be less noticeable.

Apply the paint to walls with a wide, exterior brush or use a medium-bristle dustpan brush, which you may find easier to manipulate.

Alternatively, use a nylon pile paint roller. Where a surface is very textured, choose a shaggy, exterior grade nylon roller which will get into crevices and which is tough enough to withstand the abrasive nature of the surface.

When planning quantities of paint, remember that a highly textured surface, such as pebbledash, will take almost twice as much paint as a smooth, rendered surface.

It is not advisable to paint external brickwork. It seldom looks good and, once applied, the paint cannot be removed as it soaks into the pores of the brick. Poor quality brick is best rendered or given a Tyrolean finish – a spattered mortar effect – using a special machine which can be hired.

Flat roofs Areas of flat roof, such as those over extensions and porches, are best treated with a bitumen rubber roofing compound. Even if felted roofing appears to be in reasonably good condition, apply a coat of compound to extend its life. Make sure the roof is free of dust and debris before applying the compound with a wide, cheap, disposable brush. (Once used, a brush is impossible to clean sufficiently well to use again.)

As black attracts heat, you can keep the room below much cooler by giving the compound a coat of special silver paint, once it has dried. There is then no need to use stone chippings which are usually used to dissipate heat.

Storing leftover paint Decant small amounts of paint into tins of an appropriate size, to prevent the paint from drying out. Label them clearly, showing both type and colour.

Siding

Begin by coating bottom edge of each course of boards with a brush. Clear up drips immediately with your brush. Do several courses at a time.

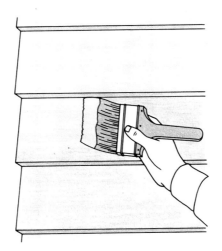

Next, paint along length of each course with short strokes of wide brush. Force paint into any cracks. To avoid lap marks, do the entire course before starting next one.

WALL COVERINGS

Because of the wide variety of patterns and styles available, choosing a wall covering can be difficult. Before selecting a covering for a particular room, consider its dominant architectural style and its furniture and furnishings; the covering should be compatible with its surroundings.

The covering's colour, pattern, texture and overall design influence a room's look. 'Advancing' warm and dark colours make surfaces appear closer or larger, whereas 'receding' cool colours make surfaces seem farther away or smaller.

Vertical stripes or patterns with an upward movement add height. Borders and friezes can be used effectively near ceilings, as dadoes and as frames round architectural elements to enhance or alter a room's appearance.

Generally, choose patterns in proportion to the room size, and if you're mixing coverings, keep the colours alike but vary the pattern sizes. Consider the whole picture, especially if rooms lead into one another. And remember that many coverings have companion fabrics and borders.

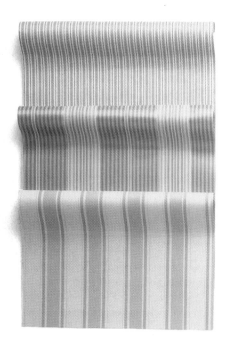

Stripes (left) are easy to match. But if the walls are uneven or out of true, the straight lines will show up these defects.

Random patterns (right) don't need to match unless one side of the sheet is shaded or darker than the other. Wall defects will not be as noticeable as with striped coverings. Good for beginners.

Small patterns (below, left) are best used in small areas, such as in a kitchen where cupboards leave little uncovered wall space, but they can also be used in large rooms with matching upholstery. When hanging sheets, some patterns will match straight across; others are drop patterns – the sheets must be staggered to align the patterns.

Large patterns (below, centre and right) are best suited to big rooms. Light colours are less likely to overwhelm the room. You may want to use a large pattern on one wall and a smaller related pattern on the other walls.

High-relief and blown vinyls (also known as Anaglyptas) are embossed. High-relief vinyls (top three) are very noticeably patterned; apply paint after hanging the covering. Blown vinyl (bottom) is raised only slightly to add texture.

Natural-look coverings include linen, hessian and grass-cloth materials. Although the textures don't need matching, the colour may vary from roll to roll. Individual rolls may also 'shade'. Before hanging these coverings, arrange the sheets to match the colour.

Exotic coverings include, from top to bottom, teapaper; ceramic chips and imitation stone (whose bumpy surfaces make it more difficult to cut clean seams) and cork, which should be hung over a lining paper. Other exotic coverings including silk and wood chips.

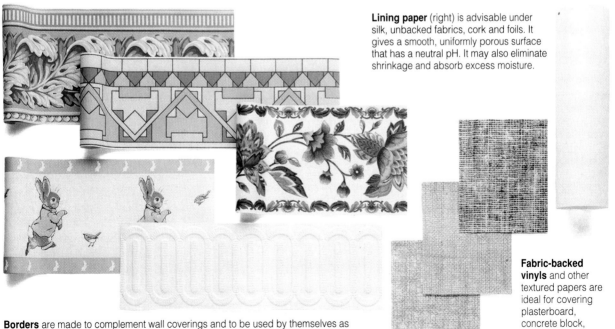

Lining paper (right) is advisable under silk, unbacked fabrics, cork and foils. It gives a smooth, uniformly porous surface that has a neutral pH. It may also eliminate shrinkage and absorb excess moisture.

Fabric-backed vinyls and other textured papers are ideal for covering plasterboard, concrete block, cracked plaster and other problem walls.

Borders are made to complement wall coverings and to be used by themselves as trim on painted walls. They may have floral designs, patterns that appeal to young children or the borders may be embossed to imitate architectural details.

CHOOSING WALL COVERINGS

Three kinds of pattern

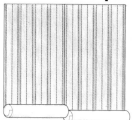 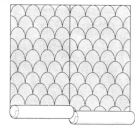 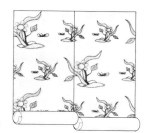

Random match Easy to hang; design either may not align or may align anywhere.

Straight-across match Easy to hang; design flows across strips when top edges align.

Drop match Harder to hang; design runs diagonally; every other strip may align at ceiling.

Creating illusions with wall covering

 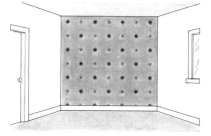

Create a cosy feeling in a high-ceilinged room by adding a wide border at the top and bottom of the walls.

Foreshorten a long, narrow room by covering one short wall; choose a pattern that is in the same scale as the room's proportions.

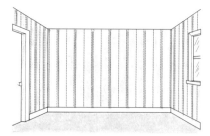 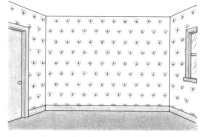

Add height to a room by choosing a vertical pattern, but avoid straight-lined designs if walls are badly damaged or out of true.

Expand a confined space, or hide wall irregularities, by covering the walls with a medium-size overall pattern.

Estimating quantity

Find the area of walls by measuring the perimeter of the room (in metres) and then multiplying by the room's height.To find the number of rolls you will need, divide the area of the walls by the area of each roll (usually 5 m²); then add one roll to allow for waste. Patterns with large repeats may require extra rolls.

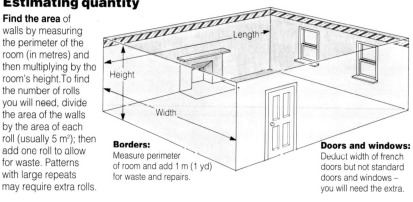

Borders: Measure perimeter of room and add 1 m (1 yd) for waste and repairs.

Doors and windows: Deduct width of french doors but not standard doors and windows – you will need the extra.

Wall coverings are categorised by the base material or ground onto which the design is printed – paper, vinyl or fabric. Often this ground provides the background colour for the design. In thicker products, the ground is laminated to a backing or substrate (duplex); whereas in thinner ones the ground and the substrate may be one and the same.

Other terms you may come across refer to ease of care and removal. Spongeable or washable coverings can be sponged with mild detergent; scrubbable ones can withstand more vigorous cleaning (p.319). In some papers, both the ground and the substrate of a strippable material can be removed, but with others only the top layer peels away, leaving what can be a lining paper on the wall.

When you go to choose a wall covering, take along fabric samples and paint chips from the area you are decorating. If you plan to mix two patterns, remember that the colours must match but the scale need not; in fact, the greater the difference in scale, the better. Even a flowered border can complement a striped covering if the colours are a good match. However, you must also consider durability and ease of installation. Many coverings come prepasted; you can either cover the back with water or soak the strips in a water trough. For unpasted wall coverings, you cover the back with the appropriate adhesive.

The packaging or the sample book should indicate the area a roll will cover. A standard roll of wallpaper contains about 5 m² (10 m × 520 mm); imperial measurements are also shown. To avoid colour variations make sure all rolls have the same batch number. To minimise variations between strips on some random-match patterns, hang them with alternate strips reversed top to bottom.

Take home sample swatches of your choices, and tape them to the wall for 24 hours to see how you like them under changing lighting conditions.

Sorting out wall coverings

Type	Description	Paste	Further information
Lining paper	Plain paper designed to cover poor wall and ceiling surfaces before painting or papering. Sold in four thicknesses	Cold-water; regular; all-purpose	Sometimes supplied in rolls twice the standard length to reduce wastage. The heavier and thicker the paper, the less likely it is to tear when you hang it
Woodchip	Two layers of paper bonded together with a sprinkling of wood chippings between them. Designed to be painted with emulsion	Heavy-duty; cold-water; all-purpose; ready-mixed	Use to cover uneven walls. Some surfaces feel abrasive to the touch and are not suitable for walls likely to be rubbed against, for example, narrow hallways, stairs and children's rooms
Standard wallpaper	A single sheet of paper with a pattern printed on it. Quality of paper varies considerably with the price	Cold-water; regular; all-purpose; ready-mixed	Cheap papers are thin and tear easily – especially when damp with paste – and are more difficult to hang than more expensive papers. Papers cannot be washed, so not suitable for kitchens or bathrooms
Duplex paper	A wallpaper – often with a relief surface – backed by another layer of paper which is bonded to form one sheet	Heavy-duty; cold-water; all-purpose; ready-mixed	The paper is strong and holds the shape of a relief well. This makes it easier to hang than other relief papers
Novamura	A foamed polyethylene with relief and a feel of fabric. Available in a wide range of colours and designs	Regular; all-purpose; ready-mixed	The surface springs back into place if it is pressed gently, and can be wiped clean. One of the easiest wall coverings to hang and strip. Paste the wall, not the covering
Relief wall coverings	Heavy paper embossed with a pattern during manufacture. The surface may be patterned, coloured or plain for painting	Cold-water; all-purpose; ready-mixed	Suitable for uneven walls and ceilings. Anaglypta is the best-known of these materials, although other manufacturers produce similar coverings
High relief wall coverings	Made from material resembling hard putty with a strong paper backing. Available in designs which include plaster daub effects, brick or stone walling and wood panelling	Lincrusta glue (for Lincrusta); heavy-duty; ready-mixed; cold-water	Lincrusta is the best-known of these materials. More durable than ordinary relief wall coverings. Soak backing paper with water for about 30 minutes before pasting. Hang as one sheet – do not crease or fold. Trim with a sharp knife and straightedge, butting joins
Vinyl	A PVC layer, with a pattern or texture, is bonded to paper. Expanded vinyls have a raised surface, foamed up by heat during manufacture, and a smooth backing	Vinyl adhesive; ready-mixed (with fungicide); all-purpose (with fungicide)	Durable and washable. Suitable for kitchens, bathrooms and children's rooms. Special adhesive required if seams overlap. Expanded vinyls need less paste than other relief wallpapers
Hessian	Available as a roll of unbacked material or bonded to a stout backing paper which helps to keep the hessian from sagging. Dyed hessian is available in a limited colour range	Heavy-duty; ready-mixed; all-purpose; cold-water	Will hide a wide range of cracks in a surface. Hang paper-backed hessian like standard wallpaper. With unbacked hessian, paste the wall, not the material. Not a matching material, so every join will show, no matter how carefully you hang it
Silk wall covering	Produced by bonding silk to fine backing paper	Cold-water; regular; ready-mixed; all-purpose	Like hessian, not a matching material, so the seams will show. An expensive and delicate wall covering not practical for walls that are likely to be scuffed and knocked
Japanese grasscloth	Made of real grasses, bonded to a fine backing paper and sewn together for strength	Ready-mixed; all-purpose; heavy-duty; cold-water	Not a matching material, so joins will always be visible. Expensive, so best used only for decorative effect – making a feature of one wall, for example. Always put the paste on the wall, not the paper
Cork wall coverings	A fine veneer of cork, stuck to a plain or painted backing paper. Holes in the cork allow the painted backing to show through, creating a colour contrast	Heavy-duty; ready-mixed; all-purpose; cold-water	Cork tiles can't be painted over, but they can be covered with lining paper and wallpaper. How easy they are to remove depends on the adhesive used to fix them in place. They can be prised off the wall with a wide stripping knife
Metallic coverings	Foil bonded to a paper backing. Fine features and many colours available	Heavy-duty; ready-mixed (with fungicide); all-purpose (with fungicide)	Use only on walls with a very smooth surface – bumps and any unevenness will show up. Paste the wall, not the covering, and take care not to get paste on the decorative side
Flocks	Velvet pile bonded to backing paper. Available in a wide range of colours and designs	Heavy-duty; ready-mixed; all-purpose; cold-water	Keep splashes of paste off the flock, as much as possible – although it should not be permanently stained by marks. Hang as for standard wallpaper. One of the more expensive papers
Special effect wall coverings	Papers and vinyls in a wide variety of designs which give the impression of real materials like wood, stone or tiling	Ready-mixed; all-purpose; heavy-duty; cold-water	Use to create optical illusions and unusual visual effects. Can be overpowering if used on more than one wall in a room. More expensive than other wall coverings

Although you can often apply new wall covering over old, it's generally better to strip off the old covering and adhesive – and if you are hanging vinyl wall covering, it's essential. If the covering is not an easy-strip, buy a commercial remover product from the wall-covering supplier or a DIY centre; follow the manufacturer's instructions.

To remove built-up layers of wall covering, or covering that has been painted over, rent a steamer from your local hire shop. Learn how to operate the steamer before leaving the store, and check occasionally during use to make sure that the water tank doesn't run dry. Follow all safety instructions included with the tool, and wear goggles and gloves.

Whatever stripping method you choose, protect the room (p.290) before starting. Lay a dustsheet on the floor and tape it to the skirting board with masking tape; then cover it with newspapers to absorb water.

If your walls are hairlined and uneven, disguise the flaws by choosing a high-relief or fabric-backed vinyl covering. Even after repairing holes and dents (pp.288-9), you may need to cover irregular surfaces with lining paper. This improves both the appearance and the adhesion of a wall

Removing wall covering

Pull down, not straight out

Strippable coverings Loosen covering at corner and gently peel each strip from wall. To remove a remaining backing paper, soak remaining substrate and adhesive for 10 minutes, then scrape with a wide stripping knife.

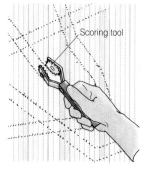

Scoring tool

Stripping with liquid remover
1. Score covering in crisscross pattern with scoring tool so that solution can penetrate to the adhesive layer. Be careful not to damage plaster or plasterboard.

2. Roll or sponge remover onto walls (or spray onto surface with a tank-type garden sprayer). Let soak into covering for amount of time specified on remover's label. When the paper bubbles up, it's ready to be stripped.

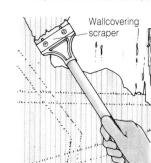

3. Soak tight spots (such as corners or narrow strips beside cabinets) by applying the remover with a plastic spray bottle.

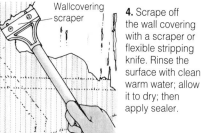

Wallcovering scraper

4. Scrape off the wall covering with a scraper or flexible stripping knife. Rinse the surface with clean warm water; allow it to dry; then apply sealer.

Using a steamer

Steamer

1. Fill unit with clean water before plugging it in. Steamer is ready to use when vapour emerges from the holes in the baseplate.

Baseplate

2. Hold steamer against (but not touching) surface for 15 sec or until area around plate is moist. Remove covering with scraper or stripping knife with one hand while steaming adjacent area with the other.

Stiff nylon brush

3. After scraping, clean the surface by scrubbing it with a stiff nylon brush. Allow the surface to dry and then apply sealer or size.

covering, and it is essential for certain delicate coverings. Leave a gap of about 2 mm (¹⁄₁₆ in) at the edges and seams of lining paper, and plan the wall-covering seams to fall elsewhere than on the paper seams.

Some surfaces should also be prepared with a primer-sealer. A sealed wall is uniform and will prevent moisture and residue from affecting the covering's adhesive. A 'universal'

primer-sealer is easy to clean up and can be tinted to match the background of the wall covering. Use it in humid areas such as bathrooms and over new wallboard, existing wall coverings that cannot be removed and surfaces that have been repaired.

You can also improve the adhesion of a wall covering by first applying liquid size to a prepared wall. In addition, size makes it easier to slide

the wall covering into place. Size is not required, however, if you use a premixed vinyl adhesive.

Wash all painted surfaces with detergent or dissolved cleaning powder. Then rinse them with clean water and let them dry.

After preparing the surfaces, paint the ceiling and all woodwork that adjoins the walls to avoid splattering paint on the new wall covering later.

Applying sealer and size

Spread sealer or size evenly over surface with paint roller or paste brush. Allow to dry for 1 hour before hanging wall covering.

After repairing painted walls, cover repairs with sealer, then wash walls.

Hanging lining paper

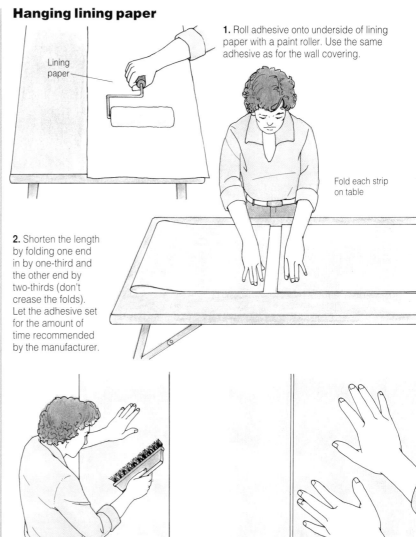

Lining paper

1. Roll adhesive onto underside of lining paper with a paint roller. Use the same adhesive as for the wall covering.

Fold each strip on table

2. Shorten the length by folding one end in by one-third and the other end by two-thirds (don't crease the folds). Let the adhesive set for the amount of time recommended by the manufacturer.

Begin at plumb line

3. Carry liner to wall and unfurl on wall as you smooth it with a 300 mm paperhanger's brush. Leave a slight space at wall edges and trim.

4. Do not butt strips at seams. Let paper dry for 36 hours, or until it does not indent when pressed with a finger.

INSTALLING WALL COVERING

Planning the layout

Plan a mismatch in an inconspicuous corner. You may start hanging at this point, or use it as an end point, beginning directly across the room and working back toward it, first from one direction, then from the other.

End point

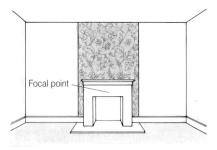

If pattern is large or room has strong focal point or wall, centre a strip (or seam) at its centre. Work outwards from both sides until you reach the end point.

Focal point

Tape marks width of strip

Level

Mark width of strip with tape on spirit level, then use it to mark strip positions round room. Rearrange guidelines to avoid awkward pattern breaks. Strips at corners should be no less than 7.5 cm (3 in) wide.

Snap chalked plumbline at starting point for each wall, allowing 2.5 cm (1 in) turn onto adjoining wall.

Before you begin, establish both where you will start and where you will finish hanging the strips, and decide how you will handle potentially awkward areas such as corners and round windows and doors (pages 316-17). To help prevent errors, pencil in guidelines to indicate the position of each strip. Because paper and prepasted strippable wall coverings will expand when wet, determine a strip's true width before marking guidelines. To do so, cut a 5 cm (2 in) strip from the roll, briefly submerge it in water, and let it expand for 10 minutes; then measure its new width.

Some wall coverings have arrows printed on the back to indicate which way the pattern should run. Decide how you want to break the pattern at the intersection of the wall and the ceiling; it's usually best not to cut through a design element, particularly if the design is strong. Remember that you'll be adding 5 cm (2 in) to both the top and the bottom of each strip for trimming at the ceiling and skirting board, so take this into your calculations. For a drop-match pattern, align the second strip to the first by eye before cutting it (facing page). Cutting a drop-match pattern from alternating rolls reduces waste; with a straight-match pattern you can cut as many strips as possible from each roll.

Check for any flaws in each roll by rerolling it in the opposite direction; this also helps to uncurl and loosen the wall covering. Plan to cut and paste two strips of covering first – then if there are no problems, continue to cut several strips at a time. Sometimes unpatterned or textured wall coverings will be over-inked and, consequently, slightly darker along one edge. To even out the colour across the wall, turn every other strip upside-down so that similarly shaded edges meet.

To hang unpasted covering, you'll need a good-sized work table and a paint roller or paste brush for applying the paste. Choose the type of paste recommended by the wall covering manufacturer, and follow the directions for mixing it; a kitchen whisk is useful for getting rid of lumps.

You can purchase a special water trough in which to wet a prepasted covering. Follow the instructions on the wall covering with regard to soaking time; oversoaking can cause some of the adhesive to wash away. An alternative to soaking a prepasted covering in a trough is to place the covering on the table and use a damp paint roller to wet the back of the strip thoroughly. Don't add any paste to a prepasted wall covering; it may be incompatible with the existing adhesive.

After hanging each strip, smooth out any air bubbles with a 12 inch paperhanger's brush (choose short bristles for vinyl, longer for paper). You'll also need a seam roller to smooth seams and edges.

As you finish hanging each strip, sponge off any excess adhesive with clean water, then dry the covering with a clean cloth. It's best to keep all surfaces clean while you're working; if you try to remove dried adhesive later, you run the risk of damaging the covering.

Cutting a drop-match covering

Cut strip from first roll (A) to length plus 5 cm (2 in) at top and bottom (for trimming), using craft knife and straightedge. Mark top with T. Weight down strip to prevent it from slipping off table.

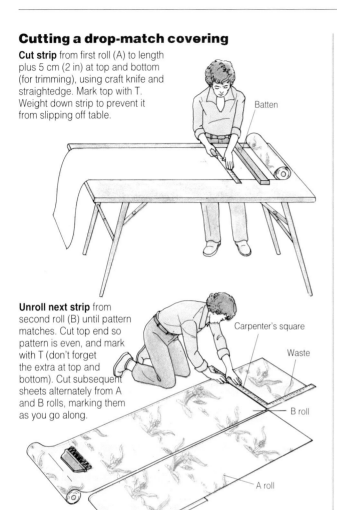

Batten

Unroll next strip from second roll (B) until pattern matches. Cut top end so pattern is even, and mark with T (don't forget the extra at top and bottom). Cut subsequent sheets alternately from A and B rolls, marking them as you go along.

Carpenter's square

Waste

B roll

A roll

Pasting the strips

Reroll prepasted covering from bottom to top (with pattern facing in), and submerge in water trough (right) for about 10 seconds. Or unfurl strip on table (see below) and wet back with saturated paint roller.

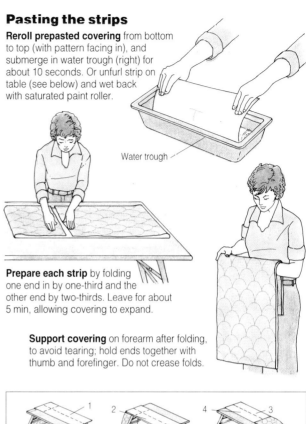

Water trough

Prepare each strip by folding one end in by one-third and the other end by two-thirds. Leave for about 5 min, allowing covering to expand.

Support covering on forearm after folding, to avoid tearing; hold ends together with thumb and forefinger. Do not crease folds.

Folded end

For unpasted covering, keep extra adhesive off work surface (where it could damage the covering) by working out from centre of strip toward surface edge, repositioning covering as shown. Make sure to paste all edges completely.

Hanging the covering

Plumb line

Align first strip against plumb line (left), smoothing the upper section first and overlapping the ceiling by 5 cm (2 in). Then release and position lower section. Remove air bubbles working from centre to edges with paperhanger's brush. To trim top and bottom, smooth paper against skirting board or coving with brush and cut with trimming knife (below).

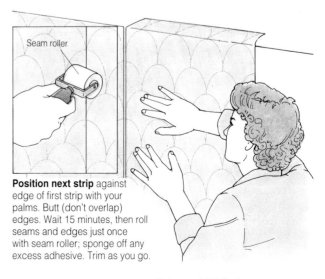

Seam roller

Position next strip against edge of first strip with your palms. Butt (don't overlap) edges. Wait 15 minutes, then roll seams and edges just once with seam roller; sponge off any excess adhesive. Trim as you go.

Paint and Wall Coverings   315

SPECIAL WALL-COVERING TECHNIQUES

Fitting around doors and windows

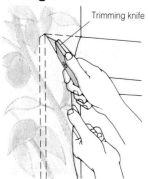

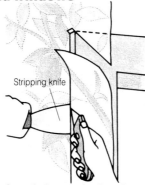

Hang strip over window or door. Cut to rough shape, leaving 5 cm (2 in) extra all round for trimming. Then make a diagonal cut from the outer corner of the frame.

Smooth the covering into place against side of frame; then trim away excess with trimming knife, guiding the blade against a stripping knife or filling knife.

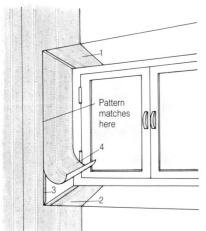

Recessed window
Let strip hang over recess. Cut horizontal line to 2.5 cm (1 in) from edge of recess; then cut and paste to upper (1) and lower (2) parts of recess. Trim at edges. Paste 2.5 cm (1 in) vertical flap around side edge (3). Cut an additional strip of covering to fit side of recess (4), making sure to match the pattern with strip on wall. Overlap this strip at upper and lower edges.

The walls of most rooms are likely to present some challenges; at the very least, you'll have to fit wall covering round one door and usually one window. Use the techniques shown here to make clean edges at windows, doors, fireplaces, built-in bookcases and cabinets. Never try to measure and precut wall covering around obstacles. It is much easier to fit when it is up, and if you make a mistake, there is usually time to reposition it before it dries.

The broad, unobstructed surface of a typical ceiling makes it relatively easy to hang wall covering there, but because you have to work overhead, the job can be tiring. If possible, enlist the aid of a helper to unfold the wet strips and hand them to you for positioning and smoothing. A sturdy scaffold (p.291) is a necessity for most ceiling work. If you plan to cover both the ceiling and the walls, do the ceiling first; otherwise you may damage the finished walls.

When you are using a patterned wall covering on both ceiling and walls, remember that you will probably be able to achieve a perfect match at only one intersection of ceiling and wall, so make this match in the most conspicuous place. Mismatches are less obvious in small, random patterns.

If you are working on stairwell walls, you may need to stand on a scaffold (p.297). While you are on the scaffold, fitting the covering to the upper part of the wall, have a helper stand on the stairs below to fit and smooth each strip to the lower part of the wall. Be especially careful not to splash water from a wall-covering trough onto a scaffold or ladder, where it could easily cause you to slip.

Where switch boxes are recessed, switch off the electricity at the mains, loosen the two holding screws and ease the switchplate forward. This will allow you to cut the paper and tuck about 3 mm (⅛ in) behind the plate. Tighten the screws and restore the power supply.

Turning a corner

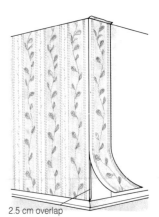

Inside corner 1. Measure from edge of last strip to corner at top, middle and bottom; cut the next strip 1.5 cm (about ½ in) wider than the widest dimension.

2. Hang cut strip, pressing 1.5 cm (about ½ in) into corner. Measure narrowest part of remainder of cut strip; mark plumb line on new wall this distance from corner.

3. Position remainder of strip with uncut edge against plumb line. Smooth covering into corner on top of 1.5 cm (about ½ in) overlap. Trim at top and bottom.

Outside corner Measure first strip as for inside corner, but add 2.5 cm (1 in) allowance for corner overlap. Plumb second wall and hang strip as for inside corner.

Covering ceilings

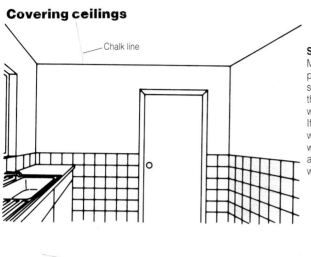

Start at window
Measure out one paper-width and snap a chalk line on the ceiling parallel with the window wall. If there are two windows in different walls, hang paper across the narrower width of the ceiling.

Hang ceiling strips
with aid of a helper, overlapping strips onto walls by 1.5 cm. Trim the covering on walls flush with ceiling. Create smooth corners by slitting covering with trimming knife and then cutting away excess (inset). Carefully smooth bubbles out of covering as you work.

Sloped ceilings Use techniques shown above, but do not cover slope and short wall with single strip. Instead, cover short wall first, overlapping by 1.5 cm (about ½ in) onto sloped ceiling; then cover sloped ceiling itself. There will always be a mismatch where sloped ceiling meets adjacent walls, but pattern can match between the strips on the sloped ceiling and where short wall meets adjacent walls.

Covering curved archways

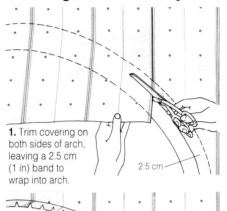

1. Trim covering on both sides of arch, leaving a 2.5 cm (1 in) band to wrap into arch.

2.5 cm

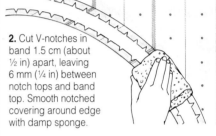

2. Cut V-notches in band 1.5 cm (about ½ in) apart, leaving 6 mm (¼ in) between notch tops and band top. Smooth notched covering around edge with damp sponge.

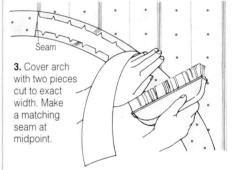

Seam

3. Cover arch with two pieces cut to exact width. Make a matching seam at midpoint.

Working round obstacles

Fixtures Cut from the seam closest to the fixture; fold covering back and then trim round fixture, using notch-shaped cuts. Press covering down and roll the seam.

Sockets and switches
Turn off power. Press an indent at corners of switch; slit the paper diagonally. Press paper to edge of switch with scissors, then trim, leaving 3 mm (⅛ in). Press in place.

WORKING WITH BORDERS

A border near the ceiling can make a room feel cosier; at dado height it makes a room feel higher. Borders can also add interest to a plain room (particularly a child's room), fill a narrow space between cupboard tops and the ceiling, or frame windows and doors. Before buying, it is best to take home samples so that you can check them with your decor and lighting.

Prepare painted walls by smoothing with fine sandpaper the area that is to be covered. Then wash away the dust. Use border adhesive to fix the border in place, unless it is self-adhesive. Apply a border over new wall covering only after the latter has dried for at least 48 hours. However, if you allow for the border while planning the wall-covering layout, you can then cut each wall-covering strip to allow the border to be inset above or within it. This method yields smoother seams, but it also takes more time and skill.

Borders are usually sold in 5 m rolls. Cut pieces the length of each wall, plus 1.5 cm (about ½ in) to wrap into the corners. To avoid awkward positioning of the design at corners or obstacles, calculate the positioning of the border before you hang it.

If the border will frame a window or a door, avoid the problem of having a one-way pattern going sideways or upside-down by selecting a random pattern. When framing with a border, mitre the corner seams, as shown. Use only an adhesive recommended by the border manufacturer.

Hanging a border

At ceiling and floor, mark width of border around room, using pair of compasses. If ceiling line or skirting board is irregular, use a level (right); trim excess from top or bottom.

For dado height, mark guideline round room 75 cm (about 30 in) from floor, using level or straightedge to keep line even. Install border so that lower edge falls on line.

Guideline

Bottom of border

75 cm

Wet or paste border, depending on type (p.315); then fold accordion-style for several minutes. Fold loosely; do not crease the folds.

Paperhanger's brush

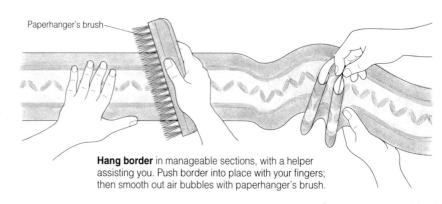

Hang border in manageable sections, with a helper assisting you. Push border into place with your fingers; then smooth out air bubbles with paperhanger's brush.

Making tight seams

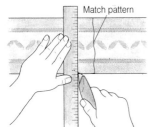

Match pattern

Butting seams 1. Overlap ends; cut through both layers with a trimming knife and a straightedge.

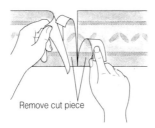

Remove cut piece

2. Remove cut pieces of both layers. Smooth ends in place with sponge; wait 15 minutes; then roll seam smooth.

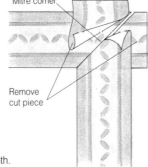

Mitre corner

Remove cut piece

Seam roller

Mitre-cut corners by overlapping pieces, then cutting through both layers at 45° angle (left). Remove cut pieces of both layers, and roll seam smooth (below).

CARING FOR WALL COVERINGS

Clean wall coverings twice a year and follow the manufacturer's directions.

Wash scrubbable coverings with a brush and mild detergent. Washable coverings can be lightly rubbed with a solution of water and mild detergent applied with a damp cloth or a nearly dry sponge. You can vacuum some cloth and flocked wall coverings with a brush attachment, but delicate ones, such as silk or hessian (p.311), are best cleaned by a professional. Commercial cleaning solutions are also available for various types of wall covering.

Whichever product or technique you choose, first test-clean a small patch in an inconspicuous area to ensure the cleaner won't stain or damage the wall covering.

Many stains on nonwashable coverings can be removed with either an artist's eraser or the centre of a slice of bread, rolled into a ball of dough. Stroke the eraser or dough downwards against the wall covering, overlapping strokes until the stain lifts off. As the cleaning agent picks up dirt, turn it to expose a fresh surface.

To remove grease or wax, cover the stain with blotting paper or paper towels, and iron over it on low heat for several seconds. Repeat, using clean paper each time, until the spot is gone. If this doesn't work, wipe the stain with a clean cloth dampened with white spirit. If, after ironing, the colour from wax crayons remains, rub it off gently with moistened baking soda on a damp cloth.

Stains that can't be removed any other way may be patched (below). Whenever you redecorate, save extra wall covering for this purpose; but remember that as ageing causes fading, a patch is bound to differ slightly in colour to the installed wall covering. Use ordinary premixed wallpaper paste or seam adhesive for patching.

Loose or torn seams and edges

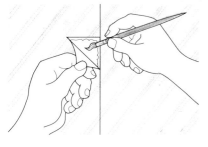

1. Brush adhesive onto wall surface and underside of covering. Press covering into place and hold for several minutes.

2. Smooth flat, and remove any excess adhesive with a slightly dampened sponge. Roll the join after 15 minutes to make sure it is firmly fixed.

Fixing bubbles

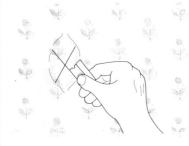

Slit bubble in X-pattern with razor blade, fold back edges and tweezer or brush out any grit. Insert adhesive as shown at left; then smooth with sponge.

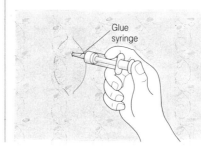

Glue syringe

For glue syringe (often available in a kit), first make small slit with razor blade. Press out air; inject adhesive. Smooth area with seam roller or sponge.

Patching a hole or stain

Remove loose paper and cut a matching patch, 7.5 cm (3 in) larger than damaged area. With a stain, apply a stain block first.

Tear the patching paper into an irregular shape so that the edge is chamfered or 'feathered' all round.

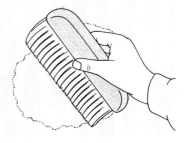

Apply paste to the patch and smooth it down over the damaged area, taking care to match the pattern exactly.

Paint and Wall Coverings   319

FLOORING

More resilient than stone or tile, wood flooring has a natural, warm appearance that enhances almost any home. It is sold in blocks, strips and planks (either solid or laminated).

It is often sold unfinished, which requires sanding and finishing, but it is also available prefinished. The final look of the floor depends on which wood you choose: the type of flooring (planks, strips or blocks), the species and grade of the wood and the finish. Because fire regulations require some internal finishes to be incombustible, speak to a qualified flooring specialist before making your selection. Be sure to describe the intended use of the flooring as well as the kind of visual finish that you want.

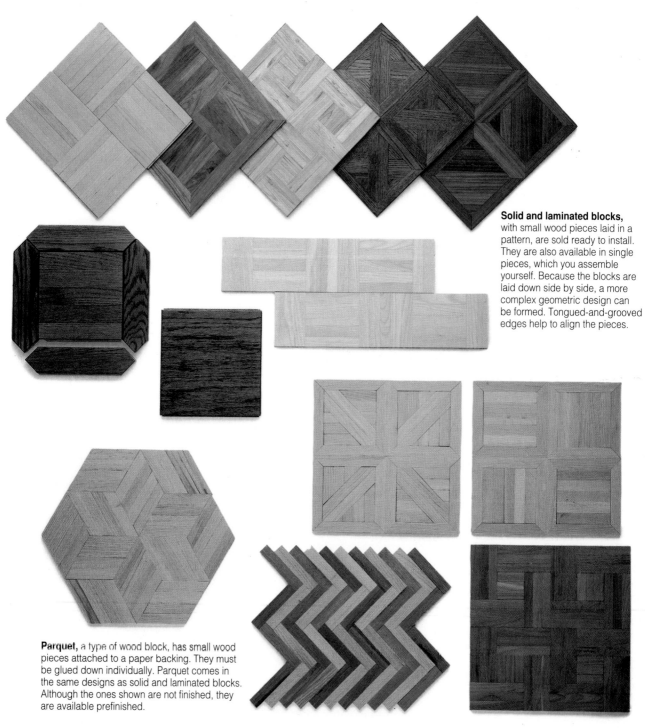

Solid and laminated blocks, with small wood pieces laid in a pattern, are sold ready to install. They are also available in single pieces, which you assemble yourself. Because the blocks are laid down side by side, a more complex geometric design can be formed. Tongued-and-grooved edges help to align the pieces.

Parquet, a type of wood block, has small wood pieces attached to a paper backing. They must be glued down individually. Parquet comes in the same designs as solid and laminated blocks. Although the ones shown are not finished, they are available prefinished.

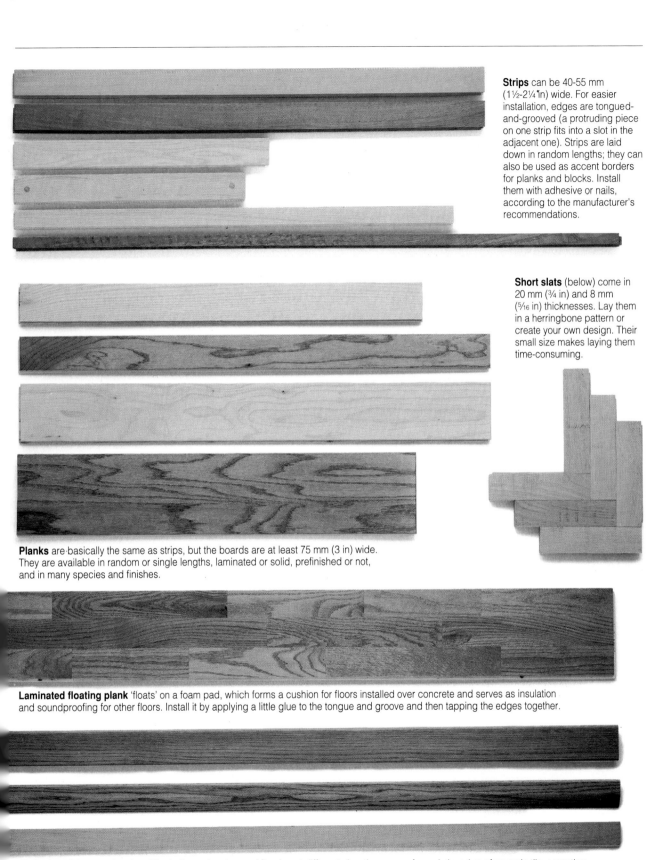

Strips can be 40-55 mm (1½-2¼ in) wide. For easier installation, edges are tongued-and-grooved (a protruding piece on one strip fits into a slot in the adjacent one). Strips are laid down in random lengths; they can also be used as accent borders for planks and blocks. Install them with adhesive or nails, according to the manufacturer's recommendations.

Short slats (below) come in 20 mm (¾ in) and 8 mm (⁵⁄₁₆ in) thicknesses. Lay them in a herringbone pattern or create your own design. Their small size makes laying them time-consuming.

Planks are basically the same as strips, but the boards are at least 75 mm (3 in) wide. They are available in random or single lengths, laminated or solid, prefinished or not, and in many species and finishes.

Laminated floating plank 'floats' on a foam pad, which forms a cushion for floors installed over concrete and serves as insulation and soundproofing for other floors. Install it by applying a little glue to the tongue and groove and then tapping the edges together.

Reducing strips create a transition between two types of flooring at different elevations: one of wood; the other of ceramic tile, carpeting, vinyl or another wood. These strips are useful where two rooms, such as a dining room and a living room, flow into each other.

RESILIENT FLOORING

Because it is affordable and easy to install and maintain, resilient flooring is a good choice for bathrooms and kitchens. Resilient flooring is usually made of vinyl (the actual vinyl content varies from product to product). It is available in 225 and 300 mm square tiles and in rolled sheets that are up to 2.4 m wide. Flooring tiles are either solid vinyl or a vinyl composition; the latter resists stains better. Sheet flooring has a base layer topped with a vinyl resin or, for added scuff resistance, a vinyl resin-urethane or vinyl resin-melamine finish; it may be cushioned with a high-density foam.

Designs with texture and colour variations are better at concealing seams, scratches, substrate irregularities and dirt.

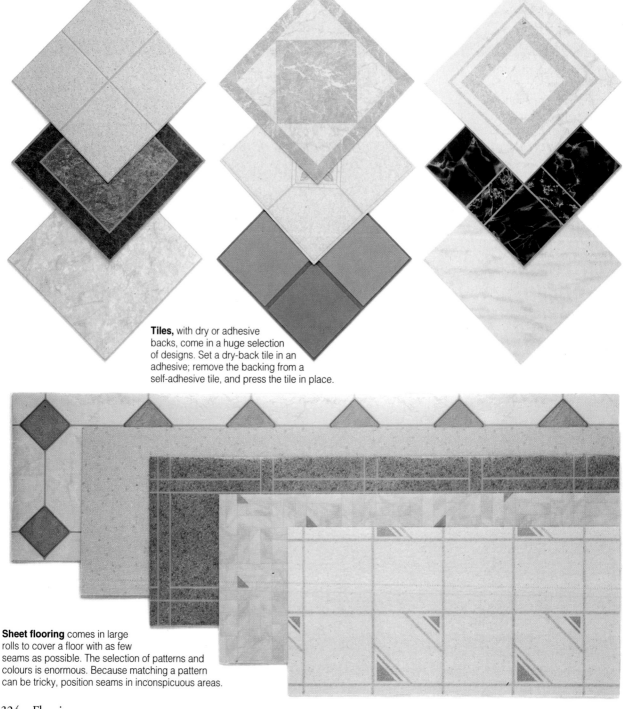

Tiles, with dry or adhesive backs, come in a huge selection of designs. Set a dry-back tile in an adhesive; remove the backing from a self-adhesive tile, and press the tile in place.

Sheet flooring comes in large rolls to cover a floor with as few seams as possible. The selection of patterns and colours is enormous. Because matching a pattern can be tricky, position seams in inconspicuous areas.

Before laying wood or resilient flooring or ceramic tile, make sure the surface beneath is flat, smooth, stable and structurally sound. If it is not, the new flooring may crack or buckle in time.

The existing floor need not be made absolutely horizontal to prepare it for a new covering. Many floors in older houses tilt or sag because of settling, and if the condition is not severe, new flooring can usually be installed over the old with satisfactory results. But be alert to sagging caused by structural damage. Have an architect, surveyor or engineer examine subflooring, joists and other framing that appears to be weak or decayed.

To prepare an existing subfloor or a finished wood floor, vacuum and clean it thoroughly and reseat any protruding fasteners. Then walk over the entire floor, bouncing on it as you go. Squeaks signal loose flooring and springiness indicates weak support underneath.

Also check the floor for bumps and hollows. Uneven wood flooring can be sanded (pp.332-3), but often the best way to obtain a flat, smooth surface is to cover it with liquid floor-levelling compound, a latex filler available at DIY and flooring centres. Choose a compound that is compatible with the subfloor and the new flooring adhesive. Mix the compound according to the manufacturer's instructions, and follow any safety precautions.

Both resilient flooring and ceramic tile can be covered directly with new flooring, but apply a floor-levelling compound first if the surface is uneven. Before applying compound or any new flooring to a concrete slab, perform a test (right) to check for excess moisture seeping through the concrete.

Caution: Never sand or remove existing resilient flooring unless you are absolutely certain that it does not contain asbestos. If it does, the dust created would be hazardous. Before removing even loose resilient flooring, call your local environmental health office for advice on safe handling techniques and regulations.

Checking for flatness

Use straightedge board or long level to find bumps and hollows more than 3 mm (⅛ in) high; sand or fill. If possible, level raised flooring by refixing or removing it.

Stiffening a springy floor

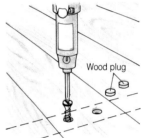

Eliminate squeaks by driving glue-coated shims between joists and flooring (far left). Do not use wedges; they will lift flooring. If repairs cannot be made from underneath, fasten loose flooring to joists with screws from above (left); fill holes with wood plugs.

Close a long gap between flooring and warped joist by nailing a 50 × 100 mm (2 × 4 in) batten along upper edge of joist (right). Brace springy joists by fitting rows of wood or metal cross-strutting strips at 2-2.5 m intervals (far right).

Applying floor-levelling compound

Spread levelling compound with trowel or wooden float. For concrete slab, first do a moisture test (inset). Clean and sand a small area and cover it with multipurpose vinyl adhesive. Fit a patch of resilient sheet flooring, hold it in place with masking tape. Remove after 72 hours; if adhesive is still wet, moisture is seeping through slab.

An underlay provides a smooth, flat surface for all types of new flooring. It gives extra support for heavy materials such as ceramic tile, provides a good nailing surface for a solid wood floor and can also provide moisture resistance.

Choose an underlay that is appropriate to the type of flooring you wish to install; be sure that it is thick enough to cover any uneven areas and imperfections in the subfloor.

Before installing new flooring, consider trying to reduce moisture and increase the comfort of the inhabitants. For example, if the floor is over a suspended floor void, lay 1200 gauge polyethylene film over joists to act as a vapour barrier. If the floor is above a living space, add a layer of insulation to reduce the amount of noise.

Existing floors Some types of flooring can be installed directly over existing flooring; however, you should always remove any carpeting and make sure that the floor is clean, dry and grease-free. (Consult a flooring contractor or a building professional to determine the specific requirements of the underlay you have chosen.)

Underlay panels can be installed directly over flooring that is dry, flat and securely attached to the subfloor. Adding an underlay and the new flooring will raise the overall level of the floor. If the difference is pronounced, you will need to install threshold reducing strips and cut doors and frames as necessary (p.329).

Caution: Resilient flooring can create hazardous dust and waste when it is removed. To be safe, contact your local authority environmental health office for advice on finding a reliable asbestos removal contractor.

Removing skirting

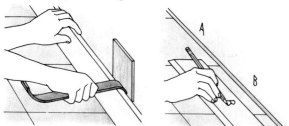

Prise skirting gently from wall with a pry bar or stiff-bladed putty knife; work gradually to minimise chipping or splintering. Protect wall with scrap wood (left). Label pieces and wall areas with matching letters to simplify reinstallation (right). If skirting is old and damaged, or if splintering and chipping are unavoidable, consider replacing it.

Installing plywood underlay

Place panels so surface grain is 90° to joists. Stagger end joints. Leave 3 mm (⅛ in) between panels and 12 mm (½ in) between panels and walls. Nail panels through joists (located 40 cm apart). Fasten every 15 cm (6 in) at the joists at panel edges and every 25 cm (10 in) at inner joists.

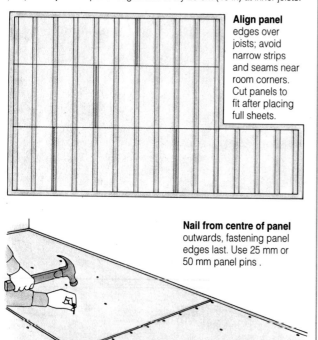

Align panel edges over joists; avoid narrow strips and seams near room corners. Cut panels to fit after placing full sheets.

Nail from centre of panel outwards, fastening panel edges last. Use 25 mm or 50 mm panel pins .

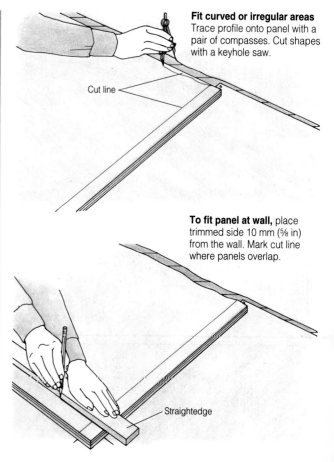

Fit curved or irregular areas Trace profile onto panel with a pair of compasses. Cut shapes with a keyhole saw.

Cut line

To fit panel at wall, place trimmed side 10 mm (⅝ in) from the wall. Mark cut line where panels overlap.

Straightedge

To prepare a floor for ceramic tile or wood parquet, use two layers of 6 mm exterior-grade plywood; for other wood flooring and for resilient flooring, use one layer of 6 mm hardboard as underlay.

When installing plywood underlay, always leave a small gap between the panels and between the walls and the underlay, to allow the panels to expand or move, and leave the gaps unfilled.

Concrete slab Parquet, laminated strip and plank flooring, ceramic tile and all types of resilient flooring can be glued with adhesive or mastic directly to dry, sealed concrete (p.325). Never glue down planks or strips of solid wood as they need to be able to move as the wood expands and contracts.

If the concrete slab is below ground level, you will need to provide a moisture barrier, as shown on the right.

When laying solid wood flooring, embed short lengths of 50 × 100 mm (2 × 4 in) timber, called battens, in mastic as shown at right. Strip or plank flooring up to 100 mm (4 in) wide can be attached to the battens. If you want to support wider planks, you will need to attach a plywood underlay.

If you are laying ceramic tiles, spread thinset adhesive and lay in it a moisture barrier of polyethylene which has been specifically designed for this purpose.

Exterior concrete slab Ceramic tile can be laid over an exterior concrete slab if it drains well and has been laid with the correct expansion joints (pp.206-7, 212-13). Make sure that it slopes sufficiently to allow rainwater to drain off, away from the house or any other structure.

Installing hardboard

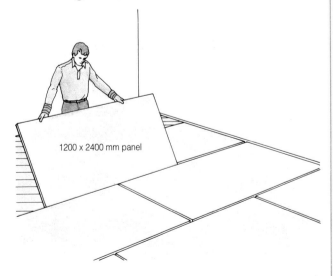

Position panels, textured side up, with seams slightly apart, staggered, and not aligned with subfloor seams. Allow 10 mm (⅜ in) gap at walls. Fasten to subfloor every 150 mm (6 in) with panel pins. Cut panels by scoring with trimming knife against a metal straightedge; fold along score to snap the board.

Preparing a concrete slab

1. Clean a slab when it is completely dry, and, if necessary, even it out with levelling compound (p.325). Then use a notched trowel to spread waterproofing mastic. Start at far corner and work towards doorway.

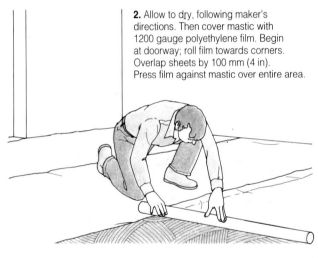

2. Allow to dry, following maker's directions. Then cover mastic with 1200 gauge polyethylene film. Begin at doorway; roll film towards corners. Overlap sheets by 100 mm (4 in). Press film against mastic over entire area.

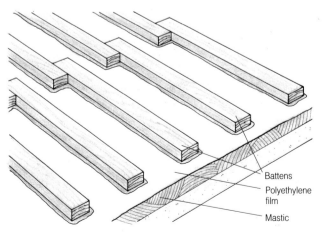

Battens
Polyethylene film
Mastic

3. To attach battens, spread runs of mastic onto polyethylene at 30 cm (12 in) intervals and at right angles to the direction of the finished flooring. Embed battens in mastic, overlapping them by 10 cm (4 in). Add a 6 mm (¾ in) underlay for planks wider than 100 mm (4 in).

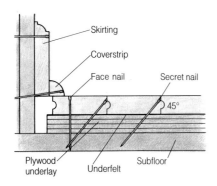

Skirting

Coverstrip

Face nail

Secret nail

45°

Plywood underlay

Underfelt

Subfloor

Strip and plank boarding require a strong support system that will hold the fastenings securely; the flooring can run either at right angles to, or diagonally across, the floor joists or screeds. Leave a 20 mm (¾ in) expansion gap between the flooring and the two walls that run parallel with the flooring.

First of all, find out how square the room is and how parallel the walls are. (Some variation is likely; cut and taper pieces to fit as described.) To determine how close to square the corners are, measure between the diagonal corners

(p.149); to locate unparallel areas, measure between the walls that will be parallel with the flooring strips. Variation between the end walls matters less because you can cut the ends to fit.

To align the flooring accurately, string a baseline on the floor parallel with the intended direction of the floorboards. In a small or average-sized room, locate the baseline close to the longest or most noticeable wall; in a room over 6 m (20 ft) wide, locate the baseline near the centre so that the flooring can be installed by working outwards from it in each direction.

Measure between the baseline and the wall every 30 cm (12 in) or so. If the wall is bowed, use a keyhole saw to shape the first course, or row, of boards. If the room is less than 25 mm (1 in) out of parallel, taper the last course; if more than 25 mm, divide the variation between the first and last courses. Mark the pieces that need tapering (p.326); then saw the boards to the correct taper. To make the adjustment less obvious,

plane the grooved edge and the tongue (or deepen the groove) of pieces in several courses. Fit the shaped pieces where least noticeable.

Select the straightest pieces for the first two or three and the final three or four courses. Slightly warped boards can be prised into place; check severely warped boards for straight sections that can be cut off and used.

Face-nail the first course of flooring, its grooved edge towards the wall, with a row of 40 mm wire cut nails driven vertically 25 mm (1 in) from the groove; don't nail through the groove. Before finishing, sink the nails with a punch and fill the holes. Continue fastening the first course by secret-nailing it at an angle through the tongued edge and into the bottom of the floorboard and the subfloor (the face and blind nails are staggered); drive these heads flush. Secret nails are hidden when the next board is put in place. Blind-nail all but the final courses. Face-nail the last two courses.

Getting started

Locate baseline Near each corner of the wall where you will begin installing boards, measure and mark the width of your flooring plus 20 mm (¾ in) for expansion joint.

Roll out underfelt over the plywood underlay, overlapping pieces by 10 cm (4 in). Felt minimises squeaks in the flooring.

Stretch string between nails driven into baseline marks in each corner. Test-fit first strip parallel with baseline. Mark irregular areas.

Lay out several courses before nailing Stagger joints by at least 150 mm (6 in) from course to course. Avoid clustering short boards and creating patterns like 'staircases' and H-joints. Strips at ends of courses should be at least 200 mm (8 in) long.

Fitting pieces

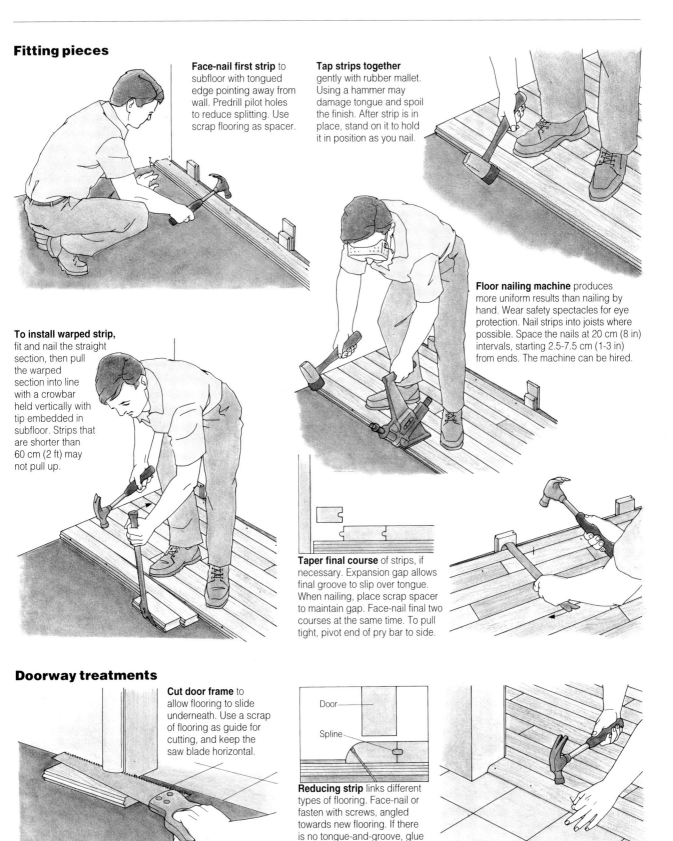

Face-nail first strip to subfloor with tongued edge pointing away from wall. Predrill pilot holes to reduce splitting. Use scrap flooring as spacer.

Tap strips together gently with rubber mallet. Using a hammer may damage tongue and spoil the finish. After strip is in place, stand on it to hold it in position as you nail.

Floor nailing machine produces more uniform results than nailing by hand. Wear safety spectacles for eye protection. Nail strips into joists where possible. Space the nails at 20 cm (8 in) intervals, starting 2.5-7.5 cm (1-3 in) from ends. The machine can be hired.

To install warped strip, fit and nail the straight section, then pull the warped section into line with a crowbar held vertically with tip embedded in subfloor. Strips that are shorter than 60 cm (2 ft) may not pull up.

Taper final course of strips, if necessary. Expansion gap allows final groove to slip over tongue. When nailing, place scrap spacer to maintain gap. Face-nail final two courses at the same time. To pull tight, pivot end of pry bar to side.

Doorway treatments

Cut door frame to allow flooring to slide underneath. Use a scrap of flooring as guide for cutting, and keep the saw blade horizontal.

Door

Spline

Reducing strip links different types of flooring. Face-nail or fasten with screws, angled towards new flooring. If there is no tongue-and-groove, glue a spline into routed grooves.

Flooring   329

Laying a floating floor

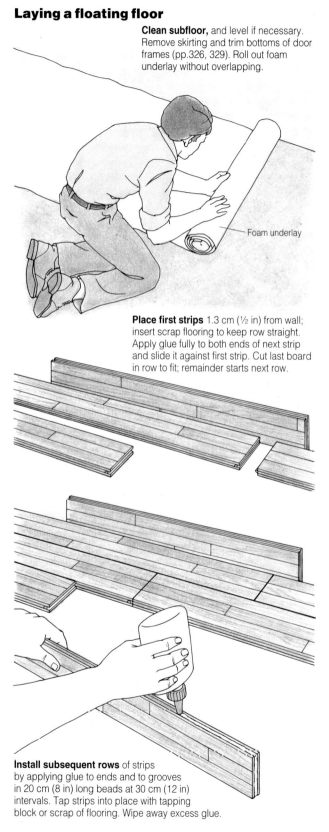

Clean subfloor, and level if necessary. Remove skirting and trim bottoms of door frames (pp.326, 329). Roll out foam underlay without overlapping.

Foam underlay

Place first strips 1.3 cm (½ in) from wall; insert scrap flooring to keep row straight. Apply glue fully to both ends of next strip and slide it against first strip. Cut last board in row to fit; remainder starts next row.

Install subsequent rows of strips by applying glue to ends and to grooves in 20 cm (8 in) long beads at 30 cm (12 in) intervals. Tap strips into place with tapping block or scrap of flooring. Wipe away excess glue.

The easiest type of flooring to install is laminated strip flooring. It requires no nailing; you either glue the pieces to each other, creating a floating floor, or embed them in mastic applied to the subfloor, creating a glue-down floor.

To prepare for a floating floor, flatten the subfloor with floor-levelling compound (p.325); then cover it with a layer of foam sheeting supplied by the flooring manufacturer. On a concrete slab, place a layer of 1200 gauge polyethylene sheeting beneath the foam as a vapour barrier.

A glue-down floor also requires a flat subfloor, and if the floor is below ground, a layer of polyethylene sheeting set in mastic. If the floor is concrete, dry and above ground, you can glue most types of laminated flooring directly to it. But if the slab is at or below ground level, first glue down a sheet of polyethylene film and install a subfloor of battens and plywood underlay. Then lay the flooring in mastic on the plywood. (For more on preparation, see pages 325-7.)

Parquet patterns may look best only when running in a certain direction; arrange a dozen or more squares on the floor as a test. Parquet, like ceramic and vinyl tiles, requires two perpendicular baselines that act as guides for the alignment of the tiles. Follow these lines precisely when laying parquet – the tiles are often not exactly square.

For best results, use the special installation tools, materials and adhesives recommended or supplied by the maker. Tools include tapping blocks and crowbars designed for fitting strips into place without damaging their tongued edges or disturbing the mastic, and a trowel with precisely notched edges for applying the mastic. Cork, available in rolls or 300 × 300 mm tiles that must be cut to fit, fills an expansion gap that is needed between the flooring and the walls.

Mastics vary in their content, but all require a waiting period after they are applied; the length of time depends on the type. Mastic is ready to accept the tiles when it has become tacky. It stays that way for a specified time; set the tiles during this open period. Trowel mastic over only as much area as you can tile in that time.

Caution: The solvents for many mastics are toxic and may be flammable. Follow the maker's safety precautions.

As you work, select squares randomly from several cartons to maximise colour uniformity over the entire floor. Before kneeling on newly laid squares, cover them with a plywood sheet. This helps to embed the squares and prevents them from sliding apart. Before the mastic hardens, walk on each square or roll it with a rolling pin to make certain the squares adhere completely. Finish the floor except for the perimeter; trowel mastic onto this area only after all the tiles have been cut to fit.

Caution: Trim parquet by hand or with a band saw or jigsaw; a table saw or a radial arm saw will cause kickback.

Allow new flooring to harden for 24 hours or as long as the maker suggests. Then cover the gaps with skirting, and fit a reducing strip where different floorings meet (p.329).

Layout for parquet

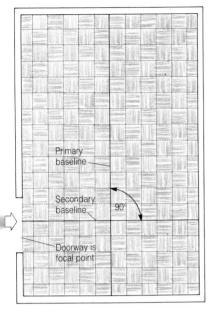

Primary baseline

Secondary baseline 90°

Doorway is focal point

Set out primary baseline parallel with longest wall. Mark secondary baseline at 90° angle to primary line. They should cross at focal point or room's centre. To check corner for squareness, measure 30 cm on one line, 40 cm on other; distance between must be exactly 50 cm – or any other 3-4-5 ratio.

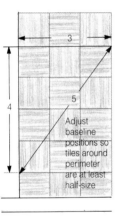

3

4

5

Adjust baseline positions so tiles around perimeter are at least half-size

Complete half of room; repeat for second half

Work in one quadrant at a time

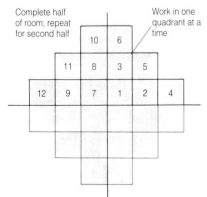

		10	6	
11	8	3	5
12	9	7	1	2	4

Starting where baselines cross, lay tiles in a pyramid pattern, placing them next to baseline and tile or in a corner formed by two tiles. This technique ensures straight rows.

Installing parquet

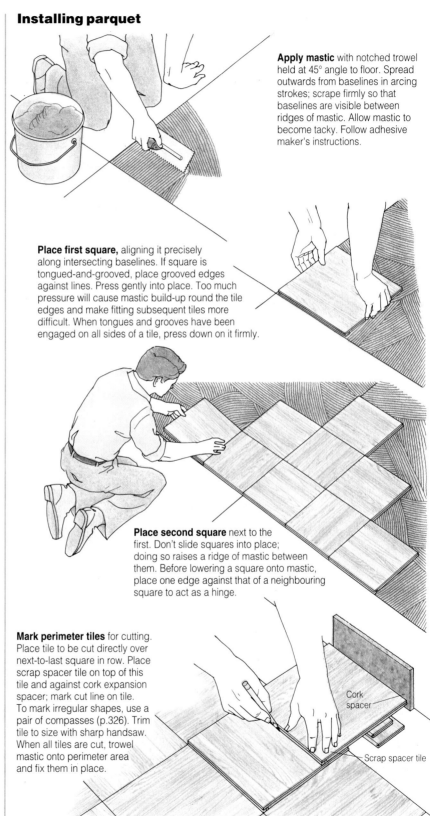

Apply mastic with notched trowel held at 45° angle to floor. Spread outwards from baselines in arcing strokes; scrape firmly so that baselines are visible between ridges of mastic. Allow mastic to become tacky. Follow adhesive maker's instructions.

Place first square, aligning it precisely along intersecting baselines. If square is tongued-and-grooved, place grooved edges against lines. Press gently into place. Too much pressure will cause mastic build-up round the tile edges and make fitting subsequent tiles more difficult. When tongues and grooves have been engaged on all sides of a tile, press down on it firmly.

Place second square next to the first. Don't slide squares into place; doing so raises a ridge of mastic between them. Before lowering a square onto mastic, place one edge against that of a neighbouring square to act as a hinge.

Mark perimeter tiles for cutting. Place tile to be cut directly over next-to-last square in row. Place scrap spacer tile on top of this tile and against cork expansion spacer; mark cut line on tile. To mark irregular shapes, use a pair of compasses (p.326). Trim tile to size with sharp handsaw. When all tiles are cut, trowel mastic onto perimeter area and fix them in place.

Cork spacer

Scrap spacer tile

Floors made from solid wood that is at least 2 cm (¾ in) thick can be restored several times during their lifetime by sanding off the old finish and applying a new one.

Thinner floors and some parquet flooring can usually only be restored this way once or twice.

Laminated flooring has a thin surface layer, and sanding will probably expose the backing underneath; which is why it is usually sold prefinished.

Sanding a floor is a big job that must be done carefully. Rather than using an ordinary belt sander or a disc sander attached to an electric drill, which can easily gouge the wood, hire three large power tools – a drum sander, a special disc sander called an edger, and a buffer.

The drum sander does the bulk of the work; the edger sands the perimeter of the room and wherever the drum sander cannot reach; the buffer prepares the sanded floor for each finishing coat. These machines must be handled carefully to avoid gouging the wood. Have a salesperson show you how to load and operate them and make sure you have plenty of sandpaper available.

Before you begin sanding, take everything out of the room and seal all interior openings to contain the dust. Then inspect the floor for protruding nails, staples or tacks and remove them. Glue down any large splinters.

Sand the entire floor with coarse aluminium-oxide sandpaper. Then vacuum the floor and sand it again with medium aluminium-oxide paper. Vacuum again and sand the floor with fine aluminium-oxide sandpaper. Then fill any cracks and flaws in the floor with filler. When it has dried, sand the floor with the buffer.

Next apply either a stain or the first coat of finish. When it is dry, polish the surface with the buffer, and then thoroughly vacuum the floor and wipe it with a tack rag. (For how to make your own tack rag, see page 164.) Repeat the process until you have applied as many coats of finish as necessary.

Caution: Follow the manufacturer's instructions exactly. Non-water-based products are toxic, and even water-based versions can be harmful.

Ventilate the area well and wear safety goggles, a respirator and rubber gloves. Extinguish all pilot lights and switch off stoves and electric motors to avoid an explosion. To prevent exposure to fumes, inhabitants should stay away from the premises for at least 24 hours after the finish is applied.

For more on sanding, staining, and finishing wood, see pages 164-9.

Sanding direction

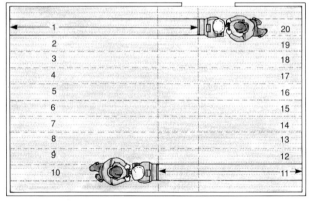

Move parallel with grain of strip floors. Begin near door; cover two-thirds of room length by moving sander back and forth. To reverse, retrace your steps without turning machine. On forward cuts, overlap previous pass by 5-10 cm (2-4 in). When ready to sand final third of floor, switch off machine and turn sander 180 degrees. Overlap the sanded area by 60 cm (2 ft).

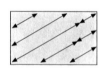

Sand parquet floor with medium-grit paper at 45 degree angle, using similar sequence as for strip and plank flooring.

Make second pass with fine grit at 90 degrees to the first pass, starting at the diagonally opposite corner.

Final pass with extra-fine grit should be parallel with room's long walls. Finish off sanding with a buffer.

Wood floor finishes

Finish type	Durability	Application	Upkeep and repair
Polyurethanes	Oil-based type is extremely durable; water-based type has fair durability. Both have excellent water resistance	Brush on with lambswool applicator. Oil-based type dries in 12-24 hours, is easier to apply. Water-based type dries in 2-4 hours; spread carefully to avoid surface bubbles	Damp-mop to keep floor free of grit. Never apply wax or cleaner containing oil. Sand dull floor; recoat with new finish
Varnishes	Moderate durability and water resistance. Avoid spar (marine) varnish, which is too soft for flooring	Spread with brush; usually needs 3 coats. Water-based type dries faster than solvent or oil based types but may raise wood grain. Keep room dust-free until dry	Dust often to remove grit. Apply wax to protect against moisture. Most repairs require stripping and refinishing
Penetrating sealers	Fair durability; strengthens and seals wood but does not protect surface	Easiest finish to apply. Spread with lint-free cloth or lambswool applicator; let stand for a time (see directions); then wipe off excess	Dust often to remove grit. Apply wax to protect against moisture. To repair, sand and apply new finish or refurbisher

Sanding and filling

Gradually lower moving drum of sander while pushing tool at start of forward motion. Walk evenly to avoid rocking sander from side to side. Near end of pass, raise drum gradually, pushing sander as far forward as possible; then to continue, begin walking backward while gradually lowering drum. Place cord over your shoulder.

Start edger while it is off the floor. Gradually lower the tool and move left to right in small overlapping circular strokes. Overlap the edger into area covered by drum sander. In areas too narrow for drum sander, such as a cupboard, move edger in zigzag pattern but parallel with wood grain.

Hand scraper removes old finish beneath radiators and below cabinet toe kicks. Follow with hand-sanding to blend with other sanded areas.

Push filler across floor with wide filling knife, forcing it into cracks. Work from corners toward centre of room. Remove excess filler from floor as you go, to avoid interfering with subsequent sanding. Most filler dries hard in an hour.

Finishing

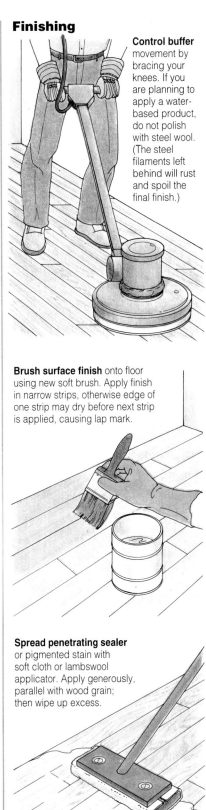

Control buffer movement by bracing your knees. If you are planning to apply a water-based product, do not polish with steel wool. (The steel filaments left behind will rust and spoil the final finish.)

Brush surface finish onto floor using new soft brush. Apply finish in narrow strips, otherwise edge of one strip may dry before next strip is applied, causing lap mark.

Spread penetrating sealer or pigmented stain with soft cloth or lambswool applicator. Apply generously, parallel with wood grain; then wipe up excess.

RESILIENT AND CERAMIC TILE FLOORS

Installing resilient and ceramic tile is similar to installing parquet flooring and ceramic tile countertops. The floor must be flat, and an underlay is needed for support (pp.325-7).

Resilient tiles are usually made of vinyl, come in a wide range of colours and patterns, and are usually 300 mm squares. In addition, accent tiles – which may be larger or smaller or in different shapes – are available. With these you can create borders or design your own patterns. Resilient tiles can usually be removed by heating them with a hot air gun. This allows you to change accent tiles to update the floor's appearance, rather than changing the entire floor. However, do not remove existing tiles if there is any chance that they contain asbestos (p.325).

Most resilient tile is fastened by gluing it to the floor with special adhesive. (The tile manufacturer or dealer will specify which kind to use.) Some tiles are self-adhesive; their backs are coated with contact cement covered with paper or plastic film. Remove the covering just before installation. Both types of tiles must then be pressed down firmly to secure them. To make sure you have not left any air bubbles smooth the tiles with a soft broom or a rolling pin. Prick persistent bubbles with a panel pin.

Ceramic floor tiles are similar to those used for countertops and walls but are generally larger and stronger. Proprietary adhesives, for use with these tiles, come in conveniently sized

Planning a diagonal layout

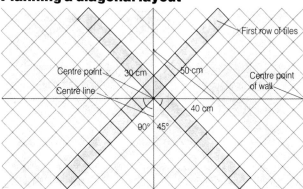

Draw a plan on graph paper, letting each square represent a tile (add grout spaces for ceramic tiles). Find the room's centre point by snapping chalk lines between the centre points of opposite walls. To check 90° angle, mark out from centre point 30 cm along one line, 40 cm along the other. Distance between two marks should be 50 cm. If necessary, adjust by redrawing one centre line without changing centre point. Bisect 90° with carpenter's square for 45° angle; check with adjustable square.

Border of tiles placed parallel with walls simplifies trimming when a room is out of square.

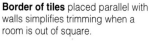

Position first row (without adhesive) along a 45° line. If necessary, adjust the row without changing its angle so that the end tiles are equal in size and at least half a tile wide. Mark additional guidelines every 60 cm (2 ft). Mark the border with a separate colour to avoid confusion.

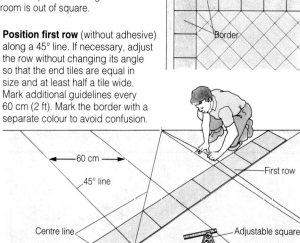

Installing resilient tiles

Remove backing from self-adhesive tile, or spread tile adhesive with notched trowel (facing page). Lay tile in place without twisting, using edge of adjoining tile as a 'hinge'.

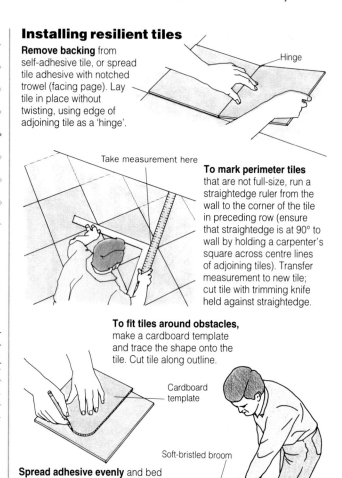

To mark perimeter tiles that are not full-size, run a straightedge ruler from the wall to the corner of the tile in preceding row (ensure that straightedge is at 90° to wall by holding a carpenter's square across centre lines of adjoining tiles). Transfer measurement to new tile; cut tile with trimming knife held against straightedge.

To fit tiles around obstacles, make a cardboard template and trace the shape onto the tile. Cut tile along outline.

Spread adhesive evenly and bed tiles firmly by smoothing over the tiles with a soft-bristled broom or a rolling pin. Make two passes with broom, one at right angles to the other. Be sure to cover entire floor.

plastic tubs. Follow the manufacturer's instructions. For more information on choosing, cutting and repairing ceramic tiles, see pages 254-9.

Tiles are usually laid either parallel with the walls or at a 45° angle to them. When laying them parallel, use the same method as for parquet floors (pp.330-1), but allow for the width of grout joints with ceramic tile.

Where a room is significantly out of square or has many obstacles, adapt the layout method on pages 328-9.

Select one wall as a focal point, mark a baseline two or three tile widths from it, and then proceed with a parallel or diagonal layout.

Tiles can help to hide a room's defects – vertical lines seem to make a room longer; a border makes it appear smaller. Hexagonal tiles should be laid with their sides, not their corners, parallel with two opposite walls.

Whatever the layout, work first on graph paper. Estimate the amount of tile you need based on the size of the

room and that of your chosen tile (plus any grout joints), adding 10 per cent extra for breakage and for future repairs. Test the design first by doing a dry run on the floor, adjusting it if necessary to compensate for obstacles and the room's dimensions.

Be careful not to apply adhesive over areas that are too large to cover with tiles before the adhesive hardens. Similarly, never apply more grout than you can spread easily and clean before it begins to set.

Laying ceramic tiles

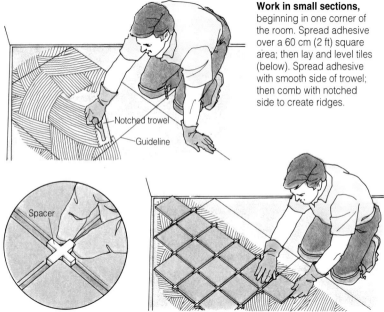

Work in small sections, beginning in one corner of the room. Spread adhesive over a 60 cm (2 ft) square area; then lay and level tiles (below). Spread adhesive with smooth side of trowel; then comb with notched side to create ridges.

Notched trowel

Guideline

Spacer

Lay tiles in adhesive, fitting them in place with a slight twist to spread the adhesive; remove excess from joints with knife. Place spacers at corners to maintain uniform gap between tiles (inset). Never walk on newly laid tiles.

Level tiles and spread adhesive by hammering against tiles with a 50 x 100 mm (2 x 4 in) batten covered with carpet or thick towelling. To raise a tile that is too low, prise it up, apply fresh adhesive to the back, and reset the tile.

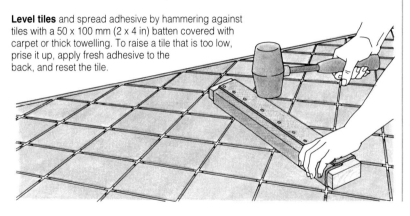

Grouting and cleaning the tiles

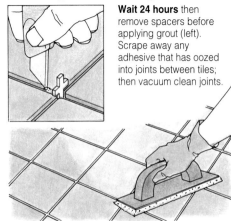

Wait 24 hours then remove spacers before applying grout (left). Scrape away any adhesive that has oozed into joints between tiles; then vacuum clean joints.

Spread grout over tiles with rubber grout float held firmly at 30° angle. Wipe away excess immediately by scraping with float held nearly perpendicular to floor.

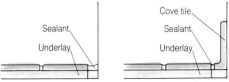

Cove tile

Sealant

Underlay

Sealant

Underlay

Apply sealant, not grout, in expansion joints such as the joint round the perimeter of the floor (left) or where cove and floor tile meet (right). Use a sealant gun to push flexible waterpoof sealant firmly into the joint.

Clean tiles before grout dries. Wipe several times with sponge squeezed nearly dry (rinse sponge often); then remove hazy residue with clean towel.

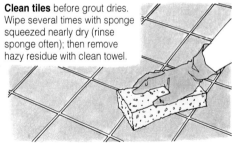

Laying the flooring

1. Ventilate the area well. Unroll flooring starting at longest unbroken wall. Allow excess to curl up at edges; adjust sheet so pattern is square to walls.

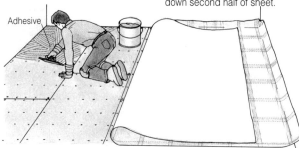

Adhesive

2. Fold back half of sheet, without creasing, to expose underlay. Apply adhesive to floor with notched trowel; immediately press down sheet. Fold back other half of sheet, cover rest of floor with adhesive, and press down second half of sheet.

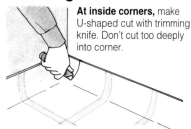

3. Flatten sheet with soft bristled broom or rolling pin to spread adhesive and remove bubbles. Work from centre of floor outward.

Usually made of vinyl, resilient sheet flooring comes in many different colours, patterns and textures. Quality and prices vary; premium grades have a durable top, or wear layer, that disguises underlay flaws.

Most sheet flooring is available in rolls of up to 2.4 m wide. Whenever possible, select a width that allows you to cover the floor with a single piece. Sheets can be joined, but it is difficult to match patterns and textures at a seam. If a seam can't be avoided, plan it so that it will occur in the least conspicuous area.

You can apply sheet flooring over almost any smooth hard surface, even over existing resilient flooring. To flatten or strengthen the underlay, see pages 325-7.

The flooring manufacturer will specify whether the flooring should be laid using the full-adhesion method shown here or whether it should be laid loose. To loose-lay flooring, follow the steps shown here to position and trim it, but leave a 6 mm (¼ in) gap along the walls and do not apply adhesive. Then secure the edges as directed by the manufacturer.

Resilient flooring can be difficult to manipulate. Avoid bending it sharply as you lay it, or it may crease or rip. Even after it has been rolled, fully adhered flooring usually develops bubbles, caused by gas escaping from the adhesive. If these have not disappeared within a week, prick them with a pin in an inconspicuous spot and then press the flooring flat.

When moving heavy items over resilient flooring, lay down a sheet of thin plywood or heavy cardboard to protect it. Clean flooring often with a mop that is only slightly damp as it is not waterproof. Special cleaners recommended by the flooring manufacturer will preserve or restore a glossy finish.

Trimming

At inside corners, make U-shaped cut with trimming knife. Don't cut too deeply into corner.

At outside corners, use a trimming knife to make vertical slits through excess flooring.

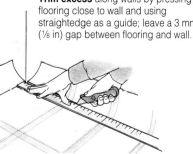

Trim excess along walls by pressing flooring close to wall and using straightedge as a guide; leave a 3 mm (⅛ in) gap between flooring and wall.

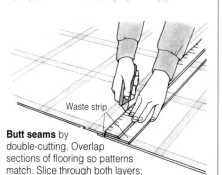

Waste strip

Butt seams by double-cutting. Overlap sections of flooring so patterns match. Slice through both layers; remove waste strips above and below.

Finishing touches

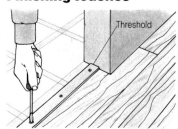

Threshold

Cover flooring at doorways and where flooring meets different material. Cut aluminium cover strips to precise length and fix with matching countersunk screws.

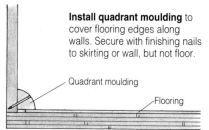

Install quadrant moulding to cover flooring edges along walls. Secure with finishing nails to skirting or wall, but not floor.

Quadrant moulding

Flooring

Strip and plank flooring

Drill holes with a flat bit at each end of damaged area. Chisel out board.

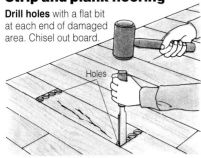

Cut to length a new strip of tongued-and-grooved flooring; reverse board and remove lower lip of groove with chisel, saw or plane.

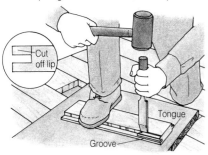

Fit tongue of new board into groove of adjacent floorboard. Tap into place with mallet and scrap block; fasten with nails. Finish to match floor.

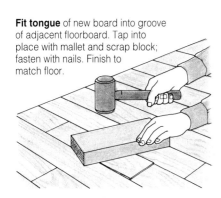

To increase the time between major refinishings, sweep or vacuum floors frequently to remove grit and wipe up spills promptly to avoid stains. For general cleaning, use commercial cleaners recommended by the flooring manufacturer or installer.

On wood floors, avoid water-based products. On floors finished with polyurethane, don't use cleaners containing any kind of oil, grease, or solvent. Synthetic floor finishes – such as Swedish finish and acrylic – resist penetration by most liquids. On the other hand, floors finished with shellac, lacquer, conventional varnish and wax are easily damaged by almost any liquid that is allowed to remain for more than a few minutes, especially liquids containing solvents such as alcohol.

To repair minor scratches in a non-synthetic finish, rub the spot with very fine steel wool (No 0000) and then apply a dab of paste wax. Extensively damaged or stained finish may have to be stripped and replaced. To repair a synthetic finish and the finish on resilient flooring, use only the products and techniques recommended by the flooring manufacturer.

You may be able to sand or bleach stained wood flooring; if not, or if floorboards are splintered or broken, the damage must be removed and patched, as shown (far left).

Lighten stained ceramic tile grout with special cleaners, available at tile suppliers. For instructions on sealing tiles and grout and repairing damaged ceramic tile, see pages 257 and 259.

In resilient flooring, small gouged areas can sometimes be patched with a paste made of grated flooring material and clear nail polish. Grate resilient flooring only if you are certain that it does not contain asbestos (p.325). However, you will usually get better-looking results by patching the area.

Parquet tile

Drill holes from corner to corner to slightly less than the depth of the tile. Chisel away all sections.

Scrape off old adhesive; then apply new layer and fit replacement tile in place.

Resilient tile and sheet flooring

Soften adhesive with a hot air gun; lift off the damaged tile and scrape off adhesive. Apply the new adhesive and fit the new tile in place.

Patching sheet flooring:
1. Place a patch on top of damage, aligning pattern precisely. Tape in place; then cut through both layers with a trimming knife.

2. Remove patch (below) and set it aside. Heat and prise away damaged flooring and adhesive as you would for a damaged tile.

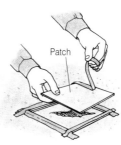

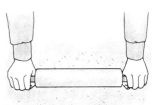

3. Spread new adhesive, using notched trowel. Fit patch into place; then press flat with rolling pin.

You will save time, money, energy and a lot of frustration if you think a project through and carefully plan each step before beginning. For almost any undertaking, large or small, you will benefit by drawing up your plans on paper. A good set of plans lets you see what tools you'll need and helps in estimating the amount and cost of the materials you'll use. It also helps you to see the complexity of the entire job, so that you can determine whether or not you'll need professional help.

Drawing up plans Begin by making a sketch or diagram of the project. It need not be elaborate – simply clear enough to illustrate what you mean to do, showing all the parts and indicating the materials you plan to use. You can make simple outlines of the parts and use heavy dots or Xs for the nails, screws or bolts.

Then, to ensure accurate results, transfer the sketch to graph paper, letting each square on the paper equal 30 cm (1 ft) or some other simple measurement. Or use measuring tools to draw the plans to scale.

To make a full-size pattern from a small picture or drawing, use a pantograph (p.19), or draw a grid of intersecting lines over the original drawing and transfer the design onto graph paper square by square. It pays to be thorough and accurate.

When designing furniture, consider the average person's comfort and use standard dimensions. Also be sure to leave enough open space around each item (pp.340-3).

For large projects, if you don't want to draw your own plans, you can alter existing ones, purchase books of ready-drawn plans or copy plans from magazines. There are also specialist monthly magazines which feature plans, while some offer a plans service. It can help to cut pieces of card to represent furniture and fittings. These small pieces can easily be moved about inside a grid floor plan to find the best arrangement. Also available in some stores is computer software for designing a kitchen or bathroom. Some DIY centres provide personalised computer planning.

Outlining the steps Once the plans for a project are drawn up, think the whole job through and make a list of the major steps. Put the steps in order, break them down into substeps, and number the steps and substeps.

When planning a large project, break it down into a series of small, manageable projects (see below). This allows you to plan your purchases, organise your time and spot any specialised work that goes beyond the level of your skills and requires a professional. Checking through the steps, make a list of all the tools you will want to have on hand. Then study the steps and the plans to determine the amounts of materials you will need (pp.344-7), including fasteners and other hardware.

Other considerations For safety, be sure to line up one or more helpers if the project will involve carrying or working with materials that are heavy or awkward to handle. Also, plan and set up a space, either in your workshop or on site, for working on the project and storing the materials.

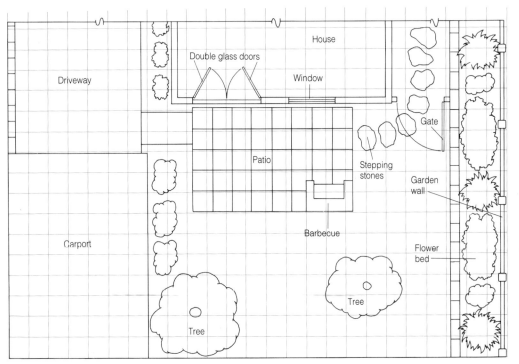

Begin a large project, such as adding a patio to your house, by drawing up a plan. Using the plan as a guide, break the project into a number of smaller, more manageable jobs, such as laying the patio floor, putting in the flowerbeds, building the barbecue and adding the stepping stones. Then, in order to see what tools and materials you will need, break each of these smaller jobs into self-contained steps. For instance, divide the patio floor job into laying out the area, excavating the topsoil, adding the gravel and mortar, laying the stones and adding the grout. Finally, do the work in a logical sequence, suiting your budget, your free time and the time of year.

If a project is going to generate a lot of waste materials, decide in advance how you will recycle or dispose of them. For a major project, hire a skip. For smaller jobs, take rubbish to your nearest waste disposal centre.

Remember that materials such as oils, paints, lacquers and varnishes, as well as thinners, strippers and other solvents, are flammable or toxic; some are hazardous to the environment. Use them according to the instructions on the labels, seal empty containers, wrap any remaining sludge in newspaper and seal it in a plastic bag or container, and take the packages to a disposal centre. If in doubt about safe disposal, get in touch with your local authority for information on how to dispose of this type of waste properly.

Rules and regulations Before you start on any large project, check to see whether you will be bound by any regulations. You can do this through the planning department at your local authority. Building work, including extensions or new garages, changing the use of a home, erecting new fencing or anything which could affect neighbours, may involve planning permission. Structural work, choice of materials, protection against damp, insulation, fire precautions, work on chimneys and flues, drains and drainage will probably be controlled by building regulations.

No work should be undertaken until all the necessary permissions have been obtained.

Write out in detail – and draw sketches – of what work you have in mind, then arrange an appointment, probably with a building control officer. The alternative is to employ the services of a local architect, who does all the negotiating on your behalf and get the necessary permission.

Some home owners are deterred by the cost of employing an architect, but his or her knowledge of the work and personal contacts with reliable contractors, if some of the work is to be done for you, can save you a lot of money in the long term.

Hiring a contractor

The skills section of this book shows you what is involved in working with various materials, demonstrating all the basic techniques and some advanced ones. It can also help you to assess what's involved in any projects you may plan and determine your role in them.

If, after assessing the job's complexity, you decide to undertake a large project that involves work you don't feel comfortable doing, consider hiring a contractor to do part or all of the job. For example, for the patio project shown on the facing page, you might serve as general contractor and do some of the work yourself, but hire a labourer to excavate the soil, an electrician to install the outdoor lighting, and a plumber to put in the garden sprinkling system.

To find a contractor, make a list of names by talking to your friends and relatives who have had similar work done, by looking in *Yellow Pages* and by calling local building and construction organisations. Contact several of the contractors who do the type of work you need, asking for references from customers who have used their services recently for a project similar to yours. Call the referees and ask to look at the work. Narrow your list to those contractors with good references. Check to see if they are affiliated to a recognised association or federation – most of which have a recognisable emblem or logo.

Finally, ask two or three of the contractors to bid on the work, giving them drawings and specific information on the materials you want. (Most contractors will provide their own materials because part of their profit is derived from the discount they receive from suppliers.)

When the quotes are in, study them carefully and choose the contractor you think is best for the job. But remember, the lowest bid is not always the best, because contractors may cut corners to bring down the price.

For your protection, get everything in writing. The contract should include start-up and completion dates, a detailed account of the work to be done, the type of materials to be used (including the brand names, if important), how and when the site will be cleared, procedures for making changes in the original plans, warranties and termination conditions.

Be sure to include the full cost of the project and a schedule of payments. Never pay everything up front; it's common to make a down payment of no more than one-third the total cost, several payments as the work progresses and a final payment when everything is completed and you have approved the work.

Your contract should also include a lien waiver clause, requiring the contractor to show proof that suppliers and subcontractors have been paid so that you cannot be sued for nonpayment of bills. Get the contractor to obtain all necessary permits and take full responsibility for following the local codes. Ask to see proof of damage and liability insurance from all contractors and subcontractors.

Once the work begins, keep an eye on its progress and quickly bring any problems to the attention of the contractor – not his workers. If you want to make a change in the plans, ask how it will affect the total cost of the project and get it in writing. Making a small change may necessitate expensive changes elsewhere. For example, to add a light fitting an electrician may have to run an extra circuit at great expense, but he might not tell you until he presents the bill at the end.

When the job is finished, examine it carefully before making the final payment. Never pay for work that has not been done.

STANDARD MEASUREMENTS FOR TABLES AND CHAIRS

When designing furniture and arranging it in a room, it's best to follow the general space requirements that have been established for the average person. A table or desk must be the proper height, for example, to eat or work at comfortably. In addition, allow sufficient space for people to pass easily through a room or to walk or work around the furniture.

DINING TABLE SIZES – shown in millimetres

	People	Minimum	Average	Ample
Square tables	2	600 x 600	700 x 700	750 x 750
	4	750 x 750	850 x 850	900 x 900
	8	1100 x 1100	1200 x 1200	1300 x 1300
Rectangular tables	2	600 x 700	600 x 750	700 x 800
	4	700 x 1100	850 x 1200	900 x 1300
	6	850 x 1200	900 x 1500	1000 x 1800
	8	850 x 1800	900 x 1800	1000 x 2300
Round tables	2	600	650	700
	4	800	900	1100
	6	1100	1300	1400
	8	1400	1600	1800

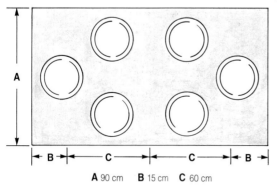

A 90 cm **B** 15 cm **C** 60 cm

Coffee table must be within easy reach of someone seated on a sofa or in an armchair but far enough away to allow enough leg room.

Dining table and chairs must be at the right height for comfort. The diagram (above left) shows an average-sized table for six. The chart directly above gives other common sizes. The drawing below gives standard heights and the minimum space needed for passing when a chair is pulled out.

55 cm minimum

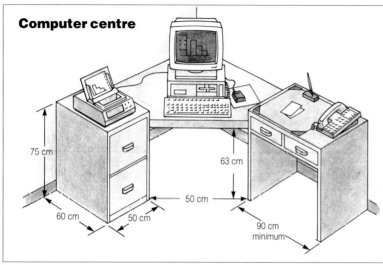

Computer centre

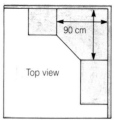

Top view

By building your computer centre into a corner, you gain more room for the monitor and keyboard, and provide a partial wraparound workspace that lets you work with a minimum of movement.

Either build or buy the elements for a computer centre. In the arrangement shown, the centre table, for the keyboard (and monitor), is 12 cm (5½ in) lower than the rest because that is generally a more comfortable height for typing. The area on the right can be reserved for writing, and the printer can be placed on the left. Reverse for a left-handed worker.

STANDARD MEASUREMENTS FOR STORAGE AREAS AND BEDROOMS

In planning storage space, always take into consideration the size of the people who need access to it. Some standard measurements are given here, but you may have to change them to suit the needs of individuals. For example, you might build low shelves in a child's bedroom but put high ones in another room for storing harmful materials out of the reach of young children. If you add extra-high shelves, use a step ladder or step stool to reach them. Bookshelves should be shallower than cupboard shelves, and they should not be more than about 90 cm (36 in) long to sustain the weight of the books without sagging. When furnishing a bedroom, remember to leave enough space for dressing and moving about.

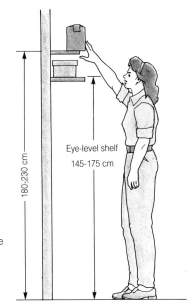

Eye-level shelf
145-175 cm

180-230 cm

A 60 cm   **B** 85 cm   **C** 125 cm

Shelves (right) should be within reach of everyone who uses them without having to stand on tiptoe. Make high shelves shallower than lower ones.

Cupboards (left) hold more if packed tightly; buy or build an organiser. Install rods for hangers at least 30 cm (12 in) from wall.

Allow access space in front of cabinet doors or drawers (below).

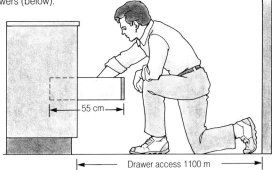

55 cm

Drawer access 1100 m

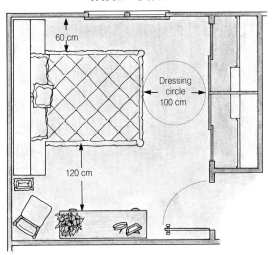

60 cm

Dressing circle 100 cm

120 cm

200 cm

Bedroom wall unit (right) can frame any bed. King-size beds usually measure 150 cm x 200 cm; double beds are 135 cm x 190 cm and single beds are 90 cm x 190 cm. Allow 50 cm between twin beds. The amounts of space shown round the bed (above) are minimums.

Perhaps more than any other parts of your home, the kitchen and bathroom benefit from careful planning. A well-designed kitchen can put everything at your fingertips and dramatically reduce the time you spend preparing food. A carefully laid-out bathroom ensures maximum comfort and avoids cramped spaces that cause you to bang your knee or stub your toe. You might also consider installing a hand-held shower and grab bars at convenient heights for anyone who might be unsteady on their feet. If someone in your household is confined to a wheelchair, you may want to make some of the adjustments shown below and on the facing page.

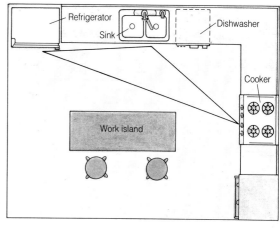

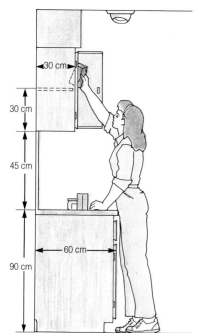

Base cabinets in kitchen are deeper than the wall cabinets, and so the top shelves cannot be as high as shelves with no obstruction below them.

Leave crouching space in front of a low oven (below) or a cabinet with swing-out doors.

Work triangle that puts the sink, refrigerator and cooker at its three corners is the most efficient arrangement for a kitchen. A U-shaped work triangle is shown in the layout on the left, and an L-shaped kitchen with a longer, narrower work triangle is shown above. When planning a kitchen, be sure to leave enough counter space between the three points for preparing food, serving and cleaning up, but make the length of the legs of the triangle short enough to minimise walking. Never place a heat-making appliance, such as the cooker or dishwasher, next to the refrigerator.

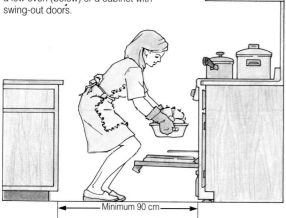

Minimum 90 cm

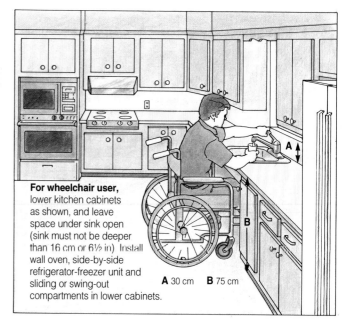

For wheelchair user, lower kitchen cabinets as shown, and leave space under sink open (sink must not be deeper than 16 cm or 6½ in). Install wall oven, side-by-side refrigerator-freezer unit and sliding or swing-out compartments in lower cabinets.

A 30 cm **B** 75 cm

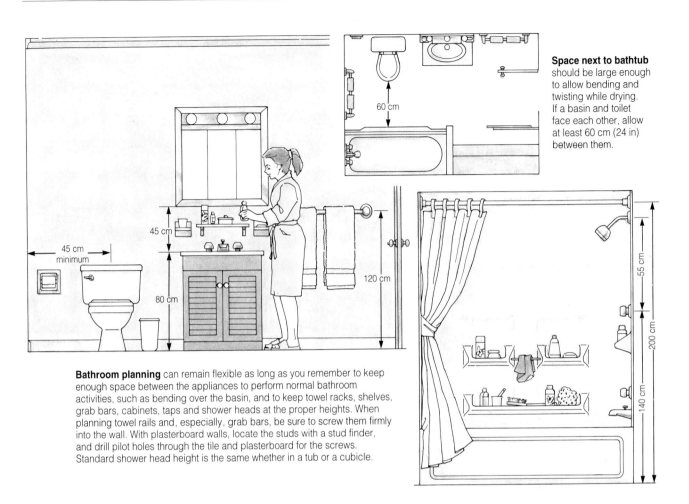

Space next to bathtub should be large enough to allow bending and twisting while drying. If a basin and toilet face each other, allow at least 60 cm (24 in) between them.

Bathroom planning can remain flexible as long as you remember to keep enough space between the appliances to perform normal bathroom activities, such as bending over the basin, and to keep towel racks, shelves, grab bars, cabinets, taps and shower heads at the proper heights. When planning towel rails and, especially, grab bars, be sure to screw them firmly into the wall. With plasterboard walls, locate the studs with a stud finder, and drill pilot holes through the tile and plasterboard for the screws. Standard shower head height is the same whether in a tub or a cubicle.

Bathroom for handicapped needs more grab bars and a hand-held shower. You should also lower the medicine cabinet and position it beside the basin (right). Leave enough space next to the toilet to park a wheelchair, and a circle of space at least 1.5 m (5 ft) across in the centre of the room to turn the chair freely (below).

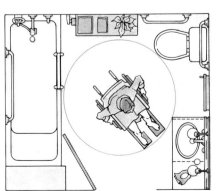

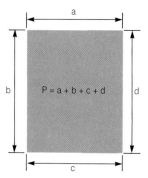

Perimeter of (distance round) a rectangle, triangle or other straight-sided shape is found by adding the lengths of all its sides.

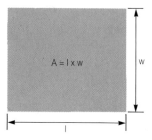

Area of a rectangle is determined by multiplying its length by its width.

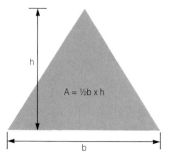

Area of a triangle is found by multiplying half the length of its base by its height.

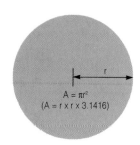

Area of a circle is determined by multiplying the square of the circle's radius (half the distance across the circle) by π (3.1416).

Once you have drawn up plans for a project, begin compiling lists of the materials and hardware you will need. First consider the nature of the project. How much will it be used? Is it to be permanent or temporary? Will it be visible or hidden, utilitarian or decorative? Should it match or contrast with existing materials? Is it going to be indoors or outdoors? Will it be used by children or a handicapped person? Have you set yourself a budget?

With these factors in mind, choose the type and quality of materials you want to use and, if applicable, pick the finish (paint, stain or natural) you wish them to have.

After you have decided on the types of materials, you will need to estimate the quantities. For materials that have to be installed in straight lines, such as pipes or skirting, simply measure the length needed. For materials that will frame or border, measure the perimeter or circumference of the piece or area to

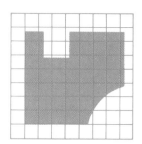

Sketch complex areas on graph paper, letting each square on the paper equal 1 cm square or 10 cm square. Add up whole squares and those more than one-third filled.

be enclosed. For many other materials, you'll need to calculate either the area to be covered or the volume to be filled. Use the formulas illustrated here to make these estimates. Then determine the amounts of materials you'll need based on these calculations.

When using any formula to help you to estimate quantities, remember to compute similar things. For instance, don't multiply millimetres by centimetres, or inches by feet. Convert them all to the same unit of measurement first.

Some materials are estimated and sold in several ways. The most common are given in the pages that follow. If you want to be sure how a material is sold, telephone the supplier.

The best way to organise an estimate of the materials required for a job is to break the job down into its individual steps (p.338), recording the type and quantity of the materials needed at each step. List every item required for building or installation, including hardware, fastenings, packing material or sealants and abrasives. Also list any tools that you may have to buy or hire.

A rule of thumb when estimating materials is to add 10 per cent to allow for miscalculations, errors, damage and waste, and also to save for future repairs. Once you have determined the quantities, multiply the amount by the cost per unit to find the total cost of the materials.

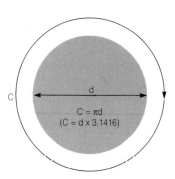

Circumference of (distance round) a full circle is found by multiplying the circle's diameter (the distance across it) by π (3.1416).

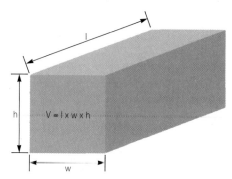

Volume, or cubic dimension, of a square or other rectangular space is determined by multiplying the length by the width by the height.

TABLE 1: Nominal and actual sizes of timber — **Nominal size in millimetres** (Actual size in brackets)

Thickness	**12.5** (8)	**16** (12)	**19** (15)	**22** (18)	**25** (21)	**32** (27)	**38** (33)	**50** (44)	**75** (68)	
Width	**25** (21)	**50** (44)	**75** (68)	**100** (94)	**125** (119)	**150** (144)	**175** (168)	**200** (193)	**225** (215)	**275** (270)

Timber and boards are supplied in set sizes and if you design a project so that the measurements fall within these set sizes, you can save a lot of waste. For example, if you still think in imperial sizes, and you want your fence to be 6 ft high, the pieces will have to come out of 2.1 m lengths, involving a great deal of waste. Change the fence to 5ft 10¾ in high, and your pieces will come out of a 1.8 m length with virtually no waste.

Bear in mind that it is very easy to oversize your timbers. Look at how manufacturers make units and you will be surprised at the small sections used, especially when frames are strengthened by sheet materials. Changing from a 25 × 50 mm section to 25 mm square will halve the cost of the timber. But where structural work is involved, always seek professional advice as to the correct sections to use.

Grading Timber is graded by the number of knots and other small defects it has. Explain the project you have in mind to your timber merchant and he will advise on the right grade.

Rough sawn or planed? For rough framework and most outdoor projects such as pergolas and fencing, timber is supplied rough sawn, and it is sold by nominal size. When timber has dried, these sizes may be a fraction smaller.

For more accurate work, or where timber is to be finished in some way, planed joinery softwood is available, often referred to as PAR or planed all round. Here, sizes will be smaller by the amount removed by planing, though the size quoted will be the nominal one. For example, it will be shown as '100 mm (4 in) Nominal'. Table 1 gives the difference between nominal and actual sizes. Table 2 shows the most common softwood sections. Hardwoods are usually supplied PAR and can vary in both dimension and in the sizes available.

Sawn softwood is supplied in basic lengths, starting at 1.8 m and rising by 300 mm increments to 7.2 m.

Buying hardwoods These woods must be chosen with care, in order to avoid adding to the destruction of hardwood forests which are under threat (p.130).

Sheet materials come in set sizes, so when planning a project, arrange components on graph paper to work out which sheet size is most suitable. Often, a slight change in design can save considerably on cost.

Plywood There are various grades – the quality of the faces of the ply will affect price. For rough construction work, shuttering plywood is most economical. For locations where damp is involved, choose WBP grades (weather and boil proof). For extreme exposure use a marine plywood. For flooring, choose a shuttering grade with one good face. The most usual size is 1220 × 2440 mm (4 × 8 ft), in thicknesses from 12 to 30 mm.

Chipboard is not as strong as plywood. Its main use is for flooring. Most grades are for internal use only, though a weatherproof board is available. The most common size is 1220 × 2440 mm (4 × 8 ft) and it is available from 12 to 30 mm thick.

Hardboard Standard hardboard is for internal use only. Oil-tempered hardboard is denser and stronger, and can be used outdoors. The most common size is 1220 × 2440 mm (4 × 8 ft) in 3.2 and 6 mm thicknesses.

Medium density fibreboard (MDF) More commonly used for furniture making, it has largely replaced chipboard. Standard size is 1220 × 2440 mm (4 × 8 ft) and comes in thicknesses of 2 to 25 mm.

Storing timber Timber and boards will normally be supplied with a set moisture content. Before using them indoors, store them in the area where they are most likely to be used, so that they can adapt their moisture content to the environment. This will help to minimise the risk of warping.

TABLE 2: Softwood – basic sawn section sizes at 20% moisture content

Thickness (mm) / Width (mm)	16	19	22	25	32	36	38	44	47	50	63	75	100	150	200	250	300
75	x	x	x	x	x	x	x	x	x	x							
100	x	x	x	x	x	x	x	x	x	x	x	x	x				
125	x	x	x	x	x	x	x	x	x	x	x	x					
150	x	x	x	x	x	x	x	x	x	x	x	x	x	x			
175			x	x	x		x	x	x	x	x	x					
200			x	x	x		x	x	x	x	x	x	x	x	x		
225			x	x	x		x	x	x	x	x	x	x				
250				x	x		x	x	x	x		x	x			x	
300				x	x		x	x	x	x		x	x	x			x

In addition to wood, you may have to estimate the amounts needed of various other building materials and hardware. Some of the most common items are discussed below.

Bricks To estimate the number of bricks you will need for a project, calculate the surface area of the wall to be built – multiply its length by its total height to get square metres.

If the wall is to be half a brick thick (102 mm) and standard-sized metric bricks (215 × 102 × 65 mm) are to be used, allow 60 bricks per square metre. For a one brick thick wall (215 mm) allow 120 standard metric bricks per square metre. Add an extra 5 per cent for breakages during handling.

Builder's merchants sell bricks in whole pallets of 400-500 strapped together which will be off-loaded by mechanical hoist mounted on the delivery lorry. For safe handling, once the strap has been cut, never stack these packs one on top of the other because they could collapse, causing severe damage or injury.

Remember that if you have to handle unpalleted bricks, such as when you need a half pack of bricks, they will take more time to unload and are at greater risk of chipping and wastage.

Concrete and concrete blocks Concrete is sold in cubic metres. The volume quoted by ready-mix concrete suppliers is that of compacted concrete, after laying and vibration, not the loose volume, which is larger. Calculate the area in square metres and multiply it by the thickness in millimetres. Divide this result by 1000 to get the number of cubic metres of concrete required. For example, if you want a 12 × 8 m slab, 100 mm thick, multiply 12 × 8 × 100 and divide by 1000. The answer is 9.6 m³, so buy or mix 10 m³ to be safe.

Walling blocks are sold by the square metre. The standard face of 450 × 225 mm sells at 10 blocks to the square metre, and the smaller, modular face (400 × 200 mm) sells at 12½ to the square metre. To calculate the number of aerated blocks you need,

find the area of the wall in square metres, subtract the area of any holes or openings and add 8 per cent for block cutting and breakage. If you are using aggregate blocks, 4 per cent extra is enough, as they are less liable to break on site than aerated blocks.

Concrete pavers Manufactured concrete pavers come in different sizes and shapes; some interlock. Check with the supplier for actual sizes and refer to the company's brochure for the coverage that each design gives.

There are so many designs and sizes of paver that there is no general rule for calculating the number you will need. Most manufacturers include edging pavers or edging kerbs with their range, to complete their designs.

Paving flags Flags used for a patio or walkway can be made of concrete or natural stone and have regular or irregular dimensions. Squares and rectangles are available in various sizes from 225 mm (about 9 in) square up to 900 × 600 mm (3 × 2 ft).

Thickness varies from 32-75 mm (about 1½-3 in). The most popular size is 450 × 450 × 35 mm thick.

Many ranges of concrete paving include a variety of coordinating sizes which allow a random laying style, reminiscent of old-fashioned natural stone paving.

Reclaimed natural stone paving is sold either by the square metre or tonne. Paving sizes and thickness vary, and it is often best to let the natural dimensions of the material dictate the precise layout of the area to be paved.

Finishes Labels on the containers of paints, stains and other finishes indicate their coverage – the area that quantity of finish should cover.

In general, to calculate the amount of finish you'll need, divide the total area to be covered by the coverage indicated and multiply the result by the number of coats you plan to apply. For large areas such as walls, deduct for doorways, windows and other large openings (p.285).

If the surface to be painted is

unusually porous, as in concrete block or new plasterboard, allow 25 per cent more paint for the first coat (usually a primer). If you are applying a light colour over a dark one, you will need to apply a thicker coat or an extra coat.

Wall coverings Wallpaper and other wall coverings usually come in standard rolls around 10 m long by 530 mm wide (about 5 m²).

To estimate the number of rolls you need, calculate the area of each wall and subtract the area of french doors, but not standard doors and windows – you will need the extra. Divide the result by five (the number of square metres on the roll) and then, to be really safe, add one extra roll to the total, to allow for mistakes or problems. To estimate the number of rolls you will need for a ceiling, multiply the length by the width in metres and, again, divide by five.

Borders are also usually sold in 5 m rolls. Measure the perimeter of the room in metres and divide by the length of the roll.

If your wallpaper is not prepasted, buy all-purpose paste in powdered form and mix it, as instructed on the packet, to suit the type of wallpaper you are using. It can also be used as a sealer or sizer and will contain a fungicide. Estimate how much you will need as you would with paint.

Laminates Plastic laminate, for kitchen worktops and cabinets, is sold in sheet form, in 1220-1525 mm (4-5 ft) widths and 3050-3660 mm (10-12 ft) lengths, but it is easier to buy it as a ready-cut component from a DIY centre or joinery manufacturer.

Acrylic sheets are available from 2 to 25 mm thick. Sheet sizes can range from 2000 × 1500 mm to 3030 × 2030 mm but suppliers often sell smaller pieces. Calculate the area to be covered and order accordingly.

Glass You can buy glass cut to order or buy a large sheet and cut it yourself. If you are buying glass to replace a broken windowpane, measure the cracked pane, if possible, or measure the length and width of the inside of the window frame. For ease of fit, cut or buy a piece of glass 3 mm (⅛ in) smaller than the maximum opening. For a large, expensive piece of glass or mirror, it is best to give the glazier the responsibility of taking the measurements, particularly if it must fit an opening that may not be perfectly square.

Glass blocks are available in a standard thickness of 80 mm, with some available in 100 mm. The faces are nominal 115 mm, 190 mm, 240 mm and 300 mm squares, and there are also rectangular blocks. They allow for a 10 mm joint.

Precast glass block panels are available, but take into consideration their considerable weight when planning to handle them.

To determine the number of glass blocks needed, measure the height and width of the structural opening, less 10 mm, then divide by the nominal size of the chosen glass block plus the 10 mm mortar joint. Alternatively, contact the supplier, who will calculate the quantities for you, according to the size of the opening.

Floor coverings Rolls of sheet vinyl flooring come in three widths: 2 m, 3 m and 4 m. Buy enough to cover the area with about 75 mm of overhang on each side for trimming. The width ordered will of course be governed by the greatest width of the area to be covered. Any area wider than 4 m will require two widths, in which case try to position the join in an inconspicuous place, such as under a sofa or bookcase.

Be sure to get enough to fill alcoves or to cover any areas which extend beyond the main floor. Colours of rolls can vary slightly, which can make it awkward to try to match rolls later.

Vinyl floor tiles come in 300 mm (approximately 12 in) squares. Some 9 in squares are available. Ceramic tiles come in a variety of sizes, including rectangular, hexagonal and octagonal shapes. They are all usually sold by the box, but sometimes they are sold by the piece as well.

To calculate the number of pieces you will need to cover a large area with tiles of the same size and colour, divide the area of the space to be tiled by the area of a single tile. If you are planning to lay tiles in patterns involving mixed sizes or colours, lay out the design on graph paper (p.338) and count the number of tiles needed in each size and colour. Add 10 per cent for waste for ceramic tiles, a bit more for brittle tiles or tiles laid in a diagonal pattern, and less for the others. Then divide the number of tiles needed by the number of tiles per box to determine the total number of boxes required.

When buying ceramic tiles, be sure to check them before leaving the supplier: they are very susceptible to breakage during delivery and storage. Also make sure that batch numbers match – otherwise you may find that colours are not quite the same.

Hardware and other items When estimating the materials you will need for a job, include hardware, adhesives and other materials.

Buy enough nails or other fasteners for joining pieces or mounting them on walls, and don't forget anchors or toggles for use in cavity walls.

If you are joining pieces with nuts and bolts, remember to include any necessary washers. Be sure to buy suitable nails and matching trim for wood panelling.

When replacing a windowpane, include the glazing sprigs and universal putty that hold the glass. And don't forget hinges, brackets, latches and knobs or pulls, if needed.

Consult your drawn plans to make a good estimate of all the hardware you will need. Fasteners get lost easily and nails bend if not driven properly, so it's a good idea to buy more than you will need for a job; you can always save the extras for future repairs and other jobs.

Nails may be measured in inches or millimetres. The more popular sizes of nail are generally available in small packs, but larger nails are cheaper when bought by weight. The number you get, in a given weight, depends on the length of the nail (see chart below).

Nails are finished in bright mild steel, blued or black iron, or galvanised for outdoor use. There are many types of nail and it is important to choose the correct type (pp.98-99).

Other fasteners, including screws, are generally sold in small bubble packs or in larger boxes. The number of pieces is marked on the package.

Buying Nails by Weight

Approximate number of nails – metric sizes per half kilogram, imperial sizes per pound.

Length of nail		20	25	30	40	45	50	60	65	75	90	100	125	150
	mm	20	25	30	40	45	50	60	65	75	90	100	125	150
	in	¾	1	1¼	1½	1¾	2	2¼	2½	3	3½	4	5	6
Round wire nails		1950	890	585	375	300	180	140	135	77	50	40	27	16
		1765	800	460	350	275	165	135	125	70	45	35	25	15
Oval wire nails			1275	760	460	325	230	160	110	60	44	33	22	16
			1150	670	425	300	210	150	100	55	40	30	20	15
Clout nails		540	375	360	270	160	130		90	75	42	38		
		500	340	320	250	150	120		82	70	38	35		
Cut floor brads					200	160	130	100	76	50				
					184	150	120	90	70	45				
Plasterboard nails				350	285									
				310	260									

CONVERSION CHARTS

Throughout this book, metric measurements have been used, except where a tool or type of hardware is still sold in imperial measurements. However, because many people find it difficult to use metric measurements, the editors have included, wherever possible, the imperial equivalent of any metric measurement. This page of conversion charts and formulas for converting measurements from imperial to metric, and vice versa, will make your project easier.

How to convert units of measurement

Imperial to metric

	To convert	into	multiply by
Length	inches	millimetres	25.4
	inches	centimetres	2.54
	feet	metres	0.3048
	yards	metres	0.9144
Area	square inches	square centimetres	6.4516
	square feet	square metres	0.0929
	square yards	square metres	0.836
Volume	cubic inches	cubic centimetres	16.387
	cubic feet	cubic metres	0.0283
	cubic yards	cubic metres	0.7646
	fluid ounces	millilitres	28.41
	pints	litres	0.568
	gallons	litres	4.55
Weight	ounces	grams	28.35
	pounds	kilograms	0.45359

Metric to imperial

	To convert	into	multiply by
Length	millimetres	inches	0.0394
	centimetres	inches	0.3937
	metres	feet	3.2808
	metres	yards	1.0936
Area	square centimetres	square inches	0.155
	square metres	square feet	10.764
	square metres	square yards	1.196
Volume	cubic centimetres	cubic inches	0.061
	cubic metres	cubic feet	35.315
	cubic metres	cubic yards	1.308
	litres	pints	1.76
	litres	gallons	0.22
Weight	grams	ounces	0.0352
	kilograms	pounds	2.2046

Conversion table for linear measurements

Metric	Imperial	Metric	Imperial
1 mm	¹⁄₃₂ in	34 cm	13½ in
2 mm	¹⁄₁₆ in	36 cm	14 in
3 mm	⅛ in	37 cm	14½ in
6 mm	¼ in	38 cm	15 in
10 mm	⅜ in	39 cm	15½ in
13 mm	½ in	40 cm	16 in
15 mm	⅝ in	42 cm	16½ in
2 cm	¾ in	43 cm	17 in
2.5 cm	1 in	44 cm	17½ in
3 cm	1¼ in	46 cm	18 in
4 cm	1½ in	48 cm	19 in
5 cm	2 in	51 cm	20 in
5.5 cm	2¼ in	53 cm	21 in
6 cm	2½ in	56 cm	22 in
7 cm	2¾ in	58 cm	23 in
7.5 cm	3 in	61 cm	24 in
8 cm	3¼ in	66 cm	26 in
9 cm	3½ in	71 cm	28 in
9.5 cm	3¾ in	76 cm	30 in
10 cm	4 in	81 cm	32 in
11 cm	4¼ in	86 cm	34 in
11.5 cm	4½ in	91 cm	36 in
13 cm	5 in	96 cm	38 in
14 cm	5½ in	99 cm	39 in
15 cm	6 in	102 cm	40 in
16 cm	6¼ in	107 cm	42 in
17 cm	6½ in	112 cm	44 in
18 cm	7 in	117 cm	46 in
19 cm	7½ in	122 cm	48 in
20 cm	8 in	127 cm	50 in
21.5 cm	8½ in	132 cm	52 in
23 cm	9 in	137 cm	54 in
24 cm	9½ in	142 cm	56 in
25 cm	10 in	147 cm	58 in
26 cm	10½ in	152 cm	60 in
27 cm	10¾ in	157 cm	62 in
28 cm	11 in	163 cm	64 in
29 cm	11½ in	168 cm	66 in
30 cm	12 in	173 cm	68 in
32 cm	12½ in	178 cm	70 in
33 cm	13 in	183 cm	72 in

The publishers acknowledge the contribution of the following people and organisations in the creation of the original edition of this book.

PROJECT EDITORS
Sally French
Robert V. Huber

PROJECT ART DIRECTOR
Judy Speicher

SENIOR ASSOCIATE EDITORS
Carolyn Chubet
Fiona Gilsenan
Theresa Lane

SENIOR ART ASSOCIATES
Marisa Gentile
Morris Karol
Carol Nehring

COPY EDITOR
Katherine G. Ness

EDITORIAL ASSISTANT
Tracy O'Shea

DESIGNER
Virginia Wells Blaker

ART ASSISTANT
Jason Peterson

PRODUCTION COORDINATOR
Jessica Mitchell

CONSULTANTS
Daniel Basovitch
Bob Buteyn
Victor DeMasi
Phil Englander
Charles N. Farley
Allan E. Fitchett
George Frechter
Eugene Goeb
Wayne Hawk
Walter Kurzmann
Peter Legnos
Jim McCann
Tim McCreight
Charles McRaven
Susan Moore
Americo Napolitano
Gerald Persico
Lawrence D. Press
Meryl Prichard
Henry H. Printz
Michael Raffio
Michael Sapienza
Seth Stem
Bob Wilcoxson

INDEXER
Sydney Wolfe Cohen

WRITERS
Roy Barnhart
Beverly Bremer
Mark Bremer
Joseph Haviland
Barbara Mayer
Laura Tringali
Joseph Truini
John Warde

RESEARCHERS
Beverly Bremer
Mark Bremer
Theo Dominic Corbin
Willard Lubka

ARTISTS
Sylvia Bokor
Mario Ferro
Ray Skibinski
Robert Steimle
Robert Steimle, Jr.

PHOTOGRAPHERS
Michael Molkenthin (principal)
Richard Felber
Deborah Denker (cover)

PHOTO CREDITS
Andrite Wondrastone
Distributing Co., Inc., p.203 (all)
W. Cody/West Light,
p.202 (bottom, left)
The Family Handyman,
p.287 (top 3)
R.D. Werner Company, Inc.,
p.83 (extension ladder)

Aberdeen's Magazine of Masonry Construction • Adjustable Clamp Company • Advanced Technology Inc. • AIN Plastics, Inc. Allcraft Tool & Supply Company, Inc. • American Clamping Corp. • American Machine & Tool Co., Inc. • American Saw & Mfg. Company American Stone and Supply, Inc. • American Tool Companies, Inc. • Ames Lawn and Garden Tools • Andrite Wondrastone Distributing Co., Inc. Armstrong World Industries Inc. • Arrow Fastener Company, Inc. • Ball & Ball • Barrasso & Sons, Inc. • Richard J. Bell Company Inc. S.A. Bendheim Company Inc. • Black & Decker • Boise Cascade Corp. • BP Chemicals, Inc.-Filon Products • Brass Accent by Urfic, Inc. Brick Institute of America • Bridge City Tool Works, Inc. • C&A Wallcoverings • Central Hardware & Electric Corp. • Central Supply Inc. Colonial Bronze Co. • Concrete Paver Institute • Congoleum Corp. • Albert Constantine & Son, Inc. • CooperTools Delta International Machinery Corp. • Ray Donarski • Tom Doyle • Dremel Power Tools • Eldorado Stone Corporation • Empak Company Fibre Glass Evercoat Co. Inc. • Flexi-Wall Systems • Florian Glass • Formica Corporation • Freud, Inc. • Garden State Flooring • Garrett Wade Company GB Electrical, Inc. • GE Plastics • Glen-Gery Corporation • The Glidden Co. • Grinnell Concrete Pavingstones • Grizzly Imports, Inc. Hafele America Co. • Hager Hinge Co. • Harris-Tarkett, Inc. • Hebron Brick Supply Co. • HEWI, Inc. • Hitachi Power Tools U.S.A. Limited Hi-Way Concrete Products • Hyde Tools • Ilco Unican Corp. • Inter Design Inc. • International Wallcoverings Ltd. • The Irwin Company Ives: A Harrow Company • Johnson Level and Tool Manufacturing Company • Jolie Papier Ltd. • Kentile Floors Inc. • Kentucky Mill Work Kentucky Wood Floors, Inc. • Keystone Retaining Walls Systems Inc. • Kwikset, A Black & Decker Company • Lasco Panel Products, Div. of Tomkins Industries Inc. • Laticrete International • C.R. Laurence Company Inc. • Lazon Paints & Wallcoverings • LBI, Inc. • McFeely's • Makita U.S.A. Inc. Mannington Floors • Marion Tool Corp. • Marshalltown Trowel Company • Middletown Plate Glass Co. Inc. • Milwaukee Electric Tool Corp. Monterey Shelf, Inc. • Benjamin Moore & Co. • Mosaic Supplies • Musolf Distributing Inc. • National Concrete Masonry Association National Manufacturing Company • National Oak Flooring Manufacturers' Association • National Particleboard Association National Wood Flooring Association • New Hippodrome Hardware Corp. • NicSand, Inc. • Owens-Corning Fiberglas Corp. • Padco, Inc. Paxton Hardware • Pfister Industries • Pittsburgh Corning Corporation • Plexi-Craft Quality Products Corp. • Porter-Cable Professional Power Tool Corp. Potlatch Corporation • Power-Flo Products • PPG Industries • Red Devil, Inc. • Cynthia Rees Ceramic Tile Showroom Rickel Do-It-Yourself Home Centers • Ridge Tool Company • Rio Grande Albuquerque • Robbins Inc. • Roofing Industry Educational Institute Roysons Corporation • Ryobi America Corp. • Sandvik Saws and Tools • S-B Power Tool Company • Schlage Lock Company • Shur-line Inc. R&G Sloane Manufacturing Co. • Solo Metal Works Ltd. • South Street Ready-Mix Concrete • Stanley Tools The L.S. Starrett Company • John Sterling Corp. • Stone Products Corporation • StoneWall™ Landscape Systems, Inc. • Structural Stone Company, Inc. Tahran Painting & Decorating Center • Target Products Inc. • TECO/Lumberlok • 3M Do-It-Yourself Division • Tremont Nail Company Triangle Tool Group Inc. • Unicorn Universal Woods Ltd. • Unilock N.Y. Inc. • Vaughan & Bushnell Mfg. Co. • Vermont American Tool Co. V.T. Industries, Inc. • Wallcoverings Association • Wedge Innovations • R.D. Werner Company, Inc. • Wilde Tool Co., Inc. Willson Safety Products • Ralph Wilson Plastics Co. • Wood Moulding and Millwork Producers' Association F.W. Wostbrock Hardwood Floor Company, Inc. • Wright Products Corp.

ORIGINATION Rapida Group plc PAPER Smurfit Condat, Neuilly, France PRINTING & BINDING BPC Consumer Books Ltd, Aylesbury

40-430-1